INHERITANCE

The Story of Wake Forest Debate, 1835-1930s

Cover Photo Credit: Photo Courtesy of the ZSR
Library, Special Collections & Archives

1911 Wake Debate Council
Top Row – C. T. Murchison, J. R. Carroll, E. A. Harrill; Bottom
Row – I. C. Woodard, G. W. Johnson, J. P. Tucker, Chairman

ISBN:
979-8-9915753-0-0 *Hardcover*
979-8-9915753-1-7 *Paperback*

INHERITANCE

HISTORY *of* WAKE FOREST DEBATE

1835-1930s

Allan Louden

CONTENTS

ACKNOWLEDGMENTS

The long-anticipated detailing of the history of the Wake Forest Debate began in earnest long ago, in the summer of 1989, when Wake debater Thomas Allen (Round Rock, TX) received a research fellowship and teamed up with me to begin months of archival work, detailing one hundred and sixty years of debate at Wake Forest. Many years later, when time allowed to finish the book, those efforts were foundational.

Jarrod Atchison, as he always does, surpassed every standard of backing. His sympathetic counsel, idea development, editing, and authoring of the critical section on the mystery surrounding Coach Zon Robinson's disappearance in the late 1930s were outstanding. Jarrod's historical instincts emboldened my own.

John Llewellyn, a dedicated colleague, consistently exceeded expectations with his support. He generously lent his local editing skills to the full manuscript three times, often raising thought-provoking questions and providing entertaining anecdotes that enriched the content. John's active appreciation for his peers is a rare quality.

Many more have contributed to gathering materials, including digging through ledgers in search of "topics debated" and insights into the debater's celebrations and troubles. Chris Miller and later Frank Robinson, Jr. undertook this tedious task day after day, each bringing their unique skills and dedication. Former wake debater and now professional historian Adam Tomasi shared detailed historical research, adding depth to the work.

The archive staff members of ZSR Library were invaluable, kind, and patient. Tanya Zanish-Belcher, the director of Wake's Special Collections and Archives, was helpful in numerous instances. Her staff, particularly Rebecca Peterson May, Emily Houlditch, and Megan Mulder, seemed to carry the burdens of my frequent and obtuse requests and questions. The Staff at Wake Forest Historical Museum near Old Wake Forest were most helpful with their time: Sarah Soleim, Carolyn Rice, and Terry Brock.

Several other Archives, including the Southern Baptist Historical Library and Archives in Nashville, National Archives and Records Administration, Maryland, Elon College and other academic Library staffs, the Wake Forest ROTC Library and Archive, and an assembly of University Archives online. Commercial archives such as *Newspapers.com* were invaluable.

Special tribute is due to Andrew Canady, an Averett College Professor of History, VA, who is authoring a definitive book on Wake Forest University and its historical relationships with slavery. His suggestions on race issues were beneficial, materially modifying the tone and content of the race chapters. Jenny Puckett also provided a model for researching Wake's history and gave kind counsel.

Ammar Basha completed our household duties with skill and care and assisted throughout, clearing the time needed for the seven months of revisions possible. His was a constant and not easy task.

As always, the community in which one mentally resides provides invaluable encouragement and moral support. My "Wellness Committee," consisting of Alessandra, Andrew, Candice, Cynthia, Jarrod, Meg, Nate, and Ron, played significant roles in motivating me. Their unwavering support was a constant reminder of the importance of community in academic pursuits. My departmental colleagues also contributed to significant conversations that enriched this work.

Unquestionably, the decades of Wake Debaters have been a significant part of my life, filling it with challenges, laughter, and inspiration. Their contributions have shaped my career in ways I could never have imagined. My daily journey was filled with engaged, smart, young arguers. In the end, working with debate was always about the debaters. In many ways, the book is an epistle to them, reflecting their passion and dedication. Each, in their unique way, has contributed to the larger mission of the Wake Forest Debate.

PREFACE

Inheritance: The Story of Wake Forest Debate, 1835-1930s

Our image of 19th and 20th-century Wake Forest debaters is of a serious-minded young man, attentive and engaged, ardently making a reflective point about policy or literature in one of the two dusty literary halls. While this image would describe some of the fellows, the debate societies were comprised of young folks who likewise gave way to horsing around. As one writer explained, the students indulged their youthful high spirits "to relieve their boredom induced by too heavy a diet of philosophy, literature, religion, or even politics."[1]

Academic C. W. Lomas noted: "Most of the recorded minutes of literary societies ... are humdrum and colorless accounts written in meticulously correct form, and beautiful although not necessarily legible script.[2] His description accurately reflects what was found with the ledgers of Wake's Philomathesian and Euzelian Societies.

As he suggests, the recorder occasionally reveals humor, at times spicing up the minutes with a pithy drawing. Reading between the lines, one sees not the buttoned-down preacher-to-be but the young men charged with merriment, indiscretion, and laughter. From the outset, the young men in the late-night halls, debating life and society, were by turns creative, ambitious, devout, lazy, and always particular characters.

---

[1] Lomas, C. W. (1953). The lighter side of the Literary Societies, *Quarterly Journal of Speech*, 39, page 45.

[2] Lomas, C. W. (1953). The lighter side of the Literary Societies, *Quarterly Journal of Speech*, 39, page 45.

G. W. Paschal, *History of Wake Forest College,* Vol. I-III.

This first volume is tasked with sculpting an authentic historical record. Logging history, in part, satisfies this fundamental objective, yet it chances to ignore the students' everyday lives; these are often valuable stories that have been largely untold. This manuscript seeks to integrate both goals by recounting a history grounded in the debaters' lives.

To bridge this gap, a concerted effort was made to present the events from the students' perspective, recounting their experiences and the impacts of trends and happenings on their lives. Occasionally, an individual is spotlighted to provide a personal touch to the narrative. Still, it is to be remembered that they are just one of many, not a definitive representation of all debaters. The central aim is to humanize these individuals by making their stories accessible and relatable.

The author has high praise for George Washington Paschal's authoritative three-volume *History of Wake Forest College.* His accuracy and thoroughness impress readers and researchers, who have independently confirmed much of his record. Paschal's fidelity is to be expected as he experienced a considerable swath of the history covered in his volumes as an observer and participant. Paschal was a former student (1889-1892), a long-term faculty member (1911-1940), and always an active participant in Society life.[3]

Paschal's *History of Wake Forest College* has remained "the gold standard" account of Wake Forest from inception to 1943. His work has influenced the storylines of the University's histories across most subsequent authors. Not without justification, many draw literally from his work with an almost hagiographic deference.

Of course, with any history, there is always more. The narrower focus of these volumes on Wake Debate allows a revisiting of Paschal's archive, rounding out many stories and, on occasion, offering alternative evidence or interpretations. Differences emerged when the materials examined for this volume, such as full archives of state newspapers, were not readily available to Paschal.

By design, most of Paschal's work was not consulted before gathering records for this project. This decision avoided prejudicing the research by absorbing a prior orthodoxy. As a result, this work is a unique construction, not a derivative. Paschal is returned to later when writing, supplementing, and at times correcting choices made here.

On rare occasions, this approach has allowed modest corrections to Paschal, but more often, it has provided an opportunity to tell the "Rest of the Story." Two apparent instances include expanding the "Murder at Eu," the Reconstruction-Era arrest by federal marshals of a Euzelian debater pulled from the hall during a debate, and the reclaiming of a lost story of one Deacon, the most famous US aviator of his times, the "Flying Parson," Belvin Maynard, who captured the first Continental airplane race and was highly honored on Wake's Society Day, 1919.

There is an unending tension in the construction of these volumes, particularly Volume 1. Every detail cannot be included; the material must be compressed to manageable sections. Yet considerable detail is needed for a true historical record. Some may find that this volume has too many particulars. The intent was to choose what was needed to

---

[3] He did his graduate study at the University of Chicago. https://www.ncpedia.org/biography/paschal-george-washington. Paschal's contributions to Wake Forest and the Societies, particularly the Philomathesians, will appear throughout this volume. A typical example is when he addressed the Phis, relaying their history as "a continual drama of sacrifices, hard work, obstacles, pathos, and humorous episodes." *Old Gold and Black*, February 17, 1934, page 1. In one of his chatty newspaper columns, President Charles Taylor reported that the young Professor Paschal summered in Chatham, "devouring Greek classics and watermelons."

preserve historical context. In the writing, errors of too much detail and too little undoubtedly occur across various segments.

There are, at times, apparent redundancies in the recounted records. Care was taken not to present stories multiple times, yet occasionally, a reminder is necessary to capture the historical moment accurately. There is a sense in which recurrence is the very material of tradition. At times, these reminders evoke relationships, intended and unintended. When events unfold in apparent repetition, for example, the sequential Intercollegiate Debates across various opponents, an earnest effort is made to offer distinct material with each instance.

The nature of publications often changed across the extended volume's landscape. Researching debate history before the 1870s, and even more so before the Civil War, must rely on few sources. Newspapers, while notable, had not developed as they would by the 1870s, and local public messaging was not preserved. As a result, some sections may feel attended to disproportionately. The early 20th century, for example, is richly documented internally in college publications and externally in scores of newspapers.

The reader will find "mistakes" in spelling, punctuation, and lists that are unevenly interposed within quoted materials. Materials were logged *as they appear in the original text.* Minor corrections were allowed when they aided the flow, but in a manner mindful of sustaining the author's intent.

Many notes that add context and color to the narratives were found in the societies' journals. The societies' minutes were faithfully recorded in oversized leather-bound ledgers that foretold permanence. The minutes, of course, until the century before the invention of the typewriter were patiently written in often-elegant cursive. Most Society Secretaries did a praiseworthy job, often readable, with only some difficult to decipher. Also, language differences added challenges; for example, certain letters, such as "S," which resembled an "F," and spelling varied, as did some sentence structures. Nonetheless, a rhythm is found when reading the minutes, and the reader gains in interpretive know-how. Most ledger entries from 1835 to the late 1940s were, page by page, reviewed to develop the topics debated in society meetings, presented in volume 3 of this series.

In the Wake Forest tradition, the reader will encounter 20th-century debate with a more literate understanding of those who constructed the world in which we now reside.

AN INTRODUCTION

Wake's Oratorical Tradition

Long before we played football, edited publications, acted, or sang – in fact, almost before we studied, we of Wake Forest talked. —Ed Wilson, The 1943 *Howler*

Edwin Wilson anonymously penned the above phrase in the 1943 *Howler*, a mantra embraced by generations in the Wake Debate Community. The refrain captures a 190-year tradition, from 1835 to the present, that has sustained Wake Debate's mission and import.

Less well known than the original passage, "Long before ... we of Wake Forest...," was an accompanying sentence that added, "The college was still a bawling child, and the first Administration Building was still unoccupied when two handfuls of students met and gave birth to two literary societies, the Philomathesians and the Euzelians."[1]

---

[1] *Howler*, 1943, page 115. Philomathesia was a popular name derived from the Greek Philomath, which means "a lover of learning." Over thirty societies were named in some version of Philomath. For example, the Philomathean Society at the University of Pennsylvania was founded in 1813. At Willamette (OR), the Philomathean Society was incorporated by the Oregon Territorial Legislature in 1856, and the Philermenian Society was established at Brown. Philomathesian societies were formed in Indiana in 1930 and at Wabash in 1934. Porter, D. (1954). The Literary

The *Howler's* 1943 editor, Ed Wilson,[2] penned analogs for each student group comprising the yearbook's section; he chose to identify the debaters with their extended history. Ed Wilson, who would soon depart for WW II as part of the "Greatest Generation," likely was rushing to meet a deadline, but his poetic prose permeated each entry, especially the one for debate.[3]

The tradition of public speaking was central to Wake Forest's self-identity, a nexus that recurs throughout this volume. The thematic continuum of "Wake Forest and public speaking" appreciably captures the College's public presentation for the first hundred years. Debate and the societies imprinted students' lives almost daily. This shared vision, its very sameness, is the fabric that bonds Wake Forest Debate history.

Investiture

The Wake Forest Institute opened in February 1834 with twenty-five students, and by September, the number had risen to seventy.[4] These came "for the most part from the homes of planters, many of them well to do..."[5] Samuel Wait was the first principal of the Institute and held the position for eleven years.[6]

The Baptist Church's need for a more educated clergy and more literate laypersons compelled that "The main purpose of the Wake Forest

---

Societies, in *a history of speech education in America*. Karl Wallace, Editor, page 242; Mother Euzelia stood with the fields of Literature and Science.

[2] Ed Wilson shared endless contributions across generations of Wake Debaters. He was himself a debater in the 1940s. He will reappear in the volume on numerous occasions. Dr. Wilson passed away on March 14, 2024, at the age of 101.

[3] Wilson's words reflected a characterization of Wake's self-concept. A decade earlier, in 1934, the *Wake Forest Alumni News* printed, "Long before Wake Forest College was known for her good football teams, saying that a man was a graduate of Wake Forest was equivalent to saying that he was an effective public speaker." *Wake Forest Alumni News*, May 1934, Vol. 3, No. 4, page 18; Wilson's secondary phrase appears to be a lending from Dr. Wm. Hooper, chairman of the Baptist committee on education, in an 1886 commentary on the Semi-Centennial Anniversary.

[4] *The Biblical Recorder*, February 13, 1884, page 2.

[5] Paschal, G. W. (1935), *The History of Wake Forest College,* Vol. I, page 159.

[6] Wait actively served on the Wake Forest Board of Trustees, usually as chairperson, for nearly twenty years after his presidency. He concluded his career as President at the newly founded Oxford Female College (1850-1857), located 30 miles north of Wake Forest. https://www.ncpedia.org/oxford-college.

Institute was to train leaders of the denomination, especially ministers."[7] The influential *Biblical Reporter*, founded two years before Wake Forest in 1833, often served as the college's early voice.

Wake Forest Institute.

AT the meeting of the Trustees of the Wake Forest Institute, it was Resolved that the laws, stipulating the amount of students' pocket money and the trading in stores, be repealed, it was furthermore Resolved, that the amounts due each student for labor, be hereafter paid them at the expiration of each and every month.

The school will re-commence on the 1st Monday in February next, the annual expense at the Institute is $100—the one half of which is required at the beginning of each session, say 1st February and 1st July. The Trustees are happy to state that the College building, will be in readiness, by the beginning of the 1st term, that they have obtained the services of Mr. Geo. Ryan as steward, whose experience and persevering habits, they hope will give general satisfaction. Done by order of the Board,

W. ROLES, Sec'y.

Jan. 11.　　　　115-3t.

Although growing swiftly, the entire statewide Baptist enterprise probably only numbered about 30,000 members at the college's inception.[8] Josiah W. Bailey's Founders' Day Speech at Meredith College in 1927 describes the early Baptist situation as even more of an uphill climb, suggesting there were, at the time, fewer Baptists. "The Commonwealth was sparsely settled. The means of communication and transportation were primitive. The number of Baptists did not exceed 17,000, and the number of churches did not exceed 200. Their ministers were, to a large extent, uneducated. Once a month preaching was the rule."[9] Wake's founding was motivated by education and, fundamentally, religion.

From the Baptist's point of view, the school's birth, pursuant to State Baptist Convention resolutions, was obtained after a bruising battle in

---

[7] Blanchard, D. D., *The Biblical Recorder*, June 3, 1936.

[8] *The Biblical Recorder*, February 4, 1884.

[9] *The Biblical Recorder*, February 16, 1927.

the legislature.[10] "... The prejudice that had existed long before in the minds of certain men in power in North Carolina by which men were imprisoned and otherwise punished for no other crime than they were Baptist, showed its cloven foot by pressing upon the literary infant in such a way, and with such force as to nearly rest the life out of it."[11]

Literary societies were partly formed to fill the students' empty space. A student's day was dominated by a severe curriculum, rigid labor, unrelenting obligations, and religion. The Societies offered a welcome reprieve.

The formation of Wake's Literary Societies took place in an era of many societal inducements. The larger culture was absorbed in public deliberation and educating a better citizenry. Nearly every college sprouted two active Societies upon its founding. Southern institutions were no exception.

Societies were popular in colleges, particularly in northern schools.[12] As schools came into existence, the campus context invited literary engagement. A social historian, Thomas Harding, discusses why the New

---

[10] President Truman characterized the founding in his address for the Winston-Salem groundbreaking ceremonies on October 15, 1951. "The bill granting a charter to Wake Forest came up for final passage in the North Carolina State Senate. Without this bill, the college could not have been founded. Yet, the vote was a tie, 29 to 29, and the bill passed only by the deciding vote of the presiding officer... Think what this means. If there had been one more negative vote, there might never have been a Wake Forest College."

[11] *The Biblical Recorder*, February 13, 1884, page 2.

[12] According to some sources, the history of literary societies begins in the colonial period as early as 1716. Wake undoubtedly was aware of these earlier starts. Although the records indicate that college literary and debating societies existed early in the 18th century, the first student associations appear to have been largely religious. The earliest mention of such religious organizations found in Cotton Mather's diary from April 20, 1716, read: "A society of pious and praying youths, at the college, I will study which way I may be useful to." Another Society of "Young Scholars" was organized at Harvard, its articles of 1723 revealing that it called itself the Private Meeting Club. Its chief concerns were religion and "Love, peace, and unity with one another." By 1719, however, the Spy Club at Harvard stipulated in its constitution "that there be a disputation on two or more questions at every meeting, one part of the company holding the affirmative, and the other the negative part of the question." Potter, D. (1944). *Debating in the Colonial Charter Colleges: And? history survey, 1642 to 1900,* Bureau of Publications, Teachers College, Columbia.

In the 1800s, the debates moved from disputation to more extemporaneous discussions. By the 1830s, when Wake Forest joined the Literary Society movement, in some cases, debates became impromptu exercises, with the topics announced in advance. The constructive speeches and, certainly, the rebuttals were extemporaneous in nature.

England schools developed early debating societies. The rationales for the South were not different:

> Some of the influences which led to the organization of such societies were the following: ... they offered respite from the classical curriculum; they were an opportunity for fraternal gathering; as the one extracurricular activity where they could release youthful enthusiasm and energy; they were the only available means by which experience in [public] speaking could be obtained with occasional differences.[13]

ORATORY IS SOVEREIGN

The societal popularity of oratory wholly fit Wake's Literary Societies' design for training men to become ministers, teachers, or lawyers, those who wished to learn the art of public speaking.[14] The Societies offered a place of belonging, accompanied by status and honor. Fredrick Rudolph remarked in his voluminous history of American colleges: "The fact that the highest and almost the only extracurricular honors attainable by college students lay in the field of oratory and debating helps to explain certain of the characteristics of Southern Leadership in the years ahead."[15]

Oratories were arguably first introduced publicly with the creation of Anniversary Day in 1854, nearly 20 years earlier than the introduction of public debates in 1872. In reality, public presentations of oratories had occurred since the school's very origin. The earliest audiences were confined to the immediate college community, students, and faculty, with a smattering of town folks.

---

[13] Harding, T. S. (1971). *College Literary Societies: The contribution to higher education in the United States, 1815-1876*, Pageant Press International Corporation, New York, page 88.

[14] A more pessimistic view was advanced by academic E. H. Wilds, who detected that the public speaking aspect of Societies faded in the early 1800s. He concluded, "It is true that there are still literary societies to be found, but these are mainly in colleges where fraternities are forbidden, and they are largely social in character. They have very little influence in the cultivation of pubic-speaking ability." Wilds, E. H. (1916). Public Speaking in the early colleges and schools. *Quarterly Journal of Speech*, Vol. 2, page 36. Wild's take on a "vanishing public speaking mission" failed to describe the soon-to-be-established Wake Forest Societies or much of the South.

[15] Rudolph, F. (1962). *The American College and University: A history*. University of Georgia Press.

In their first year, 1835, the societies sponsored a campus celebration of Independence Day. Along with food and fireworks, the 4th of July celebrations featured an Independence Day speaker, who was chosen in alternating years between societies. When the "Institute" became Wake Forest College, several orators from each society presented holiday performances in their respective halls.

Individual orators in the Anniversary Day era were rigorously selected and boisterously honored. Most years, newspapers printed an overview of each senior commencement orator and, later, those who addressed Society Day. One pre-Civil War newspaper, in 1854, illustrates the way summations were exhibited in print, sometimes reviewing up to ten speakers in full detail:

> "Enthusiasm" was the subject selected by Mr. John C. Patterson, of Orange. The unassuming modesty of this speaker at once awakened a sympathetic cord in the breasts of his hearers, and they listened with delight as he discoursed on this powerful element of success in popular oratory. Clear expositions of the true definition of 'Enthusiasm,' disrobing of that wild, unsolid fanaticism with which too many blend it, give evidence of a nice, discriminating mind and the capacity for eliminating new thoughts, and of insulted genius.[16]

The valedictory address delivered at the same graduation by Mr. Thomas H. Pritchard was assessed as that of a "gifted young orator," christened "the melting tear, the heaving bosom, the burning, thrilling language, all gave assurance of a soaring heart as he gave a sad farewell to his revered *Alma Mater*."[17]

For another five years, 1848-1854, the societies took turns providing a speaker to celebrate Washington's Birthday.[18] This practice ended with the creation of Anniversary Day. The celebration, surrounding events, and public invitation buoyed the event until it became the most important campus day of the year apart from Commencement (see Chapter 8 – Anniversary Debates – Place, Heritage, Social Opening).

---

[16] *Spirit of the Age* (Raleigh), June 14, 1854, page 2.

[17] *Spirit of the Age* (Raleigh), June 14, 1854, page 2.

[18] Paschal, G. W. (1935), *History of Wake Forest College*, Vol. I (based on entries in the Society Minutes).

PROGRAMME
SENIOR SPEAKING,
WAKE FOREST COLLEGE, N. C.
FRIDAY EVENING, OCTOBER 22, 1886, 7:30 O'CLOCK.

J. J. LANE, Marlboro County, S. C.
Subject—Opposition Solidifies Character.

E. H. BOWLING, Durham county, N. C.
Subject—Dixie's Heroines.

D. O. McCULLERS, Clayton, N. C.
Subject—Patriotism.

D. A. PITTARD, Granville County, N. C.
Subject—Utilize the Powers That You Have.

WALTER P. STRADLEY, Oxford, N. C.
Subject—The Industrial Craze.

J. B. CARLYLE, Robeson County, N. C.
Subject—Our Republic.

In the 1880s *The College Bulletin* recorded Senior Speakers and Thesis topics

From the beginning, Commencement speakers, initially all seniors, were to present a proper oratory as their graduation requirement. In some early years, declamations were presented alongside original orations. The tolerance for sitting through long speeches, lectures, and sermons was truly admirable. It was the entertainment of the day.

Soon, too many graduates necessitated limiting the number who could speak. By the 1880s, the number of speakers was fixed at ten. For four years beginning in 1869, the number of speakers allowed shrunk to four, although the number who spoke varied. The faculty selected those who spoke at graduation.

Most of the speaking training took place in the ornate Society halls. In addition to the biweekly debates, every student in their literary work was obliged to speak often. *The Wake Forest Student* in 1893 recorded purpose and practice:

> The college supplies the nourishment for the mind and requires that it shall be taken, or the student cannot long remain here, and the Literary Society furnishes the place for its independent exercise, and requires that it be taken where mind shall wrestle with mind and the conflict shall be mental, and that the honors of this field shall

be awarded to the mind which has the most muscle, greatest activity, and has succeeded best in cultivating the graces of oratory and in mastering logic and rhetoric. Students were required to debate, write, and deliver Junior speeches and other addresses, write compositions, and practice declamation.[19]

The first oration was delivered by a student, James Dockery, before the Philomathesian and Euzelian Societies on July 4th, 1835, and focused on intellect's ability to advance mankind. He began his address with the common topical element that "now" is the best of times. He said, "The present era is far in advance of its predecessors in the development of the intellectual powers of man. The march of mind has become proverbial. Mind is now employing its noblest energies in the investigation of the theories and systems of past generations; whatever cannot abide the test of experiment, a principal of truth, it fearlessly rejects. Bold innovations in the Sciences and Religion, and Government, are projected and advocated."[20]

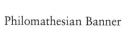

Philomathesian Banner   Euzelian Banner

---

[19] *The Wake Forest Student,* July 1893, Vol. 12, page 495.

[20] James C. Dockery. Oration delivered before the Philomathesian and Euzelian Societies, July 4, 1835. Untitled.

Senior speeches and theses were of such importance that their announcement would be registered in the *Wake Forest Bulletin*. *The* 1886 *Bulletin,* sharing the rules of graduation, logged, "All candidates for regular college degrees are required to deliver four original addresses of not less than 1000 words each, or submit to the faculty, in lieu thereof, an equal number of an original thesis of not less than 2000 words each; provided that, by this substitution, the number of addresses on any occasion shall not be less than eight, nor shall they be more than 12. In case of disagreement among candidates in making the substitutions, the questions are tied up by the faculty, by law or otherwise."[21] A touch convoluted.

Publically presented evening oratories were closely covered in the papers and celebrated with uncritical fête. *The Chatham Record* covered Mr. M. A. Jones' 1880 anniversary Day speech: "With impressive thoughts, together with the bright conceptions of the great end of life, he transported, as it were, the entire audience, into the true atmosphere of intelligence, and showed, in glowing terms, that 'he lives longest who thinks most and ask the noblest questions.'"[22]

On occasion, a critical comment broke through. In a review that was careful to distinguish content and presenter, *The Wake Forest Student* editor judged, "Mr. J. R. Carlisle ... giving as his subject 'The Lost Cause'... "In the opinion of some, was unfortunate in his subject, yet he gave us a treat."[23]

Over more than a century and a half, four primary settings dominated public oratory, openings which increasingly served as an effective voice on behalf of the college. Initially, the focus was on faculty-required Senior Orations, followed closely and often in tandem with Commencement Senior Orators. For multiple decades, before the administration appropriated the occasions, Anniversary Day and Society Day were under the full purview of the two literary societies. They invited the main speakers, ruling the campus calendar with the featured intellectual and social events of the fall and spring seasons. The events also provided the impetus for inviting alumni, the State's elite, and women from Meredith and Oxford to the campus for oratories, debates, and celebrations.

---

[21] *Wake Forest Catalog, 1886, page 27.*

[22] *The Chatham Record* (Pittsboro, North Carolina) February 26, 1880.

[23] Walter P Stradley, Editor, In and About the College, *The Wake Forest Student*, March 1887, page 283.

In due course, Anniversary Day became Founder's Day, later merging with Society Day, which the societies found difficult to finance and manage; with their blessing, it moved to more of a holiday and less a Society commemoration.[24]

THE ORATIONS ENDURED

In 1895, Mr. J. A. Tolar introduced Mr. Carey Newton of Wake Forest, N.C., as the Philomathesian Society's Anniversary Day orator. His subject was *A Pound of Flesh*. He explained:

> When I was a newish I dreamed of being an orator, when I was a Soph. I longed to be an orator; when I was a Junior, I worked to be an orator, and when I became a senior, I shrank at being an orator.[25]

Drawing from 1912 *Howler*

As the young Newton concisely captured, the orators (and the College) matured across their spans. A solid consensus existed that the institution

---

[24] See chapters 8-10 for full accounts of Commencement, Anniversary, and Society Day events.

[25] *The Patron and Gleaner* (Lasker, NC), Feb. 28, 1895, page 1.

and the societies considered Wake Forest as the State's, and perhaps the South's, premier speaking preparation center. An 1883 *The Biblical Recorder's* commentary offered the rhetorical framing that stipulated the school's character:

> Reviewing the history of the college, while it has always been one of moral and intellectual grandeur, yet in the past seven years especially, the college has grown to be one of the most commodious and prominent institutions of its kind among Baptists in the South... But perhaps nothing else more than in the faithfulness and excellence of her students does Wake Forest excel, and doubtless consists as much in the quality of the oratory of her students as in any other thing. [26]

This enthusiasm prevailed throughout much of the literary society's history through the late 1930s. Dr. H. M. Poteat, speaking to a Euzelian Society annual "smoker" in 1931, exclaimed, "The characteristics of a speaker today are the same as in the days of Cicero and are to stand up, to speak up, and shut up."

Perhaps with intentional humor, the same paper added, "Dr. Poteat explained that there was a great need for speakers today, that though he couldn't think of what they would say, speakers are always used for road and bridge openings and numerous other public and political functions. The point is, continued Dr. Poteat, "that speaking is still one of America's favorite indoor and outdoor sports." [27]

The core themes of student oratories were commonly patriotic and chauvinistic. The 1935 Society Day oratory, for example, offered by P. B. Nickens (Phi) was entitled *Monuments*, in which he cited the Parthenon as "a monument of supreme art" and the Statue of Liberty as "the embodiment of one of the highest conceptions of mankind." The speaker went on: "We have here in Wake County a monument surpassed by none—it was established by the North Carolina Baptist Convention in 1834." The enthymeme invoking Wake Forest was apparent. [28]

---

[26] *The Biblical Recorder*, February 21, 1883, page 2.

[27] *Old Gold and Black*, September 10, 1931, page 1, 2.

[28] Pres. Poteat and G. W. Paschal, along with other faculty members, selected the orators for the evening, as they did almost every year. One orator, Johnny G. Ray, spoke on the economic side of the racial question.

1905 Panoramic Campus View, 1905 – A Christmas
Postcard sent by President W. L. Poteat

As expected, there was much flag-waving in the public oratories, often presented to eager audiences. They strongly reflected a regional alignment. As with any group, the young society member talked about the ideas that reflected their concerns.[29] The most enduring post-Civil War theme was the South's looming recovery of spirit, pride, and livelihoods. No less than sixty-two titles address a burgeoning South, while twenty-five spoke directly of North Carolina's resurgence. Several versions of the "New South" rising again were uttered at the campus events.

Along with debates, oratories routinely presented topics drawn from ongoing social and political episodes. In a Phi section, the debate portion of the program misfired when two participants failed to show up, yet the oratories saved the day. For the record, one of the topics for the March 1928 evening was described: "Mr. Daniels pointed out in his speech the sterling characteristics of Mussolini acclaiming him 'The Savior of Italy.'"[30]

---

[29] For all available public oratory topics, see Volume 3 of this debate series, *Milestones*, Entry 5: Wake Forest's Oratorical Tradition: Senior Orations, Anniversary Day, Society Day, & Commencement 1835-2021.

[30] *Old Gold and Black*, March 24, 1928, page 1. More generally, the types of essays delivered in the meeting recitations are as expected. On April 20, 1903, for example, Junior orations talk on *The French and American History* – May 1, Meadows, *Changes Wrought in the South by the Civil War* – May 12 *The North Carolina Boy* – *The Old and New* – *Changes in Rural Life* – *Mountains* – *Arbitration* – *The Salvation of World Problems*. In April 1902, Mr. Privette presented his oration, *State Pride or Why We Should Be Proud of our Nation State*, and Mr. Johnson followed with *Stonewall Jackson, the Patriot and Soldier*. Twenty years later, not much had

As the embroidered oratory of preachers and politicians, having to project without microphones, gave way to a more natural, grounded presentation, many alumni expressed their fear that the oratorical foundations were being lost. One academic of the period wrote:

[W]hen older alumni of southern institutions come together at commencement, they sadly lament a something gone out of the platform exhibitions... [They] recall a time when college students "could speak," as they say. "Your boys write better English, discuss more up to date subjects than we use to; but they simply can't speak." "Why," continued he, "they don't know how to make gestures, they don't feel what they say, and they have no voices."[31]

The Wake Forest Student pushed back in response to the awakening alumni criticisms earlier in 1895, when editor Th. Page Briggs, Editor, answered back:

There are alumni of Wake Forest who are always lamenting the fact that the societies are not what they were in the old days. Well, if the speeches of the sixty-first Anniversary represent the spirit, I, for one, am glad that the times have changed... The great trouble with our pessimistic brothers... is that they allow their imaginations to almost deify some old-time speaker, comparing his present oratory with that of a schoolboy. Is that exactly fair? Nine out of ten of their heroes, I fancy, would fare badly in one of the "new-fangled" debates.[32]

T. E. C.[33] sent a dispatch to *The Charlotte Observer,* which conveyed a defense of what constitutes *suitable* oratory, offering a rather spirited

---

changed in student oratories. "The annual junior-senior oratorical contest of the Euzelian Literary Society was held in the Eu Hall Tuesday night, with W. H. Ford, Atlanta, winning first place with the oration, '*Jesus in Modern Life*.'" *Old Gold and Black*, March 23, 1931, page 1; It was not until the late modern era, in the 2000s, that topics became more personalized, sharing of identification, such as the 1992 Hannah Britton's, *I had to go to South Africa before I could go to East Winston.*

[31] Snyder, H. N. (1904). The College Literary Society, *The Sewanee Review*, Vol. 12, January 1904, page 78.

[32] Th. Page Briggs, Editor's Portfolio, *The Wake Forest Student*, 1895, page 332.

[33] The authorship is unclear, but the dispatch does provide a detailed and lengthy description of the 1886 Anniversary Celebration at Wake. Reading the coverage in its entirety is worth the time. *Charlotte Observer*, February 23, 1886.

rejection of the 1886 "contemporary empty oratorical form" in favor of an old-style voice that would not only save oratory from itself but pave the way for a Southern renaissance, his words command:

> At 7:00 PM, an audience assembled in the Wingate Memorial Hall to hear the orations of two young men who were to represent their respective societies... The orators today express the power of logic but ignore beauty. The true elements of delivery are naturalness and earnestness, which were exemplified in their highest and most complete form by the old orators. The present habit of speech, reading, has destroyed these and left us the bare skeleton of speech without life. The two great needs to make an orator equal to the age are profound study and a revival of moral courage and genuine faith. The spirit of true oratory, Mr. White thinks, will yet be revived and shall be instrumental in demolishing the tyrants thrown in establishing universal freedom. This true spirit of oratory will be the means of bringing the southern people again into prominence, as in the days of Virginia's glory.[34]

A scholarly summary of the disputes about a "suitable" oratorical style was offered in the 1904 *Sewanee Review*, describing literary society oratory immediately before and after the Civil War, a merger of the new and old rhetoric. Even though the excerpt is a bit long, it layers an understanding of turn-of-the-century Southern rhetorical practice:

> At their best, these elements [gesture, feelings, voice] brought a charm of stately attitudinizing, graceful action, moving and winning appeal to the emotions, and range and power of vocal expression; at

---

[34] *Charlotte Observer*, February 23, 1886, page 4.

their worst, affected extravagance, brazen and clanging rhetoric, and the sound and fury that signifieth nothing. This baser expression of college oratory has, unfortunately I think, ruled in our conception of the general type of the older product of the college literary society, and made it a mockery and a byword. But it should be steadily kept in mind that the literary societies formally aim to develop the orator, and that the orator was the hero of the campus in the unfeeling wonder of admiring audiences.

… It should be remembered too, that in no other part of the world the speaker gets as many glittering rewards, and no people were more sensitive to the charms of voice, emotional appeal, and graceful action than in the people of the South. Every State, every district, every community, every crossroad had more than one man whom the people heard with your gladness, and upon whom they were willing to confer honors and offices of trust for his speaking… and furnished ideals potent enough to make the college literary societies seem the most practical part of the college course. Hence it flourished as a training ground of the rhetorical, declamatory debater and speaker, and he became in general estimate the consummate flower of college life…[35]

Rarely did an evening debate draw attention beyond the campus confines. However, buried in the Richmond Dispatch in 1889, a quip offered a swipe at another college's integrity: "At Wake Forest College last night, in the literary debate of the societies, the side which championed 'civil service' won. The other side would have won if one of its champions had not charged that one of the civil-service men had boasted that his speech was not original."[36]

PRAISE AND CRITICISM OF ORATORY

The campus perspective held Wake Forest as a centerpiece for training orators, an unforgiving declaration luminous with pride. An alum, J. B Powers, wrote in 1893, "Truly, they [The Societies] are the speaker factories; and with their aid, Wake Forest College can take any young man

---

[35] Snyder, H. N. (1904). The College Literary Society, *The Sewanee Review*, Vol. 12, January 1904, page 78.

[36] *Richmond Dispatch*, February 13, 1889, page 22.

who is made of the right material and develop them into a thinker and an orator. Such a man can push his own way to recognition without the intrigues of demagogues to help him into position."[37]

The 1884 *Wake Forest Student* reinforced the positive: "*It is in the societies that oratory is cultivated.* "Here, 'steel meets steel,' mind is brought into contact with the mind, and the most powerful efforts of each are thus called forth. The rules of logic and rhetoric learned in the too often dry text books are put into practice in the literary societies... In the department of oratorical training, the literary societies are simply of inestimable value."[38]

1907 **Newbie** (*Howler*)

A March 1893 *Wake Forest Student* summed up an elemental educational mission of the College, an oratorical "from 'rags-to-riches' conversion, from back-woods to accomplished speakers and leaders, achieved through rigorous Society training. The 'plainly clad young men, fresh from the farms of North Carolina' are reborn in the literary halls. Initially awkward, making mistakes in grammar and pronunciation following debates, their critics dealt mercilessly with them."[39]

The Societies were steeped in the practicality of their training. Occasionally, they took up debate topics, celebrating and interrogating the tradition. On the 14th of June, 1872, the Phis considered, *Is oratory an art?* They adjourned the meeting without deciding the

---

[37] J. B. Powers, M. D. (Alum), *The Wake Forest Student*, 1893, Vol. 12, page 496.

[38] A. M. R. (1884). The year 1892, *The Wake Forest Student*, February, Vol. 3, page 50-51; *The Farmer and Mechanic*, also in praise of public speaking training, added: The public has a right to expect men holding "sheep-skins" that they be able to tell what they know, and yet how many scholars mumble and fall down if they attempt to preside even a ward primary or church meeting... Every man, at one time or another, feels the need of being able to give expression to his opinions in conversation or conference, and yet many of the wisest among us have neglected to cultivate the talent – and their State and communities have lost leadership that would have been a power for good. *The Farmer and Mechanic*, February 16, 1904, page 4.

[39] *The Wake Forest Student*, Vol. 12, March 1893, page 497; Thirty years later, the member remained committed to training public speakers.

question. At the next meeting, they voted "oratory is an art," Affirmative 14, Negative 10. Thirty years later, in the cold of February 1900, they contested a question examining their purpose. The affirmative prevailed 12 to 8 on the topic: *Oratory is on the decline.* The Euzelians did not debate a topic that directly considered oratory's role.

The refrains celebrating Wake Forest's oratorical distinctiveness continued until the next century, even as hints of fading glories accompanied the praise. Gradually, the overall critique reflected more a disappointment than a passion for former eras since drained from the once glittering halls. *The Wake Forest Student* offered:

1907 **Senior** (*Howler*)

> A single visit to either society hall would reveal... there seems to be very little interest taken in the debates by those who participate in them. Often men simply stand on their feet and say words long enough to keep from being fined. Others, more gifted, depend on the inspiration of the moment to give them something to say and make very little preparation. Sometimes, not one man in five who is on duty will be present; in all told, there was not a quorum at the meeting. Those who are present seem to have little interest in the proceedings of the meeting... The program is hurriedly gone through before 9 o'clock.[40]

Rufus Weaver wrote an article about an alumnus of Wake Forest inquiring about the societies' activities, specifically debate. It is noted that the debates have devolved into speeches that "were carefully written, memorized and then declaimed...Once the liveliest and sharpest intellectual combat upon the college arena, the debate has diminished into puerile declamation full of sophomoric eloquence."[41] *The Wake Forest Student* elaborated on the home front's debating practices:

---

[40] *The Wake Forest Student*, May 1909, Vol. 28, page 799-800.

[41] *The Wake Forest Student,* Vol. 12, March 1893, page 213.

Whether we wish to admit it or not, the Philomathesian and Euzelian Literary Societies of Wake Forest, long the heart of college
work and the rallying points of all loyal alumni, are now noticeably
failing to maintain the standard of speaking set in former years,
when debates would continue to midnight or until some professor
was dragged into the hall to decide a question too closely contested
for the student judges.

Oratory is gone. What we hear bears more resemblance to the monotonous rasping of grasshoppers or the tuneless chirp of crickets.
Debating has degenerated into a bombastic battle between speakers
whose supply of ammunition has not been augmented by a careful
study of the question under fire.[42]

Criticism of the in-hall debating that questions the educational product
of the societies or, more pointedly, "what it means to debate," does not
end or begin at the turn of the century. The societies were undergoing a
makeover, a part of an ongoing cultural dialogue.

In the Year of Founding

It is tempting to envision Wake Forest's formation as isolated in geography
and beholden to an insular circle of Baptist identity. This description would
not be wholly inaccurate,[43] yet this did not mean the Wake founders were
apart from the world. They were manifestly touched by what surrounded
them. These pioneers played key leadership roles at the college and across
the State and region.

When Charles E. Taylor, one of Wake Forest's most impactful presidents, was called upon to address the Seventy-Fifth Anniversary of the

---

[42] Editor's Portfolio, *The Wake Forest Student*, November 1917, page 122-3.

[43] The countryside surrounding the nascent campus was inhabited by yeomen farmers
and their families, cultivating small farms with a tenacious self-sufficiency. NCPedia,
Close to the land: North Carolina in the Victorian Era, 1820-1870, https://www.
ncpedia.org/waywelived/victorian-era-north-carolina-1820-1870; Even after the Civil
War, there was relatively isolation. In 1865, "on the east side of the railroad tracks,
there was only pine forests and some farms. And it was a long and dusty or muddy
mile south to board the trains or get the mail." *The Wake Forest Gazette*, Just a little
History: How Wake Forest went from corn to town, https://wakeforestgazette.com/
just-a-little-history-how-wake-forest-went-from-corn-to-town.

Founding of Wake Forest College, he took up the topic *The Times and The Men*. He instructed:

> We can now travel safely and in comfort from New York City to Florida in a single day. But in the early 30s of the last century, a man starting on such a journey would make his will and leave his household weeping as he departed.
>
> To form an adequate estimate of the courage and faith prudence and sacrifices of the men who founded our College, we must, if possible, have a clear vision of the setting of the Stage upon which seventy-five years ago, the curtain rose.[44]

Taylor marveled at the decade in which the College was founded, appointed with "numerous discoveries and inventions,"[45] and the first "flowering of the best in Victorian literature."[46]

---

[44] Charles E. Taylor, The Time and the Men, *The Biblical Recorder*, May 26, 1909, page 4.

[45] Taylor cites, among others, "…that Faraday made the experiments whose success rendered possible the subjugation of electricity for light, heat, and motive power, and that Liebig discovered chloroform. In 1932, Morse proved that electric telegraphy was possible. Cyrus McCormick, in 1834, was perfecting in Rockbridge County, Virginia, the reaper, which was to revolutionize agriculture and multiply loaves to hungry millions. In 1836 Colt invented his revolver and Ericsson first applied the screw to navigation. Iron was first galvanized in 1837 by Crawford, and rubber first vulcanized in 1839 by Goodyear. In the same year, Daguerre made the first photograph. In eighteen forty, Grove showed the gleams of the first incandescent electric light and water for the first time gushed from an Artisan well."

[46] In literature, he offered that the contemporaries with the College's founding "were the foremost in English literature during the last half of the nineteenth century; there would spring to your lips the names of Thackeray, Tennyson, the Brownings, Dickens, Carlyle, George Eliot, and Ruskin."; During these same years, Taylor reminded his audience that "Charles Darwin, Alfred Russell Wallace, Thomas H. Huxley, and Herbert Spencer were in patient silence doing the work which was to revolutionize the thought of the world as radically as did the Copernican hypothesis." Charles E. Taylor, The Time and the Men, *The Biblical Recorder*, May 26,

Andrew Jackson was entering his second term as president. Taylor denounced, in a less-than-sympathetic hue, Jackson's reign that overlapped the Institute years: "This man of iron will, unassailable integrity and vigorous, though unpolished intellect, had, less than two years before, brought to naught the Nullification Act of South Carolina. And the stormy waves stirred by the clash between the Palmetto State and the hero of New Orleans were still rolling angrily throughout the land."

President Taylor's history recounted Jackson ushering Wake into the "Panic Sessions" of Congress, where "the three great statesmen, Webster, with the majestic presence of an Olympian divinity, Calhoun, master of all the enginery of logic, and Clay, charged with magnetic power to influence men were united in policy and action. But in vain, they sought to batter down the inflexible purpose of the President." He describes an economy shattered by Jackson's carving out the National Bank.[47]

The realities bordering the newborn Institute were a composite of the early days. Some may quibble with Taylor's historical constructions but not with his essential conclusion that Wake's survival was a miracle. Of the hundreds of institutes established in this period, a mere handful survived. Taylor noted that in the year of Wake's founding, 1834, its ecology was awash in strife and uncertainties:

- General Scott was repressing a movement of hostile Indians at Chicago, a small village on the shore of Lake Michigan.

- Among the fifteen thousand Baptists of this State, including the Anti-Missionary and Free-Will membership, the period was one of strife and schism.

- Dissatisfaction between Western and East North Carolina had reached its culmination, and the Legislature called together the notable Convention of 1835, which radically changed the Constitution of the State.

1909, page 4. Charles E. Taylor, The Time and the Men, *The Biblical Recorder*, May 26, 1909, page 4.

[47] "Wheat, always a reliable barometer, fell from one dollar to sixty-two cents a bushel. Private capital, ever sensitive, speedily retired from circulation. Loans commanded 30 percent of Interest. Manufactories were closed, and thousands of operatives were deprived of employment."

- It was in this year, 1834, that under the leadership of Clay and Webster, the Whig party was formed.

- The educational condition of the State in 1834 may be inferred from the fact that sixteen years later, when the public schools had been in operation for ten years, one white person in every seven, over twenty-one years of age, could neither read nor write.

- There were barely 380 miles of railway in the whole country. In North Carolina, there were none. In addition, public highways were in some seasons almost impassable.

- In North Carolina, David L. Swain was the chief magistrate of the 738,000 people who at that time lived in the State. Of these, 472,000 were white.[48]

The scene was set, beginning a tradition that would flourish beyond the imagination of the young students or their founding elders.

THE BOOK'S PLAN

Historical eras are not tidy events; their beginnings and endings blend and often cross many decades. An author must make choices when presenting history and finding sensible anthologies. This volume chronicles nearly one hundred years of Wake Forest history, divided into fifteen chapters that reflect the times and trends. Necessarily, chapters at times overlap and, on occasion, may appear redundant. In those instances, the over-coverage is intentional, chosen to maintain the integrity of each segment.

Collectively, the chapters narrate the history of Wake's Debate Literary Societies from 1835 to around 1930.

The initial Chapters (1 through 4) trace Wake's societies' founding, purpose, student lives, and debating practices. The societies' prolonged responsibilities for publications and maintenance provide insight into the debaters' daily lives.

Until the turn of the century, debating was relegated to society hall exercises, a few joint appearances on campus, and public events. The encompassing Intercollegiate Era began with Trinity's stirring and curious

---

[48] Charles E. Taylor, The Time and the Men, *The Biblical Recorder*, May 26, 1909, page 4. The year 1835 also marked the birth of Samuel Clemens (Mark Twain) in Florida, Missouri.

initial debate series in 1897 (Chapter 5). It continued when scores of campus debates were held or attended across the country into the late 1930s (Chapter 6).

Commencement offered the principal public oratory outlet from the earliest times, Chapter 7. In 1879, the meeting debates entered the public eye with the Anniversary Day Debates and later by the Society Day Debates (Chapters 8 and 9).

Chapter 10 outlines the transportation story that enables the first meaningful break from solely on-campus debates.

Chapters 11 and 12 survey the influential cultural backdrop that crossed every debating epoch: the question of race, which was visibly exacerbated following the Civil War and persisted decades into the 20th century.

By the end of the 1920s, tournament debate began to complement and eventually displace the Intercollegiate era. Chapter 13 documents the inception of coaching and tournaments; Chapter 14 confirms the tournament hosting on campus; and Chapter 15 documents the motivations and conflicts that paved the way from a Literary society-centered world to the contemporary interscholastic debate framework.

The hope is that the reader may find intriguing surprises in every chapter—a configuration of lost "famous" alumni, murderous intrigue, romance and longing, and odds and ends of absorbing details. It is hoped that this exploration is accomplished with the requisite historical integrity.

CHAPTER 1

Literary Societies – Wake Forest's Fortitude

Founding the Wake Literary Societies

Literary societies were the heart of campus life for nearly a century. Wake Forest's debate narrative inescapably infiltrates the College's history in countless ways.

The height of the Societies' activity and financial influence was the early 1900s. As the student newspaper, the *Old Gold and Black*, noted in 1922, the Societies were the "standing sponsor of the *The Student*, *Howler*, Declamation Contest, Intercollegiate Debates, Society Day and Anniversary Day."[1]

Suffice it to say, the Euzelian and Philomathesian Literary Societies ... had an imposing place in college life. Yet, the vast majority of their span occurred before the 1922 watershed year.

This chapter offers an imperfect tour of an origin story for Wake's Literary Societies, as historical records offer differing details. Simply, the purpose of this chapter is not to engage those discrepancies but to give a broader sense of how the Societies originated and offer a glimpse into the lives of the pioneer Wake debaters.

---

[1] *Old Gold and Black*, February 17, 1922, page 1; Scholar David Williams observed that Societies "were significant enough in the campus communities to constitute a real force. Students were caught up in the activities of these organizations to the extent that the faculty sometimes complained that the duties of college work were of little importance in comparison with participation in the societies."

TABLE 1: Literary Societies' Founding at Institutions
with which Wake held Intercollegiate Debates[2]

William and Mary	1750

Followed shortly by Yale 1753, Princeton 1769, Dartmouth,
and Columbia 1802[3] (Harvard's Spy Club forms in 1721)

University of North Carolina	1795
Randolph Macon	1834
Wake Forest	1835
Trinity (Duke)	1824, 1827
Virginia	1825
College of Charleston	1828, 1831, 1833
Davidson	1837
Emory	1837
Richmond	1855
Furman	1860
Baylor	1865
Mercer	1897

---

[2] Comprehensive list of Literary Societies' founding. https://en.wikipedia.org/wiki/List_of_literary_societies. By the nineteenth century and certainly by the founding of Wake Forest College, societies had strong foundations at prominent colleges throughout the United States. Potter, D. (1944). *Debating in the Colonial Chartered Colleges; An Historical Survey, 1642 to 1900,* Bureau of Publications, Teachers College, Columbia, page 239. Some argue that the first collegiate literary and debate society appears to have been the Spy Club of Harvard in 1722, yet earlier instances are also suggested. UNC started very early in 1795 with the Debating Society, parent of the Dialectic and Concord Societies, featuring debating, exposition, reading, speaking, and parliamentary procedure. Porter, D. (1954), The Literary Societies, *A History of Speech Education in America.* Karl Wallace, Editor 1954, page 242.

[3] Columbia – Philolexian 1802, Peithologian 1806; Dartmouth – United Fraternity 1786, Society of Social Friends 1783; Princeton, American Whig 1769, Cliosophic 1770; Yale – Linonian 1753, Society of Brothers of Unity (1766), Calliopoean 1819. Simpson, L. (Summer, 1977), The Development and Scope of Undergraduate Literary Society Libraries at Columbia, Dartmouth, Princeton, and Yale, 1783-1830, *Journal of Library History (1974-1987), 12,* page 219.

The Biblical Recorder nurtured the Institute from its influential pages in the founding days. It wrote in 1908:

> The first steps toward the founding of Wake Forest College by the North Carolina Baptist State Convention were taken in 1832. The Board of Trustees was appointed in 1833. The school was opened as Wake Forest Institute in the farm carriage house in February 1834 with sixteen students and one teacher. By Charter, in 1834, the Legislature approved the Institute. The first class graduated in June 1839 and numbered four men. From these small beginnings, often against heavy odds.[4]

The Baptist Church was fragile at the founding of Wake Forest. Maybe 30,000 Baptists populated the entire state. *The Biblical Recorder* was finding sea legs of just having published two years.

Who other than G. W. Paschal has the authority to tell the Literary Societies' advent story? His story begins in the very first session when the students organized a debating society, which they call "The Polemic Society."[5] While few improved upon Paschal's history, many borrowed liberally.

Earlier accounts, however, preceded his tome. *The Biblical Recorder*, for instance, in 1884, presented a period account of a founding day celebration. "By 11 o'clock a.m., quite a respectable audience had assembled in the chapel... The congregation united heartily in singing, "Praise God, from whom all blessings flow."

---

[4] *The Biblical Recorder*, September 2, 1908, page 1; Samuel Wait described the school's Baptist origins in an essay on the History of Wake Forest, which he penned: "Only a year or two before the Baptist State Convention was formed, another attempt was made to provide more effectually for the spread of the Gospel, particularly in North Carolina. This was a very timid beginning. It was called, I think, a "Benevolent Society." It was, probably, at the second anniversary held in Greenville, Pitt County, N. C., In March (or April), 1830, the Baptist State Convention of North Carolina was organized. By previous appointment, I preached the introductory sermon.... Never in my life have I seen manifested a better spirit than was exhibited on that occasion." Samuel Wait, The Origin and Early History of Wake Forest College. *The Wake Forest Student*, September 1982, page 12.

[5] Paschal, G. W. (1935). *History of Wake Forest College*, Vol. I, page 147. The Eus debated the exact topic once in their history, while the Phis tackled the "thorny issue" twenty-two times. Both Societies showed a fondness for numerous topics, for example, beginning in the mid-1870s, continually pitting the generalship of Washington versus Robert E. Lee.

J. S. Purefoy – 1870s
Treasurer of the board of trustees.

The Rev. J. S. Purefoy was introduced, speaking to the subject, "The College, its Birth." He said, "three good and true men from the north, namely: Samuel Wait, John Armstrong and Thomas Meredith... laid the foundation upon which the Baptist State Convention and Wake Forest College now stand.[6]

At the school's inception, Dr. Wm. Hooper, chairman of the Baptist committee on education, recommended the purchase of land to establish a manual labor school:

Unanimously the Convention deem it expedient to purchase a suitable farm and to adopt other preliminary measures for the establishment of a Baptist literary institution in the state on the manual labor principle.

---

[6] Semi-Centennial of Wake Forest College, *The Biblical Recorder*, February 12, 1884, page 2.

Rev. Samuel Wait was the first Principal of the Institute and held the position honorably for eleven years before resigning. At the meeting of the Convention at Union Camp Ground in November 1835, the convention passed that the "Baptist State Convention transfer all their rights and titles to the lands of Wake Forest Institute to the Trustees of said Wake Forest Institute. This was done and the deed was made to the trustees of Wake Forest Institute."[7]

Hooper introduces more of the creation story—Legislative authorization—via an extended metaphor of birth and raising a child:

It was during this session of 1833 and in 1834 that we obtained from the Legislature of our State a charter for our school. The Majority of the Commons on the final passage of the bill was quite respectable, but in the Senate there was a tie and Mr. Wm. D. Mosley, in his lasting honor... gave the casting vote in our favor... I must say, without the Hon. Wm. D. Mosley, our newborn child would surely have been crushed to death.

The trustees who became the foster mother of the baby came here, destroying its precious life by administering an overdose of paregoric. Although composed of the very best persons of our denomination, they were not used to nursing infant institutions. They put board at:

$5 dollars per month, 10 months	$50
Latin and Greek tuition $2 per month, 10 months	20.00
English branches $1.50 per month, 10 months	15.00
Washing 75c per month, 10 months,	7.50
Total	92.50

Labor of students, three hours a day, 3c an hour, 250 days at 9 cents, $22.50, which left only $70 for all expenses of a student for a year... Crops failed expenses were heavy and the income not much more than half meeting the expenses, the babe was found to be in a still state.

Strong stimulants and cataplasms had to be employed. Yes, the manual labor system had to be abolished. The horses, mules, cows,

---

[7] Semi-Centennial of Wake Forest College, *The Biblical Recorder*, February 13, 1884, page 2.

farming utensils, etc., had to be sold out at auction. Board and tuition had to be raised to living rates. In 1838 a new chapter was obtained, and the school arose up out of his long slumber, to find that its name had been changed from Wake Forest Institute to that of Wake Forest College in 1838.[8]

As the focus is the student's founding experience, personal remembrances, and testimonials are offered. Of course, the leadership interacted intimately with the students, helping define the enterprise. The College's First Lady intercessions directly stamped the Societies' beginning. Evident religiosity was the cultural standard, especially in institutions such as Wake Forest. Letters from the societies and Sarah, Samuel Wait's wife, sketched the morality underwriting the Literary Societies.

An August 1835 letter from the Philomathesians to Sarah Wait assured her that their societies were "founded upon the broad principles of Christian morality." They then promised to "employ our best efforts to cultivate all the principles which may secure honorable distinction and to do good and communicate [which] is the noble duty of man"[9]... Sarah Wait wrote that her gift of three pieces of satin white ribbon was "a small token of regard for your association and proof of my sincere desire that its members may attain the highest degree of moral excellence and mental cultivation."[10]

In 1836, April, the Philomathesian minutes reflect the discussion leading to establishing the societies homes:

The officers of the Philomathesian and Euzelian societies met at Prof. Armstrong's room for the purpose of adopting some measure, by which the Society rooms in the College building might be chosen with equal satisfaction to both societies. After consulting on the subject it was unanimously agreed, that East, and West rooms should be written in two separate sheets of paper of the same size, and

---

[8] Semi-Centennial of Wake Forest College, *The Biblical Recorder,* February 13, 1884, page 2.

[9] Williams, T. J (2002). *Literary Societies at Wake Forest College,* Honors Thesis History, Wake Forest, 2002, page 10; Wait Papers, Folder 2/214.

[10] *A Book of Correspondence of the Philomathesian Society,* Literary Societies, WFRG 6.2. All correspondence to the Philomathesians was rewritten into a record book and preserved in the university archives. There are no records of the original letters.

quality, and that these seats be sealed, and delivered to Mrs. Ann Eliza Wait (Pres. Samuel Wait's daughter), and that she be requested to present the one to the Euzelian Society, and the other to the Philomathesian Society. After tea, the societies formed a procession separately, and marched in front of the house of the President Wait, where the letters were to be received. They were presented. The Philomathesian Society received the sheet with the East room, and the Euzelian the West room.

Sarah and Samuel Wait

Academic G. R. Lyle penned in 1935 an insightful sketch of literary societies in the 1850s, describing their shared cultures, aristocratic quality, and genuine comradery:

Strangely enough, there were many things to dampen the enthusiasm of the most ardent members. Their activities were restricted by a crabbed asceticism; they were blighted by the deadliest gentility; dramatic production was regarded as an "unwholesome weed that deserved no tending"; and the expense of furnishing society halls, collecting libraries, and arranging the programs was considerable.

And yet, curiously enough, the students often did things in good taste, with vigor, originality, and humor...These youngsters could have done worse things with their time. [11]

David Porter's historical recounting suggests, "The company of his fellow scholars was practically the only legitimate avenue of escape from the academic routine... It is to be expected, therefore, that societies featuring jovial companionship as well as student-directed opportunities for parliamentary practice, oratory, declamation, debate, literary efforts, dramatic 'productions,' and reading material all relatively free from faculty censorship and, usually, protected from 'prying eyes by high walls of secrecy.'"[12]

Throughout the history of Wake's Societies, the minutes had an ordered rhythm, in part dictated by constitutional requirements, prescribing the conduct and order of business at meetings. Typically, meetings were convened twice a week. The first conducted the society's business, offering honorary membership invitations, inviting commencement and Anniversary speakers, conducting elections, inducting new members, offering and debating resolutions, receiving committee reports, selecting event managers and top honorees, and assigning fines. Assignments for upcoming debates, orations, and declamations were also parceled among the members. The second and usually more raucous meeting would unbridle the speakers often resulting in turbulent debate.[13]

---

[11] Lyle, G. R. (1934). College Literary Societies in the fifties, *The Library Quarterly: Information, Community, Policy*, Vol. 4, page 492-493; David Porter's account of early Literary Chapters captures their appeal to students yearning for some independence: "When judged by modern standards, however, the colonial student, despite his closely supervised schedule, did not lead a particularly strenuous life. But unless he strolled within the bounds or indulged in the mild forms of exercise not on the banned list, he had few approved methods of consuming his surplus energy. The company of young ladies was usually forbidden during college sessions. Organized athletics was unheard of. And even the privilege of reading contemporary periodicals, much less current fiction, was denied him because the ordinary college library contained few, if any, "authors who have a role within the last 30 years." Porter, D., (1954), The Literary Societies, *A History of Speech Education in America*. Karl Wallace, Editor, page 238.

[12] Porter, D, (1954), The Literary Societies, *A History of Speech Education in America*. Karl Wallace, Editor, page 238.

[13] Philomathesian and Euzelian Minutes, ZSR Library Archives, Wake Forest University.

The records were kept in good order since the first session. "Every committee reported, and the report was recorded. A vote of thanks was recorded for every person who showed them any favor. Between the two societies, there existed the most dignified, formal, and courteous relations. The records show that they continually thanked and counter-thanked each other."[14]

It is also true that despite the societies' collaboration and "mutual thanking," from the outset in 1835, jealousies were manifest. In the second semester of existence, disagreements focused on membership disputes. By semester's end, the Phis appointed a committee "to hold a private conversation with two of our members who had left our body in order to be united to the Euzelian Society."[15] The poaching of the other societies' members was at least officially settled after some hurt feelings.

Even as the Literary Societies had to engage in many cooperative dealings (e.g., Commencement, Fourth of July), often obliquely, the minutes reflected ample competition. For example, the Phi minutes of May 23, 1839, "reported that we have endeavored to discharge the important duties devolving upon us to the extent our very humble [request]; but can only say that the comt. of the E. Society has refused to confer with us for reasons known only to themselves, and consequently, our time of session will be the same."[16] There was forever a bitter fight for new members and competing stratagems to attract them.

Even *The Biblical Recorder,* in the Societies' first semester, 1835, recognized the rising rivalry:

A very unhappy state of things existed among the students during the latter part of the last term. The two societies absorbed all feelings and all interests. Jealousies arose, and then antipathies and hostilities were carried so far that violent prejudices divided brethren of the same profession. This state of things became quite alarming, and

---

[14] Dr. E. W. Sikes, an undated entry in *Wake Forest Bulletin* as reprinted in the *Howler,* 1909, page 114.

[15] Philomathesian Minutes, May 3, 1835. In the next meeting, May 10, the minutes reflect that the "committee appointed for the purpose of having an interview with those going gentleman who withdrew from the Phis for the purpose of uniting themselves with the Euzelian Society, gave quite a favorable account of one of the delinquents."

[16] Philomathesian Minutes, May 23, 1839.

the question frequently occurred, *Tantaene animis caelestibus irae?*"
(Are there such angers for the heavenly minds?)[17]

An armistice came about through shared obligation in the aftermath
of the great religious revival of 1835. Still, throughout the remainder
of the nineteenth century, the halls of the two societies resembled two
armed camps.

At the first celebration of Anniversary Day in 1854, as there were
only orations, the societies were pitted against each other, and hostilities
came out into the open. When the public debate was added in 1872,
precaution was taken to arrange the speakers so that a member of one
society might have as his colleague a member of the other. "Under any
other arrangement, there would have been danger of a much more serious
battle than one of words."[18]

The Institute Years

Wake Forest's Institute years, pursuing the short-lived Manual Labor
model were structured so that students earned a portion of their expenses
doing the physical tasks of farming. As A. G. Headen 1909, an alumnus
of those years remembered:

> Students, as a rule, were not admitted under 12 years of age, but
> I was so near 12, I was allowed to enter, consequently one of the
> youngest pupils. At the time Wake Forest was a Manual Labor
> School, it was pretty hard to go out to work in hot afternoons,
> therefore we had a great deal of afternoon sickness. I remember so
> well being called before the president for failure to attend to some

---

[17] As quoted in the 1926 *Howler* (page 170.) Original from *The Biblical Recorder*,
September 16, 1835.

[18] *Howler*, 1926, page 170; Older and wiser members tried to admonish the Newbies
toward less competitive behavior. Phi elder W. Solomon "addressed a few very appropriate remarks to the younger members of the society, reminding them that their
duty was as members of this body, and suggesting to them the deportment that should
be observed toward the members of the Euzelian Society." While the minutes do
not indicate that intersociety rivalries resulted in inappropriate taunting or uncivil
conduct, it seemed, on occasion, the elders wanted to rein in youngsters' enthusiasm.
Philomathesian Minutes October 11, 1845.

agricultural duty; my excuse was that I was sick; he inquired if I ate my dinner, and I had to say, 'Yes, sir,' for I had eaten, and while I was not feeling well, my sickness was not serious enough to prevent me from joining in something more pleasant than work. After that, when I wished to be excused, I did not eat dinner.[19]

We turn to another remembrance of the Institute years, offered by an alumnus, fifty years after attending. William Bond's 1835 recollection bares often staggering disclosures. Without malice and with much love for Wake, he writes what, to modern readers, might appear as an exposé:

In due time we reached our journey's end and presented ourselves before the faculty—President Wait and Prof Armstrong... After some examination to indicate the classes to which we should be attached, we were duly enrolled as students and assigned to the occupancy of a large room in one of the shanties erected in Oak Grove, about two hundred yards from the site of the College buildings afterward constructed. The said shanty was not ceiled or plastered—it was very open and airy. If my memory serves me right, it was not completed as a winter residence, though it was better than some of the others, which were merely log huts.

> ## Wake Forest Institute.
>
> AT the meeting of the Trustees of the Wake Forest Institute, it was Resolved that the laws, stipulating the amount of students' pocket money and the trading in stores, be repealed, it was furthermore Resolved, that the amounts due each student for labor, be hereafter paid them at the expiration of each and every month.

President Wait impressed my youthful mind very favorably. He was tall and dignified, invariably wore spectacles, but always looked *over* instead of through them. Though his demeanor was kind and fatherly, there was something in his manner which showed that he would stand no *foolishness* as to work or lessons. Prof. Armstrong was fat, corpulent and bold—the very picture of good humor—and

---

[19] A. G. Headen, Early Days at Wake Forest. *The Wake Forest Student*, 1901, page 86.

seemed to take quite a fancy to me, which doubtless was owing to the fact that I was the youngest of all the students there.

During my first session, I was a classmate of President Wait's daughter, and really think I should have fallen in love with her but for my fear of the old gentleman. She was a pretty girl, full of fun, and so smart in getting her lessons as to be an overmatch for most of the class. I remember her mother as one of the kindest ladies I ever met.

An idyllic sketch of Wake Forest, the first known, around 1850, the only building for 40 years takes center stage village.

I was so young and small that, at my first public examination, I had to stand in a chair to reach the blackboard and work out my sums. Most of my roommates had mastered the difficult science of pipe-smoking. I am determined to add that to my accomplishments. So, one night I borrowed a pipe, took a good hearty smoke, and soon was the sickest boy in the world—thought I was going to die—I can truly say it was the only time in my life I have ever wanted to die.

A short distance from our residence, in a quiet nook, near a ravine and pond, was a considerable patch of bushes and sprouts, made famous as 'Pleasant Grove.' Being the delightful locality to which Pres. Wait escorted all culprits whose ways could not be amended by moral suasion, for the more cogent discipline of corporal castigation. It was near enough for the shrieks and screams of the sufferers to have a salutary effect in curbing our natural propensity for wrong-doing.

The manual labor part of the exercises occurred in the afternoon, from two to five o'clock. I have no doubt that farm labor in the hot sun, at three or four cents per hour, was very helpful, but certainly not very conducive to the mastery of long lessons at night. On many occasions whilst studying, my head would drop on the table before me, hoping to catch a few moments rest, and I would fall asleep.

WM. E. Bond, Edenton N.C Feb. 4th, 1887[20]

A number of observers found ample reason to trumpet the virtues of the young students' labor (a sentiment unlikely shared among the work crews). For example, the Rev. T. Meredith's 1837 address before the Literary Societies declared the virtues of the young student's "passion for working the Institute's fields." "[T]he very hardships which are experienced in our manual labor schools, are to be enumerated among their greatest advantages... Is there to be found in all the gentle amusements to be witnessed on college greens, an academic growth, which can compare with the manly refreshing, renovating exercise to be found in these fields?"[21]

Life at the Institute was settling in by 1836 when the *Weekly Raleigh Register* acknowledged the reception of the campus catalog. It indicated one hundred twenty students, the newspaper certifying the Institute was in "flourishing condition."

The experiment of the manual labor system for North Carolina has been fairly tried, and the Trustees are satisfied that it is not only

---

[20] *The Biblical Recorder*, February 16, 1887, Vol. 52, No 34, page 1; Bond's "not ceiled shanty" was described on the 75th anniversary as the following: "The Institute slave huts were used instead of dormitories and an old carriage house served as a lecture room." *The Charlotte Observer*, February 12, 1909, page 4.

[21] *The Weekly Standard*, April 26, 1837, page 2.

feasible, but that the happiest results may be anticipated. There is not a solitary student on the sick list, which proves that by the training to habits of industry and physical labor, health of body and vigor of mind are cultivated together.

The system of government is paternal. The... instructors and students partake of their food from the same table. An education is furnished to the youth of the Institute for precisely what it costs the Trustees to furnish instructors, board &c. which is $100 per annum, subject to the reduction of the student's labor.[22]

The manual labor system that asked students to bring to campus "an Axe and Hoe" was to be short-lived.[23]

G. W. Paschal suggested that before the Civil War, "the students had little time or opportunity for social life except among themselves. Their only vacant period in the week was Saturday afternoon, five full days being given to recitation and study, and Friday night and Saturday forenoon to the work of the Literary Societies. In the College sessions, there were no holidays."[24]

An account of campus life four decades later was extended by long-term Law School Dean, Needham Gulley, then, in 1875, a freshman. Late in his long career, he gave a 1941 Chapel address poetically entitled *Leaves in The Unwritten Book of The History of This Locality*. Gulley shared:

He left Clayton, NC as the only passenger to Raleigh. The train arrived near campus the next day, he and five other 'newish' arrivals stepped off into the red mud, a result of the January thaw... On North Main Street, which is Faculty Avenue, there were a mass of weeds and a narrow wagon trail which led north.... There were only two houses on the right side of the street... On the left side were a few dilapidated cottages and the old Brewer home.

---

[22] *Weekly Raleigh Register* July 5, 1836, page 3.

[23] "Every student was to provide himself with an axe and a hoe, a pair of sheets and a pair of towels. Further he was to labor three hours a day under the direction of a scientific farmer, and be subject to the control of a principal teacher who was to be a minister of the Gospel." Paschal, G. W. (1935), *History of Wake Forest College*, Vol. I, page 70.

[24] Paschal, G. W. (1935). *History of Wake Forest College*, Vol. I, page 459.

On the other side of the railroad were the railroad warehouse and the Reid house. The only other building on that side of the road was the Adams store, where the former Law School Dean made his first purchase, and where he paid as high as $0.50 for a gallon of kerosene oil, which provided the only light of the night.

Particularly amazing is the fact that Dr. Gulley still remembers the names of most of the Negroes who lived in various dwellings scattered over the locality. He mentioned John Smith, the bellringer, and he knew the names of the janitors and others, whether or not they were connected with the college.

In 1857, when Kelly arrived, around the campus was a wooden fence built to keep out the livestock roaming around the vicinity. There was only one building located where Wait Hall is now. The wings of the structure were used for dormitories, while the center was utilized as a chapel.

Dr Wingate, who was president, taught English language and literature, history, ethics, logic, and other subjects. Professor Mills, mathematics, had six classes a day. Prof Taylor, teacher of Latin, had five recitations in each class.[25]

Another alumnus, J. B. Bagley, added to the pre-Civil War aura: "One summer there was a long tent built that could accommodate all at once. This was quite an addition to the comfort of things, and everyone was pleased with it until the hogs in the yard learned that when the bell rang something to eat was in the tent."[26]

On the 99th Anniversary of Wake Forest's founding, the invited address was presented by J. Melville Broughton, then an important Raleigh attorney and, subsequently, the 60th governor of North Carolina from 1941 to 1945[27]. In an address laden with commendations on Wake Forest's first 100 years and wishes for the next 100 years, Broughton interrelated the story of Wake Forest's political founding.

---

[25] *Old Gold and Black*, March 7, 1941, page 1, 4.

[26] Bagley, J. B. (1899). Early Days of Our Institution. *The Wake Forest Student*, 1899, page 635.

[27] Broughton also was elected to the US Senate in 1949 but passed away two months into office. Broughton's contributions are discussed in depth, Chapter 14 – Tournament Hosting in the Pre-Shirley Era.

☞ We regret to state that Judge GASTON, owing to his unexpected delay at the North, and the present pressure of business, finds himself unable to deliver the address before the two Societies at Wake Forest Institute on the 25th inst.

WM. T. BROOKS, Sec.
of the Euzelian Society.

The Raleigh's *News & Observer* recorded that Broughton reminded the audience of " a dramatic scene in the North Carolina General Assembly on December 21, 1833, when Wake Forest obtained its charter from a hostile legislature. William Moseley, Speaker of the Senate and University graduate, broke a tie vote in casting the deciding ballot in favor of a charter for 'Wake Forest Institute.' "In this connection," he said, "it is noteworthy to observe that five years later, when an application was made to the assembly to amend the charter, changing the name to 'Wake Forest College and enlarging its powers, no opposition was encountered.

Yet, a *News & Observer's* précis captures the modesty of the founding intentions, "The founders never aspired to build an institution with great dimensions; they dreamed of and planned a small College of superlative quality, where young men could receive training for leadership under Christian auspices."[28]

The 4th of July Celebration

In the early years, during the Institute period, the societies' big event was the July celebration. The minutes reflect their cooperation in planning and hosting the event. They shared expenses on supplies (18 bottles of lemon syrup, nine dollars), printing tickets, and music (which cost two dollars).[29]

---

[28] *The News & Observer*, February 1, 1933, page 7.

[29] Philomathesian Minutes July 13, 1835; In November 1835, they "Resolved as it is necessary that an address be delivered before the two Societies, at the laying of the cornerstone of the principal building of the Institute, the committee of three be appointed to confer with the Euzelian Society concerning which society shall appoint the orator." Philomathesian Minutes, November 21, 1835; Euzelian Minutes, July 15, 1868. In the very early days of the college, while diversions were few, events took

"A letter was received from the Euzelian Society conferring on the Philomathesian Society the honor of electing an orator for 4 July next, which favor was kindly received. They proceeded to an election of the orator for the Fourth of July which terminated by the choice of Mr. Dockery."[30]

An 1835 description of the 4th of July celebration, in the *Weekly Raleigh Register* gives insight into not only the patriotism of the day but also the manner in which students embraced the rare holiday on their calendar. One gets the sense that Mr. Armstrong, conceiver of the Societies, orchestrated the rituals that would prevail for nearly a century. The paper recorded:

> The sun not quite raised his brilliant above the horizon, the iron-tongue summoner tolled long, and loud for martins. In a few moments all the dormitories sent forth their occupants, and a living string was seen pouring into the temporary Chapel from all quarters. After Prayer, the beloved President, the Rev'd. Mr. Wait gave some wholesome advice to those under his fatherly protection and dismissed them with a blessing. All was now bustle and activity; students were seen walking forth in their holiday apparel, smiling faces, and decorated with the ribbon or badge of their respective Societies. Carriages with "nature's last best," Equestrians and Pedestrians in groups soon swelled into a little multitude; friends met friends, parents, their children, guardians of their wards...
>
> At about eleven o'clock, the Philomathesian Society... was drawn up in military array in front of the dwelling house and presented, a

---

place that became part of the campus mythology. During the Wake Forest Institute period, "the Eus and Phis witnessed an outdoor play, which dealt with the tribulations of a fair maiden captured by Indians and her rescue by George Washington. The Indians, we are informed, seem strangely civilized, for their password was, "Watchmen, what of the night?"

[30] After a winning speech, "A committee of arrangements was instructed by the society to solicit from Mr. Dockery the interesting and eloquent oration he delivered on 4 July, for publication. Resolved: That the committee be authorized to have 500 copies of it published in pamphlet form. This meeting resolved the use of subscriptions to pay for the pamphlet. A later meeting in October indicated the committee raised $16.50, which appeared sufficient. Evidently, it was not, and later in the same meeting, it was referred to as a small amount. The committee was appointed to raise more money as it had only raised $12. The fundraising proposition was carried forward. On November 21, the minutes recorded that they had secured enough funding to publish the pamphlet.

scene I shall not easily forget. At the word of command, every head was uncovered, for at that moment, Mrs. Wait, the lady of the President of the Institute, made her appearance on the balcony, attended by the President of the Society, and Mr. W. to present the banner. [31]

Mrs. Wait delivered the following remarks to the students convened below her portico. The day's pageantry is rendered in heroic display by the *Weekly Raleigh Register*. Mrs. Wait begins:

In committing to your protection, the banner of the Philomathesian Society, permit me to express my sincere desire that all the members of this Association, many of who have become highly distinguished in the Arts and Sciences, and Literature; and may you ever cultivate all the principles of the Gentlemen, the Scholar, and the Christian.... You are among the first Sons of the Wake Forest Institute. Its future character, in a great degree, rests solely with you. Act nobly; and become its pride and its glory.

Her speech concluded with 'every hat waving in the air.' Soon, the Phis retired, and the Eus formation gathered for their banner presentation. A parallel address was then presented, concluding go forth "to explore new fields of knowledge in the regions of unsullied felicity."

After blessing the banners, the two Societies formed into lines and marched to the Grove, 'music playing and silken standards floating gaily on the fitful breeze. The procession was closed by the Orator, Readers, Presidents, and Clergymen.' As soon as the procession reached the waiting crowd, the notables ascended the rostrum to take their seats, 'the two ranks faced each other,' The Philomathesian Society marched to the right, and the Euzelians to the left, thus enclosing the whole assembly with their ranks. The banners were again presented, the Declaration of Independence read, and the Oratory of the day engaged.

The Rev. Mr. Armstrong, one of the Professors requested the ladies to keep their seats until the students returned, to conduct them to the dining hall. The procession was again formed and returned to the house, in the order in which it came: The Societies returned and with the gallantry worthy of the most refined days of chivalry, march

---

[31] *Weekly Raleigh Register*, July 28, 1835, page 2.

and counter-marched on either side of the fair ones who were formed into a procession consisting of from one to two hundred, who may well lay claim to being called the *Flowers of the Forest!* On arriving at the entrance of the Hall, the banners were bent over and formed an arch, under which the ladies marched, in my opinion, in better order than the young aristocracy of creation. [32]

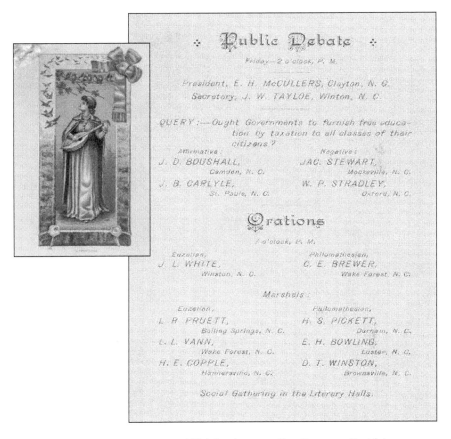

1886 Anniversary Day Program (inside)

Four years into the Institute's existence, the Fourth of July celebration commanded the state press. One paper uncritically wrote, "A desire to preserve harmony, to add to the general enjoyment, to discuss all exciting topics seemed to be the governing principle." They continued:

[32] *Weekly Raleigh Register*, July 28, 1835, page 2, 3.

The dinner was …handsomely gotten up, and very abundant, which is 'Saying a good deal when we state that it was partaken by nearly a hundred Ladies, and perhaps twice as many of the other sex.' Regular toasts were prepared and presented for the occasion. Toast three confirmed "The Heroes of the Revolution – May the flame that was kindled by their noble spirits diffused its light and warmth throughout the civilized world, and toast four confirmed The Union of the States, it must and shall be preserved, while toast ten noted education as 'One of the main pillars on which rests the stability of a free Government, it should be supported at public expense.'[33]

After 1837, the 4th of July celebration was discontinued as the school closed in June, a month before.[34] Yet a post-1837 newspaper offers full accounts of the 4th of July celebration, including 1839. In that year, in addition to reading the Declaration of Independence, a unique twist was a reading of the Mecklenburg Declaration of Independence.[35] Some North Carolina patriotism joined the public proclamations.[36]

Early Campus Life – Settling in

Academic life at the College was strenuous and closely overseen by demanding professors. Discipline was strict, and some offenses were handled

---

[33] *Weekly Raleigh Register*, July 9, 1838, page 1.

[34] Paschal, G. W. (1935). *History of Wake Forest College,* Vol. I, page 156.

[35] "The Mecklenburg Declaration of Independence is the name given to a document allegedly produced on May 20, 1775, when the residents of Mecklenburg County declared themselves "free and independent people." The declaration did not surface until 1819, 44 years after the event, when it was published in the *Raleigh Register* at the behest of U.S. senator Nathaniel Macon." A century of debate about its authenticity pitted regional pride against historians, driving the political mix. "The Mecklenburg Declaration …most certainly never existed. However, the Mecklenburg Resolves were a genuine and bold set of anti-British resolutions adopted by Mecklenburg County residents on May 31, 1775, a full year before the Declaration of Independence was penned in Philadelphia by the Continental Congress. The Mecklenburg Resolves denied the authority of Parliament over the colonies and set up basic tenets of governing." https://www.ncpedia.org/mecklenburg-declaration.

[36] General Daniel S. Crenshaw was the orator of the day. One paper described him as delivering "with great animation, and the orator completely threw himself into the subject." *The Weekly Standard*, July 24, 1929, page 3.

simply by expulsion. Morning prayers were held daily, and mandatory worship services took place each Sunday. From the outset, the primary recreational activities were centered in the Literary Societies, which dominated campus social life.[37]

Early on, the Societies' sway encompassed the ability to impose their will on the Board of Trustees. Of course, some of their ample influence was little more than the familiarity within the Wake Baptist community. David Hughes, a student historical chronicler, found:[38]

There was a time when the Philomathesian Society faced a problem … of getting new members. In 1854 the Eus gained 19 members at fall enrollment, while the Phi's got only one. In the following spring, the Eu's took 20 to the Phi's eight.

The Phi officers supposed that the cause of this was the greater number of Eu's on the faculty. Four professors belonged to the Euzelian Society; none were Phi's. To correct the situation the Society sent a resolution to the Board of Trustees in June 1856:

". . . Be it resolved by the Philomathesian Society, That... the Board of Trustees is hereby memorialized to correct as near as possible the evil now presented to their consideration by granting this Society an equal representation in the Society as soon as practical."

The resolution brought about the resignation from the faculty of one of the Eu professors. It still, however, left the Phis with only one representative. The Trustees corrected this with the replacement of the resigned Professor with one that belonged to the Philomathesian Society. This satisfied the Phi's, and the societies settled into their routine of weekly debates and speech contests.[39]

In 1844, the Phi Minutes revealed some outsized ambition. They appointed a committee to draft a memorandum for the Legislature, petitioning that body to incorporate their Society. Philomathesian Minutes, 1844.

---

[37] Wake Forest Historical Museum, Founding of Wake Forest, https://. Wakeforestmuseum.org/2013/07/17/Our History/. Society Members had Short Christmas Breaks. In 1870, the Phis had in-hall debates on December 23 and December 30th.

[38] Some would argue the relationships were almost "familial" among the educated Baptist fellowship.

[39] Phis Had Membership Problem in 1850s, Hughes, D., *Old Gold and Black*, October 24, 1955, page 2.

Prior to the Civil War, village life continued with predictability. The paucity of materials expressing the student voice in those thirty years is understandable. Immediately after the War, until the mid-to late-1880s, the community was mostly withdrawn and impoverished. In the early 1880s, however, a sense of the college again coming into its own began to suffuse the campus atmosphere. With hype and satisfaction, in 1887 *The Biblical Recorder* boasted:

Wake Forest on Thursday registered more students than on any opening day in all the years of its history… 'Better than before,' is saying of which the Baptists are fond… 'Old friends are best.' The saying contains the idea of progress and as applied to Wake Forest College, it represents a fact. On the first day of last September, 106 registered. Now there are present 155. The indications are flattering. The institution enrolled 201 students last year.[40]

The Biblical Recorder also involved itself in some "recruiting:"

It is in the interest of every Baptist boy, who can, to attend Wake Forest College. The statement needs no explanation to the observant. There he has the opportunity to contact and friendship with men who in the future are going to have right much to do and to say about North Carolina affairs… Especially is this true of a Baptist. In the expansion of our denominational work, much reliance is placed upon the intellectual laymen and minister who yearly step from the rostrum of Wake Forest. [41]

The young men entering college were divided according to their geographic location in North Carolina. If one was from the West, he naturally became an Euzelian, and if he were from the East, he would be a Philomathesian.[42] It was a fight between the two regarding which could get the most members.[43]

---

[40] *The Biblical Recorder*, September 6, 1887, page 2.

[41] *The Biblical Recorder*, September 6, 1887, page 2.

[42] William Pate, Changing Times: Debaters Won, Rode Athletes' Shoulders In 1909. *Old Gold and Black*, February 21, 1955.

[43] *Old Gold and Black*, November 24, 1922, page 1.

For perhaps ninety years, "…the societies were, in many respects, little republics, possessing a student-centered and a student-administrated discipline complete with awards and punishments, carefully guarded rituals, specifically prescribed but easily amended exercises, and, comfortable and even elaborate quarters."[44]

Welcome To the Hamlet

Following the Civil War, "The student coming to Wake Forest in August 1866, got off the train at Forestville, for there was then no station at Wake Forest, and it was against orders for trains to stop there to let off even crippled persons."…He came to the only store in town, that of the Rev. Purefoy but usually kept by his wife, in a building later used for dormitories and called 'Paradise,' but now removed, to form part of the Wake Forest Hotel on the south side of the same block... On further, next the railroad was the house…which later was the home of Dr. W. L. Poteat and family but at that time vacant."[45]

Thus, society members renewed Wake's life after the War. The next chapters tell the story of the societies' work until the turn of the 20th century, including their debating practice until the Intercollegiate era emerged.

> **62. For the further protection of Wake Forest College.** [Forbids the sale of liquor within three miles, and forbids circus or other performances, within the same distance, without consent of the Facul-

January 1849, *The Raleigh Register*

---

[44] David Porter, D. (1954). The Literary Societies, *A History of Speech Education in America*. Karl Wallace, Editor 1954, page 256.

[45] Paschal, G. W. (1943). *History of Wake Forest College*, Vol. II (1865-1905), page 34; The Purefoy hotel's benefactor was Rev. J. S. Purefoy, who served as pastor in numerous North Carolina communities from 1842 to 1889. He was Wake Forest's college trustee, financial agent, and benefactor; his most important actions were in the early years of the Civil War, at which time he saved the institution by withholding sizable investments in Confederate bonds. Hargis Taylor for NCPEDIA, https://www.ncpedia.org/biography/purefoy-james-simpson

CHAPTER 2

Debater's Society Life – 1866-1918

Campus and Society Life

From sensational to tiresome, debating in the society halls continued habitual for the sixty years, bridging from the Civil War to World War I. Recognizable student cohorts ambled through the old Administration Hall building, seeking professors or classes, finding solace in the confines of their debating halls. This chapter looks at the normally unrevealed and, at times, unrivaled daily routines, ranging from calamity to practical day-to-day management.

STUDENT LIFE

Chapter 1 chronicles accounts of "flesh-and-blood students" and their endeavors in the pre-Civil War years. This chapter seeks to add to our appreciation for how debaters viewed their world from the late 1860s to the modernizations of the 1920s. In what ways was their world organized? What might a normal day offer? And which big events defined these years?[1]

We begin with the recollections of a "farmer-neighbor," a central figure across decades of campus change. We will return to this individual when his death galvanized the campus and State. His narrative takes us back

---

[1] Far too many events, lectures, music recitals, club meetings, and shenanigans occurred on campus to be recorded here. The purpose is not to exhaustively report but rather to provide characteristic markers, often rich fusions, of events from the students' lives.

to the beginning of Institute days, in part contrasting with post-Civil War campus life.

Crenshaw was a prosperous farmer whose homestead was situated two miles from Wake Forest.[2] In the late autumn of 1908, the editors of *The Student* made their way to his farm, where Mr. Crenshaw sat them down and told them his story as a student at Wake Forest:

> My father, William Crenshaw, was for a very long time the first Treasurer of the College. He lived at the old place near the mill about half a mile from the Country store and furnished students with supplies, for there was no store in Forestville then.[3]
>
> I was twelve years old when I entered college. I started school during the week and boarded at a cheap reception house or ate with the other students under canvas out-of-doors. Accommodations were very crowded. The students roomed around in houses not yet completed. I was the first student to register.
>
> The only dwelling house on the campus was Dr. Calvin Jones' private house. The Institute held large classes in a dozen different places – one, for instance, the old carriage house. The doctor's offices were used as recitation rooms. The old Jones house stood near where the dormitory now stands, and Dr. Wait moved into it. The road from Forestville came through the middle of what is now the campus, which was then all planted in corn.
>
> The students had to do manual work on the farm for three hours every evening... Two little frame houses were built after the College started at the north and south end of campus. Prof. Armstrong and Mr. Wall roomed in one of them. Wall and Armstrong slept together, and as Wall was a great snorer, his snoring disturbed the learned Prof. Armstrong. One night when the snoring had kept him awake for hours, Armstrong could endure it no longer. He laid violent hands on his bedfellow, exclaiming, 'Wake up, wake up, you've been calling hogs all night.' Farmer Wall rolled over and answered, 'And I haven't found one hog, either.'[4]

---

[2] He was known for attending every State Fair since its inception (41 years).

[3] Forestville, located one mile south, was the main town to purchase daily items and engage in activities like collecting mail or catching trains. For a full description of Forestville in Wake's early history, see Chapter 10 – Planes, Trains, and Automobiles – Transportation Recasts Debate

[4] *The News & Observer*, January 29, 1910, page 5.

Dedication

TO

MAJOR JOHN M. CRENSHAW,
THE FIRST STUDENT TO
REGISTER AT THE OPENING OF THE COLLEGE IN 1834,
WHOSE UNFAILING GENEROSITY AND
CONSTANT SOLICITUDE FOR ITS WELFARE HAVE MEANT
SO MUCH TO WAKE FOREST,
THE EDITORS BEG TO DEDICATE THIS VOLUME
AS A SMALL TOKEN OF THEIR
APPRECIATION

MAJOR JOHN M. CRENSHAW.

Regarding the routine of daily life, Crenshaw noted that the students studied by candlelight... And used green shades for their eyes. Organized athletics weren't in sight, so amusements of "bandy,"[5] "hop-scotch," etc." filled the off-time. He observed, "The boys dressed as well as the average people. Their Clothes were made at home and their garments were cut short in order to save cloth and money."[6] He also shared that, "The Dormitory, the first college building, was built by Capt. John Berry. The work was done by slaves."[7]

The Phis called a special meeting the day following Crenshaw's passing, adopting a resolution that began with "Whereas, Major John M. Crenshaw the first student to matriculate at Wake Forest at its opening ... and the first student to join the Philomathesians Society..."[8] He died in his "stately colonial Mansion," at 88 years of age.

---

[5] Bandy is a game similar to ice hockey. A team is composed of from 8 to 11 players who wear skates, using a curved stick to hit a ball. Https://www.britannica.com/sports/bandy.

[6] *The News & Observer*, January 29, 1910, page 5.

[7] *The News & Observer*, January 29, 1910, page 5.

[8] The cemetery became one aspect of honoring in 1910 an established long-term member of their community, Major John M. Crenshaw. The newspaper's account described that "About a year ago, Major Crenshaw requested that the Philomathesian Literary Society of Wake Forest College bury him, and in keeping with this expressed wish, this society will attend his funeral in a body, the pallbearers being selected from its membership." *The News & Observer*, January 29, 1910, page 5. At Major Crenshaw's funeral, the Charlotte paper reported that "practically the entire student body and faculty attending." *The Charlotte Observer*, January 31, 1910, page 8. His portrait in Philomathesian Hall was draped in black crepe.

1916 – Howler

There is a paucity of student narratives from this epoch. Newspapers were beginning to buzz, but the campus was still sheltered. Also, student publications that became the conserver for the students' stories were decades away from launch.

By the turn of the century, however, these circumstances had markedly altered; Wake was fully on the media's radar, and a bundle of students' publications were taking shape. The historical record became more robust.

President Taylor argued in 1903 that shortly after the turn of the century, not only was the campus changing but so too were the learners. He observed, "Numbers do not make greatness. Quality is more than quantity in a true estimate of any student body... More and more, the young men who knock at our doors prepare for real college work in college classes."[9]

One might imagine that if you polled students at the turn of the century, they would have reported that their lives were commonplace, routine without adventure. They would have, of course, been infinitely loyal to their Wake Forest experience. Still, complaining is to engage in the most ordinary conversational practice. Complaints were grounded in daily routines, as their lives were somewhat prosaic, dominated by academics and religion.

Living within these sheltered habits was the lifestyle many sought, especially believers who held that being an eremite served Wake Forest. President Charles Taylor wrote in the North Carolina Baptist Almanac in 1883, extending a description that rendered Wake Forest a sanctuary. "The town of Wake Forest and the surrounding neighborhood are as free as any in the country. Intoxicating liquors... cannot be sold, given or conveyed to a student without permission in writing by the faculty.

---

[9] Taylor, C. E. (1893), *The Biblical Recorder*, August 12, page 5. Taylor further chronicled, "Examinations are ended. Students are scattered to their homes. The 'rising bell' rests from its unwelcoming summons from snug slumbers on cold winter mornings. The Full Term is finished... A good term on the whole."

The proximity to the Capitol of the State affords many of the advantages without the moral dangers of city life."[10] It is not hard to imagine that contemporary assurances to Wake parents share some of this rhetorical authority.

In the early 1900s, President Taylor was inclined to write short letters or columns for various newspapers. An open letter, concurrent with the start of the 1902 Fall term, reflects the conversational manner of his outreach:

> One more week—from the day when this paper is published—the Fall term will begin. Wednesday, August 27. That is the date. I am careful to set it down here, because some young men seem to forget the exact time of opening, and, to their own disadvantage, come in a day or a week after the machine reinvestment started.
>
> The signs are not lacking of the near approach of session-time. The buildings have been scoured into readiness for occupancy; the campus walks are being rid of the grass and weeds, which never take vacation; professors are returning from their various outings.[11]

As freshmen have from time immemorial, newbies entered college with great uncertainty. To compound their naivety, they were often hazed. Naturally, the debating societies were at the center. The Societies had long agreed to rein in hazing. Everyone "opposed hazing," but it persisted.

President Taylor worked throughout his long tenure to forbid hazing. Near his retirement, he again took up the crusade. In *The Biblical Recorder*, 1903, he wrote that hazing is: "Marred mainly by the altogether unjustifiable efforts of a few students to have 'fun' at the expense of freshmen. No malice, of course, in this sort of thing. But wrong all the

---

[10] Taylor, C. E. (1896). History of Wake Forest College, *The North Carolina Baptist Almanac*, Published by *The Biblical Recorder*, Raleigh, page 10.

[11] Taylor, C. E. (1902). News and Notes Wake Forest, *The Biblical Recorder*, August 20, page 2; The new campus life could be puzzling for some, yet some solutions were easy in that era. "S. Powell, Esq., a very intelligent and promising young man of Columbus County, was on Saturday brought to the Lunatic Asylum for medical treatment. Mr. Powell was a student at Wake Forest College, and the first indication of his failing mind was discovered by the Professors of that College in February. Believing the disorder to have been the result of hard study, his parents were advised to take him home and put him to manual labor, which was accordingly done. The experiment proved highly beneficial, and strong hopes for his recovery were entertained." *The Raleigh News*, June 17, 1872, page 1.

same. And, when you think about it, cowardly, for Fair Play is usually not invited as a participant in hazing."[12]

In 1906, high-profile hazing cases were reported in the news. The Naval Academy faced congressional investigation led by future Senator North Carolina's W. W. Kitchen, an 1884 Wake graduate. Kitchen threatened to expel every cadet from the Academy.[13] A Naval Academy student was court-martialed the next month, with others expelled earlier after the hearings.[14] The controversy was long-lasting, and apparently, hazing was controversial at another Academy, as the Phis in 1901 debated the topic, *The hazing at West Point should be abolished?* The students split, Affirmative 15 to 12.

President Grover Cleveland stood up to his critics, a popular campus view.

When politics visited the quiet village, the campus was often a centerpiece for the action (undoubtedly a welcome break from mathematical calculations). One 1892 newspaper offered a surely inflated account of

---

[12] Taylor, C. E. (1903). *The Biblical Recorder*, December 23, page 5.

[13] *The North Carolinian*, January 11, 1906, page 5. William Walton Kitchin, an 1884 Wake Forest graduate, six-term US Representatives, and apparently a successful North Carolina Governor (1909-1913), helped encourage the Wilmington insurrection of 1898, a violent coup d'état by a group of white supremacists. W. W. Kitchen is the older brother of future Wake Forest President Thuman D. Kitchen (1930-1950). https://wakespace.lib.wfu.edu/handle/10339/28113.. https://wakespace.lib.wfu.edu/handle/10339/28113. They did not seem to share generations or political viewpoints.

[14] *The North Carolinian*, February 1, 1906, page 6.

the election night celebration but illustrates, in part, what the student debaters experienced. One presumes the Tuesday night debate session was postponed. The winner, Grover Cleveland, Democrat, was popular on campus, as he was across the conservative South. Newspapers, moreover, were highly partisan. The *Durham Globe* observed in its headline, **The Students and Citizens Have a Grand Jollification.**

> The greatest demonstration ever seen in the little town of Wake Forest was made here to-night over the election. The campus was one blaze of oil barrels and continuous roar of anvils, guns and pistols. Every kind of firearm was up for hours. The students and citizens and surrounding countrymen formed a procession of half a mile long, each bearing aloft his torchlight and banner. The grand procession of enthusiastic Democrats both young and old, besieged every professor's house and demanded the speech from the faculty, all Democrats, happily responded to the lusty calls. There has never been such an outpouring of political enthusiasm in the history of the village.[15]

Many students were "zealous politicians" from the school's inception. "Occasional debates were held in a hall labeled the 'House of Representatives,' where political questions were discussed and in which members of both Literary Societies participated."[16] What is striking in Norwood's remembrance is the two societies joining in political discussions outside Society confines, sufficiently routinized to earn a nickname. Yet, in no other reference did we find this debating forum mentioned.

Often, the paper or other student publications poked fun at the debaters. In 1913, the Howler quipped that student Roberston, debating on war and liquor, retorted, "Well, I am a preacher, but I had rather have my stomach full of liquor than bullets."

The 1909 *Howler* added an aside:

Dr. Stewart: "When did Mr. Wheeler show signs of insanity?"

Morris (Wheeler's roommate): "In his preparation for the Friday night debate."[17]

---

[15] *Durham Globe*, November 12, 1882, page 4.

[16] Norwood, J. H. (1889). Wake Forest in 1840 and in 1889. *The Wake Forest Student*, Vol. 9, October 1889, page 3, 4.

[17] *Howler*, 1909, page 169.

The literary societies' debates were not always identified as stimulating. That same year, 1909, the *Howler* featured a parody of society life, offering resolutions that implicitly reveal how the societies were rule structured at the turn of the century.[18]

100 Resolutions

ℭ ℭ ℭ

WHEREAS, Messrs. Dailey, Koontz and Williams, Chas. T. Bell, O'Brian and Battle have seen fit to bore their respective societies at each session, therefore be it Resolved, That the members of these societies provide special sessions so that these bores may rid themselves of superfluous oratory and debate.

RULES AND REGULATIONS GOVERNING THESE SESSIONS.

1. That these meetings shall be optional for the members of the societies.

2. That there shall be two meetings a month-the first and last Tuesday night of each month.

3. That these meetings shall be held in the rear end of the Chemical Laboratory.

4. That the speakers shall be allowed to select their own questions for debate.

5. That the president of the newish class shall preside over these meetings.

6. That each speaker may occupy the floor as long as he wants to on his first speech but must speak for three hours or be fined five dollars.

7. That each speaker shall be allowed two hours on miscellaneous.

8. That a fine of ten dollars shall be imposed upon anyone of the speakers for nonperformance of duty.

9. That the president shall receive in payment for his services from all fines imposed.

---

[18] *Howler*, 1909, page 178.

THE WAKE FOREST DEBATER

108

1910 *Howler* Parody on Society Meetings

10. That for failing to pay any of these fines the owner shall receive the censure of his society and not be allowed to run for office in the society.

11. That the president shall appoint a committee of three to solicit funds throughout this and other states to pay for the GAS used at these meetings.

12. That a medal, costing not more than twenty-five cents and not less than fifteen cents, be given to the one who speaks the greatest number of hours during the college year. This medal shall have engraved on one side the name of the winner and on the other side the following motto:

> Sic semper tyrranis. By dingibus.
> Ego summus taurus meae Societatis sum!

Debaters were no longer the epicenter of campus social life, but for many students in 1938, speech competition was still a meaningful outlet, and some achieved campus fame. They brought forth activities of every stripe to secure stellar members. For example, the *Howler* revealed the

Philomathesian recruiting strategy: "The college golf course and the lake furnish the scene for the first frolic given for prospective members. At the Society's annual Smoker, NC Attorney General Seawell spoke."[19]

Four years later, the Phis and Eus "will each present a one-act play on Dec. 10 in the Wake Forest High School Auditorium. The plays will be given in a competitive spirit, each group trying to produce the best play."[20] Four years later, the Phis participated in the All-Campus Sing and attended a commencement oration on "Christ in Modern Life."[21] Campus singing became a regular fare for the societies.

Literary Societies continued to function at a brisk pace in the '30s. A typical example is a 1931 program for the "Euzelian Annual Smoker," held at Eu Hall.

SMITH   DEATON

Leonidas Smith and Harold H. Smith were awarded degrees of special distinction at Pi Kappa Delta Nat. Honorary- 1932 – They had to win 60% of their debates over three years.

Dr. Hubert Poteat, a well-known professor and master of Latin on the Wake Forest faculty, will be the principal speaker of the evening.

---

[19] *Howler,* 1938, page 160.

[20] *Old Gold and Black*, November 20, 1942, page 1.

[21] Philomathesian Society, *Howler,* 1948, page 172.

Dr. W. L. Poteat, Pres. Emeritus, Dr. A. C. Reid, Prof. of psychology and probably other members of the faculty who were former Euzelians are expected to be present.

In addition to Dr. Poteat's address there will be a three-minute talk on "The importance of literary society training in a man's education," the speaker to be selected.

The short debate of the typical Euzelian style will consist of arguments both pro and con, with the query, *That all the debts between nations contracted as a result of World War, including reparations, should be canceled.*[22]

Most frequently, the same individuals who occupied the Society membership also traveled to Intercollegiate debates and tournaments, placing informal stresses on the more staid meetings.

To counter this, societies upped the ante, sometimes with temporary success. The 1931 Euzelians, as reported in the *Old Gold and Black*, began their New Year's work with "Hubert E. May and Donald G. Myers saying 'yes' and 'no' respectively to the question, *Is the emergence of woman from home a regrettable feature in modern civilization?* This type of debate is seldom used in the regular debate sections, and it has created quite a little interest." Mr. May won the decision.[23]

The 1933 Wake debaters parlayed their skill into social outlets as well. "Amid a setting of soft lights, sweet music, and beautiful girls, some 200 Wake Forest men enjoyed the hospitality of their merit of the 'sisters' last Saturday night from eight till eleven." Debating gave way to more amorous pursuits in this humorous bit of "news."

Then came the highlight of the evening. The ladies of Meredith had heard, in some way, that Wake Forest was noted for its famous

---

[22] *Old Gold and Black*, September 26, 1931, page 1.

[23] The balance of the meeting was equally noteworthy. "M. H. Tadlock told of the situation in Japan with China and England placing a boycott on all Japanese articles. *British Democracy on Trial* was discussed by H. H. Deaton. Thompson Greenwood gave an account of the number of very small inventions that had brought their inventors enormous sums of money. The most popular toy of the present day, the Yo-yo, was mentioned. Wyan Washburn asked several questions and answered them under the subject, "*If we had a Dole?*" [for the unemployed]. Closing the program H. H. Jones gave a timely report on "Our Young People." Mr. Jones still has faith in the young people of modern times." *Old Gold and Black*, January 9, 1931, page 1, 4.

debaters, and demanded a demonstration. And that demonstration was given by none other than George Washington Smith Woody and Ebenezer Joshua (Happy) Bowers. These distinguished gentlemen presented one of the most elaborate and intellectual discussions ever to be heard in Wake County. The query was Resolved *That Columbus did more for America than Washington,* and the historical knowledge displayed by these gentlemen was amazing. However, at a very critical point in the discussion, it was announced that refreshments will be served to those who were not interested in the debate, and so that was the end of that.[24]

In this period, a letter from Pres. Poteat to the Board of Trustees sought support for a new social science building and placed as a centerpiece of the appeal the great needs of debaters, promising to do something about their situation. Poteat authored:

The equipment for the literary societies is grossly inadequate for so large a student body. On occasions which demand full membership attendance it is impossible for all to get into their respective halls and many of those who do enter sit flat on the floor. The brilliant record of their representative's intercollegiate debates in public life is one of the chief distinctions of the college, and it cannot be unwise for you to go to the full length of your resources in providing adequately for this work.[25]

1911 Wake Forest Campus

---

[24] *Old Gold and Black*, October 10, 1933, page 6.

[25] *The Wake Forest Student*, November 1916, Vol. 36, page 109. The Societies were requested to raise $15,000 each for a total cost of $80,000.

RELIGION

When Wake Forest was founded, the Institute was a fully absorbed religious institution. The societies, organized by Hiram K. Person and James C. Dockery, divided the students into the Phis and Eus. "The division between the two groups destroyed religious life and the unity of the college. Soon after, a 'society for missionary inquiry' was organized, passing a resolution stating 'that the spiritual interest of those with whom we associate are infinitely superior to all other considerations.' The students realized their error and began attending student prayer meetings. On August 30, they met in the chapel and established the church, of which Samuel Wait was pastor."[26]

The Biblical Reporter, itself a young publication, describes the fledgling gathering celebrating the first campus baptisms. The central figure is none other than President Wait.

> A number of the young gentleman of the Institute, the subjects of the late revival, have been baptised. Baptismal seasons are generally rich in incidents and happy in their influence on the Christian spirit, but this today awakened had so many delightful associations…A band of young men of cultivated intellect, of elevated views, preparing for active usefulness in life, would under any circumstance command the wise and good….
>
> The place of baptism was about three hundred yards from the house, when the brethren had constructed an artificial pool of some considerable extent. The declivity on both sides is very gentle and affords a view of the whole surface of the water to two or three thousand people…

---

[26] The historical accuracy of this foundation story is, at best, uncertain; Not everyone characterized the school as gripped in religion, arguing the college kept separate, religion and curriculum. A letter writer, an unidentified Wake faculty, referred to simply as "A Friend of Learning," wrote in December 1843 in *The Newberian and The North Carolina Advocate,* maintaining, "Wake Forest College is not sectarian in its character. It has not been got up to make partisans to a sect, but to extend the benefits of education… [I]t has been resorted to by young men of every variety of religious sentiment…Religious services are regularly performed, and those who lead them are Baptists, but in all other respects the course of study and training are just the same as they are in those institutions which are not under the patronage of any particular denomination. *The Newberian and North Carolina Advocate*, December 16, 1843.

Second "Great Awakening" a religious revival extending from 1800 to Civil War

An address was delivered by Mr. Armstrong...The young men were then led down into the water and baptised by Mr. Wait. What added very much to the imposing appearance of the ceremony, was the black robes in which all the young men were arrayed. There was more dignity and grandeur and solemnity in this ceremony than I had ever witnessed before... May the great head of the church continue to smile on Wake Forest Institute.[27]

As indicated in the last chapter, Samuel Wait and his wife Sarah's letters clarified the literary societies' spiritual grounding. An August 1835 letter from Philomathesians to Sarah Wait assured her that their societies were "founded upon the broad principles of Christian morality."[28]

The religiously affiliated Wake Forest leadership held tight that Faith was essential to the college's footing. Concurrently, they were champions of science and coherent progress.

---

[27] *The Biblical Recorder*, October 21, 1835, page 3.

[28] Williams, T. J. (2002). *Literary Societies at Wake Forest College*, Honors Thesis History, Wake Forest, page 10, quoting Wait Papers, Folder 2/214.

Other schools also traversed the paradox of religion and science. In 1838, the Davidson College President would warn: "Remove the restraints and sanctions of religion, and talents in intellectual attainment can't stay the demons of human depravity." In 1852, at Wofford College in South Carolina, its first president remarked: "We have no faith in the capabilities of mere intellectual training." Finally, at Trinity College in 1868, the president wrote: "Without religion, a college is a curse to society."[29]

Historian Frederick Rudolph observed these early currents, "The college as construed by the officials, he suggested, might neglect intellect in the interest of piety. It might adhere to a regimen of discipline so constraining that the joys of the world were neglected in the interest of preparing for life in the next. It might ignore the body, but be captivated by the career of the soul."[30]

Revivals and religious recommitments were periodic throughout the college's history. An example is in 1914 with President Poteat leading the effort:

On Sunday afternoon, September 25, in a meeting called for that purpose, President Poteat, at the request of the faculty, read a paper on *How to Make Wake Forest a More Efficient Christian College.* Seventeen faculty members were present, and seven participated in the discussion.... A week after it began, "the movement, tentative at first, settled into a series of regular services in the chapel. In the number who were brought under its gracious influence and in its effect upon the people of the town, the meeting was probably unequaled in recent years.[31]

In a year of many transitions, including the end of mandatory membership in 1922, the overlay of religion was ubiquitous in campus thought. The paper celebrated the selection of the President of the Anniversary Debates, a law student, and the Secretary, a preacher, the attractive combination of "Law and Gospel."[32]

---

[29] Rudolph, F. (1962). *The American College and University: A history.* University of Georgia Press, page 139.

[30] Rudolph, F. (1962). *The American College and University: A history.* University of Georgia Press, page 136.

[31] *Bulletin of Wake Forest College,* 1914, page 246.

[32] *Old Gold and Black*, February 19, 1922, page 1.

Revivals on and off campus, tents and all, were common. In 1934, for example, both sections of the society decided to discontinue meetings during revival week, and members were exhorted to attend the services.[33] The same deference happened in other years.

Many pressures challenged the promise of realizing the school's religious mission; typically, funding was the top need. Much earlier, a newly appointed Latin professor, Charles Taylor, was charged with raising funding for the school. During his northern trip in 1883, he produced a letter of appeal to a New York audience, pinpointing illiteracy as the enemy of reading God's word. Charles Taylor, seven years later Wake Forest's President, spoke directly of Wake Forest's necessity. "Religion, to succeed, simply had to do better." He laid out the practical realities:

> The returns of the last census reveal the startling fact that nearly one-third of the white people of North Carolina cannot read or write. Still more startling is the other fact that the number of whites who cannot read or write is greater by 25,635 than it was in 1870. The masses of the people of North Carolina, white and black, belong to the Baptists more than to any other denomination. There are more than 100,000 white Baptists in the State. For much of this illiteracy, therefore, we are, as Baptists, responsible.

Is any College in the Union confronted by a work of more magnitude and importance than Wake Forest, the Baptist College of

---

[33] *Old Gold and Black*, February 24, 1934, page 6.

North Carolina? The only way to reach illiteracy is from the top downward. This Institution must be enabled to cheapen tuition and double its work.[34]

Of course, the societies debated religion, even though, as historian Thomas Harding maintained, generally, "The questioning of orthodoxy was not debated in the halls.[35] The four-year-old Philomathesian Society, in its 1838 minutes, discusses a topic selection proposal. The revised Constitution article reads, "All subjects of interest, except controversial subjects on *religion*, shall be open for discussion."[36]

As Harding put it, "They were conscious of religion yet were not close to it." His sentiment undoubtedly characterized many students and faculty, yet an encompassing norm was simply not to openly question "proven" Christian doctrine.

As Paschal observed, early regulations of both Societies forbade the discussion of controversial religious questions, yet that "restriction did not apply to questions about atheists and Roman Catholics, and Mormons."[37]

---

[34] Twenty-five percent of the graduates of Wake Forest College became ministers. Of the 2,365 college graduates, 673 have entered the service of the Master in home or foreign fields. Since 1847, facts show that 43% of the service is in foreign fields. Thirty-nine have been sent to China since 1847. Wake Forest supplies about twice as many students to the Southern Baptist Theological Seminary as any other college. *The Wake Forest Student*, Vol. 2, No. 5, January 1883, page 231.

[35] Harding, T. S. (1971). *College literary societies: Their Contribution to Higher Education in the United States 1815-1876*, Pageant Press International Corporation, New York, 1971, page 98. However, there is an implied orthodoxy in a topic debated on June 8, 1839: *Should any person who dismisses the being of a God be allowed to hold any office or a place of trust*, or *Should there be a prohibition in the Civil Service?* They were decided in the negative.

[36] Philomathesian Minutes, September 9, 1838.

[37] Paschal, G. W. (1935). *History of Wake Forest College,* Vol. I, page 547; Topics not developed by Paschal included: The Euzelians in 1854 and 1858 considered, *Should the Mormons be allowed to hold offices in the United States?* rejecting their candidacy 25 to 7 and 26 to 7. Between 1855 and 1892, the Philomathesians, six times, discussed the resolution, *Ought the Mormons to be expelled from our country?* They agreed in the first five instances, changing their vote the sixth time the topic was debated. Catholics took their turn as well. In 1941, the Eus seemed to agree that Catholics could hold office but not necessarily vote. The Eus discussed Catholics nine times, the most curious being in 1880, *In the elements of paganism there is more evil than in the elements of Catholicism*. Negative 11 to 39. The Phis debated Catholicism eight times, mostly about social exclusions. An intriguing version happened just as war

Multiple chapel calls of the early years not only acted as an assembly but also as a religious reminder. Mandatory Chapel dictated a daily segment of student life until relatively recent times. For decades, attending chapel daily was mandatory, with speeches by faculty and religious leaders and occasional lectures by outside secular figures.

The chapel had assigned seats; if you were in yours on time, you would not be marked absent. Missing twelve Saturday Chapels over the year resulted in a suspension from the college. Chapel attendance also carried a grade that "reckoned in determining distinction at graduation."[38] Passive resistance to mandatory chapel remained an element of student life throughout, from Institute Days until the practice was abandoned. In 1944, chapel mutiny became especially open.

> The president of the college himself would call the roll and check those absent. The next day he would call for the reason why they were absent, some of the culprits would go meekly up to the old gentleman and, knowing that he was hard of hearing, would say, 'Doctor, I was not SICK yesterday,' and he, hearing only the one word, would reply, 'well my boy, if you were sick, I suppose I shall have to excuse you.'

---

was closing the school. In 1860, the query was: *Does Roman Catholicism prevent the dissemination of knowledge among the masses?* Decided in the affirmative 13 to 2.

Most religious topics remained generic. The Phis in 1870 considered, *Does Christianity diminish human happiness in this life?* (Negative 20 to 9) and in 1867, *Which has the greater cause of the advancement of liberty, persecution or Christianity?* (Affirmative 5 to 4). Or an entertaining debate in April 1859: *Is the legal profession compatible with Christianity?* (Affirmative 15 to 8). Later, twice in November 1906, *The Bible should be taught in the public schools of the U.S.* (Negative 3 to 2; Negative 4 to 1).

In 1898, the Eus tussled with *Is true civilization the result of a pure religion?* (Affirmative 18 to 12). Twice in 1901, they argued the resolution: *False systems of government have caused more misery than false systems of religion* (Negative 26 to 22; Negative 8 to 99). The first topic seemingly endorsed the prevailing creed, a stance which was less clear by the 1900s with the "false systems" resolution.

An odd topic in 1853 seems to ask the colleges to be religiously neutral, leaving those decisions to the individual student, who might elect more religious participation. The inelegantly worded topic read, *Would a system of College education neither providing for nor prohibiting religious exercise, but having it optional with students during the suspension of College duties to attend religious worships whenever they might see proven, be better than the present system?* was decided in the negative 11 to 7.

[38] *The Wake Forest College Bulletin*, 1927-1928, page 34-35.

NOWADAYS, we merely flatly refuse to go to chapel or have few scruples about the reasons we give for absences.[39]

Other distractions and busier lives rendered attendance as optional as possible. Students' latitudes for cutting chapel were limited, but ever resourceful, the students kept the pressure on to lessen, change, or fully end Chapel. That was not the case for the faculty, who, for many reasons, missed the service. The *Wake Forest Student* of 1910 issued a 'faculty attendance chart with the maxim "What is sauce for the goose is sauce for the gander."

Effective measures are taken to ensure the presence of the students at chapel, but of late, we have noticed with pain an increasing laxness on the part of the faculty in this regard. We have gone to the trouble of collecting the following horrifying statistics, the publication of which we earnestly hope will redound to the soul's good of our revered professors..."

The *Wake Forest Student* asked the faculty, "Will they call the office of THE STUDENT on the twenty-third of this month...to explain." The listing of Chapel absences contained all the faculty, including President Taylor. Some notable pillars in college history and Wake Debate were called out. [40]

Carlye	11
Gulley	6
Paschal	12
Poteat	3
Royall	4
Taylor	11

---

[39] In the early 1960s, "an estimated fifteen hundred students signed a petition declaring that mandatory chapel was 'anachronistic'" and that it failed utterly to contribute to the educational aims of this university." The last Chapel was held on January 14, 1969. Wilson, E. G. (2010). *The history of Wake Forest University*, Vol. V: 1967-1983, page 45.

[40] *Wake Forest Student*, December 1911, page 282.

DEALING WITH DEATH

In the first eighty years of Wake's existence, disease, infection, and accidents were real and constant threats. Society minutes were periodically interrupted with resolutions honoring a member who had passed, undoubtedly sober occasions. By the late 1830s, a young male of 20 had a life expectancy of just under 40 years.[41.]

Six and half decades after the Institute's founding, in the years covering the Wake-Trinity Debate, the average life expectancy in the United States in 1900 was 47 years for white males[42] compared to nearly 79 years in 2018 for all Americans.[43] The average expectation was likely lower in the South.

The early Wake Literary debaters were intimate with the fragility of life, most likely confronted with the death of one or more brothers during their college years. This section is offered to give insight into how these understandings were handled.

In the third year of the Institute's existence, *The Biblical Recorder* noted that Charles R. Merriam, a native of Vermont, aged about 23 years, died at the Wake Forest Institute.[44] They wrote, "Brother Merriam has been connected with the institute, we believe, from its commencement; and has been a uniformly sincere and devoted friend. The disease in which he died was a painful and protracted one, which he bore with Christian fortitude and resignation."[45] Merriam "laid in State" at the home of Pres. Wait.

The precision of language and sentiment in the short student's remembrance is remarkable. Mr. Dockery, the society's former president, arose at the meeting and addressed the society with words suitable and began the resolutions list with:

Whereas we are painfully reminded of the uncertainty of human life. God in his wisdom and providence has seen fit to call away from

---

[41] https://www.ncbi.nlm.nih.gov/pmc/articles/PMC2885717/.

[42] https://www.seniorliving.org/history/1900-2000-changes-life-expectancy-united-states/.

[43] http://fortune.com/2018/02/09/us-life-expectancy-dropped-again/.

[44] *The Biblical Recorder*, April 19, 1837.

[45] Typical of period death portrayals were descriptions of peaceful repose and coming to terms with God. See Faust, D. G. (2008). *This Republic of suffering: Death and the American Civil War*. Vintage Civil War Library, Vintage Books, NY.

this scene of things one of our own members Charles R Merriam has exchanged mortality from fertility. His spirit has soared to regions of ineffable loss. Charles Clark R. Marriam was a member of this society, and active colleague, and our first president.

Resolutions often prescribed members' expected obligations (attendance, attire) and how their concern for the passing would be expressed in *The Biblical Recorder*, newspapers, and with the families of the deceased.[46] As one would expect, help was offered as needed. The October 1902 Philomathesian minutes indicated, "Mr. Baker has typhoid fever and that the doctors say it is very necessary to send him home today. The regular order businesses are done away with, and a committee is appointed consisting of Messrs. Fowler and Collier to see that Mr. Baker is carried safely home."

Both societies often extended resolution condolences to alumni and families. Exceptional energies were extended for professors who passed away, often during the school year. For instance, "Whereas God in his providence has cut short at the dawn of the useful career, the life of our beloved Prof. C. C. Crittenden" and resolved thirdly, "that these resolutions be spread on the minutes of each society; a copy of such to the family and the Wake Forest Student and The Biblical Recorder for publication."[47]

Sometimes, the language used to describe the departed's circumstances was distinctly memorable. The student commemoration in the July 1, 1871, Philomathesian Minutes shared, "Whereas, the relentless tyrant has again entered our midst, and plucked from our ranks one of our most beloved brothers. C. M. Seawell departed this life on the 14th..."[48] Charles Seawell served as the society's president in the spring of 1869.

Soon after the Institute was given college recognition, an impactful 1842 death took place with the passing of James E. Laughinghouse. It was evident from the previous two years minutes that he was a central player in society work, often tapped to serve on committees, debates, and as an officer. The minutes recorded:

---

[46] For example, in 1875, a member's death prompted the selection of six pallbearers, with each member required to attend the funeral. Euzelian Minutes, May 24th, 1875.

[47] Euzelian Minutes, May, August 1903.

[48] Philomathesian Minutes, September 23, 1871.

As a society bound together by the thoughtful ties of friendship and a spirit of intellectual brotherhood, we deeply feel the rupturing of those fraternal ties, which have endeared us to our fellow member James E. Laughinghouse... as an officer of our society we feel ... his loss, and from the many virtues of his heart, the purity of his intentions, his gentle and conciliatory demeanor--channels of his imagination – the brightness and activity of his mind– the sincerity of his friendship, and from the great zeal he always manifested our affairs, we have lost a brother indeed.[49]

The society adopted unanimous resolutions immediately after Laughinghouse's death, promising... We will march in solemn procession with the corpse to the grave to superintend the funeral services, and we will wear the badge of mourning for sixty days. The 3 o'clock funeral sermon would be preached by the Rev. Samuel Wait, with the order of procession as follows: 1. The corpse. 2. The relatives of the deceased. 3. Students. 4. Faculty and their families. 5. Citizens of the place. 6. Visitors.

The death of young Laughinghouse was noted prominently in *The Weekly Standard* newspaper in Raleigh, which was written as part of an extended obituary, an ode not only to the departed Laughinghouse but also to learning's merits:

At Wake Forest College, on Monday morning, 7th, after a brief illness, Mr. James E. Laughinghouse of Pitt County, aged 21 years and 7 days. But a few days since did the lamented deceased, buoyant with hope and animation, mingle among us and participate in the same scenes of pleasure ... But now, he is no more. His radiant spirit, freed from its fettered dust, has winged its way to another and brighter world... Nothing is left to us but the melancholy...

James Edward Laughinghouse's
Tombstone – Wake Forest Cemetery

---

[49] Philomathesian Minutes, December 3, 1842.

...Early having imbibed those moral and religious sentiments which it is a father's pride and a mother's fondness to inculcate, he never for a moment strayed from that path of moral rectitude and high-bearing which brightened with parental example.

...To these happy traits in his character, he added the guiding influence of a high moral taste and a superior mind... which in their full development would have honored the institution with which he was connected and also the literature of the country.

...His great energy, force, and decision of character was proverbial "with all he constantly fed the youthful vigor of his studious mind with the lessons and experience of history..."

"He wing'd the shaft that quiver'd in his heart."

The canker-worm of a pulmonary disease never ceased its depredations, until he fell a victim to its ravages... Around the brightest of his promises, has death drawn the sable drapery of the tomb.[50]

Laughinghouse's importance and memory were so durable that as late as 1875, the Philomathesian minutes would consider the advice of putting up railings around his grave by name.[51]

A feature in *The Wake Forest Student*, 1954-1955, told the story of the Old Wake Forest Cemetery, containing the gravesites of many early Wake Forest students. Shirley Mudge's account extends the Laughinghouse narrative:

At the top of the hill in the oldest section of Wake Forest Cemetery stand two large tombstones, staunch reminders of the prosperity once enjoyed by the two college literary societies. Clustered around the big stones marked Euzelian, there are three small markers each engraved with the initials and the Eu insignia. Around the Philomathesian stone there are four small stones, to engrave like those of the Eu's and two with no markings at all. Buried in those bare, unkept plots are five known, possibly seven, Wake Foresters who lived, studied, and worked on the campus. They were men who spoke and debated enthusiastically in the society halls, men who lived when loyalty and devotion to the societies with integral part of

---

[50] *The Weekly Standard* (Raleigh), November 16, 1842, page 3.
[51] Philomathesian Minutes, April 3, 1875.

every student's college life – 'the Golden Age' of the Philomathesians and the Euzelians.

A legend once surrounded the death of the first society member to be buried in Wake Forest. It was said the death of James Edward Laughinghouse, a Phi from Pitt County, occurred when he fell from a window in Wait Hall, which was under construction at the time, but the story has since been proven entirely without basis. Records show that Laughinghouse was a student in the college and an officer in the Philomathesian Society when he died in 1842, but the actual cause of his death and the reason for his burial at the Wake Forest are unknown.[52]

The tombstone first placed on the grave of Laughinghouse was large and flat with black sides in the concrete top. Some Wake Forest town people still remember the marker and why it was eventually removed. It seems that on Sunday afternoons young couples, for lack of magnolias and benches perhaps, would stroll out to the cemetery and sit on the tombstone to do their courting. By some, this practice was considered a nuisance, or maybe not quite proper, so the Big Stone was replaced by a small marble slab.[53]

On occasion, the societies passed resolutions in recognition of the death of a member of the sister society. In a small student body, the members of the society undoubtedly shared classes and social lives with their opposite society's members.[54]

---

[52] Mudge, S. (1954-1955), They buried them here, *The Wake Forest Student*, Vol. 70, No. 2, page 20.

[53] Mudge, S. (1954-1955), They buried them here, *The Wake Forest Student*, Vol. 70, No. 2, page 21. The others buried include The Rev. Benson Cole, a Phi., who had the position of a tutor at the college. The three men whose graves are located in the Euzelian plot died between 1857 and 1877, those prophetic years surrounding the Civil War. James D Holloman was the first to be buried; little is known about him. The second, Robert Brewer Jones, died at the age of 41. As a youth, he volunteered for service in the Mexican War but was found to be suffering from tuberculosis and was dismissed. He entered Wake Forest in 1849 as a ministerial student. In 1866, his health made him unable to carry on his work. Jones paid a visit to Wake Forest, which had just reopened from the Civil War and found himself, quite unexpectedly, appointed agent for the college. The third Euzelian, John Lamb Prichard, who died in 1877, was a major player in the society records.

[54] Philomathesian Minutes, November 10, 1845.

Resolutions were often issued in response to the deaths of former society members. In 1850-1851, there were several such citations.[55] Most of these recognized had to have been young because even if they had joined the society in its inaugural year, 1835, 1850 was only 15 years removed.

Another aspect was the often-ignored gravesites near campus. Of special concern were those of the Society brothers. The mechanisms for keeping the gravesites refreshed deteriorated with time and memory, often forgotten. Decades after the repairs were promised, the student newspaper observed, "Another of the discarded bylaws stated that 'each year the Pres. shall appoint a freshman, who shall clean off the graves of all Philomathesians buried in the local cemetery.' This provision has been disregarded for years."[56]

Notes in 1871, in response to losing a brother, inscribed "as 'the way of death must be trod by all,' the loss of our brother should remind us that we too are every day near the grave."[57]

REBUILDING AFTER THE CIVIL WAR

The shelling of Fort Sumter on April 12, 1861, marked the beginning of the Civil War. North Carolina seceded from the Union on May 20, 1861.

Only 1,087 students had matriculated from the opening of the Institute in February 1834 until the suspension of the College for the Civil War in 1861.[58] The post-war recovery, continuing through the turn of the century, bit by bit spawned a newfound campus full of students and assurance.

Following the Civil War, the college went through a period of rebuilding, reestablishing institutional honor, and restoring confidence. When returning to campus, the debating societies provided a crucial refuge, providing a familiar *home* from which to rebuild.

---

[55] For example, the Philomathesians drafted a resolution "in memory of Dr. Leroy Strayhorn of Carroll County Tennessee, an old member of the society." It was submitted with "humility and reference to this affliction dysfunction of an all-wise and gracious Providence." Philomathesian Minutes, March 8, 1851.

[56] *Old Gold and Black*, April 1, 1933, page 1.

[57] Philomathesian Minutes, March 18, 1871.

[58] Paschal, G. W. (1935). *History of Wake Forest College*, Vol. I, page 176.

Wake Forest 47th – Pickett's charge at Gettysburg

In the Reconstruction era, the campus literary societies were largely silent as they worked through their postwar wounds, rebuilding membership. Circumstances would dictate there was little appetite for a public face; the world outside Wake Forest was also in post-war turmoil.

As President Charles Taylor reflected, "Few who have not personal recollections of the period have any idea as to the financial condition of the people of North Carolina, for several years after the close of the Civil War. Not only was money scarce, but the country was in so discorded a condition as to render it very difficult to make anything which could be sold, whether in fields or factories."[59]

Governor Zebulon Vance delivered a lecture on June 7, 1866, before UNC's two literary societies during commencement. His account of life after the Civil War gave the sentiment of North Carolinians when Wake Forest was reopening. He spoke on "The Duties of Defeat," calling for "a sincere acceptance of the decisions of the war, loyalty to our governments... and education of our children."[60]

---

[59] *The Wake Forest Student*, 1911, page 348.

[60] Franklin Shirley is quoting Vance's UNC Address. Shirley. F. R. (1962), *Zebulon Vance, Tarheel Spokesman*, Heritage Printers, Inc, Charlotte. Vance was Wake Forest's Commencement speaker in 1872 and 1888.

Vance's vivid narrative describes:

With her homesteads burned to ashes, with fields desolated, with thousands of her noblest and bravest children sleeping in beds of slaughter; innumerable orphans, widows, and helpless persons reduced to beggary and deprived of their natural protectors; her corporations bankrupt and her own credit gone; her public charities overthrown, her educational fund utterly lost, her land filled from end to end with her maimed and mutilated soldiers; denied all representation in the public counsels, her heart-broken... [61]

The Rev. J. D. Hufham, referred to as the leading member of the Baptist convention, in a post-war speech, described realities that beset North Carolinians and Wake Forest:

In 1865 there wasn't seed corn 20 miles of Brawley. The 'burners' had swept away everything as with a broom of destruction, and between Raleigh and Fayetteville delicate women kept their children to live on parched corn. Wake Forest College had been gutted. There stretched out before us a scene of desolation. Our people were brave. They said: 'we will rebuild our Jerusalem. * * * My heart grows tender with every recollection of Dr. Wingate. In the days of hardship his wife said, "go out and preach the gospel."[62]

President Wingate was tasked with overseeing the exceptionally challenging passage, which he devoutly fulfilled. "Dr. Wingate, as agent, in 1854 and 1855, raised about 35,000 and in 1856 was elected president. In the first year of his administration, 1860, the college did not meet his expenses, but it did meet expenses in 1861. The war came and Dr. Wingate had to struggle hard to keep the boys from going into the Army. Many of them left and joined the Army without going home." [63]

The college reorganized... Dr. Wingate's great task was to determine how the faculty could be sustained.

---

[61] Shirley, page 63, quoting *The Duties of Defeat*, An Address by Zebulon Baird Vance (Raleigh, 1866), page 5.

[62] *The News & Observer*, December 14, 1897, page 2.

[63] Rev. W. R. Gwaltney, Semi Centennial of Wake Forest College, February 4, 1884. *The Biblical Recorder*, February 12, 1884, page 2.

The Societies also adjusted to the war, most often joining the Confederate Army, but they also attended to issues central to their post-war continuation. In the immediate window before North Carolina entered the war, the societies moved to preserve their beloved histories. In 1862, the Euzelian Society resolved that its records should "be placed with Mrs. —— for safe-keeping till we meet again."

The Philomathesian Society ledger entry (pictured below), dated January 27, 1866, was perhaps written by Dr. W. R. Gwaltney.[64] Another entry recorded, "Thanks are thereby tendered to Mrs. Foote for the kindness she displayed in keeping the hall in order during the war, Resolved that thanks are thereby tendered to Prof. W. G. Simons for recovering books from the hall (to keep the Yankees from getting them) for safekeeping."[65]

Following the war, students would slowly return.[66] A Phi student, W. R. Gwaltney, celebrating the Society's return in 1866, presented a war lament that endured in the student's mindset for many decades:

Euzelian Hall
January 1?th 1866
After a lapse of time from 1862 to 1866
The College having resumed its exercises the
Euzelian Society organized by a meeting of old and new
members to the number of 9. Old members. W. B. Royall,
John B. Brewer, & A. F. Purefoy. New members (on record).
The Society went into the election of officers.
For President W. H. Pace
[illegible] Pres J. B. Brewer.

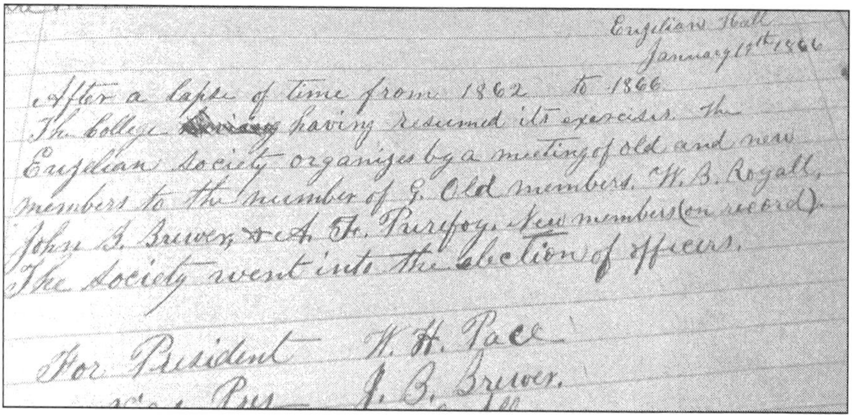

> What a blessing it is that we are permitted to meet in this magnificent hall and become members of this time-honored society. Only two old members were again assembled, and it is heartwarming to think that many of the noble founders and perpetuators of this association

---

[64] *Howler*, 1909 page 114.

[65] Philomathesian Minutes, February 23, 1866.

[66] Chapter 4, "Debating in the Literary Societies," provides further attention to Civil War debate topics.

are, some, of them, filling honorable grave on Virginia's soil, while we are proud to know that many of them are filling those honorable stations in life which the Almighty has so wisely ordained.[67]

All the school's students but five were eventually conscripted into the Confederate Army. At the war's end, sixty-seven Wake Forest students had lost their lives, only two professors were available to teach, and the campus buildings were in disrepair.[68]

Duncan C. McGuougan—"so young, so talented, some kind…"[69]

John Woodard, former Wake Archivist, refined slightly different numbers, but it was still an extraordinary toll for a school so small. Woodard wrote, "I have found 333 people from Wake Forest who served in the war. 44 died in the war-battle casualties, but some of them could have been sick."[70]

When the war came, students enlisted en masse; by the fall of 1861, only 30 students were in residence. By the spring of 1862 students enlisted from the college directly joining local units, while others went back to their hometowns to join units there.[71]

Philomathesians moved to abandon their constitutional law to keep the Hall open on Wednesday evenings, presumably because of a lack of membership. Still, at their meetings, they would have speakers on various subjects.[72] "The Chair [president and vice president absent] appointed officers to fill vacancies open by members who have left…"[73]

---

[67] Phi Minutes, January 27, 1866.

[68] Wake Forest Historical Museum, Founding of Wake Forest, https://wakeforestmuseum.org/2013/07/17/our-history/.

[69] Philomathesian Minutes, February 1, 1862.

[70] "The great disposer of human events has seen fit, in his wisdom, to call from our circle our most beloved and esteemed brother Isaiah Crudey, who fell victim to disease while listed in the defense of his nation's cause." Philomathesian Minutes, October 26, 1861.

[71] For the War, 1861-1865, Approximately 42,000 North Carolinians lost their lives in the Civil War. North Carolina sends the most men and suffers the most casualties of any Confederate state. *Winston-Salem Journal*, Nov 23, 2012. https://www.journalnow.com/news/local/archivist-probes-wake-forest-civil-war-connections/article_911349e0-35b3-11e2-a53c-0019bb30f31a.html.

[72] Philomathesian Minutes, April 19, 1860.

[73] Philomathesian Minutes, September 21, 1861.

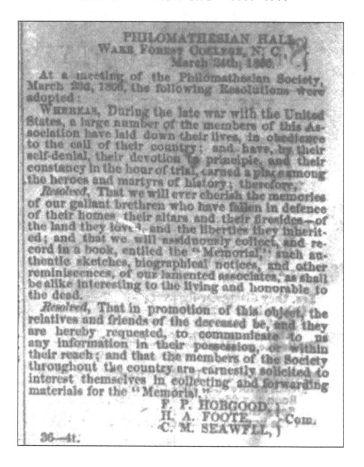

An 1866 Philomathesian Resolution honoring their "gallant brethren who have fallen, heroes and martyrs," calling for contributions for a "Memorial" Book.

An outpouring of mourning, recognition, and remorse followed the Civil War. The minutes of both societies contained references to their war dead for many years. A March 1866, Philomathesian meeting adopted a resolution to the "Fallen Heros" and their cause. Part of their resolution spoke to a particular view of sacrifice: "Gallant brethren who have fallen in defense of their homes, their altars and their fireside-of the land they love and the liberties they inherited."

"Whereas. During the late war with the United States, a large number of students laid down their lives, in the call of their country; and have by their self-denial, their devotion to principle and their constancy in the hour of trial won a place among the heroes and martyrs of history."[74]

In another meeting, they also promised to "assiduously collect, and report, in a book called the 'Memorial,' such authentic sketches, bibliographic notices, and other reminiscences..." for the fallen.[75]

The campus was derelict but largely physically untouched by the war. Almost no information remains about a hospital established on the Wake Forest College campus at some point during the Civil War. We know several huts were built on the campus; the 1838 building was used as the students and many professors were away fighting."[76] "The one building was used as a wayside hospital... It was right there on the main railroad line. They were getting casualties from (the battles of) Gettysburg and Antietam."[77]

There has indeed been an attempt at destruction, but it has failed. The political system of 1787, constructed by our forefathers, stands now firm, compact, complete and perfect—just as it came from the builders' hands. It was constructed not for eighty years only, nor yet for a period of civil war only, but for all alternating conditions of peace and war, and for all ages and all time.

Speech of Sec. of State, William Seward
The Weekly Standard, May 30, 1866.

Even as enrollment struggled, the college reopening was greeted among the faithful with optimism. Alumni and friends were encouraged

---

[74] Philomathesian Minutes, March 25, 1866.

[75] *The Biblical Recorder*, April 19, 1866, page 4; They were to request the "Parents or relatives of former members of this Society who have been killed during the war, to send the name of the place where they were killed, the date and some monument to be displayed in the Hall." Philomathesian Minutes, March 16, 1866. No later mentions suggested these righteous intentions happened.

[76] https://wakeforestgazette.com/just-a-little-history-wake-forests-three-hospitals/, "Some of the few homes that existed then may have been pressed into service. The wounded soldiers arrived by train on open flat cars. Those who died would probably have been buried in the Wake Forest Cemetery, but they cannot be found there now."

[77] *Winston-Salem Journal* Nov 23, 2012, https://www.journalnow.com/news/local/archivist-probes-wake-forest-civil-war-connections/article_911349e0-35b3-11e2-a53c-0019bb30f31a.html.

to recruit new students, especially overlooked talent. President Taylor rejoiced, "The session opened at Wake Forest last Monday. A note, received on that day, informed us that the old students are returning more promptly than usual, and a number of new students is large. Pastors at all friends of education should help the boys who want to go, and help them start. Yes, thousands of obscure voices would become great men, if anyone would give them a start."

DEBATER AND CHAIRMAN'S GUIDE.

In the period immediately after the War, the Philomathesians combined business and presentational debate meetings; except for called meetings, they met once a week.

The war also had curricular impacts beyond the pared-down offerings. Pro-regional sentiment suffused campus thinking and occasionally impacted instruction in the pre- and post-war years. Before hostilities broke out, the Board of Trustees, in the 1856 meeting, offered the following directive: "The Faculty was instructed to discontinue as a textbook The Elements of Moral Science by Wayland; as the said book contains sentiments unsound and at war with one of our domestic institutions."[78]

Wayland's voice, offering gentle moral objections to the institution of slavery, was to be banned. In widely republished advice, the *Petersburg Democrat* suggested that the faculty "procure the able work of Dr. Wm. A. Smith on the *Philosophy and Practice of Slavery*, in place of 'Dr. Wayland's *Elements*.' They will find the former contains sentiments *sound* and *not* at war with domestic institutions of the South."[79]

---

[78] *The Spirit of the Age*, June 25, 1856, page 2. In Wayland's 1837 influential book, he observes, "for if the gospel be diametrically opposed to the principles of slavery, it must be opposed to the practice of slavery; and, therefore, were the principles of the gospel fully adopted, slavery could not exist. (page 212).

[79] *The Semi-weekly Standard*, November 1, 1856, page 3.

Many decades after the war, the narrative increasingly focused on rebuilding a "New South," largely framed in economic opportunity. This rhetorical transition is documented elsewhere in this volume through the oratories presented and debate topics addressed. The passage to confronting issues of color would take several additional decades.

The idea of the debating society was, in some ways, even more important following the war. Nationally, debating societies were again on the upswing, including in the South. One popular publication of the era, the *Dime Debater Guide,* perhaps self-serving, shouted:

> Never was such an institution [debating societies] more necessary than at the present time, when the conflict of opinion is shaking society to its very base, and new ideas are germinating in the mind of every citizen who has an interest in his day or generation. The ordeal is upon us – not only the ordeal of government, but of society itself ... [E]very lad in the country is about preparing himself for the duties of citizenship by becoming familiar with the forms, and skilled in the weapons of debate.[80]

Debate may help "free the bond of history," but the process was painstaking. Mr. Gerald Johnson's article "More Excuses," which appeared in the February issue of *Harper's Magazine,* wrote, "Few things can contribute more to the moral ruin of a man than to give him a reasonable excuse for every sort of fault and frailty. The greatest misfortune that this Civil War and its aftermath brought to the South is the fact that it has provided her with such an excuse for over 60 years."

Managing the Society Halls

GENERAL HALL MAINTENANCE AND IMPROVEMENTS

A running theme of the Societies' meetings was maintaining and improving the meeting halls, the signature expression of their purpose and status. Maintenance and acquisition routinely comprised the business meetings; capital acquisitions received more agreement than how to pay for the improvements.

---

[80] *The dime debater and chairman's guide: Comprising suggestions for the formation of Debating Societies*, New York, Beadle, 1869, page 9-10.

Euzelian Hall 1897 – Heck-Williams Building

Emblems of status and governance dominated their acquisitions. In 1846, the Phils added the Declaration of Independence.[81] Shortly, in 1849, the acquisition of a new rostrum, the Hall centerpiece, engaged the Philomathesians in numerous meetings. The final product replicated the rostrum in the Commons Hall in the State House in Raleigh, "painted in the nearest style."[82]

---

[81] Philomathesian Minutes, February 6, 1846.

[82] Philomathesian Minutes, December 1, 1849:

To Wm M. Ashley for building rostrum	$108.
To Painter for painting of rostrum	$10.00
To trimmings for same	$13.55
To board of painter one week	$ 1.15
Total	$133.30

Pride in the Halls did not abate throughout the society's history. Much later, in 1931, a student writing in the campus newspaper answered his question, extolling the society halls: "The question may be asked as to why and how an organization of a voluntary nature has been so successful. Perhaps a visit to the assembly hall the Euzelians will be in itself explanatory. The room is richly furnished with heavy rugs, chairs, and draperies. At one end is an old clock of English design with wooden works

In the mid-1870s, *The Biblical Recorder*, in a cheerleader role, reflected on the place of meeting halls in the Societies' folklore. "The halls of the societies are the most costly and best furnished debating halls in the South. The choice selection of books, the elaborate furniture, and admirable rules the government tells us that young man of taste and culture hereto had for their management."[83]

From early on, the members forfeited a great deal to boost their hall's brilliance. As Paschal pictured the scene, "The meeting place of the society represented many sacrifices on the part of those who want to see a beautiful hall. $300 was subscribed by its members to purchase a rug when there were less than 50 men in the society."[84]

Controversies over upgrades could extend for months. In 1848, one committee naively suggested that the panels of the library doors be painted a mahogany color, and that other parts of the library and the rostrum be painted a Birdseye Maple."[85]

The "painting committee" and painting committee replacements extended across an immense number of meetings, plagued by indecision and procedural delays. At one point, the chairman "requested to make an excursion into the country to use all means in his powers to find a painter."[86] Twenty days later, in a special meeting called, two members were appointed to accompany each other to Raleigh to procure a painter.[87] Apparently, getting someone who could paint mahogany was harder than one might expect. One meeting later, it was moved "that Mr. Lewis be

---

in using weights for spring. Hanging on the wall are a number of large portraits of a few of the great men who have wrought so mightily and well and have gone into all parts of the world to become famous alumni of Wake Forest. What group of students would fail to be impressed with the lives and works in such manner as W. B. Royall, former Wake Forest president; E. M. Poteat, erstwhile poet and educator; Thomas Dixon, orator and playwright; or H. A. Brown, saintly Winston-Salem minister (sic), constantly being brought to their attention." *Old Gold and Black*, May 2, 1931, page 4.

[83] *The Biblical Recorder*, January 14, 1874, page 2; Much later, in 1931, the Phis bragged that "the outstanding object in Phil Hall is a 16-foot mirror directly in front of the speaker stand. Before this the new orator usually trembles; but practice soon permits him to face boldly not only his own reflection, but any audience offered him." *Old Gold and Black*, May 9, 1931, page 4.

[84] *Old Gold and Black*, February 17, 1934, page 1. (G. W. Paschal's words).

[85] Philomathesian Minutes, March 11, 1848.

[86] Philomathesian Minutes, April 29, 1848.

[87] Philomathesian Minutes, May 19, 1848.

authorized to go to Raleigh in place of Mr. Russell to whom the Pres. of the Institution refused to grant permission, for the purpose of obtaining a painter. Mr. Lewis declining the appointment."[88]

A special meeting was called four days later in which "Mr. Allen stated the object of the meeting is to take into consideration the altering of the color suggested for the door panels, mahogany to maple whereupon a motion to the effect that the door panels be painted a darker maple than the rest of the Library.[89] Finally on May 25, "the work has been executed for the sum of seven dollars exclusive of material and board of workmen."[90] Who knew collective action can be so confounding?

Daily maintenance did not fall to the society members. After the Civil War, "servants" (former slaves) were employed by the young gentry for sustenance pay. The Phis' minutes recorded, "Mr. Weatherman states that servant George can be hired to dust the hall during the session for $3.00 dollars."[91] A year later, their minutes recorded that "Mr. Hunt reports hiring a Negro to clean the hall at 12 ½ cents per week. (Approx. $2.20).[92] In November, Mr. Hunt … reported that they have hired a servant to clean the halls… at the cost of $15 on the part of each society.[93] A month later, the Committee reported hiring Negroes, offering "$25 to take care of the Hall."[94]

Minutes generally became more active when a larger capital outlay was required (and sometimes the smallest of expenditures). The sections that follow lightheartedly exploit their records for carpets, roofs, stoves, and lights. They also implicitly reveal the organization's working structure and day-to-day worries debaters confronted.

---

[88] Philomathesian Minutes, May 20, 1848.

[89] Philomathesian Minutes, May 20, 1848.

[90] Philomathesian Minutes, May 25, 1848: Hiring a painter added up. Ever frugal, that same year , the secretary moved that the cake of lead and the oil left from painting the Hall be sold… instructed to ask three dollars for it." Philomathesian Minutes, June 1848.

[91] Philomathesian Minutes February 23, 1867.

[92] Philomathesian Minutes, October 5, 1868.

[93] Philomathesian Minutes, November 15, 1868.

[94] Philomathesian Minutes, December 9, 1868. Before the Civil War, "servants," and on occasion, a free Black man would have worked on campus, which included keeping the buildings clean. The "servants" were perhaps owned by the community members residing in the Town of Wake Forest, working in the evening or on a Sunday. I am indebted to Andrew Canaday, Professor at Averett University, for his insight on slavery questions.

1909 Postcard – Philomathesian Hall – Heck-Williams Building

Much earlier, in 1873, a major expense was replacing curtains. The $78.93 outlay would be equivalent in purchasing power to about $2,065.79 in 2024. Expenditures in the 1880s ranged from purchasing 48.25 yards of calico to cover chairs[95] to expending $59.69 on life-size busts of Washington, Clay, Webster, Calhoun, and 3/4 life-size busts of Milton and Dickens.[96]

The year 1919 saw the society called to a special meeting by the president to sign a note for $1000 to secure sufficient funds, freeing up money for the costs of repairing the hall.[97] A less expensive suggestion was made in 1935 that Demosthenes' bust be improved and that the other busts be similarly treated and displayed at the society's meetings.[98]

The societies bearing much of the improvement costs led to their beseeching the College for support, with some success but little direct contribution by Wake administrations until after the 21st-century demarcation. A 1934 request illustrated, when "action was taken to have

---

[95] Philomathesian Minutes, February 28, 1880.

[96] Philomathesian Minutes, December 29, 1883.

[97] Euzelian Minutes, May 24, 1919.

[98] *Old Gold and Black*, February 23, 1935, page 1.

an investigation made about the possibility of the college sharing in the expense for repairing the chairs of the society. Several classes have been meeting in the society hall and the sexton reported that many chairs needed repairs badly. The College has been paying some rent for the use of the rooms."[99] Little did they anticipate the 1934 fire and the construction of a new campus buildings.[100]

A student, Rev. Charles Harris, from that era (Anniversary Debater 1933) wrote in a letter that each [Society] had its own elaborate room on the upper floor of the administration building when it burned in 1934, the plans for the new building provided for equally elaborate rooms. One alumnus wrote, "The important thing was the college provided prime space and funds to encourage the practice of speaking in public and thinking on one's feet."

CARPET: WARMTH, BEAUTY, AND HEADACHES

Early on, the membership seemed consumed with what was underfoot. Carpeting added warmth in cold winter meetings, but it also connoted a certain sophistication and status. In Phi's new hall in 1840, a meeting was called, entertaining a motion that the committee purchase a carpet for $350, a sum nearly twice the society's working annual budget. A Phi August meeting in presenting the budget indicated they paid Mr. Punify $326 for the carpet, but they also had expenses for drapes, books for the library, and printing the commencement address, creating a considerable deficit. Through subscriptions (additional dues), the carpet and books were directly subsidized.

Subsequent meetings of the Philomathesians established committees to install the carpet, considered and rejected any excuses for not being able to do the work, and used rollcall to identify those responsible "to attend to the brushing of the carpet."

A year later, in June 1841, the treasurer reported that Purify was still owed $78.20 (there was no explanation for the discrepancy from

---

[99] *Old Gold and Black*, February 24, 1934, page 6; The society hall chairs were more than chairs. Decoratively carved, they were a major feature, offering bragging rights for the halls. Many chairs survived and are stored on the main campus and at the Wake Forest Historical Society in Wake Forest, NC.

[100] The burning of three main campus buildings is discussed more in Chapter 13 – Intercollegiate Era Gives Way To Tournament Debates.

the previous year). The carpet also dominated in what became an annual problem: who would be appointed to roll it up and brush it before Commencement?

Keeping highly traversed areas clean absent a vacuum was a recurrent test. The standard solution, of course, is to pass a rule. The Phi By-laws of 1858 explicitly state, "No member shall spit on the hearth or carpet or be allowed to smoke tobacco in the Hall." Rules are often hard to enforce.

The repeated problems of the carpet and replacement came up again in 1872. After discussing how to sell the old carpet, the need remained to remove it. The motion offered was that twelve be appointed to take up the carpet and sweep the floor, presuming it was a multi-person task. The cleverness of the motion was that "all the names of the members be put into a hat and 12 be drawn."[101] No record was made of the happiness of the twelve who drew the short straw.

ROOF LEAKS, DECADES OF DRIP, DRIP, DRIP

As early as 1841, the Philomathesians and Euzelians colluded "relative to the stoppage of the leaks over our respective Society Halls" and took the issue to the College's Executive Committee. The Executive Committee was cooperative, but the leaks were not.

Another joint committee of the societies was formed after the executive committee passed the buck back to the societies, arguing it was the societies' responsibility that someone should stop the leaks, and resolved that each of our societies do so.

An ongoing problem, leaking roofs in the society halls, dominated the long series of meetings. At almost every meeting for months, it seemed that the Philomathesians would appoint yet another committee to meet to see what could be done about the leaks.[102]

---

[101] Philomathesian Minutes, March 1, 1873.

[102] From Philomathesian and Euzelian Minutes, 1841-2.

The societies did jointly try. In winter 1849, the Phi minutes reported, "The committee to attend to covering the roof deemed it unsafe, on account of the almost incessant rains, to take the old covering from the roof but felt bound to do something to stop the leaks. After mature deliberation and advice, they procured a paint intended to prevent leaking of metallic roofs."[103]

The roof problem seemed intractable. In January 1871, the Philomathesians did not have much luck convincing the faculty to take care of it. Their minutes reflected, "We saw Prof. Taylor, and the faculty insisted that we should have the halls treated by some means but that they (the faculty) would not assist."[104]

Almost immediately after the completion of Wake's only building for the first forty years (The College Building—later renamed Wait Hall), and the societies occupied their new meeting areas, there were issues with the roof. Paschal's elongated account classically captures what the debaters faced in preserving their beloved halls:

> The halls suffered greatly from a defect which was common to the entire building: they were under a leaky roof; already on January 25, 1840, when the Societies had been in their halls barely three years, the Euzelians were representing to the faculty that the roof needed repairs. In February 1842, both Societies joined in a complaint of the same kind. Finding no other way of having the repairs made the Societies bore an expense of eleven dollars in having the worse leaks stopped. The investigation made by the Societies showed that the roof was irreparably bad; the roofing was zinc, which it was all but impossible to keep from leaking; the Trustees were expecting to cover the building anew. The College, however, was so much embarrassed with debt that the new roof was not put on until after June 1857, when the Trustees, declaring that repairs on the roof were indispensable, ordered that a new roof be put on and the zinc be sold in part payment. In the meantime the leaks were causing constant trouble despite numerous repairs both by the Societies and a standing local committee appointed by the Trustees for the purpose,

---

[103] Philomathesian Minutes, February 26, 1849.

[104] Philomathesian Minutes, January 8, 1871; In 1874, the Euzelians were still "appointing committees" to confer with the faculty in respect to the condition of the roof over the Hall." Euzelian Minutes, May 23, 1874.

October 1, 1844. Portions at least and perhaps all were covered with shingles over the zinc, and once and again coats of sand and tar were applied; the fretted Societies stopped holes and did what else they could, calling Professor White, who was then in charge, into conference, and talking over the dilapidated condition of the roof. But with all the patches the roof continued to leak. Perhaps the halls suffered more from these leaks than the other parts of the building, since they were immediately under the roof, which was broken in the center by the belfry. The leaks were ruinous to their costly carpets, curtains, and other furniture, and their books. Time and time again both Societies remonstrated. In April 1845, the Euzelians interrupted a subscription they were making for money to buy a new carpet and returned the money already collected to the donors, fearing that promised repairs on the roof would not be made or would be of no avail.[105]

The issue of leaky roofs was never fully resolved; nearly 50 later, and in another building, the Philomathesian minutes would record, "Mr. Whitfield moved that the committee be appointed to ascertain what is necessary to be done in order to prevent the ceiling of the hall from leaking."[106]

"IT'S COLD" – A WORKING STOVE

Remembering the horse and buggy days of society life, President Poteat recalled, "There were nights when we debated until one a.m. in a room so cold I had to wrap my feet up in my coat. Our debates concerned the past alone, since we had no contemporary literature... Sometimes a debate which begins at candlelight did not end until midnight or after, and that, too, in a room in which there was no heat from a fire stove."[107] Debates were held weekly, which meant cold temperatures from October in the fall until April of the Spring term.

In 1873, upon the motion of Jay Denmark, the improvement committee was authorized to put up the stove between now and next Friday

---

[105] Paschal, G. W. (1935). History of Wake Forest College, Vol. I, page 504-505.

[106] Philomathesian Minutes, March 27, 1896.

[107] *Old Gold and Black*, November 7, 1931, page 1.

night. A vote was called on whether to even have a stove in the hall, with the affirmative prevailing with the roll call recorded for stove 23, against stove 6.[108]

The minutes from December of the next year, 1874, reflect the ongoing discussion about obtaining a stove for the meeting hall. Prof. Simmons offered suggestions relative to the purchase… The group decided to meet in Prof. Simmons' recitation room for the debate until the cold weather was over.[109]

Evidently, a purchase was successful, and there was heat for the remainder of the winter. Mr. Wilson reports having purchased one load of wood, which cost $1.00. By mid-April, the former society president A. C. Dixon was able to move that "the stove be removed from the Hall… till next fall."[110] A couple of years later, the fuel source changed, and the Internal Improvement Committee was authorized to purchase a half-ton of coal.[111]

Stoves naturally require upkeep. In 1877, a week after appointing a committee to deal with the stove, the Phis appointed a committee to polish the stove and remove the grease from the carpet. The stove was polished, but they did not undertake to remove the grease from the carpet. They informed the members that they had cleaners who decided not to clean the carpet for fear of removing the color.[112]

In 1886, a special feature of the Anniversary Day was "a handsome new banner which the Society purchased only a few weeks before. The Phi Hall has recently been re-frescoed, and the Eu Hall beautified by the addition of a new pretty stove."[113]

Maintenance was always a concern, and at the turn of the century, apparently, wood was again an option. "Assistant trea. is instructed to draw 75 cents to pay the Sexton for wood & 45 cents to pay Mr. Sherwood for stationary… On motion the vice president is empowered to appoint a committee to see about getting a new stove.[114] It was mid-January

---

[108] Philomathesian Minutes, 1873.

[109] Philomathesian Minutes, December 6, 1873.

[110] Philomathesian Minutes, March 21, 1874; On April 20th, 1891, a meeting was called that ordered "the senior class to move the stove. Those that do not comply are fined one dollar each," a sizable sum. Euzelian Minutes, April 20, 1891.

[111] Euzelian Minutes, December 30, 1876.

[112] Philomathesian Minutes, February 17, 1877.

[113] *The Charlotte Observer*, February 23, 1886, page 4.

[114] Philomathesian Minutes, November 27, 1900.

1901; a year later, the minutes indicated that "the new stove has been bought and will be here in the course of ten days."[115]

A 1933 constitutional change argued by the Phis produced a sarcastic reference to the former "stove days." The writer intoned, "Obsolete by-laws provided that in cold weather, the Sexton should be fined $.50 if he failed to build a fire in the society's stove. If these fines could be collected, the society would probably be able to build a new gymnasium for the college"[116]

Paschal wrote that the first heating plant (1914) "provided steam heat for the dormitory, Wingate Memorial Hall, the old College Building and the Library until the present heating plant was constructed in the summer of 1924."[117]

LIGHTING THE NIGHT

Debating by candlelight and later gas-lit lamps, was the reader's reality for the first several decades of campus life. Debating deeply into a shadowy night, paper and faces opaque must have contributed to some astonishing matches but also frustrated written assets. And so, the endless attempts to improve Hall lighting.

Paschal observed, "Among the first purchases of each Society were a half dozen candlesticks; on May 5, 1836, the Philomathesians ordered the purchase of four pairs of snuffers." The Societies bought candles in five-pound lots, using candles for more than ten years. He observed, "Sometimes they had trouble in collecting the candlesticks since members would use the candles to light themselves back to their rooms and forget to return them."[118]

---

[115] Philomathesian Minutes, January 12, 1901.

[116] *Old Gold and Black*, April 1, 1933, page 1.

[117] Paschal, G. W. (1948). *History of Wake Forest College*, Vol. III, page 211.

[118] Paschal, G. W. (1935). *History of Wake Forest College*, Vol. I, page 508; Philomathesian Minutes, October 17, 1868. The Phis appropriated $.65 for candles.

The saga of lighting the hall continued for decades, absorbing many a meeting. The issue of being able to see to debate in winter meetings saw the first significant improvements with the introduction of the gas lamp. The lamps were better but far from perfection.

In 1850, keeping a room lit with gas lamps required considerable effort: filling, lighting, relighting, and cleaning. Gas lamps were a bother to light and had to be lit every time the room was in use. At one meeting, it was "ordered to pay Mr. Peace $2 for attending to our lamp session."[119] The lighting process also proved expensive. In August of the same year, 1850, "Mr. Faircloth moved the society to purchase two gas lamps which were rejected" as too expensive.[120]

However poorly, gas lamps soon lit the society's night. Paschal witnessed, "It took some time to change their lamps from "fluid-burning" to "kerosene burning," and lamp chimneys were constantly breaking and burners wearing out."[121]

Less than a month after Wake Forest re-opened, in the shadow of Civil War scarcity, the eternal question of lighting was addressed, "The committee on lights reported that in as much as fluid was too costly, they thought it proper to state... that we had better be [adopting] burners for kerosene oil."[122]

The kerosene lamp, invented in 1853, greatly improved efficiency. Ignacy Lukasiewicz of Lviv popularized a variety of kerosene lamps, including the Argand lamp with its glass chimney and wick.[123] It would gradually replace the gas lamps in the assembly halls. However, it must have been a very measured shift, as the change over remained unfinished two decades after the War.[124]

---

[119] Philomathesian Minutes, June 8, 1850.

[120] Philomathesian Minutes, August 1850.

[121] G. W. Pascal, *The History of Wake Forest College,* Vol. I, page 56.

[122] Philomathesian Minutes, February 3, 1866.

[123] https://www.bing.com/search?q=argand+lamp+history&PC=U316&-FORM=CHROMN.

[124] Philomathesian Minutes, March 8, 1866.

On October 8th, 1887, the Euzelian Society moved to elect an officer whose "duty it shall be to light the lamps in the pathways of the Dormitory Building promptly at twilight on each night and then extinguished at 11 o'clock P.M. Second, that said officer shall hold his office for the term of one year and be relieved from his Society dues as remuneration for his services."[125]

The fixation on lighting continued through the late nineteenth century, often with interesting sidebars:

1867—Mr. Jones states that he can get the lamps fixed for four dollars.[126]

1874—The Treasurer is instructed to purchase one lamp, three reflectors, three chimneys, and two gallons of oil. Mr. Bagley moves that the assistant treasurer be instructed to pay seven dollars for sashes.[127]

1875—J. L. Britt moved the Internal Improvement Committee be authorized to purchase a number of reflectors and braces necessary for the lamps in the passage.[128]

1877—There being sufficient funds to allow the Sexton to purchase 5 gallons of oil and to buy a dozen boxes of matches.[129]

Each society also attempted to enhance the Hall's elegance by obtaining ornate chandeliers. Chandeliers would also greatly improve the hall's lighting. These items were costly and hard to locate without traveling considerable distances.

Apparently, discussing the acquisition of chandeliers began early, just as the Civil War was nearing. In late 1861 and 1862, the quest for a chandelier appeared in a few minutes. The consensus seems to be that an appropriate channel could be found in Richmond.[130]

---

[125] Euzelian Society October 8th, 1887; Earlier, in 1871, one fix tried to keep lamps functional was to "elect a Sexton to perform [the cleaning] duty allowing him one half of his sessional fee." Philomathesian Minutes, November 19, 1871.

[126] Philomathesian Minutes, February 23, 1867.

[127] Philomathesian Minutes, June 20, 1874.

[128] Philomathesian Minutes, January 12, 1874.

[129] Philomathesian Minutes, March 3, 1877.

[130] Philomathesian Minutes, January 25, 1862.

As societies reformed following the War, in 1866, a student moved to purchase a chandelier, but the motion was rejected. "Mr. Wicks moved that the recording secretary be authorized to write to New York inquiring about the price of chandeliers. The motion carried. The corresponding secretary was instructed... to write to all the old members of the society from 15 years previous asking them to contribute to buying the new chandelier. The motion was carried."[131] Abject poverty and displacement from the War possibly rendered this effort unsuccessful.

Two years later, in June 1868, a motion was again made that the Society purchase a chandelier. The procurement was "left discretionary with the purchaser providing he got for the hall what kind of chandelier it shall be." At the same meeting, the Phis "moved that any person who may be going up north, be requested to bring us descriptions of various kinds of chandeliers together with the price."[132] Eventually chandeliers were secured.

The chandeliers of kerosene lamps hung from the ceiling were exchanged for lamps making their own gas, which proved very unsatisfactory. Decades later (1891), the chandeliers were replaced, and the society voted to lend the old chandeliers to the skating rink.[133]

In 1902, electricity, another radical shift in lighting, was being considered. The same year as the last Trinity Debate, Phi minutes reflected, "Nothing definitely has been done but that the electric lights will cost

---

[131] Philomathesian Minutes, September 25, 1866.

[132] Philomathesian Minutes, June 21, 1868. In 1879 a chandelier was acquired with the help of Dr. Simmons of the faculty to refurbish the library. Paschal, Vol. III, page. 144.

[133] Philomathesian Minutes February 7, 1891.

a great deal."[134] Two years later, the changeout had not happened, as there had been an extended debate about how to obtain gasoline lamps in the hall.

A year later, in 1905, a meeting authorized the improvement committee to purchase new lights for the Society hall.[135] Two months after that resolution, in January of 1906, "Gentry gave notice that weeks hence that the resolution should be introduced concerning the regular dues plus the expense of the lights that each man should help pay.[136]

In 1906, "Mr. Josie E. B., as one of the committee on the Internal Improvement, was granted the right to buy lights for the Society and to pay as much over Fifty dollars ($50.00) as he saw fit."[137]. In March, "Mr. Josie was 'paid for lights the sum of one hundred and 25/100 dollars, to be handed over to the workmen who put in the lights."[138]

Reliable electric lighting debuted in 1910. In 1909, the charter of the Town of Wake Forest was amended, and the town was renamed Wake Forest; the new charter gave the town the authority to sell bonds to build a generator and electric system.[139] Wake Forest College soon tapped into the system.

In the end, *Let There Be Light.*[140]

---

[134] Philomathesian Minutes, 1902.

[135] Philomathesian Minutes, November 4, 1905,

[136] Philomathesian Minutes, January 30, 1906.

[137] Philomathesian Minutes, January 30, 1906; Later, by motion, Mr. Josie was given two dollars ($2.00) with which to go to Raleigh to see about lights. Soon, a motion instructed the internal improvement committee to arrange with the company from whom the new lights were purchased to take them back if the society wished and confer with the Phi Society committee to see if they care to pay half in light plant." Euzelian Minutes, February 23, 1906.

[138] Euzelian Minutes, March 31, 1906; Of course, debates continued whenever funds and control are in play. Even in the 1950s there would be complaints regarding lighting, this time about the bill. The minutes grumbled that the usual light charge of approximately $1.50 was $9.50 for the month. "And this was due to the *Howler* photographer using the hall to take pictures." Euzelian Minutes, November 13, 1950. They then sought to bill the *Howler*.

[139] https://www.wakeforestnc.gov/planning/historic-preservation/history-wake-forest.

[140] Genesis 1:3.

CHAPTER 3

Maintenance and Mementos:
Residing in the Societies

Administrating the Literary Societies

THE SOCIETIES' COMMITMENT

An 1893 editorial celebrating the education afforded by the literary societies inadvertently makes an early and indirect critique of the exaggerated styles favored by oratory compared to debate, which preferred logos as its foundation. The *Wake Forest Student* editor Rufus Weaver wrote:

> The man who expresses himself clearly, concisely and forcibly, talks naturally and earnestly, is the true debater. His preparation begins in his habits of thought and conversation. His reading is necessarily wider and more voluminous than the one who just writes his speech. His analysis of material in hand and his proper arrangement are limited only by his mental capacity and judgment... when he does secure the floor, he may not impress his audience as an orator, but he will do more damage and secure their attention by his lucid reasoning and unanswerable argument. Such preparation develops the reasoning powers, prepares the young debater for any conflict of mind against the mind that the future forces upon him, gives character and expression to his delivery, and fits him to be, in his truest sense, an argumentative debater and the orator of eloquence and power. [1]

---

[1] *The Wake Forest Student*, 1893, March, Vol. 12, No. 6, page 314.

The Farmer and Mechanic, a prominent Raleigh newspaper for three decades, published a 1904 feature that said much about how the public saw Wake Forest's impact on the state's imprint. The writer provides an ode to Wake Forest, the state's academic center for debate and public speaking:

> Wake Forest wisely places much emphasis upon the work of the literary societies. Young men are encouraged to write and speak, and the weekly debates are the chief objects of interest in college life... The public has a right to expect of men holding 'sheep-skins' that they be able to tell what they know, and yet how many scholars mumble and fail if they attempt to preside over even a ward primary or church meeting. At college these men have 'boned' hard and mastered the course but have neglected to cultivate the one thing that will give them the power to lead in their communities – the ability to express themselves well in public.[2]

A new era began for the Societies in 1879, when they moved into their new halls in the second story of the Heck-Williams Building, the Philomathesian Hall on the north and the Euzelian Hall on the south, assigned by lot. They were leaving the narrow halls under the roof of the Old College Building for quarters, amply large to accommodate easily 100 students each.[3]

Although before 1869, there was no restriction on the number of students the Eu's might initiate, they usually maintained a membership equal to half the student body. According to the General Catalogue, which records the membership of both societies, about nine-tenths of the 1,087 matriculants in 1869 were active members of a society. Four hundred seventy-three were Euzelians.[4]

The Literary Societies would provide Wake Forest students with a debating home for 100 years. Expansive activity would crown the century's growth. This chapter examines the structure, management, and rigors of running the organizations. Before the reader worries that this chapter's contents might be hum drum or commonplace, be assured

---

[2] *The Farmer and Mechanic*, February 16, 1904, page 4.

[3] Paschal, G. W. (1943), *History of Wake Forest College*, Vol. II, page 369.

[4] Joe Killian, Euzelian Society Changed Much in Years, *Old Gold and Black*, October 10, 1955, page 2.

some of the richest stories illuminating student life are to be found in their routines.

DAILY MANAGEMENT

The societies were the nexus of campus life, attracting a precocious class of new members each year, some indubitable in their self-concept. Describing an earlier glory day, a 1944 writer claimed, "A day or two before college opened each fall, zealous upperclassmen stationed themselves at neighboring railroad points in order to intercept the incoming freshmen and imbue them with the spirit of 'Dear Old Mother Euzelia' or 'Philomathesia,' as the case may have been."[5]

Throughout their history, literary societies' characterizations had their ups and downs. The Phis and Eus were surrounded by critics and cheerleaders who argued for improvement or lamented times gone by. Such accounts of the societies' place and consequence chronicle their circumstances through the eyes of the period's participants. Firsthand accounts, while unique, of course, also retain a teller's bias.

1922 Arial Campus View – 1922 – The Year Mandatory Membership Halted

---

[5] Literary Societies Have Old-Time Glamour, *Wake Forest College Alumni News*, October 1944.

Very early in their first decade, the early 1840s, the minutes of the Philomathesian society became especially stilted; the numbers attending meetings dropped precipitously low, and the minutes reflected few motions and even less enthusiasm. The topics debated in this period were arguably repetitive, obscure, and lacked thought-provoking content. Both inductions for new members and nominations for honorary members seemed to be down, but one highlight was the new membership of a student named George Washington.

The Philomathesian meetings regained their enthusiasm in the late 1840s, with more members attending and lively debates. But holding young people's attention for long evenings and early Saturday mornings remained a struggle. The society petitioned for faculty to affirm changing the Saturday morning meetings to a weeknight, and keeping the meetings intact was the intention of the resolution in 1849, "Resolved, that no member be allowed to leave the Hall without relief by vote of the House."[6]

The 1926 *Howler* entry described the leadership and, more touchingly, the fellowship the societies represented. This account, told with full embellishment, captures the strength that held the societies tight:

Another valuable feature of the societies...was the business meeting. This was a pure democracy. It was here that the character of the men became known. If one was a weakling, he could not conceal it; if he had the qualities of leadership, they soon became manifest; if he was lacking in moral fiber his fellows found it out. One's society mates also knew his financial status; if he had money, they used him with a will where individual expense was involved; if he was a poor fellow struggling to make his way through college, they were lenient and sympathetic and sometimes able to help. The society chastened every member with its firm but reasonable discipline... There was a mutual loyalty which was not forgotten outside the society hall.[7]

Competition for prestigious positions such as an Orator for Society, Anniversary, and Commencement Speakers was highly competitive by the late 19th century. Memberships had risen, and the positions were at the pinnacle of their acclaim. Every office and duty had elected positions. In

---

[6] Philomathesian Minutes, October 7, 1849.

[7] *Howler*, 1926, page 170.

addition to the long list of regular offices prescribed by the Constitution, sometimes elections offered special positions.

Elections were often ruckus. To maintain decorum, in 1874, the Euzelians' Minutes reflected that in June, they banned any Euzelian member from electioneering for themselves.[8] Nine years later, in 1883, bending to reality, they removed all rules against electioneering from their Constitution. Referring to this, the society president stated, "Whereas we believe it impossible to prevent electioneering, and that our laws on the subject are cumbersome and ineffective, therefore resolved . . . that all laws be removed."

Elections would choose a wide range of positions. For example, in the Spring of 1902, "the Anniversary Orator, Mr. Fowler, was elected having received 51 votes." The same gathering also designated the First Debater, the Second Debater, the Editor and Second Editor of *The Wake Forest Student,* the Secretary of the Debate, the fellow responsible for addressing new members next year, the summer custodians, and other positions.[9] Deciding officers undertook a full day's work.

The role of the Sexton included keeping everything in working order, the go-to person when something needed to be done. The Philomathesians resolved in 1900 that "the Sexton be allowed to move from place to place in the hall without permission from the president or leave the hall without permission from the society."[10] Everyone else was restricted.

The custodian's duties were to oversee the society hall and all property belonging to the Society (e.g., the revered banner). The supervisor's job was to sit at the president's left to explain membership to those initiated and report those not in membership compliance.

Some posts were not as glamorous as even the Sexton or Library sorter. One meeting logged, "Mr. Battle tenders his resignation as doorkeeper."[11] It must have been a strict job.

In December of 1905, the Euzelians added an archivist to their officers, charged with preserving the records. They were to collect, in addition to the regular society minutes and bookkeeping, "also newspaper reports of the anniversary commencement exercise, all the debates, and any other

---

[8] Euzelian Minutes, June 6, 1874.

[9] Philomathesian Minutes, May 12, 1902.

[10] Philomathesian Minutes, October 13, 1900.

[11] Philomathesian Minutes, March 1896.

exercise in which the Society takes part. Also, all invitation tickets issued, all circulars, commencement programs, catalogs, YMCA or athletic announcements, or other matters pertaining to Wake Forest College."[12]

The surplus of positions is illustrated in the reported winners of the 1925 Philomathesians officers tally, indicating how institutionalized the organizations were (note the elected Phi President was later to become the debate coach and all-around University Renaissance man, A. Lewis Aycock).[13]

President, A. L. Aycock
Vice-president, B. N. Barnes
Recording Secretary, F. H. Malone.
Asst. Rec. Secretary, V. R. Brantley
Supervisor, S. A. McDuffie
Asst. Supervisor, M. D. Blanton.
Correspondence Secretary, C. B. Earp
Financial Secretary, B. M. Squires
Treasurer, R. P. Downey
Registrar, J. T. Gaskell
Auditor, O. L. Norment
Chaplain, R. Carlton
Assistant Chaplin, B. O. West
Doorkeeper, W. E. Bowman
Assistant Doorkeeper, W. A. Reid
Senior Critic, O. L. Norment
Asst. Senior Critic, A. D. Hurst
Junior Critic, A. B. Peacock
Asst. Junior Critic, D. S. Haworth
Sexton, J. L. Reid

Society could also look forward to the elected junior and senior critics. The 1902 Philomathesian minutes reflect that "the critics of the senior and junior oratory's offer their opinions of the essays as soon as the speakers are done, and that they report to the supervisor if for any reason they know that the essay is 'not of his own composition.'" The member would be fined one dollar.

---

[12] Euzelian Minutes, December 1905.
[13] *Old Gold and Black,* October 9, 1925, page 1.

When the society's size became unwieldy, with multiple officers for each of the increased number of sections, the number of officers was purposely contracted. In their February 1903 meeting, the Eus passed a resolution abolishing assistant officers, joining two divisions, divided into six sections, meeting on Friday night only.[14]

Meetings were tightly managed throughout, as reflected in their ledgers. They followed the prevailing constitutional provisions to the tee. The 1888 Phi constitution, with its fixed provisions, served as the organization's prescribed script.

TABLE 1: 1888 Philomathesian Constitutional Provisions

1888 – Philomathesian Constitution – The society's meeting format was precisely structured and largely enforced; the minutes were read sequentially in accordance with the bylaws of the group. Representative bylaws, Article II, published in 1888.

Sec. 1. The presiding officer shall call the house to order	Sec. 14. Committees may report.
Sec. 2. The role shall be called.	Sec. 15. Resolution shall be in order.
Sec. 3. The chaplain shall offer prayer.	Sec. 16. Motion shall be in order.
Sec. 4. New members shall be elected and initiated.	Sec. 17. Miscellaneous business shall be in order.
Sec. 5. Query for two weeks shall be read	Sec. 13. Unfinished business shall be in order.
Sec. 6. Query for one week shall be read.	Sec. 18. Disputants for two weeks, one week hence shall be appointed.
Sec. 7. Query for debate shall be read, discussed, reread and decided.	Sec. 19. Selection to read composition shall be appointed.
Sec. 8. Critics shall report.	Sec. 20. Section to declare, two weeks hence shall be appointed.
Sec. 9. Role shall be called.	Sec. 21. Composition shall be read.

---

[14] Euzelian Minutes, February 21, 1903; The Societies were becoming too large to effectively operate and meet increasingly diverse interests (e. g., publications). All the sections, however, continued debates. The Thursday Night Section of the Phis in 1932 debated *Resolved, That Will Rogers should be elected president of the United States. Old Gold and Black*, January 23, 1932, page 3.

Sec. 10. Resolutions shall be in order.	*Section 22. Composition critics shall report.*
Sec. 11. The presiding officer shall call the house to order.	*Section 23. Disclaimers shall disclaim.*
Sec. 12. The role shall be called.	*Section. 24. Critics shall report.*
Sec. 13. Unfinished business shall be in order.	*Section 25. Custodian shall report.*
Sec. 14. Committees may report.	*Section 26. Financial Sec. shall report.*
Sec. 15. Resolution shall be in order.	*Section 27 Roll shall be called.*
Sec. 16. Motion shall be in order.	*Section 29. Proceedings of the meeting shall be read.*
Sec. 11. The presiding officer shall call the house to order.	*Section 28. Supervisor shall report.*
Sec. 12. The role shall be called.	*Section 30. Chaplain shall offer prayer.*
Sec. 13. Unfinished business shall be in order.	*Section 31. Adjournment shall be in order.*

The 1888 Constitution was not especially forgiving. It mandated, "After prayer the members shall resume their seats and remain in them until the motion for adjournment is decided and distinctly announced by the Chair."

A striking bylaw in the 1888 Constitution Article 6 Section 2 reads, "Any member for gross and ungentlemanly conduct, or contempt of society may be expelled on impeachment by a vote of two-thirds of the whole number of members." A crossed-out and penciled insertion of "on impeachment" was deleted, and "treasonable remarks" were added. Much earlier, in 1836, the Phi minutes noted five resolutions were introduced to expel from all connections with the society," five members for being "guilty of an ungentlemanly conduct." The nature of the offense was unnamed in the minutes.

Fines were also constitutionally mandated to preserve secrecy. One Phi provision invoked: "Every member of the Philomathesian Society be required to pledge his sacred word and honour to observe with the most in violent secrecy all the proceedings of that body during the process each shall place his hand on the Constitution and by-laws and say I do solemnly promise in the presence of all here on my sacred word and honour to keep secret all the proceedings of the society." In March 1838, the Philomathesian imposed a fine of five dollars, which, in today's terms, is closer to a $150 fine.[15]

One could appeal fines, often successfully when accompanied by a plausible excuse. But an appeal, even among friends, did not work every time. One meeting must have been interesting on a long December evening when the society did not find an answer to the apology letter satisfactory, and the society unanimously censured the member.[16]

The Philomathesians' Constitution in 1914 illustrates alterations to earlier versions, but also is an enigmatic continuity of the basic document, which over the decades held its character. Provisions, e.g., "every member of the Society having equal rights and privileges" and "every student of Wake Forest College is eligible for membership," lived on.[17]

Finances

From the beginning, finances were front and center in the Society's ledgers. As the organizations matured and took on more responsibilities, their financial woes became more serious until after the turn of the century with the addition of several student publications and the increasingly extensive Anniversary and Society days and Intercollegiate debates, financing issues became acute, leading to sharing arrangements

---

[15] Earlier postures via secrecy were sterner. In the mid-1870s, the Phis appointed a committee to ferret out "who has been revealing the Secrets of the Society." By the turn of the century, the strict adherence to strict secrecy regarding society work had begun to erode, and many instances of openness were occurring earlier. A 1909 editorial in *The Wake Forest Student* called for ending "holding meetings secretly. There is nothing but debates going on in either hall and the character of these debates could not be injured by allowing visitors for the Hill and from the opposite societies to attend them." *The Wake Forest Student*, Vol. 28, May 1909, page 801. "It would improve debating, checks on abuses, and society competition." Philomathesian Minutes, September 1905.

By 1931 few things were secret. In prior years, "No outsider was allowed to know who the officers were. Admission to the meetings could not be obtained except by giving the password, 'sentram.'... Those alone who have taken the initiation can be revealed the meaning of 'sentram.' Loyal Philomathesians continue to guard carefully the significance of the mystic word." *Old Gold and Black*, May 9, 1931, page 4.

[16] Philomathesian Minutes, December 2, 1843.

[17] Philomathesian Minutes, September 7, 1876.

with the student body and the College administration. The collateral loss was the Societies' loss of control.

This short accounting of the societies' finances does not intend to provide a considered history, but rather to share a flavor of the categories of finance issues that confronted the students during the first hundred years.

The financial beginnings were understandably strained. In the year the societies formed, 1835, a report on the books was provided, which indicated the society had a total of $180.97,[18] One-dollar subscriptions raised most of their account. The expenses were also high, including $63.46 for the identifier banner, music for the Fourth of July, and some books for the library. They still owed a balance for printing the Dockery oration.[19]

The 4th of July celebration became more formal three years later, with added expenses. The Address by the Rev. Thomas Meredith was authorized to be published in 400 copies, delivered at the commencement, and presented to the Wesleyan society.

The minutes accounting laid out income and expenses.

Monies collected and paid in 1836	$85.36
Monies collected on fines and fees	$34.30
Monies collected on various subscriptions	$79.10
Borrowed A. Parfrey	$23.50
Total¶	$222.26
Paid for books	$150.00
Paid for curtains, Etc.	$25.75
Paid for Oration	$22.50
Paid for Celebration	$ 0.00
Paid for Tickets	$ 2.00
Paid for Crape (death)	$ 2.50
Total	$220.75

The ongoing saga of trying to collect fines and dues infused the society minutes. In their first year, the Phis adopted a provision to coax fee collection. They voted "that if a member fails to pay his fees within six

---

[18] In adjusted terms, the Society balance sheet would be about $3,200 in 2022.

[19] The expenses incurred in hosting the 1st Fourth of July celebration are detailed in Chapter 1.

weeks after their due, he shall… be deprived of the use of the library for four weeks."[20]

In the early 1840s, the audit committee reported cash on hand to be $128, the amount to be paid out during the term of $114.70. The societies worked at the margin. Establishing the library and keeping the halls in order also consumed resources. During this period, however, there were fewer fines assessed. That could reflect perhaps the inability to pay fines, or maybe students were less disorderly (although there is no reason to believe that to be true). Students of this early era often came from modest means, even as they were among their community's elite.

Just after the Civil War, in February of 1868, an audit showed a balance of $141.25, In those years a sizable figure. Nonetheless, money was tight for decades after the war. Nearly ten years later, in 1875, a member was authorized "to buy one ream of paper for the society's use, also to buy 1 gallon of oil." In 1877, paper was a relatively expensive commodity.[21]

In a special 1905 meeting, the Constitution was waived by motion, and Mr. Fairfield was paid $1.25 per 5 yards of ribbon for use during the inauguration of Pres. Poteat. When H. W. Poteat became Wake's president, his son H. M. Poteat was then president of the Euzelian society.[22]

Debt collection was an ongoing mission. A Philomathesian tactic employed in 1874 asked the chairman of the finances committee to write to old members who are in debt to the Society, sending bills and requesting payment.[23] This post-graduation collection of dues and fines was most likely lackluster, or forgotten altogether.

Occasionally, the groups would enact programs aimed at helping alumni or current members. In 1874, the Philomathesians authorized "that 1/10 of the funds hereafter received by the society from whatever source, be reserved as a standing fund for the education of indigent

---

[20] Philomathesian Minutes, March 15, 1845.

[21] The minutes of the Euzelian Society were kept in a recycled store record ledger from New Bern, North Carolina, dated 1816. The minutes filled the remaining space on pages where the store's accounting did not fill an entire page.

[22] The society minutes often recounted expenses and income as reported by the treasurer but also regularly offered notes of individual charges, however small, several of which are illustrated elsewhere in this chapter. An example of these reports is a 1919 entry, "paid to Mr. Curry $8.00 for one box of oranges – $4.00 for one-half box of lemons, $2.00 for 4 pounds of grapes total of $14.00." Euzelian Minutes, March 8, 1919.

[23] Philomathesian Minutes, December 12, 1874.

members of the society for whose education there is no other provision."[24] The resolution goes on to specify the awardee had to be
recommended as a beneficiary by two-thirds of the society and with
good academic promise. The funding would be secret, presumably not
to embarrass the student, and they would be asked to pay back after
graduation.[25]

There could not have been much funding to distribute to deserving
members. Although likely unrelated, two years later, near the end of
the 1876 fall term, the Eu's auditing committee reported the Society's
balance as $3.74.[26]

The Society's financial manager presented fees of $810.67 for the 1886-
1897 year.[27] The fees were steep in the year that Wake Forest held its first
Trinity Debate. Converted into current value, this amount represented
Society memberships of about $26,500 and change today. Even in the
mid-19th century, Wake Forest catered to a certain elite. In the 1842 Phi
minutes, it was moved and passed that no member be allowed to pay
the debt of another member of the society; the reason for this policy was
not enumerated in the minutes.[28]

In 1888 the groupings had become more financially sound. Except for
Grover Cleveland's loss in his reelection attempt, the year would have
been a good one from the students' viewpoint. On March 24th, 1888,
the Euzelian Society resolved to buy gold-headed canes for each member
of the graduating class. The canes are engraved with the name of the
student, his degree, the year of graduating, and the words "Euzelian
Society." The cost of each cane is less than $5.00.[29]

The college was often in financial straits and was not a ready source
for the societies to tap. As late as 1848, President Taylor narrated, "the
liabilities of the Board had reached the sum of $20,000. Some were in
despair, and even hinted at the final abandonment of the enterprise."[30]

---

[24] Philomathesian Minutes, February 21, 1874.

[25] Philomathesian Minutes, February 21, 1874.

[26] Euzelian Minutes, November 7, 1876.

[27] Philomathesian Minutes, February 27, 1897.

[28] Philomathesian Minutes, 1842.

[29] Euzelian Society, March 24, 1888. Translates to about $160 today.

[30] Charles E. Taylor, 1896, History of Wake Forest College, *The North Carolina
Baptist Almanac*, Published by *The Biblical Recorder*, Raleigh, page 8.

The 1909 *Wake Forest Student* lists expenses and earnings for 1834-1835 students: tuition, board, sundries, stipend earned, and candles for light, dominate.

Yet the actual tuition for the college remained modest throughout, aimed at providing access to enable a trained ministry. The shortfalls were often of crisis proportion; finances were only righted by substantial donors (e.g., the Bostwicks of Boston) or good economic times with increased enrollment. At times, the margins of survival were so close that meeting faculty salaries was known to lapse.

According to *The College Bulletin*, in 1906, students paid only $14.50 when they graduated, and the "tuition fee ($25) is due in advance. No charge for tuition was made against students who are ministers or sons of ministers of the Gospel.[31] In the same year, food in a student boarding-

---

[31] *The Biblical Recorder*, July 1, 1903, page 13. In 1903, in an open letter, President Taylor wrote, "This item is very important. Tuition fees henceforth will be $25 per term instead of $30...Instead of the "incidental and library fee" ...a cash Matriculation fee of $10 will be collected ...Including ministers and minister's sons.

house would cost $1.75 per week, while a furnished room for two, with fuel, was $10-$20 each year (only $14 per year in the college dormitory). Books are estimated at $10, laundry at eight dollars, and lights at three dollars.[32] For much of the school's history, low fees were intentional, allowing students with moderate means to attend.

Rather than the societies tapping university resources, the reverse happened, as with President Poteat's letter to the trustees in 1916 seeking support for literary societies.[33] The respective committees in the literary societies voted that the society would contribute $15,000 toward the erection of a new building which would contain new society halls. Pres. Poteat said the building would cost $80,000, and the two societies were asked to contribute $30,000.[34] Presented in person to the Euzelian and Philomathesian Societies, President Poteat proposed that they cooperate to erect a Young Men's Christian Association building.

To the Philomathesian and Euzelian Societies, Wake Forest College: Wake Forest, N. C., September 15, 1916.

Gentlemen: In the report which I had the honor to present to the Board of Trustees of Wake Forest College in its annual session last May the following passage occurs:

The equipment for the literary societies is grossly inadequate for so large a student body. On occasions ... it is impossible for all so much as to get into their respective halls, and many of those who do enter them sit flat on the floor. The brilliant record of their representatives in intercollegiate debate and in public life is one of the chief distinctions of the College, and it cannot be unwise for you to go to the full length of your resources in providing adequately for their work... A new building for the societies and the religious forces of the College is an urgent necessity. It would not only serve directly the needs of these important features of our enterprise but also release valuable space for classrooms. It is not impossible that

---

[32] *College Bulletin,* 1906-1908, page 33.

[33] *Bulletin of Wake Forest College,* 1916, page 179-180.

[34] *The Charlotte Observer,* December 5, 1916, page 11. Much earlier, Philomathesians adopted resolutions, essentially kicking off a fundraising campaign to build a new Hall. The campaign was unsuccessful, wiped out, like much else, by the Civil War. Philomathesian Minutes, April 6, 1850.

the funds for such a social-life building will be provided without any financial obligation on your part, if you will authorize it.

The Board of Trustees did authorize such a building. I beg now to lay before you formally the proposition upon which the College seeks your cooperation. ... The amount of money needed for this building and its maintenance is $80,000... to inaugurate a campaign to secure the remainder of the proposed $15,000 contribution by each of the societies.

I have the honor, gentlemen, to be   Very respectfully yours,
                                        William Louis Poteat, *President.*

This financial quest did not come to pass, as other building projects intervened, and the societies ultimately lacked the assets. Meanwhile, the financial pressures assumed by expanded society functions (e.g., new publications) began to erode the budgetary distances between college and society. In 1904 a source would lament, "A major expense, of course, was *The Student,* and the recently established *Howler,* but also major expense was the invitations for the various events including commencement and anniversary day debates. They also had to finance the hosting of our participation in the Richmond ($40 November 1904) and other intercollegiate debates. On occasion, the societies had to go to the reserve funds." It would still take nearly twenty years before substantial cost-sharing took hold.

By 1922, both societies had taken the tracking and collection of assessments, subscriptions, and fines seriously, eventually transforming into full finance departments with secretaries and treasurers. Both societies operated similarly. At the beginning of the fall term, each member was advised on the aggregate of regular dues and when they should be due. Others were appointed to keep track of fines on a weekly basis, and delinquents were reported to the censor of the society, who then operated to enforce collection.[35]

---

[35] *Old Gold and Black,* February 17, 1922, page 2; Also, in 1922, under the tutelage of trustees and officials of Wake Forest College along with several members of the alumni, some economic stability was established. This plan was "known as a Sinking Fund of the Euzelian and Philomathesian Societies... The purpose and plan of the fund was to establish a permanent savings department for the two organizations... According to the latest report for the gentleman in charge of the funds now on hand, there is approximately $15,500 in the treasury, the amount being divided

By 1922, an *Old Gold and Black* survey found that opinion held that "the societies are accomplishing little in the way of their original purpose, and in the opinion of many of the students, have become the means of financing college publications and social functions of the year."[36] There was a worry that they had lost their mandate to teach all students public speaking. Attempted returns to emphasizing debating failed to revive the societies; the "serious" debaters were hosting other schools and soon were off to tournaments.

Yet the Societies' financial overstretch by 1922 could not be ignored, doubtless contributing to the end of mandatory membership and transfers of publication control.

Fines

The preferred, and likely effective method for ending hijinks, was to fine rule breakers. Not all students were of means, and fines had consequences for their financial well-being. Collecting fines also became an essential part of societies' budgetary health. Every financial statement recorded the fines assessed, who paid, and who was delinquent.

Thomas Harding's historical account of Literary Societies summarized: "Fines were a vital part of the proceeding of all societies. The relative importance of these fines is better understood when it is realized that during this era, the real value of money was high. Board and room for a collegian could be obtained for $10 per month, labor could be hired for $.50 per day."[37]

Fines were not a perfect fix, of course. While not a Wake Forest instance *per se*, a Missouri Society is illustrative of an era: "Despite the purchase of a new rug, members of the society persisted in spitting on the floor. A system of fines broke down when the membership continually remitted them on appeal, and even the installation of spit boxes furnished

---

almost equally between the two societies. Almost a third of that amount is invested in Liberty Bonds and other government securities." *Old Gold and Black*, February 17, 1922, page 2, 3.

[36] *Old Gold and Black*, January 27, 1922, page 1.

[37] Harding, T. S. (1971). *College Literary Societies: The contribution to higher education in the United States 1815- 1876*, Pageant Press International Corporation, New York, page 96.

only a partial solution."[38] The Wake Forest societies encountered similar difficulties in maintaining the beautiful carpets in their halls, as referenced later in this chapter.

Many of the fines were aimed to conduct an efficient meeting, a highly valued skill, but many of these instances point to a more human side of young men's hijinks. Although the meetings and debates were conducted with a high level of formality, as judged by today's standards, nevertheless, while admonished not to laugh, one imagines many instances of hilarity. The following Table 2, edited more for interest than representativeness, contributes a sense of what the rules hoped to regulate in different eras.[39]

TABLE 2: Decorum in the Hall – Fines

Leaving chair without permission; Leaning back in chair; Being absent longer than 10 minutes	Fined $.10	August 1840[40]
Lying down on two chairs.		September 1840[41]
Absent himself from the meetings three times in succession without an adequate excuse	Fined five dollars ($180 today)	November 1841[42]
Remaining seated during the prayers.	Fined $.25	May 24, 1868[43]

---

[38] Lomas, C. W. (1953). The Lighter Side of The Literary Societies, *Quarterly Journal of Speech*, *39*, page 48. Original, Minutes of the Athenian Society, University of Missouri, *Passim*, 1850-1861. The 1888 Phi constitution prescribed fines for "any member who chews tobacco in the hall, spit upon the floor."

[39] The process of identifying fines levied was through examination of the duplicate societies' ledgers (minutes). Fines were not systematically searched. Only segments of the minutes were examined. Fines over the years were repetitive and, for the most part, codified in their Constitutions. The fines noted in Table 1 were selected for their representativeness, but also at times for their unique human interest. Several are undoubtedly outliers.

[40] Philomathesian Minutes, August 1840.

[41] Philomathesian Minutes, September 1840.

[42] Philomathesian Minutes, November 1841.

[43] Euzelian Minutes, May 24, 1868.

Appending a handkerchief to Another's coattails while speaking.	Fined $.25	March 7, 1874[44]
Any permanent writing with anything but ink.	Fined $.50.	August 13, 1874[45]
Bringing a cane into the hall and using it.	Fined $.25	February 6, 1875[46]
Playing with a paper doll baby.	Fined $.25.[47]	February 13, 1875[48]
Rolling a ball across the floor during session.	Fined $.25.	May 8, 1874[49]
Playing marbles in front of the chapel	Provided Euzelians passed.	May 19, 1876[50]
Calling for the Question unreasonably	Fined $.25.	August 23, 1876[51]
Sitting in an unbecoming position.	Fined $.25;	April 17, 1880[52]
Moved to fine every gentleman who is brought up for laughing and confesses.[53]	Motion Rejected.	September 25, 1866
Wrestling after a debate in the hall.[54]		June 21 1842 June 2, 1860s
Lying on the floor (irreverent conduct).[55]		April 3, 1869

---

[44] Euzelian Minutes, March 29, 1884.

[45] Philomathesian Minutes, August 13, 1874.

[46] Euzelian Minutes, February 6, 1875.

[47] This would be a $6.40 nowadays.

[48] Euzelian Minutes, February 13, 1875.

[49] Philomathesian Minutes, May 8, 1874, "Were they rolling to each other? Were the speakers boring?"

[50] Philomathesian Minutes, May 19, 1876.

[51] Philomathesian Minutes, August 23, 1876.

[52] Euzelian Minutes, April 17, 1880.

[53] Philomathesian Minutes, September 25, 1866.

[54] Philomathesian Minutes, June 2, 1860.

[55] Euzelian Minutes, April 3, 1869.

Placing a hat on a bust.[56]	Fined $.25.	March 29, 1884
Making a "peculiar noise."[57]	Fined $.25.	April 5, 1884
Consulting a dictionary during a debate.[58]	Fined $.25.	October 17, 1885
Wearing a false mustache.[59]	Fined $.25.	January 23, 1886
Answering "Yes" instead of "Aye."[60]	Fined $.25.	January 28, 1893
Putting a cap on in the hall.[61]	Fined $.25	April 8, 1893
Entering the Hall in Athletic suit.[62]	Fined $.25	May 6, 1893
Leaning head against the clock, sighing, wearing a sweater in a ball, scratching Cook's head[63]		March 7, 1903
Reading over Patton's shoulder, eating peanuts in Hall[64]		November 12, 1903

Each society's constitution offered long and detailed sets of statutes. For example, the 1888 Constitution, Article 8 begins with this prologue, registering what constituted finable offenses:

Fails to address the President by his official title or leave blinds open or Windows up on leaving Hall, or is absent from Society longer than 15 minutes, the time prescribed by section C, or fails to return

---

[56] Euzelian Minutes, November 30, March 29, 1884.

[57] Euzelian Minutes, April 5, 1884.

[58] Euzelian Minutes, October 17, 1885.

[59] Euzelian Minutes, January 23, 1886.

[60] Euzelian Minutes, January 28, 1893.

[61] Philomathesian Minutes, April 8, 1893.

[62] Philomathesian Minutes, May 6, 1893.

[63] Euzelian Minutes, March 7, 1903.

[64] Euzelian Minutes, November 12, 1903.

key to the officer from whom borrowed within four hours, or is absent from any rollcall during a meeting of the Society, or laughs, or otherwise disturbs Society; or if a member whose duty it is to speak on question fails to speak five minutes, or if a Junior or disclaimer uses manuscript or book while speaking, or unless all the chairs are occupied, if any member occupies either of the two sofas during the session of Society, or leans his head against any wall, window facing, window blind, or door facing of the Hall, or calls for the division after the President has rendered his decision, shall be fined 25 cents.

It continued: "kicks or shakes the door seeking entrance, or fails to write a one half page or its equivalent as an evaluator, or fails to write and read before the Society 300 words as an original composition.

Constitutional provisions could be unforgiving. Some provisions evoking fines were perfectly clear:

Section 15: Not more than three members at the time shall be allowed to retire to attend to a call of nature. No other member shall be allowed to retire for the same cause, unless one of the three has returned or 15 minutes have expired.

Section 16: No member shall be excused from Society on Saturday morning to do any regular college work, or to fill any engagement with any professor, for a conference in regard to such work before 10:30 o'clock. No motion to excuse any member on such excuse shall be considered by the President.

By 1902, the fines were heavy. Recorded in just two Euzelian meetings, fines included $.25-$.50 for laughing aloud, lounging, talking, shooting toothpicks, throwing hat, groaning, punching a man in the ribs, tripping a man, and being unprepared for one's duties.[65] Maybe the debaters in the hall had become more raucous, or the fines were a means of revenue generation.

The primary thrust was to regulate behavior during meetings. Sometimes, these admonishments seemed minor, yet they rose to full society consideration, as with "Mr. Duffy moves for the society retract all it has said derogatory to Mr. Toss's character.[66] Or when Mr. C. moved,

---

[65] Euzelian Meeting, November 22 and 27, 1902.
[66] Philomathesian Minutes, March 12, 1870.

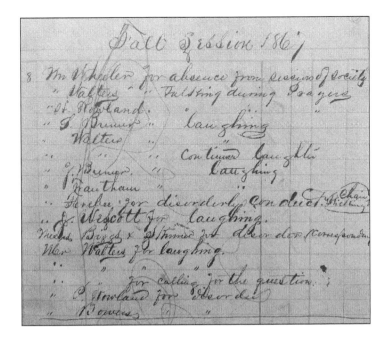

The 1867 Philomathesian meeting must have gotten the giggles.
Multiple fines were assessed for Laughing. Finding laughter in the
direct post-Civil War years was undoubtedly welcomed.

the doorkeeper ascertains who has the impertinence to trouble us by knocking at our door.[67]

On rare occasions, this deliberative effort involved resolving quarrels among members. In June 1872, a special Monday evening meeting was called, "The object of the meeting is to reconcile the difficulty arising between the members Mr. Herring and Kivitt... Statements having been made by each of them, the matter being discussed among the members.[68] But the matter was not settled.

A more formal resolution was adopted at the next meeting, June 8. It read, "Whereas Mr. Kivitt has been guilty of conduct which reflects discredited not only upon himself also upon the Philomathesian ... The conduct of this gentleman toward Mr. Herring was wholly uncalled for and deserving the severest reprimand of every member of the society.[69]

---

[67] Philomathesian Minutes, March 12, 1870.

[68] Philomathesian Minutes, June 3, 1872.

[69] Philomathesian Minutes, June 8, 1872.

Provisions were made for appealing fines by anyone who believes himself unjustly fined. Pleas were routine and often successful, not helping the treasury but aiding relationships.[70] Lying in an appeal could result in greater punishments[71], usually a figurative banishment. That form of separation on such a small campus often meant leaving the fold.

Rarely, a member would be expelled from the Society for "ungentlemanly conduct." The specifics of what was "ungentlemanly" were noticeably absent in the minutes. With great rarity, a proposed new member was not affirmed.

Even more rarely, a member would resign. Sometimes, resignations were accepted. Inviting someone back who had strayed was likely. In 1846, "the minutes recorded" a letter from Mr. Chovin asking... "That a committee be appointed to" consult with the gentleman and endeavor to bring him back to the society..."[72]

Any student of the institution was eligible for active membership, provided he was not a member of any other society. Originally, faculty members were permitted to become members of the society but were exempted from taking an active part.

In addition, early in 1842, the Eus made provisions for the reception of transient members, "any gentlemen of good character," who were elected and introduced to all members. These transients were free from charges and society fees. This provision seems to have been made for the benefit of residents of the vicinity who desired the advantages of the society. Few ever became transient members.

For some time, the conditions and terms of membership were not clearly defined or understood. This led to dissension, and some dissatisfied members offered their resignation. Because this misunderstanding

---

[70] Around 1914, the President appointed a "leave of absence committee." The student petitions would be heard assuming all fees and fines of the applicant had been paid, and the excuse was reasonable.

[71] At a Saturday morning meeting in April of 1906, the Euzelians presented for consideration, in part, the following resolve: That any member denying a charge when a member has direct proof that he is guilty of the offense, the said gentlemen shall be reported for contempt of Society. Euzelian Minutes, April 7, 1906.

[72] Philomathesian Minutes, November 21, 1846. In a subsequent meeting, "the committee appointed to wait upon Mr. Chapin and endeavor to turn him from his purpose, have used all honorable means to do so without effect." And he was dismissed. Philomathesian Minutes, November 28, 1846.

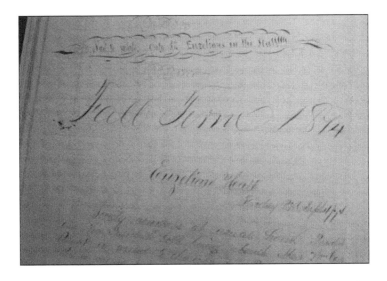

An embroidered note appears at the top, reading:
"Sorry to relate, Only 12 Euzelians in the Hall!!!!"

culminated in chaos, a committee was appointed in 1836 "to draw up a code of laws for the moral government of the society."

Fines and expulsion were the penalties for violating the code. One of the most rigidly enforced regulations stated that "any Member who shall play at any game of cards, or Who shall be guilty of uncleanness will be expelled." These laws, proving either unnecessary or inoperative, were soon repealed.

In the early 1900s, fines began to increase, the staple fine of $.25 that characterized most of Table 2, was sometimes sprinkled with the princely sum of $.50. Increasingly, finable offenses were organized by the amount of the fine; the insertion of the one-dollar category covered serious offenses that were largely unknown or unenforced (e.g., any member using any unfair means, such as electioneering, to improperly obtain the passage of a question or motion).

New categories were added as needed. For example, the business manager could be fined one dollar if *The Wake Forest Student* or *Howler* failed to make a report, as the societies became the purveyors of student publications. The severe fine of five dollars was reserved for any member elected as a Marshall and failing to serve or commit "a capital felony or do any act for which by the laws of the land he might be convicted and sent to jail or to the penitentiary."

Regulating Behavior on Campus

That societies regulated members' involvement in meetings and debates is to be expected. What is rather surprising is the degree to which they were responsible for each student's daily campus life.

In 1880, the Euzelians passed a resolution obligating each member to report if they saw anyone defacing the college hall.[73] Years earlier, "Mr. Thompson and Mr. Battle were fined for throwing eggs in and about the college."[74]

Protecting the campus at times sounded severe. In May 1875, three individuals were chosen as a vigilant committee "to keep order and unworthy persons from entering the College passages."[75] During the 1880s, "numerous petitions from the societies to the faculty asked, for instance, that the sheep and cows be kept off the campus."[76]

Mr. Bullock, Phi, was fined $1.00 for urinating out of the window. Others were assessed for the same or similar offenses. Two Euzelian students in 1884 were levied $1.00 for urinating near the College Building.[77] One account recorded a society member being fined for peeing out of a third-floor window in the Society Hall. In blending the mundane and the profound, an extension of the same sentence in the ledger's official minutes was celebratory of Stonewall Jackson's memory.

In 1905, the Euzelian Society boasted that, in addition to its many contributions to campus life, it tried to assume the self-imposed task of caring for the dormitories and campus grounds. Before the late 1890s, the faculty managed the dorms. The students initiated a "sanitary campaign," which forbade even throwing an apple peel on the grounds. The claim was that their spirit of cooperation prevailed among the students and was conducive to better student-faculty relations.[78]

---

[73] Euzelian Minutes, January 31, 1880.

[74] Philomathesian Minutes, May 16, 1874.

[75] Euzelian Minutes, May 22, 1875. It is thinkable that the general societal poverty created vagrancy.

[76] *Old Gold and Black*, February 17, 1922, page 2.

[77] Euzelian Minutes, February 9, 1884. They also were not tolerant: "any person spitting out the window be fined $.25," Philomathesian Minutes, 1842.

[78] Euzelian Minutes, 1904. Full control of the dorms in the end remained with the faculty. Also, Paschal, G. W. (1935), *History of Wake Forest College,* Vol. I, page 491.

The societies even adopted a role as the campus enforcement agent. One incident reported, "A student was molested last Thursday night by stones being cast into his room through the window and we believe such conduct to be uncharacteristic of a gentleman, as it was intended to do to him a private injury, which the perpetrator feared to do boldly and openly, but rather taking advantage of the darkness of the night, to conceal his dastardly act..."[79]

The standard of decorum for intersociety conduct was also enacted. The very first class of Philomathesians "resolved that any member who shall act so as to disturb the other Soc. while in session shall be subject to a fine of $.50.[80] It should also be noted that in a community so small, the students were close friends. [81]

In some matters, they had a level of control over their members that the faculty could never maintain. "The faculty could not keep the students from trampling the grass, or going to the train, or tearing down rustic benches or marking or defacing by whittling and carving college furniture and buildings, from spitting on floors of chapel and classrooms and halls, and library, or keeping firearms, or throwing water from the windows, but the Societies had little trouble with enforcing proper regulations about these things." [82] The faculty learned to work with the Societies, and, knowing the sharp rivalry between Societies, maintained a neutrality toward them.

LONG-TERM COMMITMENTS

From the outset, the societies undertook long-term obligations that chronicled campus life, sustained a public voice, and supplemented their debating. The following section explores three commitments that span their lengthy existence. The theme is the tenacity by which the societies reigned, even as some dark days plagued day-to-day life.

---

[79] Philomathesian Minutes, February 20, 1847.

[80] Philomathesian Minutes, November 21, 1874.

[81] "Societies often sparred on recruiting members, which was the organization's life-blood. The minutes occasionally reflected a dispute between the societies, accusing one another of violating the accord between the groups. For example, in 1870, the Phis accused the Eus of taking a member in "before regular time." Philomathesian Minutes, October 15, 1870

[82] Paschal, G. W. (1943), *History of Wake Forest College*, Vol. II, page 369.

Library

In their very first year, the societies focused on acquisitions for their libraries After calibrating their net worth, the Philomathesians passed a resolution in November 1835 "that all the money remaining in the treasury be passed over to Prof. Armstrong and that he be requested to purchase for the use of the society, such books as his best judgment shall dictate."

Initially, an $800 order for books was placed.[83] The book shipment's arrival, as Paschal details, "…was a great event in the institution; great crowds gathered round the box, even before it was opened, and when the lid was off and the bautiful (sic) new volumes laid out, they could not restrain their expressions of admiration, while those nearest would not make way for those in the rear, some of whom had to wait another day before getting to see and handle the volumes."[84]

As was the standard for the day, "Prof. Armstrong was charged with obtaining the books and then paid back." The list of purchases from the April authorization read:

Robertsons works three volumes	$6.00
Shakespeare's works two volumes	$6.00
Boswell's Johnson two volumes	$4.25
Johnson's works two volumes	$4.25
Berks works three volumes	$6.50
It's All Nations eight volumes	$10.00
French Revolution six volumes	$8.00
Goldsmith's works one volume	$1.75
Scott's works one volume	$1.75
Milon and Geyte one volume	$1.75
Herber and Hannah one volume	$1.75
Burns works one volume	$1.75
	$51.75[85]

---

[83] $800 in 1836 is equivalent in purchasing power to $26,530.49 today. Armstrong received the funding guarantee at the end of 1835; we assumed purchases were made in 1836.

[84] Paschal, G. W. (1935), *History of Wake Forest College,* Vol. I, page 524.

[85] Philomathesian Minutes, April 30, 1836.

Societies purchased works of fiction, history, politics, and science and made them available to society members. As historian Fredrick Rudolph summarized, the Societies' library served as an educational opening to a wider world. "Besides the curriculum, the extracurricular was of such dimension...as to materially recast the intellectual life of student learners."[86]

American fiction and English literature were first welcomed to campuses by literary societies with their libraries and student magazines.[87] That literature promoted learning more than a colorless curriculum with its ecclesiastical underpinnings.

The Wake President and faculty embraced the Societies in almost every way. No hints of flattening student inquiry appeared beyond that associated with routine joint acquisition plans. Indeed, choosing volumes exhibited the faculty and students' faithfulness to religion, yet the collections became more worldly as the years unfolded. The College was righteously religious but also embraced learning to its full extent.

Works of ancient Latin or tomes laying out mathematical methods were expected in a college education, but fiction was not advised for the "educated class." In addition to forbidding socialization with "young ladies," early prohibitions asked the students to refrain from reading contemporary works that were not in the school library.[88]

Through rare, the Societies' libraries explored beyond the classical, even as the selection process was conservatively assembled to ensure that the books were of "the highest literary merit." Each constitution accordingly required a committee for book selection and often invited the faculty for references.[89]

In their meeting jousts, debaters often weighed literature's worth. Faculties had long sought to "protect" students from low-level literature. Curious students welcomed a more enlightened mélange, especially for

---

[86] Rudolph, F. (1962). *The American College and University: A History*. University of Georgia Press, page 137.

[87] Rudolph, F. (1962). *The American College and University: A History*. University of Georgia Press, page 143.

[88] Potter, D. (1944). *Debating in the Colonial Chartered Colleges; An Historical Survey, 1642 to 1900,* Bureau of Publications, Teachers College, Columbia, page 239-40. Timothy Williams adds, "There exists, however, no evidence that their libraries contained controversial titles" although Williams provide no evidence for this claim. Timothy J. Williams, *Literary Societies at Wake Forest College*, Honors Thesis History, Wake Forest, 2002, page 7.

[89] Paschal, G. W., (1935). *History of Wake Forest College,* Vol. I, page 525.

leisure reading. Between 1858 and 1891, the Philomathesians debated ten times some versions of the topic: *Should students indulge in reading novels?* Eight favored reading novels. The Euzelian topic in 1839, the Institute's fourth year, cut to the nub of religion and the Enlightenment: *Is the tendency of novel reading destructive to morals and literature?* The answer was affirmative, and the topic was only debated once more in 1941 by the Eus.

BUILDING THE COLLECTION

As noted earlier, the Phi and Eus' emphasis on their respective libraries occurred at the outset. In mid-March 1837, the Phis appropriated $60.75 for acquisitions, a princely sum at the time.[90] Only a year earlier, in April 1836, the Philomathesians approved the purchase of several books, including a full encyclopedia set, for the real sum of $50.25, or $1360 in current exchange.[91]

In the same year these purchases were authorized, the Philomathesian Minutes provided a long list of donated books, including James Burgh's 1797 book *The Art of Speaking*. The book went through many editions. The donation to the Wake Forest Institute Library did not survive, possibly because the Literary Society men too often consulted it.[92]

The full title was *The Art of Speaking. Containing an essay in which are given rules for expressing properly the principal passions and humors, which occur in reading, or public speaking; and lessons taken from the ancients and moderns; Exhibiting a variety of matter for practice.* The book opening reads: "That Oratory is an art of great consequence, will hardly be questioned in our times, unless by those (if any are so ignorant) who do not know, that it has been taught, and studied, in all countries, where learning has been found, ever since the days of Aristotle."

The library received many books from alumni and friends. Most business meetings included a short list of books purchased or contributed

---

[90] Philomathesian Minutes, March 4, 1837. This section presents examples of contributions and acquisitions but is not intended to be representative of the scores of transactions that would have occurred with the societies prior to Wake assuming library management. Paschal provides names of major contributions and contributors in his *History of Wake Forest College*, Vol. I.

[91] Philomathesian Minutes, April 30, 1836.

[92] Philomathesian Minutes, March 19, 1836.

to the library. Notes of thanks were ordered, and totals spent were recorded.[93]

Later in 1916, a state senator made a notable enough contribution that it was reported in *the Fayetteville Weekly Observer*: State Senator A. D. Ward, provider of the Ward Medal for the Best Commencement Address, "presented the college library with a set of books on Southern Literature costing $75."[94]

Acquisitions were a recurrent element in business meetings. Oddly, the committee chair reported that, in 1873, "no books have been purchased during the term.[95] It may have been a particularly lean year.

The availability of materials that the members could obtain for the library was limited, but the Societies soon found avenues. In 1840, the Phi Society authorized bidding to obtain copies of the *North American Review,* the oldest literary magazine in the nation, founded in Boston in 1815. They were successful in purchasing 12 at the cost of $10, "a savings of five dollars, exclusive of their postage." They were to be added to the library reading room.[96] In 1845, the pre-Civil War Phis subscribed to the *Democratic and Whig reviews.*[97]

Euzelian minutes in April 1874 recorded a motion authorizing the chairman of the

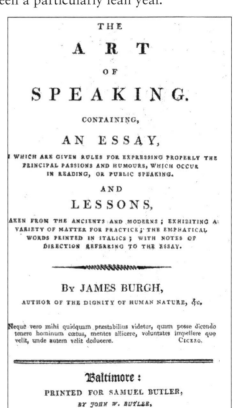

[93] Philomathesian Minutes, March 10, 1849; Euzelian Minutes, March 21, 1874.

[94] *Fayetteville Weekly Observer*, March 8, 1916, page 2. A. D. Ward was a Wake Trustee.

[95] Philomathesian Minutes, June 21, 1873.

[96] Philomathesian Minutes, March 1840.

[97] Philomathesian Minutes, November 23, 1845.

book committee to buy the book *Bible Looking Glass*. The committee reported on April 18 that they had received the book for $3.75, a hefty expense.[98] Religious treatises were not an uncommon purchase. In some instances, faculty and others were assigned as agents charged with acquiring books, often because of their distinctive access.

Sometimes the purchases (or failures to purchase) had political overtones. Soon after reconvening following the Civil War, the Phi Minutes (1868) discussed a motion relating to the book *The Life of Stonewall Jackson*. As one might expect, the group who later entertained the motion to replace the picture of Judge John Owen, a former governor, with the portrait of Stonewall Jackson to hang in their hall[99], decided in favor of buying the book.[100]

The membership had a penchant for books venerating its war heroes. As late as 1906, Mr. Ashcroft presented the society three, including, *Yesterday To-day and Forever*, $2 00; *Life of Gen. Lee*, $5.00, *History of the War Between States*, 2 vol., $9.00.[101]

In 1928, the small sum of $157.93 was appropriated for new books in the library.[102] By this decade smaller amounts were provided as the primary financial support had moved to the college.

[98] Euzelian Minutes, April 4, 1874.

[99] Philomathesian Minutes, September 5, 1874.

[100] Philomathesian Minutes, June 7, 1868.

[101] Euzelian Minutes, April 14, 1906.

[102] *Wake Forest Bulletin*, 1928-9.

MANAGEMENT

The libraries were an evident source of pride, curated and coddled. Yet they were similarly an uninterrupted provocation in managing their upkeep.

Before 1878, when the Societies' libraries were handled in one account... much of the activity centered around acquiring, reordering, shelving, reclaiming non-returned books, and monitoring returns before more books would be lent.[103]

Rules seeking to establish an "obtainable" library etiquette for the membership were rife. Circulation issues persisted the whole time. In only their second year, 1836, "Each member on borrowing books from the library" was asked "to put on a temporary cover, and in failing to do so shall be fined 5 cents."[104] Books were, after all, valuable and valued.

In 1840 the members seemed to be in the mood to account for their library missteps. In a March meeting, it was "... carried that any member taking any book at the library for anyone who may not be a member, shall be responsible for it for as if he had taken it out for himself and shall be entitled to only one volume a week for such a purpose."[105] Struggles in keeping the library in order only increased with more members and procurements.

On their shelves were found encyclopedias, dictionaries, and other books of reference, and temporarily, the library's literature on subjects proposed for debates by the literary societies.[106] For Hall shared preparation materials, "Debate literature and material was placed on reference in the library two weeks before each debate to prevent any excuses for being unprepared to speak... No slackers and kickers are wanted in society work this year."[107] Much earlier, in 1871, the minutes recorded, "the speaker was fined $.25 for getting a book during the debate." Those serving as the evening's critics were allowed to get a book from the library.

---

[103] *The Weekly State Chronicle*, June 11, 1886, page 1.

[104] Philomathesian Minutes, October 1836.

[105] Philomathesian Minutes, March 1840; Soon after the Civil War reopened, in May 1868, a Philomathesian meeting discussed whether to allow the faculty access to books in the library. Faculty access seemed to vary across decades.

[106] *Wake Forest Bulletin*, 1912.

[107] *Old Gold and Black*, October 6, 1928, page 2.

Payments for the library were an ongoing concern. Preserving the books, new acquisitions, and improvements were, at times, overwhelming responsibilities; often, the librarian or assistant librarian was seen to resign their post. A committee report of the 1871 Philomathesian meeting concluded, "Several of our books need binding but owing to the impoverished condition, the treasury committee did not think it advisable to have it done."[108]

The societies' sole ownership of the libraries shifted in 1879 when the Board of Trustees proposed to the Societies a handsome hall in the Heck-Williams building in exchange for their library volumes. The hall would be for the use of the Societies should they place their libraries under college monitoring, to be run by the faculty and students. The Societies accepted the proposition, and the "College Library," as it was named, contained 8,000 volumes with a 50,000-book capacity. At this time, the Wake Forest College Library was the largest in North Carolina.[109]

Thomas Pritchard, the student responsible for adding public debates on Anniversary Day, wrote brightly about the library in 1882. The centerpiece is the Reading Room, "in which nearly all of the papers of the state and many of the leading newspapers and periodicals of this country and Europe are found. The reading Room is open for two hours, and the Library one hour each afternoon...A library fee of $1.00 per term is collected from each student to be applied to the improvement of the Library."[110]

Publications

The Wake Forest Student was the eldest of the three major society publications—the monthly literary magazine, a weekly newspaper, and a Yearbook. The literary magazine, initiated in 1882, provided robust commentary on college happenings and student life. After over forty years, in 1932 the format was altered amid changing "news" alternatives, featuring almost exclusively humorous and literary work.

The Wake Forest Student began innocently enough when a small pamphlet was brought out secretly in the form of a sheet of paper and tacked

---

[108] Philomathesian Minutes, February 4, 1871.

[109] *The Wake Forest Student,* Vol. 1, 1882, page 61.

[110] Pritchard, T. H. (1882). Brief History of the Literary Societies of Wake Forest College. *The Wake Forest Student*, February 1882, Vol. 1, page 62.

to a tree in front of the old administration building. It was said to be distributed "on the dark of the moon by the sophomore class, and devoted to the interest of fresh, faculty, and fools."

The *Student's* sharp parody of campus life was the entry point for student publications. The second publication, the Howler, did not receive official recognition until twenty years later, 1903. The youngest of the college publications, a newspaper, the Old Gold and Black, was founded in 1916.111 Before these more formal methods of informing the school, outreach took the form of pamphlets in the early years.

PAMPHLETS

When resources allowed, the societies published the addresses as pamphlets when sponsoring high-profile speakers. Wake Literary societies took up the practice with passion, publishing as tracts the addresses of every anniversary speaker, save two, until the Civil War.[112]

Pamphlets served the educational function of Literary Societies, but perhaps more prominently they were the Societies' calling cards. Publication conferred status on the sponsoring organization and thereby on its members.

Obtaining a speaker's manuscript and arranging its printing was a considerable task. The difficulty of funding

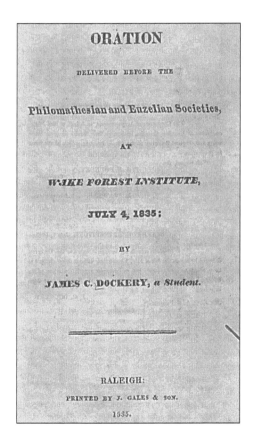

[111] *The News & Observer*, May 7, 1934. Special Issue on 100th Anniversary of Wake Forest.

[112] Paschal, G. W. (1835). *History of Wake Forest College*, Vol. I, page 562.

these pamphlets likewise was a never-ending issue. Disagreements over how to pay for the booklets and their distribution often dominated business meetings long into the night. Typically, the default solution in these funding questions was to assess member's subscriptions that they then paid.

Pamphlets were placed in the Societies' libraries and often distributed widely. Several copies were given to each faculty and society member. In chilly November 1838, in the Institute's fourth year, the society "tendered thanks to Weston R. Gales Esq. for the highly interesting, instructing, and eloquent address delivered the day before to the societies." In the Philomathesian minutes, they "believed others will read it with the same intense interest with which we listen to his delivery." They elected to print 800 copies of the address.[113] This printing may have been less costly as it was produced in the offices of Gales' own *Raleigh Register*.[114]

One example suggests the difficulty of collecting enough funding and producing sufficient copies for wide distribution; the minutes, in this case, reflect the money dues needed to publish the Rev. Meredith's 1837 address.[115]

---

[113] Paschal speaks to similar financial pressures in publishing Commencement speeches: "To publish these addresses, usually about 1,000 copies, was often very costly, especially if the address was long, the expense ranging from forty to one hundred dollars, but reaching the latter amount only when the printer took advantage of the polite young men who did not like to offend by getting prices beforehand. When the addresses had come, neatly stitched into regulation pamphlets, from the press, the Society that was publishing them would provide the other Society with a liberal number, present each member of the faculty with five or ten copies, send ten to twenty copies to the author, put a dozen or more in the Society archives, and distribute the remainder among its own members, who sometimes would find sale for them at five or ten cents a copy." Paschal, G. W. (1935), *The History of Wake Forest College*, Vol. I, page 561-562.

[114] *An address delivered before the Philomathesian and Euzelian Societies of Wake Forest College* by Weston R. Gales, printed at the office of the *Raleigh Register*, 1839; Weston R. Gales was the editor of the influential *Raleigh Register* and later Raleigh's mayor. In the preserved pamphlet Gales tips his hand early, "The dawn of liberty has ever been preceded by the rays of science; that where the faculties of the mind have been bound by the shackles of ignorance and superstition, there [is] oppression." Gales believed, "The language of the newspaper was the public conversation of the country." He opposed sensationalism of newspapers' crime coverage. https://www.ncpedia.org/biography/gales-weston-raleigh.

[115] One of the three purposes of the Baptist State Convention, stated in the constitution that Meredith drew up, was "the education of young men called of God to the ministry." Wake Forest Institute received his staunch support. In its first year,

The amount for printing the address	$35.00
Collected on subscription	$19.50
Remaining due on subscription	$ 7.40
Amount collected and subscribed	$26.90
Yet lacking to the amount	$ 8.10
Receive since the report was made out	$ .50
Leaving wanting to the amount	$ 7.60[116]

In 1842, Phi minutes reflected the oft-repeated difficulty of paying for the printing of manuscripts. The minutes recorded that Mr. Cotton's address made a sale of 33 copies, leaving 46 copies in their possession. The motion was offered to "take the remaining copies of the address to Raleigh next winter and distribute them to the honorary members of the society in the legislature."[117] In the same meeting, they talked about the charge of $50 to publish 600 copies of Mr. Childers' oration. Only 255 were sold.[118]

THE WAKE FOREST STUDENT

Thomas Dixon, the soon-to-be-well-known novelist, as Corresponding Editor, along with fellow editors, W. H. Osborn and Charles Smith, give birth to *The Wake Forest Student* in 1882. It was literary and populated by campus news until its temporary discontinuation in 1928. When the magazine reemerged in 1932, it had changed its nature to primarily a literary-humorous publication.[119]

---

he was the chair of mathematics and moral philosophy, and in 1838, he was elected president of the board of trustees." Meredith was far ahead of his time in his concern for the education of young women. In 1838, as chairman of a committee, he offered a resolution urging the "convention to establish a female seminary of high order... modeled and conducted on strictly religious principles but ... as far as possible free from sectarian influence." The convention adopted the resolution but took no steps toward carrying it out. Sixty-one years later, in September 1899, the Baptist Female University opened its doors, and in 1909, it was renamed Meredith College. https://www.ncpedia.org/biography/meredith-thomas.

[116] Philomathesian Minutes, November 1837.

[117] Philomathesian Minutes, 1842.

[118] Philomathesian Minutes, October 1837.

[119] *Howler*, 1936, page 156. *The Wake Forest Student* was also temporarily suspended from 1924 to 1925, but it continued from 1926 through 1928, when it was discontinued again in 1932, only to be revised in multiple versions over the years, as a literary magazine.

The Wake Forest Students'
roots began earlier in February 1877 when the Euzelians
adopted a motion requesting
the editor of *The Biblical
Recorder* include a weekly
column written by one person
from each society.[120] A month
later, in March, W. L. Poteat
was chosen as the editor of the
Euzelian Society to write the
Wake Forest Column.[121] The
future Wake Forest President,
however, graduated and took
formal leave.

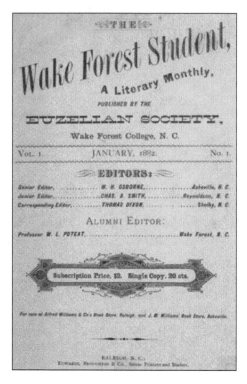

The following semester, E.
M. Poteat, W. L.'s younger
brother, begins to attend Euzelian Society meetings.[122] He
became a Euzelian man and,
in 1881, drafted resolutions that selected a group of men to compose
the *Wake Forest Magazine*.

November 26th, 1881, E. M.'s brother, Professor W. L. Poteat, was
selected as the faculty editor for *The Wake Forest Magazine*.[123] A month
later, *Wake Forest Magazine* was renamed *The Wake Forest Student*. [124]

The Wake Forest Student prevailed as a leading campus voice for
around forty years. The publication was substantive, disseminating
major essays, literature, poetry, and campus gossip, often from the
student's point of view.[125] Published monthly during the school year,

---

[120] Euzelian Minutes, February 24, 1877.

[121] Euzelian Minutes, March 10, 1877.

[122] Euzelian Minutes, June 9, 1877.

[123] Euzelian Minutes, November 26, 1881.

[124] Euzelian Minutes, December 10, 1881.

[125] Not an atypical program, the content of a 1917 issue was listed in the campus
newspaper: *On New Year's Eve* (verse), Roscius; *Thomas Jefferson* (Essay), A. C.
Reid; *To A Portrait* (verse), W. B. Sinclair; *What is Coming* (sketch), J. A. MacK-
aughan; *Twilight* (verse), E. J. Trueblood, *The Non-Slaveholders of The South* (essay),

it functioned as the college's informal history for much of this period. During President Taylor's administration, *The Wake Forest Student* "was the medium of the college students and faculty for the publication of their production, except for the annual college catalogue and occasional bulletins."[126]

The Wake Forest Student was often in arrears. In the Spring term of 1900, for example, receipts were $588.58, disbursements $562.67, with the balance on hand of $25.91[127], in sharp contrast to when the societies' entire operation, including Commencement and Anniversary and Society Days expenses, was in the $200 range.

It was apparent to *The Wake Forest Student* editorialist that when Society membership was no longer mandatory, there would be uncertainty about the future of the Society Day, Anniversary Day, and their publications, as the societies would be financially unable to sustain them. They would have to be "financed through some other agency."[128] Presumably, the college's Bursar.

Some students pushed back, believing that "*The Student* as a literary magazine should continue to be fostered and championed by the literary societies."[129] But the die was cast. In April of 1922, as mandatory membership ended, the Faculty accepted the Societies' request to forgo their financial responsibility while leaving the management of debates and publication of *The Wake Forest Student* with the societies, and putting *The Howler* on the basis of financial support from the student body.

The relationship between exercising their editorial freedom and with faculty was not always smooth. A Euzelian motion in 1906 read:

> In order that further conflict between editorial staff of the Student and the Faculty may be ended for the present time, BF moved that the manuscript for *The Student* for the remaining three months of this term be left in the office of the president to be handed by them to some member of the faculty and we think it best on account of

---

R. E. Hurst; *Stick to It* (verse), E. F. Cullom; *Saint Francis of Assisi* (sketch), C. P. Hening; *Clouds and Sunshine* (verse), W. B. Sinclair.

[126] *Old Gold and Black*, May 24, 1946, page 2.

[127] Philomathesian Minutes, September 15, 1900.

[128] *The Wake Forest Student*, January 1922, page 305.

[129] *The Wake Forest Student*, April 1922, page 240.

the present unpleasantness that it be handed to some other than the present alumni editor.[130]

The nature of the kerfuffle or its "resolution" were not aired publicly; at least, our inquiries did not unearth it.

Following the periodical's 1928 suspension, it moved away from being a publication of record, a role increasingly assumed by the *Old Gold and Black,* to becoming a literary outlet. It also took on a more humorous tone, harking back to its beginnings, lampooning college life in pamphlets nailed to a tree. The faculty and administrators protecting the school's reputation were less amused. By this time, they held the purse strings.

The Wake Forest Student's status became dubious in 1933. The College newspaper headline scolded:

Publication is Suspended in Meeting of Committees
The Student, Literaty-Humorous College Periodical, will appear No More
COMMITTEE TO REDUCE COST OF PUBLICATION
Students will Hold Meeting to Vote on Refund of Seventy-five Cents

The accompanying article states, in part, the Dean's reasoning, which the paper reported as saying "that the content and character of the present *Student* reflects the type of sentiment that the college cannot afford to sponsor." The statement was cryptic, but someone had been offended. The pivot in the article was to characterize the change as a move to protect students from the seventy-five cents general fees each semester to support *The Student.* A student referendum might be called, and the five-dollar fee to support the *Howler* was threatened to be dropped.[131] The publication reappeared in October of 1933, evidently without faculty censorship.

HOWLER

The first *Howler's* preface wrote that the *Howler* was founded as a "publication of the student-body, edited and printed by students for students, to this passing and unsubstantial record of college life we dedicate this,

---

[130] Euzelian Minutes, March 31, 1906.

[131] *Old Gold and Black*, Feb 11, 1933, page 1.

the first volume of "The Howler, hoping that we have made a substantial record of the collegiate year 1902-03."

For decades, the *Howler* functioned as the record of student life, faithfully accounting for the events and organizations of campus life.[132] In the late 1960s, in the grip of the Vietnam conflict and a rapidly changing domestic landscape, along with publications following the artistic cultural flair into Avant-garde commotion, the *Howler* ceased to be a reliable publication of record.[133]

In its years of greatest influence, the *Howler* expanded upon and largely replaced the reflection in *The Wake Forest*. Prior to the official *Howler* in 1903, the only record of college life, outside of *The Wake Forest Student*, was the "Old Howler," vocal "tree bulletin" board.

About once a month, the students would gather around the tree and read a treatise known for representings college life in a "jocular way." The "New Howler" acknowledged in the precedent version that sometimes the jokes were a "little shady," and the new version would "add more dignity and strength."[134]

The Yearbook *Howler's* first
Illustration – 1903

---

[132] Each class and organization was able to report their annual highlights. On occasion, they approached their constituency with a clever bit of whimsy. The *Wake Forest Student* editors wrote, "Since the Howler board of editors sent out their card requesting a vote for each student on the most popular, the handsomest, the ugliest, etc....not a few of the handsome ones have brought out their Anniversary suits to aid them in the race."

[133] The *Howler* corrected many of the 1990s "cultural excesses," favoring artist layout at the expense of preserving a record, but now the publication was faced with the daunting task of seeking an audience for its content.

[134] *Howler*, 1893, Preface.

Like other publications, the *Howler* scrambled to pay the bills. Almost yearly reminders were circulated, chiding the students to do their part and purchase that year's installment. Typical is a 1904 prompt, "Last year, much to the discredit of the student body, the number of boys buying an annual was pitifully small. This in a large measure accounts for the great debt which the editors contracted."[135]

Others praised. *The Biblical Recorder* observed, "We had received 'The Howler.' – The Wake Forest Annual for 1903. The title will stir the memories of many an old student. ... we have heard that two students, Messrs. Sherwood and Camp are backing this enterprise, having put $600.00 in it. This sort of "patriotism" commends applause...Its price is $1.00. Everyone should buy a copy.[136]

OLD GOLD AND BLACK

The last of the societies' publications was The *Old Gold and Black*, which may have roots older than the other two student outlets. An article mentions a potential precursor in 1849: "Sailing gaily forth under the title, *The Saturday Review*," ... solicited contributions of "witticism, of criticism, and burlesques on the student, faculty and condition in college."[137] The *Old Gold and Black*, however, was not officially sanctioned until 1916.

---

[135] *The Wake Forest Student*, Vol. 23, January 1904, page 252.

[136] *The Biblical Recorder*, May 20, 1903, page 5; E. L. Sherwood is the same individual debating in the 1902 first Richmond Intercollegiate Debate; unfortunately, they were not winners.

[137] *Old Gold and Black*, November 18, 1921, page 1. "Publication" was accomplished orally, a student reading it aloud..." Picture a college lad of the period perched upon a stump, his face ambushed behind his whiskers, wearing extremely baggy "breaches." The review, it appeared, "'flourished for a few months." A similar effort was tried with *The Critic* in 1859. These reported publications were not verified in this research and the Wake Archive office also was unable to find evidence of the "publication" (orality unpreserved).

Old Gold and Black, Vol. 1, No. 1. Founded January 19, 1916

The early years were somewhat rocky. In the publication's third year, the Euzelians, in March of 1919, "appointed a committee to investigate the books of the business manager of the *Old Gold and Black*, with a view to deciding the advisability of discontinuing." The committee reported that the cost of paper was enormous. The chair appointed a committee to confer with a similar committee from the Phi. Society and the faculty to consider the advisability of discontinuing the paper.[138]

After having been suspended for six months, *Old Gold and Black*, "the weekly bearer of the college life at Wake Forest college, promises to put an appearance this week. The publication, which was once a private enterprise, and later published by the athletic Association, has proved a failure, financially in the past; but its future is assured as it has been made an organ of the Euzelian and Philomathesian literary societies, and will now be put on a solid financial basis."

That financial certainty took time, yet the paper emerged as the vital campus voice, holding sway for seven decades. If events, people, and organizations were covered in the *Old Gold and Black,* they *were* Wake Forest.

UNIVERSITY DEBATERS' ANNUAL

The *University Debaters' Annual* was not a Wake Forest publication, yet it deserves mention as an important moment in Wake Debate. The Annual served as an influential nationwide model for debating for twenty-plus years,[139] an authority that also touched the Wake squad. The publication

---

[138] Euzelian Minutes, March 1, 1919.

[139] https://the3nr.com/2021/06/16/the-evolution-of-plans-in-policy-debate-part-1-the-early-history/.

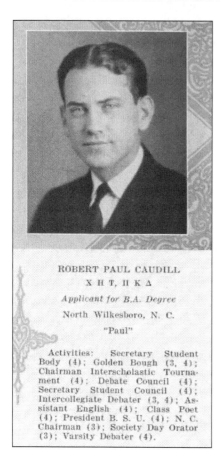

ROBERT PAUL CAUDILL
Χ Η Τ, Π Κ Δ
Applicant for B.A. Degree

North Wilkesboro, N. C.

"Paul"

Activities: Secretary Student Body (4); Golden Bough (3, 4); Chairman Interscholastic Tournament (4); Debate Council (4); Secretary Student Council (4); Intercollegiate Debater (3, 4); Assistant English (4); Class Poet (4); President B. S. U. (4); N. C. Chairman (3); Society Day Orator (3); Varsity Debater (4).

debuted with a 1914-1915 edition. "Debaters and coaches considered it a great honor to be included, and the handbooks were the key to learning how to gather information proficiently and distill it into arguments."[140]

Characteristic of the series, the 1920 volume featured eight nationally drawn intercollegiate debates, each with an introduction, an affirmative and negative brief, the first, second, and third affirmative and negative speeches, rebuttals, and bibliographies for each resolution. The first volume featured debates between the University of Washington and Harvard on *The suppression of propaganda for the overthrow of the United States Government* and the University of Redlands and Leland Stanford Junior University on *Compulsory arbitration of railway labor disputes.*[141]

R. Paul Caudill,[142] the winner of every debate award available at Wake, had one of his debates published in the 1928 volume of the *University*

---

[140] Keenan, C. J. (Fall, 2009). Intercollegiate: Reflecting American culture, 1900-1930, *Argumentation and Advocacy*, 46, page 94.

[141] Keenan, C. J. (Fall 2009). Intercollegiate: Reflecting American culture, 1900-1930, *Argumentation and Advocacy*, 46, page 94.

[142] R. Paul Caudill, born in Dockery, N.C., in 1904, was the author of over 25 books. He was the fifth generation in his family to be a Baptist minister, enjoying an influential career in Southern Baptist circles. Dr. Caudill was 97 years old and pastor emeritus of First Baptist Church of Memphis. He obtained his Ph.D. from Southern Baptist Theological Seminary in Louisville, Ky. At the First Baptist Church of Memphis, he began a ministry for the deaf in the city and established a Chinese Baptist Church. In his retirement years, he preached regularly at the Shelby County Penal Farm and was instrumental in building a chapel on the grounds. He was a

Debaters Annual.[143] The debate featured Wake versus North Carolina State College, discussing the topic: *Unanimous jury, Three-fourths jury vote in criminal trials.*

Honors and Awards

HONORARY MEMBERS

From the outset, the Philomathesians and the Euzelians welcomed honorary members and guest speakers to various events. One letter from Rich O. Britton accepting his honorary membership with the Phi's apologized for being late in the return of his letter, he wrote "The evening previous to my leaving home for the mountains of Virginia, where my family had gone for the benefit of their health, I intended to have answered it immediately on arriving at the place of my destination, but I was severely attacked with the Bilious Fever [severe indigestion], which can confined me to my bed for some time, which was the cause of the delay..." The letter reveals health uncertainties that accompany most of the college's history, yet an invitation was rarely unheeded.[144]

Both societies' constitutions allow persons of distinction to be for election as honorary members. A reading of the societies' minutes suggests that nearly all nominated were approved; hardly a year passed without each society selecting a score or more. The Euzelian records indicate that by 1840, they had elected 58 honorary members and 332 honorary members by 1860.[145]

The Philomathesian Society decorously debated in March 1844 whether *It would be in the interest of the U. S. to admit Texas into the union*, with the affirmative winning by a narrow margin, 10 to 9. At the same meeting, Mr. Langford read a letter from Samuel Houston

---

trustee of Baptist Memorial Hospital for 30 years. In the summers, he traveled to mission fields, engaging in evangelistic work. He led First Baptist to build nine chapels in Africa and a hospital in Bangalore, India.

[143] Phelps, E. M. (1927-1928). *University debaters annual: Constructive or rebuttal speeches delivered in debates of American Colleges and Universities during the College year, 1927-1928.* New York, the H. W. Wilson Company, (pp. 305-346). The published debate featured North Carolina State University and Wake Forest.

[144] Society Correspondence, 1836.

[145] Euzelian records, 1835-1860.

Samuel Houston, first (1836-1838) and third (1841-1845) President of the Republic of Texas. He played a key role in the annexation of Texas by the United States.

accepting honorary membership in the society.[146] In the year of his induction as a Philomathesian in 1844, Houston was in the last year of his second term as President of the Republic of Texas.

Samuel Houston's letter read:

My Dear Sir,

I have had the honor to receive, after a long delay, a note from the proper officer of the Philomathesian Society at Wake Forest College, tendering me, in the most flattering terms, the valuable distinction of honorary membership without body.

I beg you, in return of this mark up the two partial considerations to offer to the members of this Society in a most grateful acknowledgment and to assure them that they have, individually and collectively, my best wishes for their happiness in life and success in the ennobling pursuit to which they are dedicating so many precious hours.

The time will come when the best interests of Society and country will claim something at their hands. May they never be found wanting! Let them learn early the duties and obligations of an American citizen (and how superlatively glorious is that name!) North Carolina herself does not lack a model for her sons. The memory of Macon, the pure and incorruptible, will lead them on to the acquisition and practice of every virtue that can adorn the man, the patriot and the statesman.

On this continent, too, the fields of literature, science and the arts are to a great extent unbroken. Their resources are rich and varied. Talent and learning may develop them with an advantage.

With pleasure I accept the proposed membership and on becoming a Philomathesian, I beg to express the hope that, though widely

[146] Philomathesian Minutes, March 17, 1844.

separated, we all may be closely united in the common task of doing in our respective spheres, all the good we can towards God, our country and our fellow man.

With feelings of deep regard for the prosperity and usefulness of the Society and the young gentlemen, its members.

> I am, Sir,
> with most respectful salutations
> your obt. servt
> Samuel Houston

Two years later, in 1846, in a book Houston enclosed to the society: "Presented to the Philomathesian Society of Wake Forest College, North Carolina, by their friend and fellow member, Washington City, June 5, 1846." Houston's inscription was within the book *Report of Exploring Expedition to the Rocky Mountains in the year 1842 and to Oregon in North California in the years 1843-44,* an influential treatise on westward expansion written by Capt. J. C. Fremont.[147]

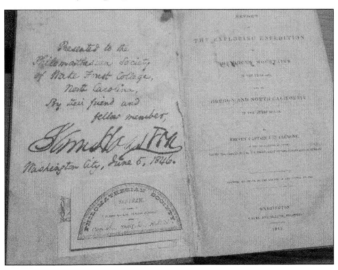

"Presented to the Philomathesianb Society of Wake Forest College, North Carolina, by their friend and fellow member," Samuel Houston, Washington City, June 1846.
In Exploring Expeditions of the Rocky Mountains by Capt. J. C. Fremont

---

[147] John C. Frémont, Republican politician, American explorer, military officer, and US Senator from California lost the 1856 Presidential election (Electoral College 174 to 114) to James Buchanan, whose election was a harbinger of the coming Civil War.

In the early years, honorary members were drawn from both Northern and Southern politicians. In the first round of honorary membership accepted by the Phis, (1835), Henry Clay expressed his pleasure in receiving honorary membership and added his "fervent hopes for" the "welfare and fame" of the societies. Daniel Webster also wrote, from Boston, thanking and accepting the Philomathesians as "brethren."[148] Prior to the Civil War, major national figures, representing Whigs and Democrats, Anti and pro Slavery politicians, were invited, an openness that came to a close as the War approached.[149]

During the mid-1800s, "the Euzelian Society elected soon-to-be President James K. Polk as an honorary member, and the president's letter of acceptance is one of the rare possessions of the society."[150] Polk addressed the Euzelian Society on 15 June 1842 with warm appreciation and acceptance of honorary membership. He emphasized the importance of "the association of young Gentlemen and the organization of Societiez (sic) such az (sic) I understand yourz (sic) to be" within American colleges and universities.[151]

In the immediate aftermath of the Civil War, honorary membership entered a provincial period. The Societies felt it safe to show their preference for men and things Southern. In selecting gentlemen for honorary membership, they elected Lee and not Grant.[152]

---

[148] Henry Clay and Daniel Webster in *A Book of Correspondence of the Philomathesian Society*, ZSR Baptist Historical Collection, Z. Smith Reynolds Library, Wake Forest University, Winston-Salem, North Carolina. The Philomathesians favored Clay so much that, when they debated whether he should be the next president, it prompted an anonymous jokester scribbled within the margins of the query book, "yes by jolly!" as reported in Timothy J. Williams, *Literary Societies at Wake Forest College*, Honors Thesis History, Wake Forest, 2002, page 12.

[149] Distinguishing aside: Daniel Webster (Dartmouth), Henry Clay (Richmond), and John Calhoun (Waddel School, GA, Yale) each attributed their skills for public careers to their early Literary society days. Hellman, H. G. (1942). The Influence of Orators on Public Speaking, *Quarterly Journal of Speech*, 28, No.1, page 11, 12.

[150] *Old Gold and Black*, February 23, 1935, page 1. Efforts to locate the letter in the ZSR Library collection were unsuccessful.

[151] Euzelian Correspondence Box, Literary Societies, WFRG 6.2. As reported by Timothy J. Williams, *Literary Societies at Wake Forest College*, Honors Thesis History, Wake Forest, 2002, page 12.

[152] Paschal, G. W. (1943). *History of Wake Forest College,* Vol. II, page 57-58. They also subscribed to Mr. Hill's magazine. *The Land We Love* was a magazine published monthly in Charlotte from May 1866 to March 1869. Founded and edited

After the War, 1886, the Phis presented a resolution offered by Mr. Oliver "to erase names of honorary members who are 'radicals,' which is laid on the table."[153]

There were some rejections, although a rebuff of a nominated honorary member remained extremely rare. An 1872 Phi meeting rejected an honorary member, likely for "political" reasons." "The motion to elect Mr. DA Jenkins of Raleigh (State Treasurer) as an honorary member of our society was rejected."[154] Although not indicated in the minutes, identification with the Republican candidate during the Reconstruction era was just too much baggage.[155]

Occasionally, one of the student's professors would be tapped for membership. In 1900, the Phis elected Professor Crittenden as an honorary member. Prof. Crittenden worked closely in support of the societies.[156] When the young Prof. Crittenden passed away three years later, the "Resolution of Respect" was jointly signed by three members of both the Euzelian and Philomathesian societies.[157]

In the college library, still preserved, are letters of acceptance from many famous men in history. The Phi records hold one from Henry Clay in 1835, "Gentlemen: I have received your favor communicating the wish of the

---

by ex-Confederate General Daniel H. Hill, it reflected interests, tastes, and beliefs as a Southerner and an academician, NCPedia https://www.ncpedia.org/land-we-love.

[153] Philomathesian Minutes, August 7, 1868.

[154] Philomathesian Minutes, October 12, 1872.

[155] https://www.ncpedia.org/biography/jenkins-david-aaron, NCPedia's historical brief of Jenkins concluded that "When the Civil War was imminent, he was unquestionably loyal to the South, but he foresaw the inexpediency of secession and was opposed to it. During the conflict he was, as a magistrate, exempt from active field duty. After the war, he became identified with the Republican party, holding the view that the interests of the people could best be served by their taking an active part in politics and seeking, by their influence, to temper and restrain the excesses of those in power.

[156] From Paschal, G. W. (1943). *History of Wake Forest College*, Vol. II, page 506. Professor C. C. Crittenden, a professor with the School of Pedagogy. "His life and his service at Wake Forest College were both brief. He was nearly twenty-eight years old when he came to the College in September 1900, and he died on April 23. 1903, after an attack of influenza. On July 23, 1901, he married Miss Ethel Taylor, daughter of President Charles E. Taylor."

[157] Philomathesian Minutes, April 25, 1903. Additional tributes also were presented, including W. B. Royall's in *The Biblical Recorder*, "In the cause of popular education Prof. Crittenden was an ardent worker. His interest in the schools of the community, white and colored, was genuine and practical." April 29. 1903, page 5.

Philomathesian society of the institute at Wake Forest to place my name on the list of its honorary members. Greatly obliged by the friendly sentiment toward me which promoted that wish, I take particular pleasure in seeing to it, and shall feel honored by the association of my name with those in the memory of the society..."[158]

A century later, during the first week of October 1946, Pres. Harry S. Truman was made an honorary member of the Philomathesian Literary Society. The 1947 yearbook boasted in the Phi writeup that famous honorary members showed the society's prowess. "The Phis didn't stop with President Truman as it also "voted to send letters invitation to such persons of contemporary promise as Clare Booth Luce, Carl Sandberg, Robert Frost, Winston Churchill, Walter Lippmann, Dwight Eisenhower, and Richard Wright, among others.[159]

The selection of Richard Wright, Negro novelist, shattered a century-old precedent that had forbidden the bestowing of honorary membership upon any Black person. There was only slight opposition to the selection of Wright.[160]

Individuals were suggested because of some outstanding accomplishments in the field of literature or world affairs. Mrs. J. A. Webb of New York, also among 1947 nominees, was a unanimous choice of the Philomathesian Society because she is the only living person known to have been named for the society.

The Phi's broke a tradition this year in choosing among those selected for invitation to honorary membership, Mrs. Philomathesia Fold Webb."[161] According to facts related at the meeting, "Mrs. Webb's father was one of the first members of the Phi Society, having entered Wake Forest 100 years ago this fall, 1857. He and three sons, all of whom came to Wake Forest and likewise affiliated with the Phi's. Mrs. Webb was the first girl in the family, and because she could not attend what was then a strictly

---

[158] Hughes, D. (1955). Phis had membership problem in 1950s, *Old Gold and Black*, October 24, page 2.

[159] *Howler*, 1947, page 18.

[160] *Old Gold and Black*, October 11, 1946, page 5.

[161] *Howler*, 1947, page 117. The Euzelians also had a namesake, Mrs. Euzelia Dunn Fort. She was born Euzelia Dunn in 1871. Her uncle John Ray bestowed the name Euzelia, who regarded his college society most highly. William Pate, *Old Gold and Black*, November 16, 1953, page 4.

men's school, her father bestowed upon her the name Philomathesia, so that she might still be a "Phi."[162]

MEDALS

For over a century, the awarding of medals to the top society performances helped define a sense of reward, solicited public recognition and triggered alumni interest. Each class received community acclaim when publicly saluted at graduation.[163]

In the pre-Civil War decades, societies were full of pomp and circumstance, displays not limited to commencement. In 1851, for example, they resolved:

> We should have some badge of distinction more perfect and permanent than the one we now have by which the members may be distinguished, and which will answer for a marked distinction between the members of the Society and the world, when they have assumed the attitude of an active and manly life.
>
> Therefore, let it be unanimously resolved that the Philomathesian Society do away with the badge of white ribbon usually worn on commencement occasions and substitute the strip of gold to be made in the shape of the Greek letter Phi, with a sentence inserted in the main stem of the letter.
>
> "Resolved that we be aware of this badge through life." It also suggests that the Euzelians do the same.

The resolve was awash with hubris.

Regalia's importance never fully abated. In January 1910, the Euzelians entertained the adoption of a resolution to be submitted to pass as a law of the State of North Carolina. It asked for legislation protecting the Euzelian Society pins, badges, and medals from people wearing them who are not and have never been in the Society.[164] We did not find evidence

---

[162] *Old Gold and Black*, October 11, 1946, page 5.

[163] *Old Gold and Black*, May 19, 1950, page 3. The names of medal winners can be found in the chapter "Wake Forest's Oratorical Tradition" in Louden, A., & Atchison, J. (2022). *Milestones: Defining Lists of Wake Forest Debate 1835-2022*. Library Partners Press. It is not a full or systematic listing but captures many winners.

[164] Euzelian Minutes, January 16, 1910.

that the legislature took up the issue, but it further suggests a certain audacity. In fairness, their expression emanated from the Literary Society world they inhabited, the world they were experiencing

Medals, especially in the late 1800s and early 1900s, were a focal symbol of achievement among one's peers. In memorials or introductions, the speaker's college exploits were often recounted as "the winner of the Dixon or White Medals," much as one would recall an athlete's number of championships today.

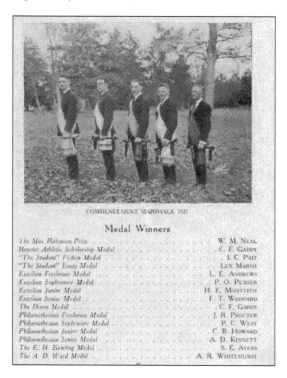

The *Howler* 1921, Metal Were Prominent

Remarkably, the issuing of medals was suspended in 1889. According to the records, they were not given again until 1893.[165] The monthly *Wake Forest Student*, the only campus outlet, is left to discern why.

---

[165] An exact date on which medals were again awarded is difficult to establish. One looks to newspaper accounts of commencement exercises. *The Biblical Recorder*, June 17, 1891, begins its report with "Monday was class day. This exercise has taken the place of the competitive debate for medals."

Almost in passing, it shared, "In May ...the societies had passed resolutions abolishing their medals. The advocates of the measure to abolish argued that offering medals to encourage special work "smacks of the academy," that strife and hard feelings were engendered, and that it was a sordid motive to work for "a little piece of gold."[166] They became the victim of their own importance.

When the oratory and debate medals were ended, a student editor, writing in *The Wake Forest Student* in 1889, bemoaned their end, arguing that there would follow a lessening of Society's success. His reasoning was founded on human motives.

> We may surprise some by saying here at the close of the scholastic year that the Literary Societies at Wake Forest College ought, in our opinion, to re-establish their medal system, with, perhaps, some changes.
>
> The Societies are magnificent engines for their special work, but of what service can the most splendid engine be, even though painted in the most gorgeous colors, if its fly-wheels and pistons are idle? We believe that we have never witnessed a poorer year's work by the Societies than the one that is just drawing to a close, yet some very good work has been done. Opinions may well differ as to whether or not the abolition of the medals has been instrumental in bringing about this result. But you may talk of and decry the sordid motive of working for "a little piece of gold," but the fact remains that the hope of a prize and public mention as the successful competitor in a contest serve as stimulants to a large number of students.[167]

---

[166] *The Wake Forest Student*, Vol. 8, October 1888, page 21. The resolutions "prevailed in the societies, and at their meeting in June, the Board of Trustees of the College, on the recommendation of the Faculty, abolished all the medals awarded in the department of college work." Nine medals were eliminated, and the Monday evening Declaimer's prize was also eliminated.

[167] C. G. Wells, Editor's Portfolio, *The Wake Forest Student*, Vol. 8, June 1889, page 384. In later years, there were some neophyte moves to curtail medals, such as in 1902, but little came of those efforts. "There was honestly a lively debate going on eliminating the sophomore oratory medal, a resolution is presented that "it is unjust to discriminate against any one class"; therefore, we would "no longer offer the battle for oratory to the junior class." Philomathesian Minutes, September 1902. Of course, the students were not guileless as the "siren of the gold medal" suggests. One beguiling student captured what they all knew, "A young man comes to college, works for a medal, wins it, and when once he has the glittering gold hung to his watch

Another student commentator longingly supported the medal restoration "We want to see again ... the old-time rush of students to the College Library on Saturday of each week. We want to see them bear away arms full of old and dusty records... We want to see the flicker of the midnight lamp as the eager student bends to gather knowledge that will be worth gold to him in the afterlife."

The medals were restored after the drawn-out lull, with additional medals being inserted over the years with more and more recognition for top achievers. First established in 1914, a freshman was acclaimed as displaying the greatest debate improvement. The contest was the first of a few similar competitions in which the societies offered medals to the men who showed the most skill in debating and oratory in the Sophomore, Junior, and Senior classes.[168]

Pres. Poteat and G. W. Paschal and another faculty member selected the 1926 finalists, as they did almost yearly. One orator, Johnny G. Ray, spoke on *The Economical Side of The Racial Question*.[169]

An important medal for more than half a century was the Thomas Dixon Senior Oratory Award. Competition was fierce, often with scores participating in the Euzelian Society tryouts. In 1905, for example, the Dixon Senior Oratorical Contest included Mr. W. E. Goode, *The Russian Peasant*, Mr. J. B. Anderson, *Americanism and American Traits*, Mr. Edward Long, *Newspapers of To-day and To-morrow*. The decision committee headed by faculty members Royall, Gorrell, and Lake retired to make the decision, selecting Mr. R. D. Covington, who spoke on *Some Dangers to Our Republic*.[170]

---

chain or around his sweetheart's neck, if perchance he has one, he says to himself, "Behold! I have conquered the whole world; I'll sit down and weep because there are no more worlds to conquer." Alas! Poor fool: soon he needs to weep sure enough." Ek. Sam., *The Wake Forest Student*, Vol 9, December 1889, page 95.

[168] *Old Gold and Black,* April 13, 1918, page 1, 8; A few medals came and went over the years. Later, some medals were named after donors or to recognize individuals of importance. For example, the "John E. White Orators Medal" given by Dr. John E. White of Atlanta shall be awarded to the greatest skill in the orator, and the contest shall be open to all classes in the Society's pay (given in at least 1917).

[169] *Old Gold and Black,* November 6, 1926, page 1.

[170] Euzelian Minutes, May 12, 1905. Even as late as 1930 – Society Day tryouts...were unusually spirited, especially in the Euzelian society, where ten aspiring orators took 10 minutes each to offer a satisfactory solution to world problems like peace, education, science, and world peace. *Old Gold and Black,* November 21, 1930, page 2.

A less-well--remembered award was sponsored by A. D Ward from 1909 to 1940, honoring the featured student selected to speak at Commencement. [171] Eugene Worrell was the last winner in 1940, as he was awarded the "A. D. Ward Medal for best Oration of Senior Class."

Medal awards ended when there were no recipients available. The *Old Gold and Black* sighed, "For the first time in over a century, the Philomathesian Literary Society will offer no medal in debating at annual commencement exercises since all nine men scheduled to appear in traditional speech contests backed out last week." A late '40s student, Edwin Wilson, became a player in the transition.

> The debates, in which freshmen and sophomores usually participate, was slated to take place last Thursday night. But on Thursday night there were no debaters in the Phi Hall. Joe Leonard, Pres. of the society, later explained, "We won't be able to have the debate since there is no one to debate." [He listed the names of those who pulled out].
>
> Members of the literary society who backed out of the planned debate gave various reasons for the retreat. "I had too much work," said Ed Wilson. He expressed the attitude taken by a majority of the other men, although one Phi attributed his reason for not debating to general indifference." [172]

So ended a long, proud tradition of publicly recognizing debaters. Other means of featuring these participants would be forthcoming.

---

[171] His medal continued until Ward's death in 1940. Senator Ward's Wake affiliation was long-standing. A. D. Ward had been the president of the Board of Trustees at Wake Forest. The "Ward" label reappeared on occasion in the '60s and '70s. It had no formal connection to the award proceedings later and presumable was no longer financially supported. The 1950 contestants included some famous Wake Forest debate names: Betty Pringle, Lamar Caudell, Ed Christman. and Pat Murphy. Ms. Pringle spoke on the topic, *A Defense of Women*. *Old Gold and Black*, May 5, 1950, page 3.

[172] *Old Gold and Black*, May 11, 1940, page 4.

CHAPTER 4

Debating in the Literary Societies

Debating in the Societies

Reconstructing the Debate Hall atmospherics can only be imagined. Minimally one recognizes that the levels of formality changed over time. In general, meetings had a formality of form and function unfamiliar today. The assemblies also ricocheted from stifling formality to unruly hilarity. After all, the debaters occupying the Hall were not automatons but rather young men of serious temperament, gleeful cutups, ambitious, and sometimes indolent. Their escapades were more or less an open secret.

Societies held weekly debates, a fidelity that held true over most of the organizations' years. Exceptions were uncommon. On occasion, a debate cancellation occurred because of "too much business" (e.g., decorating the hall in preparation for commencement or taking account of an unprepared debater who was subsequently fined). Debates would also be canceled for revivals, examinations, and public events.[1]

---

[1] In the first year of designing constitutions and bylaws, the Philomathesians met every fortnight (two weeks), a practice they shortly abandoned for weekly meetings, then two meetings per week, one for speaking and one for business. While this chapter focuses on debating practices of the societies, they also engaged in literary events as part of their mission. For example, in 1906, it was newsworthy for the Raleigh *News and Record* to share, "The Wake Forest Literary Club met with Dr. and Mrs. William L. Poteat last night. The meeting was a pleasant one. The subject was 'Dickens as an Educator.'" The *News and Record* (Greensboro), April 8, 1906, page 3.

Dr. Henry Jones was a lifelong faculty member (thirty-five years, from 1924 to 1959) when an enterprising student elected to interview him about debating in the early days. This excerpt yields a feeling of how an evening of debate might progress. Dr. Jones is the same figure who stepped off the train into a night of celebration after defeating Randolph Macon in 1909[2].

> Dr. Jones...recalled the intense debate contests, the official critic who sat with his big dictionary and passed judgment on each contest, the very beautiful Tom Dixon metal for debating – Dr. Jones had this metal – and Dr. Hubert Poteat's eloquent interpretation of the Euzelian banner.

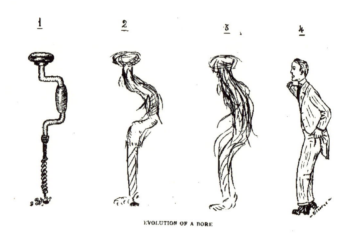

EVOLUTION OF A BORE

1910 *Howler* illustration "EVOLUTION OF A BORE"
offers a commentary on Society meetings.

"Our training," Dr. Jones remembers, "came not through instruction but practice. Of course, we were criticized on what we said. but in the societies, we learn first to talk."

"Sometimes speakers got to be dull," said Dr. Jones. "When this happened, the speaker could expect to hear a steady groaning from the rear. Of course, students who were caught groaning would be fined, but it was hard to catch the guilty ones." Dr. Jones smiled

---

[2] The 1909 debate and celebration are featured in Chapter 6: Intercollegiate Debate Goes on the Road.

when he remembered speakers who were inspired to greater heights of oratory when their audience began "groaning."

Dr. Jones also recalled the trick members could play if they didn't care to fulfill their society's debating requirements. A rule of the society required that a member be fined for not meeting his debating obligations if he happened to be within a certain distance of the town at the time. Some members would take long walks out of town to keep from debating.

Dr. Jones did not claim any special recognition from his early debating years. Nor attributing his activity in debating to "ambition," Dr. Jones modestly stated that "one was expected to participate in the societies."

His first interest in debating, he recalled, came in the little one room schoolhouse where he attended grammar school. One evening it was announced that the debating society was to be organized.

Curious, little Henry Jones attended the proceedings. Everyone was present and he sat beside his friend Kemp "and watched the speech being made. The query for the evening, he recalls was: "resolved, that that the negro should be colonized." Henry turned to Kemp.

"What's' colonized Kemp,'

"It means pack em' up and send em' overseas," said Kemp.

It began to look as if everyone was going to speak that night. young Henry turned again to his friend.

"Do I have to make a speech, Kemp?" Kemp told him he was supposed to. Henry squirmed.

"I can't make a speech, Kemp."

"You got to, boy," Kemp replied. If Kemp said so, Henry knew he must. So when his turn came little Henry Jones stood up and walked to the speaker's platform and made his speech. When he returned to his seat, he asked Kemp how he did.

"Pretty good boy," his friend replied, "but you got on the wrong side."[3]

Establishing order in the hall and setting expectations required law-making for the meetings. March appeared to be the "regulatory

---

[3] William Pate, Changing Times: Debaters Won, Rode Athletic' Shoulders in 1909, *Old Gold and Black*, February 21, 1955, page 2.

month." On March 20, 1840, the Phis passed: "That during prayer, every member shall either stand or kneel. Resolved further, that the supervisor shall take cognizance of every breach of ungentlemanly and unchristian-like conduct and report the same to the President."[4]

Societies strictly enforced the rules, presumably allowing all speakers sufficient time to address motions. Speakers were restricted to two speeches of no more than 15 minutes. In the 1840s, the Philomathesians passed a motion that allowed a member on the floor the third time with the President's permission.[5] In the same meeting, a member was fined "for rising to speak before the views of the silent members were called for."

In 1844, the Philomathesians passed a rule extending the 15-minute limitation on speaking time to 30 minutes.[6] The bylaws also required members to speak to issues. It was never clear, other than if fines were assigned, that times were strictly enforced. With few members in the early years, longer speaking times could be accommodated.

Of course, the 30-minute limit did not last; one can imagine meetings becoming interminable. "If each of the disputants used the maximum time on the first round, the six had spoken for three hours. At the end of that time the fray had just begun, for there were usually many who had become interested and were ready to do battle in defense of their views. Accordingly, no one need be surprised that the conflict which began at candle-light often did not end until midnight or after, and that, too, in a room in which there was no heat from fire or stove."

Speaking times (and even order) have continually changed over the decades. As membership grew, speaking durations shrunk. In the 1938 minutes, Mr. Baxter, a Phi, was fined for speaking more than 15 minutes. Speeches remained somewhat lengthy, a frustration to those members who wanted their individual contributions to the evening's conversation to be heard.[7]

Despite the long evenings and dry repartee, Paschal was comfortable in assessing:

---

[4] Philomathesian Minutes, March 20, 1840.

[5] Philomathesian Minutes, August 1840.

[6] Philomathesian Minutes, February 3, 1844.

[7] Several small variations occurred over the years, for example, "The motion of Mr. Foote it is ordered that one-third of the members here be required to speak at least five minutes on each query – fine $.25." Philomathesian Minutes, September 20, 1868.

Evidence is abundant that the work of the Societies was cheerfully done even though the debates were often protracted beyond midnight. The members not participating except as listeners sat through the long hours. with no audible murmur, except now and then one would fall asleep and snore...

At times also the minds of the members went wool-gathering in more pleasant ways. Seemingly taking notes for a speech they were in reality fashioning phrases to put in letters to their sweethearts, or writing complimentary words about young ladies of their acquaintance. The secretary having to observe a proper decorum as he faced the seated members often used the pages of the record book for neatly boxed-off statements like these, from the Euzelian Society minutes of February 4, 1882: "Oh! for a glance at that beautiful black hair, one sweet word from those cherry-red lips, above all a look from those lovely brown eyes."[8]

The meetings pre-assigned members their turn to present declamations and debates, yet occasionally, the speakers arrived unprepared, often leading to fines and, from time to time, a substitute speaker. The March 1841 Phi minutes read, "Mr. M. Grandy was expected a dissertation [original essay] and failed to read one. Mr. Grandy also failed to disclaim. Mr. Dawson was absent."[9]

Debate winners in the Philomathesian and Euzelian Hall debates were chosen in three ways. For most years, the present members voted, offering a plurality victory. The Societies moved to panels of students in later years. Public debates typically graced events with invited distinguished panels. On a few occasions, the audience was invited to vote.

In the first decade of the twentieth century, the regular meeting debates moved from membership voting to judge panels, presumably for reasons offered in a 1903 Euzelian resolution:

Whereas it has been impossible to obtain a just decision of our debates and whereas a just decision will create a deeper interest in

---

[8] Paschal, G. W. (1943). *History of Wake Forest College*, Vol. II, page 366.

[9] Philomathesian Minutes, March 1841; In the 1870s, members had to do an original composition. They were often given five weeks' notice before the presentation, while the debaters received two weeks and, in some periods, one week. Failure to perform resulted in a fine of $.50.

the debates. Resolved that the questions in the debate be decided by judges.

Resolved 2nd: That the number of judges consist of five members of the society chosen without class distinction to be appointed by the presiding officer of each meeting.

Resolved 3[rd.] That the judges shall cast their votes by ballot and the decision be announced by the president.[10]

It was enacted, and the first Eu panel debate was on whether it *Is best for the U.S. to build and maintain a large Navy.* Two debates on the topic followed in two different meeting sections. The first was an assembled vote, negative 20 to 8, and the second debate was decided with the new panel rule, 5 to 0 for the affirmative. The Phis began utilizing a three-member panel in 1907, continuing until at least 1937.

"Until 1922, the Societies were regarded as an organic part of the College…Friday night and Saturday after chapel service were given over to them. During these years, they assumed the responsibility of keeping a check on the whereabouts and conduct of their members who constituted all the students.".[11]

The Hall resounded with debates, some profound, many little more than a single notch in forming the participant's character. In one mythical debate, an alumnus and future governor found himself debating both sides of the resolution at hand. An Interview with Governor Broughten uncovered:

It was a dark cold night in January 1909. The snow was down to the limbs of the magnolias on the Wake Forest campus, and the wind was piling the flakes against the historic buildings of the college. There was little sign of life on the campus and only an occasional student scurried through the storm.

---

[10] Euzelian Minutes, 1903.

[11] Paschal, G. W. (1943), *The History if Wake Forest College,* Vol. II, page 365. In 1922, speaking time was restrained to accommodate burgeoning membership. "The members of the societies are required to debate once every fourth week…Each section of both societies have eight men on to debate-Four each side. In this way every man gets a chance to speak every fourth week in the month, instead of every second week as has been the custom… heretofore they were required to speak at least three minutes and allowed seven for both. Now they are allowed thirteen minutes for both speeches," *Old Gold and Black*, October 10, 1922, page 1.

1919 Campus View

Two sets of windows above the library were brightly lighted though, an activity that couldn't be halted by a snowstorm was taking place in the halls of the Euzelian and Philomathesian Literary Societies. Attendance was a bit below the usual hundred and 50 in the Eu Hall, but the show would go on. An important debate on United States trade had been scheduled, and four of the societies top-notch debaters have been pitted against each other. The quartet were called to their places at the front as the session was opened; only one man responded. Sensing a program disaster but determined to give this man his chance, the president called on him to speak.

Tall and lanky, the massive black hair pushed back from his forehead, this young fellow, who looked to be about 19, took his place at the front of the hall. Easing into a fine conversational tone with naturalness and sincerity he told in a straightforward fashion why the United States should endeavor consistently to extend its trade throughout the world. Then he sat down, his fellow students applauding.

The president, mechanically following parliamentary procedure, called for the absent opposition to take the floor. The black-haired young orator who had just finished his speech rose once again and took over.

At the end of 10 minutes, he concluded: "for these reasons, the United States must adopt a policy of strict economic and commercial isolation in regard to Europe and the Orient. A program of trade-extension would be disastrous."

His listeners incredulously rebuked themselves for having ever allowed themselves to think world trade should be fostered, and three judges retired from the hall.

After 20 minutes of fierce debate among themselves, the judges returned to point out which was the young debater's better self. The session was adjourned, and the men trudged through the blizzard to their rooms.

"That debate of yours did pretty well tonight, Dutch," commented Hubert Jones to Melville Broughton once the pair reached their room.

Modestly brushing aside the remarks, the man who today became the governor of North Carolina sat down at his desk and began work on the next article for the college publication.[12]

Presumably, one prevailed in the Broughton versus Broughton debate, although the newspaper account did not reveal whom, leaving the ending an enigma. Broughton's own account is less generous. He debated as a freshman, "the judges solemnly took the matter under consideration and announced that both speeches were of an inferior quality and that they were unable to make a decision as to relative merits. Consequently, the matter was allowed to stand as a tie."[13]

Broughton's contributions to Wake Debate continued his whole life. As an undergrad, he served on the debate council and was editor of *The Wake Forest Student*. He routinely returned for Anniversary Day celebrations (presenting the Literary Address at the 99th celebration). He donated "a beautiful loving cup" for the high school tournament in the '40s, ending with his career as a US Senator. His son, J. Melville Broughton, Jr., won an on-campus campaign debate and became student body president in 1943.[14]

---

[12] Neil Morgan, A College Leader Who Becomes Governor: Melville Broughton Found Time for All Phases of College Life, *The News & Observer*, January 9, 1941, page 20.

[13] *Wake Forest Alumni News*, March 1944.

[14] Further details on Broughton's long involvement in Wake Debate are provided in Chapter 13 – Early Tournament Hosting.

Literary Debate Procedures and Practice

DEBATING SCHEDULES

In their second year, the two societies formed a committee to consult the faculty to obtain "permission" to change the day of the week the societies met. Apparently, obtaining faculty permission meant President Wait gave his approval "to whatever the Societies may deem proper." Pres. Wait, in deference, was politically astute, as arguably were the students for asking.[15]

Over time, the campus' powers became more hierarchical, increasingly "rule-bound." As with any leading group, the instinct was to maintain but also with an impulse to reform and modernize. Naturally, changes almost always impacted schedules and regular gatherings.[16]

For a period, rather than assigning two affirmative and two negative speakers, the members could volunteer for the side of the resolution they wanted to support. On occasions, the debates would be unbalanced, with six-to-one speakers on the respective sides. The fashion didn't last long; deciding winners became complicated, and establishing the query's balance was fraught.[17]

The selection of debaters or topics could occur first, but most often, both were announced at a business meeting, selected by the President, a committee, or through rotation.

Many variations of debates and speaking rotations were tried. Some were offered only to be defeated, such as an 1895 motion to change the calendar every three weeks, having ½ of the society debating on Friday and ½ debating on Saturday. It was rejected 41 to 22.[18] Another

---

[15] Philomathesian Minutes, October 1837.

[16] Philomathesian Minutes, October 1837; The debates were carefully provided for in such a way that every member of the Society should have a part in his turn. To manage the debate, the Societies appointed certain members, called disputants, to be in charge. Paschal, G. W. (1935). *History of Wake Forest College*, Vol. I, page 536-538.

[17] In the recorded meeting debates for the Euzelians, as few as 'one representing only one side' also occurred. A 1916 debate considered *We should have two years of military training for all high schools in the United States* (3 to 2 Affirmative) had nine affirmative and eight negative debaters, and on October 24, 26, 1917, debating *That the single land tax advocated by Henry George is practicable*, (3 to 2 Negative) found twelve affirmative and eleven negative speakers participating.

[18] Philomathesian Minutes, December 8, 1895.

method passed in 1895 involved the society breaking up into even parts alphabetically, with one group debating on Friday night and the other on Saturday night.[19]

As the school grew in numbers, so did the membership of the Societies. The Phis were said to have over two hundred active members, and in 1897, they went to three weekly meetings. The Phis reported that "the plan is working well, and each member is doing about twice as much work as before."[20] They kept faith in members' regular debate participation, although maintaining that key signature was increasingly strained.

In the same meeting, the resolution was proposed to go from five to four sections per week as the sessions were too small and they were not doing "their best possible work." Five weekly meetings were briefly adopted to accommodate debates for the many members. The multiple meetings lasted in part of the 1910s and '20s but were difficult to sustain. Assignments to meetings became controversial, and coordinating the multiple instances of a topic consideration on varying nights of the week was confusing. The burgeoning membership made maintaining each member's regular debating schedule more difficult.

Even with the thriving memberships, the maintenance of active debating norms, to the credit of the members' patience, generally held. The 1914 By-Laws of one society provided that the assembled were "divided into two sections, as nearly equal as possible," the first meeting on Friday night and the second session on Saturday night. Members were now (section 2) required to fulfill "the duties of each member to speak either to the debate (or disclaim) once every two weeks, and for each member to disclaim three times during the year." Time limits were also prescribed, and debaters were allowed two speeches, the first of seven minutes and the second of three minutes.

JOINT DEBATES

As belligerent as the relationship between the two societies often was, recurrent talks of joint appearances happened. Of course, the important joint appearance was the Anniversary Debates which for years featured mixed-paired teams.

---

[19] Philomathesian Minutes, December 14, 1895.

[20] *The Wake Forest Student*, 1895, page 277.

Various proposals, as with the 1874 plan for a unique venue and mood, popped up. The Phi's recommended "A joint debate in the College Chapel. The nature which shall be comic for the entertainment of the public."[21] We did not find mention of any joint humorous interlude taking place.

Additionally, in the same year, Mr. A. L. Dixon moved that a committee be appointed to work with the Philomathesians on a joint debate between the societies.[22] In September 1875, it was resolved that a committee of three be appointed to ask the Euzelian Society to cooperate with us in making arrangements for a public debate in the chapel four times a year.[23]

Mr. Dixon offered an elaborate set of rules for the joint debate.[24] The debates did not materialize. There may have been too much bureaucratic complexity to support the elaborate structure or a lack of sustainable

---

[21] Philomathesian Minutes, May 19, 1874.

[22] Euzelian Minutes, February 21, 1874.

[23] Philomathesian Minutes, September 25, 1875.

[24] Resolved that we meet in joint debate with the Philomathesian Society four times a session. The first meeting to be held on the first Friday night in October, the second on the first Friday night in December, the third on the first Friday night in March, the fourth of the first Friday night in May, and that it be governed by the following laws.

I.   The meeting shall be held in the chapel.

II. One half of the members of both societies shall constitute a quorum.

III. The officers shall be the President, vice president, secretary and the two disputants to be elected by the Societies in the regular session whose term of office shall continue to meetings.

IV. The President for the term commencing October 1874 shall be elected by the Philomathesian Society and Vice Pres. by the Euzelian Society. The president for the term commencing March 1875 shall be elected by the Euzelian Society and Vice Pres. by the Philomathesian Society and secretary by the Philomathesian society, thus alternating for all succeeding terms. Each society shall elect a disputant.

V.   It shall be the duty of the president to preside at the meeting of the society, preserve order, and enforce Mell's parliamentary rules.

VI. It shall also be the president's duty to appoint a committee of four, two from each Society, at the beginning of each term whose duty shall be to select queries for discussion and to report at each meeting the query for the next meeting. He shall also appoint at each meeting the members, five from each society to open the discussion of succeeding debates. In the division of speakers, he shall not appoint more than three members of each society on the same side. After those appointed have finished speaking, the question shall then be open to the miscellaneous discussion, the silent members having the preference. He shall also at the beginning of each term appoint a doorkeeper to serve during his term.

VII. It shall be the duties of the vice president to preside in the President's absence.

VIII. It shall be the duty of the secretary to record all proceedings of society to be read at each succeeding meeting.

enthusiasm. Certainly, these joint debate series were not meant for the public's inclusion, as rule XI states, "None but active members and honorary members of both Societies shall be admitted to the meeting."

At the beginning of the last decade of the 19th century, the 1890 *Wake Forest Student* noted, "The University has commenced to hold a series of public debates. The societies arranged to have eight of them. "Too few men have been taking an active part in the debates. We believe these public debates will create a new interest in society work and cause more men to participate."[25] Each of the four sections of the society will elect a representative for each public debate. Thirty-four men will take part in a public debate. Members of both societies and the people of the town will be invited to attend...[26] although some may have occurred, again, we did not see evidence that these happened or were sustained.

Weekly debates in the society halls became less frequent in the late '30s. Often, they were competitive tryouts for public events—Society and Anniversary Day, Freshman-Sophomore Debaters, and Intercollegiate Debates—or held faux debates and entertainment fare. [27]

DEBATING STYLES DEBATED

Wake was aware of nationwide debate programs and particularly interested in the Ivies. A 1908 essay re-published in *The Wake Forest Student*, "Public Speaking at Harvard University," offered a six-page essay describing the Harvard model for debate councils, Intercollegiate Debate, Commencement, and elements of coaching. The guidance included an endorsement of the non-scripted clash and a model more in tune with

---

IX. It shall be the duty of each inspector to note all violations of the laws of his respective Society and report the same to his Society in regular sessions.

X. No member shall speak more than twice on any question, limiting both speeches to ten minutes each.

XI. None but active members and honorary members of both Societies shall be admitted to the meeting.

XII. Each Society shall bear its proportional part of all expenses incurred.

XIII. All questions shall be decided by a majority vote of the members present. Philomathesian Minutes, 1874.

[25] *The Wake Forest Student,* November 1914, page 140.

[26] *The Wake Forest Student,* November 1914, page 140.

[27] These choices and pressures are more fully explored in Chapter 14, The Intercollegiate Era Gives Way to Tournament Debates.

their meeting debates that would, in time, reign in intercollegiate debates. The adapted advice from Harvard's model included:

> The Debating Council appoints a coach for the two terms, usually he is an old 'Varsity debater' himself. For three weeks he is training his men as carefully as a football coach ever put his team through. Nearly every afternoon or night through the practice of about three hours. None of the speeches are written, not even those for the final debate. Each debater speaks first on one side and then the other. The coach puts up every case he can imagine, he puts all sorts of interpretation upon the query that he thinks could occur from teams of the other University and makes his men meet these cases and interpretations.[28]

Effective debate, at least in this new intercollegiate model, involved the synthesis of argument and audience adaptation in a way that balanced reason with the application of persuasion. Students, it was argued, needed to focus less on the technical skills associated with style, memory, and delivery and instead focus on those topics more directly relevant to Invention: the analysis of controversy, the articulation of arguments, and the crafting of an appeal that "fits" an audience.[29]

"These skills of good oratory in debate are acquired naturally and almost unconsciously, a thing which cannot be said of the student who tries to make an orator of himself by declamation or acting."[30]

As argumentation became more formalized, a 1915 report on debating proposed, "Knowing syllogisms, and categories, and the what-nots of formal logic is not sufficient. The student must actually synthesize his evidence into a clear, coherent argument, which will tend to convince the audience, the judges, and even the opponents."[31] This training may

---

[28] *The Wake Forest Student*, October 1908, page 92.

[29] McCowan, J. (2017) Renewing a "Very Old Means of Education": Civic Engagement and The Birth of Intercollegiate Debate in The United States. *Speech and Debate as Civic Education* Edited by J. Michael Hogan, Jessica A. Kurr, Michael J. Bergmaier, and Jeremy D. Johnson, The Pennsylvania State University Press, page 47.

[30] Freeburg, V. O. (1915). Debating in the college curriculum, *The English Journal, 4*, page 581.

[31] McCowan, J. (2017) Renewing a "Very Old Means of Education": Civic Engagement and The Birth of Intercollegiate Debate in The United States. *Speech and Debate as Civic Education* Edited by J. Michael Hogan, Jessica A. Kurr, Michael J. Bergmaier, and Jeremy D. Johnson, The Pennsylvania State University Press, page 47.

be made convenient by the preparation of briefs.[32] This 1915 mention of prepared pre-research, or briefs, is the first mention in this treatise.

The campus debating societies were conscious of debating practice controversies and trends. The advent of national journals and dialogues, especially in the late 1910s and '20s, assured the debaters were not insular. However, reactions to outside controversy did not always make a difference in the debates staged on society meeting nights or later in tournament practices.

An early controversy that would be mulled for decades dealt with debating both sides of the topic. Historian W. R. Nichols claimed that debaters should engage in advocacy, to which they personally agreed. Nichols' counsel was not especially relevant for the frothy post-Civil War topics (and presumably many serious topics). Nichols warned against contingent principles. He wrote:

The tendency of debate now to be centered on argument over ... The requirement that a debater be prepared to take both sides of the question. The debates of the old literary societies surely had their weaknesses, but one of them was not being the blatant encouragement to relativism. In the old days, human beings debating on issues

---

[32] Freeburg, V. O. (1915). Debating in the college curriculum, *The English Journal*, 4, page 579-580.

about which they felt deeply, and their appeals were to the whole nature of man, not only to his ability to recognize evidence.[33]

That debates should encourage taking both sides blew up with the entry of national figures:

In 1913 Theodore Roosevelt unleashed a vigorous attack on the notion that college debaters should be trained to debate both sides of an issue... "I emphatically disbelieve in it as regards general discussion of political, social, industrial matters. What we need is to turn out our college young men with ardent convictions on the side of right... William Jennings Bryan came to Roosevelt's support in this attack on scientific relativism, on the view that all matters were unsettled, open, free from conviction until thoroughly and scientifically studied and argued. This distinction between belief and fact, between persuasion and argumentation, is essentially the distinction between the old college and new university. It was the distinction between a certain morality, a world of settled conviction, a regard for the whole man, between these and a moral neutrality, a world of unsettle and conviction, a regard for man as mind.[34]

The reverberation of national controversies reached the North Carolina campus. An influential 1920s sparring emerged over whether teams should have coaches. Some lamented the "crime of giving instruction in solely the coaching system." They argued, as C. S Warren encapsulates, that the "preparation of a few selected students by short-term methods for single occasions to make an exhibition or to win a victory." corrupted the reason for coaching.[35] One wonders how concerned Aycock or

---

[33] Nichols, W. R. (1937). A historical sketch of intercollegiate debating: III. *Quarterly Journal of Speech, 23,* 259-278.

[34] Frederick, R. (1962). *The American College and University: A History.* University of Georgia Press, page 451-452.

[35] Warren, C. S. (1922). The crime against public speaking, *Quarterly Journal of Speech Education,* Vol. 8, page 138-144. Warren's stance is now amusing for what this author wrongly describes and what he "gets right." He finds coaching in "Intercollegiate contests" a crime. The coach's reputation is at stake... He has to take the chance of accident, sickness, or total collapse among his pupils. He has to take the chance of meeting an opposing coach who is his inferior. He has to take the chance of meeting foul play. He has to take the chance of biased judges. And he has to take the chance of satisfying standards of judgment that have never yet been formed."

Quisenberry were as they lined up students for the next tournament; we imagine little.

George P. Baker, of Harvard debate fame, also predicted, perhaps accurately, that this new form of debate competition might evolve into a "highly developed special form"—an "intellectual sport"—that would become increasingly disconnected from public discourse.[36] He concluded that "constant vigilance" would be necessary "if some of the past evils of athletics are not to creep into this intellectual sport."[37]

A familiar complaint raised by the late 1900s, was the speed that debaters favored. An *Old Gold and Black* editorial complained:

> For some inexplicable reason our debaters have grown to think that the prime requisite of rebuttal is speed, and that the rejoinder is the one opportunity given in the course of the debate for the speaker to poke the audience in the ribs and get some natural or acquired wit out of his system. The fallacy of such a policy is evident. What is the object of the rejoinder? It is the hand-to-hand combat where the bayonet may be used legitimately... Fast speaking is only permissible as long as it conveys the thoughts well. When it fails to do this the audience forgets the speaker's fighting words and rather takes the attitude that he is speaking for their delectation.[38]

We would counter, "Welcome to tournament life." There also was considerable controversy regarding the appropriate degree of coach intervention in constructing speeches. See for example, Lane, F. H. (1916). Faculty help in intercollegiate contests. *The Quarterly Journal of Public Speaking*, Vol. 1, No. 1, page 9-16.

[36] Harvard professor George P. Baker illustrates some faculty responses to intercollegiate debate. Baker was instrumental in teaching debate and argumentation at Harvard during this boom period and influential among coaches.

[37] McKown, J. (2017). Renewing a "Very old means of education": civic engagement and the birth of intercollegiate debate in the United States. *Speech and Debate as Civic Education* Edited by J. Michael Hogan, Jessica A. Kurr, Michael J. Burgmeier, and Jeremy D. Johnson, The Pennsylvania State University Press, page 48.

[38] Editorial, *Old Gold and Black*, March 1, 1919, page 2. The editorial argued for focusing on only argument as the answer to speed. "The average debate at Wake Forest allows not more than four minutes for the rebuttal. This gives the speaker enough time to attack not more than one point. If he is to successfully tear down the arguments set forth in that one point. In the past we have noticed the debaters giving about one minute or less to each of the various points advanced by the opposing side, and then bidding them God-speed. The result is that the speaker really fails to demolish his opponent's argument, but rather side-steps the issues. The judges then

We are reminded of Ross Smith's caution for debaters who talk too fast. Paraphrasing his refrain: "*Speed* is the number of ideas communicated per minute that matter."

VARIED PRACTICES AND RESULTS

"By the middle of the nineteenth century, almost all the major societies provided that decisions be reached reflecting the merits of the debate." Yet with human auditors, there is never a clean break, and decisions were rendered on the merits of the debate and queries assessed.[39]

There remains a question of how to interpret the decisions of the observers or judges: as sentiment toward the resolution or merely their assessment of who debated better. It is likely that many votes were a commentary on a resolution's content, as speakers often choose to defend a personal viewpoint. Sometimes, the voting could simply reflect loyalties and friendship ties with those presenting.[40]

In 1843, the Phis adopted a resolution requiring the "President, at each regular meeting, to give a written decision on the question then discussed." Furthermore, the president was required to give a valedictory address upon leaving office. Non-compliance was to be fined.[41] The requirement apparently proved too burdensome. A month later, the society members rescinded the new rules and waived any fines "incurred by the law by the President."[42]

The meetings concerned training younger members, yet the top-speaking public debate slots were often filled with familiar names. The ability to break through to a "public" slot became increasingly remote as the

---

naturally form the opinion that the debater knows very little about the subject and judge him accordingly."

[39] Porter, D. (1954). The Literary Society, In Karl R. Wallace, Ed., *History of Speech Education in America*, page 248.

[40] At several points in this volume, topics debated are reported along with the end-of-debate vote. At times, we infer that the decision reflected the group's opinion. This should be viewed with some skepticism for the reasons noted. The 2-1 and 3-0 panel decisions of the Euzelians are in this category, but one assumes they were more reflective of the debate than personal preference. However, popular opinion trends can be faithfully traced, suggesting that the meeting's decision often reflected their viewpoint, particularly on then-current public policy questions.

[41] Philomathesian Minutes, September 15, 1843.

[42] Philomathesian Minutes, October 28, 1843.

organizations grew. Designed to feature and prepare younger debaters, 1911 saw the first Sophomore-Junior Debates. They were conducted with substantial falderol for three years until they merged into the new Society Day in 1914.[43]

THE FIRST DAYS OF SCHOOL – LEGGING NEWISH

The young debaters were not always treated with full embrace; echoes of a distinct pecking order abounded. There developed a year-long informal initiation into the group. The newish, or first years, had to earn their stripes. The Euzelian secretary penned the amusing poem of the Newish angst in struggling to win the freshman metal in 1903.

> The "Newish's" hearts are beating fast
> The senior center with eyes steadfast,
> Listening to the newish roar
> And thinking it an awful bore.
> But still the "Newish" thundered on,
> And still the weary seniors beyond.
> They are through at last the seniors go
> There'll be joy for one – for others woe.
> Euzelian Hall is quiet within
> Each vote Newish" thinks "I'll Surely win,
> But when the metal to Jones was given
> He considered this little less than heaven.
> He sends a message to a certain "made,"

---

[43] *The Wake Forest Student*, November 1911, page 157.

"My glories now will never fade."
I brought the freshman metal down
And am the greatest "orator in town."
Though when the news came, "you all done well"
The other "Newish" think they have played in "h-ll."

Composed by W. H. Price

Two years later, in 1905, Josiah Francis wrote a somewhat dismissive poem[44]. His poem (truncated here) outlines a characterization of the Euzelian's "newish contest" speakers and mood. The newish speeches were to be endured.

The newish contest! All set still, We heard that it was coming.
The woods and calls rocks and hills,
Had heard that speech of Dunning.'
The Dutchman Jones denied his points,
And next came giant Bunn,
But with "sought off" words and shaky points
Our Creasman spoke 'em some.
The Newish quaked, chief Weathers came;
"That metal must surely be mine."
The "Sophs" did grand, the fuss went out.
That speech was "shore fine."
Shakeup' yer' dry bones, here's Willie Jones,
"Ducky" Murray beat the air, he laid it off,
He pawed big holes in the carpet
"the metals mine call! I saw it shine!
Alack: a day, the South's all right!
Ye distinguished Seniors, mark it!
No runs, no hits, no errors made,

1903 – Newish – *Howler*

---

[44] Poetry was a preferred mode of expression during this period.

The "newish" had yet to score:
A sawed-off man, a speaker I trow
"Bufe" Williams, I think they call him,
But for shaky bones and frogs in the throat,
Not that: but the Seniors appalled him.
and the noble Seniors retired what they did
was not to be known some like that I guess
But they returned and said: Brown's the man."
Says the newish, "Aint the seniors a mess. Not here Mary"
Society adjourned, the newish went home
Save the one, he went to the station
"I'm something I guess, peck it off on the wires
It will need no explanation."
Approved and "bored" adjourned 11:10

PEACE ORATORICAL CONTEST

Anti-war sentiment has often occupied a place in America's dialogue, usually in cadence with wars past or anticipated. In March 1892, *The Wake Forest Student* first mentioned the Intercollegiate oratorical contest, which began at the annual meeting of the Teachers' Assembly.[45] The

---

[45] *The Wake Forest Student*, March 1892, Vol. 12, page 241. Anti-war movements influenced the establishment at the end of the 19th century. "Prominent politicians, academics, authors, and businessmen who had moral concerns about the Spanish-American War formed the Anti-Imperialist League in June 1898 to protest the annexation of the Philippines as a violation of American ideals. The debaters had debated Cuba, the Philippines, and the implications of American expansionism on scores of occasions. https://www.history.com/news/anti-war-movements-throughout-american-history; The contest was a subset of a much larger national peace movement. The Intercollegiate oratorical peace contest started before the onset of World War I in 1906. It was founded by academics at Goshen and Earlham colleges to "promote peace-oriented activities among faculty and students." By 1912, the year North Carolina and Wake Forest entered the competition, the International Peace Association had conducted an Intercollegiate and interstate oratorical contest" involving "at least 300 undergraduates from many colleges and some 16 states." In 1937, Professor Zon Robinson announced that tryouts to represent Wake Forest in "the finals of the State Peace Oratorical Contest will be held tonight at 7:00 PM in the Social Science Building. The winner will represent Wake in the state finals (High Point College). Prizes in the State Contest will be $50, $30, and $20." The tryouts coincide with the observance of Peace Day on the campus. *Old Gold and Black*, April 22, 1937, page 1.

Peace Oratorical Contest was another venue for the debaters to apply their speechmaking skills.

After an inexact two years of organizing, the "four leading male institutions of the State" (Wake, Trinity, Davidson, and Guilford) worked to create the Intercollegiate Oratorical Contest "to be held at each annual meeting of the Teachers' Assembly. Addresses were to be original and limited to fifteen minutes each," with a medal. The program will "supply a much-needed incentive to the study of oratory throughout the State no one will question."[46]

Wake consistently participated in the Intercollegiate Peace Oratorical Contest. In 1924, contestants boasted to the *Old Gold and Black,* "Wake Forest men have won the prize for the last three years in succession. The debate Council is anxious to get the best possible material in the preliminaries in order to pick a man and oration that will make it a string of four successive victories."

The judges were to consider memory, voice, distinctiveness of utterance, argument, gesticulation, and general effect. Wake Forest was allowed to enter up to four participants who were to advocate on behalf of "some settlement of differences between nations." The winner in 1924 would receive a cash prize of $75.[47]

Wake Forest speaker H. T. Wright was crowned the fourth consecutive Wake winner speaking on *A Vital League,* advocating the League of Nations.[48]

In February 1924, the *Winston-Salem Journal* encouraged contributions, and presumably, the opportunity to serve as a host city reminded

---

[46] *The Wake Forest Student,* March 1892, page 241. "Widens the horizon of their under-graduates and causes them to look beyond the four walls of their Alma Mater." *The Wake Forest Student* refers to the Intercollegiate Oratorical Contest held at Morehead City in July 1895. I. M. Meekins won the medal over Trinity and A & M at the oratorical contest. *The Wake Forest Student,* July.

[47] $1377 in today's currency. The sum certainly would have covered tuition and living expenses. Tuition in 1924 was a modest $25.00/semester. *Bulletin of Wake Forest College* [1906-8], page 32. The *Bulletin* advised, "No charge for tuition is made against students who are ministers or the sons of ministers of the Gospel." One enterprising student, W. C. Stephenson, recounted, "I decided that I would take the agency for a gas lamp which was guaranteed to give a better light than electric lights. It sold for a reasonable price. In a few days of work at Christmas season, I sold 15 and made enough profit to pay my [Wake] tuition for one semester." *Winston-Salem Journal,* January 13, 1924, page 2.

[48] *Old Gold and Black,* May 2, 1924, page 1.

readers of what is as important as athletics. "We should be equally alert to secure intellectual contests, especially one of the magnitude of this, in which every men's college of consequence in the state is expected to participate."

MODEL LEGISLATIVE ASSEMBLY

In the early 1920s, societies became interested in speaking and debating in a legislative environment. A 1922 Eu meeting passed, "at the suggestion of the president, the question as to making our section of society similar to a kind of legislature was brought up and passed." And that they did so is reflected in later meetings in which resolutions were not debated but rather bills were introduced in the "mock legislature" debated and taken to vote.

Perhaps in lieu of formal debates, discussions were held about bills before the North Carolina assembly; for example, in 1922, the Eus argued, "The General assembly of N.C. do enact: *That divorce be granted in N. C. on the ground of adultery only.* The bill failed to carry by an 18 to 9.[49]

The students met in the 1938-1939 season of the Model Legislative Assembly to "pass on official laws for Tarheelia, a mythical state. In addition, Wake Foresters Eugene Worrell and Bedford Black were elected president of the State Senate and Speaker of the State House of Representatives, respectively. Black repeated his accomplishment on a larger scale in April, when he was elected Speaker at the National Student Congress, held in conjunction with the Pi Kappa Delta debate tournament in Topeka, Kansas."[50]

In the early '40s, North Carolina hosted student legislatures in which Wake Forest students played a major role in the competition; the students

---

[49] Euzelian Minutes, March 2, 1922; other examples of the "legislative" debate format debated in regular hall meetings: March 9, 1922 – *The governor of North Carolina shall have the power to veto any bill passed by the Gen. Assembly. The general assembly may, however, pass any bill over the governor's veto by a two-thirds majority in each house.* (The bill was defeated by a vote of 11 to 10), March 23, 1922 – *Grant members the privilege of smoking, chewing, etc.* (Passed 11 to 7.), March 30, 1922 – A *"Resolution to Congress of the U.S. recommending a passage of a national lynching law."* (Failed to pass 8 to 6), April 27, 1922 – *Change the governor's salary from $7,500 to $10,000.* (Passed.).

[50] *Old Gold and Black*, September 24, 1938, page 1.

were almost exclusively debate team members. "The 15 men will present a bill to *Return the entire state of North Carolina to prohibition*...Billy Windes, Wake Forest debater, will introduce the bill on the floor of the Senate, and Burnette Harvey [also a star debater] will present the measure to the House. "[51]

Resolutions Debated[52]

Several sets of debate topics appear in *Milestone, Defining Lists of Wake Forest Debate: 1835-2022,* Vol. 3 of this series. The chapters provide the Euzelian and Philomathesians topics debated in the weekly meetings, including the vote by the students assembled and, in later years, the panels' decisions. Another chapter provides the public debates, recording the societies' panel decisions and, on occasion, total audience votes.

As suggested earlier, the criterion these decisions represented was not always clear. Patterns exist with various topics, suggesting that the students often voted according to their opinions regarding a question. In some cases, the panels and membership were guided by judging standards they had collectively adopted: judge according to the goal of "educationally" grounded objectivity, favoring those "who did a better job debating." It is also reasonable to assume, in a room of alliances and close friends, that topic votes on occasion reflect relationships more than arguments.

---

[51] *Old Gold and Black*, October 24, 1941, page 1.

[52] G. W. Paschal's chapter on Debate topics in *History of Wake Forest College,* Vol. I, pages 540-558, provide considerably more detail, with analysis and listing of topics debated. He also quickly addresses the selection process, further detailed later in this volume. What appears in this section regarding topics is more supplemental to his work but seldom with overlapping content. Additionally, the records unearthed for this project are not always in accord with Paschal's accounts of topics. As noted in the text portion of this chapter, Paschal's claim that the societies conspicuously avoided the Civil War, while more often the case, had many notable exceptions. Additionally, Paschal claimed that the first question for debate upon regrouping was in the Euzelian Society, *Was Bonaparte a blessing or a curse to France?* and in the Philomathesian Society, *Which deserves the more honor, Columbus for discovering America or Washington for defending it?* Our examination of the ledgers shows that the Euzelians debating on April 19, 1861, addressed *Which most deserves our censure, Cortes for his treatment of the Mexicans or Pizarro for his treatment of the Peruvians?* (Affirmative 8 to 7). We agree with Paschal about the Phi topic.

The age-old issue of eliminating bias in judging debate has been evident throughout, just as it is today. The general recommendation was that a debate should be judged on argumentative merits. The debaters early on, in April 1848, however, were less pristine. A member introduced the criterion that "the weight of argument and not our beliefs influence us in voting on questions debated in the Society." The gentleman's motion was rejected.

* * * * * * *

How different were the queries of the early days? There was no wrestling with trusts, railways injunctions, ship subsidies, or war reparations, as would later become common. The first resolution discussed in the Euzelian Society was *That there is more pleasure in the pursuit than in the possession of an object.* The unsystematic decision favored the negative.[53]

Without a doubt, there was rigidity and repetition in the topics voiced. The Eus debated, in some form, *Whether the death of Caesar was beneficial to Rome,* twenty-five times (The Phis thirty-five times). The Phis were more concerned with *Was Elizabeth justified in putting to death Mary Queen of Scots* (forty-five time, the Eus twenty-nine times).

Mary, Queen of Scots was the Scottish Queen from 1542
until he forced abdication in 1567. Combined the Eu and
Phis debated her fate at least seventy-five times.

---

[53] Dr. E. W. Sikes, in an undated entry in *Wake Forest Bulletin* as reprinted in the 1909 *Howler,* page 114.

Beginning with the mid-century Anniversary Debates, the public events topics were "hackneyed and outworn subjects... It was not until 1882 that questions involving practical, economic factors and the public policy of our own country began to get their innings."[54] The topic of the day was, *Is the system of suffrage conducive to the best interest of the Republic?* The question, decided in the negative by the chapel assembled with a majority of 70, indicates a conservative crowd's response.[55]

In the middle decades, many topics were rotated from the questions selected by the query committees and approved by the Societies. Soon, both Societies had query books with some three hundred queries each on almost every conceivable historical or current subject, except that controverted religious subjects were disqualified.[56]

The Query Book, affording predictable, safe topics, was used extensively after the Civil War, although not exclusively. In January 1869, as the new term began, the Philomathesian's minutes noted this action by Mr. Wicks who "moved that the Query Committee be vested with the power to examine the Query Book and reject or cancel such queries as in their judgment are bad ones."[57] Some housekeeping was in order and was undertaken periodically.

An 1875 Phi resolution asked that no queries be selected from the query book. Presented topics would be selected by consent of the disputants and two-thirds of the members present.[58] The weight of too many member decisions likely led to retaining the sedate Query Book topics.

There were rare instances in which a seemingly whimsical topic would be bandied about. Almost tongue-in-cheek, the students gathered in 1878 considered, *Did Jacob Neds steal Ned Jacobs's pocket-knife?* A clever take-off on a popular multi-blade knife or an equally popular folding

---

[54] *The Wake Forest Student,* March 1898, page 470. After the turn of the century, frequent topics supported women's education, voting, and emancipated social roles, all within the context of the times. The 1882 date for the introduction of partisan/political topics is not correct. Examples go almost to the beginning of the debate on such content. *The Wake Forest Student's* conclusions are an overstatement. Substantive issues were debated throughout, especially in the early institute and years that followed shortly thereafter.

[55] *The Daily Review,* Wilmington, 1882; Attitudes regarding via suffrage, especially in Society debates, changed trajectory to an accepting stance by the turn of the century.

[56] Paschal, G. W. (1935). *History of Wake Forest College,* Vol. I, page 536-7.

[57] Philomathesian Minutes, January 30, 1869.

[58] Philomathesian Minutes, May 15, 1875.

wooden children's toy. The negative prevailed 12 to 25, who knows what that meant.

Paschal wrote, "...beginning from 1879, books were now much easier to handle and consult, and for the first time, newspapers and periodicals were made readily available for students. The result was that the queries for debates were soon changing to matters of current interest. Of course, the change was piecemeal. The Societies continued to discuss *Which was the better general, Hannibal or Scipio.*"[59]

Many of these "less-practical" topics were themselves appealing inquiries. One recurring theme stood out. The Eus debated an aspect of *Happiness* twenty-two times and the Phis Twenty-nine times; topics focused on life's meanings. For example, *Is a married life happier than a single one?* (1841) or *Does the uneducated man enjoy more real happiness than the*

---

[59] Paschal, G. W (1835). *The History of Wake Forest College*, Vol. I, page 371. We found topics on political and social issues considerably earlier than Paschal suggests, a date he links to the starting of the Anniversary Debates, 1872.

educated? (1848), or more esoteric, *Is a private life happier than a public life* (1835). Finally, one shared by everyone, *Do the summer or winter season affords the greatest amount of happiness* (1850).

Repetition also occurred in historical comparisons and foreign policy debates of the day. The Philomathesians were obsessed with Annexations (Texas, Mexico, Canada, Philippines, Hawaii, and most often, Cuba), debating whether the United States ought to (or already had) join in the colonization of the world. They experienced more than twenty debates on the subject. The Euzelians debated Cuba an additional fifteen times, favoring annexation but also considering Cuban independence from Spain and the United States.[60]

Their topics reveal that members were interested in a multitude of subjects. They were typically drawn to serious topics arising from world events and the intellectual curiosity of the period.[61] The relationship to the "nations of the world" tended to be aggregated with such topics as *Backwards nations should be controlled by progressive nations* (Phi. *1904*).[62] The Eus, also in 1904, considered and rejected the motion (Negative 5-0.). Although a panel vote does not prove anything, across topics, the impression is that members seemingly rejected being an overlord nation.

--*-*-*-*-*-*

The following sections reflect on four topic domains: Reckoning with the Civil War, World War I and II, Education, and Alcohol Regulations. The arenas are not commensurate in importance or temporal scope, yet each helps explain how topics developed and the contestations the debaters faced.

---

[60] Policy topics in the "foreign" arena were geographically Euro-centered, but seldom framed in contemporary terms. The Eus and Phis each considered topics regarding France over twenty times. This, however, was almost entirely historical. Likely, the often-repeated Napoleon discussions were approached with a tedium. Over a hundred debates analyzed English history and the Irish over 20 times. A few other countries were considered, with Greece being most favored, but singularly as ancient history. It was often debated whether *Greece or Rome was the greater country.*

[61] Harding, T. S. (1971). *College Literary Societies: Their Contribution to Higher Education in the United States 1815-1876*, Pageant Press International Corporation, New York, page 98.

[62] January 15, *Negative 8 to 10; January* 16, 1904, *Negative 13 to 10.*

RACE, CIVIL WAR, RECONSTRUCTION TOPICS

Topics often reflect the social and political conditions of the era in which they are debated. Unavoidably, debaters approach those issues from the perspectives of their lives. Given our current identifications, we would appropriately find specific earlier topics debated and positions taken as abusive. Yet, the offending rhetoric would have been customary in the debater's historical context. Discussions of Race render these era-related differences especially difficult, yet they are the decades-long historical record of Wake's being.

Consider an often-debated topic: *Do savage nations possess a full right to the soil?*[63] Through the 1800s and into the 1930s, "A strong consensus held that people came packaged in neat categories such as 'civilized' and 'fit,' 'primitive' and 'deviant" The fittest human beings squarely on top."[64] The underlying assumptions of fundamental differences and inherent superiority were largely viewed as a given, as with these illustrative topics: *Will Africa ever become a civilized country?*[65] and *Was the African race designated by our Creator to be slave or freeman?*[66]

Yet debating these topics prompted the debater and audiences to question underlying societal conventions. The selection of topics and compelling two-sided debate suggest that racial inferiority was not universally held. Opinion was heavily weighted with Southern sympathies, yet as with the present, in the 1800s, society was mixed in its political sentiment.

In the trying days following the Civil War, societies generally guarded against political entanglements. As Paschal summarized: "No questions on the last war or on current political events ... were proposed for discussion. Even economic and social questions were carefully dodged... During these years, most of the questions debated were historical questions of a past age."[67]

---

[63] Philomathesian Minutes, December 1872. The decision for the debate was Affirmative 14, Negative 5, arguably an enlightened position for the times.

[64] Charles King, the anthropologist who upended the 'science' of white supremacy. *Washington Post*, August 2, 2019. https://www.washingtonpost.com/outlook/the-anthropologists-who-upended-the-science-of-white-supremacy/2019/08/01/.

[65] Euzelian Minutes, September 7, 1839.

[66] Philomathesian Minutes, October 23, 1873, Decided Affirmative 11 to 8. Nine years after the Civil War, slavery was still seen as appropriate.

[67] Paschal, G. W. (1943). *History of Wake Forest College,* Vol. II, page 57.

Determining whether Mary Queen of Scots and Charles the First were justly executed was not offensive. "It was safe to discuss the actions of those whose tombs were already shrines, but it was thought dangerous or inexpedient "to call into question the acts of men like Stanton and Thad Stevens or Governor Holden, to try to determine the justice of Andrew Johnson's impeachment, or to have any view on the Thirteenth, Fourteenth, and Fifteenth Amendments to the Federal Constitution."[68]

There were deviations, which are explored below. An early exception was the debate on the first of October 1869, about whether *the former slaves benefited from their freedom.*

A telling topic with many variations was whether there was *Any difference in the amount of happiness between the most savage being and the most civilized.*[69] In 1841 this query likely reinforced the "Happy Negro/Slave" stamp, but it may also have suggested that the "veneer of civilization' Southerners presented was not always definitive.

A 1904 *The Wake Forest Student* editorial likely reflected the general attitudes toward race at the turn of the century. They wrote, "The 'So-called 'Race Problem' has been the theme of so much flighty oratory, the rallying cry of the politician and the demagogue, the all-absorbing question for the debate in literary societies, and yet solution in the eyes of many is as far from being realized as ever... No *coup d'etat* will reap a satisfactory solution, ...the final settlement will come alone through the ameliorating influence of time."[70]

The student column continued with a message that rejected any responsibility by Whites and argued things only improve when Blacks are free to pull themselves up by their bootstraps (As Whites did). He argues that Blacks' desire for suffrage will only happen when it is fully restricted. Denying voting privilege as the means for extending voting access seems a transparent contradiction.

There is a corresponding responsibility laid upon the Southern white man: racial antipathy must be put away, and the utterances of radical reformers must be checked. The time is come for conservative men to take the lead. The disenfranchisement of the Negro,

---

[68] Paschal, G. W. (1943). *History of Wake Forest College,* Vol. II, page 58.

[69] Philomathesian, September 19, 1841, essentially a tied vote.

[70] C. P. Weaver, Editor, *The Wake Forest Student,* April 1904, Vol. 23, page 465.

while seemingly an untoward event, will eventually work out for him his salvation, for his desire for suffrage will cause him to deplore his present condition, and dissatisfaction is the mother of amelioration. The task of helping him shake off the shackles will then fall into willing hands, and the way to citizenship will be made easy for him.[71]

A more generous read would see Weaver suggesting Blacks voices need make the case, a process not reserved for unsympathetic Whites.

As noted, some Wake histories have suggested that topics regarding race were essentially void in Society debates. There is some truth to the claim relative to the broader corpus; in the 1870s, both societies concentrated on literary byplays. Yet race topics were addressed on many occasions; in addition to those mentioned below, debates were held discussing race questions of the day, usually with the anticipated Southern view prevailing.[72]

Other debates that took place included: *Is slavery as practiced in the United States incompatible with the spirit of free institutions?* Decided for the Negative (1836)[73]; *Is slavery consistent with the principles of a free government?* Decided for the affirmative (1838) (Phi).[74], *Has freedom been beneficial to the Negro* (1869), Negative 16 to 9; *Race segregation is the only solution of the race problem,* The decision recorded in minutes ledger as "Negative; Negative; Negative" (1920).[75]

Before the Civil War's closure of the college, as students left to join the North Carolina brigades[76], the societies remained shy about debating slavery, with the exceptions noted. As the membership shrunk and the

---

[71] C. P. Weaver, Editor, *The Wake Forest Student*, April 1904, Vol. 23, page 467.

[72] Race topics were on occasion proposed, but not often selected for hall debates. Among a list of proposed Eu topics was the following: *Is the negro race constitutionally inferior to the white race?* The topic was not among those selected. Euzelian Minutes, September 13, 1851.

[73] Philomathesian Minutes, May 28, 1836

[74] Philomathesian Minutes, February 15, 1838.

[75] Three Phi Debates, *January 19, 28, & 31, 1920.*

[76] To maintain membership in the 1850s, and before the full clouds of the Civil War gathered, the societies "added to the accepted literary functions of debate and literature have been investigations in the current accomplishments in the various arts, studies of great music, pertinent college occurrences from a literary point of view, and creative work." Hughes, D., Phi's had membership problems in the 1850s, *Old Gold and Black*, October 24, 1955, page 2.

war was waged, the topics returned to historical form rather than reflecting current happenings. For example, for the fourth time, on April 11, 1862, the handful of reminding Phis debated, *Was Washington a greater general than Alexander the Great?* Affirmative 3 to 0.

The Euzelians mostly moved to safe topics, yet they debated on April 11, 1862, nearly a year after Fort Sumter fell and eleven months after North Carolina's succession,[77] by then the pressing topic: *Would the raising of the blockade be productive of more benefit than injury to the Southern Confederacy?* Ayes 7, Nays 0. The vote reveals that few members remained in session.

The Phis, debating longer, wondered in September 1861, *Has the downfall of Republics been more owing to the want of wisdom in their legislations than the decline of morals in the people?* (Affirmative 3 to 2.) This judgment confirms that it is sometimes easier to blame institutions than those who compose them.

The general avoidance of slavery and war topics may have been a denial of the unfolding politics or simply wanting to avoid controversy. Yet, the meetings show a much more concurrent and controversial resolution selection list than those that eventually reached the floor. These likely solicited some fiery disagreements. In one meeting in December 1861, over half a year *after* North Carolina had seceded from the Union,

---

[77] The North Carolina convention in Raleigh seceded from the Union on May 20, 1861. Nearly twenty years later, in April 1881, the Phis debated: *Were the Confederates justifiable in firing the first gun at Fort Sumter?* The assembled voted on behalf of the cannons, Affirmative 27 to 9.

the Philomathesian query committee offered a set of challenging topics. Included were:

1ˢᵗ Should North Carolina, independently of the actions of any other State, have seceded with South Carolina from the U. S.?

2ⁿᵈ Which is superior as a conservative element in government, the numerical or the concurrent majority?

3ʳᵈ Did South Carolina act prematurely in seceding from the US without proposing a concerted action with her Sister States?

4ᵗʰ Is it patriotic to sacrifice personal honor for one's country?

5ᵗʰ Was the doctrine of nonintervention unfavorable to the South?

9ᵗʰ Should the South as a separate nation devote itself entirely to the planting interests or growth in its manufacturing system?

10ᵗʰ Was the Mason and Slidell case a breach of international law?[78]

The final topic debated was historical: *Was Napoleon justifiable in sanctioning the death of the Duke of Enghien?*[79], a debate just two meetings before the college suspended operations. The last meeting sadly announced no new disputants or topics to be debated but provided for a caretaker for the hall and safe storage of the society's records in Petersburg, Virginia.[80]

---

[78] Philomathesian Minutes, December 7, 1861. The Mason-Slidell case, "The Trent Affair" was a diplomatic incident in 1861 that threatened a war between the United States and the United Kingdom. The U.S. Navy illegally captured two Confederate diplomats from a British ship; the UK protested vigorously. The United States ended the incident by releasing the diplomats. Topics addressing race were, on occasion, proposed before the Civil War but not often selected for hall debates. Among a list of proposed Eu topics, a decade before the War, was: *Is the negro race constitutionally inferior to the white race?* The topic was not among those selected. Euzelian Minutes, September 13, 1851.

[79] Philomathesian Minutes, April 26, 1862, Societies were not always bound to the query book, as the above suggests. Paschal claimed, "At times, some rash query committee would propose to add to the list of debatable questions one such as, *Was the murder of John Wilkes Booth justifiable?* and *Has the government of the United States the right to interfere with the actions of any State?*, but they were uniformly rejected."

[80] Philomathesian Minutes, May 6, 1862; As the war commenced, the Phis debated until May of 1862, the topics, some inconsequential, some pertinent, involving fewer and fewer students. The Eus' last debate was over a year before the Phis ceased. It contested on March 29, 1861, *Should the practice of taking oaths be abolished?*

TABLE 1: Race Topics in the Three Years Before Entering the Civil War

1859, April 23 – Philomathesian: *Has any one of the United States a right to secede from the Union?* Negative 11-8.	1859, August 5 – Euzelian: *Would a dissolution of the Union be beneficial to the South?* Negative 16-5.	1859, August 20 – Philomathesian: *Has the institution of African slavery been beneficial to the U.S.?* Affirmative 11-8.
1859, September 3 – Philomathesian: *Which would be more dangerous to the South, a dissolution of the Union or the abolition of slavery?* Negative 13-4.	1859, November 26 – Philomathesian: *Is slavery an evil offense?* Negative 7-3.	1860, August 18 – Philomathesian: *Has the institution of African slavery into the United States been beneficial?* Affirmative 10-6.
1860, November 2 – Euzelian: *Will African slavery be perpetual in the United States?* Affirmative 9-4.	1861, February 28 – Philomathesian: *Which would be more dangerous to the South, a dissolution of the Union or an abolition of slavery?* Negative 8-4.	1861, August 2 – *Should the union of a state with a federal union be for an indeterminate or a fixed period of time?* Affirmative 5-1.

As noted earlier, Paschal suggested the Societies felt it safe to show their preference for men and things Southern.[81] Yet there were intermittent efforts to "come to terms" with the reality of the War's abrupt after-effects. Table 2 indicates hall debates in the three years after the college reopened.

Decided in the negative, 9 to 3. The topics dodged the unfolding war but were nevertheless of substantive content, not wholly hollow as has been suggested in Wake histories. As the Civil War commenced, the number of students in the society meetings dwindled to sometimes under ten. Minutes began to record resolutions such as "Whereas information has reached the Society of the death of Willie P. Mangum who was slain while gallantly defending the honor of his State..." Philomathesian Minutes, August 31, 1861.

[81] Paschal, G. W. (1943). *History of Wake Forest College,* Vol. II, page 58.

TABLE 2: Race Topics in the Three Years Post-Civil War

1866, May 17 – Philomathesian: *Should North Carolina have seceded in May 1861* Affirmative 8 to 2.	1866, June 3 – Philomathesian: *Has the Negro been benefited by his freedom.* Negative, 7 to 4.	1866, November 16, 1867, November 16, Philomathesian: *Should the Negroes be colonized?* Negative, 16 to 11, 10 to 4.
1867, February 9 – Philomathesian: *Is resistance to government ever justifiable?* Affirmative, 10 to 3.	1866, November 10 – Philomathesian: *Ought the conscription law have been passed in 1862.* Affirmative 10 to 4.	1868, March 8 – Euzelian: *Has freedom proven beneficial for the Negro.* Affirmative 13 to 3.
1868, March 11 – Philomathesian: *Is the Negro benefited by his freedom?* Negative 11 to 10.	1868, September 25 – Which has greater cause for complaint Indian or Negro? Affirmative, 12 to 5.	* The Indian vs Negro's plight was debated by the two societies nearly thirty times. In related Indian topics, the Eu debated fairness to Indians and the Phi more concerned with deportations of tribes to the West.

Discussing racial issues did not end in three years; variations continued for the next sixty years. Some topic choices were not as veiled as often happened, with topics focused on who should have the right to vote. Typical would be an Eus' 1862 topic, *Ought the right of suffrage to be limited to those who can read and write?* (Affirmative 2, Negative 3). Sometimes, the limitation was linked to property ownership. The Eus argued the question of universal suffrage or specific restriction thirty times (the Phis forty).[82]

A stunningly direct inquiry was taken up in 1899, the year of the second Trinity debate, *Suffrage should be taken from the negroes in the Southern States* (Negative 22 to 18). The same topic advocating stripping Blacks of the vote, in January 1900, was agreed for the Affirmative 50 to 11.[83]

---

[82] By the 1890s, suffrage topics focused primarily on Women's right to vote, particularly for the Philomathesians.

[83] A serious effort was made to find the vote and wording of the A&M resolution. The records were most likely destroyed in a fire.

Although unnamed in the resolution itself, post-Reconstruction and solid-
ifying Jim Crow attitudes were openly discussed.

The *Progressive Farmer,* a Winston, North Carolina newspaper[84], also
in 1900, noted in an editorial the respective responses of the Wake Forest
and North Carolina Agricultural and Mechanical College for the Colored
Race Literary Societies to a topic they both debated on changing the North
Carolina Constitution to restrict black suffrage.[85] The editorial derided a
proposed amendment, which imposed literacy tests to vote.

The *Progressive Farmer* approached, with more than a little invective, the
story involving North Carolina A&M and Wake Forest debating societies.

At a Wake Forest College society debate some weeks ago, we were
informed, the opponents of the amendment won. On the other hand,
at a debate held by one of the literary societies at the Colored Agricultural and Mechanical College in Greensboro a few days since the
subject discussed was the amendment and, singularly enough, the
affirmative won.

It would be noted that section for the proposed Constitutional
Amendment reads as follows: "Every person presenting himself for
registration shall be able to read and write any section of the Constitution in the English language," etc. We suggest that the next Legislature specify what Constitution the voters must read – the Constitution of North Carolina, of the United States, of Kamchatka, or the

---

[84] Winston and Salem do not merge until 1913, so the paper cited here carried only
the "Winston" moniker.

[85] Agricultural and Mechanical College became North Carolina A&T in 1967. North
Carolina Agricultural and Technical State University, the first land grant college for
people of color in North Carolina, can be traced back to 1890 when the United States
Congress enacted the Second Morrill Act. The Literary Societies at NC A&T were
Eclectic and Collegian, their respective Society Presidents in 1900 were: Eclectic, C.
C. Hunter, and Collegian, E. S. Plummer. *Fifth Annual Catalogue of the Agricultural
and Mechanical College for the Colored Race 1898-1899,* page 54. Life on campus
in 1900 was still highly regulated. NC A&T's Rules and Regulations (Bulletin 1900)
began thusly: "1. The signal for rising will be given at 6 a. m. Dressing and arranging
rooms, 6 to 6:30 a. m. Morning prayers, 6:30 to 6:45 a. m. Study, 6:45 to 8:15 a. m.
Breakfast, 8:15 to 8:45 a. m. Class work, 9 a. m. to 1 p. m. Dinner, 1 to 2 p. m. Class
practice work, 2 to 4 p. m. Recreation, 4 to 6 p. m. Supper, 6 to 6:30 p. m. Study, 6:30
to 9 p. m. Prayers, 9 to 9:30 p. m. Retiring signal, 9:45 p. m. Lights out, 10 p. m."
*Sixth Annual Catalogue of the Agricultural and Mechanical College for the Colored
Race, 1899-1900,* page 15.

Constitution of the State Tobacco Growers Association! A little light would be appreciated."[86]

Surprisingly, the first intercollegiate debate between NC A & T and Wake, for which we can find a record, was in April 2019, 119 years after this account of perspectives on the literacy amendment resolutions.

Hall debates after the turn of the century remained in sympathy with Southern standards but increasingly sought out enactments of the "New South" economic expansion. Following the Civil War, the topics are more general, as detailed above, reconciling, or rejecting the War's implications.

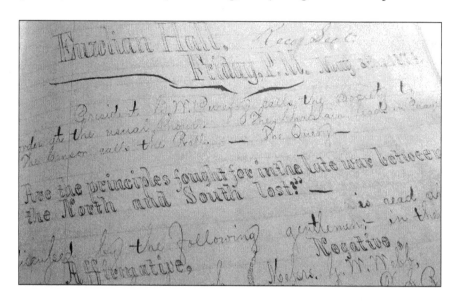

Some of the queries discussed until the wee small hours by the Philomathesians were: *Resolved, that slavery is incompatible with the American ideals of democracy.* This was a constant debate subject from the time of organization of the societies until after the war. Incidentally, this question provoked such furor and feeling in the Euzelians that they were forced to abandon it for more peaceful, if less exciting, discussions."[87] Earlier in October 1904, the Euzelians did not agree with a topic from a potential list to speak on, that *Congress should take some action to prevent lynchings in the South* (Negative 5-0).

---

[86] *The Progressive Farmer,* February 6, 1900, page 2.

[87] *Old Gold and Black,* February 17, 1934, page 1, 2.

The Eus' actual topic the week following the passed-over lynching topic still teemed with racial undertones. Twice on October 21 and November 11, 1904, the Eus' two respective meetings tackled, Resolved: *That in the so called "Yellow Peril" there is no danger to the power and civilization of the great nations of Europe.* Nov.11, Affirmative 4 to 1.[88]

For evident reasons, debates presented to the public were not as abundant as in-hall contests. Debates to a general audience do not begin until 1887. The pre-Civil War debates on slavery paralleled the national debate unfolding for the 26 years from the school's inception to the beginning of hostilities.[89]

Chapter 12 – Debating Race Before Their People, pays attention to public debates and offers a more detailed probe of the fare presented.

TABLE 3: Public Debates on Race

1887	Anniversary Day Debate – *Was the introduction of the Negro into the United States productive of more good than evil? The affirmative audience voted 133 to 33.*
1903	Anniversary Day Debate – *Deportation is the best solution of the Negro problem in the United States.*
1903	Intercollegiate Debate – Richmond – *Deportation is the best solution of the Negro problem in the United States.*
1904	Intercollegiate Debate – Richmond –*The advanced nations should control, for the world's benefit, the territory occupied by backward races.*

---

[88] Other topics included: Was the South justifiable in fighting the late Civil War? (1880) Affirmative: *Was the late Civil War beneficial to the South?* (Debated four times, Negative 20 to 10, Affirmative, 22 to 10, Affirmative 11 to 10; Affirmative 7 to 5, 1897.) **Has the American Civil War resulted in greater good for the country than evil? Affirmative 8 to 10; 12 to 9, 10 to 11.** (1905), and *That the results of the Civil War were more beneficial than detrimental to the South.* Negative 3 to 2; April 6, 7 (1905) and Negative 3 to 2 (1906).

[89] Representative topics previewing the impending War include: *Is it probable a disunion will ever take place between the Northern and Southern States?* (September 1844, Affirmative 6 to 5; March 1845, Negative 7 to 4; September 1848, Affirmative 10-5.; August 1852, Affirmative 15-14.), *Has a State the right to secede from the Union?* February and May 1851, Negative 19 to 10, Negative 13 to 3; April 1859, Negative 11 to 8; *Should the disunion of the Union be beneficial?* Affirmative 15 to 14, August 1852, and *Should the North reject the annexation of Texas into the union, and would the South be justifiable in seceding?* (February 1839, Negative).

1924	Society Day Debate – *Congress should be authorized to enact a uniform marriage and divorce law, with intermarriage between races prohibited.* Negative.
1965	International Public Debate – Britain – *The American dream is at the expense of the American Negro.*
1983	International Public Debate – Britain – Resolved: *This house would ban the Ku Klux Klan.*
1986	Public debate – High Point regional – Resolved: *That the United States should disinvest its economic holding from South Africa.*
2006	Campus Faculty Debate – Resolved: *Why are our schools re-segregating?*
2014	International Debate Rwanda – Resolved: *The United Nations should be obligated to intervene militarily in situations of genocide and grave human rights abuse.*

THE ANTI-WAR IMPULSE

In the World War I years, foreign policy disputes clustered around the impending and post-war problems, ranging from, *The present adminis-tration of the U.S. should warn all Americans not to travel on armed mer-chant ships* to, later, *The U.S. should adopt the League of Nations Cov-enant.*[90] In early 1915, the topic inquired if *Germany's present methods of warfare were justifiable,* decided in the negative each time. [91] As the war ensued, the Phis asked in April of 1917 that the *United States should send an army to the front to cooperate with the Allies.* Both societies, in a joint debate, explored one of the War's great military strategic disputes, a prelude to the two-decade hence D-day invasion, whether *Europe can be invaded by Sea.*

---

[90] The Phi debated the League over ten times, the Eus four.

[91] Other pre-WWI topics included: 1915 – *America should prohibit the shipment of ammunition of war to belligerent nations.* January 1917 – *A system of compulsory military training should be adopted by the United States.* February 1917 – *The United States should adopt a system of universal military service.* (Eu debated the draft four times, Phis seven, with mixed verdicts).

After the bloody conflict concluded, debates happening around the country and on campus unveiled a formidable isolationist influence. Debates between the two World Wars " marked topics addressing World peace, disarmament, the League of Nations, and war debts.[92] A reactionary topic asked should *The Allied nations adopt a long-range policy of control over the Axis nations.*

After the turn of the century, world events, as with society in general, were imposed on debaters. One strain of discourse was the extensive antiwar sentiment that followed World War I and preceded World War II. The tone was reflected in Cloyce Tew's impassioned address before an audience of the state's elite, with whispers of the impending World War. The fervent young debater's words continue to reverberate through our shared history. The speech below is edited heavily yet retains vivid imagery and masterful rhetorical composition.

The newspaper account, where one can find his speech verbatim, shared that Cloyce Tew, a Raleigh boy, came home from Wake Forest with the degree Bachelor of Science, two gold medals, and a diamond-studded pin, awarded for four years of intercollegiate debating. His oration Friday, entitled *War,* was delivered before the 1927 graduation.

---

[92] Examples include: October 1915 & March 1917, *The U.S. should participate in the world league to enforce peace., Will regional alliances bring world peace? The United Nations organization should be immediately strengthened into a sovereign world government.* Aff., and in the war year 1917, *The U.S. should participate in the World League to enforce peace* (Phis, eight times, generally endorsing.), January 1918, *All the nations now at war should agree to a gradual system of disarmament at the close of the world war* (Phi ten times, Eus four), and beginning in 1932, *The U.S. should cancel the Allied debts contracted during the World War* (Phi four, Eus once).

Mr. Pres., Ladies and Gentlemen:

Nothing has ever been settled by war – which could not have been settled by some other way. There never was a war that was not an indictment against the human race. The fact that we still have war shows our weakness in our depravity; and proves that we are still uncivilized and yet in the jungles...

Prior to 1917 we hoped that our people were a least a little wiser than other people of the world; that our goodly land, our high pretenses, our hopes, and fears had caused us actually to grow and burst the shell; but such was not the case – for we abandon our high ambitions extinguished our lights, call back our vanguards, turned around and took up the barbarian's method of the past. We abandon our treaty plans and dreams of peace and adopted the method of the ancients and help to make again the world a slaughter pen.

And so, we joined with 14 of the greatest nations of the earth in a desperate war——more gigantic, more bloodied, and foolish, and more wicked than any war that has preceded it. We were not fighting... against ignorance or immorality, not fighting against diphtheria, that chokes our little children to death; not fighting tuberculosis... not fighting to find relief for cancer or leprosy, nor any of the evils that beset the race but fighting people of our own kind, who kneel before the same shrine and worship the same God... I submit to you in all candor that the men who were killed in this war, when they turned their pale faces toward home, wife and children and died were innocent of its cause...

It has been estimated, that if all the dead, as a result of the last war, were placed end to end, a pedestrian could walk a distance equal to the total mileage between New York and San Francisco and return, stepping every foot of the way upon a bloated bodies of war dead, and yet we said that our honor caused us to put these men to death...

We passed recently a child labor law, preventing the little children of this country from being abused by working in manufacturing establishments and shops—and yet we killed millions of innocent men in order to make the Kaiser sorry—and thereby left millions of children fatherless to cry themselves to sleep at night, uneducated and uncared for... "These little ones without being the least responsible for the horrors of war, are suffering with hunger, pain, loneliness and bewilderment, utterly ignorant of the cause of their suffering. ...

…War lowers all our standards and threatens the very existence of humanity. It has caused as many drops of blood to be shed along the Mediterranean as there are drops of water in the sea; it has caused many teardrops on this side of the Atlantic as there are drops of water in the Amazon; it has reduced to putrid flesh grinning skeletons, bleached and withered bones the youth and flower of every age and land; it has disgusted humanity with itself, made religion a farce and prayer a mockery.

Why should human beings call on God for mercy when they will not show mercy to one another? Millions of men in this last war were on their knees in the trenches praying to God for mercy—while at the same time looking over embankments trying to blow out the brains of their fellow men, trying to make their wives widows and their children fatherless…

It is astonishing to think that in spite of the fact that Jesus of Nazareth, the founder of the Christian religion, declared in his Sermon on the Mount, "Blessed are the peace-makers"—an element of the American people—in certain newspapers and moral cowards as well as some organizations, make it appear that he, who in a faithful fateful hour, prefers peace to war is a traitor to the country in which he lives. I long to see the time when our… statues will be representations in marble of civil and not military leaders; our historians will eulogize statesmen instead of warriors…

Does not loyalty to Jesus' way of life, demand that we should renounce war as unchristian, futile and suicidal, and realize that in love and spiritual processes are forces mightier than military weapons, and that the most certain means of overcoming evil is found in the spirit of the crucified Nazarene, who said 'love your enemies.'

Is not love more powerful than hatred? Do we not believe that the cross is mightier than the sword? The challenge is clear—only believe. With faith… America can… break the thralldom of war… But as yet America has turned a deaf ear to those who are desperately sick of war and who passionately long for its abolition. At such an hour as this, can it be that it is to America, the reproach of the Master comes ringing down the ages, "On ye of little faith."[93]

---

[93] *The News & Observer*, Sunday, June 5, 1927, page 4 (Sports Section).

EDUCATION

Expectedly, students settled into educational surroundings soon turned to topics moving their lives. Well over a hundred Philomathesian topics dealt with aspects of education, as did fifty-plus Euzelian debates. In the early years, the general value of obtaining an education, and especially higher degrees, was debated, weighing the merits of being affluent or educated. The fifth and final Trinity Debate in December 1901 queried whether *North Carolina should adopt the principle of compulsory attendance in her public schools.*

The trending argument called for extending general education to all North Carolinians. Toward the turn of the century, the topics asked if the State should provide free elementary and secondary schools, an issue much more favored by the Euzelians. The Eus were also more likely to debate education and suffrage.

Early in their existence, the Wake boys undoubtedly held traditional attitudes regarding roles open to women, yet the Society members were more open-minded than the topics they articulated. For instance, in 1847, the Eus responded to a debate on educating women: *Do high literary attainments tend to make a woman unfit for performing domestic duties?* Their verdict was a decisive no, 22 to 4.

In addition, the Societies were generally supportive of accentuating women's education. Thirteen times, the Phis debated a version of a May 1860 query: *Is the education of females as much entitled to the consideration of our enlightened people as that of males?*[94] Presumably, this subject was in their topic rotation, but the fundamental question was openly contested.

The Phis directly debated the value of coeducation over ten times, and the Eus, six. Initially in opposition in the 1890s, campus opinion shifted to strong support for coeducation, as well as public funding of primary and secondary schools. By the 1930s, the emphasis had altered to the narrower question of Baptist schools, as public institutions had previously included female students. The topic on Society Day in 1930 was resolved: *That the Baptists of North Carolina should make their colleges coeducational.* Part of the debate concerned merging Wake Forest

---

[94] Decided in the affirmative 8 to 4.

and Meredith; a possibility whispered about but never taken close to a conclusion. The affirmative won.[95]

Later, curricular issues, often specific to college life, became popular and familiar today, pitting "liberal arts" against "applied occupations." In 1883, a refined version was debated: *Should students, while pursuing a course of literary education, study with reference to a particular profession?* (Affirmative 24 to 15). The table below gives a sampling of other education topics debated. A favorite is whether money from *"rich people" would corrupt the college mission,* debated in 1907.

TABLE 4: Debated Curricular Issues

Should a man receive a medical diploma without a classical education? Phi	January 30, 1847	Affirmative 22 to 10.
Ought a student in college direct his studies with reference to a particular profession? Eu	March 18, 1859	Tie 17 to 17 vote, Chair decision for affirmative.
Ought college students to study politics? Phi	November 19, 1841	5 to 9.
Should W. F. College have a five or two-month session? Phi	May 31, 1872	Affirmative 7 Neg 12.
Time required for getting a bachelor's degree shall be two years instead of four; And the time required for the bachelor's degree shall be three years instead of four. Eu	Oct. 9, 1903, Nov. 20, 1903	2nd Debate -Negative 4 to 1.
Admissions to college should be by examination only. Eu	November 6, 1903	5 to 0
Southern colleges should accept the so-called "tainted" money from billionaires. Eu	April 5, 6, 1907	Affirmative 5 to 0; Affirmative 5 to 0.

---

[95] *The News & Observer,* November 24, 1930, page 4. April 1, 1930, December 11, 14, 1923, and May 4, 1933, the Phis debated, Resolved, *That Wake Forest and Meredith should be combined.* They voted Affirmative. There were also some "humorous" topics, such as the November 17, 1932, *Meredith College being detrimental to the wellbeing of Wake Forest.* No ruling.

The study of ancient classics is a needless waste of time. Eu	November 29, 30, 1912	Negative 3 to 2; Negative 3 to 2.
College courses should be entirely electives. Eu.	January 24, 25, 1913	Negative 3 to 2
All colleges and universities should require four years of academic work before admitting students into their professional schools. Phi	November 25, 1937	Affirmative
Does the prosperity of the college depend more upon the execution of the faculty than the deportment of the students? Phi	October 11, 1845	Affirmative 15 to 14.
Baptist senior colleges in the state of North Carolina will have coeducation. Eu	November 7, 1931	Coeducation was debated many times
Ought a student in college direct his studies with reference to a particular profession? Eu	March 18, 1859	17 to 17 Tie, Chair decision for Affirmative

In 1927, the faculty debated before a chapel assembly, to the delight of the students, arguing the query: *Should the letter system be adopted in grading?* The third speaker, debate coach Dr. Quisenberry, smartly asked if a teacher knows the exact value of the question he is asking. Mercurially, he questioned the value of the grading process itself; he added, "If he [the faculty] knows the value of the question, does he know the value of The Wake Forest Students answer?"[96]

ARDENT SPIRITS

In 1856, the Euzelian minutes noted a debate held in the Hall: *Has war been more destructive to mankind than ardent spirits?* The ledger entry indicated, "After the debate had been prolonged till very late hour during which time there was an unusual display of eloquence and exhibitions of the genius, which rendered in the discussion exciting, entertaining and

---

[96] *Old Gold and Black*, February 19, 1927, page 1.

instructive, the poll was taken in the question cited in the Affirmative Ayes 21, Nays 6."[97]

"Ardent spirits" could be found just off campus if one was willing to overlook the law and school rules. Just maybe, some young men succumbed to the lure.

The Phis debated evil spirits as a social threat and reviewed the virtues of the State of North Carolina regulating liquor twenty times and the Eus, eight. Prohibition was deliberated throughout the pre-and post-Civil War Prohibition Movements, especially during the early 20th-century movements, which rendered NC dry, and later when the 19th Amendment enacted prohibition. Religious influences were heavily felt, permeating campus thought. While many rustled up local liquors, others took temperance seriously, perhaps a sizable majority.

The Temperance Movement was long-lasting, starting in the early mid-1800s and not losing impetus until the Prohibition Amendment was repealed in 1933, over a hundred years later. North Carolina "retained its antiliquor law for four years after the nation passed the Twenty-first Amendment ending Prohibition."[98]

In a called meeting on March 7, 1870, the Philomathesian Society agreed "to the use of our Hall that the Temperance Society may be organized in it."[99] Mr. Bland, Phi President, stated, "The Temperance Society is going to have a party in the college building about Christmas and moved that the hall be open as the location."[100]

In a letter in *The Biblical Recorder*, June 15, 1881, regarding its prohibition efforts, R. A. P. Colley,

---

[97] Euzelian Minutes, April 25, 1856.

[98] NCPedia, https://www.ncpedia.org/temperance-movement.

[99] Philomathesian Minutes, March 7, 1870.

[100] Philomathesian Minutes, December 11, 1875.

Pres., and Ed. S. Alderman, Sec. (presumably of the State Prohibition organization) wrote to Wake's Literary Societies:

> Last evening will long be remembered by the students of Wake Forest College as one of the most enjoyable occasions during their stay at college. The two Literary Societies met in joint session at 7:30 p.m. to discuss the question: Resolved, That it is the duty of every North Carolinian to support the present prohibition movement.
>
> ...The prohibition movement has taken a deep hold upon the citizens and students of this place. They are awakened to the importance of the movement, and the discussion last night showed that the students were in earnest., the meeting was characterized throughout by a soberness... They look upon it as one of the greatest blessings that can befall our commonwealth, and have resolved to one and all, to give their voice and influence for prohibition during the coming summer.[101]

However lively the debate, one must assume the students' "enthusiasm" for some "ruling out" spirits did not extend to the next summer.

Prohibition pressures in North Carolina remained powerful. The same year as the 1881 debate, the NC General Assembly authorized a referendum for statewide prohibition. "The result was the crushing defeat of temperance proponents by a vote of 166,325 to 48,370. Yet the issue was not dead. Prohibitionists went to work in their own communities, and by 1900, they had eliminated legal liquor sales in many rural areas and small towns by means of local referendums." Wake Forest was dry by this time.[102]

John R. Jones' 1909 Senior Thesis dealt with prohibition, likely his first Affirmative for that year's Anniversary debate. "This nation can no more endure half drunk and half sober, half 'wet' and half 'dry,' half license and half anti-license, than it could half slave and half free. The good people of this nation will not compromise... For in American blood, it is written, 'A question is never settled until settled right.'"[103]

---

[101] *The Biblical Recorder*, June 15, 1881, page 2.

[102] The Democrat party becoming decidedly dry, the outlawing of rural distilleries "all but dried up all but the state's 80 towns with populations of 1,000 or more." NCPedia, https://www.ncpedia.org/temperance-movement.

[103] John R. Jones, April 20, 1909. Senior Thesis

The 1917 season also saw a debate with Randolph Macon on the merits of prohibition. Wake, in opposition, won, shunning alcohol and framing the central issue as one of "state's rights." "It is not a moral issue but one of politics."[104] In 1926, Wake hosted the University of Arizona, debating *That this House condemns the present system of prohibition in the United States.*

The Arizona debate was largely framed in economic metrics, with the classic arguments of the government's right and capacity to regulate.[105] The last speaker concluded with a quotation from Lyman Abbott: "The progress in prohibition is far more a result of changes in men than changes in legislation…" Let the conflict go on from State to State and raise the glad song, 'The Nation's Going Dry,' not at the point of a bayonet… But by the sovereign ballot of the American freemen."[106]

The 1927 Founders Day debate was "well attended by professors and students alike." Euzelians on the Negative, B. T. Henderson and B. W. Walker scored a two-to-one victory over Phis, G. N. Ashley and G. F. Johnson, debating the question, Resolved, *That the Volstead Act should be modified so as to permit the manufacture and sale of light wines and beers.*"[107] The debate hinged on disparate interpretations of public opinion regarding prohibition.

The Volstead Act was meant to help secure enforcement of the 19th Amendment and was itself controversial. Naturally, the debaters took it on. In the first debate of the school year, "Larry Eagles… won a decision for the affirmative over W. H. Ford and D. A. Pickler. H. H. Deaton was the other affirmative speaker for the query, Resolved, *That the Volstead*

---

[104] *The News & Observer*, April 10, 1917, page 1.

[105] For those interested, a full transcript can be found in *The Wake Forest Student*, 1926.

[106] *The Wake Forest Student*, April 1909, Vol. 27, No. 7, page 559-574.

[107] *Old Gold and Black*, February 5, 1927, page 1. The National Prohibition Act, known informally as the Volstead Act, was an act of the 66th United States Congress designed to achieve better the 18th Amendment (ratified January 1919). https://www.britannica.com/topic/Volstead-Act; After the passage of the 18th Amendment in 1919, the society debate shifted to considering altering the Volstead Act to make exceptions to full prohibition. In 1927, the Eus were reported to have hosted a lively encounter, the affirmative holding that wine and beer were said not to be harmful, and "if they could be sold, they would take the place of the poisonous whiskey that is now being consumed in such amazing quantities" despite prohibition. The negative reasoned the political will did not exist to weaken prohibition. It also would bring back "open saloon with all its evils … workmen are going about their tasks with clear minds."

Act should be changed so as to permit the manufacture and sale of beverages containing not over 4 percent alcohol by volume. "If the debate can be judged by the interest, Thursdays was a good debate. Eagles indeed convinced the audience that it is easy to get intoxicating drinks in a very short time."[108]

By 1931, students' attitudes toward alcohol had loosened noticeably.

According to Jamie McKown, in this intercollegiate era, "no longer were debates viewed merely as performances demonstrating the educational accomplishments of students. Debate was now serving society by providing in-depth analysis of important issues for a broader public audience. Debate had become its own form of directed civic engagement."[109]

---

[108] *Old Gold and Black,* October 3, 1931, page 4; The Intercollegiate debates provided a practical venue for distilling liquor topics. In 1927, seven debates with other colleges were held on this topic.

[109] McKown, J. (2017). Renewing a "very old means of education": Civic engagement in the birth of intercollegiate debate in the United States. In J. Michael Hogan, J. A. Kurr, M. J. Bergmaier, and J. D. Johnson, *Speech and Debate as Civic Education* (pp. 36-52). Pennsylvania State University Press, University Park, Pennsylvania, page 46. He assigned community influence to the 1920s, but we would argue that the debates were equally influential in their first decade, the 1910s.

ADDITIONAL THEMES

The following is an assortment of "topic stories, sometimes amusing, sometimes deadly serious, debated in the Society halls. Some departures are innately curious and are presented as such. For nearly eight decades, topics were debated, providing endless examples to be unearthed. Herein is a selection of some of the issues.

1874—The Euzelians were conversant with the social world outside Wake Forest's gate.[110] They took up political and social issues, addressing, for example, *Are the Grangers productive of good to the country.* (Affirmative, Yeas 12, Nays 4).[111] The Granger movement grew out of a farmers' lodge, the Patrons of Husbandry, founded in 1867 by Oliver Hudson Kelley. While employed by the Department of Agriculture, Kelley toured the South and was struck by the enslavement of Southern farmers to outworn methods of agriculture. He believed the situation could best be remedied by an organization that would unite farmers.[112]

1895—Debate queries often foreshadowed future trends. An examination of Philomathesian records revealed that the question discussed three years before the Battleship Maine was blown up in the Havana, Cuba harbor (1898) was: *Should the United States interfere with Spain's treatment of Cuba?*[113]

1927—A birth control debate was argued in terms both more retro and more enlightened than some held today. In a December

---

[110] Several signs indicated the debating societies were aware of national activities. This awareness extended to debate-theory questions; some issues continuing into the next century. For example, the 1893 *Wake Forest Student* shared, "We notice that the American colleges are beginning to see the necessity of keeping up their debating societies. The debate seems to have fallen into disuse in some of our important institutions, but such a blunder cannot long prevail in our land. The debating societies must live as long as our institutions do. John Gore informed his peers that "'A New England Debating League' has recently been formed, consisting of the following institutions: Brown, Wesleyan, Tufts, Bates, Boston University, and Boston College." John Homer Gore, Editor, *The Wake Forest Student*, 1893, page 341.

[111] Euzelian Minutes, June 5, 1874.

[112] Grange Movement, https://www.encyclopedia.com/history/united-states-and-canada/us-history/granger-movement, June 17, 2019

[113] *Old Gold and Black,* February 17, 1934, page 2.

meeting, the Euzelian debate topic, though not formally recorded, dealt with "the age-old question regarding the dissemination of the knowledge and means of birth control... The discussion waxed hot during the whole hour, with neither side giving nor accepting quarter. An active offense and resistant spirit were manifested by the belligerents, and every point gain, or lost was the result of heated controversy."

The winner, the affirmative, Steele and Benfield, pointed out some of the "evils that would result from the lack of means of birth control, showing that the weakest portion of our race comes from large families." The negative held that birth control "would be wrong morally from a social, natural, and physical standpoint."[114]

1928—The Phis had fun with the censorship of motion pictures, considering *That state censorship of motion pictures should be adopted in the United States.* Perhaps with tongue-in-cheek, perhaps by conviction, the affirmative observed there was "An increasing desire of the youth...to attend shows, and many of them were, of such type that was greatly embarrassing to both boys and girls...a great number of the present-day crimes could be traced back to the immoral picture...The negative "forcibly attacked" stating that the theatre had to bear the blame for many unjust crimes. "This is the only loophole for the lawbreakers." It sounds like the sides are in agreement. The affirmative won.[115]

1930—At various periods in the history of literary societies, societies took their purpose of exploring the literary more seriously. Undoubtedly, participants might have heard these topics differently than today, so maybe with minimal irony, the following program unfolded on April Fool's Day. "L. O. Munn gave a brief character sketch of Lord Byron and discussed his poetry. A pleasing declamation was given by T. S. Lawrence on the subject of 'Meditation.' The evening's excitement undoubtedly improved with the debate, *That Wake Forest and Meredith should be combined.*"

---

[114] *Old Gold and Black*, December 7, 1927, page 1.

[115] *Old Gold and Black*, March 10, 1928, page 1. "Due to the training school at the church, it was voted to dispense with the rebuttals."

The popular side seemed to have the advantage" in that the affirmative was victorious.[116]

1931—An *Old Gold and Black* headline teased the issue of separation of church and state. The resolve was, *That a preacher's activity in politics are detrimental to his Christian leadership as a preacher,*

EU SOCIETY DISCUSSES
PREACHER AND POLITICS
Preacher's Place Declared To Be
In Pulpit and Among His Workers

The affirmative side argued:

The purpose of religion and preachers was in the pulpit and among his workers, that his duty was to preach the gospel, and that if he did all this he would have no time for things as corrupt as politics. The negative deplored the present state of politics and stated that in a thing so vital as the election of our government officials, there should be an element of religious influence. The negative explained, however, that a preacher was not to use sermons in politics, but that his leadership be maintained by his personal right to vote and using that vote wisely. The negative speakers were awarded the decision.[117]

1936—One particularly interesting resolution found its way to the debating floor, as European powers maneuvered prior to World War II. The resolve at the Wake Church, Founder's Day/Anniversary Day 102nd celebration, was *That Italy is justified in pursuing a policy of armed conquest of Ethiopia.* The Phis gained victory by showing that Ethiopia needs European supervision, which Italy is best qualified and most fully justified to administer. "Italy gained only the crumbs of the colonial spoils," asserted a Phi debater,

---

[116] *Old Gold and Black*, April 5, 1930, page 1.

[117] *Old Gold and Black*, March 28, 1931, page 1. Also, as a part of the program, C. H. Stroup gave an oration, *A Dissertation on Surplus Time*, and a comical reading, *The Chivalrous Shark*, which was read by F. U. Fletcher. A three-minute speech on *Why Married Women Should Not Be Allowed to Teach in the Public Schools of North Carolina* was made by Bill Patton.

"and so has as much right to take over Ethiopia as other nations had in the past to seize their possessions."[118]

1937—Debates in the halls continued regularly throughout the 1930s, mostly on hot issues of the day. Right on cue, both Societies held debates on Franklin Roosevelt's plan to "pack" the court with "New Deal" friendly judges. "The cradle of Liberty is still rocking, six weeks after it was set in motion by President Roosevelt's surprise announcement of his intention to increase the membership in the Supreme Court in the event that incumbent judges over three score and ten don't choose to retire.[119] Amid the applause of those present, the student judges gave their decision to the negative in both societies."[120]

The *Old Gold and Black* conducted campus interviews about court packing, soliciting Greek Professor and historian G. W. Paschal, "I am for the plan because I think that it is the only way in which New Deal measures can be realized. The method purposed is strictly constitutional; the evil to be corrected has been recognized by two of the greatest Republican presidents, Taft and Roosevelt, and does not involve any danger of a dictatorship." Those frustrated with the court's intransigence might have a "much more violent reaction at the next election."[121]

By the 1930s through the 1950s, the programming of the society meetings became much more idiosyncratic, with the hope of building membership through more interesting programming. Some would say the societies' offerings were chaotic.[122] They were, however, in the flow of the times and an ever-more-variable world.

As the years progressed, societies held fewer and fewer debates. Jamie McKown summarized, "The well-documented decline of literary societies in the late nineteenth century had brought with it a decline in society

---

[118] *Old Gold and Black*, February 1, 1936, page 1.

[119] *Old Gold and Black.*, February 27, 1937, page 1.

[120] *Old Gold and Black.*, February 27, 1937, page 4.

[121] *Old Gold and Black.*, February 27, 1937, page 1.

[122] Where, in a topic taxonomy, would one place this November 1943 topic: *The centipede suffers more from athlete's foot than the giraffe from sore throat.* Negative it was, presumably the giraffe suffered more (or, as likely, the negative side better handled the "argument").

debates. College and university publications from the period consistently worried that interest in literary society participation, as well as the quality of the debates they produced, were waning. Campus debates generally were not well attended, and they were criticized for their excesses of oratory and elocution.[123]

HERE ARE THE BOYS WHO TALK — THEY'RE DEBATERS

Above you see the entire Wake Forest debate squad as the camera man caught them in a deep mood. In fact, it is that mood of concentration which only a debater can assume. They win honors left and right, and are one of the most industrious groups on the campus. But we've still got a surprise for you, dear reader, and if you'll be so kind as to turn to page four the thrill of a lifetime awaits you.

HERE ARE THE FOUNDATIONS OF ORATORICAL FAME

Yes, you're right. This is a study of limbs. After admiring the entire picture, we decided to put on a drive for the aid of Brooklyn Girl Scouts, so we divided the photo. If you will promise not to turn back to the first page, and will name each one of the squad, correctly you will be given a free trip to Rolesville. Be sure to sign a pledge, and enclose a ten dollar bill with each list of names you enter. All entries should be addressed to Mr. John Polanski. His decision will be final. Contest closes today at noon.

A 1939 *Old Gold and Black* issue utilized humor to note the Debate Squad; the two pictures, comically captioned, were found separately on pages 1 & 4.

---

[123] McKown, J. (2017). Renewing a "Very old means of education": Civic engagement in the birth of intercollegiate debate in the United States. In J. M. Hogan, J. A. Kurr, M. J. Bergmaier, and J. D. Johnson, *Speech and Debate as Civic Education* (pp. 36-52). Pennsylvania State University Press, University Park, Pennsylvania, page 40.

CHAPTER 5

Intercollegiate Debate Launches

The First Intercollegiate Series – Wake vs. Trinity

The three following chapters recount Wake's debate activities during the Intercollegiate Debate Era, which ran from 1897 through the late 1930s. The first of these three chapters begins with Wake's early entry into Intercollegiate debating, revisiting Wake's first debate series, a five-year Thanksgiving Day festivity with Trinity College.

The "Intercollegiate Debate Era" unfolds as opportunity, transportation, and funding come together in the emergent surroundings of easier travel, maturing collegiate institutions, and a more mobile and resourced audience. The country was experiencing a learning awakening that transformed the outreach and purpose of literary societies in general and colleges in particular.[1]

---

[1] The extension of college debate to a greater public was contemporaneous with the Chautauqua Movement of the early 20th century. https://en.wikipedia.org/wiki/Chautauqua. In the Midwest, "nearly every town had its own Lyceum by the end of 1830s," Clayton, M. K. (1987) Making the American prophet: Emerson, his audiences, and the rise of the culture industry in Nineteenth-Century America, *American Historical Review*, 92, page 604. "Skilled oratory and the practiced eloquence of traveling lecturers undergirded the prominent 'Lyceum and lecturing movement the Midwestern United States' and impressed young and eager audiences." Lauck, J. K. (2022). *The Good Country: A history of the American Midwest 1800-1900*, University of Oklahoma Press, page 58. These movements were soon copied in the South and particularly in the Carolinas.

THE INTERCOLLEGIATE DEBATE ERA

1897-1903 – Single school series – Trinity, Richmond

1903-1913 – Single School Series – Furman, Mercer, Davidson, Randolph Macon, Baylor

1914-1918 – Two School/Year Series – Baylor/Davidson, Richmond (2)/Randolph Macon, R-M/Baylor

1919-1923 – Three Debates a Year– Combinations of Emory & Henry/Randolph-Macon/Baylor; Colgate/ Davidson/Mercer/Baylor; Okla Baptist/Davidson/Stetson/Marysville/Union/William Jewell

1924-1926 – Multiple Debates Scheduled – Mercer, Charleston, William & Mary, Oklahoma Baptist, Furman, Davidson, Baylor, Pittsburgh, Arizona, William & Mary

1926-1938 – Single Series and Regional Tours. A few scattered after 1938.

In 1905 and 1907 Wake Forest did not engage with another college.

The Wake Forest debates began simply enough as a one-on-one series orchestrated around the Thanksgiving and Easter holidays in association with Raleigh and Greensboro's Chambers of Commerce. For the most part the programming engaged in home-and-away events. Wake would organize Anniversary and Society Day contests on campus, the societies debating between themselves, but most debates with other institutions were held in regional population centers, primarily Raleigh. Debates were often hosted on other schools' campuses or in regional centers like Atlanta and Birmingham. Several Raleigh colleges were the site of debates when hosted by Wake, the most frequent being Meredith College.

Around 1917, Intercollegiate Debating began to expand. As *The Wake Forest Student* reported, "Wake debaters had never met more than two colleges in one year, and until recently, never more than one in a single year." One student publication commented that Debates were never scheduled except when they felt almost sure of winning.[2]

The Debate Council played a pivotal role in shaping campus life for most of this period. It was composed of members of each society; later, a

[2] H. E. Olive, *The Wake Forest Student*, January 1917, Vol. 36, page 226.

faculty representative was added. It is unclear when a council was formed to oversee debate governance, although references were found as early as 1908. Informally, the Council was formed when the societies named representatives to negotiate in tandem with Trinity. The Council was at its height in the active years before World War I, certainly including 1911 to 1914.

In 1913 *The Wake Forest Student,* which printed an official college directory, listed the Debate Council, chaired by Roland S. Pruitt, at the top of the page immediately under Pres. W. L. Poteat, LL.D. The Student Athletic Association did not appear until the fourth slot.

Of course, this listing is not definitive evidence of influence but is consistent with the importance and deference the Council commanded. Its central mission, inventing and investing in the Thanksgiving and Easter productions, was praised by *The Wake Forest Student*, who argued that its work was no easy task.

> The centrality of the Debate Council in managing the intercollegiate debates can hardly be underestimated. It was their responsibility to negotiate the schedule of debates for the coming year, and as we have seen elsewhere, it was easier said than done, sometimes requiring pressure, sometimes diplomacy, sometimes begging, sometimes an assuredness.

By the end of the 1930s, tournament debates began to supersede individual contests. Not surprisingly, the tournament debaters were also members of the Debate Council, a redundancy that further eroded the Council's role since, in the era of tournaments, a "scheduler" was not as central. Also, maintaining long tours was expensive and the audiences had largely disappeared. For the students, there were increasingly other ways to escape campus, and the debaters themselves found tournament competitions more challenging, entertaining, and educationally helpful.

It was not easy to schedule opponents. Those institutes who signed a contract tended to be in the same rank, most often small liberal arts schools with religious affiliations. Except for Trinity (Methodist) and Davidson (Presbyterian) in the early years, and often beyond, the Intercollegiate opponents shared Wake's Baptist affiliation. Wake did not, or was not able to, schedule large public universities, although these debates were happening, such as with the University of North Carolina versus

Georgia or Texas. Wake's options, including Pittsburgh and Arizona, enlarged toward the end of the era.

Often, institutions were unwilling to meet Wake Forest in debate, or that was how the home institution viewed endeavors to negotiate with potential opponents. They did not want to risk losing to a small upstart. *The Wake Forest Student* editor Tyram Hunter characterized the Wake Forest College record as one of its "swallowing men on the arena and capturing trophies." Potential opponents offered a myriad of excuses. As Hunter saw it, "some of them have just made previous arrangements to debate other institutions; some belong to Debate Leagues and could not meet us; others have 'sworn off from debating; and one beloved sister institution, inasmuch as it had all to lose and nothing to gain in debating a small institution,' flung back contemptuous Goliath sneer, 'You're too little.'"

Earlier that year, *The Wake Forest Student* lamented:

> Our literary societies have drunk the... intoxicating drought of victory until they are beginning to see the landscape evolve like a merry-go-round. In debate, Wake Forest to-day stands supreme; everybody denies the statement, but strangely enough, nobody but Davidson has the nerve to try to disprove it, and Davidson ought not to count, for a Presbyterian, to quote Wake Forest eminent chief Bobbitt, 'would cross Hades on a rotten rail if anyone told him he couldn't.'
>
> The Azure world is not the company we desire; we want to debate, and what are we to do?... The Debate Council this fall has challenged 15 colleges and universities from Missouri to Virginia, and from Pennsylvania to Louisiana, and every case, except one, we received a polite note expressing regret that their schedules were already filled when Wake Forest's challenge arrived.[3] Seemingly, the acceptance was overridden by an athletic team's concern.

One could argue that the Wake community had an inflated sense of itself, but its claim to debating prowess represented more than wins and losses, which were ample; it was part of Wake's very fabric. Wake's identity was not that of David facing Goliath but as a formidable competitor in the Intercollegiate sphere.

In the 1910s and '20s, Wake's societies had grown large, and the opportunities to participate in a public debate remained limited. Some

---

[3] *The Wake Forest Student*, Vol. 30, No. 2, November 1910, page 162.

members could go for four years and never get to join in an intercollegiate debate.[4] Most often, reliance on "two or three men of prestige and slightly more ability in their class" precluded wider participation.

In part, the debate council of 1918-19 came to the rescue and began scheduling multiple debates, adding Baylor and Colgate, renewing some like Randolph Macon and others to the schedule. By 1924, many tours and public debates were added; they no longer had the charm of uniqueness.

1903 – Raleigh at the beginning of the Intercollegiate Era
Approximate Population 17,000

Until the turn-of-the-century, Wake Forest was a sleepy place, at least for the students tethered by classes and means. *The Farmer and Mechanic*, a Raleigh newspaper, penned in 1904, "Wake Forest is regarded a college village – and nothing more, but the visitor here sees a growth of population ...felt elsewhere in the State.[5] Not until 1917 did Wake

---

[4] Debaters filled many other prestigious roles, Marshals, Secretaries, etc.

[5] A Message to Wake Forest, Editorial Correspondence. *The Farmer and Mechanic* February 16, 1904, page 4.

Forest have twenty faculty members, including Pres. Poteat, as well as the professional programs.[6]

Notwithstanding its relative physical isolation, the Wake community was exceedingly aware of intercollegiate debates as early as 1895.[7] A note in *The Wake Forest Student* referenced the annual debate between Yale and Princeton, noting the December 6 date and the question to be discussed Resolved, *That in all matters of State legislation of a general character, a system of referendum should be established, similar to that now established in Switzerland.*" It was announced in the same issue that "There will be an inter-collegiate debate between the University of Georgia and Emory College on May 15th."[8]

Consideration for intercollegiate debates was not just limited to the eventual opening Trinity-Wake series. As early as November 3, 1900, Phi minutes note ambitions to take part in debates with Randolph Macon and Richmond. "Mr. Weaver reports that Mercer would consider a debate between Wake Forest and Mercer."[9] Wake, however, did not finalize agreements or pursue other options until the collapse of the Trinity debates.

The intercollegiate debating series became the pinnacle of nonathletic extracurricular activity on campus. Student editorials suggested that intercollegiate debates had become a barometer of the intellectual health of the institution and the quality of its education. Likewise, being selected to the intercollegiate team became one of the highest honors a student could aspire to.[10]

Additionally, "As debaters maneuvered into the world, they visited places that were completely new to them, college towns and big cities

---

[6] Four attended the University of Richmond. Getting outside the bubble generally meant you were a professor of anatomy. The faculty included future president Thurman D. Kitchin, Wake historian George W. Paschal, and President Poteat's son Hubert, a 1906 graduate and debater. Librarian Mrs. Ethel Crittenden was the lone female representative. In addition to the primary faculty, there appeared to be six instructors and perhaps fifteen assistants who helped with teaching.

[7] *The Wake Forest Student,* 1895, page 144.

[8] *The Wake Forest Student,* 1895, page 277.

[9] Philomathesian Minutes, November 1, 1900.

[10] Jamie McKown, J. (2017). Renewing a "Very Old Means of Education": Civic Engagement and The Birth of Intercollegiate Debate in The United States. In *Speech and Debate as Civic Education* Edited by J. Michael Hogan, Jessica A. Kurr, Michael J. Bergmaier, and Jeremy D. Johnson, The Pennsylvania State University Press, page 41.

where they were greeted by marching bands, feted at buffet luncheons and smokers... Perhaps most lustrous was the unchaperoned train travel. Thus, for many of the young men, even those of privileged backgrounds, intercollegiate debate held elements of real adventure..." This exposure could influence a student's beliefs and ambitions and give him the confidence to venture beyond where he grew up.[11]

By 1912, forty-one of the existing forty-seven states boasted colleges and universities with debate teams.[12]

*_*_*_*_*_*_*_*

We turn next to the era's opening salvo, the formative Trinity-Wake Debate series. Debate and Wake Forest were about to be transformed. What follows is not only a historical accounting of each Trinity Debate, but also collectively reveals the emotional reactions, negotiations, and changing self-concepts the Trinity series fashioned. Each debate has its own tale.

The First Intercollegiate Series – Wake vs. Trinity

1897 – FIRST WAKE – TRINITY DEBATE

1897, November 25 – Intercollegiate debate – *Ought the systems of water–works, lighting, and streetcars to be operated by the city for its people, or by private individuals?*
Trinity, Affirmative, J. B Needham, H. M. North & S. A. Stewart; Negative, Wake: C. H. Utley, A. B. Cannady & T. Neil Johnson.
Wake was the winner.

Wake Forest's first intercollegiate debate was held in Raleigh in 1897 with Trinity College. This was a little ahead of the time when Yale, Harvard, and Princeton formalized their intercollegiate triangular debates in 1908,

---

[11] Keenan, C. J. (2009). Intercollegiate: Reflecting American Culture, 1900-1930, *Argumentation and Advocacy*, 46, page 82.

[12] Keenan, C. J. (2009). Intercollegiate: Reflecting American Culture, 1900-1930, *Argumentation and Advocacy*, 46, page 81.

although they informally debated before that year.[13] A Wake Forest grad-uate working on his MA at Harvard debated in the 1906 Princeton Harvard showdown.[14] Some have suggested the Wake Forest-Trinity series was among the earliest contests in the South.[15]

Trinity began as a Methodist school for young men in Randolph County, North Carolina, and later, in 1859, adopted the name Trinity College. In 1897, after spirited competition among cities, Durham was selected, and the school moved at the invitation of local tobacco finan-ciers. Trinity prospered in Durham, and in 1924, with the establishment of the Duke Endowment, the trustees changed its name to Duke as a memorial to contributor James Duke's father. [16]

Mr. T. Neil Johnson, a student at Wake Forest who later became Pro-fessor of Bible at Meredith, "set a movement on foot here to have a debate between Wake Forest and some other college of the State. A debate was accordingly arranged between Wake Forest and Trinity, and Mr. Johnson was chosen as one of the speakers to represent his college."[17]

---

[13] "Yale began to debate competitively in the 1890s, with ad hoc debates against Harvard. E. R. Nichols puts the first intercollegiate debate with Harvard Yale in 1892, Nichols, E. R., (1936). A historical sketch of intercollegiate debating: *The Quarterly Journal of Speech*, 22, 1936, page 213; "A more formal association of Ivy League debaters began in 1908 when Harvard, Princeton, and Yale agreed to hold three annual debates, known together as Triangulars. Debaters at each college fiercely competed before their faculty members for the coveted slots. These were high-caliber debates: overflowing audiences watched each debate, and judges and presiding offi-cers included university presidents, mayors, U.S. Court of Appeals judges, and even the former U.S. president Grover Cleveland. The public avidly watched the debates, and they were reported widely by newspapers like *The New York Times*." History of Yale Debate Association, Http://www.Yaledebate.Org/History.html.

[14] *The Wake Forest Student*, Vol. 31, No. 8, May 1912, page 750; *Daily Princetonian*, Vol. 30, No. 126, November 14, 1905, page 1.

[15] In the same year, 1897, North Carolina debated Georgia on the question of the *US acquiring Hawaii. The News & Observer*, December 24, 1897, page 6.

[16] Duke University: A Brief Narrative History, https://library.duke.edu/rubenstein/uarchives/history/articles/narrative-history.

[17] *The North Carolinian (*Raleigh), April 1906, page 8. "The other speakers for Wake Forest were Rev. A. B. Cannady, now in the Southern Baptist Theological Seminary, Louisville, Kentucky. And Rev. C. H. Utley, pastor of churches at Wilmington." The fame of the original Trinity debaters endured. Over thirty years later, the school newspaper published a piece by G. W. Paschal – W. F. Intercollegiate Debates – which updated, "Mr. Johnson had a varied and most honorable and useful career. He was the first State superintendent of the North Carolina Baptist State Convention Sunday schools. He has several university degrees and is now a missionary to Japan. Mr.

The introduction of intercollegiate debate at Wake Forest created an expanding interest in debate and a revival for the Societies. As with other parts of the country, as rhetorical scholar Jamie McKown examined, "The well-documented decline of literary societies in the late nineteenth century had brought a decline in society debates. College and university publications from the period consistently worried that interest in literary society participation and the quality of the debates they produced were waning. Campus debates generally were not well attended, and they were criticized for their excesses of oratory and elocution. This led to a concurrent deemphasis on 'oral expression' within the curriculum."[18] The resurgence of intercollegiate debate after the early 1890s reversed this trend. "Debate now became one of the most venerated extracurricular activities."[19]

Intercollegiate debate developed in parallel with the introduction of football (1888, First WFC football) and escalated for similar reasons: the allure of competition, the identity with school spirit, and a media drawn to the contest: "While intersociety rivalry had generated interest in past debates, this paled in comparison to the enthusiasm generated when colleges competed against each other."[20] In the intercollegiate debate era, at least in the early years, students traveled to be in attendance, cheering heartily for their school's debating heroes.

The debate was portrayed as comparable, a balance to the unfolding "sport-as-king." The term "student athlete" was first encountered when researching the first Trinity debate. The author provides a mature call for a didactic balance between the roles.

> We take such contests as evidence of the fact that the athletic tendency has not militated against that spirit of intellectual contest which should characterize the literary work of a college... The time

---

Cannady started life as a lawyer in Florence, S.C., but later turned to the ministry and now is in Florida." *Old Gold and Black*, January 21, 1928, page 2.

[18] McCowan, J. (2017). Renewing a "Very Old Means of Education": Civic Engagement and The Birth of Intercollegiate Debate in The United States. *Speech and Debate as Civic Education* Edited by J. Michael Hogan, Jessica A. Kurr, Michael J. Bergmaier, and Jeremy D. Johnson, Pennsylvania State University Press, page 36.; See Chapter 14 – Transitioning from Society Life for a more in-depth discussion of curriculum development and debate practice.

[19] McCowan, page 40.

[20] McCowan, page 40-41.

has been when the product of the college was either a scholar or an athlete, and when there was no such thing as the student-athlete. We are glad to see an increasing, earnest effort on the part of college authorities to develop the well-rounded man. Upon this development depends the hope of our country; and so it is that we believe that, in addition to the football team, there should be sent forth such men as will represent Trinity and Wake Forest in the coming debate. In no State in the South are the literary societies better sustained than at Trinity and Wake Forest, and we can promise all who ttend the debate that something highly entertaining, interesting and instructive is in store for them.[21]

One newspaper put it much more succinctly, "It appeals to reason and mind rather than to muscle in the realm of athletics. It causes no broken bones"[22] Another applauding securing the debate concluded, "This is about ten thousand times better than football."[23] At the outset, debates and athletic matches were spectator sports, one comfortably indoors.

The enthusiasm was not confined to Wake Forest or Trinity's campus but also reflected the growing passion across the country for intellectual contests. A University of North Carolina alumnus captured this rising phenomenon well in an essay entry titled "Intellectual Contests," likely accompanying the second Trinity-Wake debate euphoria:

The growth of apreciation (sic) on the part of the public of inter-collegiate debates, as distinguished from the craze over the athletic contests, is receiving special considerations as well as commendation of the press. We believe it was our university [UNC] and the University of Georgia which began the revival of this feature... which was probably followed by Trinity and Wake Forest colleges, and the public approbation thereof, has been expressed both by the interest of the people attending the debates and favorable comments of the press. In referring to this, the New York Evening Post says:

"Moreover, these contests, which cut no figure to speak of with these of the student body or the general public when the athletic craze was satisfied, are steadily growing in importance and interest

---

[21] *The Wake Forest Student*, October, Vol. 17, No. 1, 1897, page 128-129.

[22] *The News & Observer*, November 26, 1897, page 4.

[23] *The Raleigh Times*, November 15, 1897, page 1.

with both classes. More young men, for instance, entered the competition for Yale for placement on the 'team' which will meet Princeton next week than in any previous season since the rise of the meeting at New Haven. Large audience potential is based in Philadelphia, Chicago and other cities."

A Debate at Raleigh, N. C., On the evening of Thanksgiving Day, between representatives of Trinity and Wake Forest colleges in that state, clearly showed that both students and outsiders are now interested in such intellectual encounters. There were delegations of 100 and 200 associates of the contestants, although one of the institutions is seventy-five miles from Raleigh; the largest Hall in this State capitol, crowded with hundreds of people, were turned away for lack of room.

The treatment of this event by the press of Raleigh illustrates the return of sanity in the public mind as clearly as it does the rising standards for athletics and the colleges themselves.[24]

The city rolled out the red carpet for this year-defining event. Consistent with the holiday and the times, the coverage contained a decidedly religious tone and a pointedly Christian perspective. After all, it was Thanksgiving. Selected excerpts from *The News and Observer* illustrate, beginning with a devotional headline.

GIVE THANKS UNTO THE LORD
People of Raleigh Have Cause to be Grateful¶
AND TAKE A HOLIDAY SERVICES THAT THE
CHURCHES THIS MORNING
SUMPTUOUS FEAST FOR THE DAY
The Intercollegiate Debate Between Wake Forest and Trinity's Students
This Evening at The Academy of Music.

The News and Observer was not shy in proclaiming reasons for Raleigh to be thankful.

To–day is a day of rejoicing, of Thanksgiving, and the people of Raleigh will generally recognize it as a holiday. The people of few

---

[24] *The Morning Post* (Raleigh), December 3, 1898, page 4.

cities in all the land have more cause for gratitude on this day of national Thanksgiving.

No great fires have consumed the property of the city, no epidemic has swept away its inhabitants. The health record of the city was never better, and the financial failures can be counted on the fingers of one hand and have some digits left.

All this time the city has been building up and extending its bounds; churches have been erected, schools have prospered, hospitals and homes for the unfortunate have been enlarged and endowed. Surely the Lord has blessed us..."[25]

The city of Raleigh, the main centerpiece for Mid and Eastern North Carolina, went all out for the Thanksgiving holiday, during which an athletic event and debate were featured. The town in 1900 was a bustling residence for 13,643, while the Wake Forest College town recorded 823 souls. Randolph County's Trinity had a meager 274 residents.[26]

The debate owned Raleigh for the day, and the city's events moved to accommodate. In one of numerous event stories, *The News and Observer* reminded citizens of the grand plan:

In deference to the debate between the Trinity and Wake Forest students, the teacher's recital for Peace Institute which had been arranged for Thanksgiving, was given last night.

Thanksgiving services of the Presbyterian, Baptist, Methodist, and Christian churches will be held at the First Baptist Church at 11 o'clock.

The colored people will hold their Thanksgiving services at Shaw University. The sermon to be preached by the Rev. James Dean, of Florida, now presiding elder of the Newbern district.

In the afternoon there will be a game of foot-ball between Shaw University and St. Augustine, at Athletic Park.

Of course, some elaborate and swell dinners will be served at the two hotels – the Yarborough House and the Park. Their menus are something wonderful, and the feast such as they will furnish to-day will make a bright oasis in the desert of a boarder's life.

---

[25] *The News & Observer*, November 25, 1897, page 5.

[26] *Census Bulletin*, Washington DC, No. 39, January 22, 1901. The North Carolina population was 1,808,810, a 17.1 percent increase in 10 years.

The good housewives of the City of Oaks embellish when making preparations for the event... the pantries are teaming with good things and the small boys of the households are saving up their appetites so they may accommodate unheard of quantities of turkey and cranberry sauce and eat innumerable pieces of pie.

CHAS. H. UTLEY,
Wake Forest.

Then to-night, as a fitting close for the day's festivities, comes the intercollegiate debate between Trinity and Wake Forest colleges, which we hold at the Academy of Music, beginning promptly at 8 o'clock.[27]

Wake Forest sent about 125 students, and a special train brought large numbers from Trinity. There were many from Oxford and other learning institutions. The Peace and St. Mary's girls were out in all their beauty. Reduced rates were given on all the railroads.[28]

President Chas. E. Taylor, professors Brewer, Gorrell, and Poteat were among those who came out from Wake Forest yesterday afternoon to attend the Wake Forest Trinity debate.[29]

The hometown *News and Observer* poured forth multiple headlines following the debate, loudly exalting the event's importance.

---

[27] *The News & Observer*, November 25, 1897, page 5. The article furthermore stated, "All state offices were closed, and no official business will be transacted during the day. The banks and many of the principal stores in the city will not open. At the post office Sunday hours will be observed. The Sheriff's office will be closed from 11:00 AM until 4 PM, and Sheriff Jones will celebrate today by giving his jail boarders a safe fine, Thanksgiving dinner. The Sheriff will give to each a plug of tobacco and a bag of smoking tobacco to gladden their hearts."

[28] *The Semi-Weekly Messenger* (Wilmington), November 30, 1897, page 5.

[29] *The Press-Visitor* (Raleigh), November 26, 1897, page 1.

WAKE FOREST WON
The Inter-Collegiate Debate Last Night.
DEEP-WATER MEN THE FINEST ORATORS
Both Sides Had Hundreds of the Friends Present
The Enthusiasm as Great as it Ever Was at a Football Game

Feelings ran high as the debate progressed and in the drawn face and gleaming eye of the collegian in the audience you could read of the intense yearning for success that was flaring up in his bosom, and when a speaker would score a point, his fellow students would go into a frenzy of applause. Those in the gallery would rise to their feet and with waving hats and swaying bodies set up such a hurrah as was never heard before... "This beats football all the hollow," remarked a great lover of the game, after one of the best speeches and wildest scenes of the night.[30]

The people of Raleigh thoroughly enjoyed the occasion... "Come again, we like your new athletic contest of mind against mind.

A. B. CANNADY,
Wake Forest.

Wake students Charles Utley, Albert Cannady, and Thomas Johnson defended the negative on the query, *Ought the systems of Water Works, Lighting, and Street Cars be operated by the city for its people, or by private individuals?* Each speaker gave a twelve-minute speech and spoke for seven minutes in rejoinder. The judges were President Dinwiddie of Peace Institute, Prof. Hugh Morson of the Raleigh Male Academy, and Capt. S. A. Ashe. "Three better judges could not have been selected," the paper noted.[31]

---

[30] *The News & Observer*, November 26, 1897, page 4.
[31] *The News & Observer*, November 26, 1897, page 4.

The Hon. C. H. Mebane, State Superintendent of Public Instruction, served as moderator and welcomed the audience, calling the debate a "rich intellectual feast that was about to spread before them."

The Raleigh News & Observer embellished the event's flavor:

Many a time in recent years has this city been stark, staring football mad on Thanksgiving Day, but at no time has college spirit and enthusiasm run higher than it did yesterday and last night. Great crowds have gone out to witness these games, but none greater or so appreciative as that which listened to last night's debate. Many victories have been lost and won here on the athletic field by one or the other of these institutions, but none half as glorious or that will be so long remembered as was the decision of last night's contest of brain against brain and oratory against oratory.

It was a great intellectual battle--nobly was it fought and worthily won and no battered athlete on the football field ever had cause to be so proud or was ever such a hero in the eyes of the world and his comrades as were the three men who won the victory for their college. The shades of Wingate and Craven would have rejoiced had they heard the scions of their respective institutions contending for intellectual mastery before that great audience.[32]

The next morning President Taylor remarked at chapel prayers that it was the finest debate he had ever heard, and he had been hearing debates for thirty years or more."[33] A gentleman who heard the Trinity-Wake Forest debate suggests that Wake and Davidson hold the debate at Davidson and discuss the same question. Wake Forest will now be the "child's mother college of the state for debates to be held here sometime next spring."[34]

The celebration did not end in the hall. "Quite a number of the students failed to recover from Thanksgiving in time to attend recitations the next day. This may have been due to the extremity of rejoicing over the victory of the debaters at Raleigh; far be it from *The Student* to accuse any man of celebrating too gloriously. But since Thanksgiving Day, certain Seniors seem to have learned the meaning of the word *ostracized*."[35]

---

[32] *The News & Observer*, November 26, 1897, page 4.

[33] *The News and Record*, November 28, 1897, page 6.

[34] Around In The City, *The Press-Visitor*, November 26, 1897, page 1.

[35] T. H. Lacey, Editor, In And About College, *The Wake Forest Student*, 1897, page 32.

Collateral damage was reported in other sectors as well. Mr. H. G. Griffin, baggage master on numbers 11 and 12 on the Southern, conducted the special train run from Durham to Raleigh for Thursday afternoon's Wake Forest-Trinity debate. Just before the train left Raleigh and returned to Durham, Mr. Griffin had his foot painfully mashed. He got caught in some way between the wheels of the car. He was carried to Rex Hospital.[36]

The judges, Dinwiddie, Morson, and Capt. Ashe, in making their decision, graded each speaker on four things: Force of argument, literary merit, oratory, and capacity for rejoinder. The averages of the three speakers on each side were then added together and the side's average thus obtained the Wake Forest mark was the higher.[37]

The Academy was crowded long before the debate began by a captive audience, and the college young man from the rival institutions was very much in evidence.

The first speaker on the affirmative, *Mr. J. B. Needham* (Trinity), "made a good speech and produced a favorable impression.

"The municipal operation of public works by cities," he said, "has been such a success wherever tried that the mere fact that question was being debated in the South indicated that this section was about 50 years behind the times..."

J. B. NEEDHAM,
Trinity.

There is nothing more dangerous to our liberties to-day than those soulless corporations. They have their slimy fingers on our ballot boxes. As long as we allow corporations to dominate there can be no liberty.

Needham lamented "In North Carolina we have private ownership, and then Robinson's circus comes along the water is already so yellow that his fakirs don't have to put any coloring matter into

---

[36] Around In The City, *The Press-Visitor,* November 26, 1897, page 1.

[37] *The Raleigh Times,* November 26, 1897, page 1.

their fancy lemonade." There is nothing more dangerous to our liberties than "these soulless corporations."

Mr. Utley , and *Mr. Cannady* for negative Wake Forest countered that cities' control of public works "meant more public offices and thereby the power of the political machine would be increased and the opportunities and temptations to bribery and corruption made greater and more dangerous." Utley added, "Every city has its Tammany." Some might find reflections of current political thinking in Albert Cannady's claim that "Government Ownership is prescribed as a panacea for all evils of society. This utopian idea is socialistic and originated in the brain of a dreamer. Socialism and democracy are antagonistic."[38] Cannady added, "The government has no right to come in and compete with its own citizens."

In summary, Trinity offered, "New York is one of the most corrupt cities in the world, and yet her water supply is one of the best in the world...It will not get the public works in the hands of politicians, but it will get them out of the hands of self-seeking corporations." Mr. Stewarts' splendid speech won great applause as he closed the case for his side.

Mr. **T. A. Johnson** (Wake) was the last Wake speaker. Based on the German model, which he characterized as "rapid" socialism. He asked, "What is socialism? It is the government putting in its panel and doing for a fellow that which he ought to do for himself. Oh, but they say the people want government ownership. Of course, they do. I'd like to know something the people don't want. Their argument won't hold water, but I must admit, it holds a good deal of gas."[39]

At the debate's conclusion, at 11 o'clock, the judges retired and came back with a decision in favor of Wake Forest.[40]

A euphoria permeated the campus following the Trinity-Wake Forest event in Raleigh. Editorials ran in *The Wake Forest Student,* that such events among state college men should be frequent and permanent. "Such

---

[38] *The News & Observer*, November 26, 1897, page 4.

[39] *The News & Observer*, November 26, 1897, page 4.

[40] And why not end with a little controversy? "It was reported here yesterday that Wake Forest had taken an unfair advantage in his debate with Trinity, in that it had put on as debaters two post-graduates when it was understood that only undergraduate students were to participate. This report, *The News & Observer* is informed, is entirely without foundation. All the debaters on both sides were undergraduates. *The News & Observer*, November 27, 1897, page 8.

contests," an editorial argued, "are in every way preferable to physical encounters."[41]

This celebratory veneer does not imply the quality of the arguments were better. In fact, it looks as if the speakers, and one could credibly say Wake on the negative side, appealed to deeply held political bias more than to a reasoned calculus of the problems, economic or social.[42]

1898 — SECOND WAKE — TRINITY DEBATE

1898 November 24 – Intercollegiate debate – *Resolved, That the United States should not adopt a policy of territorial extension.*
Wake, W. F. Fry, J. C. Owen & Walter Johnson; Trinity College, H. M. North, J. M. Flowers & S. A. Stewart.
Trinity Won, Metropolitan Hall, Raleigh, NC, Headline: "Trinity Covered Herself with Glory," The Morning Post, November 25, 1889

The successful Thanksgiving debate in 1897 led to campus enthusiasm. Describing the second Wake-Trinity intercollegiate debate, *The Wake Forest Student* editor entered… "The immense audience which the debate drew shows better than words can express, how much the people of the State appreciate such literary battles. Even after the large Metropolitan Theatre had been packed and crowded, galleries included hundreds of people who could not get standing room, were turned away."

> The success of the joint debate between Trinity and Wake Forest… surpassed the anticipations of its promoters, proved that the experiment met the hearty approbation of the people of the State, and showed that nothing stands in the way to make the movement a permanent feature of college life.

So summarized *The Wake Forest Student,* which quickly added, "It was shown that an abundance of college enthusiasm could be manifested and that people were more willing to attend such contests than other forms

---

[41] *The Wake Forest Student,* January 1898, Vol. 17, page 305.

[42] A nearly full and considerably more nuanced text can be found in *News & Observer,* November 25, 1897, page 1.

of inter-collegiate encounters. The occasion was marked by the utter absence of any ill feeling either between the contestants proper or the students of the respective colleges."[43]

The editor was on to something as the intercollegiate debate age flourished at Wake for three more decades. As Wake faculty member W. G. Paschal assessed, "To give some idea of the interest in debating in those days, I quote from a contemporary account: 'The Wake Forest-Trinity debate held in Raleigh Thanksgiving evening (1898) was given up by the people of the State, of all denominations as being the greatest literary treat they ever heard."[44]

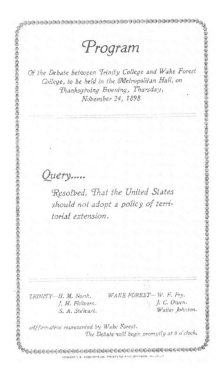

Program

Of the Debate between Trinity College and Wake Forest College, to be held in the Metropolitan Hall, on Thanksgiving Evening, Thursday, November 24, 1898.

Query.....

Resolved, That the United States should not adopt a policy of territorial extension.

TRINITY—H. M. North.   WAKE FOREST—W. F. Fry.
          J. M. Fishwers.   J. C. Owen.
          S. A. Stewart.   Walter Johnson.

Affirmative represented by Wake Forest.
The Debate will begin promptly at 8 o'clock.

Paschal describes the Hall as overflowing. The same Hall in which Wake Forest held their public debate with Trinity University would months later entertain the "The king of oratory Charles B. Aycock," or as historian H. Leon Prather writes, "the Democratic Moses, who would lead North Carolina out of the chaos and darkness of 'Negro domination.' As he did throughout the campaign, Aycock mesmerized a standing-room-only crowd at the Metropolitan House in Raleigh, pounding the podium for white supremacy and the protection of white womanhood.[45]

---

[43] R. C. Lawrence, Editor, *The Wake Forest Student*, Vol. 17, January 1898, page 305-306.

[44] W. F. Intercollegiate Debaters, G. W. Paschal, *Old Gold and Black*, January 21, 1928, page 2. Paschal's column provides what became of many of the early Intercollegiate debaters and shares their career paths.

[45] The Ghosts of 1898: Wilmington Race Riot. *The News & Observer*, Friday, November 17, 2006. His involvement in the Wilmington Race Riots is documented. He also became known as the "Education Governor" for advocating improvements to North Carolina's public schools. https://en.wikipedia.org/wiki/Charles_Brantley_Aycock.

Aycock spoke frequently and convincingly for the Democrats' white supremacy campaign. Two years later, he was elected governor by what was then the largest margin of victory in the state's history (Gov. 1901-1905). During his campaign, he led the fight for a "suffrage amendment," which disenfranchised blacks.[46] Aycock's election as governor less than a year later provides a commentary on the times in which the Wake-Trinity debates took place.

The local commentary, perhaps not surprisingly, is much brighter. It captures part of how citizens wanted to see their lives, and not without justification. Such accounts expose the complexities and contradictions inherent in people's lives. *The Morning Post* (Raleigh) chose a rosy picture of Trinity and Wake for its readers.

.H. M. NORTH,
Trinity.

The annual debate between Wake Forest and Trinity last night adds to the already high repute of those institutions, and was not only pleasing to the friends of each, but increases the pride of the citizens in both. It was indeed a Battle Royal between bright young men who evinced aptitude as well as ability, and careful aptitude as Trinity won the victory, but it was after a very hard and close contest. The victors have cause to be proud of their success, but that if you can have the consolation of knowing that when Trinity went under the wire they were at its throat-latch.

Last night's debate was the best evidence of this bond work these two institutions are doing for our State we have witnessed – it was the handicraft of the Masters... the young men showed that they are of the stuff of which men are made – real men, an article of which the market is by no means overstocked.

---

[46] https://www.ncpedia.org/anchor/governor-aycock-negro.

This is but another evidence of the splendid work and influence of Wake Forest and Trinity, affording an object lesson which cannot be lost to the public.[47]

The Thanksgiving evening debate addressed the pressing national question: *US Expansion and what to do with territorial acquisition following the Spanish-American war, Cuba and the Philippines among others.* Some readers will appreciate reading the full debate transcript with its more nuanced and in-depth arguments surrounding the territorial acquisition vs. territorial integrity debate. The excerpts below have a certain "think-about-it" spectacle bias.[48]

Trinity had the affirmative (against expansion), and Wake Forest the negative (for expansion)[49]

Affirmative – Mr. H. M. North – Trinity

"We said emphatically that we did not want Cuba and Puerto Rico, etc. We violate a moral obligation… "Manifest destiny" does not demand that we violate the fundamental principles of our government.

For government cannot be manufactured. Our treatment of the Indians shows what will be our treatment of the new people we shall conquer."

Negative – Mr. W. F. Fry – Wake Forest

"The Constitution lends its influence to the side of expansion. It has been in no less than 11 times, beginning with Louisiana in 1803 and finishing with Hawaii in 1897. Congress has reorganized expansion as constitutional four times: Texas when that annex by joint resolution in 1844; 70 islands in both oceans have been occupied under resolution in 1856; similar by Midway Island, in the north Pacific was annexed in 1867, and Hawaii in 1897. The Supreme Court has in numerous instances declared the constitutionality of annexation.

We need territory in every part of the world. Our commerce must go everywhere, and where goes our commerce, our Navy must go. Think of Dewey's plight when the war was declared; turned out of

---

[47] *The Morning Post* (Raleigh), November 25, 1898, page 4.

[48] See a full transcript at *The News & Observer*, November 25, 1898, page 2 or *Morning Post,* November 25, 1889, page 5.

[49] *The Morning Post*, November 25, 1898, page 5.

China's harbors, he was a wanderer far from home; he had nowhere to go; he had to conquer or die, and he conquered him a home..."

Affirmative – Mr. John Flowers – Trinity[50]

"We may seek to hide expansion under the indefinite phrases of 'obligation' and 'destiny.' It is contrary to the nature of man to spend his resources upon inferior peoples unless he thinks there is to be a pecuniary reward... Expansion does not pay... If we make them free, as we promised to do, we will have their trade, and if we annexed Cuba and Puerto Rico, we will incur the expenses of governing them for a trade that we would get anyway... France, Spain, and Italy stand bankrupt for no other reason than their dependencies."

Negative – Mr. J. C. Owen – Wake Forest

"That we would denigrate into imperialism... is contradicted both by reason and experience. Our people are opposed to imperialism for themselves and all others. They declared against it in unmistakable terms in the Revolution. Eight times have they extended their time, and every time imperialism was unthought of.

What is the United States? A system of self-government. If this is true, then to extend the United States is to extend self-government. Is self-government imperialism?"

Affirmative – T. A. Stewart – Trinity

"The essence of this question is whether our government is adapted to the needs of races whose hues vary as the rainbow and whose stages of civilization range from supercilious Aguinaldo[51] down to the monkey that is just lately dropped his tail. It behooves us not to become unstrung with ecstasy of power or drunk with the wine of conquest. How are we to govern our heterogeneous assortment of

---

[50] Six years after this event, Trinity debater John Flowers's body was returned to the States from China, where he was a rising star with the American Tobacco Company. "The circumstances of his death make it a particularly sad one. He was among strangers, was taken sick with smallpox, and died in hands of his Chinese nurses. He had entered Trinity at the age of seventeen. He won several speaking metals from Hesperian Literary Society." The *Richmond Times-Dispatch*, February 19, 1905, page 17.

[51] A Mexican Christmas Bonus.

herbivorous, omnivorous, and pestiverous (sic) humanity scattered around the globe? There are but three possible ways. First, admit our new territories as States. Second, make colonies of them, allowing the natives to manage local affairs. Third, place over them a military government. The first two methods are out of the question, and only the military method is practical. When we attempted that, difficulties will arise, threatening our very civilization.

The fourth companion of the flag is international entanglements... We have at home 50 million foreigners who can scarcely read. We have the liquor problem, the sediment problem, the Negro problem, Tammany Hall, gas rings, labor strikes, etc. We have trouble enough at home without roaming the seas in search of the woes of humanity."

Negative – Mr. Walter Johnson's – Wake Forest

"Our manufacturing interests grow every census... the world's astounded at the variety and perfection of their labor-saving devices, our coal is inexhaustible. Our mines supply half the world's silver and gold Our farmers, miners, operators and capitalists all suffer if we do not extend our commerce just as fast as we can.

1899 – Wake Debaters, A. R. Dunning, O. L. Powers, A. W. Cooke

The East is opening up for our articles. India is already open: China with 400,000,000 subjects is awakening to the needs of Western products – a great event to commerce."

The article's author offered further comments on the oratorical model. The newspaper man admired, "A most praiseworthy feature of the debate was the total absence of any spread-eagle oratory or straining for pretty phrases. The young gentlemen had evidently not written out carefully tuned speeches for the occasion but had informed themselves on the merits of the question and trusted to the occasion for suitable words. The result was that none of the speeches were at all dull or tiresome, in which respect they differed admirably from much of the college oratory a few years ago."[52]

Some Wake enthusiasts were less charmed by the style, embarrassed as we were about losing to Trinity. They lashed out at their home-team debaters. One irate witness, writing in the State Baptist's *Biblical Recorder,* delivered a scolding:

The Wake Forest men were childish in their illustrations, ineffectual in putting their arguments and ludicrous in their ribald, crude, farcical and wholly uncalled for efforts to ridicule their opponents. Their arguments were as good, if not better than those of their opponents, but these defects destroy their force. Of debaters on such an occasion a fair degree of the grace for culture is required. Ridicule, ribaldry, far-fetched illustrations and disjointed mental processes, and every speaker save Mr. Flowers, who himself all but fell into the same unhappy way. I'm scared of the argumentative features of the debate. A true debater will make no reference to an opponent; he makes his speech on the question into his audience. Of oratory, none was heard.[53]

---

[52] *The News & Observer*, November 25, 1898, page 2; Selected Rejoinder Excerpts. Mr. Flowers (Trinity): "Alaska is a lamentable spectacle of American extension. Not an American institution can be found in all Alaska." Mr. Owen (Wake): "We will expand on the broad and noble principles of freedom and religious liberty – to do for them as we do for ourselves. Whenever Anglo-Saxons have expanded, they have done so with…benefit to the annexed", Mr. Stewart (Trinity): "We have only extended in our past to homogeneous people and contiguous territory. We have annexed all that natures boundaries intended we should…We have caused twenty-four Republics to spring into existence."

[53] A Baptist loss to a Presbyterian school was too much for the writer quoted. The author demolished the Wake debaters for losing. It is not clear the source, but the

1899 – THIRD WAKE – TRINITY DEBATE

1899, November 30 – Intercollegiate debates – *Resolved, That the United States Senators should be elected by popular vote.*
Trinity, Affirmative, S. A. Stewart, S. S. Dent & J. M. Flowers; Wake Forest, Negative, A. R. Dunning, O. L. Powers, & A. W. Cooke.
Wake Won: Judges, Rev. Dr. Eugene Daniel, pastor of the First Presbyterian church; Rev. Dr. T. D. Bratton, Rector of St. Mary's School, and Hon. R. H. Battle, one of the leading lawyers in the State.

The rhythm of the debates was established by 1899. Each school's representatives, meeting in Raleigh, codified the event, announcing the topic and sides.[54] Post-debate coverage also had a familiar feel, "perhaps as never before… Every inch of space in the building was filled with people and still hundreds had to go away without so much as even getting a peep in at the door."[55]

The stakes on campus were exceptionally high, and the students' energy and focus were devoted to beating Trinity. One student said, "Every day, different faculty members receive letters urging them to incite the boys to increase their efforts to defeat Trinity and bring home the cup."

Program of the Debate

Between Wake Forest College and Trinity College, to be held in the Academy of Music on Thanksgiving Evening, Thursday, on November thirty, on eighteen ninety-nine.

Query:

Resolved, That United States Senators should be elected by popular vote.

| TRINITY | S. A. STEWART. S. S. DENT. J. M. FLOWERS. | A. R. DUNNING. O. L. POWERS. A. W. COOKE. | WAKE FOREST |

Affirmative represented by Trinity.
The Debate will begin promptly at eight o'clock.

---

loss was discussed multiple times in periodicals. *The Biblical Recorder*, November 30, 1898, page 4.

[54] "The committees [sic] composed of J. M. Flowers and S. A. Stewart, from Trinity, and D. M. Stringfield and G. A. Foote, Wake Forest, met in Raleigh last Thursday and arranged the terms of the inter-collegiate debate…The debate will be held in the Academy of Music, Raleigh." *The Progressive Farmer*, October 3, 1899, page 3.

[55] *The News & Observer*, December 2, 1899, page 8.

The debate is not to be laughed at, as one who has ever engaged in any kind of contest well knows. Boys, be unanimous in your support of the speakers, and your part is done. Remember, it is not you, not the Philomathesian Society, not the Euzelian Society, but the College, which will be represented in Raleigh Thanksgiving evening."[56]

The coverage of the third Wake-Trinity debate segment took a different turn than the previous years. What follows are excerpts substantially edited. For a richer transcript, see *The Farmer and Mechanic* (Raleigh), December 5, 1899, page 6. It provides an archetype of how, at the turn of the century, the media valued and promoted public debates, especially those of the colleges.

The Farmer and Mechanic (Raleigh) opens with its multitiered head-lines designed to draw story readers. Following is verbatim coverage from the daily.

WAKE FOREST TAKES BACK
DEBATER'S CUP

Trinity Lost the Trophy Last Night

A VERY FINE DEBATE

Wake Forest Said It Should Be Done Indirectly By The Legislature As Now, and the Judges Said Wake Forest Argument Was Best.[57]

...This was the third contest, Wake Forest having won the first and Trinity the second of the annual events. The victory last night makes the Baptist boys the guardians of the hard-won trophy for the ensuing year.

...Each inch of standing and sitting room in pit and galley was occupied, and such an audience! Special trains from Wake Forest and Trinity brought down several hundred people yesterday afternoon and the brains and beauty of Raleigh grace the occasion.

The shout that went up at the close of each of the speeches of the young champions was something never to be forgotten. The yell of the college boy when he hollers for his institution is as no other yell. It is longer, louder and has more genuine, unforced

---

[56] *The Wake Forest Student*, November 1899, page 99.

[57] *The Farmer and Mechanic* (Raleigh) December 5, 1899, page 6.

human enthusiasm in it. Both sides hollered last night, and when finally, the judges announced the victors, the sound that went up from Baptist boys was a triumph for the human lungs – and nobody enjoyed it more than those who were partisan of neither side. Certainly the occasion was a clear and sufficient vindication of those who contend that intellectual combat can arouse the same enthusiasm and interest as the contests on the diamond and the gridiron.

S. A. STEWART.
(Trinity) Union County.

Affirmative – Mr. S. A. Stewart – Trinity College.

We would have two houses and the relations between the Senate and the States would not be disturbed. The Senate would still represent the States in their political capacities. Nor would the system of checks and balances on which the two-house idea is founded be disturbed. Senators would still represent the State as a whole, while the Congressmen would represent only his district.

A purpose for which the Senate was created – equal representation of all States in the upper house – would be better secured than now. Do you know that fives States are today without equal representation in the Senate, owing to inability of their Legislatures to elect? Did you know that in the last seven years fourteen states have been denied equal representation owing to the dead-locks in legislatures? If the people elect them, then these legislative dead-locks will be things of the past.

So great has become the power of the corporations over the Senate, that stock boards are often regarded as the most essential Senatorial equipment; the Plutocracy, the uncrowned king, stalks boldly into the Senate cut, there to further his unhallowed ends. The Senate now contains many men of great wealth, some – an increasing number – are Senators because they are rich. A year or two ago there were twenty-seven millionaires in this Senate almost every third Sen. a millionaire...

The people elect directly their state law-makers, their governors, their Presidential electors, the most of their State officers and in some instances their judiciary. In every state the tendency is to give the people complete and direct sovereignty in selecting their law-makers. Have they proved unworthy of this trust? 100 years of experience has demonstrated that the people are safest repository of power and responsibility for all progress.

Negative – Mr. A. R. Dunning – Wake Forest.

The present system of electing Senators has stood the test for 110 years. It has served the country well, and it may be changed for no superficial or temporary reason. The necessity for changing should be palatable, of considerable weight...

"Sirs. You may bring forth more than a little passing trouble or incidental blunder to radically overthrow a system fathered by Washington, developed by Jefferson and Hamilton, nurtured by Webster, Clay, and Calhoun, and honored by over a century of usage. No cry of political soreheads or platform-makers will ever suffice...

ARCHER R. DUNNING.
(Wake Forest) Aulander, N. C.

The proposed plan, in its very nature, is radical to the last degree... If carried to their logical results would lead to election by popular vote and majorities of the president, the judiciary ...It would result a complete overthrow of the whole scheme of the Senate and in the end of the whole scheme of the National Constitution.

Mr. S. S. Dent – Trinity

Political power and political responsibility should go hand-in-hand. The Senator represents the people, he should be elected by the people…commercial and money classes do not need this power to protect them from the people, yet widely the people do need it to protect them from the money powers.

S. S. DENT,
(Trinity) Jefferson, N. C.

Mr. O. L. Powers – Wake Forest.

The House and Senate were intended to be different, and to secure this end their methods of election must differ. Change does not always mean improvement.

Cities and their foreign populations would control popular elections, their votes outweighing the balance of the rural sections. The seething foreign population in the north and west, the illiterate Negro voter of the South are forces to be reckoned with. I deny that popular elections are free from corruption. If evil arises once in a while under the present system of electing Senators it is not the fault of the system but of the low standards of the people. They cannot be trusted in moments of excitement. The voice of the people is not always the voice of God.

There must be somebody to stand between the unreasoning madness of the mob

OSCAR L. POWERS.
(Wake Forest) Pender County.

and the unjust demands of the discontented. The Senate was created for this purpose.

Mr. J. M. Flowers – Trinity

Legislatures should be chosen to legislate, not to elect Senators. The present system results in one of two evils: it either secures the election of United States Senators on State issues or the election of legislation on national issues.

Mr. A. W. Cook – Wake Forest

All evils of the present system would reappear in the system proposed... In every Republic, there is some check upon the prejudices and radical tenden-

JOHN M. FLOWERS.
(Trinity) Taylorsville, N. C.

cies of the people. The Senate is the check of conservatism and stability. It will eliminate the State... and destroy the last vestiges of States rights.[58]

At the close of the debate, the judges retired and consulted for a quarter of an hour... Dr. Eugene Daniel announced the decision in favor of Wake Forest. He created much merriment with his anecdotes of the Irish Judge who is always confused by hearing both sides of the question and so gave his decision as soon as he had heard one side.[59]

Students may have followed the arguments closely but, in their write-up, seemed more preoccupied with getting off campus and mingling with the college women of Raleigh. As suggested, many found more entertaining leisure than the Meredith reception. The headline in *The Wake Forest Student* read: **AND WHAT SHALL we say about the debate? "What debate?"** – Why the Thanksgiving debate, to be sure. The students' interests were aired:

---

[58] *The Farmer and Mechanic* (Raleigh) December 5, 1899, page 6.

[59] *The Farmer and Mechanic* (Raleigh) December 5, 1899, page 6.

On Thanksgiving noon, Mother Earth bore a placid smile on her face, and the sun poured his gladsome light down to cheer us on to victory. Yes, it was a beautiful day; and, as a consequence, over 200 of the loyal, all in holiday attire, pulled out of the station at 2 o'clock. Arriving in Raleigh at three, we amused ourselves for a while by "seeing the sights" of the great city. But the crowning feature of the day was the reception tendered the Faculty and Students of Wake Forest College by the young ladies of the women's college. Many did not go, but we think that the consciousness of what they missed is punishment enough for them. Someone made the knightly remark about the fair maidens who made the occasion charming for so many; "the tender buds of North Carolina's womanhood appeared in all their radiance and beauty."[60]

Students were, of course, taken with the victory. "Powers, Dunning and Cook covered themselves with glory, not of the variety that lasteth for a day, but endless and infinite. When Dr. Daniel... announced that Wake Forest was the victor, pandemonium reigned for a time. During the interval, The Professor ceased to be stern, the Senior to be lordly, the Sophomore to be sarcastic, and the Fresh to be verdant. The most sober came back intoxicated – with *joy*, of course.[61]

When reading the argumentative account of the debate, it would be easy to suggest that Trinity, not Wake Forest, provided superior reasons and should have won the debate. Of course, this newspaper's account cannot fully communicate style and nuance, always a genuine part of any decision, but the manifest claims seemingly weighed affirmative. This takeaway may be no more than a bias for our times and how the election of Senators played out in history. And we may give insufficient credence to the notion that centers of power should serve as a check on the populist mob. And, of course, as we will discover shortly, when the series blew up, it just might have been a home-court advantage in selecting judges.

When researching the literary societies' public debates, topics, and sides (see Milestones, Vol. 3), a pattern develops in which the side that wins the larger proportion of debates is negative. It is easier to appeal to the known and to speculate unchecked on potential dreadful outcomes.

---

[60] *The Wake Forest Student*, January 1900, page 263-264.

[61] *The Wake Forest Student*, January 1900, page 264.

Drawing a sample of major public debates—Anniversary, Society Day, Intercollegiate Debates—the breakdown favors the negative 55 to 41 affirmatives. It seemed that often Wake found itself arguing the negative.

1900 – FOURTH WAKE – TRINITY DEBATE

1900, November 29 – Intercollegiate Debate – *Resolved, That the South Carolina dispensary system is unwise.*
Affirmative, Trinity, Affirmative, J. T. Liles, W. H. Wanamaker & F. S. Cardin; Wake, Negative, S. S. Flournoy, W. A. Dunn & H. E. Flack. Trinity was the Winner.

Four years after Trinity-Wake Forest's annual duel started, the gathering had statewide stature. Sunday's show became more institutionalized and was greeted with less animated press coverage. The event hall was filled, and the winner enjoyed notoriety, yet the details of the argument and composition were no longer reported in detail.

Nonetheless, the holiday continued to be popular. In the month before the upcoming 1901 debate, the Raleigh Chamber of Commerce appointed a committee to "consider the advisability of charging an admission fee to the future – Trinity Wake Forest debates."[62] On the committee was Judge Thomas Womack, who would later appear as a judge for public debates on campus. It is unclear if the measure was realized.

Prior to the debate, students tried to boost enthusiasm… let us board 'the special,' and one solid body, on Thanksgiving Day go to Raleigh with the determination to inspire our speakers and win the cup."

Newspapers published schedules of a broader range of church

Dr. Willis Richard Cullom

---

[62] *The Wake Forest Student*, editorial, 1901, page 99.

services, train schedules, the football game, and Meredith's reception for Wake Forest and Trinity students.[63]

Public discussions turned more to civic improvements than who carried the day's debate. *The Farmer and Mechanic* coached, "Raleigh's need of an auditorium was again felt last night. More than five hundred people were turned away and 1800 people were packed into a hall that could comfortably seat only 1200... It is to be hoped that the next Thanksgiving, Raleigh will have an auditorium that will be fully equal to large crowds that attend these debates."[64]

An unusual tradition became folklore following the debate. Perhaps it was in the third or maybe fourth debate [Maybe fifth, see below], during the enthusiasm of the welcoming home crowd, it was said that a faculty and a goat had graced the Wingate Chapel stage. A student's recollection incorrectly remembered sequential wins in the debates so perhaps the story itself could be dismissed. It's just that the rumor, and cultural references to the incident, continued for decades on campus.

Sloane Guy, in an alumnus memory, said, "It is enough to strain anyone's credulity to believe a statement in the *Wake Forest Student* for the year 1908 [65] to the effect that Dr. Willis Richard Cullom rode 'across this (Wingate Memorial Chapel) stage on the back of a Billy goat!'

Of course, the attendant circumstances must be taken into consideration. For them, we turn to Dr. J. W. Lynch, Dr. Cullom's associate in the Department of Religion for the past fifteen years. Wake Forest had just

---

[63] *The Morning Post,* November 29, 1900, page 5.

[64] *The Farmer and Mechanic* (Raleigh) December 4, 1900, page 4.

[65] I could not verify Prof. Cullom's with the goat as appeared in the 1908 *Wake Forest Student.*

won its second consecutive debate [no consecutive wins happened] with Trinity. This victory meant that Wake Forest won permanent possession of the cup.[66] This passage suggests that the student's recollections were of the fifth debate.

When such a notable victory was won, it was customary for the faculty to join the students in celebrating. No one, certainly, believes that Dr. Cullom rode the goat. The faithful reporter of the event records that Dr. Lynch, usually the master of ceremonies for these affairs, merely pointed his finger at Dr. Cullom and announced that he was demonstrating such hilarity that he could "visualize" Dr. Cullom riding the goat.[67] Dr. Lynch said, "I can envision' Dr. Cullom riding that goat across the stage!" Now the question is, did Dr. Cullom ride that goat across that stage?"[68]

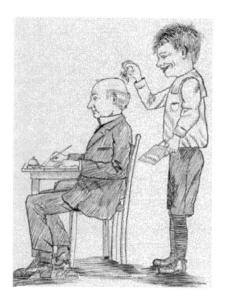

Howler Drawing Characterizing
Students with Faculty – 1912

Another student, Jack Sawyer, later remembered the story more ambiguously. "It seems that once after a particularly notable debate victory, the debaters were met at the depot by the students en masse, and a huge reception was held. The spirit of the festivities grew higher and higher with everyone cutting capers. As a mascot, there was a goat on the stage."

Despite the dearth of public clamoring for debate details, the students themselves maintained a passion for the event. Society debaters scrambled and clawed to be the college's ambassadors. Fifteen contestants, "all of whom made

---

[66] The Trinity Cup survived and is displayed in the Carswell Hall lobby.

[67] Sloan Guy, Pioneer Bible Teacher: Trainer of Ministries and Professor of Religion, Dr. Cullom, Memorial issue, *The Wake Forest Student*, 1938, Vol. 54, page 12.

Dr. Willis Richmond Cullom was a long-time Religion Faculty chair and one of the most venerated professors in the college's history. In the Memorial issue *of The Student,* he is featured alongside N. Y. Gulley, B. R. Sledd, and J. W. Lynch, each a legacy in Wake Forest history.

[68] Memorial issue, *The Wake Forest Student*, 1938 Vol. 54, page 17.

excellent speeches," gathered in the small campus chapel in mid-October tryouts. Professors Carlisle, Royal, and Sledd selected six to take part in the second preliminary.[69]

Joseph Adams, Jr., Editor of *The Wake Forest Student* during the 1900 turn-of-the-century debate, wrote from the perspective of a student who boarded the train, celebrated in Raleigh's Thanksgiving setting, and returned home to offer a boisterous welcome for the team "cheated" of their victory. The student's excitement and worries are palatable in his narrative.

Thanksgiving Day dawned cloudy and cold. All the forenoon the campus and streets were deserted. At 2 o'clock it seemed that the whole college was gathered at the depot. There stood the *Special* waiting until all could get tickets. Soon we were off to Raleigh at the rate of nearly a mile a minute with 250 happy students aboard. The "hurricanes" came out and stared open-mouthed at the whirling mass of cars, dust, yells, and college songs. And now, almost before we knew it, we were in Raleigh and on our way to the Baptist Female University.

Never was there such a gathering of charm and beauty. But to spoil our happiness it seems that the faculty of that institution had gotten together and invented an electrical apparatus for ringing off visitors at the appointed hour in quite a scientific manner. At the striking of six this plotted apparatus was put in operation, an electric bell, in a dignified manner, announced to the noisy crowd that the time of departure was at hand. With dismay the faculty watch the failure of their cherished plan, and diving below, soon the noisy clang of the supper bell put the assembled knights to rout.

An hour before the appointed time the sidewalk and street in front of the Academy of Music were so densely packed that no carriages could pass. When the doors were finally opened a terrible rush for seats took place, and in five minutes the large hall was crowded. Now for half an hour the audience must wait. During this time there was a vocal contest carried on between the students of the two rival institutions. Yell followed yell, each louder than the last, increasing in volume until the roof was in fair danger of being lifted bodily

---

[69] *The Wake Forest Student*, December 1900, page 184.

from its support. It is with some pride that we say, that although Trinity yelled loud and well, still in this respect, she was completely outclassed by Wake Forest. The familiar old yells:

> Chick-a-go-ruck! Go ruck! Go-re!
> Chick-a-go-ruck! Go ruck! Go-re!
> Hi! Ho! Hi! Ho! W. F. C.! W. F. C.! – Tiger and
> Raw! Raw! Raw! Whoop-la Vee
> 'Or et noir and W. F. C.!

1900 – Wake Forest – S. S. Flournoy & W. A. Dunn

Made the walls of the old Hall echo, then re-echo. By the motion of their arms, and the swelling of their cheeks, the band seemed to be playing, but no other evidence was given.

Suddenly the whole audience rose to their feet and burst into united applause as the speakers came out on the stage and took their seats.[70]

---

[70] Joseph Q. Adams, Jr., Editor, In and About the College, *The Wake Forest Student,* October 1900, page 253.

Wake lost the debate 2-1, the general complaint being that the judges were swayed by oratory and not the quality of arguments, which should have been the decision point. Sounds familiar.

A grand ovation awaited the representatives upon their return. The college *en masse* met them at the train. In the melée of trumpets, horns and tin pans. The judgment day would have passed unnoticed. Born upon the shoulders of their comrades, the debaters were carried to a wagon elaborately decorated with old gold and black, and pulled by the students themselves. In front of the post office most of the faculty were found assembled. They were mounted upon the stone campus wall and there they addressed the debaters and students. The general sentiment expressed was that the injustice had been done to Wake Forest, and that our debaters had nobly won a noble victory, if they had not brought back the Cup.[71]

1901 – FIFTH WAKE – TRINITY DEBATE[72]

1901, December 6 – Intercollegiate Debate – *Resolved, That North Carolina should adopt the principle of compulsory attendance upon her public schools.*
Wake, Affirmative, – William Albion Dunn, J. C. Little & O. P. Dickinson; Trinity: Negative, C. L. Hornaday, L. I. Howard & W. H. Brown. Wake Won; The debate was postponed a week due to illness of two Trinity Debaters.

From time-to-time newspapers find pleasure in correcting a sister's publication mistake. Having provided nonstop coverage of the Wake Forest Trinity debates, *The Progressive Farmer* commented, "The Statesville Landmark says: 'Wake Forest College won in the debate between representatives of

[71] Joseph Q. Adams, Jr., Editor, In and About the College, *The Wake Forest Student*, October 1900, page 253.

[72] "This question was agreed upon at a conference of representatives of each college held at the Yarborough House in this city yesterday at noon. The students who represented the colleges in the meetings were Mr. W. A. Dunn, Mr. O. E. Dickinson for Wake Forest, and Mr. L. B. Howard and Mr. E. A. Cranford for Trinity. *The Progressive Farmer*, October 15, 1901, page 3.

that college and Trinity in Raleigh Friday night. This is the third successive victory for Wake Forest in similar contests.' In this latter statement, the Landmark is in error. Having attended each debate, we know that Wake Forest won in 1897, 1899, and 1901, and Trinity in 1898 and 1900.[73]

Each successive debate in the series commanded less press as the event became part of the scenery. It was left to the Raleigh *News & Observer* to offer the boisterous headline celebrating the Wake Forest victory and employ the hyperbolic style of the era to describe the debate, only the flavor of which is presented here.

THREE TIMES THE VICTORY HAS GONE TO WAKE FOREST
A Great debate upon the question of compulsory education in North Carolina
AFFIRMATIVE CAPTURED THE SILVER TROPHY
Deafening Cheers Greeted the Victors.
IT WAS A MAGNIFICENT AUDIENCE

All Raleigh was represented in the vast throng that gathered in the Academy of music last night.

It was a gala occasion, and while the lower floor had a touch of soberness because of the garb of the gentlemen, the gallery was a garden of color and loveliness, filled with handsomely dressed young ladies representing the educational institutions of Raleigh, some schools attending in a body.

The colors of the two colleges flew side by side in friendly rivalry in the audience. When the curtain rose... it was an inspiring sight that greeted the eyes of the young orators on the stage. Every seat occupied, all aisles crowded and a volume of applause sending the hot blood of anticipation to the cheek, for as it would well again it would mean victory for one and defeat for the other. Would the "Blue" of Trinity or the "Gold and Black" or Wake Forest wave in victorious breeze of applause...[74]

The debate between Wake Forest and Trinity was postponed from Thanksgiving night to the next Friday night, with two Trinity representatives

---

[73] *The Progressive Farmer*, December 17, 1901, page 3.

[74] *The News and Observer*, December 7, 1901, page 5.

being ill from the effects of vaccination.[75] The football game between A&M and Davidson was also an unintended casualty. "But for the sharp, biting wind, which made it seem intensely cold, the crowd at the game would have been twice as large as it was, the postponement of the Trinity and Wake Forest debate, which was to have been held last night in the city, also cut off a large crowd of college boys from those two institutions who would have been here."[76]

Some of the 1901 Commentary was still plaintive about losing the fourth debate to Trinity. An invested student regretted, "We do not mean to criticize the judges, nor have we for one moment entertained the idea they decided contrary to their convictions; however, we deem it admissible to state that we do think the judges went beyond their function in allowing their personal knowledge to enter into the decision."[77]

As with most complaints, they were not groundless. In announcing the decision for Trinity, the lead judge spoke:

I am required by my colleagues to perform a difficult duty. The decision that arrived at is not unanimous, but is acquiesced in by one and is the judgment of the other two judges. The rules require the decision should depend upon the arguments and not oratory. We are chiefly embarrassed by the fact that the question was argued from two different points of view, consequently the judges have been compelled to rely largely upon their own knowledge of the state of affairs in South Carolina. Prohibition and the dispensary are totally different. But without entering into the argument, I say, that while Wake Forest indicated greatest merit in oratory, we must yield the Palm for argument, and hence the cup to Trinity.[78]

The Biblical Recorder counseled acceptance of the decision but weighed in with a bit of derision: "We could wish that future debates might be judged upon the whole presentation of a side, rather than simply upon

---

[75] *The Biblical Recorder*, December 4, 1901, page 2. The Wake debaters were described for years later as J. D. Little, now of the Indian territory, Mr. O. P. Weathers, of Wilson, and A. Dune. *The North Carolinian*, April 19, 1906, page 8.

[76] *The Morning Post*, November 29, 1901.

[77] Timberlake, E. M., Editor's Portfolio, *The Wake Forest Student,* January 1901, Vol. 20, No. 4, page 241.

[78] *The Commonwealth* (Scotland Neck, NC), December 6, 1900, page 2.

A postcard circa 1900 shows Fayetteville Street, Raleigh

argument, since reasoning is but one element in public speech. Already, the unwholesome tendency to decide upon argument alone is manifest. Every speech but one—that of Mr. Dunn—would have been improved in delivery if it had been simply read from the manuscript."[79]

In addition to the judges being slaves to the argument instead of oratorical flourish, rumors accounting for the host school winning every debate did not imply exactly that the "fix was in," but there was an appearance.[80]

A Wake Forest student warned of the corrosive nature to the series' credibility if the host continued to win every debate. He wrote in *The Wake Forest Student,* "Already a general impression has gone throughout the State that an alternating process is in operation, which decides these debates not according to merit but according to the year for the one or the other college to win…The impression must be corrected, and it is for the students of Wake Forest College to prove that the report is

---

[79] *The Biblical Recorder*, December 5, 1900, page 8.

[80] An account of one debate judge, the evening of the fourth debate, could lead one to question objectivity. "Among the visitors who came to Raleigh to hear the Trinity–Wake Forest debate was Rev. John W Stagg, D. D., who acted as one of the debate judges. Dr. Stagg has recently accepted the call of the synod to undertake the raising of $300,000 as the 20th Century fund for education." The article focuses on his "Herculean effort" to build Davidson and the Presbyterian church. *The Farmer and Mechanic*, December 10, 1901, page 4.

erroneous by showing the people of the State that the Cup can be won for two successive years by the same institution."[81]

The students knew full well that the host institution selected all five-judge panels and subsequently won the debate. Collusion was not the reason, but there may have been subtle identity factors at work. In subsequent intercollegiate debate contracts, provisions were made for panels to be selected and approved by both programs.

TRINITY TERMINATES THE DEBATE SERIES

The *Morning Post* headline announced the scoop of the day in September 1902:

WILL NOT CHALLENGE – No More Debates
Between Trinity and Wake Forest.

The abrupt announcement caught the Wake debate community by surprise. They did not know of Trinity's much earlier decision to cancel the debate series. After a yearlong discussion, the Trinity Literary Societies voted on September 19 to withdraw from the Wake debates. A special report to the *Morning Post* on September 20 revealed:

> At a meeting of the Colombian and Hesperian Literary Societies of Trinity College held tonight the annual debate between Trinity College and Wake Forest College was abolished. Trinity will, therefore, not challenge Wake Forest for another debate.
>
> This action has been in contemplation by Trinity for some time. Reasons given are that in one year Trinity would choose 12 men from whom to select judges, in the next year Wake Forest would make the choice of 12. For this reason, it is alleged the debates have grown to be one-sided affairs, the college selecting the judges always winning. Trinity decided that as Wake Forest now holds a cup it was the proper time to decline to make a further challenge."[82]

Others found that Trinity's withholding their withdrawal was an act of generosity. One newspaper wrote "It is learned that Trinity … would

---

[81] *The Wake Forest Student,* December 1901, page 162-163.

[82] *The Morning Post,* September 20, 1902, page 2.

have taken the steps last year but for the fact that the Methodist boys did not feel he could honorably abolish the debate with the cup in their possession. So far as Trinity is concerned the cup will remain with Wake Forest."[83]

Announced in papers on the 20th, the Philomathesian ledger recorded on the same date the election of Mr. Foster to go to Raleigh at the proper time to make arrangements for the annual Thanksgiving debate with Trinity College."[84] After learning the circumstances, the societies rapidly pivoted, and a week or two later the society elected Mr. Fowler to act in conjunction with the Eu's to arrange a debate with Richmond College.

The Phis and Eus voted on October 11 to hold a joint meeting to discuss the Trinity situation and "appoint a committee to confer with the other society and faculty to arrange a debate with some other college."

Incredulity regarding the news of Trinity's retreat echoed across the state's editorials. Even *The Biblical Recorder,* weighed in, scolding Trinity. "What's the matter with the Trinity boys? Why is it that college contests have to be abandoned every few years? The University of North Carolina is out with the colleges in respect to athletics, and the colleges are out with one another in respect to debates. Get together, men."[85]

Also provoked was a public defense of the Trinity debaters. In one Raleigh paper the argument begins with denial, soon turns to a defense of their withdrawal, and returns to the "flawed judging" excuse. Trinity stood for justice.

> Item sent out from Durham telling of the breaking of the annual debate between Trinity and Wake Forest Colleges, it seems that Wake Forest accuses Trinity of leaving inferences that were not true. The story was not sent out by anyone connected with Trinity. It was late at night when the societies adjourned, and I secured the best report possible at that time. I did not mean to reflect on any of the judges or either of the colleges in what I sent out. The truth is that the debate was broken off because it began to look farcical when the honor of winning alternated each year. The Trinity societies thought that it would be best to stop the debate... The societies deliberated

---

[83] *The Semi-Weekly Messenger* (Wilmington, NC), September 26, 1902, page 6.
[84] Philomathesian Minutes, September 20, 1902.
[85] *The Biblical Recorder* (Raleigh), October 1, 1902, page 6.

Trinity College Hesperian Literary Society minutes, Motion
to withdraw from Wake series, September 19, 1902.

about the matter for more than a year. I have since learned that as a
matter of fact the judges were not all Methodists or Baptists but all
were selected by one college this year and the other the next. This
arrangement was not satisfactory and the debate was broken off.
This much is set in justice for all concerned.[86]

---

[86] *The Morning Post*, September 23, 1902, page 3. Author undisclosed, feels like the
newspaper's opinion.

The Wake students were annoyed but, more importantly, affronted that Trinity had secretly discussed withdrawal months before sharing that information. An aggrieved editorial in *The Wake Forest Student* offered the Wake perspective while lightly lobbying for continuing the series:

The students of Wake Forest are surprised and disappointed at the action of the Literary Societies of Trinity, by which the Annual Thanksgiving Debate with us has been abolished, surprised at the reason they give for discontinuing the debate, and disappointed because we are not to have another opportunity of meeting them in an intellectual engagement. We can only say that, while Trinity has a perfect right to withdraw from the contest at any time she chooses, it does look rather bad for her to say that the reason she does so is because of the partiality of the judges. It is true that the college that selected the judges has always won the cup, but it is equally true that the judges have invariably been men of the highest standing in the State, and members of neither denomination. We are sure that, with possibly one exception (and then evidently in Trinity's favor), these men have always decided the debates to the best of their ability, and according to the rules of the contest. We have never complained to Trinity about the decision of the judges.

But, leaving all of that out of consideration, there are other ways of selecting judges, and if Trinity wanted to meet us this year, other arrangements for obtaining judges might be readily devised and agreed to. Besides, when Trinity debates with any other institution, such as Wofford, or Vanderbilt, or Randolph, she knows that there will be the same, if not more, chance for partiality than there was in the Trinity-Wake Forest contest.

The decision was not the greatest good that came from the debate to either college. These contests have been the means of training scores of young men to think and speak with accuracy and impressiveness before the public; they have produced a spirit of generous rivalry between two institutions of learning; and we believe that they have also had an educational value to the State at large. We hope that Trinity will reconsider her action-Let us have the debate, no matter which college wins.[87]

---

[87] Editorial, *The Wake Forest Student*, October, Vol. 22, No. 1, 1902, page 45-46.

The sixth debate in the series was off the table. Ironically, others seemed willing to step into the void and debate Trinity. *The Richmond Times-Dispatch*, in what some might see as a brazen spot of journalism, offered, "Trinity can honorably decline, should Wake Forest desire the contest to take place as usual, which doubtless she will, judging from an editorial in Sunday's Post, lamenting the action taken by Trinity's societies, and expressing a desire that they should reconsider the matter. Trinity wishes to have a debate with some Virginia school of like standing, and if a contest can be arranged to take place in Richmond sometime in the latter part of November."[88]

The idea for another Trinity and Wake Forest intercollegiate debate was always in the air but did not happen for nearly 30 years. An article in 1910 discussed the revival of the Trinity debate program and Trinity's completed scheduling of intercollegiate debates with Suwanee College and others under consideration. The article states "until more is heard from these colleges the matter of the Wake Forest debate will be held in abeyance."[89]

The next joint debate appearance occurred in 1927 at the Peace Institute in Raleigh in which there was a Wake and a Duke debater paired together on each team, perhaps a symbolic reconciliation. More likely the acrimonious end of the turn-of-the-century series would have been long forgotten.

Spurred on by the Trinity debacle, the "Golden Age" of intercollegiate debate was about to launch.

* * * * * * *

THE JOINT DEBATE
Arranged Between Wake Forest and Richmond.
To Be Held in Raleigh Thanksgiving.

So read the headline in the Raleigh paper confirming that a substitute debate partner had been secured. It did not take long for representatives of Wake and Richmond to gather and arrange a replacement debate. Raleigh's *News & Observer* reported that "Messrs. E. B. Fowler and

---

[88] *Richmond Times-Dispatch*, September 24, 1902, page 3.

[89] *The News & Observer*, September 24, 1910, page 8.

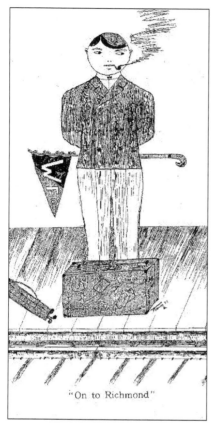

"On to Richmond"

J. B. Huff, of Wake Forest, and Mr. B. Percy Alley, of Richmond College, met at the Yarborough House and drew up an arrangement regulating the debate.... A debate *to grant independence to the Filipinos.*

The city had prepared to host Trinity and Wake and easily substituted Richmond. Even an afternoon football game between A. and M. College and Richmond was arranged for which the city anticipated "there will be a big crowd here on that day."[90]

Several papers announced the negotiated rules. They interestingly addressed the very concerns that ended the Trinity Wake series, including the basis for withdrawal, judge selection ("The number of judges for the debate shall be limited to three; one selected by each college, and these two to select the third"), and criteria for reaching a decision ("The judges shall decide the question on the merits of the arguments produced").[91]

As they declared, **"On to Richmond."**

[90] *The News & Observer,* October 15, 1902, page 5.

[91] *The News & Observer,* October 15, 1902, page 5.

CHAPTER 6

Intercollegiate Debate Goes On The Road

Emerging from the Trinity entrée, Wake Debate took to the trains, aggressively scheduling home-and-away audience debates. The era of public forums was coming into its own. Richmond was first up for the Debating Deacons. The heart of the intercollegiate era was about to play out for the Wake Forest debaters over a 30-year span.

Seemingly, the best way to tell the Intercollegiate Debate story is as it was experienced, through individual encounters. Some of these convenings altered how the school saw itself, some dominated the campus social agenda for weeks, and most made Wake participants statewide celebrities.

In the early years, two or three debates were held annually. Years later, the number of debates grew rapidly with more funding, better transportation, and more debaters needing accommodation. The opponents initially were schools with Baptist traditions located along a railroad. Also scheduled were in-state schools of like tradition, beginning with Trinity and Davidson.

Long tours with many opponents became the norm in the mid-1920s. The latter stage was highlighted by debates with high-profile prestigious opponents, particularly Colgate and Baylor. For the concluding years, geography was no longer a controlling factor, as Arizona, for example, graced the campus.

This chapter records the adventure, excitement, and occasional debate segments, as argued, that depict the intercollegiate contests with Wake's major rivals.[1]

---

[1] A detailed listing of all the of the Societies' public debates can be found in Vol. 3 of this series, *Milestones: Defining Lists of Wake Forest Debate* (2023).

"On To Richmond" (1902-1904,
1915-1916 (4), 1926, 1929, 1931, 1941-1942, 1947-1948)

Following the collapse of the Trinity-Wake Forest series, the students moved fast. "Meeting with Richmond's debaters, R. H. Willis, W. B. Thraves, and John W. Kencheloe, at the State House, Raleigh, the envoys agreed on debates featuring two debaters, a departure from the normal team of three students. They would be judged by three judges, one selected by each college with the third selected by the first two. The loving cups were to be presented by Raleigh Chamber of Commerce."[2]

The Richmond debates, along with a football game, would anchor the city's holiday events, seamlessly following the Trinity series. Wake Forest and the state of North Carolina awaited the event and a big win. The first Richmond debate, however, would turn out differently.

1902 – FIRST RICHMOND DEBATE – RALEIGH

"The committee, in considering delivery, argument, and composition of the debate in rendering its verdict, unanimously awards the victory to the able representatives of Richmond College," so announced Judge H. G. Cotter, unleashing the visitor's salute.[3]

The News and Observer, swept up in the tumult, recorded: "It was a scene that defies description. Flags and ribbons were swinging in the air, the audience was on its feet, cheers and college cries echoed, and everywhere there was noise and clamor, for strangers had come into the state and in the capital had won the trophy from an institution native to the soil." A sizable contingent of Richmond students and citizens had taken the train to Raleigh."[4]

---

[2] The earlier account suggested they met at a prominent Raleigh Hotel, not the Capitol. Perhaps they met at both. The story next to this front-page lead reported President Theodore (Teddy) Roosevelt admonishing a South Carolina Congressman for objections to the appointment of an African American candidate. Teddy Roosevelt wrote in his response, "I cannot consent to take a position that the door of hope, the door of opportunity, is to be shut upon any man, no matter how worthy, purely upon the grounds of race or color. Such an attitude would, according to my convictions, be fundamentally wrong." *Richmond Times-Dispatch*, October 16, 1902, page 9.

[3] *The News & Observer*, November 28, 1902, page 1.

[4] *The News & Observer*, November 28, 1902, page 1.

E. J. SHERWOOD,
RICHMOND DEBATER.

JAMES ROYALL,
RICHMOND DEBATER.

Of course, with Richmond winning the first Thanksgiving Day affair, which the papers reported as being "heard by fully 2000 people," the crowd had every reason for celebration much in the style that Wake would display in Richmond the following year."[5]

The evening's question was Resolved: *That American honor demands that we grant independence to the Philippines*, the affirmative "championed by J. W. Kinchaloe and Lena Lacey, of Richmond College and the negative by James Royall and Edwin Sherwood, of Wake Forest."[6] The Raleigh newspaper would update its northern brethren in a "special dispatch" to the *Richmond Times*, leading with the often employed weather metaphor of the period: "The almost incessant downpour rain which characterize weather conditions here yesterday has passed off, and to-day donned clear and considerably cooler, so that there was in every prospect now for a practically ideal Thanksgiving day, and great crowds at both the Richmond college against the Agriculture and Mechanical College

[5] *The Richmond Times-Dispatch*, November 28, 1902, page 1.

[6] *The Richmond Times-Dispatch*, November 27, 1902, page 1.

foot-ball game and the Wake Forest-Richmond college debate are expected here to-morrow."[7]

After the "surprising" first Richmond debate loss, there was at least good-spirited joshing about the debaters' "mistreatment" by Richmond. A *Wake Student* editor alluded to some resentment, writing, "Last year, at Raleigh, with all personalities and ill-feelings cast aside, we enjoyed a debate of the highest order, our two representatives vieing [Sic, vying] with the Wake Forest of Virginia."[8]

In an editorial, *The Wake Forest Student* manager, H. E. Craven, responding against a "sore loser" charge expressed by some, promised to take the high road:

> The first Richmond College-Wake Forest debate has come and gone, and the trophy is now in captivity in the enemy's territory. Hence, there is little to be said about the debate. but we do want to say a few things: First, the debate was conducted on a high order, above the plain of personalities, and above mere quibbles about words and isolated, irrelevant facts; Second, we fought hard and lost; Third, we have no complaint to make of our representatives, of the Richmond debaters, or of the judges, and although one or two reports may have gone out to the contrary, the student body and the college are not responsible for the private opinions of any one man. Wake Forest accepts the decision of the judges in a manly spirit. There has been less kicking this year than ever before, and we believe that we are learning the lesson of taking a defeat without murmuring.[9]

Even the statewide *Biblical Recorder* weighed in, "We congratulate them, and all the Virginians. give us another chance." Of course, the editorial call for gracious restraint would not prevail as controversy over fairness and judging seemingly always perseveres.

Throughout the intercollegiate period, societies were responsible for producing the debates – invitations, judges, travel, and sundry expenses – persistently creating a monetary hardship for the always financially strapped clubs. As at other public events, the Eus and Phis elected

---

[7] *The Richmond Times-Dispatch*, November 27, 1902, page 1.

[8] Gaston S Foote, Editor, *The Wake Forest Student*, October 1902, Vol. 23, page 53.

[9] *The Wake Forest Student*, Editor's Portfolio, H. E. Craven, December 1903, Vol. 22, No. 3, page 172.

marshals to oversee the Raleigh evening, from decorations to seating the audience. The elected position of Marshal was highly valued and visible, and the students' names were always of high mention in newspaper coverage. Typically, in the 1880s and 1890s, a full-page *Howler* was dedicated, picturing that year's marshals.

In November 1903, the Philomathesian minutes recorded a motion by Mr. Fleming "that the society refused to pay for the dress suits of our Marshals at the Thanksgiving debate. After some discussion, the second to the motion was withdrawn. Mr. L. then moved: we pay for the dress suits of our marshals and nothing else. The motion is carried."[10] Haggling over how to pay for the Marshal's expenses at the Thanksgiving debate in Raleigh continued for two months. The resolution required detailed proof from the assistant treasurer and an offer of $30 to cover the expenses.[11]

1903 – SECOND RICHMOND DEBATES – RICHMOND

In the second debate at Richmond, Wake chose the affirmative for the question, *That deportation is the best solution of the negro problem in the United States.* Richmond, as the host, chose the topic, and its two literary societies, Mu Sigma Rho and Philologian, met in the Richmond president's office and hashed out the topic, "offering the best field for a fair and spirited debate."[12]

---

[10] Philomathesian minutes, November 22, 1903.

[11] Philomathesian Minutes, January 10, 1903.

[12] The *Deportation of Negroes* debate at Richmond was not preserved in a way I was able to discover. Newspapers only announced participants, the topic, the Wake win, and headlines coupled with what felt like the "more important" result of the football

Wake Forest was represented by J. W. Whisnant, "the calm, argumentative debater," and J. N. Lofton, "the fiery, eloquent orator. Such a combination proved too worthy steel for the Richmond college debaters, and they went down amid the blood of the arena."[13]

Making the trek to Richmond became the highlight of the holiday.[14] *The Wilmington Messenger* reported that "the president and faculty and 150 students from Wake Forest college will go to Richmond Thursday to see the football game and also to hear the debate Thursday evening... Three special cars from Wake Forest will be in the train, and the cars will be decorated."[15] The fare was "placed at the low rate of $2.50 ... "those who desire to do so can take sleeper on the return."[16]

According to *The Morning Post*, Wake's faculty and students were to be joined by more than fifty of the most prominent young ladies in the city. "Notify the chaperones that they are expected to join the special train, which will be why there are special features of the train. It will be a great trip, and being personally conducted by Mr. Gattis, there is every assurance that will afford for its patrons probably the most delightful trip that has ever been made from Raleigh.[17]

After being feted by the Richmond president-led reception following the debate, the happy warriors boarded the train for the return home. The Raleigh paper provided an account of the arrival festivities, which they deemed "a well-planned and enthusiastic celebration."[18] The

---

match. The same topic, Deportation, was used at an Anniversary celebration in 1903, and compelling excerpts from that debate are provided in Chapter 12 – Debating Race Before Their People. The third Richmond debate, "*Advanced nations should control, for the world's benefit, the territory occupied by backward races*, was preserved in the local North Carolina papers.

[13] *The Wake Forest Student*, Vol. 22, February 1903, page 195.

[14] Students who lived any distance could not always go home for the holidays as classes were scheduled immediately following the holidays. "The College announced that exercises will be suspended on Thanksgiving in light of the great battle that night between representatives of Wake Forest and Richmond College." *The Times Dispatch* (Richmond), 1903, November 25.

[15] *The Wilmington Messenger*, November 27, 1903, page 5.

[16] *The Morning Post*, November 7, 1903, page 6.

[17] *The Morning Post*, Nov 22, 1903, page 6. Mr. Charles H. Gattis, the popular city ticket passenger agent of the Seaboard Air Line, *The Morning Post*, November 7, 1903, page 6.

[18] The BOYS ARE LIONIZED (Special to *News & Observer*), *The News & Observer*, November 28, 1903, page 4.

enormity of these events in students' lives, from community to politics, becomes apparent.

> They were not allowed to put a foot to ground, but were carried on the shoulders of their comrades to a decorated hack and walked in a jiffy up to Leigh Hall by a team of spirited and shouting bipeds. Dr. Walter Sykes was master of ceremonies. The hall was packed, a large number of ladies of the hill being present. The debaters presented the loving cup to Pres. Taylor, who responded on behalf of the college. Then followed speeches from Dr. Lynch and the members of the faculty through the entire list present. The Hon. E. Yates Webb, representative and congressman from the Ninth District, was called out and expressed his hearty sympathy with the happiness of his alma mater. The debaters made the concluding speeches. The student band contributed to the brightness of music to a very interesting and memorable occasion.[19]

And from "A little girl who lived on the hill."[20]

> Hurrah! Hurrah! we won the cup,
> And it's here, we hope to stay;
> Old Richmond had to give it up,
> And let us take it away.
> To Whisnant and Lofton we give the praise
> They're the ones who save the day;
> Three cheers for both we gladly raise,
> But them we can ne'er repay[21]

1904 – THIRD RICHMOND DEBATE – RICHMOND

The third 1904 Richmond intercollegiate debate undertook the topic *That the advanced nations should control, for the world's benefit, the territory occupied by backward races.* Although not as unashamedly racist as the "deportation of the negro problem" debated the year before, more than a little chauvinistic racism resided in the topic. The troubling thought of the

---

[19] *The News & Observer*, November 28, 1903, page 4.

[20] "Lived on the hill" refers to regular Township of Wake Forest residents.

[21] *The Wake Forest Student*, Vol. 23, February 1904, page 268.

Special Train

....TO....

**WAKE FOREST
Feb. 12, '04**

Leave Raleigh 6:30 p. m.
Arrive Wake Forest 7:00.
Leave Wake Forest 12 night.
Arrive Raleigh 12:50 a. m.

**FARE: 55c.
For the Round Trip**

Account celebration of Wake Forest
College Literary Societies February
12th.
For information apply to

C. H. GATTIS, C. P. T. A.
Raleigh, N. C.

age was not out of the debaters' awareness, as revealed in their arguments. Even as the assumptions underlying the topic were largely unchallenged, still an awareness of the injustices undergirding "colonialism" was voiced.[22]

The campus mood, however, was less one of reflection and more of carnival. With the full hype of a sporting event, delight reigned prior to the debate. *The News & Observer* described the Thanksgiving affair "as one of the most important in many respects of the college year—Richmond is to be met and defeated."

To ensure they could overpower the hall's atmospherics, a "large body of students over 200 warmed up on campus, meeting in "Memorial Hall last night to practice the college songs and yells. After a few interesting speeches on the history of former debates with Trinity, Richmond and Furman, the boys got down to business, making the large hall ring with new life."[23]

In the midst of these closing scenes, with just as much vim and vigor as they had at the beginning, Wake Forest students were crying out, one voice asking the question:

"What's the matter with A. and M.?"
"She's all right," this from 100 voices.
"Who says so?" by the solo.
"Everybody." by the crowd.
Whose everybody?"
"Wake Forest," and then a prolonged cheer.[24]

---

[22] See Chapter 12 – Debating Race Before Their Public, where some of the debate's claims are presented.

[23] *The News & Observer,* November 22, 1904, page 3.

[24] *The Wake Forest Student,* December 1904 Vol 24, page 193.

This laurel for A. and M. was for its victory over Clemson college football, but the Wake Forest beaux varied "Baptist University" and "peace institute" now and then, where the girl smiled, applauded, and did some cheering in return.[25] Wake's yearbook pleaded, "we were glad to have the B. U. W. girls visit us, and we took great delight in entertaining them. girls, we want you to come again next year."[26]

The *Howler* yearbook section, "History of Newish Class," was bois- terous in recounting the Raleigh debate: " It was a grand affair for us... we are going to elect Messrs. Olive and Patton honorary members of our class for saving our cup from them foreigners."[27]

Becoming one of the debaters on stage was a competitive and elongated process. Nine finalists tried out for the debate in addition to the two who graced the stage. Being selected was a striking local accolade.[28]

There were warning signs of what was to become the grand community event, and it was not a debate. *The Chatham Record* observed, "These inter-collegiate debates are very important to the participants and are enjoyed by all who hear them. and yet they attract nothing like as large crowd as does a foot-ball game!"[29] The competition for spectators would become a serious concern in a few years.

The Richmond three-year series (1902-1904) was about to come to an abrupt halt. Wake Forest apparently pulled the plug, as the Phi's 1905 minutes indicate that the object of their meeting was: "to bring before the society certain letters from Richmond college objecting to our refusal to meet them in further debate for the cup given by the Chamber of Commerce." The literary societies were ready to move on and, in a November 11 meeting, indicated, "Mr. Picot was paid twenty-five dollars ($25.00) to pay expenses as [his] committee to meet the like committee from Mercer, to arrange the debate.[30] The next Richmond debate would not happen until 1915.

---

[25] "The building was packed with nearly all the Wake Forest students, who had taken a special train, and nearly 300 young women from the Baptist University here were on hand to cheer them. The *Graphic* (Nashville, NC), December 1, 1904, page 8.

[26] *Howler*, 1905, page 58.

[27] *Howler*, 1905, page 58.

[28] *The News & Observer*, November 2, 1904, page 1.

[29] *The Chatham Record*, December 1, 1904, page 2.

[30] Philomathesian Minutes, October 28, 1905.

Joseph C. Patton and Alfred H. Olive – Richmond Debaters – 1904

The following intercollegiate debate was not with Mercer as the Philomathesian's negotiators anticipated. Instead, two years later, it was in 1904 with Furman University. Furman, a sister Baptist college, had issued a challenge, which, with the help of the faculty, became the selection. Apparently, the Wake Forest faculty had proposed and passed a resolution to only allow one debate in a year; no debate was held that year with Richmond.[31] The faculty restrictions would not last a year; after 1906, the Deacons were about to routinely board trains to participate in multiple debates.

1915-1916 – LATER RICHMOND DEBATES

The Richmond series was renewed 11 years later, in 1915 and 1916, in a newly cooperative atmosphere, with a touch of the experimental.[32] Two debates were held each year on the same evening, a double-barreled

---

[31] *Greensboro Daily News*, April 17, 1906, page 3.

[32] The Richmond student newspaper, *The Collegian*, admonished all Richmond students. "Next year four men will be chosen to represent your College against Wake Forest—only four, but every student in the Societies who has any ambition for these honors should begin now to train for them. There must be training and practicing… and remember, in all you think and do to keep this before you—Wake Forest must be defeated next year." *The Collegian*, Vol. 1, No. 16, April 16, 1915.

gala: one in Richmond and one in Raleigh. Their fans would have to track, via telegraph, the winners from each distanced venue. The events played out, as ordered, in Wake's favor. Over the two seasons, Wake won all four debates, which became bragging rights on campus and in state newspapers.

The student newspaper, the *Old Gold and Black,* was not shy in offering a "certain" description of the debate and debaters. The article claimed, "Wake Forest debaters exhibited the same ease of delivery, the same confidence in themselves, and the same force of argument characterizing almost every debater that has represented the college in such contests... each successive speech was hurled hot and unmanageable into the hands of their opponent." Richmond was described as competent as "lacking teamwork."[33]

"The winning of either of two contests will be sufficient to take the series, and there is every hope that our recently-selected representatives will end the whole affair in a blaze of glory and 'make assurance doubly sure' by victories on both sides of the query." In essence, the essay argued that the Societies remained relevant and there were still men willing to do 'that merciless, effective work ... who, "while their companions slept," (Longfellow may be taken literally) 'were toiling each upwards in the night.'"[34]

In May 1915, a resolution was passed by the literary societies declaring that some sort of recognition be given to the winning intercollegiate debating teams. "Our athletic heroes have had 'W's' given them for a long time. Those who toil in the wee small hours, preparing themselves to hold up Wake Forest's debating record, should be given equal recognition... there is plenty of room for both athletics and debating; there is no reason why Wake Forest should not excel in both."[35]

Despite no shortage of tributes, the debaters did not receive "athletic" letters. The Richmond debate participants were awarded pins for their achievements at the spring commencement exercises.

---

[33] *Old Gold and Black*, April 29, 1916, page 1.

[34] *Old Gold and Black*, February 26, 1916, page 2.

[35] *The Wake Forest Student.* May 1915, Vol. 34, page 598. Another state paper suggested the importance the campus placed in these events. The announcement that Col. J. Brian Grimes, North Carolina's Secretary of State, would preside over the debate pleased Wake Forest. Col. Grimes was one of the foremost exponents for North Carolina, his presence as the presiding officer added auspiciousness to the occasion. *The Charlotte Observer*, April 1, 1915, page 10.

THIRD INTERCOLLEGIATE DEBATE

BETWEEN

Richmond and Wake Forest Colleges

THURSDAY EVENING, NOVEMBER 24, '04

RALEIGH, NORTH CAROLINA

A decade later, in 1924, the Eus and Phis, "In an effort to place debating on par with athletics," decided the men who make the College debating teams "may have the choice of a slip-over Sweater with a monogram having the society seal superimposed.[36] A small diamond would be inserted into the pin if a student made the team three times. Each Society passed the motion unanimously... "The societies will award debaters letters just as the athletic Council awards athletic letters. The society seal across a monogram will distinguish the debating and athletic honors." [37]

The original evidence that offered proof that a letter was awarded was a 1927 Raleigh *News & Observer* photo (below). The team of eleven festooned in letter sweaters is presumably assembled on the steps of the Wake Forest Wait Hall. More conclusive evidence was the 1926 sweater preserved at the Wake Forest Historical Museum.

Despite the apparent "Golden Age" of Society influence, as evidenced by awarding a Letter Sweater, an *Old Gold and Black* editorialist in 1916 raised a flag, alarmed by chatter suggesting the possibility that the Board of Trustees... would eliminate the Societies[38] "just as with athletics, which the Board was rumored to be considering for elimination, there would be repercussions." He envisioned a "furor, equal to that aroused by the heated athletic mass meeting, will be provoked."

The authors were realistic enough to allow that 1916 was not the former golden age; Wake as an isolated campus no longer existed; it was

---

[36] *Old Gold and Black*, February 29, 1924, page 1.

[37] *Old Gold and Black*, February 29, 1924, page 1.

[38] Discussions before the Board of Trustees happened, but most concerned allowing the addition of letter fraternities around 1905, which were rejected.

WAKE FOREST VARSITY INTERCOLLEGIATE DEBATE TEAM

Circa 1927 *Debate Lettermen*, Back Row: G. N. Ashley, B. W. Walker, C. B. Vance, R. E. Wall, J. L. Carlton, Front Row: W. W. Cahoon, W. C. Whitley, C. E. Weston, D. S Haworth, Elmer Cloer (four public debates, two Debate Councils), G. F. Johnson.

no longer the serene "primeval and communistic state of existence" as the former eras were described in the editorial.[39]

The Board did not eliminate athletics or societies. Yet, the latter had ceded public attention to sport and were about to concede much of their remaining weight when student membership was no longer required six years later.

*_*_*_*_*_*_*

The Furman Rescue
(1904, 1925-1926, 1928, 1930, 1933, 1940)

Not surprisingly, intercollegiate debates, particularly those hosted in Raleigh, where students could attend, were not just about the "elevated" reasons often voiced (e.g., the college's public exposure or notions

---

[39] *Old Gold and Black*, February 26, 1916, page 2.

of educating the public) but had rather more "direct" motives. The 1903 account seems preoccupied with romantic adventures, which undoubtedly composed an unofficial travel plan.

[November] means …a Thanksgiving debate in Raleigh, at which a thousand dancing eyes, representing half as many fair damsels, are the observed of all observers. It is said there is only one debate, but in reality, there are a great many, and the intercollegiate affair only serves as the hub around which the other debates revolve. The other debates are masculine-feminine, strictly private, with impromptu speaking, and no judges. It is surprising sometimes how eloquent some bashful, blushing lad will become under the stimulus of a beaming pair of eyes. sometimes it is victory, and sometimes it is defeat, but whichever it may be, it is always a joy.[40]

The "fill-in-the-gap" debate with sister institution Furman in 1904, discussed *Resolved, that the expansion policy of the United States government is for the best interest of its people.* The debate was held at

Presbyterian College in Charlotte, NC. The *Charlotte Observer's* geographic lens reflected its affinity with both communities. The paper's account supplies insight into the appeal and mechanics of early intercollegiate debates, as well as recounting the racist claims consonant with the times.

Arthur S. Gillespie's Debate Letter Sweater. One of his honors was debating in the South Carolina-Georgia Tour in 1926. Courtesy of the Wake Forest Historical Museum, Wake Forest, NC.

By the striking of the hour, 8 o'clock, set for the beginning of the exercises, the college auditorium was comfortably filled by a cultured and interested audience. The ladies were out in all of the glory of the new Easter clothes and the applause they frequently gave indicated that their favors were about equally divided.

---

[40] *Howler*, The College Calendar, 1903, page 127.

Though some delay was caused by the nonappearance of Col. Hoyt, of Greenville, S. C., who had been selected by Furman as a judge. Finally, it was decided to ask J. Q. Adams to serve in his stead. During the wait, the Wake Forest students, about 50 of whom were present, gave several college yells, ringing in "Wake Forest," "Charlotte," "Presbyterian College," "Elizabeth College." "Furman University" and the "Tar Heels." This pleasantry took well with the audience and prepared the way to a hearty reception of all the debaters.

Before the debaters were introduced the presiding officer explained ...that the judges in reaching their decision, should be governed by the following percentages: composition, 20 per cent; delivery, 20 per cent; argument 60 per cent.[41]

The debate asked if America wanted to become a colonial power. The debate, framed in economic terms, revealed itself as soundly grounded in cultural racism.

Wake speaker Phillip C. McDuffie argued that "we as a nation now depend upon other nations for the continuation of our present prosperous conditions. We must sell our surplus products and buy the things we do not produce. This can only be done by expansion.

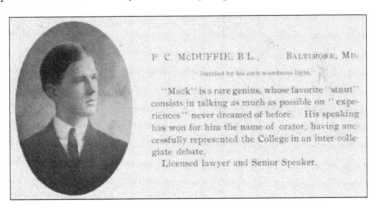

What kind of expansion are we pursuing? Not the old imperial policy of Rome, but one that spreads the national influence to every nation under the sun. Not a policy of greed, but one that will secure to America the commerce of the world."

---

[41] *Charlotte Daily Observer*, April 5, 1904, page 5.

Mr. Vass from Furman argued on the negative, "Do we realize what we have? A people inferior to our people, and with many but poorly curbed passions. Surely our purposes cannot be other than benevolent. Now, will not these islands come into competition with Americans? Will the American live on the low wages of the Filipino?"

One of the heroes of the early intercollegiate era, Alfred H. Olive of Wake Forest, argued, "Expansive policy is nothing new. The English people have always been an expansive people; and it is unconscious obedience to this cosmic law that we must go forward... We have one-fifth of the world's population; one-seventh of the world's territory; but one-third of the world's wealth. We find as a mathematical certainty that one man in America, judged by production and consumption, is equal to 10 men abroad."

The newspaper observed his speech was much more reasoned when pointing out that the Louisiana Purchase was condemned as "the greatest curse that can befall our republic."

Furman's Langston reasoned, "This change from our former policy of peace to our present policy of imperialism is due to our sudden acquisition of great wealth... It has caused us to choose hatred instead of love; slavery instead of freedom, and empire instead of republic."

In rebuttals, one of the debaters from Furman offered that the US had no right to govern the people without the consent of the governed. Wake Forest's R. Olive retorted to Langston by asking:

If we should consult the negroes in South Carolina as to the manner to which we govern them? I am here to say that if I am forced to discuss this question, I shall certainly take the side of my South Carolina friends. and if he had been in South Carolina from 1868 to 1876 and had seen the negroes in their imprudence yet under the protection of the United States Government, he would think as I think.... I am now leaning upon a stick, the result of four years of that war; but if I had it to do again, I would go gladly."

Prof. Brewer... said the argument of the young man for Wake Forest was in line with the Col.'s way of thinking and was in line with Wake Forest's argument.

The judges appeared. Rev. J. Q. Adams announced their decision, as follows: "We find the affirmative won on composition and acclamation, and the negative won on argument."

"But which one?" demanded a voice in the audience.

"Well, you have heard our statement," replied Mr. Adams.

"Which won the most? said someone, amid an uproar.

"The affirmative!" said Mr. Adams. and the house went wild with enthusiasm.[42]

The Furman debate series did not resume until 1925, and then with a much more conciliatory tone. *The Biblical Recorder* praised, "We're always glad to hear of its intercollegiate debate. It is a contest of brain rather than brawn. It is a mental exercise which is profitable to the young men in their afterlife. They get accustomed to hearing their own voices, and the rejoinders train them to think rapidly and speak extemporaneously. This debate was very much enjoyed by those who attended. while our visitors lost the decision, they made many friends during their sojourn in Raleigh."[43]

A year later, *Old Gold and Black's* commentary on the Southern Tour week identified Furman University as the leading Baptist institution in South Carolina. The commentary claimed, "You might well call the two institutions first cousins; Dr. W. L. Poteat, president of Wake Forest, and Dr. E. M. Poteat, for 15 years president of Furman… are brothers."[44] Wake and Furman would debate many more times over the coming years.

--*-*-*-*-*-*

Ordering Procedures with Mercer
(1906 (2), 1908, 1914, 1921, 1924, 1926-1928)

On December 7, 1905, Euzelian society's minutes announced securing an agreement with Mercer for a three-debate series. The negotiations after the Trinity falling out had tightened the details surrounding the debates. The Mercer agreement illustrates agreements reached across most schools with whom Wake held public debates.

Promoted by Wake students and fawning newspapers, the early intercollegiate era began to cement Wake Forest's external and self-image

---

[42] *Charlotte Daily Observer*, April 5, 1904, page 5.

[43] *The Biblical Recorder*, April 15, 1925, page 7.

[44] *Old Gold and Black,* April 24, 1926, page 1.

The debate committee of WFC and the debate committee of Mercer University hereby agree to hold a series of three debates under the following conditions:

I. Debate shall be held at Raleigh, NC on Easter Monday, 1906. The second at Macon, Georgia on Thursday Thanksgiving Day, 1906 and the third Atlanta Georgia on Easter Monday of the year 1908.

II. All expenses of the debate, except those of the visiting team, shall be borne by the local institution in the first two debates; the railroad expenses of the third debate shall be shared equally by the colleges.

III. All the local arrangements and the charging of the mission shall be left with the local institution, and it in the case of the Atlanta debate, shall be determined by future agreement.

IV. Receipts from admission charges, if made, shall be used to defray local expenses, and any surplus shall be divided equally.

V. The college alternate in selecting subject of debate. The subject must be announced to the other college five months before the date of the debate. The choice of sides rests with the college to whom the subject is announced and this choice must be made known within two weeks of the time of receipt of the speeches one of 20 min. duration and the other of five min. The first series of speeches shall be opened by the affirmative and shall alternate between the affirmative and the negative speakers. The second series shall be in the same order so far as to sides of the debate are concerned, but either side, may if it chooses, vary the order of his speakers. There shall be interval between the first and second series of not more than five min, during which none of the regular debaters shall consult.

VIII. A debater? is allowed to interrupt another debater only in case of misrepresentation of an argument or mis-statement of fact.

IX. The alternate from the visiting college show shall act as Secretary, and both alternates and shall act as timekeepers. The presiding officer shall be chosen by the host.

X. At the conclusion of the debate the judges without any consultation, shall determine their decision and submit them in writing without signatures to the presiding officer who? shall announce the vote.

XI. The award shall be made independently of the merits of the question and is based solely upon the merits of the debate, the decision going to the side that excels in argumentation.

XII. Each contest shall be judged in the cited way by three judges who shall be disinterested persons, not connected with the institution and any relation, and chosen in the following manner. At least two months before the contest colleges shall alternately submit a list of 15 persons nominated as judges, from which number the other colleges shall report back, within two weeks, a list of at least six in order of preference. The first three available to act will be selected. In case less than three are available another list shall be prepared in like manner.

as the site for public address training... Bragging rights, comparable to athletics, became influential in the institution's *amour propre*. A student previewing the noteworthy Mercer debates proclaimed:

> Wake Forest cannot boast of money, magnificent buildings, or fine equipment, but her jewels are her men, and the distinguishing characteristic of her men is that they can *speak*. That is not merely a legend of the past but the reality of the present. time and again in recent years have her men gone against colleges and universities in various states, and in all those debates only once has she failed to keep Old Gold and Black ever waving high."[45]

The questions surrounding judging persisted. Randolph-Macon served as a model: the host institution selected the judges from a list of 15 nominated names not affiliated with either college. The non-host institution held veto power, narrowing the list to six, hoping to obtain three prominent but unaffiliated celebrities. If three could not be cajoled into judging the debate, an honor in social circles, a new shorter list would be developed. The judge's instructions were explicit. The signed agreement expressed, "the award shall be made independently of the merits of the question and solely upon the merits of the debate."

Arrangements were left with the host school, which were extensive due to being part of a major Thanksgiving Day civic celebration. Wake hosted first in Raleigh, Mercer in Macon, and the third debate in the "neutral" site, Atlanta... Arrangements included negotiations with the city's Chamber of Commerce, obtaining an appropriate venue, and preparing all the invitations, tickets, and receptions. They were not inexpensive affairs. The third debate, remote from both hometowns, required splitting costs, including train transportation, as specified in the agreement document.

1906 – FIRST MERCER DEBATE – RALEIGH

The calendar year 1906 featured two debates with Mercer, the first held in Raleigh on Easter in the academic spring term and the second, opening the fall semester, hosted by Mercer in Macon, Georgia.

---

[45] *The Wake Forest Student*, November 1906, Vol. 26, page 149.

The debate series immediately commanded interest. Newspapers wrote of the intense preparation for both Wake and Mercer debaters. One quoted a letter from Mercer: "There is now at Mercer healthful enthusiasm and genuine loyalty, the literary societies have experienced rivals, and the Mercer spirit of oratory is regaining its place. No single cause has contributed as much perhaps in this direction than the Mercer-Wake Forest debate."[46] The letter continues to ensure Wake knew that Mercer was undefeated in debate, as was Wake, making the contest definitive.

"Nearly every Wake Forest student was here and a great many citizens of Wake Forest and adjoining towns." The Academy of Music began to fill early, though there was not so large a crowd as usual due to the admissions fee that was charged because of the overcrowding of the academy in previous debates and because of the expense of the debate."[47] The assessed fee was 25 cents. Admission was free for Baptist University for Women, Peace Institute, St. Mary's, and Wake Forest college students.[48]

Ultimately, the local newspapers recorded "a great victory for Wake Forest with the speeches on both sides truly powerful, free from the usual sophomoric rhetoric, presenting facts and arguments proving conclusively their respective claims."[49]

---

[46] *The Raleigh Evening Times*, March 31, 1906, page 2.

[47] *The News & Record*, April 17, 1906, page 3.

[48] *The News & Record*, April 8, page 3.

[49] *The North Carolinian* (Raleigh) April 19, 1906, page 8; Each speaker had 20 minutes for their first speech and five minutes for rejoinders, separated by a five-minute intermission. During the entire discussion, one paper suggested that the "Wake Forest boys," whenever they had a chance, "would give college yells and sing college songs" in support of the debaters. *The North Carolinian* (Raleigh) April 19, 1906, page 8.

Oddly, little about the debate's content was reported in newspapers. The topic discussed was whether *Southern States should encourage foreign immigrants admitted into this country to settle within their borders.* In their reporting, the reception, hosted by Dr. and Mrs. W. L. Poteat, was featured and described as "one of the most enjoyable social occasions of the season."

Each [invitees] was given a pamphlet in which were blanks to be filled out in a musical romance. It was arranged by Mrs. Hubert Poteat. Mr. Poteat would call out the number and the question and the guest was to guess and write in the pamphlet after the number, called the answer, which would be the name of the song.

All the guests repaired to the dining room, where several courses of refreshments were served. The dining room was decorated with poppies, ferns and other flowers, interspersing with the college colors. Before leaving, the club sang the old song, "Here's to Wake Forest" and the new song, the words of which were recently written by Dr. G. W. Paschal.[50]

1906 – SECOND MERCER DEBATE – MACON

The Raleigh Times, 1906 headline extolled:

Joy of Victory at Wake Forest
Mercer Again Defeated in Field of Debate
By Wake Forest's Best
The Greatest Triumph, Says Pres. Poteat, That the College Has Ever Won
A Holiday Granted to Give Student's Full Opportunity to Enjoy the Victory[51]

(Special to the Evening Times)

Wake Forest College, and the Wake Forest campus, and in fact the whole town, is ringing with cheers this morning. The good news that Wake Forest has won the Mercer-Wake Forest debate, held in Macon, Ga., last night, was received early this morning, and the

---

[50] *The News & Observer,* 1906 April 27, page 5.

[51] *The Raleigh Times,* November 30, 1906, page 7.

old college bell began ringing forth the good news. Cheers could be heard at an early hour at the various eating clubs and boarding houses—cheers for the men who won the debate, Wake Forest representatives, Messrs. Fred F. Brown of Asheville, and Walter H. Weatherspoon of Durham. College spirit is running high, and at this writing the college song can be heard on the campus.

President Poteat was greeted with thousands of cheers as he approached the Wingate Memorial Hall for Chapel exercises. At the conclusion of the service, he said: "We were in Raleigh last night and about 12 o'clock heard the good news through the Associated Press dispatches. The dear boys who have won this sweet victory for us will come into our arms tomorrow about noon... I consider this the greatest victory won in the history of the college."

At the conclusion of the chapel exercises hundreds of students passed into the president's office, begging him and the other members of the faculty to give a holiday on account of the victory. nothing else would do, so the holiday was granted.[52]

The dispatch promoted that this victory (and the year before) were the only two defeats Mercer had ever suffered. Before the debate, they admitted to some uneasiness that the decision might not have gone Wake's way. After all, the debate was "in a far-away state, where the sentiment was practically all for Mercer and the judges from Georgia."[53]

In previewing the second Thanksgiving Day debate in the Macon City Auditorium, *The News & Observer's* South Carolina correspondent sent an entry that "revealed" how the debate was portrayed in Macon. The rendering "is not only of interest to alumni and friends of Wake Forest, but to the people of North Carolina as a whole, for the debate is not only between two colleges, but debaters represent in a way the two states."

The reporter warned that the South Carolina paper elevated the Mercer representatives' abilities "as speakers of more than ordinary ability, the many honors as debaters they have won being enumerated, and the article concludes that they stand a good chance of winning the question."

---

[52] *Greensboro Daily News,* December 1, 1906, page 8.

[53] *The Raleigh Times,* November 30, 1906, page 7. The judges of the debate were Chief Justice Cobb of the Supreme Court of Georgia, Professor Johnson of Emory College, and the Honorable Mr. Fleming, ex-Congressman.

The hometown newspaper alert included Mercer's suggestion that the stylistically inflexible Wake Forest debaters should work to directly engage with the debated question.

The Wake Forest debaters of the previous year "little is known of them, except like all Wake Forest men, they are eloquent speakers. That, indeed, seems to be their strong forte. Mercer's history of debating is very different. Little attention beyond the ordinary rules of expression is paid to delivery. Mercer's ideals demand that the debaters produce in advance ideas on their subject. As the debate is to be decided upon argument alone, every indication points to a victory for Mercer, unless the Wake Forest debaters could sweep the judges off their feet by appeals to sentiment delivered an eloquent, persuasive oratory.[54]

The hometown newspaper from Raleigh naturally defended the Wake Forest win from a year earlier. "Everyone who knows anything of the speakers sent by Wake Forest knows that their speaking contains the element of clear facts... Those who heard the debate in Raleigh last year with Mercer will testify that it was won by Wake Forest because the arguments and not the oratory surpassed the speakers from the former

J. B. Weatherspoon, super-debater, entrant Mercer debates, as well as the 1906 Anniversary Day Debates, Wake's well-spoken conservative

---

[54] *The News & Observer*, November 18, 1906, page 13.

institution." This exchange illustrates the passion surrounding debates and highlights the pedagogical issue of eloquence versus content simmering, if not in debate training, nominally in public expectations.

The campus victory celebration departed from the customary litany of speakers. The salute started with Oscar J. Sikes and Junius L. Allen's description of the debate itself, "How it was done." The entrée was followed by the faculty (Gulley and Carlyle), members from each class (Senior, O. R. Mangum, Junior, J. C. Newell, Sophomore, E. E. White, and Freshman, W. S. Britt), with J. L. Bennett of the Medical class, A. L. Fletcher of the Law class. Uniquely, the speeches closed with Mercer alumnus William D. Upshaw (more on Upshaw below), as well as responses from the debaters themselves, Mr. F. F. Brown and Mr. W. H. Weatherspoon.[55] One has to hope the speeches were short, but, given the era, they likely were not.

The freshman representative was remembered in the *Howler*: "We beat Mercer on Thanksgiving in debate, and you ought to have heard Britt speak! He just put the 'rousements' on and naturally tore things up. We didn't know he was so good."[56]

According to *The Wake Forest Student*, the debaters:

>...rendered a most crushing defeat of Mercer University for the second time in succession ...the boys all seemed confident and hung around the telegraph office to hear some message to bring their fondest hopes into realization. Finally, a message came at early dawn, 'we came, we saw, we conquered. easy victory—O. J. Sikes.'"

The Wake Forest men celebrated, but when the debaters returned home, the real celebration began. "They were met at the depot by every man, woman, and child in town. They were placed in the "Old Gold and Black" wagon with Dr. Poteat... went through town and up to the Chapel. The band led the wagon while the entire student body marched in classes with their banners.

"Oscar Sikes gave his version of the battle. he told of how the debaters were cheered by seeing a Wake Forest flag waved in the gallery by Angel, son of Dr. White, pastor of one of the Macon churches, and an honored son of the college.

Two people who went on the trip gave speeches describing the experience. "Mr. William D. Upshaw, editor of *The Golden Age*

---

[55] *Bulletin of Wake Forest College* 1906, page 79-80.
[56] *Howler*, 1907, page 63.

and a former Mercer student, was introduced by Dr. Poteat following his conciliatory message. Mr. Upshaw was received amid great enthusiasm. his first sentence, 'Fellow students, I am not much of a speaker, I came from Mercer,' caught the crowd." Mercer had won eleven straight debates, then lost the next two to Wake.

The evening ended with Mr. Upshaw and his two nieces placed in "the chariot and rapidly carried over the campus into the depot, where Mr. Upshaw gave the boys a few pieces of advice and a stirring farewell speech. This ended the grandest celebration of victory ever seen at Wake Forest."[57]

1908 – THIRD MERCER DEBATE – ATLANTA

Atlanta was selected as neutral ground after Wake twice prevailed over the previously undefeated Mercer team. *The Atlanta Constitution* told of the Mercer campus preparations:

The manifestation of enthusiasm at Mercer University this morning over the prospects of winning in a debate against Wake Forest in Atlanta Monday evening was of an unusually strong character, the entire college body, both students and faculty, participating. Songs, yells, and all kinds of organized backing for the students who will represent Mercer already await the beginning of the trip. Early Monday morning, more than 100 Mercer students will move out from the Mercer campus ...to the Grand Opera House... with probably the strongest following ever backing debaters from the Baptist institution."[58]

The enthusiasm was not limited to the Mercer campus. One of the Wake debaters was fully invested in the debate. He bragged, "I have a patent on my style of speaking, and there is more pull in my voice

---

[57] *The Wake Forest Student*, January 1907, Vol. 26, No. 5, page 420, 421.

[58] *The Atlanta Constitution*, April 18, 1908, page 11. By this juncture, the mechanics had been set up. Central to these early debates was the selection of the judges, which was, in part, a hangover from the Trinity experience. The Wake Forest committee "placed in the hands of its like committee of Mercer, the names of 15 men who will be eligible to act as judges of the debate. Six of these men are to be selected by the Mercurians. Then three of these are chosen by our committee."; *The Wake Forest Student*, Vol. 27, No. 8, April 1908, page 660.

than in the arms of a half-dozen men... I Am going to Atlanta with the debaters.[59]

The papers even covered the team's Atlanta departure. "Debaters Fred F. Brown, Fred T. Collins, and alternate Herman T. Stevens were off this evening for Atlanta, GA, where they go to represent Wake Forest in the Mercer-Wake Forest debate."[60] The president, W. L. Poteat ,accompanied the debaters along with Dr. J. W. Lynch, the College Bursar, E. B. Earnshaw, and Mr. J. L. Allen, about as distinguished a representation as possible for the college.[61]

Other "somebodies' in attendance merited individual announcements in the press. "Mr. I. Richard Rozier, Athletic Director and popular coach of the college ball team, with family, left yesterday for Atlanta. They will take in the Mercer-Wake Forest debate tonight in that city."[62]

The debate was so high-profile that the Macon newspaper commented, "A special car will carry up Mercer's delegation, who will use every energy in the debate."[63] Only one judge was agreed upon the day before the event: ex-Justice of the Supreme Court of Georgia John S Chandler.[64]

---

[59] *Howler,* 1908, page 39. Senior summary for Herman Stevens, an alternate for the Mercer debates.

[60] *The Farmer and Mechanic,* April 21, 1908, page 3.

[61] *The Farmer and Mechanic,* April 21, 1908, page 3.

[62] *The News & Observer,* April 21, 1908; One also had to transport the Wake Forest audience. "College Bursar E. B. Earnshaw, having communicated with Mr. C. H. Gattis of this Seaboard Railway, announced that for a number of not less than 150 students, the fare to Atlanta and return will be only $5.00 each as special rates for Wake Forest people to attend the debate on Easter Monday. The boys are elated over this generous proposition by the Seaboard Air Line." *The News & Observer* March 4, 1908; As one might expect, it was a little cheaper to train from Macon to Atlanta, a shorter distance. An ad in the *Macon Telegraph* offered a "$3.10 down trip Macon to Atlanta via Central of Georgia Railway on account of Mercer-Wake Forest debate. *The Macon Telegraph*, April 18, 1908, page 6.

[63] *The Macon Telegraph,* April 20, 1908, page 7; Mercer's post-debate enthusiasm was fully embraced: "The Tabernacle was crammed from bottom to top. Over 100 Mercer students had accompanied their representatives and the entire faculty of the institution was present, cheering as lustily as any of the boys. Besides these, the majority of the Cox college girls were there mingling their treble with the masculine base and with their eyes lighting the way for Mercer's victory. At the close of the contest, the Mercerians marched in a body to the Terminal station, yelling every foot of the way and flinging back a storm of echoing enthusiasms as their train pulled out for Macon." *The Atlanta Journal,* April 21, 1908, page 6.

[64] The accepted panel of judges included John S. Chandler, Ex-chief Justice of the NC Supreme Court, Prof. W. M. Stanton, and W. L. Lingle.

Mercer prevailed 3-0 before an audience that included "A delegation of Mercer students, a large part of the student body of Cox College,[65] a sprinkling of 'Wake Forest supporters.[66] The topic debated was *That the tendency toward the centralization of power in the federal government in the best interest of the republic.*[67]

1921-1928 — LATER MERCER DEBATES

The second 1921 intercollegiate debate "was the first meeting with Mercer in a number of years," the last Mercer debate was held in 1908, 13 years earlier.

Wake won one of the more unusual affirmative decisions while arguing for "closed shops," which required workers to join unions. This was a decidedly progressive position.

The returning Wake debaters applauded the "most cordial hospitality … the Mercer students stopped eating dinner together, and they yelled on their entrance into the mess hall, and just before the debate, there was a Wake yell and then for the home team. in his opening comments Rufus Weaver, Mercer president and Wake Forest alumnus, "welcomed them heartedly."[68]

In the early 1920s, as societies became active again following WWI, Intercollegiate Debates were pivotal on campuses. Tryouts could feature scores of students. One Wake Forest "Hall of Fame" judging panel who witnessed the Mercer audition debates, including Dr. Needham Y. Gulley, Dean of The Law School, future historian G. W. Paschal, and Wake's sitting president, W. L. Poteat.

*_*_*_*_*_*_*

---

[65] Macon, GA., Women's College.

[66] *The Atlanta Constitution*, April 21, 1908, page 14.

[67] The Atlanta papers celebrated the Mercer win. "The winners were championed by Chas. H. Garrett of Macon, and Ralph E. Bailey, of Savannah. Though always distinguished as debaters, both these speakers broke their brightest records Monday night and planted for their college one of the most substantial and luminous victories she had ever won. On the decision of the judges being announced the whole big audience rose and cheered itself hoarse." *The Atlantic Constitution*, April 21, 1908, page 6.

[68] *Old Gold and Black*, April 29, 1921, page 1.

Celebrations Reign – Randolph-Macon
(1908-1909, 1915, 1917-1918, 1921, 1927)

We often let our men debate.
Some school of speaking men.
The other speakers find their mate.
Our fellows always win.

1908 *Howler* – FROM JUNIOR CLASS POEM

1908 – AN OPENING

Four students, one selected for each society at Randolph-Macon and
Wake, met in the tiny border village of Weldon, NC, to finalize the upcoming Thanksgiving match.[69] "At last, after long and tedious searches
in various climes, we have found an institution willing to stand against
us in debate. Randolph-Macon has challenged us, and our representatives
shall meet here at Raleigh on Thanksgiving evening, where the Virginians
are expected to bravely oppose the flashes of oratory and peals of logic
that shall be hurled upon them by the Wake Forest debaters."

One Richmond newspaper exclaimed, "Wake Forest college now
stands as conqueror of practically the entire south, having met and defeated, Trinity college, Richmond college, Furman University and Mercer
University, and is now thirsting for Randolph-Macon's scalp."[70]

The rules were set, and the "faculty were forbade to provide the debaters any aid.[71] The community, as in earlier years, accommodated, including changing church schedules. The Tabernacle Baptist Church posted
in local newspapers that their services will be "The evening service will
be promptly at 7 o'clock and end at eight. thus, giving the opportunity
of attending the Wake Forest debate."[72]

---

[69] *The Charlotte Observer*, September 28, 1908, page 8.

[70] *The Times Dispatch* (Richmond), September 24, 1908, page 9.

[71] *The Evening Chronicle* (Charlotte, NC), October 13, 1909, the major public institutions were noticeably absent from the list of the conquered.

[72] *The News & Observer*, November 26, 1908.

1909 – RANDOLPH MACON – A
CELEBRATION LIKE NO OTHER

In the early days of intercollegiate debate, upon the train's return, an announcement of victory, often foreshadowed via a telegraph message, unleashed a college-wide celebration. A particularly iconic tribute was well preserved in Wake folklore, in part because one of the participants, later a Wake English faculty member, could recount with authority the happenings.

Henry Broadus Jones, B. A.

WINGATE, N. C.

"With temper calm and mild,
And words of softened tone,
He overthrows his neighbor's cause
And justifies his own."

Member of Track Team, '07, '10; Associate Editor of Weekly; Member of College Senate, '09-'10; First Debater, '10; Speaker in Wake Forest-Randolph-Macon Debate, '09; Speaker in Wake Forest-Davidson Debate, '10.

Height, 5 ft. 8 ins.; weight, 145 lbs.; age, 23 years.

It has been said since Clay, Webster and Grady passed from the stage, that the day of oratory and debate is passed. Not so. It has been said since Calhoun crossed the "Bar" that the star of logic has never since shown so brightly. Not true. For Wake Forest College has a young logician, who promises to be a power in the field of logic and debate. His manner of arriving at conclusions is unsurpassed, and his arguments remain unbroken. He is a diligent student, and in whatever pertains to the glory and honor of his college, he is always enthusiastic. He has been in two intercollegiate debates, and has won laurel wreaths of honor for himself and his Alma Mater. In almost every phase of college life, he lends a helping hand; and when he faces life's battles, we predict for him a successful career.

The 1909 Randolph-Macon, Ashland, Va., debate was perhaps unassuming, given the evening's topic which considered, *The best source for obtaining government revenues, internal taxation, or custom duties.* Yet upon the train's return, the debate details were set aside. An unbridled celebration ensued, which in many ways came to symbolize the campus receptions that preceded and followed. The participating debaters were E. N. Johnson (Phi), H. B. Jones (Eu) and alternate, D. B. Carrick (Eu).

In the early *Howlers,* each class recorded its history. The seniors of 1910 recalled the joy of another holiday debate victory. "We look back with joy to Thanksgiving night, and we can still hear the old college bell ringing out, 'another victory, won,' and the music of the pans as the howling mob woke up the town. Some of the speeches that certain members of the faculty, clad in scanty apparel, made when called from their slumbers still linger. Particularly do we remember Professor Carlyle's speech in rhyme, as is his wont, which closed with this inspired couplet:

> "While the moon is shining bright,
> Now I bid you all good night."[73]

REV. J. W. LYNCH, M.A., D.D.
College Chaplain

A seminal poem that appeared in the 1909 yearbook, *The Howler*, has endured through the years. It was penned by the College Chaplain, Rev. James W. Lynch, to honor Wake Forest debaters. Indeed, some spoken form of the ditty graced many later entertainments.

The Wake Forest Debater

* * *

(By DR. J. W. LYNCH[74])

---

[73] *Howler*, Vol. 8, 1910, page 47.

[74] The 1930 *Howler* was dedicated to James W. Lynch: "Scholarly, Cultured, Orator, Peer Among Ministers, Fearless, Unexcelled Teacher, Christian Gentleman. For 30 years a servant Of Wake Forest College as Pastor, Chaplain, Trustee, Confidential Financial Agent, Teacher."

Lynch offered a thoughtful statement acknowledging the special honor, a lyrical description of Wake Forest. "Brothers in the great outline country, I find few persons who know exactly where Wake Forest is, but I meet with many who know where her sons are, the college's known by her fruits she has 'spheres of influence' in every field of endeavor and her far-flung battle lines are holding their own. I voiced their greetings and grateful affection for Alma Mater. Her lap is not filled with gold. Some of her garments are threadbare with time and toil and are not in the fashion of the day. Her hands are still hard from the poverty of lean years, but they are open and outstretched in democratic hospitality for rich and poor alike. She is not unduly proud of her wealthy sons, nor is she ashamed. She still lives in the old homestead remote from the centers of congestion population and accumulated wealth. Her health stands by the road and she is the friend of man... The rich college will get

"His tongue is made of whiteleather,
    His words are shotted lead,
He lifts you like a downy feather,
    And stands you on your head.

"He speaks the ear off a frog,
    The hair from the 'possum's tail,
Routs the fleas off a mangey dog,
    Electrifies the pokey snail.

"He moves the cold to weep in rain,
    Or breaks an elephant's back,
He stops a Seaboard Air Line train,
    And speaks it off the track.

"Always He speaks the bark from forest trees,
    The feathers off a goose,
Breaks the spell of the Pleiades,
    And turns Orion loose.

Although hardly the only time passing trains deposited Wake debaters into the arms of a friendly flock, the return on the night of the victorious Randolph-Macon team dramatically parades the excitement and standing of debate in the early intercollegiate era. William Pate, an ambitious student with an ear to history, resurrected the event, guided by then-Professor Jones, one of the students who had stepped off the train into the whirlwind. Pate writes:

Take away automobiles, downtown movies, the quick bus trip to Raleigh, fraternities, most of the other organizations on the campus; cut drastically the activities of the athletics at Wake Forest; take away these things and life would become nearly empty for the modern Wake Forest student.

---

richer, and State institutions will grow stronger; but Wake Forest is built deep as the heart can love and highest the soul can pray. Voicing the passionate feelings of her loyal sons and devoted friends, I fling to the world the challenge: *We shall live, we shall rise, we shall command.*"

But hardly more than 40 years ago these present-day advantages did not exist... Unless a student did catch the "shoo-fly" or hop a freight to Raleigh, probably about once a year, he found himself in a small, compact, homogenous community where everybody knew everybody else and days were quiet and peaceful. That is, the days were quiet and peaceful except one evening in 1909, as it was growing dark, one of the passenger trains which passed through Wake Forest regularly began to slow. Emitting steam and smoke, it stopped at the small station.

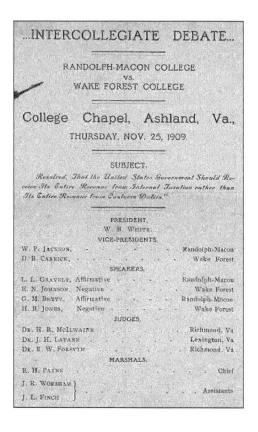

Such a rare occurrence usually excited the curiosity of the inhabitants anyway. But on this evening, there were more than just the curious onlookers; practically the whole town was there.

Luggage in hand, two young men left their seats and prepared to get off the train.... both knew why everyone was at the station. But they must have been a little stunned when a mass of clamoring people met them at the train's platform.

Jones and Johnson started to descend from the train, but their feet never touched the ground. Both young students were lifted in the air on the shoulders of husky athletes. Before them, all the way to Wingate Hall, a line of bonfires illuminated the night.

Cheers and shouts rent the night air as the two young men took a free ride to Wingate. Then the celebration in their honor began.

It was the custom in those days to celebrate victories by building a large bonfire, probably in front of Wingate... and have faculty members make speeches. ... many speeches ... made for the victory celebration last[ing] far into the night,"[75].

Jones recalled decades later the preceding year's 1908 match in Raleigh with Randolph-Macon in which Collins and Martin had participated. "Whenever the two debaters went ahead of their opponents, students in the hall would raise the chant "Collins and Martin, Collins and Martin," with all the fervor of a sports fan." [76]

Before the 1908 debate in Raleigh, President Poteat announced ... "that college work would be suspended Thursday, October 21, in order that the boys might attend the State Fair in Raleigh, "and the Randolph-Macon debate."[77]

A portion of the reception for the Randolph-Macon Thanksgiving debaters included reading a poem written by one of the ladies of the "Hill" (the newish poem).

> "What is the bell a-ringin for?" asked newish from his bed.
> "To Wake you up, to Wake you up," the other newish said.
> What makes it rings so loud, so loud?" asked newish from his bed;
> "It's for a celebration," the other newish said.
> For we've beaten Randolph Macon – you can hear the Wake Forest students shout:
> They've got a drum a-beatin' it an' runnin' all about;
> They're goin' to wake the faculty and make 'em speak, no doubt,
> For we have beaten Randolph Macon in Virginia."
>
> "What makes the bonfire burned so bright?" asked newish from his bed.
> "They wanted to tell the hurricane," The other newish said.

[75] Pate, W. (1955). Changing Times: Debaters won, rode athletes' shoulders in 1909. *Old Gold and Black*, February 21, page 2. "That evening, the college bell began to toll, and students with a wagon searched out Prof. James L. Lake, Physics, and placed him in a chair and in the wagon. From his mobile platform, Prof. Lake made the appropriate speech to happy students. This celebration lasted until midnight.

[76] William Pate, W., Changing Times: Debaters won, rode athletes' shoulders in 1909. *Old Gold and Black*, February 21, 1955, page 2.

[77] *The Evening Chronicle* (Raleigh), Oct 13, 1909, page 1.

"What makes 'em yell and holler so?" asked newish from his bed.

"Because they just can't help it," the other said.

"For we've beaten Randolph Macon, and they're marching all around,

To wake the folks, the dreaming folks, to hear the joyful sound.

There won't be much sleep tonight, because the boys have found.

That we've beaten Randolph Macon in Virginia

"How did we beat them in debate?" asked newish from his bed.

"Why, Johnson spoke and Jones he spoke, that's how it was," he said.

And have we ever beat them before? asked newish from his bed.

"Why, yes, it is a habit with Wake Forest boys," he said.

"We have beaten Randolph Macon, and this 'twas done.

We sent our boys to Ashland town and waited for the fun;

We knew that we would beat 'em and now you see we've won,

We've beaten Randolph-Macon in Virginia!"

"For we've beaten Randolph Macon, and we brought the old cup home,

And we're going on debating for all the years to come,

We have beaten all the colleges from Forest Hill to Rome,

We've have beaten Randolph Macon in Virginia."[78]

By defeating Randolph-Macon, one newspaper remarked, "Wake Forest College holds the enviable distinction of having won 11 out of 15 debates. Much attention is given to debating ... with the result that the young man preparing for the ministry are graduated better equipped, both rhetorically and mentally."[79]

1915-1927 — LATER RANDOLPH-MACON DEBATES

After a six-year hiatus, Wake again debated Randolph-Macon in 1915. These debates garnered attention, but less so, sharing attention with

---

[78] *The Wake Forest Student*, Vol. 29, December 1909, page 250-251.

[79] *The Siler City Grit*, December 1, 1909, page 2.

other major debates in the same calendar year.

Particular debaters, on occasion, drew media attention. One newspaper assessing the 1917 debate could not resist elevating to central prominence one of the Randolph-Macon debaters, a North Carolina native. They inscribed, "In the main Wake Forest debaters showed closer preparation in their argument, greater ease and delivery, and finer appreciation of the subject. But Mr. H. Bond, the closing speaker for Randolph-Macon, demonstrated splendid platform ability. Mr. Bond is

1919-1920 Debate Council

the son of Judge Bond of the North Carolina Superior Court Bench."[80]

The campus celebrations surrounding Intercollegiate Debates continued but, with the passage of time, failed to match the 1909 buckboard celebration. Some, like 1919, for example, were not without thrills: "Much excitement was caused on the night of the Randolph-Macon debate when the 'movies' caught fire. it looked like it might be the whole business part of the town would be burned up, but quick work by the bucket brigade prevents the spread of the fire.... for what could we do without the 'movies?'"[81]

*_*_*_*_*_*

---

[80] *The News & Observer*, April 10, 1917, page 1. Wake's Randolph-Macon team was its second, as the first team is off at the Baptist Southern Convention debating Baylor.

[81] *The Wake Forest Student*, 1919, page 202.

Provincial Grudge Match – Davidson
(1909-1911, 1913-1914, 1917, 1921-1922, 1924-1925, 1930)

1909 FIRST DAVIDSON DEBATE – GREENSBORO

"The preliminary contestants seemed to go into a do-or-die spirit," with ten gentlemen competing to be selected for the upcoming Easter debate with Davidson. Dr. C. E. Brewer, who presided over the preliminary run throughs, remarked at the conclusion of the exercise, "Wake Forest could put out five teams of none of which she would need to be ashamed."[82] The students forewarned, "We know the Presbyterians are not to be trifled with, but we do not expect to trifle."[83]

The first Greensboro debate was Davidson's first intercollegiate series.[84]

The year 1909 was an impactful one for the Wake Forest Debate Council. Having just concluded the Randolph-Macon series,[85] Wake initiated a three-year series with Davidson College. The natural rivalry between schools of similar cultures increased confidence, and the Davidson deal was inked, with debates set for Greensboro, Winston-Salem, and Raleigh.

Even the smallest details about the upcoming debates provided fodder for state newspapers. *The News & Observer* found it newsworthy to record that Mr. Charles Bell, manager of the Wake Forest debating team, visited Greensboro yesterday, attending to details of the Wake Forest-Davidson debate.[86] When the student selection committee reported the topic to be debated, that too earned multiple news clips[87].

Whenever possible, the papers recorded local celebrities' connections with the debates. The *Monroe County Record* dutifully reminded readers that, "Rev. R. H. Hipps attended the Wake Forest Davidson debate Greensboro... where his son Andy Hipps was one of the debaters."[88]

---

[82] *The Wake Forest Student,* April 1911, page 689.

[83] *The Wake Forest Student,* April 1911, page 670-671.

[84] *Winston-Salem Journal,* February 2, 1909, page 1.

[85] The Council also managed a second debate on Easter with Baylor University, which was definitely more weighty, but the Davidson series appeared to capture more of the imagination.

[86] *The News & Observer,* April 11, 1909, page 16.

[87] *The Charlotte News,* February 3, 1909, page 6.

[88] *Madison County Record,* April 16, 1909, page 5. Everyone who was "official" at the debate was newsworthy. The *North Carolinian,* November 26, 1908, page 5,

The *News-Record* not only singled out the "local boy does well" story but also reprinted in full *only his* speeches from the Davidson debate.[89]

Wake won the first Davidson debate, spawning many favorable headlines from the state's newspapers, especially those in the Piedmont region. For example, *The Charlotte Observer* headline boasted:

Wake Forest Winner
Presbyterians OUT–TALKED

A more modest headline adorned the *Greensboro Patriot*:

College Boys Debate
Wake Forest and Davidson Discuss Subsidy For Merchant Marine-Decision in Favor of The Baptists.

The *Greensboro Patriot* registered:

Wake Forest had the negative side of the question and while the Davidson boys made splendid arguments, the decision of the judges was not a surprise. The winning team received the handsome loving cup offered by the Greensboro Chamber of Commerce as a prize.[90]

All the speakers being greeted by the enthusiastic applause... Perhaps the Wake Forest rooters were a little more vociferous.

A special train was run from Davidson to bring, in addition

---

observed, "R. M. Proctor, son of Mr. I. M. Proctor, who is a senior at Randall Macon (Sic), will act as timekeeper for that institution."

[89] *The News-Record* (Marshall, NC), April 23, 1909, page 5.

[90] The Chamber of Commerce of Greensboro presented the cup. "Silver with gold lining... the value of the cup is $75." *The Raleigh Times*, April 14, 1909, page 2.

to the students, many friends of the college from Charlotte and other points in that section.[91]

Reflecting the period's traditions, the *Raleigh Time*s described the campus excitement that greeted the debaters upon their triumphant return. These triumphal narratives are somewhat repetitive, yet each touches a unique moment of pride and offers a distinctive peek into the campus culture. Each reported here had its own peculiarities. What other "victory story" ends with J. B. Lynch's words, *"I received the cup brought by representatives, the first line of the apostolic succession?"*

The debaters W. H. Hipps and F. T. Collins, and O. W Henderson, alternate, returned yesterday afternoon on the 5:45 and were given a miniature Roman triumph. They were carried from the station to Memorial Hall in chairs elaborately decorated with old gold and black, escorted by the entire student body.

In Memorial Hall enthusiasm ran high. Dr. C. Brewer, who presented the speakers... W. H. Hipps and F. T. Collins made appropriate speeches, presenting loving cup to the college, the principal thought being, "take it, keep it, and go on to victory."

Dr. J. B. Lynch made the speech of acceptance... "Some of you fellows wouldn't let me sleep much last night, but I got up singing this morning." ... accepting the cup, he said: "On behalf of the college, the two literary societies, the community and the alumni, I received the cup brought by representatives, the first line of the apostolic succession."[92]

1910 SECOND DAVIDSON DEBATE – GREENSBORO

Perhaps with some inclination toward the "home" college, *The News & Observer* offered its headline: **DAVIDSON COLLEGE WINS THE DEBATE—Decision Against Wake Forest A Surprise.**[93]

The second debate, also an Easter Sunday affair, was again held in the "neutral" city of Greensboro. The resolution read *That the legislative*

[91] *The Greensboro Patriot*, April 14, 1909, page 1.

[92] *The Raleigh Time*s, April 14, 1909, page 1.

[93] *The News & Observer*, March 29, 1910, page 3.

initiative and referendum should be introduced in our State government.[94] The Affirmative Wake debaters were J. B. Eller and H. B. Jones, of Randolph-Macon fame.

The Charlotte Observer, with a subtle feel for their "home" school, captured the atmospherics, awash with the compensatory debate triumph after an afternoon baseball 7 to 4 beating by Guilford College:[95]

> Fired on by crushing defeat administered its college in the athletic event of an eventful Easter Monday in Greensboro," the Davidson partisans plunged into the second Davidson-Wake Forest debate. Even before the judge's announcement, "the sting of defeat lingered in the breasts of the faithful Davidson rooters had been given a soothing panacea, for it was realized that defeat, if such much come, would not be the result of 'errors of judgment' as was charged in the afternoon."
>
> This feeling of consolation was soon turned to joy... In the great victory last night these little trifles were forgotten and the demonstration that followed was worthy of the eloquent and brilliant efforts of the four speakers, for in the rush for the speakers to offer congratulations the vanquished as well as the victors were overwhelmed.[96]

Having wrested the silver cup from their Baptist neighbors, the next year's showdown in the series was greeted with marked eagerness. One headline read **THE "RUBBER" A YEAR HENCE.**[97]

---

[94] "Each team has fifty minutes at its disposal to use as it saw fit, provided no speaker shall use more than thirty-five minutes nor either side use more than fifteen minutes in rejoinder." *The Greensboro Record*, March 28, 1910, page 5.

[95] *News and Record* (Greensboro), March 29, 1910, page 5. "In the presence of 1,800 enthusiastic supporters of the opposing colleges."

[96] *The News & Record*, March 29, 1910, pages 1, 3. The same source provides an extended recounting of the debate speeches. In a city without debate societies, two groups with the schools' home churches, the Philathea classes of the First Baptist and First Presbyterian Churches, tendered the student reception. *The Greensboro Record*, March 28, 1910, page 5.

[97] *The Charlotte Observer*, March 29, 1910, page 1.

1911 THIRD DAVIDSON DEBATE — RALEIGH

Hours before, the Raleigh opera house was filled, with Davidson people taking the right aisles and Wake Forest taking the left. The Wake Forest men entered the hall in a body just before the curtain was raised, and the seated Davidsonians sounded the signal of their coming in a ringing, complimentary yell. The audience was entertained by chants and songs ricocheting around the hall.

1911 Davidson Debate Winners
J B. Eller, R. S. Pruette, & S. C. Hilliard

A hushed expectation filled the room just before the curtain was raised at 8:45. The students and townspeople had gathered to consider whether *The Panama Canal should be fortified.*[98] What ensued was described with an inflated newspaper flourish as "a brilliant example of oratory and debate... the Wake Forest team having the best of the argument throughout."[99]

The unhidden rivalry between Davidson and Wake Forest boosted the rivalry to a "fever pitch," as another newspaper labeled the contest.[100]

---

[98] *Greensboro Daily News*, April 18, 1911, page 1.

[99] *Winston-Salem Journal*, April 18, 1911, page 1.

[100] *Winston-Salem Journal*, April 18, 1911, page 1.

There was an undertone of mutterings from the time the last spirited rejoinder had finished until the sealed decision of the judges was revealed. While the debate president was opening the envelope, there was intense silence. As he concluded, "...the supporters of Wake Forest realized the meaning; there was an outburst that was long continued and unprecedented." Wake had just won the deciding third match of the hallowed Davidson series.

"The stage was filled instantly, the Speakers were hoisted aloft, the band was drowned out... Then students and alumni joined in singing, 'Oh, here's to Wake Forest,' and if they were a little off tune, nobody cared, for the Greensboro cup was ours— the Ark had returned to Zion."[101]

SIDNEY CECIL HILLIARD........ B. A., Phi
Wake County, North Carolina.
I speak with the tongues of men and of angels.
Age 26; weight 220; height 6 feet 1 inch.
This is the biggest man of the class. Of a widespread and towering physique and weighty intellect he towers far above his fellows. In short he is a mighty man. A keen student in affairs of state, possessed of a tongue that could convince Prof. Lanman that the moon was made of green cheese, he is a debater of parts. It is told that those Davidson debaters listened with fear and trembling to the mighty roaring of his voice at the Greensboro debate, and it is a matter of history that the judges stumbled over each other to hand him their decision, and that a half hour later a fair damsel in the audience delivered him her decision, also favorable. Wherefore he has waited on his diploma with ill-concealed impatience.
On the gridiron he has used his mighty brawn in the interest of his class while the multitude looked on in wonder and amaze.
He is a ministerial student and since his Sophomore year has held down with great effect the pastorate of divers churches. His success is so clearly assured that it is useless to waste words in prophecy.
Second Debater Anniversary, '10; Chief Marshal Commencement, '10; Class Football, '10; Wake Forest-Davidson Debater, '11; Chairman Debate Council, '11-'12; Anniversary Orator, '12; Speaker Carlyle Memorial Service, '11; Delegate to North Carolina Historical Society, '11; Wake Forest-Baylor Debater, '12.

The train ride home was especially festive. "The night train was jammed to the doors. Nobody complained of the discomfort, for everybody was happy. What mattered about the track meet? Who cared about baseball anyhow? For Wake Forest still holds her old record of never having lost a series of debates, and stands once more on her old pentacle of champion

---

[101] *The Wake Forest Student*, May 1911, page 803-804.

E. B. Cox, 1916, *Howler*

debater of the State of North Carolina."[102] As the *Biblical Recorder* abbreviated, "Rah! Rah! Wake Forest!"[103]

At the Wingate Memorial Hall tribute, Dr. George W. Paschal Master of Ceremonies, Dr. F. N. Y. Gulley said there should be great rejoicing... but it brought us nearer the time that Wake Forest would lose a series for it is impossible to win always."[104]

A major player of the Intercollegiate Era was Sidney Hilliard, illustrative of an era, the hero of the Davidson and Baylor debates, and the costar at several top speaking events.[105] His yearbook summary gives a sense of the commemorative acclaim which greeted celebrity debaters.

---

[102] *The Wake Forest Student*, May 1911, page 804.

[103] In another reference, *The Biblical Recorder*, 1911, added, "the Davidson debaters did well indeed, and the Wake Forest victory was won only by fine forensic ability and debating skill of a high order."

[104] *The Charlotte Observer*, April 24, 1911, page 3; "Dr. Poteat had read before the student body the morning of the debate an invitation from the young ladies of the Philathea classes of the Presbyterian and Baptist churches of Greensboro requesting the representatives from Davidson and Wake Forest to be present at a reception immediately after the debate in the Smith Memorial Building, which invitation was gladly accepted." *Greensboro Daily News*, April 16, 1911, page 1.

[105] As with the dangers of the times, eight years after graduation, Hilliard became a victim of the Spanish Flu epidemic, "He was cut down in the flower of his manhood, a young man of striking personality and unusual vigor." He died at his home in Scotland Neck on Friday night, February 2, 1912. Hilliard graduated from Wake "with the degree of B.A. in 1882. He represented the Philomathesian Society in the Anniversary debate the year of his graduation. From 1883 to 1888, he was Principal of the Vine Hill Academy of Scotland Neck, and from 1887 to within three years of his decease, he was editor of *The Democrat* (Scotland Neck, NC). In 1887, he was licensed to practice law... He was unusual among the alumni, gifted as a public speaker, and was recognized everywhere as one of the leading men of Eastern North Carolina." *Bulletin of Wake Forest College*, 1912, page 157.

Others from the era evoked analogous luster, some more fleeting than others. A few years after Hilliard, a fairly non-descript debater was remembered in the 1916 Yearbook. Why young E. B. Cox is included here, as with Hilliard, and Murchison below, is to draw attention to the fervent and often powerful and moving language applied in this age of debater fame.

The *Howler* wrote, "What panorama could be more conducive to oratory than a bridge over a silent stream, all the stars stopped to gaze through the crisp midnight air... Lurking in every shadow? Here E. B. Cox set the air to vibrating, and he has kept it in motion ever since. Two years later the same aerial waves hurled all his opponents off their feet and gave him the Junior Debater's Medal by an easy margin."[106]

Later, in 1936, Law Senior, a debate leader whose name appears often in this volume, was revealed with an energy seldom seen today. The yearbook thundered in its Senior writeup for Claude Murchison. "When he peeps through his spectacles at you in a hot debate and balls up his big football fist and stalks up giant-like towards you, his voice sounds thrice as deep and his logic cuts keener than the ancient weapons of war. There is magic in it! You are mystified by his eloquence and imagine you hear Demosthenes by the seashore or Burke in Parliament."[107]

1913-1930 – DAVIDSON/WAKE RIVALRY RUNS ITS COURSE

Successive series with Davidson, 1913-1914, brought their own dissatisfactions. The 1913 loss to Davidson in Winston-Salem's Salem College Memorial Hall bothered more than a few.[108]

The comment section of the local paper printed an unsigned editorial. The author lectured Wake Forest, "Our friends at Wake Forest made a mistake to send their crack team against Baylor, and a raw lot against Davidson. We are told by a gentleman who was in Winston that neither team made a record of extraordinary brilliance, but that the Davidson boys literally 'mopped the earth' with the Wake Forest debaters. Perhaps

---

[106] *Howler*, Vol. 14, 1916, page 38.

[107] *Howler*, Vol. 9, 1911, page 40.

[108] Wake also lost the 1914 contest, 3-2. Had Wake tied the series, there would have been a third debate, but after winning two, Davidson possessed the winner's trophy. The Twin City paper said 2000 attended on Easter Sunday.

this little jolt will make Wake Forest somewhat more careful hereafter, and not undertake to do it all in one day. ... Wake Forest has established a great reputation as a training school for oratory. ... we hope there will never be another double-barreled debate while the world stands."[109]

The unidentified writer (who turns out to be Rev. Livingston Johnson) was answered in follow-up correspondence. Blasting away, using yesteryear's "social media," the then-powerful letter-to-the-editor, the columnist chides Johnson:

"Well, 'the blockade preacher' as you newspaperman call him, wrote that the 'glory of Wake Forest has departed,' when our boys lost a Davidson-Wake Forest debate. I couldn't see it that way. We have been debating everyone that would enter the talking match with us, and this is the first series that we have ever lost. If you heard Wake Forest and Baylor last year in the auditorium, you saw our boys were strong enough to have some glory yet, as they say, our boys 'wiped up the earth' with Baylor.

Now I didn't like what Charity and Children said about the debate that we lost. It was not a walk over. Two of the five judges voted with us. They were not Baptists and had no Wake Forest predilections. I don't know the religious faith of the others.

A divided court went against us and I don't feel that we ought to be humiliated.... I think Wake Forest has every reason to be proud."[110]

Complaints emanated from the student chorus as well. The *Wake Forest Student* noted that the debaters moaned about the debate with Davidson because they claimed Davidson shifted their advocacy several times. first, they didn't advocate a plan. Then, they advocated twenty or more.

Davidson's second speaker said: "All right, you want us to propose a method. He then proposed some fifteen to twenty or various methods, naming them so rapidly that as some said, '40 Philadelphia lawyers couldn't have taken them down. He then insisted the negative must refute them all to prove the present best of all methods."

---

[109] *Winston-Salem Journal*, April 6, 1913, page 12.
[110] *The News & Observer*, May 3, 1914, page 4.

When our debaters argued that Davidson had to advocate one plan, Davidson replied in their last speech with one plan, which, of course, we could not respond to."[111] Similar strategies featuring compound plans populated theory debates until nearly a century later (and perhaps even today).

The 1914 topic was: *That all candidates for elective offices, in North Carolina, should be nominated by a direct primary, modeled after the Wisconsin plan, instead of the convention system.* Not a debate to which one might expect students or townspersons to flock.[112] The *Winston-Salem Journal,* however, called for citizens to attend the debate, noting that the subject's importance to the community was compelling.

1916, *Howler*

The "legalized primary," they argued, was more important than academics or even the victory of one team over the other. They remind citizens "that the Democrats in session at Raleigh last Wednesday passed a resolution that next General Assembly, to enact primary law.... The method of nominating representatives of the people is of vital concern to every citizen.

The debate Monday night will be the most intelligent discussion on a primary that will be held in North Carolina this year. Davison debaters might know more reasons for legalized primary and know more about the history's primary duty than members of the next

---

[111] Jay B. Hubbell, The Open Door: The Davidson Debate, *The Wake Forest Student,* May, Vol. 32, No. 8, 1913, 679-680.

[112] The Davidson students were offered a special train at $1.50 round trip. They also saw the "Winston-Salem Baseball team, the "Twins." *The Davidsonian,* April 8, 1914, page 1.

General Assembly will know. Wake Forest debaters know more objections to the primary than can be advanced by any member of the next General Assembly. These four young men have lived the primary for the last four weeks; they have thought and talked about it during their waking hours and have, no doubt, dreamed of that night. Representatives from both colleges were at the Democratic meeting in Raleigh last week – the Davidson men to find new reasons for the primary and the Wake Forest men to pick holes in the reasons advanced... This debate ought to appeal... to every citizen who wants to be further enlightened... Our people ought to encourage such debates as we are to have Monday night by greeting these young men from Wake Forest and Davidson with a packed house.[113]

The respective Chambers of Commerce praised the Wake/Davidson debates as important community attractions, Greensboro saying: "As for the power of intercollegiate debate to draw, it is only necessary to recall the attendance at the Carolina-Washington and Lee debate several years ago, and the three-contest slate between Wake Forest and Davidson. It was a very noticeable feature of the Davidson-Wake Forest debates that the college boys came in greater numbers and with greater enthusiasm for these events than for the baseball games. It is unreasonable to believe that from these contests, a desire was created in some boys to live in Greensboro."[114]

The 1921 Davidson debate illustrates how National propositions dominated the contested topics in the 1920s and '30s. The Friday evening topic asked whether *The U.S. should cancel loans and war debts from World War I allies*. Perhaps in a retrenchment mode, Wake, on the negative, argued that the US "had performed her full share in the winning of the war and that the victorious nations had received sufficient indemnities from the central powers to make cancellation unnecessary... 'They made the fur fly'[115]... We did our part, and we expect to be compensated." [116]

---

[113] *Winston-Salem Journal*, April 12, 1914, page 12.

[114] *Greensboro Daily News*- November 1914; Dr. H. E. Rondthaler and the Winston-Salem Board of Trade now donated the trophy cup. *Greensboro Daily News*, November 1914.

[115] *Old Gold and Black*, April 22, 1921, page 2.

[116] *Old Gold and Black*, April 22, 1921, page 1.

Late in the intercollegiate period, an account of a 1929 loss to David-son discloses underlying reasons that the era was about to culminate. The *Old Gold and Black* grumbled: "This debate proved to be a success in every way except the attendance. The crowd was almost as large as usual, but far from what it should have been… The majority of the student body no doubt missed this debate willfully."[117]

--*-*-*-*

The "Big Time" – Baylor
(1912-1914, 1917-1921, 1923, 1925-1927, 1932)

Difficulty scheduling debates remained, so much so that there was con-siderable enthusiasm, institutionally and among debaters, with the an-nouncement of the debate series with Baylor University. The "Debate Council had… at last found an institution without cold feet, and we think it is a foe worthy of our best steel. Baylor University of Waco, Texas, looms large on the horizon. Wake Forest must meet her at Waco next Easter. Baylor is a large institution of some seven or 800 students. It would mean something for Wake Forest to take a cup from them."[118]

Newspaper interest in the Baylor debates was surprisingly sparse. It seems that the Easter Sunday date, shared with a Davidson debate, con-sumed much of the oxygen in the state press.

1912 – FIRST BAYLOR DEBATE – WACO

The debater representing Baylor and Wake was set to engage the timely topic—*The merits and demerits of the initiative, referendum, and recall*—in Baylor's Carroll Chapel.[119] Neither school had lost a debating series.

Baylor, not Wake, won the first debate. The next morning, the *Waco Morning News* observed, the debate"… was pitched and character of argument employed was credible, rendering the discussion the subject

---

[117] *Old Gold and Black,* March 16, 1929, page 1.

[118] *The Wake Forest Student*, Vol. 31, No. 4, January 1912, page 340-341.

[119] *Waco Morning News*, April 7, 1912, page 2.

highly enjoyable to the large audience that attended. Plenty of... pep, vim, and college spirit was on every hand."[120] Wake, having few in attendance, was cheered before the banquet repeatedly by the Baylor audience.

Following the decision in Waco, the throng rushed for the college bell. After that, [the crowd] formed a line and marched in a parade downtown. During this parade, the snake dance and other college stunts were performed before the crowd entered the cafe for a banquet.[121]

Given the significance of the Waco debate, an accounting of Wake's disappointment appeared inevitable. "Said to be the first report received from the Wake Forest-Baylor debate, from Mr. E. V. Ferguson to a friend in Wake Forest, 'we have met the enemy, and we are his'n.' The old bell didn't ring; we waited for particulars. Our forlorn hope came back raging for a second chance on neutral ground with equal backing."[122]

Another disappointed student wrote in defense of the home team, "While Wake Forest is 'up in the air' over her baseball victories, the debating banner is hanging at half-mast. It was a bitter unexpected pill that Wake Forest gulped down on Easter Monday night when the news came from Waco, Texas, that our debating team had gone down ... the loss of the victory, however, is due to no fault of our team, for it is one of the strongest that has been set out in years, and the college would not hesitate to send the same team against any college... Next year in Raleigh, an audience of thousands [will] see Baylor swept entirely off her feet."[123]

The Baylor community was magnanimous in victory and almost apologetic, at least as expressed in an extracted quotation from a Waco paper, widely reported in North Carolina papers. *The News and Observer,* for example, wanted readers to know the press of Waco had the following to say:

---

[120] *Waco Morning News*, April 9, 1912, page 4. "During the interim between the close of the debating and announcement of the decision, the Wake Forest debaters were called upon for impromptu speeches and express their appreciation for the manner in which they have been received here and of the character of the debate." A limited recounting of the arguments in the debate can be found in the Waco paper.

[121] *Waco Morning News*, April 9, 1912, page 4.

[122] *The Wake Forest Student*, 1912, page 768.; Col. Richard Wynne, Superintendent of the Confederate home (Waco); Mr. Sidney G Samuels, a prominent lawyer of Fort Worth, and Mr. H. B. Terrell, State Sen., the judges who rendered a decision in favor of the Baylor debaters.

[123] *The Wake Forest Student*, 1911, page 759.

While the Baylor men won the unanimous decision last night, it was rather attributed to the fact that her representatives had the more favorable side of the question and in the minds of the judges than to any superior qualifications on the part of the men themselves. In fact, the visitors were more experienced speakers, more polished orators and more at home on the stage, and they put up a character of debate that was forcible and enlightening. The Baylor men were much younger, but no less enthusiastic, though not quite possessing that confidence that mark their opponents from the Tar Heel state.[124]

BROWN
PRUETTE
PRITCHARD ALT.
WAKE - BAYLOR DEBATERS

---

[124] *The News & Observer*, April 18, 1912, page 1. The quotation is taken from the *Times-Herald*, Waco, TX.

1913 – SECOND BAYLOR DEBATE" – RALEIGH

Wake Forest College will meet Baylon (Sic)[125] University... in the second debate... on Easter Monday. "The nearing of time for this great intercollegiate debate makes glad the hearts of 400 Wake Forest students, 25 Wake Forest professors and thousands of college alumni. While Wake Forest has in past years never been overly successful in athletic events, it has won a reputation for debating."[126]

The question read: *That the United States Senators should be elected by direct vote of the people*, with Wake defending the negative. "The crowd must have been 2000, all of Wake Forest mind."[127].

In a sub-headline, *The News and Observer* revealed the debate's conclusion:

Baptist Topped off Successful Day by Downing Texans in Great Forensics Contest.

The following day, "The Wake Forest student body carried the winning Wake Forest-Baylor debaters and the baseball team from the depot to Memorial Hall... In the hall... shouts of triumph filled the air."[128]

"Mr. Orrick, who opened for Texas, somewhat demoralized the shining generalizations of the Tar Heels, but the victory was a duplicate of the baseball score, easily 4 to 2.[129] After the debate," "Their cup running over with the joy of two victories in a single day, paraded the [Raleigh] streets."[130]

In his second Baylor encounter, Wake rebuttalist Shaw Pruette closed in opposition to the direct election of senators. "Shaking his fist at the 'political iconoclasts,' he looked at the Baylorians and said,' you have

---

[125] In the excitement of the events, a "Special to *The News & Observer*," reprinted in *The Farmer and Mechanic*, March 25, 1913, page 5, the correspondent stated the opponent's name to be *Baylon* Univ., five times. The headline writer, fortunately, got it right.

[126] *The Farmer and Mechanic,* March 25, 1913, page 5.

[127] *The News & Observer*, March 25, 1913, page 3.

[128] *The Wake Forest Student*, Vol. 32, No. 8, May 1913, page 687.

[129] *The News & Observer*, March 25, 1913, page 3.

[130] *The News & Observer*, March 25, 1913, page 5.

called the senate the reactionary body. I'll tell you, your plan was considered in the original Constitutional Convention and, after deliberation, unanimously rejected. Our fathers built more wisely than they knew. Your plan is against American ideals, traditions and customs and those who advocate this change are themselves reactionaries."[131] Belligerence, more than reasoning, seemed to carry the day.

Amusing asides also occurred with the alternate debaters. "Each sent an alternate. J. M. Prichard came to sub for a North Carolina Baptist; if he died of stage fright, Mr. W. M. Harrell of Waco stood ready to go in for either of the others if any of the sweet girls in the gallery through a lasso over their heart of a visitor."

1914 — THIRD BAYLOR DEBATE — MACON, GA

The third and deciding debate of the series with Baylor University never happened. It received considerable newspaper coverage and was originally scheduled for Easter Sunday at a neutral site, Mercer University. Excitement radiated as the match approached.

Originally scheduled for April 14, the two schools would have to wait until May 1 for the debate. It was postponed in deference to a Furman-Mercer oratorical contest held on the Macon campus on that date.[132] Some newspapers predicted the Easter debate would feature the debates with Furman and Mercer as well as Baylor and Wake Forest. That arrangement was not sustained, and the "featured event" shifted to the May 1 alternative.

Anticipation continued to build. In late April, *The News and Observer* printed an extended column featuring Raleigh's favorite son, Carey Hunter. They remarked that at the time of the Mercer debate, the Wake sophomore had already "received an appointment to the position of assistant professor in the English department at Wake Forest" and was serving at the time of the debate [133]

One newspaper reported that the Wake debaters had passed through Raleigh on their way to Macon.[134] but were turned back somewhere on

---

[131] *The News & Observer*, March 25, 1913, page 5. The article provides a more reasoned and interesting rendition of the debate's arguments.

[132] *The News & Observer*, April 29, 1914, page 2.

[133] *The News & Observer*, April 29, 1914, page 2

[134] *The News & Observer*, April 29, 1914, page 10.

The 1914 debate with McCourey and Hunter was abandoned.
A telegram from President W. L. Poteat arrived at Baylor,
"debate canceled – Mumps epidemic at Wake."

their route "on account of the seizure of two of the Wake Forest team by mumps... The disease was epidemic in the college at the time.

An outbreak of mumps had ravaged the Wake community. The infirmary was crowded, and many students returned to their homes. In the township "a number of homes have been quarantined with a house full of students."[135]

At 7:30 A. M., Wednesday, April 29th, "the committee for Wake Forest delivered the following message to the Western Union Telegraph Company at Raleigh: 'Baylor Oratorical Association, Waco, Texas: debate must be postponed. two debators (Sic) have mumps.'" The team consisted of Mr. E. B. Cox, Mr. Carey J. Hunter, Jr., and Mr. J. C. McCourey, alternate.[136]

---

[135] *The News & Observer*, May 4, 1914, page 4.

[136] *Bulletin of Wake Forest College*, Vol. 9, No. 1, April 1915, page 168-169.

A Raleigh reporter added, "The worst came when the debating team, ready to meet Baylor University in the final and decisive battle series three, had to take their beds with swollen cheeks. That sounds funny, sometimes. It looks funny too, occasionally, but having the mumps is no joke."[137]

1917-1927 — LATER DEBATES WITH BAYLOR

The combination of World War I and a world pandemic (Spanish Flu) wreaked havoc on the scheduling of intercollegiate debates in 1918. Just before the turmoil, a new debate series was inked with Baylor in 1917. The first debate featured debaters J. B. Edwards and E. D. Banks, whose "trip carried them some 4000 miles before their return."[138] The important Easter Sunday debate with Baylor proceeded in Waco, Texas.[139] The telegram received read "Victory for Wake Forest."

At the opening of the academic year, in January 1918, the Debate Council, without its chairman due to illness, had scheduled only two late debates, one with Baylor. The expanding War moved the Council to announce, "Owing to the decrease in size of the student body, it is not deemed wise to have more than two debates scheduled."

The Debate Council also was undergoing "the misfortune of receiving resignations of its officers, who left College in response to the call of the National Government. "Under the leadership of the newly elected officers, Mr. M. T. Rankin, chairman, and Mr. H. I. Hester, secretary, the Council hopes soon to close the arrangements now being negotiated with other colleges concerning debates, and to make a definite announcement of the inter-collegiate debate program for the spring in the very near future."[140] Despite their hopefulness, no new series were introduced. The pandemic-year debates ensued because they were formerly contracted.

---

[137] *The News & Observer*, May 4, 1914, page 4.

[138] *The News and Record*, April 8, 1917, page 5.

[139] *The News & Observer*, April 8, 1917 (Sunday), page 13. A debate with Randolph-Macon occurred on the same day in Raleigh, considering whether *The United States should prohibit the manufacture and sale of intoxicating liquors. The Wilmington Morning Star* (April 13, 1917) crowed, "This double victory [Baylor and Randolph-Macon] scored last Monday evening on the forensic platform comes as a source of much gratification to the College and his supporters throughout the country." It was also the year of the first Colgate debate.

[140] *The Wake Forest Student*, January 1918, Vol. 37, page 232.

The war changed campus, as one observer wrote:

What Wake Forest lacked of being thoroughly Democratic was entirely done away with in the melting pot of the war. The spirit of good fellowship and equality was prevalent as never before... The mellow tones of the college bell gave way to the more commanding notes of the bugle.[141]

One campus reporter saw a benefit in upholding Wake's long-term claim of top-level speaking training: "Probably one lesson learned from military training was the advantage in life of being able to speak in public."[142]

Even with many debaters heading to Europe, the interest in being selected as an Intercollegiate debater remained sturdy. Serving as a headline intercollegiate debater was not an easygoing task. The open-round contest in 1918 found "about 15 candidates preparing for the preliminaries, which will be held on February 21 and 22 for the purpose of selecting three men for the Baylor team."[143]

While the student paper mourned the loss of several of her strongest debaters, there are still men in college, according to the Council, "with the ability to uphold the reputation that is been achieved on the forensic platform. In comparison with other colleges, who have likewise been weakened by war conditions, Wake Forest should be strong as ever."[144]

They asserted that, with the ability of the chosen debaters, "two victories are the natural expectation of all."[145] Wake's optimism nearly prevailed.

---

[141] Sketch of the S. A. T. C. at Wake Forest. [Student's Army Training Corps]. *The Wake Forest Student*, February 1919, Vol. 39, page 16.

[142] *The Wake Forest Student*, February 1919, page 71.

[143] *Old Gold and Black*, February 16, 1918, page 4: These tryouts were popular and rigorous. In the 1917 tryouts for the Baylor debates, the campus newspaper listed the names of 14 Eus and 11 Phis seeking to make the three-man team. Student debaters tried out for the affirmative or the negative side. Undoubtedly, there was a jockeying to select a panel that would give you the best shot.

[144] *Old Gold and Black*, February 16, 1918, page 4.; The "survivors committee" comprised H. A. Jones, Dr. G. W. Paschal, and Dr. W. L. Poteat, *Old Gold and Black*, March 2, 1918, page 1.

[145] "In the Baylor debate the negative side of the question ... will be argued by Messrs. Britt and Feezer. Mr. Britt's ability is known to all members of the Philomathesian Society and to those who heard him in the Society Day Debates of 1917. Mr. Feezor is likewise known as a speaker of the entire student body. He was one of the winning

Baylor wins in Easter Debate
Creates Tie-In Three Debate Series With Wake Forest College
GOVERNOR BICKETT PRESIDES AT CONTEST
Decision Of Judges Is Two to One For Baylor Debaters[146]

Wake Forest, affirmative, spoke on the resolution: *The short ballot system of election should be adopted in the states.* At the contest's conclusion, the marshals collected the ballots and turned them over to Governor Bickett, the presiding officer... "It is now my duty to announce that by a two-to-one vote, the gentleman from North Carolina will now have the privilege and the pleasure of congratulating the gentleman from Texas." In time, the ruckus settled in the Meredith College auditorium, and all were congratulated.

INTERCOLLEGIATE DEBATERS

F. C. FEEZOR   L. J. BRITT

BAYLOR UNIVERSITY AT ATLANTA, GA.

D. T. HURLEY

Query- Negative

Resolved, That the Federal Government should settle industrial disputes by compulsory arbitration.

Tied one and one for the series, the 1919 showdown debate was slated for a less partisan venue: Atlanta, Georgia.

The third discussion centered on *Industrial disputes in compulsory arbitration.*[147] President Poteat and his wife attended the Atlanta debate at the First Baptist Church, held the night before the Southern Baptist convention. Wake won 2-1.[148]

Research herein could not find writeups about the "most important" 1919 tiebreaker. The same is true for the doubles match with Baylor the following year, in 1920. However, the Baylor debates and others held

---

team in the Anniversary Debate of this year, besides winning the freshman medal in the Euzelian Society." *Old Gold and Black*, March 1, 1919, page 1, 3.

[146] *The New & Observer*, April 2, 1918, page 7.

[147] *The Houston Post*, May 14, 1919, page 2.

[148] *The News & Observer*, May 22, 1919, page 5.

in late April were caught in the academic void between terms, with students scattered, the campus newspaper shuttered, and state newspapers without copy.

The 1920 Baylor debaters were particularly interesting, or we presume so, as two debates were held on the same night, one in Waco and one in Raleigh. Baylor won both 2-1, which dampened headlines. Attention also was diverted to the Northern breakthrough debate with Colgate a week later.

All the 1920 Intercollegiate meetups debated *That labor through representation of its own choice should have a voice in the management of industry.*[149] By this point, the practice was for schools to use the national debate topic for their intercollegiate contests, favoring both schools' familiarity with the topic yet contributing to staid fare, lacking audience appeal.

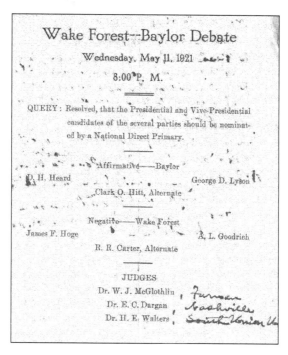

[149] For the 1920 debate, "Twenty-six men entered the preliminaries, twelve from the Phi Society and fourteen from the Eu. Also, "Yearby and Austin will compose the invading team to attack Baylor in Waco, Texas. and on the same night, Williford and Edwards will repel the invasion of the Baylor team in Wake Forest." *Old Gold and Black*, March 12, 1920, page 4.

The record with Baylor is quiet after the early 1920s, although debates still occurred regularly. The year 1925 was the exception; a "Great debate won unanimously," read the telegram from Memphis, Tennessee, where the team from Wake Forest College met the team from Baylor University before the Southern Baptist Convention."[150]

Increasingly, the major intercollegiate debates were not civic or campus affairs. For some years, Wake Forest and other Baptist institutions of the South, along with Colgate and Baylor, had staged intercollegiate debates before the Southern Baptist Convention's annual meeting each spring.

A later campus accounting exclaimed, "The last three of these [Southern Baptist Convention] have been won by Wake Forest. The three straight victories for Wake Forest are as follows: In 1923 William Jewel was met and defeated in Kansas City, in 1924, Mercer University was met and defeated in Atlanta, and in 1925 Baylor University was met and defeated in Memphis."[151] The article suggests the successes were in "no little part due to able coaching by Dr. G. W. Paschal," an early reference to formal coaching. His efforts were voluntary, in service to the students and the school's heritage.

Intercollegiate Debate Events grew... As They Faded Away (1926-1942)

1917-1939 – EXPANDED HORIZONS – COLGATE

The Phi selection for the intercollegiate debaters for the 1917 Colgate debate was intricate and competitive. The tryouts included inter-sectional debates on the topic: *That the United States should adopt a system of universal military service.* Those competing included W. H. Paschal, who failed to make the cut, just one of the prominent names in the room at the time. The judging panel included Wake's President, Dr. W. L. Poteat, along with two faculty members, B. M. Boyd and C. P. Herring.[152]

---

[150] *Old Gold and Black*, May 18, 1925, page 1. The Query was *That Congress should be empowered to override, by a two-thirds vote, decisions of the Supreme Court declaring acts of Congress unconstitutional.*

[151] *Old Gold and Black*, May 18, 1925, page 1.

[152] *Old Gold and Black*, January 27, 1917, page 1. Three months of controversy, agreements, and ultimately the tryout debates are described in what feels like a news

Preparing and anticipating hosting the "Northern Baptist College" dominated campus conversations. While hopes were high, the Deacons were to be disappointed. As one headline read:

NEW YORK DEBATERS WREST VICTORY FROM WAKE FOREST BY 2 TO 1 DECISION

Wake Forest Debaters Make Brilliant Defense of Admittedly Harder Side Colgate Speakers Evidence, Faultless Preparation and Win On High Merit

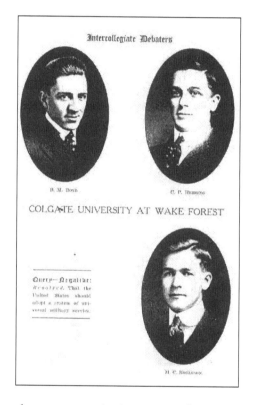

"From the time that Pres. C. E. Brewer of Methodist College, presiding, announced the first speaker until the victorious Colgate cheer from the throats of three Northern debaters two hours later greeted the decision of the judges, the audience in Wingate Memorial Hall was clouded with doubt, so strong was the argument that characterized the debate of each speaker."[153]

The student newspaper reported, "The New York State debaters scored heaviest when they "in reply to a repeated demand from Wake Forest for a definite plan," argued that was not incumbent on them..., a tactic, in various forms that would resonate through to the modern era.

Three years later, the second Colgate debate added to the folklore of always being the winners at the Southern Baptist Convention, held in

---

sequence in the *Wake Forest Student* 1916-1917.

[153] *Old Gold and Black*, March 10, 1917, page 1. This reporter could write more effectively.

1920 in Washington, D.C. The decision in favor of Wake Forest was unanimous.[154]

Entering World War I in 1917, debate schedules tended to shift away from a model of "winning is all" to ostensibly a more educational model. In January 1917, *Old Gold and Black* reported, "In the past, it has been Wake Forest's policy to try to win every debate entered. This year stress is going to be laid on the two debates held in this State, while the third is not as important in many respects, and it is probable that the third team will be sent to Waco, Texas."[155] The competitive model prevailed on the whole in the forthcoming seasons, but what winning meant had changed, no more buckboards and adoring crowds.

1925-1932 – THE CONFINES OF GEOGRAPHY END

In the mid-1920s, interest in intercollegiate debating neared its height, as measured by the number of one-on-one debates with other institutions. Longer tours—North, South, and West—with stops at three, four or more schools became commonplace.

DEBATE BY COLLEGES HERE.

Wake Forest and Colgate Meet in First Baptist Church Tonight.

An intercollegiate debate between Wake Forest College, N. C., and Colgate University will be held at the First Baptist Church tonight.

Washington alumni of Wake Forest College will give a dinner at St. Mark's Cafe tonight in honor of President William C. Poteet and the intercollegiate debaters.

---

[154] *The Independent* (Elizabeth City, NC), May 21, 1920, page 3. "The students from Wake Forest were F. C. Freezer, D. Banks and B. E. Morris. Colgate University is one of the very large Baptist schools of the north. Students were encouraged to contribute any materials they knew about the topic to help Wake's efforts.

[155] *Old Gold and Black,* January 20, 1917, page 1, 8.

The 1925 intercollegiate debating schedule introduced departures from the previous years. Several "intersectional debates with leading universities of the north, middle west, and far west" were added, ranging from Pittsburgh to Arizona. Also, the council provided "the advantage of engaging the teams of several universities ...on the same query."[156]

The debates were more experimental, employing an "open forum" format, with three debaters on each side and winners decided by an audience-shift measure. Hosting Pittsburgh in 1927, "300 students and townspeople witnessed the Deacon victory in the second open forum debate of the season. "Pres. Poteat welcomed the Pitt debaters to our unexciting

INTER-COLLEGIATE DEBATES, 1926

QUERY: *Resolved*, That this House Condemns the Present System of Prohibition in the United States.

University of Arizona at Wake Forest, N. C.

WAKE FOREST COLLEGE, *Negative*   UNIVERSITY OF ARIZONA, *Affirmative*

Won by Negative

J. S. HOPKINS   O. L. NORMENT

QUERY: *Resolved*, That the United States Should Recognize the Soviet Government of Russia.

William and Mary at Wake Forest, N. C.

WAKE FOREST COLLEGE, *Negative*   WILLIAM AND MARY, *Affirmative*

Won by ....

D. S. HAWORTH, JR.   R. E. WALL.

---

[156] *Old Gold and Black*, November 13, 1925, page 1.

town." The debate, in an open forum format, registered votes before and after the discussion. This way of dual voting shows the power of persuasion. The Wake Forest debaters won-over 68 negative votes during the argument."[157]

During this era, Wake participated in the "open forum" format sparingly. One student wrote, "Coach [Paschal] has decided that the plan is very unsatisfactory, for it is almost impossible to obtain an unbiased audience or one that is capable of properly judging a debate. It has been decided that the experiment will not be tried next year, except where other colleges requested it."[158]

Wake Forest was not the only school in North Carolina that had an active program with intercollegiate tours. As the flagship state school, UNC commanded a slightly more prestigious set of public events. One in particular, the visit by the Oxford Union in November 1925, which the *Old Gold and Black* reported "was the most important event in the annals of forensic activity to have been held in North Carolina, from the standpoint of the prestige of the two universities. Many Wake Forest students journeyed to Chapel Hill for the debate."

Wake opponents diverged from the large public institutions by heritage, happenstance, and choice, yet the program was advantageously active. The 1926-27 season of Intercollegiate Debates may well have been the height of competitive frequency.

The season, which took place primarily in the spring of 1927, running from February to late April, under the direction of debate coach Dr. G. W. Paschal, faced sixteen opponents in audience debates, five hosted on the Wake Forest campus.[159] The next fall, an exciting debate council entertained potential invitations from schools such as Pennsylvania, Texas, and Oregon, with negotiations ongoing. Wake was moving up the food chain. The actual schedule for the spring of 1928 showed an

---

[157] "Votes before the argument began were 56 affirmative and 129 negative; after the conclusion of the arguments, the votes were 129 affirmative and 61 negative. The team affecting the largest number of changes in the minds of the audience was declared the winner." *Old Gold and Black*, April 17, 1926, page 1; The Pittsburgh debaters, as one of the premier national programs, were "on one of the most extensive schedules in the history of the American forensics, meeting some 40 schools throughout the Middle States. They have warmly invited the deacons to invade Pennsylvania next spring." The voters were Wake partisans.

[158] *Old Gold and Black*, May 16th, 1928, page 2.

[159] *Old Gold and Black*, February 2, 1927, page 1.

impressive set of debates but did not include any of the aforementioned schools.[160]

As already noted, in the late 1920s, the travel schedules became more extensive with Western/Eastern North/South, Alabama/Texas, South Carolina/Georgia Tours. The incentive of "off-campus" participation may have spurred interest among students. In October 1930, the student paper recounts that 42 men had signaled their intention to compete for places on the varsity and freshman squads. How many completed the arduous tryouts – extended training and judged performance – was less clear.

Tours provided an opportunity to travel and interact as the college representatives, while expenses were on the societies' tab. Access was still limited, but prospects were clearly tantalizing. Twelve debaters and two alternates were chosen for the traveling team in 1929. The debate topic was: A *substitute for trial by jury should be adopted*. The off-campus events included:

Carson-Newman College at Wake Forest, N. C., Joe Carlton & Wade Bostic

Emory and Henry College at Louisburg, N. C., R. Paul Caudill & Luther Robinson

University Of West Virginia (Girls) At Wake Forest, N. C., Wade Brown, H. C. Carroll & D. R. McClary

Elon College At Elon, N. C., Max Griffin & J. M. Early

High Point College at High Point, N. C., Wade Brown & D. R. McClary

Howard College At Wake Forest, N. C., E. C. Shoe & R. Paul Caudill

Pi Kappa Delta Championship series of the South Atlantic Province, Joe Carlton & Wade Bostic, Championship won by Wake Forest College

N. C. State College at Meredith College, Raleigh, N. C.
West Virginia Wesleyan College at State College, Raleigh, N. C.
Wofford College at State College, Raleigh, NC

---

[160] *Old Gold and Black*, October 22, 1927, page 1.

INTER-COLLEGIATE DEBATES, 1926

QUERY: *Resolved,* That the Operation of Coal Mines in the United States Should be Regulated by a Federal Commission.

A. S. GILLESPIE   C. R. TEW

SOUTH CAROLINA-GEORGIA TOUR

Wofford College at Spartanburg, S. C.
WAKE FOREST COLLEGE, *Affirmative*   WOFFORD COLLEGE, *Negative*
Won by ....

Furman University at Greenville, S. C.
WAKE FOREST COLLEGE, *Affirmative*   FURMAN UNIVERSITY, *Negative*
Won by ....

Mercer University at Macon, Ga.
WAKE FOREST COLLEGE, *Affirmative*   MERCER UNIVERSITY, *Negative*
Won by ....

QUERY: *Resolved,* That the Federal Government Should Control and Operate the Coal Mines.

University of Richmond at Wake Forest, N. C.
WAKE FOREST COLLEGE, *Affirmative*   UNIVERSITY OF RICHMOND, *Negative*
Won by ....

T. W. BAKER   ELMER CLOER   J. T. GASKILL

Virginia Tour, R. K. Benfield, E. C. Shoe & Luther Robinson

Hampden-Sydney College at Hampden-Sidney, Va.
University of Richmond at Richmond, Va.
William and Mary College at Williamsburg, Va.

Southwestern Tour, Wade Bostic, Joe Carlton, Roy Robinson & Max Griffin

Wofford College at Winthrop College, Rock Hill, S. C.
University of South Carolina at Columbia, S. C.
University of Chattanooga at Chattanooga, Tenn.
Carson-Newman College at Jefferson City, Tenn.
Lincoln Memorial University at Harrogate, Tenn.
Emory And Henry College at Emory, Va.

Increasingly, societies were immersed in a troublesome overstretch. In 1908, the students sought administrative financial support, citing the intercollegiate debate with Baylor as being especially expensive because of the distance traveled.[161]

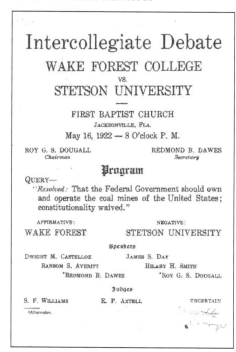

Intercollegiate Debate

WAKE FOREST COLLEGE
vs.
STETSON UNIVERSITY
—
FIRST BAPTIST CHURCH
JACKSONVILLE, FLA.
May 16, 1922 — 8 O'clock P. M.

ROY G. S. DOUGALL   REDMOND B. DAWES
Chairman   *Secretary*

Program

QUERY—
   "*Resolved:* That the Federal Government should own and operate the coal mines of the United States; constitutionality waived."

AFFIRMATIVE: NEGATIVE:
WAKE FOREST   STETSON UNIVERSITY

Speakers

DWIGHT M. CASTELLOE   JAMES S. DAY
RANSOM S. AVERITT   HILARY H. SMITH
*REDMOND B. DAWES   *ROY G. S. DOUGALL

Judges

S. F. WILLIAMS   E. P. AXTELL   UNCERTAIN

*Alternates.

The college's external organ, the *Wake Forest College Alumni News,* acknowledged the problems with financing: "Very recently, the societies have found the burden of financing the debates too great… but the society still provides most of the debaters' preliminary training. By slow degrees, conditions have so changed that it is next to impossible to get an audience of students and others of respectable size to hear even a debate."[162]

Intercollegiate events were nonetheless entrenched and would continue through the Quisenberry and Robinson tenures. As late as 1937, the "varsity debate squad today started a tour of the western part of North Carolina, where they will clash with other colleges' teams at Greensboro, High Point, Hickory, Asheville, Mars Hill, Banner Elk, and Boone. Last Wednesday the Baptist debaters met representatives of High Point College and the Women's College of the University of North Carolina. Thursday, they spoke against Lenore-Rhyne College debaters. Friday, the Wake Forest team engaged the Asheville Teachers College forensics stars, while a heavy

---

[161] *The Wake Forest Student,* November 1908; The Society needed to settle the accounts for its ambitious projects from time to time, as in 1930 when "Mr. Taylor moved that we contribute $50 more to the expenses of the debate audited trips.' This motion was carried out with the understanding that the society should be presented with any statement of the expenses incurred while on the trip. Euzelian Minutes, March 1, 1930.

[162] *Wake Forest College Alumni News,* Vol. 3, No. 4, February 1931, page 3.

day Saturday calls for the debates against Mars Hill, Lees-McRae, and Appalachian Teacher's Colleges."[163]

A letter dated April 17, 1982, from a debate alum, Lilburn Moseley, perhaps 80 at the time of his writing to the team, shows that the late tours were of import to the students. In his career, he chaired the Debate Council and debated in the Anniversary Debates, and his intercollegiate debates included wins against Pittsburgh (129 to 63, audience decision), Furman, and a bevy of schools, including Baylor, on the 1926 Southern tour.

He wrote in a May 1, 1982, letter, "Wake Forest was for me a new world of freedom, and interpretation of life that challenged every choice. I marveled today at the scholarship, dedication, the inspiration of the debate faculty."[164]

--*-*-*-*-*-*

Stories from the Intercollegiate Debate time are innumerable, and this accounting cannot extend each, but it is hoped we can preserve some of the atmosphere of the Intercollegiate Debates. The following snippets, presented chronologically, help illustrate the tone and variety of debates in which Wake Forest engaged.

(1919) The *Howler* roasted Wake debater Onslow Glenn, a participant in the **Emory and Henry** encounter: "At the Raleigh debate his arguments like Samson the Danite slew the wicked men of Gath. It is said judges tumbled over one another to render their decision, and that a half-hour later a fair damsel in the audience delivered her decision, also favorable."[165]

(1922) *Oklahoma Baptist*: "Amidst a hushed stillness that bespoke the suspense produced upon the audience by argument regarded as a very nearly evenly balanced, the three little slips of paper were collected and presented to the President, who announced that he found two for Wake Forest and one for Oklahoma... Following

---

[163] *Old Gold and Black* February 6, 1937, page 1.

[164] Lilburn Moseley, personal correspondence, April 17, May 1, 1982.

[165] *Howler*, 1920, page 39. In addition, Glenn served as Senior Class President, Society Day Orator (*The American Leader*) and Anniversary Marshal.

Senior Onslow Glenn, 1920

the debate, the president, speakers, marshal of the debate, and other invited guests repaired to the Philomathesian Society Hall, where they entertained themselves, serving refreshments and cigars."[166]

(1923) "Wake Forest began its inter-collegiate debating season here Monday by winning a brilliant victory over the strong *Maryville* college team from Tennessee. The debate was one of the best witnessed in Wake Forest for many years... [I]t must be conceded that the visitors were slightly outclassed in the art of debating by the Wake Forest representatives... The decision was two to one in favor of Wake Forest"[167]

(1923) The Wake Forest debating team, W. R. Wallace, L. E. Andrews, and M. G. Stamey...return from their Western trip this morning after having attacked and successfully captured honors from *William Jewell College* of Missouri in one of the hardest contest debates ever held before the Southern Baptist Convention.[168]

Prior to the encounter, the locals "built up" their future opponents. "William Jewell College, Missouri, is rated above any debating team among the best, having defeated Baylor University's crack team, the powerful team of Simpson College and rated above the University of Southern California so the Tar Heel Baptists have a battle royal on their hands.... William Jewell will never be able to strap the scalps of Stanley, Andrews and Wallace to their war belt."[169]

---

[166] *Old Gold and Black,* April 7, 1922, page 2.

[167] "Moyock Boy One of Winners in Debate," *The Daily Advance* (Elizabeth City) March 22, 1923, page 1.

[168] *The Biblical Recorder,* May 30, 1923, page 12.

[169] *The News & Observer,* May 10, 1923, page 5.

The Baptist Student

WILLIAM JEWELL   versus   WAKE FOREST

THE WAKE FOREST TEAM

1923 Wake Team at the Southern Baptist Convention Debate,
Nashville, TN, W. R. Wallace, L. E. Andrews, and M. G. S. Stamey.
Photo courtesy of Southern Baptist Historical Library and Archive,
originally published in Sept-Oct 1923 *Baptist Student Magazine*.

(1924) "The agony of defeat." The second year of the Tri-State
Debates featured two sets of debates, the first with the **University
of North Carolina** and **Davidson** and the second with **Charleston
College** and **William and Mary College**. An "unexpected" loss to
William and Mary led the *Old Gold and Black* to take issue with the
decision, writing, "The debate itself was obvious, to all who heard
it, of the splendid training and ability of the Old Gold and Black
warriors. Oratory flowed with startling rapidity; logic was freely
dispensed. So ably and convincingly did Andrews and Earp put
their case and drive it home that few, if any doubted a unanimous
victory. The audience was completely surprised and disappointed
when the decision went by a vote of 2 to 1 to William and Mary."[170]

(1926) With *Arizona University* opening the Wake Forest debating schedule on March 18, "the Wake Forest devotees of forensic
encounters, as well as the people in the neighboring towns, will
have an opportunity to hear what are the best debating teams in
the country. This team from the southwest has by far one of the

---

[170] *Old Gold and Black*, May 5, 1923, page 1, 6.

most distinctive records of any debating organization that has come under the observation of the Wake Forest Council since it began its negotiations for debates last fall. The closing of the contract with the debating team representing the University of Arizona marks quite an extension of Wake Forest's range of contests."[171]

"The largest audience, approximately 500, in the annals of recent Wake Forest forensic clashes attended the debate."[172] This is undoubtedly an embellishment. The audience was large, however, as they voted Wake Forest the winner, 233 to 77.

(1927) "All Things New Are Old." In a December issue, the *Old Gold and Black* chronicled an intercollegiate debate with Virginia's **Emory and Henry** College on the topic of *That the United States should revise her tariff laws so as to permit of free trade with any other nation on a reciprocal basis.* The topic remains contemporary, as did the debate move made by the Emory and Henry debaters, who argued essentially a plan-inclusive counterplan. They agreed with Wake's affirmative that the tariff laws and preference for free trade should be revised. They reserved, however, that to be workable, reciprocity was required.[173]

---

[171] Wake Forest to Debate Arizona in Wingate Hall – "Cactus Jumpers" to Meet the Deacon Debaters, *Old Gold and Black*, January 22, 1926, page 1, 3. The tendency to build up the opposing team's credentials, comparable to sports talk praising an opponent before a match, seemed proportional to the opposition's perceived status. The student newspaper noted, "On this team from the Arizona University is Richard Pattee, a senior in the College of Liberal Arts, who is a better debater. He was a member of the team which won the undisputed University championships of the FARC West last year and was the leader of the team which defeated Oxford University, England, by an overwhelming decision. The second member of this team is Fenimore Cooper, who was a member of the debate squad at Arizona two years ago and is an experienced speaker. He is the scion of the two of the most important families of Arizona and northern Mexico, being half American and half Spanish in blood. Carlton Wicart, the third member of the squad, is one of the leaders at Arizona in literary and dramatic activities. He was a member of the team which successfully invaded Oklahoma two years ago. He has recently been elected as Rhodes scholar from Arizona."

Wake Forest will send against them, two of the speakers who are alert, grasping points of reputation, and fluent in speaking, hoping to make this contest one of the largest in this section of the country. The query debated was: *That this house condemns the present system of prohibition in the United States.*

[172] *Old Gold and Black*, March 27, 1926, page 1.

[173] *Old Gold and Black*, December 1927, page 1.

(1927) Wake lost a high-profile debate to **Bucknell University** of Pennsylvania. The decision provided by the judges who apparently struggled in their decision gives insight into the tension in deciding debates between argument quality and presence. Proportionality had been changing in decision criteria for some time. The judges were quoted as observing, "The visitors held tenaciously to the validity and significance of the technical points of the query. The Wake Forest men scored a decided success, as their well-developed speeches, their use of English, and their forceful and polished delivery."[174]

(1930) "Sam Miller and Harold Deaton... hardly showed traditional southern chivalry when they knocked into the cocked hat hopes of the **Chowan** College girls for a week's holiday by defeating their forensic team last Saturday night... There were rumors that the Chowan student body would be given a holiday of a week if their team could conquer the mighty aggregation from Wake Forest. They pinned their hopes upon the oratorical abilities of Miss Mary Lou Martin and Isla Poole, and they had good reason to be optimistic in their chances for victory and vacation. The debaters were given a week or two of recess to study the disarmament question and to work up an invincible plan of attack to defeat the Wake Forest team, upholding the negative side of the query.

The students were feverishly interested, and the townsmen were just as interested in seeing whether the young ladies would win their greatly desired holiday. The auditorium at Murfreesboro was packed, something quite unusual nowadays at a forensic clash."[175] Wake won, and presumably, Chowan was left with devastating disappointment.

(1931) The **Catawba** Indians and the "Ariel Brigade" of Wake Forest College went into action on Thursday night, February 26, 1931, when representatives from Catawba and Wake Forest met in a warm-up debate.[176] Wake Forest College met the fair representatives of "the land of the sky" in a debate here last Monday night when they engaged **Asheville Normal** in a non-decision bout in Wait Hall...

---

[174] *Old Gold and Black*, March 26, 1927, page 1.

[175] *Old Gold and Black*, March 8, 1930, page 1.

[176] *Old Gold and Black*, February 28, 1931, page 1.

Wake Forest debaters engage a women's team for the second time this season... Wake Forest was defeated by the Asheville debaters last year. The contest next Monday night is to be a nonpartisan affair. "The only revenge available to Wake Forest is to defeat the girls in the minds of the audience, which will be difficult to do, considering the great advantage women have in always having the last word."[177]

1940 Farmville Female Seminary Association Debate Club
(Perhaps Dolores is seated third from the left)
Photo Courtesy of Longwood University. Archives

(1939) Intercollegiate Debates_outside of tournaments and public appearances also happened. On October 16, 1939, Eu. minutes report that "the president, James Koppel (sic), then referred to the society a challenge for a debate by the Dialectic Senate, a literary society at **North Carolina**. He announced that we would accept the challenge with no objection from the society."[178]

(1942) The farce of the entire forensics season was a debate that resulted in a challenge by **William Jewell College** as a salve to the hurt they suffered at the hands of the football team. They lost on the gridiron, and so they sought revenge via the debate squad. Their medium was a nondecision debate, which allowed both sides to give vent to the ache through their oratorical prowess.

---

[177] *Old Gold and Black*, March 14, 1931, page 1.

[178] Euzelian Minutes, October 1939.

As shown, tours and campus debates starred multiple opponents, a success that also marked the ending phase of the intercollegiate debates. One last encounter, among the era's last instances, materialized in 1941 and follows.

Under the guidance of coach Zon Robinson, a giddy collection of young debaters visited the Farmville Female Seminary Association in nearby Longwood, Virginia. One member of the traveling squad, Neil Morgan, sent home colorful accounts of tour highlights. perhaps poking a little fun at his colleague, Wes Hatfield. The Hatfield satire reveals the elements of humor in the situation but also exposes the sexist constructions of the times.

"It was a new sort of situation oratory for the quartet of deacon debaters.

And a new sort of situation for Wes Hatfield. but they would all come through. They always had.

Wavy-haired coach Zon Robinson called his men together; everybody was right there. So they huddled cautiously behind a red plush curtain which separated a small, bare stage from some 250 ultra-ultra debs in a remote Virginia finishing school. "The Southern Seminary for cultured young gentlewomen," the sign had said when they entered the Buena Vista campus. The Greek at the filling station had commented gruffly: "They dump here all the sub-debs that get too hot to handle."

Other Boys

Some of the boys from Washington and Lee had come along and they were going to put on an exhibition debate concerning aid to South America. Hatfield was supposed to argue against it, and that had been all right until he'd met Dolores. she was a ravishing little senorita from the Argentine who had been chairman of the welcoming committee and had done her job quite well – at least insofar as Wes was concerned. Coach Robinson was afraid Hatfield's arguments against South America now might sound a bit weak. The good coach remembered those few minutes in the room labeled "entertainment parlor" just after the Wake lads had landed on the seminary campus when Wes and Dolores had first succeeded in getting by themselves. They had walked upstairs to the auditorium, parted at the stage-door, and here was Hatfield. Nerves in general were on edge. Tension was high. Therefore, the huddle. and the coach's little pep talk:

"All right boys. all women are alike. and you fellows aren't scared of 'em, get out there and do some talking."

Polite Chatter

Wes Hatfield, Wake Farmville Debater

As a plush curtain screeched solemnly to the side, revealing Hatfield and the Wake man on one side and the Washington and Lee boys on the other, there was a polite patter of hands as some of the girls laid down the knitting they were doing for the British soldiers. A few of them looked up. Dolores was on the front row tossing soulful gazes at our man Hatfield.

"The South Americans are an ardent, enterprising people," Hatfield beamed at the audience, mostly Dolores.

She beamed right back in solemn agreement.

Way back in the rear, surrounded by adoring knitters but aware only of the efforts of his forensic fighter, coach Zon Robinson nodded assent. Up and on the stage the other debaters appeared oblivious – oblivious that a great struggle was about to occur.

"They need us."

If "the South Americans undoubtedly need us," Wes continued as he looked out at Argentines Dolores.

She smiled, half rebuking, half inviting.

"What is this question wondered Robinson. He was supposed to be arguing against the aid to Latin America. wonder if that crazy South American had actually got him nuts?

Hatfield was wondering the same thing. but he was about to decide.

"But girls," he said, and might as well have put it in the singular; "the question is whether we can afford to center our attention on South America to the neglect of our other interests."

And Hatfield mused about the girl back home.

Dolores' jaw, then trembled, shocked to discover that there was any question in the mind of her American as to her supremacy above all others. Hatfield saw but remained stolid. A fire burned bright in his eyes then smoldered. His shoulder straightened. He bristled with resolve. Dolores leaned forward, straining to hear his words.

"Involvement in South American affairs would be fatal to our more important interests," he shouted; "let us isolate ourselves from them, for their intentions may become disastrous."

Hatfield sat down, flushed. The sub-debs returned to their knitting; Robinson looked relieved. The other speakers stirred vaguely. But Dolores? Her blood rushed to her dark face. She stared icily at Hatfield, rose, and walked out of the hall, her back turned forever to her Americano.

The *Old Gold and Black* held strong. For Hatfield and the Deacons won the debate by a unanimous audience decision – after Dolores had left. The Wake Foresters left the seminary campus speedily and headed home.

And Hatfield?

He flicks his coat sleeve and remarks:

"Dolores? Oh, just a passing fancy."[179]

---

[179] Morgan, N. (1941). Hatfield Finds Solution; Deacon Debaters Look on: New Situation Faces WF Speakers On Virginia Journey, *Old Gold and Black,* February 28, page 4. It is fair speculation that Delores is third from the left in the Farmville photo. She likely never knew of this sophomoric story, which young men often favored at all-male schools.

CHAPTER 7

Commencement: The Orators Showcase

Commencement Commences

"From the first, the Societies claimed, as a
right, a part in all public Exercises.[1]

In the year of the formation of the Literary Societies, 1835, the societies assumed the privilege of inviting a speaker to address the annual Commencement events. In an arrangement that continued until the end of the century, the Euzelians were expected to invite the orator in the odd-numbered years and the Philomathesians in the even-numbered years.

The Literary Societies' relationship to commencement was one of individuals speaking to the assembled. Debates were not presented at Graduation as they were on Anniversary and Society Days. Yet they are closely linked, if for no other reason than that the orators, senior speakers, and senior commencement speakers were the same young men who, on weekday evenings or a Saturday, were debating in their respective halls.

Commencement was not initially greeted with the reverence later attached to the exercise. It took time for there to be graduates, and then their numbers were nominal. The hazards of returning to the home farm or small town were likely much more salient than hoping the family would be free to travel to remote Wake Forest. In the first volume of the

---

[1] Paschal, G. W. (1935). *History of Wake Forest College*, Vol. I, page 591.

History of Wake Forest College, Paschal captures his version of life in that era:

> In this period (before the Civil War), the students had very little time or opportunity for social life except among themselves. Their only vacant period in the week was Saturday afternoon, five full days being given to recitation and study, and Friday night and Saturday forenoon to the work of the Literary Societies. In the College sessions there were no holidays. In the early years the Commencements seem to have had no social features and to have been very meagerly attended. After the period of the Institute, the first notice of anything of a social nature in connection with Commencement was in 1843, when on the night of the last day a large party of ladies and gentlemen partook of the refreshments provided, and after a suitable time spent "in a most friendly manner," left at an early hour much pleased.[2]

Paschal is correct that a large-scale reception on commencement evening took a while to become part of the campus fabric, but smaller ones were held. In 1842, the year before he described the "first social," one state paper's rendition nonetheless had a charming notice worth attending to: "In the evening they gathered in the society halls for a social party sponsored by the societies. Ample provisions were made for the company, and there was besides 'the feast of reason in the flow of soul,' without the presence of intoxicating liquors." [3] It is possible the gathering was internally focused, and inviting the public to hear orations and celebrate the graduates occurred later.

It would be several years before the full regalia of tradition congeal. Commencement in 1840 appeared not as easy to plan as it was in later years; the minutes of the Philomathesian society indicated that its negotiations with the Euzelians were unsuccessful and that they would not have society-specific representatives at the commencement.

Getting a speaker for commencement was difficult. In 1840, every meeting for a month or more included letters received from those not accepting the nomination to address commencement; the societies then looked for the next person to be asked. Finally, in April of the 1840

[2] Paschal, G. W. (1935). *History of Wake Forest College,* Vol. I, page 459.

[3] *The Fayetteville Weekly Observer,* July 6, 1842, page 2.

season, they announced that W. H. Battle Esq.,[4] the newly appointed superior court judge, would speak before the societies for graduation.

The controversy was not quite resolved when, in August, the printer, Mr. Gales, offered only 300 copies of the address instead of the agreed-upon 500. After providing 100 copies for the Euzelian society and five for each faculty member, Mr. Battle received 10, and the library received many. Only then were members allowed to purchase an address copy for $.16 apiece.

Of course, early on, when there were only four graduates (1849), all were mandated to be "commencement speakers." "The Graduating Class, consisting of Messrs. H. B. Folk, W. M. Wingate, S. G. O'Brien, and R. C. Meacham entertain the audience with Addresses that would have been honored to much older heads," the *Raleigh Times* assessed.[5]

The reporter also gushed about the after-reception, "it could not fail to fill a visitor with feelings of pleasure and admiration, to see the sobriety, neatness, and order of the students." Perhaps testing credulity, he continued, "With almost universal consent, they frown upon every innovation of

1882 – Commencement Program

---

[4] William H Battle, Esq delivered an address before the Philomathesian and Euzelian societies of Wake Forest College, June 18, 1840. Raleigh; printed of the office of the *Raleigh Register* 1840. The address took upon itself the historical mission of cautioning the soon-to-be graduates, warning "them of danger, to guard them against temptation, to withdraw them from evil, to alert them to virtue, and to impress upon them the precepts of virtue and piety." For all the trouble, the speech resided in a self-piety that one must assume the students heard at each and every public gathering. Raleigh's *Weekly Standard* review embroidered, "The address delivered by W. H. Battle… Was truly a classical performance: replete with learning and clothed in the garniture of intellectual embellishment." *Weekly Raleigh Register*, July 3, 1840, page 1.

[5] *The Raleigh Times*, June 29, 1849, page 3.

the laws of their Institution and are determined to support the Faculty in their proper administration. By such a course, they have become proverbial, wherever known, for their order, docility, and manly application to duty."[6] One doubts the commentator was that naïve, as the Wake debaters were real, not manikins.

Coverage of commencements in the very early years was sparse but effusive. Press accounts typically logged uncritical praise of the speakers and inflated the importance of the occasion. In that vein, *The Biblical Recorder* enthused, "The graduates elicited particular attention from the audience, and more especially from the younger part of the fair portion, who seem particularly interested in that part of the exercises; and indeed it was not to be wondered at, for according to the concurring opinions of many older and wiser heads present, the young men of the graduating class exhibited strong marks of original and well cultivated minds, and acquitted themselves to their own honor and into that of the Institution."[7]

As with all history, commencement altered over time, just as many traditions are held to this day. The role of the societies beyond the opening resplendence (see "Procession and Reception" below) was fundamentally to invite external speakers and select the senior speakers from their memberships when it was no longer practical for each member to address the occasion.[8]

The timeline provided in Figure 1 helps visualize the evolution of student speakers at graduation, while the narrative below focuses on the external speakers brought to campus. Notice that the commentary is distinctly weighed in favor of the 1870s until about 1920. Much of the "imbalance" has to do with the nature of newspaper coverage. The era was the height of local newspapers, with most cities like Raleigh hosting five or more flourishing papers.

The religious schools and State education institutions received full coverage; the window to Wake was primarily *The Biblical Recorder*, keeping

---

[6] *The Raleigh Times*, June 29, 1849, page 3.

[7] *The Biblical Recorder*, July 1, 1848, page 2.

[8] Internal society selection processes changed often and were controversial. For most of the 18th Century, the Societies voted, and in the modern era, tryouts were preferred. In 1884, controversy erupted over how many speakers would be from each society. The Phis "Voted that the Societies be requested to appoint each six of its members as competitors for the Declamation Medal at the coming Commencement. Let it be understood that the action is for this particular occasion and not intended to indicate a permanent plan." (Letter from W. L. Poteat, Sec. of the faculty, April 18, 1884).

tabs from Raleigh. Before the Civil War and until the late 1870s, there were no internal publications at Wake Forest other than the "catalog," *The Wake Forest Bulletin*.

FIGURE 1: A Senior Orations/Commencement Timeline

Institute Years– *1865 – 1869*	One speaker selected alternately between societies to present a Fourth of July address.
Early Years	All senior class members were expected to speak unless excused by the faculty in the early years.[9] In the early 1880s, the number of speakers was fixed at ten; others in the class wrote a thesis or spoke elsewhere.
	1854 The first joint presentations of Anniversary Orations from each society became a public occasion. The Phis tried to organize a public event with a full program in 1848 but were unsuccessful. Early on, the faculty kept the commencement oratories "private."
	From 1869 to 1872, there were four Senior Speaking events a year: in the fall, October, December, Spring, March, and April. After introducing a debate on Anniversary Day, there was one in April.
	From 1868 to 1878, the Salutatory speech was delivered in Latin.
	In 1899, the number of speakers was reduced to eight from ten, which had been fairly standard until the early 1880s; before that, every student was required to produce a Senior Oration[10]. Reduced further in 1909 to six and in 1924 to four. In 1973, the Dean of the College reduced the number of speakers to three.

---

[9] 1886 *Wake Forest Catalog*, page 27, Senior Speeches and Thesis, "All Candidates for Regular College degrees are required to deliver four original addresses of not less than 1000 words each, or submit to the Faculty, in lieu thereof, an equal number of original theses of not less than 2000 words each; provided that, by this substitution, the number of addresses on any occasion shall not be less than eight, nor shall they be more than 12. Anniversary addresses may be submitted as a thesis, subject to the foregoing regulations."

[10] These were handwritten "oratories" submitted to the faculty. Often, they appear to be a recycling of earlier work, particularly 1st Affirmative speeches from debates they had participated in, often adapted as Society Day and Anniversary Day addresses.

"Senior Speaking" Ends	1900 Senior Speaking was held in December & March until 1914-15. "On April 25, 1914, the Societies passed a joint resolution, declaring that the senior speaking had proved more or less a failure and asked that it be abolished, the request the faculty granted.[11]
Orations separated from Main Commencement Day	Orations were presented on Graduation Day until 1929; after that, speeches were presented most often the day before the conferring of degrees
	1938-1956 – Committee on Literary Societies and Debate recommended speakers to the faculty. 1939 Orations were held at a separate morning event on Graduation Day. Separate-day evening events happened before and after 1939
	The first female senior orator was in 1946[12]
Selection of Senior Speakers moves to the Debate Coach	Dr. Franklin R. Shirley became the chairman of the Committee on Literary. Societies and Debates in 1951, and from then until 1972, his committee handled the selection of Senior Orators.
Student Life Selects Senior Orators	The Student Life Committee selected the Senior Orators for 1972, 1973, and 1974.
	Until 1973, the Senior Orations were held as a separate event on graduation weekend, typically on Sunday, preceding the Monday graduation. In the late 1800s, depending on commencement dates, the oratory event was on Wednesday or Thursday.
Dean's Office Selects Orators	In 1975, the Dean's office and the Assistant Chaplain took over the selection task. Top students were invited to a Senior Colloquium, where the best three were selected to speak at the Honors and Awards Convocation.

---

[11] Paschal, G. W. (1948). *History of Wake Forest College*, Vol. II 1865-1905, page 376.

[12] Ms. Easley must not have reached the final round. Two years before women could officially enroll, Nancy Easley won the Society Day Oratory in 1944, "Miss Nancy Easley, daughter of Dr. J. A. Easley of the college religion department, was chosen as Eu president during the spring elections, thus becoming the first woman to hold a literary society presidency in the history of the school. Women were first admitted to Wake in 1942.

| No longer associated with Commencement | In 2010, the finalists presented their orations at the February Founder's Day Convocation, with the winner presenting during the Honors and Awards Convocation graduation week. |
| | Senior orations are standalone events, only the finalist presenting at Founder's Day, having no relationship to commencement. |

Eventually, the number of graduates precluded each senior from giving an oration at graduation, and separate Senior Speaker events were held. The faculty were to attend these speaking events and, by their vote, select the appropriate number of commencement speakers for any given year.

From 1869 to 1872, there were four *Senior Speaking events* a year, independent proceedings from Commencement speakers... It was reduced to one set-aside day for Senior speakers each semester when the public Anniversary Debate started.[13]

--*-*-*-*-*-*

---

[13] Senior Speaking was held in December & March until 1914-15. Apparently two programs could not accommodate all graduates giving a speech to the faculty, so speakers were allowed to bypass by substituting a written essay.

In May of 1905, the Eus' introduced a motion by W. E. Goode, which read: "Whereas the members of the faculty, during past sessions, have failed to attend Senior speaking in sufficient numbers to warrant a just election of commencement, speakers, therefore it is resolved: That we the Philomathesian and Euzelian Literary Societies refuse to elect further Senior Speakers and until the faculty shall be manifest a willingness to attend such Senior Speaking in a majority. It passed a third reading and was passed to Dr. Taylor, the Wake president. Presumably, the faculty responded in the short term, but in looking at newspaper accounts of society-sponsored contests to select the graduation speakers, a loyal and relatively small group of faculty show up year after year, particularly in the 1920-1930s to judge whatever Society speaking contest is needed. Paschal and the University President were often on board.

In 1914, the final blow to Senior Speakers was struck when "On April 25 the Societies passed a joint resolution, declaring that the senior speaking had proved more or less failures and asked that they be abolished, the request the faculty granted." The Societies organized tryouts, somewhat elaborate contests that often had preliminary and finals to select the commencement speakers. Until 1929, these three winners spoke at commencement. Later, the celebration of orators took place later in the day and soon appeared on another day in the graduation week program, typically in the afternoon the day before.

By the 1870s, commencement was sophisticated enough to reach the entire state, particularly the State government in Raleigh. The developing commencement traditions that included a larger public were captured by a regional newspaper in 1881, "Thursday is always the 'big' day; this brings the day on which the graduating class delivers her speeches. Soon after breakfast, carriages and buggies begin to come in, laden with people to attend the commencement. About 9 o'clock, the train from Raleigh arrived, bringing a large crowd. At 10 o'clock, the crowd assembled in the spacious new chapel."[14]

A decade earlier, *The Weekly Sentinel* shared an especially sublime depiction of graduation: an 1871 Hallmark card. You can almost feel the welcome of the townsfolk as visitors arrive.

The old go to enjoy the literary feast prepared and to look after the young. The fairer sex are usually present, *doubtless* to encourage young men in their efforts to climb the hill of science, and they appreciate the kind of consideration of the beauties of creation, bestowed upon them as much attention as possible under the circumstances.

A pleasant ride of 15 miles over the Raleigh and Gaston Railroad, brought us to the beautiful village of Wake Forest. All was life and animation, and we were reminded forcibly of Virgil's description of the Carthaginians building their city under the direction of Queen Dido.[15]

As the trains arrive, the citizens were at the station to welcome visitors and sign them to their homes; and we here make the assertion without fear of contradiction, that no more generous warmhearted hospitable people can be found than those of Wake Forest... Students who attend the school, always retained the strongest affection for the place, and when they return, even after the lapse of years, felt perfectly at home.[16]

Graduation ceremonies lasted several days, with layers of speaking events: Declaimer, Freshman, Sophomores, Alumni and Society speakers,

---

[14] *Goldsboro Messenger*, June 13, 1881, page 2.

[15] Dido is known best as the mythical queen of Carthage who died for love of Aeneas, according to "The Aeneid" of the Roman poet Vergil (Virgil). https://www.thoughtco.com/dido-queen-of-carthage-116949

[16] *The Weekly Sentinel*, July 4, 1871, page 2.

and the Commencement Speaker. The commencement in 1881 began on Monday with the freshman engaged in a competitive declamation contest of 12 students vying for the Taylor medal, given by the wife of Prof. Charles E Taylor... The medal was unanimously awarded to W. W. Kitchen, the son of the Hon. W. H. Kitchen, the former member of Congress from the second district as the best disclaimer. One paper described, "Young Kitchen is one of the smartest boys in college, being only 14 years of age."[17]

Naturally, there would be troubles from time to time, but one would not expect the kerfuffle to include "image repair" involving a newspaper reporter and the College President. A journalist excluded from Memorial Hall in 1859 by an overflowing commencement crowd went public with his complaint in a major Raleigh newspaper:

> We were present on this occasion, but were unable to obtain a seat – no provision whatever having been made for the press.... The public invents a lively interest in the progress of our educational institutions, and naturally look to the press of the State for information related to them. The press, however, though active in its effort, is paralyzed by a want of forethought in the heads or managers of these public institutions...At Wake Forest no accommodation at all was afforded. We (the Reporters) applied to one of the Marshals for a seat but were informed that it could not be furnished. So long as the state of things is allowed to exist, it should be a matter of no surprise that meager and imperfect accounts of public events appear in our papers.[18]

The printed criticism must have connected, shortly thereafter Wake President W. M. Wingate personally, in a clever message with mockery, an "open letter" to the newspaper in response to the reporter's grumble. He offers an apologia, sort of...

> I confess I was not a little surprised to find a notice of our Commencement exercise... That one of your Reporters seriously brings us to task for our want of courtesy to the press... Your Reporter states that "he applied to one of the Marshals for a seat, and was

---

[17] *Goldsboro Messenger*, June 13, 1881, page 2.

[18] *The Weekly Standard*, June 15, 1859, page 3.

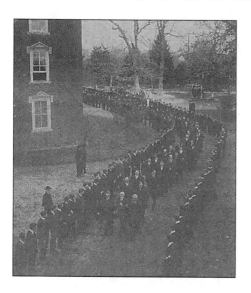

1884 – Wake Forest College faculty and trustees process through a double column of students. Photo: Wake Forest Historical Museum

informed that it could not be furnished." I could hope that he was not known as a Reporter from the *Standard* Office, but this is hardly possible since he could not then have felt aggrieved as one of the Press.

One of our marshals, I know, took great pains to seek out the gentlemen of the Press and was, in part, successful... Your Reporter, I hope, is aware, that, on account of the particular state of the fashions, the ladies now occupy the whole chapel, with the exception of the Rostrum and a few seats appropriated to the Band and the exercises during: that all the students are thrust out: that the rostrum is so crowded, that the speaker has scarcely room to pass and repast, the members of the Board of Trustees cannot sometimes find a place to witness the exercises...

Now, all this, Messrs. Editors, we regret very much. We regret the size of the Chapel, the state of the fashions, the confusion and disorder incident to so large a gathering, and most of all the slights and oversights which may unwittingly occur... Adam's fair race must be attended to, let the fashions be what they may, or storm would soon gather over our devoted heads, to which your Reporter's (with all deference) *is as nothing...*

I trust I have said enough...

Respectfully W. M. Wingate [19]

Planned events were always at the mercy of Mother Nature, however, not always in the form of inclement weather. The Spanish Flu influenced

---

[19] *The Weekly Standard*, June 22, 1859, page 3.

commencement but not "admittedly" as expected. While many other gatherings were relinquished, the 1918 graduation was held with a smattering of public attendance. In hushed tones, a 1918 *The Biblical Recorder* account described a world shaped by World War I; coverage that veered into a patriot discourse, never alluding to the concurrent flu pandemic.

The war very seriously affected the attendance upon the Commencement at Wake Forest...

The visitors who did attend the exercise, however, were richly repaid. Simplicity marks the Wake Forest finals, which was in perfect keeping with the times. The spirit of levity was absent, and solemnity pervaded the occasion, which this writer never witnessed at Wake Forest on any occasion in the past. There was no band to furnish music, and this in itself, produced a sobering effect, as it has often been said that "it does not seem like commencement until a band strikes up."

Thursday morning, another distinguished alumnus of the College spoke. Hon. E. Yeats Webb, Congressman from the seventh District, occupied a platform. Mr. Webb prefaced his speech by saying he could not deliver a literary address, but would speak on a vital subject, the one subject that is now before the American people. All were glad that Mr. Webb discussed the war, for he had been at the heart of things in this country ever since the war began and his address was filled with important and interesting facts and figures.

Mr. Webb declared most emphatically there must be no looking back until victory is won. We must carry this war on Prussian militarism no matter how long it may require, or what it costs.

Mr. Webb sounded a timely note of warning. He said we must have a great care, and the preparation for, and the prosecution of the work, we ourselves shall become a military nation... There is a danger that we shall adopt the very things we are fighting to destroy... we must never forget that we are fighting this war to win universal and permanent peace, such a peace that can only come by the destruction of the spirit of militarism.[20]

Over time, the Societies' roles in graduation lessened, driven by fiscal concerns, as the event simply outgrew their ability to administer. Eventually,

---

[20] *The Biblical Recorder,* May 29, 1918.

in the 1940s and beyond, the purposes and audience were more apart from Societies' history and traditions. As early as March 16, 1901, Philomathesian minutes proposed that the Society no longer be responsible for music at commencement.[21] Four years later, the Phis voted $50 to pay for commencement, which is surely a figure well below the event's budget.[22]

SPEAKERS

One recounting of the 1873 commencement ended with "a lecture delivered by the Rev. Dr. Hatcher, of Petersburg, Va., on *The Advantages of the Modern dance*. It was one of polished irony, exposing, as it sought, the follies of those who are addicted to the fashionable dispensations of the present day to such an extent as to jeopardize and destroy their health. The dance characterizes one of the finest experiences ever invented to engender and confirm disease. The address elicited frequent peals of laughter and the happy delivery of the speaker together with his imposing personal appearance has occasioned many well-merited complements."[23]

While Dr. Hatcher's speech was certainly unorthodox, having multiple speakers for graduation was not. Typically, these speakers were courted and invited by the Debating Societies' membership well past the early 1900s. Over time, faculty and administration incrementally assumed the role. The societies continued nominating graduation speakers until 1938. For the next twenty years, until 1956, a Committee on Literary Societies and Debate recommended speakers to the faculty. It is unclear when the administration assumed sole authority for inviting outside commencement speakers.

Initially, single speakers from beyond the campus addressed the societies on their February founding. For example, Rev. J. L. Reynolds, Richmond, Virginia, delivered the annual address for the two literary societies in 1849, generating a chaste review: "The subject, The Conquest of Knowledge, was truly a chaste and eloquent production, exhibiting much learning, the commendation of all present." [24]

---

[21] Philomathesian Minutes, March 16, 1901.

[22] Philomathesian Minutes, November 4, 1905.

[23] *The Weekly Era*, July 3, 1873, page 3.

[24] *The Weekly Standard*, June 15, 1849, page 3.

Soon, the societies selected, together and in alternating years, several speakers each year: the Baccalaureate, the Alumni Address before the Founding Societies, The Alumni Dinner Speaker, and the Commencement Address—an impressive lot.

The 1935 speakers included the "Commencement Sermon, Rev. J. B. Hipps, professor of religion at Shanghai University; graduation speaker Josephus Daniels, United States Ambassador to Mexico and Secretary of the Navy; Ovid C. Foote of Washington DC delivered the alumni dinner address, which was credited with 1000 attendees."[25]

In the early years, the selection process under the auspices of the societies, undoubtedly in consultation with the faculty and individuals with favored contacts, tended to favor ministers of major churches across the Eastern United States. Later, notable educators, often presidents at various colleges, and journalists, typically editors of influential publications, filled the invited ranks. Hardly a year passed when the speaker was not accomplished and, most often, a major public personality.

Obtaining a weighty speaker was not always easy. The Societies started months ahead, writing letters of invitation. Recorded in the Phi Minutes of December 11, 1841 – in margins described as in "Candlelight" – "a long debate ensued after losing two commencement speakers. A list of alternatives was offered in alternatives to alternatives, the pecking order in service to the shrinking timeline." [26]

---

[25] *The Charlotte Observer*, May 26, 1935, page 9.

[26] Philomathesian Minutes December 11, 1841.

A great preponderance of the selections included a Who's Who of major names of the day, often in positions of considerable influence. Some selections, in retrospect, seem odd.

One such example drew attention, appearing in 1857, as printed in the Raleigh's *Semiweekly Standard*, "We understand that the Rev. Dr. Hooper intends, in his Commencement speech of Wake Forest College on 10 June, to address the audience on this subject: 'The sacredness of human life,' and American indifference to its destruction, as exemplified,

> By the bloodshed of our public highways.
> By the bloodshed of sudden rencounters
> By the bloodshed of the duel.
> By the bloodshed of the bar to the jury box."[27]

A speech tackling provocative social policy was itself unusual, yet this speech advertised itself unabashedly in newspapers before his delivery at commencement. William Hooper was a past President of Wake Forest, 1845-1848.[28]

Four years earlier, the Societies invited a speaker to address the Literary Societies, Abraham W. Venable,[29] "The greatest talker of the age."[30] Venerable was a lawyer from the Hillsborough area and a former Congressman whose opposition to the Compromise of 1850 cost him his reelection. He was a staunch champion of State's Rights in the pre-Civil

---

[27] *Semi-Weekly Standard*, May 30, 1857.

[28] More formally, Hooper's address was titled, *The Sacredness of Human Life and American Indifference to its Destruction*, which was especially concerned about the lawlessness as represented by the violent caning of MA Senator Sumner on the floor of the Senate by Representative Preston Brooks of South Carolina, who rendered Sumner unconscious and bloody on the floor of the Senate. Sumner had just delivered a speech, "The Crime Against Kansas," in which he railed against the institution of Slavery. https://www.senate.gov/artandhistory/senate-stories/charles-sumner-after-the-caning.htm. Hooper's address elicited disapproval from certain factions as Paschal noted: "Though admitting the excellence of certain features of the address, "at one time keen in irony, at another burning in satire," on the whole the editor of the *Biblical Recorder* seemed as much displeased with it as he had been pleased with the address in which the speaker of the previous year attacked the founders of the College. Paschal, G. W. (1935). *History of Wake Forest College*, Vol. I, page 583.

[29] NCPedia, https://www.ncpedia.org/biography/venable-abraham-watkins

[30] *The Fayetteville Weekly Observer*, March 7, 1853, page 2

War period. He preached, "For success in life self-control is necessary; to attain this, self-denial must be practiced, and that too in early life."[31]

Although little is recorded about Venerable's 1853 Wake Forest speech, the *Southern Weekly Post* did note that graduates, six in number, as a whole "disclaimed well – they speak like earnest men." The article also observed that "In former years it has been too commonly the practice with young men close of college to leave and graduate at other institutions."[32] As Wake's reputation grew after the Civil War, which interrupted an ascending Wake, the flow would be reversed after a decade.[33]

> ....Wake Forest College is to have a good bill of fare next Commencement. Dr. LANSING BURROWS, of Augusta, Ga., will deliver the Alumni Address; Dr. J. B. THOMAS, of Brooklyn, New York, will deliver the address before the litterary societies; and Rev. C. A. STAKELEY, of Charleston, S. C. will preach the baccalaureate sermon.

Late in the pre-Civil War years, in 1858, the Board of Trustees opted to impose their own merits with a policy designed to enforce students not straying from the task. The board "Decided to require... the President to read a report publicly on Commencement Day, not only of the distinctions and scholarship, but of the punctuality of each student in attending Chapel and recitation exercises during the Collegiate year. This regulation, it is hoped, will have a happy effect on inducing greater punctuality

---

[31] *Southern Weekly Post*, June 18, 1853, page 2.

[32] *Southern Weekly Post*, June 18, 1853, page 2.

[33] Many speeches of note were given, and it is an impossible task to touch on many here. Some are mentioned, as with the following, for their amazing overstatement. On the fourth day of the 1859 commencement, in an afternoon session before the evening orations, the Mount Vernon Association of Wake Forest sponsored a speech by Mr. Miller. His acumen with audiences was so widely known that the reporter dismissed talking about the speech, saying that everybody already knew of its content. However, he concluded, "From what we heard expressed of it, it is regarded by very many discriminating men fully equal or superior to the orations of Hon. Edward Evertt..." *The Weekly Standard*, June 15, 1859. Everett was the "nation's leading orator" and featured speaker who spoke for two hours, bringing his audience to tears, and was followed by the more modest Abraham Lincoln's *Gettysburg Address*.

and discharge of duty."[34] No records exist of whether this on-high proclamation changed chapel attendance. It is doubtful the President opted to
obscure the congratulatory day with a distracting absentee list.[35]

When selecting commencement speakers, the societies implicitly put
their reputations on the line. Yet not all speakers picked by the Societies
were universally acclaimed. An interesting exception was the controversial 1868 selection of L. B. Olds. The New Yorker was the 1868 Commencement speaker, the first since closing in 1861.

The societies published his address."[36] The Phi Minutes discussing
this publication discloses a curious mystery surrounding the Olds Commencement Address. In an 1868 meeting, the Philomathesians "moved
to instruct Mr. Hufham to confer with publishing houses regarding the
speech of Mr. Olds. They also introduced a resolution binding society
to protect Mr. Olds"[37] Why the group felt a need to "protect" Mr. Olds
is lost to history, although clues and motives pervade the following
findings.

Coverage of the speech from one regional newspaper was expressly
positive, signaling a measured post-Civil War optimism. They observed,
"Few institutions of learning in the South have been able to continue
their operation since the surrender of the Southern armies, and it is truly
gratifying to find that Wake Forest College founded in the liberality of the
Baptists of the State, and concentrated by the prayers and tears of those
who have gone to their rest, still able to weather the storm, and gathers

---

[34] *The Biblical Recorder*, June 17, 1858, page 2.

[35] The President may have read such a list on an alternative day of graduation week.

[36] Olds, L. B., *Language as The Voice of Latitude, With the Control Over Both Sentiment and Music. An Address Delivered Before the Philomathesian and Euzelian
Societies of Wake Forest College N. C.*, June 11, 1868. The address was published at
the considerable cost of $101.00 (plus $.25 to have been delivered from Forestville),
Philomathesain Minutes October 2. Seventy-five copies were sent to Mr. Olds. In the
years before the Civil War, as was told in Volume I of Paschal's history, "nearly all
the literary addresses were published, but in all the years since the War only two, that
of L. P. Olds in 1868 and that of Z. B. Vance in 1872. Both of these were published
by the Philomathesian Society. Mr. Olds' study of *Language as the Voice of Latitude*
was considered a valuable practical contribution. As published, it fills eighty pages, at
about three hundred words on the page. Though every page is interesting, it is hard
to see how an audience could have had the patience to hear the entire address in one
sitting. The publication cost taxed the Philomathesian Society's treasury for several
years. Paschal, G. W (1948)." *The History of Wake Forest College*, Vol. III, page 265.

[37] Philomathesian Minutes, August 28, 1868.

a large and intelligent a number of our citizens together to witness his annual commencement exercises."

The commencement speaker, Mr. Olds, "has selected the influence of climate, language, and music for his theme. The address showed that much labor and research had been called into requisition in its preparation, and was of marked interest by the audience throughout, although it required about two hours for his delivery."[38] Paschal summarized his thesis as "languages are mellow or harsh according to the distance of those who speak to them from the equator, and his speech still has a scientific interest."[39]

The subject of the commencement address may have raised objections, but it was likely part of a larger picture regarding the speaker. His ethnocentrism suggested not polluting our culture with the African and other southern hemisphere cultures. He concludes, "The Northerner cannot be Southern at the same time."[40] Yet, in a speech of the same year in Raleigh, he said, "The man tearing down his own house in anger is not the one to rebuild." He counseled moving beyond the "white man's natural desire to build Reconstruction as nearly to the old order of things as possible."

While hardly moderate to the modern ear, it was likely a bold political statement in the context of the times He concluded, "The genius of the Republic seems able to bear the strain of the two classes of voters, the poor and the ignorant white man, and with the quality; cannot a third class be added, the poor ignorant Negro, without overthrow?"[41] Olds appeared with Republican speakers, likely eliciting enemies in the post-occupation period following the Civil War. As wrongheaded as we find his racist thesis on climate determinism, he also suggests some inclusions for Southern Blacks, enough to cause a stir with the majority "lost cause" opinion.

---

[38] *The indicator*, (Warrenton, North Carolina), June 19, 1886, page 2.

[39] Paschal, G. W. (1943). *The History of Wake Forest College*, Vol. II, page 32.

[40] The speech was also one of acceptance of Equator's peoples, particularly in the diversity of music, "we conceive of the swelling parts of these millions… The simple three stringed instrument of the Hottentot vibrating to the touch of relaxed thought and feeling… The rough clanging of the polar circles… Making one grand chorus epitomizing in the soft and indelicate renderings of the lament of the scattered tribes of Babel…"

[41] *The Daily Standard*, September 18, 1868, page 2.

A *Wilmington Journal* editorial was less than flattering, "I see it announced in the city papers here that one L. P. Olds has been offered the Presidency of the University. [42] ... Olds has no qualifications for the position and is universally regarded, I believe, as an erratic personage who doesn't know his own mind about anything."[43]

It is of interest that the Phis would risk what was likely at stake when inviting a known "progressive" to speak, but the Phis' support possibly had more to do with the fact that his son, Col. Frederick Augustus Olds, was a Philomathesian at the time;[44] loyalty emboldening bravery.

In another instance a decade earlier, *The Weekly Standard* greeted a speaker with praise while masking a dismissive tone with extravagant adulation.

An interesting feature on the occasion of Wake Forest Commencement was the address delivered before Euzelian and Philomathesian Societies by our friend Dr. S. S. Satchwell...[45] The theme of the Orator was "The Influence of Material Agents in Developing Man," the Dr.'s efforts must have been a complete success. The Chapel of the College was said to have been crowded with utmost capacity ... although the doctor was occupied over two hours of delivery, there was no visible evidence of fatigue exhibited by any of the audience. A person who heard it said, "Great attention to its preparation had evidently been paid by his accomplished author, who seemed to have thought much upon the subject – Many of the aphorisms were worthy of being written "in letters of gold."

Dr. Satchwell is no candidate for oratorical honors; and yet his language may be truly said to be "diffused yet terse, poetical though

---

[42] We were unable to find a reference for which university. He applied to the legislature to establish a school, which may or may not have happened.

[43] *Wilmington Journal*, December 25, 1868, page 6.

[44] Frederick Olds moved to North Carolina, became an advisor to Gov. Zebulon B. Vance, and later a newspaperman at *The News & Observer*, becoming an advocate of "social history," history about and for the people – instrumental in preserving great swaths of North Carolina history, https://www.ncpedia.org/biography/olds-frederick-augustus.

[45] A leading Public Health Doctor and researcher who helped establish the State Board of Health in Greensboro, 1879, https://www.ncpedia.org/biography/satchwell-solomon-sampson.

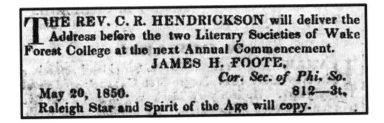

THE REV. C. R. HENDRICKSON will deliver the Address before the two Literary Societies of Wake Forest College at the next Annual Commencement.

JAMES H. FOOTE,
Cor. Sec. of Phi. So.

May 20, 1850.   812—3t.
Raleigh Star and Spirit of the Age will copy.

plain," He is none of your theoretical visionaries who hope to earn an ephemeral reputation by tickling the fancy and pandering....[46]

On many occasions, outside reviewers respond to commencement speakers, heightening the College's silhouette. Obtaining high-profile individuals impacted the school's stature in certain circles, and typically, the society selectors "shopped up," and often within circles occupied by North Carolina Baptists.

In 1878, the State Baptist newspaper was taken with Dr. Henry Mc-Donald. Dr. McDonald, born in Ireland, first landed in New Orleans as a mere youth, whence he made his way to Kentucky, where he taught school and read law. He was converted from Romanism to the Baptist faith and began to preach. He then was a pastor and professor of theology in Georgetown, Kentucky.

The *Recorder* observed, "This Prince of a man captured all hearts during the late Commencement at Wake Forest. His address before the Literary Societies was simply superb, the very best speech for such an occasion that I've heard for many years, if not the best I've ever heard. There is a wonderful charm about the man."[47]

Speakers included several U. S. Senators, including nearly all North Carolina senators and, for example, the Hon. J. B. Currie, U. S. Sen. from Alabama, 1871.[48] U. S. Senator Matt W. Ransom (NC) spoke twice, giving the Address to the Societies in 1877 and ten years later. One reporter was mesmerized, writing, "Senator M. W. Ransom, as the "silver-tongued orator from whose lips that beautiful oration, 'The Defense of the South,' first fell. Senator Ransom arose, and throwing out his cuffs, began his oration. He looked every inch a statesman as he stood

---

[46] *The Weekly Standard*, June 30, 1858, page 3.

[47] *The Biblical Recorder*, June 19, 1878, page 2.

[48] *Wilmington Journal*, May 26, 1871.

before the large audience. He was, as the negro said, "the sinecure of all eyes."[49] The acceptance of racist fare was, on the whole, unquestioned.

Notably his second appearance coexisted with a re-emerging college. *The Biblical Recorder* gave its blessing to the aging politician/orator.

> Ten years ago, we heard him in the old chapel. Those years have marked an era. As he stood before the vast audience, in the new Memorial Hall, he too, must have thought of the change, and given direction to what he said... He is sixty. The raven hair and beard is now white; there is perceptible a slight stoop in the once majestic shoulders; and there is just a little more hesitation in the nervous step... The sight of the audience served to kindle it anew; under the magic effect of his own voice, he rises on the wings of an unsurpassed eloquence... The swelling soul has transformed him.

Early Wait Hall with William Wingate and Prof. William Louis Poteat, later Wake presidents in the foreground.

When Governor Vance addressed the Literary Societies at the 1872 graduation, "Many had been in the crowd that greeted the arrival of his

---

[49] *The State Chronicle* (Raleigh), June 9, 1887, page 2.

train, deboarding as the 'Lion of the Day.'... Only by a strenuous effort, the "boys" could restrain themselves from cheering the man what was a friend to them in need."

Opening the graduation ceremony by introducing Vance, President Wingate told the audience that "it was necessary for the audience to exercise patience, as Gov. Vance was tired by his travels and must have little recuperation before his speech." *The Raleigh News* added that Vance "arrived on the morning train from Fayetteville, where he made a political speech...and traveled all night, yet he was in full trim and as much himself as if he had been caged and preserved for the occasion."[50]

Nearly fifteen years later, the then-late-term Senator Vance again addressed Commencement. At least one reporter was disappointed. "A more perfect day could not have dawned... The presence of Vance made men and women smile in expectancy. But they were somewhat disappointed. Gov. Vance was not funny. He didn't tell any jokes, but delivered a learned address, every word which he read from manuscript. The address was the ablest we've ever heard from our versatile and accomplished Senator. At the same time, it was less popular."[51]

---

[50] *The Raleigh News*, June 27, 1872, page 1.

[51] *The Biblical Recorder*, June 20, 1888, page 2. There were many prominent men at the graduation; as reported in the newspaper, the list is indeed a Who's Who of state government, educational and religious institutions in particular. Gov. Vance was accompanied on stage by Judge Fowle. The newspaper reported, "Among prominent gentlemen on the stage, we noticed Associate Justice Davis, Capt. Charles M Cook and Rev. Bayless Cade, of Louisville; Prof. J. B. Brewer, president of the Chowan Baptist Female Seminary; Prof. F. P. Hobgood, President of Oxford Female Seminary; Rev. Dr. Pham, W. H. Kitchen and W. A. Dunn, of Scotland Neck; Rev. W. R. Gwaltney, of Greensboro; Geo. W. Blount, of Wilson; Rev. John Mitchell, D. D., of Wake Forest; Dr. A. R. Van, Rev. Dr. R. H. Marsh, of Oxford; Rev. W. D., Prichard, Dr. R. R. Overby, of Camden; J. J. Lassiter of Anderson; Rev. J. B. Richardson, of High Point; Rev. N. B. Kopp of Lilesville; Geo. W. Thompson, of Wake Forest; Rev. Geo. W. Sanderlin, of Wayne; Rev. T. J. Taylor, of Warrenton; Rev. W. L. Wright, of Reidsville; Prof. Jno. C. Scars, of Thomasville; Hon. Paul Cameron, of Hillsboro; Dr. T. J. Boykin, of Baltimore, Md.; Judge D. G. Fowle, Maj. S. M. Finger, Hon. Walter Clark, Rev. C. Durham, Col. J. M. Keck, W. H. Pace, Col. P. S. Kennen, J. N. Holding, Donald W. Bain, N. B. Broughton, W. G. Upchurch, R. H. Battle, J. J. Thomas, and B. App. Montague, of Raleigh... In the audience, there were many known and prominent gentlemen from all sections, especially Wake and the surrounding counties. No one who sees the character of the men who attend the Wake Forest Commencement will ever be surprised this is our greatest prosperity." The event signaled, among others of its type, the (re)emergence of Wake Forest in the State's consciousness. A full rendition of Senator Vance's Address on Education is provided in the article.

The year 1886 brought yet another Governor to the ceremony, Gov. Scales, as well as the Chief Justice, Attorney-general, and the President of the Agricultural Society, among others. A *Richmond Dispatch* reporter observed that among the senior orators, there was the absence of allusions to Greece and Rome and more the discussion of such subjects as "strikes, socialism and other living questions of the day. This tendency toward the modern and the practical is attributed to the influence exerted by the eagerly read periodicals in the reading rooms."[52]

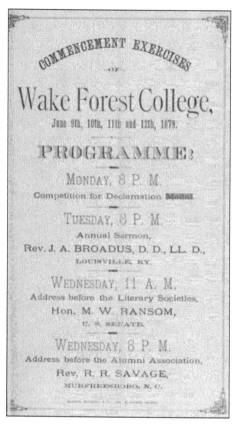

1879 – Commencement "Programme"

Gov. Scales addressed the throng and encouraged the safe observation that "Your college is now a grand success." He stated further his "peculiar pleasure that there were so many of the young men going to preach the gospel."[53]

Many others, especially politicians, graced the commencement stage. After the usual difficulties in locating the 1889 speaker, a charming accounting of a successful ask was provided, along with echoes of the Civil War shadowing the positive description.

The Euzelians and Philomathesians Societies have been fortunately looking there (The lovely Shenandoah Valley, Va., connected with the exploits of Sheridan and Jackson) for a speaker. Yet, he showed his scholarship as a college professor and president and his statesmanship as a representative in Congress. He is from Jefferson

---

[52] *Richmond Dispatch*, June 11, 1886, page 3.

[53] *The Biblical Recorder*, June 16, 1886, page 2.

County, Va., and the mantle of Virginia's statesman, Thomas Jefferson, has fallen upon him. His name is William L. Wilson.[54]

One of the traditional speeches of the middle-to-late nineteenth century was the alumni address before a banquet on the second night of the four commencement evenings. The usually conservative *The Biblical Reporter* stepped out a bit, speculating on the all-male affair in 1887. "There's a sentiment afloat which is gaining adherents rapidly, and that is, the Alumni Association becomes a little less selfish in the matter of banquet... Why is the company composed altogether of men? The presence of ladies would add greatly to the *esprit de corps* of the affair, and the speeches would be better."[55]

It is difficult to imagine the difference from today's graduation ceremonies in tone. One can hardly picture a contemporary university president giving an explicitly Christian speech. This was not the case in 1904, when, in his last graduation, President Charles E. Taylor gave the commencement baccalaureate sermon.[56]

Dr. Taylor preached on "Love," basing his remarks on Phil. 1.8-11: "And this I pray, that your love may abound yet more and more in knowledge and all discernment; so that you may approve the things which are excellent; that ye may be sincere and void of offense unto the day of Christ; being filled with the fruits of righteousness, which are through Jesus Christ, unto the glory and praise of God." Dr. Taylor showed the importance of love as a characteristic Christian virtue, that love was best when directed by knowledge and discernment.[57]

---

[54] *The Biblical Recorder*, June 19, 1889, page 3.

[55] *The Biblical Recorder*, June 22, 1887, page 2.

[56] Apparently, it was the practice that the president gave the baccalaureate address and assumed the role of campus pastor, although outside speakers were also common. Most Wake Presidents to this point were practicing ministers.

[57] *The Morning Post*, May 24, 1904, page 6; His sermon does error to a generic Christian positive tone.

PROCESSION AND RECEPTION

The graduation procession was a public moment for the Literary Societies, showing their wares: banners and sashes, marshals and guests, walkways and applause, which composed a grand entrance worthy of the occasion. In 1842, the Phi Minutes approved a resolution that "after our next commencement every member of this Society, who may refuse to march on any public occasion when the Society agreed to do so, shall without adequate excuse, be fined the sum of five dollars,"[58] an equivalency of over $100 today.

The societies provided explicit instructions for their membership at graduation. As early as 1846, the Philomathesian "Committee of Arrangements" informed the members:

> At the ringing of the bell, the students will assemble at Pres. Wait's house where the marshals will form them into two ranks according to their heights – the tallest in front, from there they will march down Elm Street in front of Prof. Brooks—thence onto Mulberry Street to Broadway, along Broadway in front of the main building turning at right angle they will march to the Chapel—the ranks will then wheel right and left and countermarch lifting hats from their heads as they pass the trustees, faculty until they pass the rear of the procession—they will then fall in immediately after the procession and march into the Chapel.[59]

In the early period, all the graduates would speak. The speaking list read:

Charles Wilmont Egerton – *Latin Salutatory*
James Dunn Huffman – *Fanaticism*
Moses Hamilton Baldwin – *Claims of Self-knowledge*
Elijah Forbes Beachum – *The Child of Nature*
Benson Field Cole– *Individual Effort Indispensable to Success*
Thomas Jackson Foote – *Perpetuity of the American Government*
Lewis Hall Shuck –*Les fausses Prediction touchant l'merique*
Henry Harvey Harris – *Female Education*

---

[58] Philomathesian Minutes, June 1, 1842.
[59] Philomathesian Minutes, May 11, 1846.

Frederick Marion Purify – *Deliverance of the Children of Israel*
Benjamin Franklin Simons – *The Necessity of a Truly American Literature*
Charles Wilmont Edgerton – *Liberty Essential to Progress*
Lewis Hall Shuck – A poem – *Joan of Arc*
James Dunn Huffman – *Valedictory Address*

The Biblical Recorder's description sets the scene for professionals at the cusp of the Civil War, 1856.

On Thursday morning, at 10 o'clock, the public exercises of the Graduating class commence by the members of the Literary Societies, Faculty, and Trustees forming a procession in front of the President's house and proceeding with accompanying music to the College Chapel. The spacious Hall was well-nigh filled with the ladies in attendance while the aisles, doors and windows were crowded with gentlemen who could not otherwise be accommodated. The president, in consecutive order, announced the names and themes of the young gentlemen, who were graduated, and who, in speaking acquitted themselves in a manner highly credible to all concerned.

The audience sat through thirteen speeches, to get to the moment when the newly installed Professor of Moral Philosophy, President Rev. W. M. Wingate, distributed diplomas and made yet another speech of closing remarks.[60]

By the 1870s, colleges were regaining energy after the mid-century devastation of their sustenance. In 1878, for example, "The marshals formed the members of the Philomathesian and Euzelian Societies into two companies under their respective banners, and after marching them single file in opposite directions so as to pass by the Chapel door, the united banners, the members of the two societies locked arms making one more round the circular walks in from the college, entered Chapel in double file, Phi and Eu marching fraternally side-by-side."[61]

---

[60] *The Biblical Recorder*, June 19, 1856, page 2

[61] *The Biblical Recorder*, June 19, 1878, page 2. A complete account of the speeches, guests, and students across the four-day graduation events can be found in this citation. Sometimes, the four days of events were not fully attended. *The Biblical Recorder* reported in 1899, "We have this morning the Literary Address by the distinguish Dr. W. P. Trent, of the University of the South, at Sewanee, Tenn. We are

These long-standing traditions highlighted the debating society's role in commencement, suggesting a formality that misses the more human stories that also occur at commencements. *The State Chronicle*, speaking to its Raleigh audience, wanted to impart the atmosphere for the readers who were not in attendance and presented an upbeat rendition:

> There may be Colleges in the country where more people go to Commencement than come here, but there is no place where everybody has a better time. There is, and always has been, the absence of formality and stiffness here that is a charming novelty and is refreshing. All day and until the evening has waned, gay groups of young folks sit in promenade about the beautiful campus, and their very appearance betrays that degree of enjoyment that is not always found even at college commencements. This year the crowd has been larger than usual. Every train that has arrived since Tuesday morning has brought charming young ladies and gallant young gents from all about, until today (Thursday) the village and grounds are filled with people, every one of whom seems to be enjoying the occasion to the full extent.[62]

One local newspaper could not resist jumping on board, tracking a local connection. *The Roxboro Courier* "heard the remark made by a competent judge that at the recent commencement at Wake Forest, a Roxboro girl was pronounced the handsomest lady attending the commencement."[63] She remained unnamed.

And it was not always about speeches and romance but more about place. The *Weekly State Chronicle* observed, "The pleasures of each recurring commencement to an alumnus of a college are not in the eloquent addresses and sermons, or in the company and music. His pleasure is in living over the old days when life was young, and the future, in his imagination, golden...Some of them were old men, and as they thought of their college days, their eyes brightened, their hearts were lighter, and they walked with a quicker step than was their wont. They were boys again."[64]

---

surprised that there is such a meager attendance. The hall is but little more than half filled. If the people of Raleigh were properly appreciative of opportunities, they would be here by the hundred." *The Biblical Recorder*, May 31, 1899, page 4.

[62] *The State Chronicle*, June 11, 1886, page 1.

[63] *The Roxboro Courier*, June 16, 1892, page 3.

[64] *The Weekly State Chronicle*, June 9, 1987, page 2.

THE BUSINESS OF COMMENCEMENT

Commencement and other holidays served as advertising for the college and societies. They struck gold when observers published glowing accounts in regional newspapers, whose flattery often seemed directed to North Carolina Baptists. The state's citizens were assured that the "through" course of instruction here is [based on] moral culture. This influence invades the whole institution and guarantees to Parents and Guardians that their sons and wards may be considered safe from contaminating influences.[65]

Beginning in 1868, the Societies issued invitations for the Commencements and Anniversary occasions, "although funding the expense somewhat burdensome."[66] The College's commencement was more than simply a rite of passage. The four days of festivity also provided the most public connection to listeners beyond the campus grounds. Markedly, in the early decades each day's speeches and ceremonies displayed traditions in which the debating societies were in evidence.

The Board of Trustees met at the beginning of the graduation week, and their debates and outcomes were routinely reported in stories chronicling the event. In addition to the standard excitement of the college's "growth and unlimited future prospects," the college's aspirations were shared statewide.

At the commencement of 1879, for example, after the death of Dr. Wingate, it was determined to erect a chapel as a memorial to him.[67] Efforts were made "toward raising funds, and before the crowd left the chapel, over $8,000 was subscribed on the spot. The building was at once begun and was completed by June 1880, at the cost of $13,000; the whole amount was raised by voluntary subscription to the friends

---

[65] *The Weekly Standard*, June 17, 1906, page 2.

[66] Paschal, G. W. (1943). *The History of Wake Forest College*, Vol. II, page 56-7.

[67] "The day after Dr. Wingate died, a cold, blustery day in March 1879, Dr. William Royall, Prof. Mills, and Dr. Taylor sat in the angle in front of the library, at the foot of the steps leading up to the Euzelian Society Hall and talked. There was a decided disposition among some of Dr. Wingate's friends to bury the body of the dead president on the campus... This Dr. Taylor opposed, on the ground that it would not be wise to set such a precedent; he suggested that the body be buried in the cemetery and that a monument be erected to Dr. Wingate's memory on the campus in the form of the sorely-needed chapel, for which Dr. Wingate has been appealing." Taylor, C. (1911). Some reflections on Ex-President Taylor. *The Wake Forest Student*, 1911, page 349.

of the college." Memorial Hall would become the home of Wake's most famous civic debates.

The first man to head the list of subscribers to the Wingate Memorial was a farmer named Leigh of Wake County, who gave $1000. This old gentleman was himself uneducated. One of the rooms in the building is named Leigh Hall in honor of him.

Newspapers praise the new chapel as one of the most comfortable meeting buildings in the state, accommodating large crowds. "It has ten windows on each side and is so ventilated at the top that the hot, impure air can escape. Even in the warmest weather, it never gets uncomfortable. It will seat over 1000 people and is situated on the second floor, rendering it airy and cool."[68]

Bringing together the flock required special transportation arrangements, often resulting from negotiations with the railroad supervisors. In 1880, "The Raleigh and Gaston Railroad will issue tickets at three cents a mile to the commencement of Wake Forest."[69] A year later, *The*

INTERIOR VIEW OF THE CHURCH

Wingate Memorial Hall, host site for several public debates

---

[68] *Goldsboro Messenger*, June 13, 1881, page 2. Another estimate placed Memorial Hall's seating capacity at 1500. *The State Chronicle*, June 11, 1886, page 1. They are not in agreement. One thousand seems to be the historical consensus on the capacity of Memorial Hall, which burned to the ground in an arsonist fire in February 1934.

[69] *The News & Observer*, May 25, 1880, page 3.

Biblical Recorder included a letter of invitation from Wake supporter T. H. Pritchard, who said the Raleigh & Gaston and Augusta Airline would sell first-class tickets for 3½ cents and second-class tickets for three cents a mile.[70]

The 1889 trains brought throngs of well-wishers. On Thursday of the Wake Forest commencement week, "an excursion train arrived from Durham containing nine coaches, with about 600 as jolly and orderly Sunday-school people as were ever seen anywhere. The excursion was from the First Baptist and the Blackwell's Baptist churches of that progressive town and were accompanied by a number of their friends... They had Durham Light Infantry Band along which discoursed the very best of music."[71]

By 1889, the round-trip prices rose considerably to 70 cents.[72] Leaving at 9:45 am Raleigh and returning at midnight, the round-trip in 1892 was 85 cents.[73] In 1902, a special offer for a train from Winson-Salem to the Wake Forest commencement was $4.80.[74] The costs and citizens' means helped define the graduation visitors' demographic.

Just as the culture of Wake Forest shifted dramatically in the 1920s, the societies' hold weakened. They might select commencement orators who would speak on a non-main event day or suggest some outside speakers but little else. By 1924, newspapers covering commencement barely made mention of the graduation orators.

An article covering commencement in the *News and Record* of the same year signaled the College's "better health" by a sports reference, "Coach Garrity Wake Forest's football flag was resurrected from the dark caverns of the sub-seller and made to fly exultingly..." During graduation week, it was excitedly noted that the school could sneak in a varsity-alumni baseball game.[75]

One tradition that remained emphasized in campus and community coverage, at least until the acceptance of female students, was a "dreamy" idealization of campus visitors. The romantic lament was particularly

---

[70] *The Biblical Recorder*, June 1, 1881, page 2.

[71] *The Biblical Recorder*, June 19, 1889, page 3.

[72] *The Morning Post*, May 21, 1889, page 6

[73] *The State Chronicle*, June 5, 1892, page 4.

[74] *Winston-Salem Journal*, May 21, 1902, page 2.

[75] *News and Record*, June 4, 1924, page 3.

prevalent in the late nineteenth-century coverage. One local 1881 news-paper observed, "Perhaps the most enjoyable feature of the whole commencement is a social gathering of young people in the library and halls of the two societies. I now write these notes: at 10 PM, the crowd is on the campus in society halls, gallant beaux promenade with beautiful girls, whispering (no doubt) soft words of love, regaled with sweet music from Keshich's First Regiment Band of Richmond, Va. ... The session closed with 181 students.[76]

From the students' viewpoint, the Anniversary Debates, which were more of a festival atmosphere under their direct control and included debates, likely became the students' preferred event. The next chapter examines the anticipation generated by the Anniversary Debates each February.

---

[76] *Goldsboro Messenger*, June 13, 1881, page 2; The commencement for students, as the text points out, was also about receptions and romance. A witness to the 1889 commencement elaborates on the venues' centrality, "the social reunions in Library, Society and Memorial halls were as delightful as ever, through the rain debarred the lover couple the pleasure of Campus promenades 'by the pale light of the moon.' So they had to content themselves with alcoves and recesses in library and hall to breathe out what the burning hearts had hid for the loved ones." *The Wilson Mirror*, June 19, 1889, page 5.

CHAPTER 8

Anniversary Debates – Place, Heritage, Social Opening

Anniversary Day Beginnings

Soon after meeting in November 1835, the Society committees from the two Societies easily agreed to pursue the idea of beginning an annual Anniversary celebration and asked the faculty for consent, which was unanimously given.

In early December of the preceding fall, it had been agreed that each Society would elect a speaker to deliver "an oration at seven o'clock on the evening of the ensuing February 14." As their first representative for this occasion, the Euzelians chose B. F. Marable and the Philomathesians Thomas H. Pritchard." [1]

"Before seven o'clock on the evening of the celebration, the Euzelians marched out of the building by the north end door, the Philomathesians by that on the south end, and to the chapel door where the files uniting marched abreast into the chapel... with much pride... they listened to the speeches of their chosen orators.

Accompanied by slim external audiences, orations commemorating the 4th of July and Washington's birthday paved the way for Anniversary Day.[2] The first iteration, which featured multiple student orations, began

---

[1] Paschal, G. W. (1935). *History of Wake Forest College*, Vol. I, page 595-596.

[2] Paschal proposed that "the early years the Commencements seem to have had no social features and to have been very meagerly attended." Paschal, G. W. (1935).

WAKE FOREST COLLEGE, FORESTVILLE, N. C.

in 1845. By November 1847, the Societies had made arrangements for celebrating Washington's birthday with an oration, each Society furnishing the orator on alternate years. The Washington Birthday celebration faded after the Anniversary observations began in 1854.[3]

Although the society's first public anniversary celebration was not "sanctioned" until February 14, 1854, anniversary observances had arisen earlier. In November 1838, the Philomathesian Society voted to celebrate its anniversary publicly on February 28, 1839, and elected Mr. A. A. Connella to make the principal address on that occasion.

On February 13 of the following year, the Phi Society, following the suggestion of a committee of arrangements, settled on February 28, "the weather in all probability will be cold and disagreeable, and our company small," voted to abandon the plan to celebrate their Anniversary, but instead to have an exhibition on April 24. For this, the Society made an elaborate program consisting of an oration, a debate, a dissertation, two declamations, and one of Garrick's farces. As they agreed, it was too big an undertaking and was abandoned.[4]

A major change in the Anniversary's impact came in 1872 when the highlight became a public debate between the Phi and Eu societies. The debate began at 1:30 and lasted all afternoon.[5]

History of Wake Forest College, Vol. I, page 459. The same pattern was likely with the early internal Anniversary gatherings.

[3] Paschal, G. W. (1935) *History of Wake Forest College*, Vol. I, page 595.

[4] Paschal, G. W. (1935). *History of Wake Forest College*, Vol. I, page 594-595.

[5] *The Herald-Sun*, April 20, 1941, page 10; The Wake literary societies may have had public debates as part of their Anniversary celebrations earlier than some other

An 1872 dispatch to *The Biblical Recorder,* a cross between a travelogue and reporting, observed in idyllic fashion the unfolding of an Anniversary Day. The author begins, "Off for the Wake Forest anniversaries. Pleasant passengers and sweet babies on the train. Cordial welcome at the college. Enjoyed a walk, a talk and a dinner with Dr. Brooks."[6] The *Recorder* describes the audience as having come long distances for the event, particularly the six adjoining counties, which in 1872 would have been the relevant geographical ambit for their readers.

The author paints the festive scene, even as his remarks embody explicit prejudice for Italy and Catholicism. He composed:

3 P.M. Large audience in the chapel. Visitors from Wake, Franklin, Johnson, Granville, Gates and Cleveland. Here is the "Italian band," not that of which the devout Cornelius was Capt., but a band of Italians: two young men playing on harps, one boy and a girl playing on the fiddles, and a man with the flute. The Romans once the noblest men and women on the earth. Now political corruption in a rotten religion having reduced them to a poor dejected state. But they made good music, and best we have heard during these 21 years in which we have been attending debates and senior speaking's (sic) in this chapel.'[7]

He also did not resist irony in his critical but affirming description of the students in attendance, the youthful future. He described:

The students are fine-looking set of young men. Their heads are so welcomed, brushed, oiled, and perfumed, and their hair is beautifully parted and curving over their foreheads. And their long boot-heels enable them to take such a high stand; but the girls also have high heels and larger piles of jute on their heads than any milliner would advise. As for gaudy sashes, gay hats, nodding plumes and brilliant bracelets, we can't begin to do the subject justice. But in spite of

---

schools. Georgia's began in 1888 when debates became part of commencement exercises. Davis, F. B. (December 1949). Debating in the Literary Societies of Selected Southern Universities. *Southern Speech Journal*, Vol. 15.

[6] *The Biblical Recorder*, February 21, 1872, page 2.

[7] Certainly, debates and oratory occurred in the chapel before, but debates were not an invited public event until 1872.

so much fuss and feathers, the young men, and especially young women, present a very fine appearance."[8]

In 1877, a reporter delighted in describing the anniversary celebration as an escape from the mundane. He wrote, "As an acquittal is to the criminal or a fountain in the desert is to the traveler, so is an anniversary to the 'college convict.' How pleasant to lay aside the dry textbooks, even for a single day, and step from your cell to enjoy the sweet nectar from the fountain of pleasure.[9]

Whatever freedoms the reporter alluded to were normally steeped in religion. W. L. Poteat's address to the Literary Societies on February 16, 1877, was unapologetically a call to the service of Christ: Life's a Battle—*Man a Soldier in It*.

The excerpt that follows provides an account of how the 1898 Anniversary Debates were received. The selection credits Thomas Henderson Pritchard for introducing the Anniversary debate idea.

Thomas Henderson Pritchard,
conceived adding debates
for Anniversary Day

For more than thirty years the Literary Societies of Wake Forest College were content to celebrate their birthdays by the delivery of orations at night and a reception immediately after. The former were delivered in the old Chapel.

The afternoon debates, which for twenty-six years had proved a pleasing feature of the Anniversaries, were inaugurated mainly through the influence of Mr. Robert Samuel Pritchard,[10] who had graduated at the head of his class in 1868. After spending two

---

[8] *The Biblical Recorder*, February 21, 1872, page 2.

[9] *The Observer*, February 25, 1877, page 3.

[10] *The Wake Forest Student* misreports the name as Robert Samuel when, in fact, the correct name is Thomas H. The other information is correct as far as we can detect.

years at the University of Virginia, he was accepted by the Foreign Mission Board in Richmond as a missionary. While he was making preparations to join Dr. Yates in Shanghai, China, and was eagerly looking forward to a life of usefulness in his chosen field, his health began to fail. He spent the winter of 1871-72 at Wake Forest, bravely struggling, by active out-door labor, to regain his strength… It was during this winter that Mr. Pritchard urged upon prominent members of the Societies the inauguration of the debate, at least as an experiment. After much discussion, joint action was taken by the Societies. The first debate was held on Feb. 14th, 1872. But before this Anniversary, Mr. Pritchard had passed from earth to heaven.[11]

Of note at the first Anniversary Debate in 1872 was the negative debater Richard (R. T.) Tilman Vann, debating in his junior year. The young men grappled with the topic of the day: *Is an increase of knowledge an increase in happiness?* The program was more philosophical, lighter than the political topics of later years.

R. T. Vann, who at 12 years of age, lost both arms in a cane mill accident, one below the elbow and the other below the shoulder. His mother died when he was five. Through the assistance of an aunt and her husband, he entered Wake Forest College, graduating in 1873 as head of his class. He later earned a Doctor of Divinity degree from Furman.[12]

His life's great vocation was rescuing the Baptist Female Meredith College from near financial oblivion. He served as college president for fifteen years, beginning in 1900. His tenure elevated women's societal access and status in many ways. He stated regarding education, "I am

---

[11] *The Wake Forest Student*, Vol. 17, March 1898, page 469-471.

[12] Vann spent his early years teaching at Baptist female institutes and serving as a pastor with several churches. He also served on the Wake Forest College Board of Trustees from 1894 to 1928. Vann rose to fame in part through his independence in public debates defining the Civil War, an early one contested on the pages of the *Wilmington Messenger*, in which Vann, while acknowledging Confederate general Jubal A. Early's valor, nonetheless rejected his "long connection with that Grizzly horror, the Louisiana lottery. The Louisiana State Lottery Company was a private corporation that ran the Louisiana lottery in the mid-19th century. It was, for a time, the only legal lottery in the United States, and for much of that time, it had a very foul reputation as a swindle of the state and citizens and a repository of corruption. The Lottery was chartered on August 11, 1868, by the Louisiana General Assembly with a 25-year charter and, in exchange, gave the State $40,000 a year. Wikipedia. https://en.wikipedia.org/wiki/Louisiana_State_Lottery_Company.

opposed to educating women as women. I am in favor of education. The idea that woman acts by intuition and man by reason degrades the woman."

He was also an executive secretary of the Baptist State Convention and was influential in saving Wake Forest president W. L. Poteat's career, arranging a series of lectures for Poteat to defend the teaching of evolution in his science class, which threatened to divide not only North Carolina but much of the South. Poteat's eloquent lecture, "Christianity and Enlightenment," in which he insisted that "manifestly science cannot discredit faith," resulted in his reclamation to serve both science and religion.[13]

As the first debate launched, Vann was simply a student debater. After the 28 to 52 votes for the negative (Vann's assigned side winning), an eyewitness account observed that "the truth is both sides are right. A knowledge of truth and virtue is an increase of happiness, while a knowledge of vice and the ways of iniquity is an increase of sorrow."[14]

R. T. Vann

The Anniversary Day audiences eventually demanded more serious topics, forgoing the playful for more "thoughtful" content. *The Wake Forest Student* provided a thorough, turn-of-the-century synopsis of the Anniversary Day events topics in 1898.

... After the first few years, in the character of the questions selected for discussion. These were, at first, for the most part, hackneyed and outworn subjects, though many can

---

[13] "Christianity and Enlightenment," Baptist State Convention; Winston-Salem, North Carolina; 1922, William Louis Poteat Collection, Wake Forest Special Collections & Archives, https://wakespace.lib.wfu.edu/handle/10339/101895. Also see Linder, S. C. (1963). William Louis Poteat and The Evolution Controversy, *The North Carolina Historical Review*, Vol. 40, No. 2 page 135-157.

[14] *The Biblical Recorder*, February 21, 1872.

bear testimony to the fact that they afforded occasion for genuine oratory and brilliant rejoinder.[15]

In the years immediately following were discussed such questions as these: "Is the Sword Mightier than the Pen?" "Which Is the Cause of More Evil, Ambition or Intemperance?" "Was Calhoun or Clay the Greater Statesman...

It was not until 1882 that questions involving practical, economic factors and the public policy of our own country began to get their innings. The first of these, regarding "Universal Suffrage"... In 1883, the bone of contention was furnished by "Foreign Immigration," in 1885, by "England versus Ireland," and in 1886, by "Free Education by Taxation."

More contemporary themes for debates seemed to favor policy issues. The following are some of the more recent subjects: A United States Railroad Commission (Phi, 1892), Election of U. S. Senators by Direct Vote (Phi, ten times, 1989-1927; Eu, six times, 1899-1917), and Government Ownership of Railroad and Telegraph lines (Phi, 18 times, 1840-1940, Eu, 14 times, 1889-1919).

Such questions... are certainly more profitable to the large audiences that hear and enjoy the speeches, being stimulating to thought and distinctly educational.

There has been a gradual improvement, not only in the questions, but also in the debates themselves... More stress is now laid on essential rather than incidental features. There is better taste exhibited in the personal references in the second speeches.

All these changes for the better are some of the outward indications – as they are the results – of the gradual expansion of the courses of study and the general improvement of the work of the whole College...[16]

Attempts to make topics more relevant, often in response to criticisms, resulted in more germane Anniversary debates. A worthy example took place in the 1906 debate. *The Wake Forest Student* explained that the Anniversary resolution about *Child Labor in manufacturing, prohibiting*

---

[15] Each of the men who took part in it have made their mark in the world—three at the bar and one in the pulpit. They were H. R. Scott, A. C. Dixon, D. A. Covington, and Bruce Williams. *The Wake Forest Student*, Vol. 17, March 1898, page 469-471.

[16] *The Wake Forest Student*, Vol. 17, March 1898, page 469-471.

the employment of children under 14 years of age in the mills and facto-
ries of the State, was of importance to the South during this era.

They reasoned that the topic "is an up-to-date question and a live
issue, one which will interest the members of our legislature during the
winter. It's a question every North Carolinian should study, as this is fast
becoming a manufacturing State, and whether or not we shall allow the
seed of our future citizens to be ground up in the mills."[17]

VANCE AI   ANNIVERSARY SPEAKERS.
WHITEHEAD   ALLEN   FOWLER   PRIVOTT   HARPER   MARTIN
SEAGRAVES, secretary   STEPHENSON, President

The public debate occurred at two in the afternoon and offered the
flavor of the era's debates, powerful and direct. In this instance, the negative concedes their opponent's ground, shifting the basis for the decision.[18]

> Mr. William E Speas – solemn, stern, earnest – representative of the
> Euzelian, was the first speaker... He spoke with confidence, for he
> knew he was throwing some hard nuts to crack at the feet of his
> opponents.
>
> In the first place, child labor is detrimental to the physical welfare
> of a child. That working the twelve-year-old child for 11 hours a day,
> or worse still, for the same link length on that night, amid flying lint,

---

[17] *The Wake Forest Student,* Vol. 25, November 1906, page 637.
[18] *Bulletin of Wake Forest College,* 1905, page 84.

in a fetid atmosphere, amid the roar of machinery, must inevitably result in slowed child's physical development.

He showed the effect of working young girls in the most delicate circumstances. Their lives must inevitably result in wrecking their physical and moral life, which will interfere greatly with their life's great calling. If the exploitation is allowed to continue, it must necessarily result in the progressive degeneration of our race, resulting violently in race suicide.

Mr. Thomas N. Hayes – clear, powerful, convincing – the representative of the Philomathesian Society, was first on the negative. When he begins in that strong voice of his, everyone listened knowing that his opponents would fare badly ere he ceased.... The faces of his antagonists were a puzzled expression as he continued... "We are not here to defend child labor or to eulogize the cotton manufacturing industry for we admit the proposition, that child labor is an evil...This question is for consideration of a remedy, not the discovery of an evil. We are opposed the commercial children of tender age.... Speaker proceeds objections not to the law's intent but rather it's workability.[19]

The Affirmative prevailed. "Dr. Poteat expressed his delight on having quite a number of members of the legislature present. The Governor would have been present had not illness prevented."

Anniversary Day Reflections – 1872-1922

The introduction of debates into the anniversary celebration added momentum when Wake Forest emerged from the Civil War's aftermath. The school regained stability and sought to find a larger role in society. Due to improved transportation and proximity to the state capital in Raleigh, the town was increasingly populated by alumni with governmental clout.

The two Societies owned Anniversary Day and would leverage that opening to the world. It was, as *The Wake Forest Student* acclaimed, "In some respects the most important event of the year. It is the one in which the individuality of the student becomes more prominent, untrammeled

---

[19] Oscar Mangum, Editor, *The Wake Forest Student*, November 1906, Vol. 26, page 643.

by rulings of Hiram[20] (sic) it is a time under the orderings and management of the students, most especially, and affords them an opportunity to try their strength, unsupported by the hands that have led them – and their weaknesses too, if youth has any.[21]

Shortly after the Anniversary debates going public, an 1877 newspaper, *The Observer* (Raleigh), captured the pattern of Anniversary debates that would hold for decades. The reporter, characteristic of the era, offers an

---

[20] Ihram is a state one enters into to demonstrate their veneration for the Sacred Precinct (Haram) around Mecca. One may not pass the boundary delineated by the Landmarks (Miqāt, pl. Mawāqīt) except in a state of Ihram.

[21] *The Wake Forest Student*, Vol. 2, March 1883, page 319. *The Biblical Recorder* added to the sentiment of student independence: "On these Anniversary days, the students assume sole charge. The faculty are in the background; and it is all the better that such is the case. Not that the instructor is not wiser than the instructed, but because he is. He prefers that this day shall be a student's day, for its completeness bespeaks his own workmanship... The joyous, rollicking, free anniversary is, therefore, the student's favorite, and has about it the sparkle and snap of youth and growing strength." *The Biblical Recorder*, February 16, 1887.

abstract of arguments presented, all while adding his own dramatic suspense:

At 2 o'clock the spacious chapel was filled with an audience which, for pretty ladies and fine-looking young men, could not be equaled anywhere but at Wake Forest.

The officers and debaters, six fine looking young men, take seats upon the rostrum... The Secretary... reads the query for... "Was the administration of Henry VIII detrimental or beneficial to England?"

Mr. W. L. Wright, of Montgomery, opened the debate in one of the most

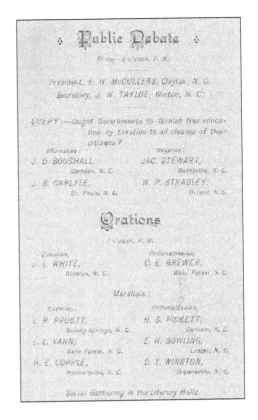

pointed philippics (sic) we ever listen to. He presents a character so hideous, selfish and polygamist, that it is hard to see how anything beneficial would come from such a ruler. Mr. Wright possesses the unusual tact of knowing how to be severe and fair at the same time, which combined with his logical reasoning, renders him a fearful antagonist in any debate.

The audience can't see how such an argument can be answered until Mr. W. E. Daniel, of Weldon, replies in a beautiful and well-written speech. He dwelt upon the disadvantages under which Henry assumed the throne, the influence of public opinion, and the events of the Reformation. Mr. Daniel, in his happy manner of delivery, put his arguments with such significance and telling force, that he leaves the audience unable to decide which way to vote.

Mr. J. G. Bunch, of Edenton, continues the debate in the affirmative with an invective oration that reminds us of the criticisms of Addison. Terse, vigorous and severe, he presents the *darkest* picture of royalty and selfishness. He censures Henry for withholding the Bible from his subjects and living a polygamist life. He completely converts us… with such logical reasoning and piquant arguments that we almost decide not to vote at all.

After rejoinders of 10 minutes by each of the speakers, the vote of the audience is taken, and the question is decided in the affirmative by the vote of 32 to 30.[22]

Moving into the 1880s, a more boastful, confident feeling emerges. *The Biblical Recorder* sang the praises of their perceived "awakening" when describing the 1883 gathering: "Old students and visitors show their appreciation by attending in such numbers as to fill to overflowing the large audience room of the Wingate Memorial, and it is difficult to obtain even standing room in the halls, library, and reading room. Reviewing the history of the college… has always been one of the moral and intellectual grandeur, yet it has been within the past seven years especially that the College has grown to be one of the most commodious and prominent institutions of its kind among Baptists of the South."[23]

The details of the 1889 Anniversary event were documented in *The Biblical Recorder,* whose reporter was in the house, along with a weighty segment of Raleigh's elite.

Many who are familiar with crowds that assemble at the College on special occasions [would think] that the gathering this time suggested a commencement crowd. A larger number of Raleigh people attended than ever before. They went out on three trains at various hours; a special train which left here at 4:30 p.m. carried, among others, Governor Fowle, State Auditor Sanderlin, Rev. Dr. J. W. Carter, and about seventy-five members of the legislature.

… The subject was, "Are the merits of the present system of free schools in North Carolina sufficient to justify the State in supporting it?"… The young gentlemen made the debate spicy and lively… It was left to the audience to decide which side made the best arguments. The majority sided with the negative.

Gov. Fowle, who was given an ovation as he entered the Hall, was called upon for his speech. He gracefully and cheerfully responded

---

[22] *The Observer* (Raleigh) February 25. 1877.

[23] *The Biblical Recorder*, February 21, 1883, page 2.

in a short, brilliant, cheering talk, in which he expressed his pride in Wake Forest as a State institution, and returned to the fact that the 1st degree of any kind ever conferred upon him was given by Wake Forest College.[24]

By the late 1890s, some observed that the debates were "stimulating and engrossing," but the orations were often "monotonous and unoriginal." The refrain was that the orations were "endured rather than enjoyed."

Periodically, however, a speech would sparkle, as in the case of John B. Spillman, a junior who spoke at the 1890 Anniversary. His oration was entitled *Israel's Political Redeemer.*[25] Paschal, in his Wake Forest History, underlined the speech for its contrast with the dull, too stylized oratories typically presented. He observed, "…an excellent address in reading as well as in hearing, for the delivery of which he took half an hour, audaciously relieving his tendency to hoarseness with sips now and then from one or another of two glasses, one containing a colorless fluid, the other red wine. Those who heard the speech will never forget it, nor the speaker."[26]

Although the orations were not as popular as the debates, the orators had one advantage over the debaters. Before the speeches, the young orators were conducted down the aisle of Memorial Hall in the midst of thunderous applause, while the debaters were deprived of this fanfare.[27]

---

[24] *The Biblical Recorder*, February 20, 1889, page 2.

[25] Harris, Nan Lacey, Anniversary Day Affair Once Was Social Event of The Year – Speaking of 1890 Anniversary. *Old Gold and Black*, February 4, 1944, page 1, 4.

[26] The speech can be found in *The Wake Forest Student*, July 1890, page 505.

[27] Not all newspaper coverage was optimistic. In 1895, the coverage of the oratories aroused some negative responses to speaker Robert Simms' language, who delivered an oratory entitled *The Crusade of the Nations. The News & Observer* offered this corrective. "He said he did not mean the crusades of history, but the March of the people whom God loves. He treated his subject with much insight into the trend of present events. *The News & Observer*, February 13, 1897, page 4.
   In a natural way, the criticism of young Simms is illustrative of how public events like the 1897 Anniversary Day oratories were part of larger cultural debates. *The Caucasian* (Clinton, NC) newspaper is an example of running with the story. *The Caucasian* was published for about 25 years and was progressive in its orientation despite its moniker. It picks up on the speech by Robert Nirwana Simms at the 1897 anniversary celebration and extols it thusly. – A YOUNG MAN'S PATRIOTIC ORATION: "The most glorious invigorating encouragement of the hope that there is to be in this great country of ours an immortal spirit of liberty and justice is the fact that the coming man – the boys in youth of today – are studying the problems which are coming up for solution, and are getting at the basic truth of the principles

The pattern of coverage of the debates fell into form, with many newspapers offering direct coverage or reprinting other papers' stories. The College and the Societies increasingly received admiring press.

One paper reported that the 1895 Anniversary celebration "was so well enjoyed by all that the Dawn light was stealing across the eastern sky when the crowd began to disperse."[28]

The positive coverage of the Anniversary Day continued for more than two decades. In 1905, on the 75th birthday, the *Farmer and Mechanic* (Raleigh) newspaper extolled:

> Oratory, fervid with the fervor of the South, argumentative with the argument of the trained mind, was the feast spread at the annual debate and oratorical exercises of a literary society at Wake Forest College today.
>
> The annual events are a great feature in the life of this college town. The hall – and it is a large one – is crowded afternoon and night. The

1905 Anniversary Officers – *Howler*

---

by which these problems must be met and solved. As evidence of this fact the CAUCASIAN takes the liberty of publishing, in this issue, an oration delivered by Mr. Robert N. Simms at the Wake Forest College Anniversary on February 22. We have not at any time seen in so young a man a greater evidence of the fire of indignation and righteous rebellion against the inexpressible 'sham' now mis-called a government of the people for the people by the people." *The Caucasian* (Clinton, NC), April 8, 1897, page 2. R. N. Simms was also the graduating class salutatorian in 1895.

[28] *The Patron and Gleaner* (Lasker, NC), February 28, 1895, page 1.

old settler is here, the young children are here, the vigorous young manhood and womanhood, the maturity of the strong and the feeble. It is a galaxy of beauty and of manliness.

Especially happy is the season for college students. Being masculine in great number, and susceptible because of the abstinence the influx of feminine frills and furbelows, common beauty of the face and form, always cause a warm glow to start in the heart throbbing and cover the face with smiles.[29]

Individual debaters often were held up for public acclaim. The 1914 *Wake Forest Student* etched, "The second debater for the negative is called. A long, slender, lean-looking fellow walks to the stand. 'Who is he? Can he speak? Where did he come from?' came the whispered question from over the hall. They did not have long to wait, Mr. R. H. Taylor poured such a volley of argument into the room, that the gentlemen of the affirmative pushed back their hair, looked in their papers, whispered to each other, and new fire flashed in their eyes... The Band played. The audience stretched..."[30]

President W. L. Poteat, the president of Oxford College and the Board of Trustees, judged the debate. The vote was split two to one in favor of the negative.

At other times, particular papers alerted neighbors of heroic contestants. The 1894 *Democrat* (Scotland Neck, NC) noted one debater because of his special background. They wrote: "The 59th Anniversary exercises of the literary societies of Wake Forest College were celebrated... One of the negative debaters was W. C. Newton of Legos, Africa." Newton is an example of the type of young man Wake was trying to produce in the 1800s.[31]

---

[29] Edward Britton, *The Farmer and Mechanic*, February 14, 1905, page 8.

[30] *The Wake Forest Student*, Vol. 32, March 1914, page 424.

[31] *The Commonwealth* (Scotland Neck, NC), February 22, 1894, page 3. "W. C. Newton lived in Nigeria for several years following the appointment of his parents and older sister by the Foreign Mission Board in 1889. His parents and sister died of 'African fever' (possibly yellow fever) after brief periods of service. Newton Memorial School, in Oshogbo, Nigeria, a boarding school for missionary children, was named in honor of W. C. Newton and his mother. Though Newton loved the African people and was deeply concerned for mission work there, it was not thought wise for him to return to the dangerous African climate when he was appointed a missionary in 1902. Instead, he went to China, where he served 37 years and later

Three years later, in 1909, an account is noteworthy as it delivers in more detail how students experienced the event. The college newspaper preceded the historical recounting with the headline:

ANNIVERSARY DAY . . . WAS SOCIAL EVENT OF THE YEAR
Bright lights, Pretty Girls, Stimulating
Speeches Marked the Day

Lights were bright in the Society Hall. Wake Forest men had waited long for this hour. The orations were over, and the speakers triumphantly bore a blushing proud girl on each arm. The doors have been thrown open between the Society Halls and the crowd roared from one to the other...

Faculty wives reigned over the punchbowl, whose contents rapidly became depleted only to be filled again. The popular girl excitedly filled out a lengthy date list, sneaking a glance out the corner of her eye to see the impression she was making on other members of her sex... She could hardly wait to get back to Meredith to tell the unlucky girls what they had missed... Her escort was proud... of his girl, proud of his rarely worn evening clothes, proud that this important social event, Anniversary Day of 1909, had been a success.

Not only did the College look forward to the day with happy anticipation, but also the townspeople of Wake Forest ... especially the young girls. People from the surrounding countryside left their farms and drove the family buggies into town. Often, the Anniversary was attended by a state legislator, a venerable court judge, or even a governor. It was an event that appealed to everyone who knew Wake Forest...

The peak of the celebration came at the social gathering in the Society Halls after the orations were finished. Here the feminine guests of the students had the chance to shine. The girl not only dated her inviter but her close friends as well. She met the faculty; she conversed with students; she showed off her corsage of American Beauty roses. The reception lasted until midnight. At this late hour,

---

joined the Baptist theological seminary in Hwanghsien... Wake Forest College awarded him the honorary Doctor of Divinity degree in 1925. Newton died at 93 years of age in 1966."

the special train could often be heard blowing its whistle for those girls who wished to return to Raleigh.[32]

Occasionally, reporting on Anniversary Day would focus on the issue debated. One instance piqued press interest in 1888. The debaters took up the argument of "laissez-faire" – "the state should let the individual alone to pursue wealth and happiness as he pleases as long as not... assail the rights of others."[33] The negative advocated the necessity of government restraints on capitalistic excess like Jay Gould and telegraph lines.

The debate topic generated newspaper backlash. A *News & Observer* column warned that a non-laissez-faire future would be dystopian.

> The reporter of the debate, conducted on the occasion of the anniversary celebration did the Negative an injustice which we cannot pass by unnoticed. The arguments of the Affirmative were stated very fully, but those on which the Negative base their defense for the most part was not mentioned. The proposition established by facts of history, which was not, and cannot be refuted, that any interference contrary to Laissez-faire leads inevitably to paternalism and that socialism, communism, anarchy and revolutions are all the children of paternalism was prove conclusively and stands unrefuted; but our reporter said not a word of these things.[34]

In 1888 *The Biblical Recorder* was teased by the laissez-faire topic. They broke in, "Any doubt as to the truth of the statement made by the Rev. Thos. Dixon, Junior, In the RECORDER some months ago, that the Literary Societies of Wake Forest College were the best school of oratory and debate in the country, must have vanished if the doubters had the pleasure of hearing the [Laissez-faire] debate and oration last Friday."[35]

Early in the century, the Anniversary event felt the pinch of inadequate venues and rising attendance. A 1902 suggested solution, which likely

---

[32] Nan Lacey Harris, Anniversary Day Affair Once Was Social Event of The Year, *Old Gold and Black*, February 4, 1944, page 1, 4.

[33] *The News & Observer*, February 19, 1888, page 1. This source provides a full account of the debate.

[34] *The News & Observer*, February 21, 1888, page 1.

[35] *The Biblical Recorder* cites the same Thomas Dixon, author of *The Clansman* (1905). See Chapter 11 – Race Permeates Wake Forest (Debate) History. *The Biblical Recorder*, February 22, 1888, page 2.

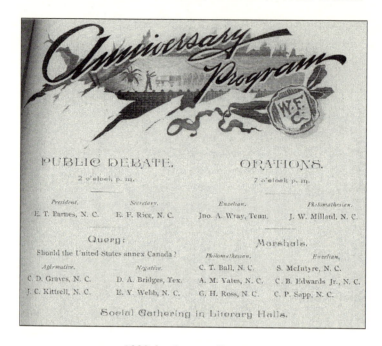

1892 Anniversary Program

did not happen, was that "the annual reception, which is usually held after the close of the exercises, will be omitted. The reason for this is a lack of time, and also, it is generally felt that we have no suitable Hall in which to give such a reception... And, too, weather conditions at this time of the year are ordinarily bad, and this makes it inconvenient for the young ladies in attendance.[36]

Now and then, the debates were criticized as tiring exercises. The assembled students and citizens, conditioned to sit for elongated periods, would show their fatigue. Alternatively, a debate, or debater, often captivated an audience.

In a "stereotyped description," the 1908 debater Fred T. Collins was singled out for his skills displayed at the anniversary program. The reporter's entry testified in a lively manner regarding Mr. Collins:

The most popular speech was that of the inimitable Mr. Collins, the most typical Irishman in North Carolina, a rough-and-tumble speaker, who had added to his inherited talent of some speech and

[36] *Old Gold and Black*, January 10, 1925, page 1.

the fine qualities of a platform orator. Mr. Collins kept his large audience in an uproar, with the skill of the word-magician turning ludicrous nonsense into what had appeared to be an invincible argument. The speaker is perhaps the most original speaker at Wake Forest.[37]

In the 1908 program, an evening of oratory was summarized by the *News & Observer*, noting an insightful speech presented by Mr. Fred F. Brown regarding the Civil War's long aftermaths in the South's psyche. His speech, fundamentally hopeful, acknowledges the region's continuing "inferiority complex," echoes of which permeated the politics of the South.[38] His topic, *The Building of the South,* reveals a South just beginning to surface forty years after the War, placing Wake Forest as a presence in the region. He articulated, in part:

The pages of Southern history are star-studded with the names of those who, in war and peace, have exercised such wisdom, courage, and foresight that their names are rightly placed in the galaxy of heroes... Tonight, we ask you to shift the emphasis to turn your gaze from those before the footlights, to look upon those behind the scenes. Those who in obscurity have patiently, quietly, wrought out the South of today.

In obedience to the advice and example of Lee, they returned to their homes and volunteered in the armies of enterprise and industry... There was no trumpet sound, no bugle call, no taunting enemy, no enthusiasm that comes from the numbers associated together. It was a supreme test of patriotism, and never did a people stand the test more heroically...

---

[37] *The News & Observer*, February 16, 1908, page 10. "Each speaker was greeted with spontaneous applause and the walls of the historic chapel vibrated and the floor shook whenever a speaker would score an important point. After being absent from the chapel some time, the judges return, and Chief Justice Clark made a brief speech that captivated the audience saying that the winners of the debate had not secured a unanimous decision, but by a two to one the negative was declared the victor. Somebody said it was the Chief Justice who filed "a dissenting opinion."

[38] Additionally, a residual sense of regional inferiority of being "Southern" was resisted in public comment but existed, sometimes reflected in defensive debate resolutions. For example, implied in the 1881 topic: *Which have furnished the more distinguished men, the Northern or the Southern states?* (Negative 10 to 42, December 16, 1881.)

Old Gold and Black, February 1917, Eight of Nine
Front Page Stories were Society/Debate Related

Along with the industrial prosperity came the political development. The political outlook in 1865 was even darker than the
industrial prospect. Yet investigations will reveal the startling fact
that the political administration of the South has surpassed in many
respects those of any other section. The robbery, speculation and
corruption methods of bosses and political machines that have characterized other sections have not flourished in the South. It is true
that in national affairs the South has not gained her lost prestige,
that she has not furnished the presidents for the nation since 1865

as she did before 1865... But who will deny that, though slowly, yet surely, we are regaining our lost prestige, winning more and more the confidence of other sections... Is there not every reason to believe that, as at no distant day, the South will again come into her own and 'The subtree will return to the Kings.'

... There are more men we know who, like Lee, returned from the conflict against the armed foe and took up the equally ardent battle against the more subtle foe – ignorance. There are more men than we know, who again likely refused handsome salaries and easy positions in another business content to remain in the schoolroom having no salaries. There are such men throughout the South, there are such men in Wake Forest.[39]

The centrality of anniversary celebrations continued strong until the mid-1920s. Just how dominant the debating societies were is illustrated by a February 1917 *Old Gold and Black* cover (above). Eight of nine front page stories concerned the debate events, tryouts, Society news and history, and even humor as with the moonlight train story from Raleigh's Meredith. The word "Debate" appears in the article copy twenty-nine times.[40]

Anniversary Day Practices

WEATHER

A recurring theme for the Anniversary Day was the strong likelihood of inclement weather. The February Day celebration was performed in the heart of winter. The weather could dash the hopes of the post-oratory stroll with your evening date, "far from the madding crowd." The weather led coverage, with rare exceptions, in every anniversary news story; the elements closer to the lives lived than in our modern impermeable world.

A sampling, especially of Anniversary debates coverage in the late 1800s, expresses the weather's supremacy in the most imaginative and delightful manner.

---

[39] *The News & Observer*, February 16, 1908, page 10.
[40] *Old Gold and Black*, February 17, 1919.

- 1885—"Day after day, the students at Wake Forest College awaited the coming of 13 February, the 50th Anniversary of the Philomathesian and Euzelian Societies. Snow fell the night before, and when day broke upon the white fields and giant forest heavily burdened with snow and ice, the snow changed into a slow rain mingled with hail. A real wintry day which rendered the glowing expectations of the College boys almost groundless."[41]

The Great Snow of 1899

Fayetteville Street in Raleigh, during the Great Blizzard of 1899.

- 1885—"Notwithstanding the clemency of the weather, the audience was large enough to make the occasion one of interest and pleasure. Among those returning was Thomas Dixon. Entertainment by the Euterpean Band of Raleigh. After the hall had been comfortably heated, the music rendered it so pleasant indoors that all seem to forget the cold, stormy blast without."[42]

- 1878—The day "Dawned with a cloudless sky. The citizens of the surrounding country came in private conveyances, and at an early

---

[41] *The Wake Forest Student,* Vol. 4, No. 7, 1885, page 309.

[42] *The Wake Forest Student,* Vol. 4, No. 7, 1885, page 309.

hour, the village was alive with people coming and going in every direction. The piazzas and porticos of the Professors' houses and other private residences were filled with young of both sexes who seemed to have a joyful time... to [bask in] the beautiful shade of the grand old oak on the campus, to lounge upon the rustic seats beneath them, and indulge in anecdote and witticism."[43]

- 1887—"The 52nd birthday of the societies was celebrated on 11 February under the most auspicious circumstances. Despite the evil weather conditions from former occasions and the ill-omened yellow flag on the present, the day dawned brightly, the wind blew briskly, and the boys went busily to and fro. This is the student's gala day, and every boy belonging to the Societies hails it with delight..."[44]

- 1888—"Friday morning came out in beautiful sunlight. The face of old Earth smiled under the warm greeting from the King of Day. All the forces of nature were combined to give Wake Forest and her history a day suitable for the occasion. The weather could scarcely have been more inviting."[45]

- 1888—"The weather was simply glorious. No correspondent ever said that about anniversary weather before. It's an original statement."[46]

- 1890—"The day before was very pleasant, and all took that as an earnest possibility of bright weather for the great occasion. But when, upon the next day, the wind was blowing a gale, and for the time the rain came down in torrents, the high hopes of the previous day gave way to deep despondency, which shone upon every face. But about 11 o'clock the cloud drifted away, the sun came out, and the day, begin so bad, ended as beautiful as anyone could have asked."[47]

- 1891—"According to the usual fatality which attends such occasions, the customary rain-storm put in an early appearance, and the fifty-six Anniversary of the foundation of the literary societies

---

[43] *The Weekly Observer*, June 18, 1878, page. 4.
[44] *The Wake Forest Student*, Vol. 6, March 1887, page 283-286.
[45] *The Wake Forest Student*, Vol. 7, No. 6, March 1888, page 263.
[46] *The Biblical Recorder*, February 22, 1888, page 2.
[47] *The Wake Forest Student*, Vol. 10, March 1890, page 254.

bade fair to become one of the gloomiest in the long catalog of its gloomy predecessors."[48]

- 1924—"For once, the weather was good, and a spring day greeted the best of beautiful maidens that came to break the dreary monotony of college life in this deserted Hamlet."[49]

- Year unidentified—"A phenomenon besides which an earthquake would have been commonplace occurred on Friday-the weather was superb! It was said, indeed, that Doctor Tom stoutly refused to be convinced that Anniversary had passed because it didn't snow."

INVITATIONS

North Carolina's political elite were invited to attend for much of Anniversary Day history. In 1901, for example, Professor Needham Yancy Gulley, future Law School Dean, then a recently appointed faculty member, "came to Raleigh yesterday afternoon as the bearer of a special invitation from the societies to the governor and other State officials, and also to the justice and officers of the Supreme Court to attend the anniversary literary societies for his college. Invitations had already been sent to both houses of the legislature. [50]

In 1889, *The Biblical Recorder* approved its invitation, saying, "... those Wake Forest boys do get up the most charming and attractive invitations that we ever saw."[51] Surrounding newspapers also received invitations. *The Progressive Farmer* (Winston, NC) "acknowledges an invitation... The card is an exceedingly fine specimen of topological art. "The programme and invitation cards, issued by the young gentlemen, are models of neatness and good taste.[52] Eight years prior, *The Farmer and Mechanic* cleverly declaimed, "The handsome Marshals send an

---

[48] *The Wake Forest Student*, Vol. 11, March 1891, page 306.

[49] *Old Gold and Black*, February 15, 1924, page 1.

[50] *The News & Observer*, February 14, 1901, page 5; NCPedia, https://www.ncpedia. org/biography/gulley-needham-yancey. Gulley would subsequently become the founder and Wake Forest Law School Dean, honored today by Gulley Drive, which traverses the lower Winston-Salem campus.

[51] *The Biblical Recorder*, February 20, 1889, page 2.

[52] *The Progressive Farmer* (Winston, NC), February 2, 1888, page 3.

handsome invitation card of the 45th anniversary."[53] Another newspaper in 1888 offered, "It is a beautiful piece of card-board, gild edged and silk trim, that lies on our desk, an invitation of the Euzelian and Philomathesian Literary Societies to attend the thirty-third anniversary of their founding. [54]

As detailed in earlier chapters, the invitations, integral to the Societies' self-promotion and prestige, were also a financial burden. It was difficult to negotiate the printing in distant Raleigh, and paper was not an inexpensive item. As late as 1906, the Euzelian minutes reflected that "Jenkins H. was paid $3.25 for 100-anniversary invitations (and $17.50 for the band to furnish Anniversary music).[55]

The societies were active in bolstering attendance. In 1906, the Eu Society voted to send the Seaboard Railroad seventy-five ($75.00) dollars to run a special train on anniversary night.[56] The invited speakers were recruited to boost the affair's favor. The 1905 address before the literary societies was delivered by Mr. Bliss Perry, Editor of the *Atlantic Monthly*, Boston, Massachusetts. Perry is one of the foremost literary men of the country, having been offered the chair of English at Harvard University.

Naturally, not all those invited accepted the honor, the most likely reason being scheduling conflicts and travel constraints. One speaker, perhaps the most in-demand of his era, was Henry W. Grady, the 38 year old Editor of *The Atlanta Constitution*, a newspaper he built into a powerful voice post-Civil War. Early in December of 1889, Grady was invited to deliver the annual address...Governor Fowle has written him, urging him to accept the invitation."[57]

Sadly, by Christmas Eve, *The News & Observer* lamented, "The people of the entire South will deplore the untimely death of Henry W. Grady whole illness terminated fatally yesterday morning... No man of

---

[53] *The Farmer and Mechanic* (Raleigh), January 22, 1880, page 108. The Marshals: E. M Poteat, D. L. Ward, Stantonburg; A. D. Hunter, Apex; O. L. Stringfield, Pender County.

[54] *The Western Sentinel* (Winston-Salem, NC), February 2, 1888, page 2.

[55] Eu Minutes, February 1906. Notes from January 1905, the year before, indicate the Society paid Mr. George A. Peck $95 to meet all expenses of Anniversary Day. A March 24 society ledger recorded "by motion Jenkins H. Was paid eight dollars for rent dress suits and three dollars for the Orchestra, totaling $11."

[56] Eu Minutes, February 15, 1906.

[57] *The Wilmington Messenger*, December 18, 1889, page 1.

the South has achieved equal distinction since the return of peace as he whose death is so truly mourned."[58]

ROMANCING THE HOLIDAY

The train slowed as it approached the depot. The crowd tensed with anticipation, for this train transported a special payload from the city of Raleigh. Young ladies from Meredith, Oxford, Peace, St. Mary's, Trinity, and Lewisburg had caught the special train. They were about to walk the campus grounds, joining the fête of oratory, debate, and boys.

For most of her first half-century, Wake Forest was an isolated rural institution, feeling more like a monastery than a festival. An all-boys school implied a certain insularity that, when combined with serious academic expectations, led students to describe their campus life as "gray." Not surprisingly, the anticipation of a free date on their calendar, that by arrangement might also include a human date, was received with exuberance.

The tale of Anniversary Day, and later Society Day, is one of romance. The welcoming of the young ladies to the fellows' campus dominated much of the commentary offered by the students themselves. Outside observers also took special notice. "There were quite a number of accomplished and popular young ladies present. I hear of a few lengthy engagements, some early retirements, and a little talk of the *sun, moon, and stars.*

A few years earlier, in 1880, an area paper *The Chatham Record* (Pittsboro, NC) observed, "At 5 o'clock, P. M., a special train arrived from Raleigh, bearing from the 'City of Oaks' a cargo of charming beauties, who sparkling eyes and rosy cheeks bespoke their cunning in 'heart stealing,' the reality which was felt by many a student where that gracious freight was summoned back by the whistle of the iron horse."[59]

---

[58] *News & Observer*, December 24, 1889, page 2; Those in the debate community may remember for decades his namesake HS in Atlanta, Henry W. Grady High School, was a foremost player in the state and national debate circuit. Now, Midtown HS, Grady HS was renamed in 2021 in recognition of racial sensitivities. Grady was more enlightened than many of his generation but was also an ardent segregationist. Flora, J. M., and MacKethan, L. H. (2001). *The companion to southern literature: Themes, genres, places, people, movements, and motifs.* Louisiana State University Press, page 390.

[59] *The Chatham Record* (Pittsboro, NC), February 26, 1880, page 2.

The train was the lifeline of Anniversary Day and the avenue for potential companionship. A 1903 Raleigh paper boasted, "Already more than 50 of the most prominent young ladies in the city have notified the chaperones that they expect to join the special party of young people, which is one of the special features of the train. No time should be lost in reserving parlor car chairs... and berths in the sleeper for the return trip. It will be a great trip, and being personally conducted by Mr. Gattis, there is every assurance that will afford for its patrons probably the most delightful trip that has ever been made from Raleigh."[60]

---

[60] *The Morning Post*, Nov 22, 1903, page 6. Gattis was the railroad's top manager for the Wake Depot. In the 1910 *Wake Forest Student*, the then-editor and future North Carolina Governor, Melville Broughton, commented, "Some of the trains are not stopping at Wake Forest on Anniversary night. Many of the students had girlfriends over from Raleigh colleges for the occasion and were chagrined at the railroad authorities being unwilling to stop the fast train and carry them back. Said he: Our most distinguished alumnus, Governor Kitchin, was one of the number who looked sadly on as the train with a rather aggravating show of speed passed through on Anniversary night. What His Excellency said is not recorded ...highly probable the words were not discreet at the moment." A Leader Who Becomes Governor, *The News & Observer*, January 9, 1941, page 20.

An 1897 poem in *The Wake Forest Student* captures the romantic whimsy and diegesis of the day.

THE ANNIVERSARY GIRL

Oh, she comes, with her ribbons and ruffles and curls,
The Bonniest, sweetest and the fairest of girls
    As lovely as maiden can be;
And Seniors and Juniors and Sophomores all,
overcome by her glasses, and loves meshes fall
    But she is not a coquette, not she.
She brightens the college, so classic and gray,
and drives the grim spirits of science away,
    With her smile so happy and free;
And while love and music enliven the scene
Of all, she's the peerless and radiant queen,
    But she is not a coquette, not she.
And when she departs, I have often heard say,
There are many fond hearts that she carries away;
    But she can't love them all, don't you see!
So she calls them all over and picks out the best,
And sometimes, I am told, she forgets all the rest
    But she is not a coquette, not she.   C. L. G.[61]

A 1903 account is particularly flirtatious; the day's rhetoric was everywhere more personal than that unfolding on stage with the debates and oratories. Among campus residents, romantic fascinations took place in a distinct pecking order, as the 1903 *Howler* captured:

February is anniversary month, at which an Oldish measures his popularity by the number of times he refuses engagements because he is "full up."[62] The new man looks on longingly and hides his disappointment with the words, "Vanity, Vanity. All is Vanity." The day comes at last, and with it, a deluge of visitors, the majority of whom belong to the fair sex. Everyone attends, but nobody knows the query for debate, nor the excellence of the speeches, save a few

---

[61] *The Wake Forest Student*, Vol. 16, March 1897, page 431.

[62] The phrase "my dance card is full" meant that a lady was popular enough to have a man lined up for every song at a dance.

sedate listeners in front. At night come the orations, and then the reception in the society-halls, where every swain becomes an eloquent orator to the small audience of one. Everybody is happy, save the taciturn man who is stuck tight as an oyster-shell in the corner, and who has remarked a half dozen times within the last ten minutes that it is remarkably warm, despite the fact that the wind howls around the window at his back. At last, the lights go out.[63]

For the newbies, however, the day held future promise as it was the one time during the Spring session when it was considered proper for the freshmen to escort young ladies about the college grounds. A more full-fledged account argues vigorously for the most "beautiful women" premise and, perhaps unintentionally, exhibits how the Anniversary participants wanted to see themselves:

If you are so fortunate as to be here and enjoy the warmth of the all-pervasive hospitality, you forget the carpet is snow in the chilly wind singing around the corner of the stately buildings on the campus.

Visitors were here to enjoy the debate and to meet friends, but the boys had eyes only for the bevy of lovely girls who graced the event... They were the "whole thing," as current slang goes. Raleigh sent out car-loads of charming belles, and if I thought they outshone the bells of other towns and cities, it is simply because it is a habit of the Raleigh girls to do this – a habit that is descended from the mothers to daughters in every generation from the time of Lafayette lingered in Raleigh because, as he said, he had not found so many beautiful women in any other town in America. But there were belles here from Richmond and other cities, from other States who vied in grace and beauty with those from North Carolina... There is a fiction here that this Anniversary occasion is held to hear a debate upon some topic of current interest and importance, and to test the ability of the best orators. And the boys are out in full force to hear the debate and the orations, and they show their interest in partisanship by plotting and thereby cheering the members of their own society... What would the Anniversary be without the reception in the girl's exclamation? It would be like the play of Hamlet with Hamlet left out.[64]

---

[63] *Howler*, 1903, page 128.

[64] *The Farmer and Mechanic*, February 16, 1904, page 8.

The ritual of affirmation, bathed in pageantry, soon gave way to more amorous quests. An 1897 account recalled, "Sweet strains were waved up from the reading room, where the drum band discoursed sweet music. In the dim corners of the library, some couples were discussing in low voices, books and authors (?). Even the 'courting gallery' was invaded by the unsuspecting damsel, ignorant of its mysteries until her escort explained them to her."[65]

Meridith Students Circa 1900

Before the trains departed, the social reception surpassed, with perhaps a scamper around campus grounds. The evening gathering spoke to alumni remembrance as well. "The reception tonight was brilliant, many of the leading Baptists of North Carolina being present, and besides the gallant numbers of students there were present handsomely gowned... Every hour was spent pleasantly... and especially was the reunion of the sons of the college, who had gone forth in the world after being prepared for his conflicts on the sacred Hill, beautiful and impressive. These "old" men had returned as to their mother, to renew the close ties of love and sympathy and interest with their college brothers."[66]

---

[65] *The Wake Forest Student*, March 1897, page 430-431.
[66] *The News & Observer*, February 16, 1908, page 10.

Not every year worked out as students hoped. In 1918, "A perfect spring day ushered in the 83rd anniversary of the founding … with nothing to mar the impressiveness and pleasure of the occasion except the lack of the usual large crowd of visitors … Something of the accustom gaiety was lacking in a spirit of seriousness seemed to pervade the atmosphere of the college.[67] Unspoken was the onset of the Spanish Flu and the drums of World War I.[68]

The year 1920 also was problematic both for the anniversary and romantic encounters, yet 1921 offered renewed anticipation. The Spanish Flu had ended most college activities in 1920. The *Old Gold and Black,* described, "Last year the celebration was marred to a considerable degree, in that an epidemic of the influenza necessitated the young ladies of neighboring colleges being placed in quarantine, and the commissioners of Wake Forest prohibiting any public gatherings other than those among students of the college."[69]

In 1919, the reporting of the debates did not seem to reflect an ongoing pandemic, perhaps due to the off-year between spikes in 1918 and 1920. *The News & Observer,* echoing characterizations from the college, reported the occasion which unfolded: "Under the most favorable weather conditions, and attended by a host of out-of-door visitors, consisting chiefly of Meredith and Oxford college girls".[70] *The Charlotte News* in September 1919 wrote, "No one of the many experts of the [US Public Health Service Service] would make a more positive forecast of the all-important

Drawing in 1912 *Howler*

[67] *Old Gold and Black,* February 23, 1918, page 1.

[68] See Chapter 14 – Early Tournament Hosting – for a more thorough discussion of the 1918-1920 Pandemic and WWI's impact on campus.

[69] *Old Gold and Black*, January 21, 1921, page 1.

[70] *The News & Observer,* February 15, 1919, page 3.

question, will there be a reoccurrence? All agreed, however, that a recurrence was not unlikely.[71]

Prohibiting women's colleges' attendance was understandable with the war and pandemic, but often, the presidents of the women's colleges could be willful in upholding standards for class attendance and exams. The "negotiations" with college presidents were, at times, protracted. "If for no other reason, the anniversary promises to be attended with its usual success because Dr. Brewer consented to permit the Meredith girls to come over on special invitation. Due to the fact that the girls have classes on Friday, they will not be able to be present for the debate in the afternoon. They will come over on number 20, commonly known as the 'Shoo Fly,' which usually arrives at Wake Forest about six o'clock."[72]

Demise of Anniversary Day Debates

The Anniversary Day, as depicted, prevailed until well after the turn of the century. With the advent of more stirring social lives, the celebration gradually lost its former social significance. On a long weekend, the drive or train ride home felt "shorter."

As early as 1912, other events, especially spectator sports, were crowding out attention formerly reserved for the Anniversary festivity. The night before the 1912 event, a Charlotte newspaper reported not the upcoming debate but that the Wake Forest basketball team "ran away with the five from A & M by a score of 50 to 3."[73]

For much of the Anniversary Day's history, the college's recognition of its founding was discrete from the major holiday sponsored by the societies, a distinction guarded jealously by the societies even as they often shared the same calendar date. Yet in February 1924, the Phis adopted a resolution proposing to turn the day into what would be known as Founder's Day.[74] This resolution isolated Society Day as the only holiday fully owned by the two societies.

---

[71] Will The Flu Return? *The Charlotte News*, September 19, 1919, page 10.

[72] *Old Gold and Black*, February 17, 1922, page 1.

[73] *The Evening Chronicle* (Charlotte), February 19, 1912, page 5.

[74] *Old Gold and Black*, February 29, 1924, page 1; Provisos included "that the college bears all expenses of the day and give a full holiday." *The Wake Forest Student*, Vol. 43, May 1924, page 398-399. One reason offered was that the anniversaries come so

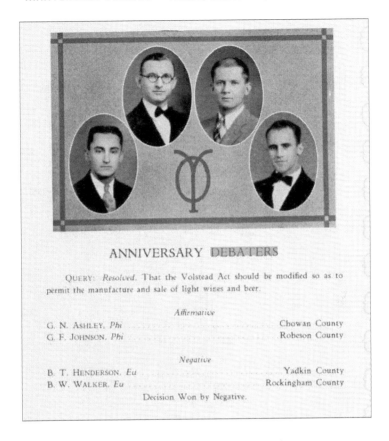

ANNIVERSARY DEBATERS

QUERY: *Resolved.* That the Volstead Act should be modified so as to permit the manufacture and sale of light wines and beer.

Affirmative

G. N. ASHLEY, *Phi* .... Chowan County
G. F. JOHNSON, *Phi* .... Robeson County

Negative

B. T. HENDERSON, *Eu* .... Yadkin County
B. W. WALKER, *Eu* .... Rockingham County

Decision Won by Negative.

The fundamental reasons lie in the fact that societies were no longer compulsory for all students and that the two holidays had become too much for societies to plan and finance. Increasingly, their energy and resources were directed to debating tours and the existing and newly established publications.

Ironically, the two largest headlines on the same front page that announced the Anniversary Day handoff to administrators were *Twenty-Four Twirlers to Pick Staff* and *Honors Lost: Blue Devils Annex Nip and Tuck Battle.* [75] What was celebrated was no longer of the 19th century.

Several traditional Anniversary Day activities continued for years, with aspects shared by the College and societies. In 1925, activities were added

---

close together, and to save the extra day for class work, the two occasions are to be combined and held on February 3, the second of the registration days for the spring term. *Old Gold and Black,* January 10, 1925, page 1.

[75] *Old Gold and Black*, January 10, 1925, page 1.

to the day, perhaps attempting to revive the festivities. Nevertheless, this further weakened the value of the orations and debate.[76] In 1925, U.S. Senator, the Hon. J. W. Bailey, was the main attraction of the Founder's Day event (see below), with debates and orations slowly shunted to other locations and times. Adding the president's annual address to the ceremony's evening portion affirmed the event as effectively an administration occasion.[77]

Gradually, society speaking events moved out of the general public purview. The open social receptions, long the highlight of the occasion, were abandoned, with the societies adopting inter-society speaking contests and evening banquets. As the administration "elevated" Founder's Day, with the social fraternities orchestrating campus activities, the societies incrementally receded to an elevated "club status."

The Societies continued to invite outside speakers. In 1928, alumnus and former Dean Dr. E. W. Sikes, then Clemson President, spoke on the *effects of education and religion on the production of wealth*. He held that education, as well as religion, more than other societal factors, lead to prosperity. Sikes reasoned that times were improving and, through a lens of prosperity, proclaimed, rightly, that the society of 1927 exhibited much less "ecclesiasticism and bigotry" than in 1827.

He was thought of as sharing an enlightened view of education and religion. On religion, he suggested in keeping with the learned of the times that "The wealth of the world is among Protestant people, not among Catholics and Mohammedans ... America, the most Puritan of all nations, is also the most prosperous. There must be some connection between the two."[78] Maybe such speech-making retained the interest of students, but one wonders.

---

[76] The afternoon 2:30 debate still occurred. The winning Affirmative defended *Prohibiting the issuance of tax-exempt securities*. By this point, debate topics depended on the national topic selected; it is no wonder the audience drifted.

[77] President W. L. Poteat, long an advocate of the societies, whose son was president of one at the time, read his report, "It is 91 years today since Samuel Wait gathered 16 boys in the swept and garnished carriage house of the Calvin Jones farmstead and opened the career of the Wake Forest Institute. How has the little one become 1000 and the small one a strong nation? In 1838, the Institute became the college, and the first college building was completed. It was 40 years before the second building was added. Now there are nine buildings." His speech was a fund-raising appeal. *Old Gold and Black*, February 7, 1925, page 1.

[78] *Old Gold and Black*, February 11, 1928, page 1.

By the early '40s, Founder's Day debates were of lessened interest among the two societies that were directly facing each other for a bevy of intersociety speaking honors. Increasingly, literary events were outside the awareness of the community or statewide audience. Invited speakers, guests, alumni, and faculty would join in, primarily for an evening banquet, but few attended the actual debate.

John McMillan and Martha Ann Allen
Top Founder's Day debaters listen to their opponent's
speeches for slip-ups. Circa 1943

As early as 1932, the physical boundaries already signaled a diminished importance. The afternoon debate was held in the Eu Hall, not the traditional Wingate Memorial (the evening oratories were in Wingate).

The Euzelian's newly elected president in 1937, John Ezell, compared the literal Founder's Day Program to a funeral, highlighting the resemblance.[79]

In 1935, the *Howler* would praise the anniversary debaters: "Running true to form, [the Societies] displayed one of the most spectacular forensic battles of recent history. Orators were wearing the oratorical colors of their societies for the last time, crowning well their labors in the societies."[80] What is notable about this account are the participants' names

---

[79] *Old Gold and Black*, February 20, 1937, page 1.

[80] *Howler*, 1935, page 141.

and sustained Wake contributors: "George Copple and H. A. Matthews bowed in defeat to the victorious Philomathesian team composed of Alfred Martin and Carl Ousley."

This is not to say that campus interest had fully subsided; the debating societies remained committed to the intersociety challenge. Debates remained locally relevant and, on occasion, were reported in college publications with some detail.

A 1936 example illustrates the changing context in which debates took place at night in the church. The excerpt is also interesting for its topic and discussion, what would be, in a historical lens, an uncomfortable defense of Mussolini's approach to occupying Ethiopia.

> The evening's feature was a debate on whether Italy was justified in pursuing a policy of armed conquest of Ethiopia.
>
> The Phi's gained the victory by showing that Ethiopia needs European supervision, which Italy is best qualified and most fully justified to administer: "Italy gaining only the crumbs of the colonial spoils," asserted a Phi debater, and so has as much right to take over Ethiopia as other nations had in the past to seize their possessions.[81]

Three years later, in 1939, the anniversary still commanded a headline extended fully across the top of the *Old Gold and Black* front page.

YES, WE'RE TO HAVE A BIRTHDAY PARTY
FOUNDER'S DAY PROGRAM OFFERS ONE GRAND PARTY
Sen. J. W. Bailey to Make The Feature Address
BIG BIRTHDAY CAKE WITH 106 CANDLES
All Alumni Chapters To Be Connected With Party By Radio

The newspaper article that followed is rich in detail and tells what Anniversary Day had become for the societies, a celebratory banquet replete with notable speakers and guests. The 1939 event, however, did usher in an ambitious new technological aspect via relay telephone.

---

[81] *Old Gold and Black*, February 1, 1936, page 1, Dr. George W. Paschal, Dr. W. R. Cullum, and Prof. Carlton F. West voted in favor of the affirmative. After the program, President Thurman D. Kitchin asked the assembled audience to stand while he read the necrology of Wake Forest alumni who had passed away during the past year. Included in this list was Captain Fowler of California, who was 102 years old when he died. He was born before his alma mater was founded but could not outlive it ... The program included J. Alfred Martin's oratory, *Let Us Return*.

A "Birthday Party," the first of its kind in the history of the college – will be the theme of Founder's Day celebration at Wake Forest this year, as school officials, alumni and students adopt a unique form of commemorating the 106th anniversary of the founding of the college, February 1, 1940.

United States Sen. J. W. Bailey, member of the class of 1893[82], will be the featured address of the occasion, as guests… sit before the large birthday cake for Wake Forest, supporting 106 candles. Through the courtesy of the station WPTF in Raleigh, the full hour of party festivity will be broadcast.

Importance of the event is brought home by the fact that the sitting US Sen. Bailey was joined by speakers as part of the 106th birthday banquet included Pres. Thurman Kitchin, Dr. R. T. Vann, former president Meredith College, and soon to be elected North Carolina Gov., Wake Alum J. M. Broughton.

And maybe his son was Anniversary Day orator – H. K. Bailey, Phi.[83]

To facilitate a "united party," relay telephone service will be installed to all sections of the state, where local chapters of the alumni will be holding their individual parties. It will be a 'Founder's Day' all over the state for sons of Wake Forest, and in all group parties, a cake will be carved· in commemoration of the school's birthday."[84]

In 1941, the "Special guests for the Founder's Day program" this year were some 200 North Carolina high school debate squads invited to attend the program by Professor Zon Robinson, debate coach.[85] The event was no longer Anniversary Day as celebrated by the Societies.

---

[82] Sen. Joshua Bailey Williams (1873-1946), a Wake graduate, also became the editor of *The Biblical Recorder*, the official weekly newspaper of the North Carolina Baptist Convention, a central influential role. The story of his career remained eventful and influential. See https://www.ncpedia.org/biography/bailey-josiah-william.

[83] Senator Bailey's son was an Anniversary Day orator, sharing the venue with Eugene Worrell. Sen. Bailey was the Anniversary speaker for a second occasion.

[84] *Old Gold and Black*, December 15, 1939, page 1. The event was divided into two days, one with the Inter-society contests and a more formal day in the church, with President D. Thurman Kitchin reading the College necrology for the year. 'Due to the registration for the second semester's work and the basketball game with North Carolina University." the evening program was abandoned. *Old Gold and Black*, February 4, 1939.

[85] *The News & Observer*, January 22, 1941, page 2.

The celebrations' association with student speaking continued to drift. By the 110th in 1944, "In an effort to make this occasion one of general interest, your oration contest was held in the Monday morning student assembly."[86] This arrangement likely went the way of morning assemblies. It is possible that the last Founder's Day debate took place in 1944. There were no later mentions of Founder's Day debates in the *Howler*.

---

[86] Philomathesians Page, *Howler*, 1944.

CHAPTER 9

Society Day Renews Campus Cadence

In their heyday, the Eu and Phi Societies were every bit the cardinal social fraternities. Without abandoning their elemental purpose of training fellow students in public speaking skills, their choices were often informed by amusement as well as betterment.

Perhaps acting more in tune with a Spring party than a public speaking opportunity, starting in 1914, they organized and hosted Society Day. The annual spring event was filled with football and day-long socials, culminating in receptions, dates, and dances, with, of course, orations. The top debaters showed off their skills not just to their fellow students but also to invited guests.

Students from Meredith College, the all-female Baptist school in nearby Raleigh, were frequent guests. The 1934 *Howler* seconded the campus war cry "More Society Days and More Ladies." The yearbook reported: "Many young maidens from Meredith were the guests of the society members. After all is said and done, the presence of girls on our campus adds color and attention to any affair."

Society Day was a relief for "beleaguered" students who were clamoring for any reason that would result in class cancellations.[1] Shortly after

---

[1] More and more, campus life became fragmented by emerging student activities. Some diversions happened due to the college president's initiative. In 1891, the Raleigh-based Southern Inter-States Exposition featured a "Wake Forest Day." The event "brought President Charles E. Taylor and almost the entire faculty and some two hundred students and many friends to the city on October 16th. The boys came through the city in grand style, making the air ring with their 'college yell.' They

EDITORIALS—
—WITHOUT A CHAPEL
—GOING TO THE DOGS

Old Gold and Black

TWENTY-TWO MEN
AWAIT INDUCTION
TO GOLDEN BOUGH

Vol. XXIII. No. 0 — Z-596　　　　WAKE FOREST, NORTH CAROLINA, SATURDAY, NOVEMBER 17, 1938　　　　PRICE: TEN CENTS PER COPY

GIRLS, GAB HIGHLIGHT SOCIETY DAY

the turn of the century, the campus remained "formal," dominated by class work. A more applied curriculum was beginning to develop, but nonetheless, the day-to-day continued its classical roots.

A Society Day holiday aimed to take advantage of spring weather rather than the often-disappointing inclement conditions reserved for February's Anniversary Day. The idea was an easy sell for the semi-isolated community of young men, who might have considered their lives as convential.

The Birth of a Holiday

The precursor to Society Day was the Sophomore-Junior Debates, first held in 1911. This event, designed to showcase and train younger debaters, was a prized affair marked by intense interest. In 1914, the Soph.-Jr. debates fused with the proposed "new holiday," emerging as Society Day. This evolution from events defined by a central debate to a full-fledged holiday marked a significant shift in the campus's social life.[2]

"The day will be set apart as a regular College holiday to be known as 'Society Day," *The College Bulletin* recorded. They also announced that Senior Speaking would merge into the "Fall Anniversary."[3] "Instead of the regular twelve Senior speakers, only four will be chosen to speak that night."[4]

State newspapers announced the new holiday invitations' arrival with the required eagerness. Raleigh's *Farmer and Mechanic* intoned, "The invitations for the First Annual Society Day ...have just been issued," they

---

admirably conducted themselves throughout their visit and made many friends for the institution." In all probability, the excursion was a public relations win, internally and externally, and an entertaining departure. *North Carolina Teacher*, Vol. 9, December 1, 1891, page 223.

[2] *The Wake Forest Student*, November 1911, page 157.

[3] *The News & Observer*, Oct 26, 1914, page 7.

[4] *Wake Forest Bulletin*, 1914.

alerted in early October. The headline, replete with delight, was:

**WAKE FOREST WILL
HAVE SOCIETY DAY**
Event on Thirtieth Rival
to The Spring Anniversary
Occasion[5]

"After the evening orations, the Berean Class[6], gave, "a delightful banquet to the visitors, the faculty, and many of the citizens of Wake Forest. It is probable that this banquet will each year give the crowning touch to Society Day."[7]

It took many hands to assemble the program, from

1915 – Society Day Officers and Marshalls

invitations to banquets, inviting speakers, securing venues, scheduling sports events, and much more. The page of the first year's Society Day officers (right, *Howler*) illustrates the respect and importance accorded these elected leaders during this period. Newspapers also carry detailed stories announcing the winners of society elections for Society Day orators and debaters, as well as attending chairpersons and marshals.[8]

The query for the first Society Day Debate was *That the right of Suffrage in North Carolina should not be restricted on account of sex.* (The panel voted 3-2 for the Negative).[9]

---

[5] *The Farmer and Mechanic,* October 14, 1914, page 12.

[6] Christians who were known for open-mindedness and reliance on the scripture to verify the truth. The Bereans were a group of Jews who converted, they lived in the city of Berea. Their name is from the New Testament. https://www.christiantoday.com/article/who-are-the-berean-christians-and-what-can-we-learn-from-them/122926.htm.

[7] *Wake Forest Bulletin,* 1914, page 43.

[8] *The News & Observer,* May 2, 1915, page 10.

[9] The General Assembly in 1920 rejected the Nineteenth Amendment extending the vote to women by a legislature vote of 71 to 41, arguing that "women suffrage would threaten the sanctity of the family, state rights, and white supremacy." North Carolina

WILLIAM BRYAN BOOE, *Phi.*

Candidate for LL.B.

CANA, NORTH CAROLINA

Age 23; Height 5' 9½"; Weight 150.

"I dare do all that becomes a man; he who dares do more is none."

In Bryan we see good qualities so intermingled that an honorable and successful future for him seems assured. Profound in the law, he was licensed last August; able in debate, he represented his society last anniversary; popular on the campus, he has a host of friends. The law and senior classes have invested him with many honors in recognition of his unusual ability. Gifted when it comes to the ladies, he shines in social gatherings as well as on the campus. His versatility, having won for him many honors here, will stand him in stead in the arena of life, where only the able and worthy rise to places of lasting honor.

Anniversary Marshal, '21; Vice-President of Summer Law Class, '21; Member of Y. M. C. A. Cabinet, '21-'22; Secretary of Philomathesian Society, '21; Member of Honor Committee, '21-'22; Member of Ex-Service Club, '19-'20-'21; Secretary of Senior Class, '22; Anniversary Debater, '22; President of Philomathesian Society, '22; Licensed Attorney, '21; Intercollegiate Debater, '22.

The affirmative argued, "the evolution of governmental affairs has brought women in direct relationship with most all functions of government...just as man's development paved the way toward all rights of suffrage, which he now enjoys... the educated and the laboring man have been allowed to vote because they were intelligent and morally fit to administer the affairs of our government and for the same reason ... Women should be given this rightful power."

On the negative Mr. J. G. Booe held that 'the different natures of men and women would not allow them to participate side by side in politics and the voting was not 'an inherent natural right.' Furthermore "if women take up the spirit of duties intended for men, she becomes a masculine woman, all of which is a result of failure in herself and home."[10] Booe's sentiment was mighty traditional.

Society Day included an afternoon athletic event, adding to the entertainment and festive side of the program. The lucky trains

would have been the final state required to ratify the Nineteenth Amendment. With ratification a *fete accompli* and thus with nothing to gain nationally by ratifying, the legislators sought not to alienate the prevailing antisuffragist sentiment at home. Not until 1971 did the General Assembly of North Carolina endorse the Nineteenth Amendment. The Wake students seemed well ahead of legislators on women's voting. https://www.ncpedia.org/women-suffrage.

[10] *Greensboro Daily News*, November 1, 1914, page 8.

would arrive from Raleigh, with the Wake fellows taking their assigned acquaintance to the athletic field.[11]

As with each rendition, the evening was filled with oratory and the crowning banquet. "The [1916] banquet was attended by nearly two-hundred girls from Meredith, the senior class from Oxford, the people of the community, and practically every student in the college here."[12]

The pattern for Society Day was soon ingrained, with only slight hiccups, one of which was World War II, until the audiences moved on to alternative venues in the late 1930s and early '40s.[13]

Society Day's Pinnacle

The Wake Forest Student exclaimed, "The fondest expectations of any sane individual were realized, in that from morning till midnight, entertainment was on every hand." The 10 AM 1916 debate held *That the United States should annex Mexico.*[14]

The heyday of Society Day was relatively short-lived. From 1914 to the mid-1930s, the event went from being the summit to merely acceptable. Students eventually had access to autos and often returned to their homes on an extended weekend.

The "Society Day window," however, was a stirring time on campus. The State migrated to the Wake Forest village to hear debates and orations and, if lucky, a student might get a kiss on the side.

---

[11] In 1916, a new inter-class track meet was added, along with shoe and sack races and other amusements. In 1917, the athletic feature was a tennis match with Elon. *The News & Observer*, October 30, 1917, page 7. "The tennis team found no difficulty in defeating Elon in the match on Society Day, all of the matches being won with comparative ease." *The Wake Forest Student*, Vol. 37, No. 3, December 1917, page 180.

[12] November 1916 *The Wake Forest Student*. The oratory titles reveal much about the combinations of optimism, constraint on the day's topics, and youthful exuberance. Mr. A. C. Reid spoke on *North Carolina's Greatest Liabilities*, C. H. Stevens considered *Divine Discontent*, G. E. Eddins explored *Americanism and World Politics*, and J. B. Davis articulated *The Anglo Saxon Heritage*.

[13] Society Day became part of homecoming week, and the college's first homecoming celebration was circa 1935. The year of the Homecoming and Society Day merger appears uncertain. Paschal pegs the establishment of "Homecoming Day" in 1935. Paschal, G. W. (1943). *The History of Wake Forest College*, Vol. II, page 380.

[14] *The Wake Foret Student*, December 1916, page 179-180; A faculty panel of Gulley, Nowell, & Jones voted for the Negative.

The student body had grown substantially by the 1920s. From what was then celebrated as high enrollments in the mid-1880s of around 160, it became 325 in 1905; by the 1920-1921 school year, 577 students registered.[15] The student newspaper admired the impending crowds in 1921. "With over 500 students in college, practically all of whom will remain on the campus, and with 1000 invitations sent out by the students to their families and friends and with the promise of a large attendance from the student body of Meredith, Oxford and Lewisburg colleges, the attendances presage a record-breaking event."[16]

President Dr. William Lewis Poteat served as Toastmaster for the evening occasion… The gathered were invited to the gymnasium, where a reception was held. The faculty and their wives composed the receiving line, which welcomed the guests.[17]

---

[15] *The Wake Forest Bulletin*, 1920-21, page 156.

[16] *Old Gold and Black*, October 14, 1921, page 1, 4.

[17] *Old Gold and Black*, October 14, 1921, page 4.

The '21 weather was also in a cooperative mood. "The little rain which fell on that day, instead of marring the occasion, was one of the causes for rejoicing, so great was the need for rain."[18]

In times past, the rivalry between the two societies was keyed to the highest pitch. It has been reported that several years ago, the two societies would not have been possible to debate because of the intense rivalry. To have Society Day, it was decided that one debater from each society should be on each side. "If the societies had debated each other, a war would have broken out on the campus before the debate was over. ... well, times change."[19] The teams were mixed in the early days of the Junior-Sophomore and Society Day debate. After 1926, the debates pitted the societies in opposition.

The prominence of Society Day was undoubtedly not the same for everyone, but a large segment of the students bought into the excitement. As one newspaper line read, "Society Day in all of its splendor and grandeur is only three days away."[20]

In the campus newspaper and among much of the outside press, every year was previewed or claimed to be the "greatest in history." A 1923 account is not an exception but is a charming instance of the Society Day coverage. The attention to detail gives insight into how the students imagined the occasion.

> Thorough preparation is going to make this year's celebration the greatest in the history of the event. Under the supervision of the college, the most competent young men have been selected for the debating and speechmaking. A program of the last degree in perfection has been mapped out.
>
> Meredith, Lewisburg and Oxford colleges will send delegations of beautiful and vivacious young ladies. The size of the Meredith aggregation of pulchritude[21] will surpass all the others, if present indications are taken for judging the number of ladies who will come over Monday. Latest reports have set the numbers that will come from Meredith at 200.

---

[18] *The Wake Forest Student*, 1921, page 180.

[19] *Old Gold and Black*, November 17, 1928, page 3.

[20] *Old Gold and Black*, November 2, 1923, page 1.

[21] Meaning, "Beauty," "allure," "heavenliness"

It has been definitely decided that the Meredith girls will come and go by rail. They will leave Raleigh on the afternoon train on Monday arriving at 6 o'clock. This will give them time to have dinner with their gallants, attend the exercises in Wingate Memorial Hall, and then be present at the reception that will be held after the exercises are over in the hall. The ladies will return to Meredith Tuesday morning.

Everything is in readiness for the day. The speakers have labored hard to get up arguments and oratory that will make the listeners glad they had a chance to hear. The homes of the faculty and townspeople will be thrown open to receive and welcome visitors. Special entertainment at the theaters has been secured to amuse those who care to see good moving pictures. The halls of several fraternities have been specially decorated and prepared to receive and serve as gathering places for those who attend the celebration.[22]

The keen planning and palpable anticipation impress almost everyone, with the noteworthy exception of "Mother Nature." The post-event story bespoke the utility of redefinition and resurgence.

SOCIETY DAY SUCCESS
DESPITE A BAD START
IN THE RAIN AND MUD

So shouted the *Old Gold and Black* headline in 1923 as melancholy swept the campus, the rain putting an almost certain damper on the arrival of the Raleigh train in time for making adequate acquaintances. "After all the planning and rushing, a week later the buoyancy that anticipated 'last degree of perfection' was washed away by a 'steady rain and plenty of mud.' The arrival of the Raleigh ladies was postponed by 'lowering skies and muddy roads' that prevented the arrival of visitors until late in the day. The weather and the absence of the expected Lady visitors was reflected in the attitude of the celebrants. It looked like a gloomy festival during the morning and afternoon. Only a few people were present at the afternoon debating."[23]

---

[22] *Old Gold and Black*, November 2, 1923, page 1.

[23] *Old Gold and Black*, November 9, 1923, page 1.

The arrival of the night train with the Meredith girls put the needed stimulus into the program...The orators addressed several remarks to the fair visitors who are not there to get the benefit... The reception held in the gymnasium after the orations was what really made Society Day social. It was the occasion at which the visitors got acquainted with each other and with the Wake Forest students. Music by the Wake Forest Hurricane Serenades played, while punch and ice cream were served, used to limber up the occasion after formality of the debating and oratory.[24]

In 1930, the debates were chased by an evening football game with Duke, a "wiener roast on the golf course and semi-formal dinner at Miss Joanna Williams." The debate itself addressed the query *That it should be the policy of the Baptists of North Carolina to make their colleges wholly co-educational.*

Superstar debaters of the era, Harold H. Deaton and his partner W. Herschel Ford, upheld the affirmative, arguing that the time for the change had arrived and the merger would save money as well. The negative, Butler Pruitt and E. Leonidas Smith, retaliated by claiming "there is a danger in mixing the sexes in college, that present-day co-education is not a success and that the North Carolina Baptists do not favor such a policy."[25] More specifically, an unanswered argument that "to admit both boys and girls would entail, among other difficulties, the necessity for additional physical equipment, which, in the light of the denomination's impending financial crisis, would result in bankruptcy."[26] The negative won a two-to-one decision. The larger Baptist congregation's opinion was indeed persuasive.

Much earlier, in 1896, in a Phi session, the debaters had visited and narrowly rejected coeducation, 15 to 14. In 1840, the Euzelians considered the topic: *Which should demand our attention the most, the education of the males or of the females?* The decision was 8 yeas and 13 nays, but given the resolution's wording, it's not clear if they voted to educate women or men as their priority.[27]

---

[24] *Old Gold and Black*, November 9, 1923, page 1.

[25] *Old Gold and Black*, December 12, 1930, page 1, 2.

[26] *The News & Observer*, November 24, 1930, page 4.

[27] Probably not surprisingly, given the debates resided among the students themselves, the Euzelians debated some form of an education topic well over 50 times, the

Unlike the governing Baptists, the students were much more favorable to a union of the colleges. A similar topic, even more loaded, had carried the day a few months earlier in April. In a spring meeting, the Phis responded affirmatively to the topic that *Wake Forest and Meredith should be combined.* Topics considering some level of unification had been debated on campus as early as 1924.

Merger sentiment gained momentum, and in 1929, the school paper's headline, spread across all seven columns, would exclaim:

POLL FAVORS CONSOLIDATION
Ninety Percent Want Damsels To Grace Campus
Meredith Girls Answer Questionaire: Show Desire For Merging
GIRLS EXPECT TO FIND LOVE HERE
Wake Men See Proposal As Uplifting To Students In Study, Dress, And Habits[28]

Of course, the issue of the merger did not take root due to one fall holiday debate. As the Raleigh newspaper noted the year after the student poll, "There is no issue whatever before the boards of trustees of the respective institutions; the decision of the judges will be the answer to the query that supplies the fireworks for the most colorful occasion on the Wake Forest College campus this fall."[29]

--*-*-*-*-*

For the first thirteen years, the members elected the debaters who represented them on Society Day. In 1927, the societies moved to choose their representatives by contest. Preliminary tryouts were held, with the final audition primarily judged by faculty. Those selected automatically became part of the intercollegiate debating team (the rest had to try out in practice debates).[30]

Philomathesians nearly 90 times. The 1846 Phis, of another male-centric era debated *The education of females as much entitled the consideration of our enlightened Republic as that of males.* Negative, 19 to 12. A half-century later, the Eus split on the 1897 topic: *Should women have higher education?* Tied 20 to 20.

[28] *Old Gold and Black*, March 4, 1929, page 1.

[29] *The News & Observer*, November 20, 1930, page 3.

[30] *Old Gold and Black*, March 19, 1927, page 1; The selected Society debaters composed the traveling team for the December debate, which included NC State, UNC, and

So this is SOCIETY DAY

The social milieu of the 1930s was considerably changed from the college's founding decades. Campus holidays remained constant, with their attendant invitations to a bevy of young ladies. Wake and sister school Meredith retained close ties, partly motivated by shared denominational roots and romantic openings, an association enthusiastically promoted by both schools' debating societies.

Two weeks before the 1930 Society Day shindig, the Wake Forest students had gone as a body "to a social at Meredith sponsored by the literary societies of the two institutions." [31] The social was partly to enable the boys to make dates for Society Day.

As noted earlier, the press releases previewing Society Day engaged in hyper-hyperbolic descriptions, predicting the best "day of days." In 1933, with Society Day's combination with Homecoming, the *Old Gold and Black* exploded, "This year's celebration is expected to reach extra-stellar heights in that not only will Saturday be a day set aside for Society Day, but, also, the day on which homecoming is to be observed. Affiliating homecoming day with the Society annual celebration a happy reunion of both alumni and students was foreseen, expanding to magnitudinous proportions the always big celebration." [32] Society Day, joined with Homecoming for six years. [33]

High Point College, *Old Gold and Black*, November 23, 1929, page 1; Some the society faithful hailed 1927 as the "new birth of Society Day." *The Wake Forest Student*, Vol. 45, December 1927, page 133. Membership had increased but so had the number of students. By 1927, the mini-revival of Society Day was more aspirational than actual.

[31] *Old Gold and Black*, November 21, 1930, page 1.

[32] *Old Gold and Black*, October 14, 1933, page 1.

[33] In this period, of course, most all alumni were Literary men.

Observing the 1933 celebration, an aspiring collegiate journalist took some literary license in *Old Gold and Black,* scripting, "When the first rays of the morning sun came across the campus of Wake Forest College today, and lighted the scene in an autumn glory, the sleepy birds that have defied the warnings of approaching winter took little note. They merely chirped a few times feebly and fluffed their feathers for another comfortable hour. Not so with the many Freshmen, Sophomores, Juniors, and Seniors of our college. No, despite the fact that last night was an active one for the Freshman, what with yelling, grading, preparing a bonfire and singing; they were up bright and early. Today is society day."[34]

Planning and executing the strategy was not always smooth. With two proud competing tribes, some tensions were inevitable. Society Day 1939 led to a public ruckus between the two societies, playing out in newspapers' front pages and testy behind-the-scenes negotiations.[35]

---

32   *Wake Forest College*   [1917-

Society Day, 1917

Society Day, the autumnal celebration of the Philomathesian and Euzelian Literary Societies, occurred on October 29, with the following program:

JUNIOR-SOPHOMORE DEBATE, 1:30 P. M.

A. J. FRANKLIN, JR., Eu., *President.*
J. I. ALLEN, JR., Phi., *Secretary.*

QUERY: *Resolved,* That the right to vote should not be restricted on account of sex, constitutionality waived.

Affirmative:
L. J. BRITT, Phi., Robeson County.
A. W. BEACHBOARD, Eu., Buncombe County.

Negative:
B. S. LILES, Eu., Union County.
D. B. JOHNSON, Phi., Bladen County.

ORATIONS, 7 P. M.

C. S. OWEN, Phi., Buncombe County: "The Call of the West."
W. B. GLADNEY, Eu., Lincoln County, La.: "Helping Hoover."
H. I. HESTER, Eu., Columbus County: "The Task of the Red Cross."
L. V. COGGINS, Phi., Chatham County: "The Passing of Kings."

Marshals:
P. E. WHITE, Eu., *Chief;* D. R. FOUTS, A. R. FLEETWOOD,
H. J. DAVIS, Phi., *Chief;* H. D. LOCKERMAN, L. Y. BALLENTINE.

---

[34] *Old Gold and Black*, October 21, 1933, page 6.

[35] *Old Gold and Black*, October 14, 1939, page 1.

The college had not consulted the societies in selecting October 21 for Homecoming, and the Societies were behind the temporal eight-ball in holding selection contests. The internal debate was on: " Two of the Society presidents say that Society Day will be postponed to November 11, while the other declares vehemently that such shall not be."

Page Acree, the Philomathesian president, decided that there was "not sufficient time to prepare the debates and orations worthy of their name." Jim Koppel, Monday night Euzelian section president, agreed. Together, they set a date three weeks later. Meanwhile, the president of the main section of the Eus, Hendlee Barnett, along with Executive Secretary Bedford Black, posted notices that tryouts would begin one week hence in time for speeches at Homecoming Day.

Realizing that Society Day could not be on two dates, the adversaries "met briefly and decided to stick by their guns. 'We are not going to break with tradition,' they said. 'Society Day should be on Homecoming Day.'" Becoming the "affirmative" at this point, Barnett and Black defended the Homecoming Day, saying that "the alumni have the right to hear the amazing Wake Forest orators and debaters."

Acree and Koppel offered their rebuttal, arguing that Society Day was not for alumni but for current members to learn from the invited speaker. Acree postulated perhaps the real reason, "if a holiday were received for homecoming, another might be attained for society activities and thus the students would get two days off instead of one!" The resolution was not apparent; Goldblatt concluded, "The enigma must be solved, and solved it will be. Perhaps they will have two society days." Lost to history is how the decision was made when the "negative" prevailed and Society Day was moved to November 11.

Combined homecoming and Society Day meant that much of the control had been ceded to the Administration, relegating the Societies to selecting debaters and speakers. The event engendered less and less enthusiasm; the *Old Gold and Black's* 1939 top headline nevertheless read, **GIRLS, GAB HIGHLIGHT SOCIETY DAY**.[36]

---

[36] *Old Gold and Black*, November 11, 1939, page 1.

Romancing Society Day

Henry Davis's essay, "A Society Day Visitor," in the 1917 *Wake Forest Student*, interprets the Meredith Women's College coeds' (and others') standing as Society Day visitors.

> The young ladies full of fun and gaiety began to crowd off the train even before the cars had ceased to move. Around the depot you will see hundreds of enthusiastic and handsome young lads ready to greet the fair maidens with a hearty welcome to their college."
>
> Oh, I'll declare I never saw such a rush – Hello James...Mighty glad to see you – no, I can carry my suitcase, James. Never saw so many boys in my life –I'll declare, we had the "moistest" fun on the train. Gee! What a pretty campus – and that *Arch*... [The student's opening comments are followed by long sections on football games and receptions, with a fragment of oratory.]

> As the train left, the boys rolled off the moving cars and yelled until the last coach had lost itself in the darkness. Now nothing could be heard but the roar of the engine. The day was over; the girls had gone, and to-morrow meant the same old thing – WORK.[37]

The 1920 campus paper's account burnished the Day: "Beautiful weather, large numbers of girls from Mere-dith, Lewisburg and Oxford colleges and many visitors from other places.... The gym-nasium was artfully decorated

---

[37] Henry J. Davis, A Society Day Visitor, *The Wake Forest Student,* November 1917, page 103, 107.

with pennants and evergreens. The presence of so many members of the fair sex contributed more than anything else to the pleasure and joy derived from the occasion. The room was very nearly filled with couples strolling about the floor.[38]

An *Old Gold and Black* sub-headline in 1935 assured with a touch of irony:

Influx of Angels from Meredith, Peace, and St. Mary's Will Make Life Worth Living for Stayed Literary Devotees.[39]

Another reporter held, "Many new men plan to attend and bring their fair friends along" to join in the "moonlit stroll under the magnolias." [40] Society Day was more than speeches and dinners; it was, at its core, a romantic departure from the mundane.

The stage was primed, but how could the migration of young women be orchestrated? The unfolding was explained in a partially "mean-boys" fashion.[41] "[T]he novel and romantic feature of the whole affair lay in the fact that these girls, for the most part, were entire strangers… It was a misfortune, when your girl came, if she was tall and ugly. It was a joke if she was fat. But it was an everlasting source of exaltation if she was a real, living queen."[42]

There were few girls in the small village, but the women's college gave hope. The trains would deliver to the campus Meredith's extra charm. After all, the arrangers were living and breathing, three-dimensional, motivated society debaters.

Naturally, Society Days evolved over the years but only incrementally. A description "ten years later" at the 1924 event reveals an alluring account, with many extra details of the tenor and shape of the typical celebration.

---

[38] *Old Gold and Black,* November 12, 1920, page 1.

[39] *Old Gold and Black,* October 25, 1935, page 1.

[40] *Old Gold and Black*, November 1, 1935, page 1.

[41] "Wake Forest, one of the few institutions which through years has refused admission to the fair coeds, is to be invaded by girls. But they are coming for only one day and coming then to add color and prestige to the annual society day…Meredith College authorities have ruled that young women of this institution who will attend the celebration must make the trip to and from Wake Forest on the train. Accordingly, there is some talk of running a special train to bring the pretty things to the village," *The Charlotte Observer,* November 2, 1923, page 3.

[42] *The Wake Forest Student,* April 1917, Vol. 37, page 357.

The story opens with the Newbie's unique posture vis-à-vis Society Day, extends with descriptive asides, including the mystery of assigning dating matchups, and concludes with a realistic assessment of Society Day's subdued future.

This is one of the few occasions when a freshman is allowed to be seen on the campus with one of the fairer sex. As a rule, a freshman's hair is in danger if he is seen with the girl and Wake Forest on any other occasion, but "now is the time for all good men to come to the aid of their college, open and especially the freshmen.

Within the last student generation sufficient interest in Society Day has been manifest to invite all the young ladies from the nearby colleges, who wish to do so, to send their names over and have a young man chosen for them and not known who their partner for the day is until they arrive on the hill.

When the train would make its appearance around the bend below the lumber yard numerous shrieks and yells would go up from the anxious Romeos, and the chief expression to be heard was "Railroad!"

Above, Oxford Female Seminary – 1850-1925 , Samual
Wait, Oxford President – 1850-1857

After welcoming the fair guests with preppy yells and the "spelling of Wake Forest" in their honor, the anxious ones (both the fair ones and the more anxious otherwise) would proceed to the fountain on the campus where the assortment would begin. There are the names of the partners that will be read out in the couple pair-off.

Happy couples would then make a quick getaway from the crowd and by chance a few of them would drop in to hear one, or at least part of one, the speeches of the debaters that afternoon. A few of the more fortunate (or unfortunate) couples would stay for the whole debate.

After the debate, from that time until the time of the evening repast, the debaters as well as the other Romeos would walk the campus with their "dearly beloved" ones that would take a little time occasionally from singing their own glory to sing the praise of their Alma Mater.

The orators at 8 o'clock would be greeted by an audience about the size of the one that greeted the debaters that afternoon. If anything, there would be a few more to hear them but the majority of the listeners would be longing for the time for the reception and the grand Promenade around the little music stand in the gymnasium to begin.

The day's jollities would come to an end with the reception in the hall followed by the call for the ladies to make their appearance at the depot. As a train would slowly crawl out from the station shed all would declare that they had had a grand and glorious time. Such was the society days in the "good old days."

Such days have ceased to be experienced at Wake Forest any longer. Society Day is looking forward to a chance to "go home" or make up some back work "that I've been planning to do for a long time."

Every Wake Forest man that desires to get the most of us on Society Day should let himself be seen on the campus that day with a young lady. Freshmen are not only ones to have a fair one to accompany them next Monday.[43]

If hosting the society day required the presence of students from adjacent women's colleges, there was often the bureaucratic difficulty of permissions from the visitor's schools. Society day was an easily shared holiday in most years, but not always. When the festive day was "in a

---

[43] *Old Gold and Black*, November 1, 1924, page 1.

groove" in 1916 a delay developed requiring some fancy footwork on the societies' part. The celebratory date had to switch a couple of times to accommodate wishes of Meredith's president Brewer[44].

"The First Trip to Meredith" – *Howler*

"A committee of the Berean Class was in consultation with Dr. C. E. Brewer, President of Meredith college, last week in regard to securing the entire student body from Meredith to attend on Friday, October 27. Dr. Brewer, owing to a holiday coming the preceding week, would not permit the girls to come on Friday. However, he has agreed to their coming on Monday, and so realizing the necessity of having girls to make the celebration a success, the Berean Class is petitioning the faculty for a change of date."[45]

Not only was the day moved, but other accommodations were also obliged. The Societies picked up the guarantee required for a special train, which left Raleigh at 2:30 PM and returned at 12:30 PM, a fairly short turnaround.[46]

---

[44] Before becoming President at Meredith, C. E. Brewer had been a Dean at Wake Forest. *The Fayetteville Weekly Observer*, March 8, 1919, page 2.

[45] *Old Gold and Black*, October 7, 1916, page 1.

[46] *Old Gold and Black*, October 21, 1916, page 1.

Presumably, not too many feelings were hurt as Wake's president greeted everyone in the evening. His comments were responded to by President Brewer of Meredith and Professor Highsmith of Oxford, who joined Poteat on the daises.

In 1925, Society Days was also moved to Monday in deference to the attendance of the Meredith women. The afternoon football game with the Richmond Blues was also moved to Monday.[47] The senior orators and debaters, musicians, and caterers moved with them.

Eight years later, the Society Day calendar dates had to be changed (twice) to accommodate Meredith. So tied with the holiday was the ability of Meredith women to attend that the date had to wait for a signoff from the Meredith Dean (By this point, the President of Meredith was not making the decision alone). "A telephone call from the Dean of Meredith College Tuesday night settled the date for the celebration of the 99th anniversary of the founding of the Euzelian and Philomathesian Literary Societies as October 21."[48]

HARD PROBLEMS —Ed Wil- ciety, confers with George Ed- were to be solved in preparation son, standing, president of the dins, Euzelian, who grits his for tomorrow's Society Day Philomatheeian Literary So- teeth over hard problems which and holiday.

---

[47] *The Wilmington Morning News*, Oct 27, 1915, page 10.

[48] Additionally, the conflict of activities at the two colleges and "the necessity of having Meredith girls on the campus to carry out the traditional events which had been for the past ninety-eight years, there was some delay in fixing the date. Through the kindness of Meredith's officials, Stunt Night, which was to have taken place tonight was postponed to a later date thus doing away with any conflict." *Old Gold and Black*, October 7, 1933, page 1.

Through the late '20s and '30s the Societies saw mixed achievements in hosting the "big day." A sizable sidebar in 1927 stole the attention from the public debate as the buses from Meredith and Lewisburg could not be there for the morning debate. "The excitement for the day first appeared to be a 14 to 7 football victory over High Point College in the afternoon. But even greater immediate excitement was when it was reported that the buses engaged to bring the Meredith girls over to Wake Forest on Saturday afternoon had "in order to avoid hitting a coming car, crashed into an obstruction alongside the road." Three of the Meredith women were injured, one of whom was hospitalized for a short period.[49]

Following the student orations, the same year, then-President Francis P. Gaines addressed the banquet goers. He scratched his prepared remarks and spoke to *The Unpardonable Sin in Higher Education*. "The unpardonable sin he declared is the attitude that some half-educated persons have in feeling that their college training gives them the right to 'high-hat' everyone else who has never been to college."[50]

Presumably, a day in which the debate was exhausted by few in attendance, a crash led to further delay, and a predictable banquet was not the most "brilliant affair" in years, but, in print, the recounting was rescued. The State papers also continued to inflate. several papers in 1933 carried a story applauding that "Four hundred young girls were escorted about Wake Forest College today by students celebrating the annual society day."[51] Undoubtedly an overestimation.

The Society Day's magic was no longer the romantic siren. Social mores and access to out-of-town adventure rendered the presence of Meredith women less momentous. In 1941, for one brief year, the girls of surrounding colleges were banned for Society Day. "For the first time in history there will be no girl guests of the Euzelian and Philomathesian members. A joint session of the two societies last Monday night resulted in a decision to rule out girls. Social emphasis will be placed this school

---

[49] *Old Gold and Black*, November 29, 1927, page 1.

[50] *Old Gold and Black*, November 29, 1927, page 1; Among his audience were literary society sponsors, which may have been much like a fraternity's "house mother." The *Old Gold and Black* reported that at this reception, "Miss Angie Dancey, Hayes N. C. Sponsor of the Euzelian society, and Miss Mildred Vogler, of Winston-Salem, sponsor of the Phi. Society was present." *Old Gold and Black*, November 29, 1927, page 2.

[51] *Asheville Citizen-Times* (Asheville NC), October 22, 1933, page 1.

year on Founders' Day, January."[52] It was a minor speech contest by this point, and the fellows could get their own dates.

Ed Wilson, future Provost, then president of the Philomathesians, indicated a more plausible reason. "Less emphasis is being placed upon Society Day than in previous years, mainly because of the lack of a football game to attract co-ed visitors."[53] Some activities, including the banquet, were moved to January and Founder's Day. Instead, a touch football game between the societies was in the works.

The "Flying Parson"

Researching the past Society Days, an enigma emerged. Why, in 1922, did Wake's president, along with a bevy of notables, launch Society Day with the solemn dedication of a bronze tablet placed at the admired Memorial Hall? Here rests a mystery to be uncovered.

With the passage of time, major tales in an institution's history can simply vanish. Wake Forest's aviator Maynard, a worthy story, is such a lost legend.

The News & Observer reported on the special dedication performed on Society Day 1922, "Just three years from the day that Belvin W. Maynard, 'flying parson' and noted pilot, spoke to visitors at Wake Forest on 'Society Day' in 1918 [1919], a bronze tablet two feet and by one and half feet was presented to Wake Forest college here today, bearing the inscription in honor of the world-famous pilot who lost his life September 7, 1922 when his plane fell to earth, destroying pilot and ending the career of Maynard in its infancy."[54]

The tablet presented was readied by faculty and friends who raised the funds. Dr. Weaver, when interviewed for the *Old Gold and Black,* said: "The most gratifying feature of the work of the committee named for the purpose of raising the funds has been the cooperation of Maynard's admirers and friends... Every penny was voluntarily contributed." The faculty voted for the bronze marker to be placed in Wingate Memorial

---

[52] *The News & Observer*, November 6, 1941, page 12.

[53] *Old Gold and Black*, November 7, 1941, page 1.

[54] *News and Record*, November 25, 1922, page 1.

Hall and for a second scholarship in Maynard's name to be established, available primarily to ministerial students.[55]

MAYNARD STIRS SOCIETY DAY CAMPUS EXCITEMENT

Society Day 1919 was promoted for its imminent excitement yet was not much different from any other year's publicity. The *Old Gold and Black* in October predicted a grand event, "from the moment the whistle blows at 2 o'clock on Monday, announcing the cross-country run, and till the refreshments at the reception that night, there will not be a dull moment."[56]

The same issue advised that a "famous sky pilot" was to visit the campus. Pres. Poteat had wired the aviator "to give, if possible, the exact dates of his arrival."[57] But the main story featured the debaters, acclaimed in the newspaper, each honored with an individual photo and a write-up for their hard work. The preview promised that Wake Forest, Meredith, and Oxford presidents would address the reception.

Little did the Wake community know that the stars would align and "from the sky," Society Day 1919 would become one of the most memorable in Wake history.

In October, the *Old Gold and Black* led with the story of Maynard's major triumph. "Our 'sky pilot' had put it across again." they laid forth:

Flying at an average speed of nearly two miles a minute, through snow, fog, clouds and rain, Lieut. Belvin W. Maynard, Wake Forest Student, called the 'greatest pilot on earth,' finished the return transcontinental trip in a few minutes less time than the flying time of his westbound trip.

A total of approximately 5,400 miles across the continent traversed... When Lieutenant Maynard landed on Roosevelt Field Saturday afternoon, he was greeted by a large crowd of admirers. The first persons to greet him as he stepped from his machine were his two little girls and his wife, who rushed across the field, amid the frantic cheering of hundreds of spectators, held back at a safe distance by special details of soldiers.

---

[55] *Old Gold and Black*, December 1, 1922, page 1.

[56] *Old Gold and Black*, October 31, 1919, page 1.

[57] *Old Gold and Black*, October 31, 1919, page 3.

Maynard was the first aviator out of the sixty-two contestants who entered to finish the high-speed serial journey, the most adventurous, peaceful air race the world has known.[58]

Rumors circulated that the instantly famous alum, distanced from his Wake days by only three years, might be in North Carolina. He could join his fellows for the big Society Day celebration if luck would hold. Confirmation was fleeting, but the "flying Parson," who was back in the state preaching, arranged to be on the Wake Forest campus.

The 1919 Society Day was indeed an enormous occasion. The hero arrived on Society Day; an occasion well understood by the pilot. Students, faculty, and the community celebrated the promising transportation advances in flight, welcoming back a former society member.

The headlines proclaimed **MAYNARD A GUEST OF WAKE FOREST**. The story recorded that "Lieutenant B. W. Maynard, with Gov. Bickett as a passenger in the De Haviland trans-continental plane, shot over to Wake Forest College, 17 miles from here today and participated in the welcoming ceremonies planned there by the students of the college in honor of their fellow student who left there a few years ago to jump into world fame."

The school newspaper reported:

With suppressed excitement, the entire student body waited the opening events of society day. Soon after the noon hour, small groups begin to gather around the railroad station and as time sped onward the throng increased to a multitude.

Some merely scanned the horizon for the first glimpse of Lieut. Maynard, flying in his de Haviland plane, while others whose minds dwelled upon other things, listened hopefully for the whistle of the special train bringing one hundred and thirty Meredith students.

Lieut. Maynard... very considerately timed his flight in order to fly over the town just as the passengers were leaving the special train. Lieut. Maynard had thought that he could land here, but upon finding the air conditions very bad and the field being rather dangerous, he deemed it best not to attempt to descent. After flying over the campus a number of times, he made a wide circle headed toward the south and soon disappeared from view.

---

[58] *Old Gold and Black*, October 24, 1919, page 1, 4.

In the midst of the debate, Lieut. Maynard, who had returned from Raleigh by automobile, entered… In honor to the man who had brought honor to Wake Forest, the entire assemblage stood up with one accord and remained as the Lieutenant had been seated. At the end of the debate, Pres. Pittman called on him for a speech, but Lieutenant looked tired, so Dr. Poteat arose and suggested that he save himself for the reception.

GOVERNOR BICKETT GETS SOME REAL THRILLS WHEN "FLYING PARSON" TAKES HIM OVER WAKE FOREST

North Carolina's Governor enjoyed his airplane ride with Lieutenant Maynard immensely yesterday afternoon until the flyer reached Wake Forest. The Governor confesses that he considered the aviator somewhat reckless in skimming down into the classic groves of the College and then gliding quickly up again. Governor Bickett is on the right in the picture standing beside Lieutenant Maynard just before they started for their "Joy Ride."

At the evening event Governor Thomas Bickett presented, "the greatest pilot on earth," who told of his flight from Mineola to San Francisco and return. Along with his narrative he paid beautiful tribute to "our destinies," as governor Bickett had termed the students of Meredith, who graced the hall.[59]

After the celebration, Maynard returned to Raleigh, along with his dog Trixie, to fly over the County fair in his North Carolina hometown of Clinton.

---

[59] *Old Gold and Black*, November 7, 1919, page 1, 4.

Governors are by their very nature politicians, and Wake Forest graduate Governor Thomas Bickett (1917-1921) happily joined in the media circus. *The News & Observer* shadowing the arrival noted:

Gov. Thomas W. Bickett climbed aboard Lieut. Belvin W Maynard's DeHavilland airplane yesterday afternoon shortly after 2 o'clock in less than 10 minutes was swooping in dizzy circles around the heads of welcoming crowds gathered on the golf links at Wake Forest, 17 miles away, to greet the winner in the trans-continental air race...

It was by the governor's insistence that he took his first air flight. Arrangements have been made to carry him over to Wake Forest in the afternoon in readiness for the arrival of Lieut. Maynard, Sgt. Klein and "Trixie" in their plane a few minutes later. But the governor insisted on flying, and Lieut. Maynard was willing. Mrs. Bickett, it appears, was not consulted, but the governor was careful after he donned Sgt. Klein's tightfitting coat, his helmet and goggles to remind someone to tell his wife how pretty he looked. [60]

Give my regards to Max Gardner and tell them go make the best governor he can," the governor called out as he crammed himself down in the seat that Sgt. Klein and Trixie usually occupy. "Trixie" wasn't a bit impressed with the honor having a mere governor occupy her accustomed place, and she put up a merry little piece of disorder as the plane took off. Then she found that Sgt. Klein had also been left behind also and took the loss philosophically.

It was an ideal day for flying. A slight wind was blowing, but the sun was warm and the sky entirely clear. For 30 minutes or more, the governor was in the air. With Lieut. Maynard, he circled about Raleigh then made a straight course for Wake Forest, coming into the golf link first from the east. Around and around the plane soared, the powerful motor roaring.

The landing field selected by Lieut. Maynard Sunday afternoon was that part of the golf links composing a sort of level Valley between two sloping hills half a mile from Wake Forest on either side of the embankment the crowds were thick. They watch the plane coming low over the treetops and then darting upward. Several times, the pilot plunged downward, as if to land, and then took

---

[60] *The News & Observer*, November 4, 1919, page 1, 2.

PARSON SETS RECORD IN AIR DERBY:
HOPES TO WIN TRANS-CONTINENTAL RACE

First Lieut. B. W. Maynard and his famous German police dog matrot,
Trialo, taken at start of flight.

off skyward again. Finally, there was a yell: "Here he comes." The big plane shot down over the treetops, almost kissed the earth, ran parallel with it for 25 yards and then as Lieut. Maynard shook his head vigorously in negative fashion, pointed his nose at the starting angle and Maynard was leaving Wake Forest...

"That flying was great," the governor said. "The only thing I didn't like was that swooping down over the treetops. That made me nervous."

Gov. Bickett wandered about in pleasantries and then gave the exercises a serious turn when he intoned on campus that evening. "I think there is just one lesson the youth of the whole State may well learn the glorious example of Lieut. Maynard: that is, that the highest courage, and the greatest efficiency come from the highest thinking and the cleanest living."

Everyone was in a celebratory mood. W. L. Poteat, president of Wake, "attributed the remarkable development of the flying machine to the demands made by the war for maximum efficiency and everything that has been a part in the enterprise...With the possible exception of the Wright brothers, Lieut. Maynard has made the largest contribution to the development of the flying machine."[61]

Wake Forest's *Old Gold and Black* exclaimed, "Hooray for Maynard! This has been the universal feeling of the entire student body at Wake Forest since news came the Lieut. Bevan Womble Maynard's trans-continental flight of last week, the first of its kind."[62]

Lieut. Maynard entered Wake Forest in 1914 and completed two years of academic work for the BA degree, after which he left Wake Forest to enlist in the aviation service and was sent to France very soon after the United States entered the war... Upon returning from France some time ago, Lieutenant Maynard came back to Wake Forest on a furlough and registered for the present session. Still, after receiving his discharge from the army and briefly resuming classes, he "was invited to participate in another race, one that made the New York-Toronto contest seem timid.

The race covered some six thousand miles, from Long Island to San Francisco. Its sixty-seven planes would land at designated points for fuel and rest. (Only flying time counted in picking the winner.) With Maynard was his pup, Trixie (wearing a Snoopy-style scarf), and his mechanic, William Klein. Their de Havilland was named *Hello Frisco*."[63]

The cross-continental dash would pluck him from obscurity. Maynard entered and won the grueling round-trip race outpacing the top flyer of the era. He became an instant celebrity with calls to perform at air shows and occupy church pulpits.[64]

Flying was immensely risky, with several pilots dying in nearly every race. Newspapers recorded the deaths[65], the passion for the races, and

---

[61] *The News & Observer*, November 2, 1919, page 2.

[62] *Old Gold and Black*, October 17, 1919, page 1.

[63] https://www.ncpedia.org/biography/maynard-belvin.

[64] Also launched were contacts with powerful sponsors. Lancaster, J. (2023). *The Great Air Race: Glory, tragedy, and the dawn of American aviation*. Liveright Publishing Corporation, New York, page 35.

[65] *Reno Gazette-Journal* (NV) October 16, 1919. Less than halfway through the Intercontinental race, the Nevada paper reported, "the death toll and the race today stood at seven, leaving 39 pilots in the contest Lieut. French Kirby, pilot and Lieut. Stanley C. Miller, observer, yesterday 'went west' when their plane crashed at Castle Rock, Utah. An article in *Aviation History Magazine* (January 24, 2018) recorded, "The cost of the race in men and machines had been high. There had been 54 wrecks and forced landings, 42 of them disabling, and nine men had died."

even landings ("He should have gone around the field again. Instead, Maynard did a dangerous-looking skid one way and then the other way and set his plane down"). Maynard became known for his speed and for opting for dangerous flying choices.

ELMIRA STAR-GAZETTE

Preacher Ahead In Air Race, Has Mishap

When the United States entered World War I, Maynard was eligible for deferment as a father and minister but elected to go to France to train those engaging the "Red Baron" [66] (Baron Manfred von Richthofen) as the dueling bi- and tri-plane aces flew over the *la champagne*.

"During his eighteen months at Issoudun, he logged more than 700 hours above the French countryside…Crowds gathered to watch him perform." Five months after the Armistice, he set a new world record for continuous loops, completing 318 in sixty-seven minutes. A witness recalled the precision with which his single-seat Sopwith Pup, tailing a thin stream of oil smoke, inscribed perfect circles that began and ended at the same altitude, as if Maynard were following 'a mechanical groove in the heavens.'" [67]

Another source claimed the loops, on Lincoln's birthday, "were at an altitude of 2,000 feet, much nearer the ground than any aviator had ever attempted before." [68] His role in the European theatre was that of an airplane tester, an extremely dangerous avocation. As the "American Army 'ace,' he faced death constantly flying the newly arrived planes before turning them over to the flight commanders." [69]

THE TRANSCONTINENTAL RACE

The broken crankshaft, the dangerous light over mountain ranges, the race through four snowstorms, the exchange of engines to ward off defeat, all these things became the exciting moments of the unfolding race. Each crisis exalted in the press was accompanied by the humble

---

[66] https://www.history.com/topics/world-war-i/manfred-baron-von-richthofen

[67] Lancaster, J. (2023). *The Great Air Race: Glory, tragedy, and the dawn of American aviation.* Liveright Publishing Corporation, New York, page 43.

[68] *Chicago Tribune*, October 12, 1919, page 2.

[69] *Chicago Tribune*, October 12, 1919, page 2.

Maynard's estimation: "As a flyer led all his contestants in the world's August race, the Lieut. Maynard talked about as informally as if they had been inconsequential details of a more or less uninteresting trip."[70]

The Mineola, New York, newspaper announced: "Lieut. Belvin W. Maynard, Victor in the Army's air race across the continent and return, the greatest aviation endurance test in history landed here at 1:50 PM" with double-tiered front-page font **MAYNARD WINNER IN GREAT FLIGHT AT MINEOLA FIELD.**[71]

The hometown New York newspaper, *Star-Gazette* (Elmira, NY), provided a riveting blow-by-blow account of the transcontinental flight, the material that would elevate the pilot to hero in the hero's own words.[72]

> Our hardships were scattered across the continent… we were tired at night, very tired. When we reached Chicago…the Aero-Club had sleeping quarters for us on the field. We did not get much sleep.
>
> The next morning, we encountered the roughest weather of the trip. We finally got to Omaha and the weather got better. The wind was against us, but we finally made Cheyenne.

---

[70] *The News & Observer*, November 2, 1919, page 2.

[71] *Star-Gazette* (Elmira, NY), October 18, 1919, page 1.

[72] A more detailed account of Maynard and others' nine-day race, with considerable detail, including remarkable technical nuances, can be found in Lancaster, J. (2023). *The Great Air Race: Glory, tragedy, and the dawn of American aviation.* Liveright Publishing Corporation, New York.

It was freezing cold at Cheyenne. Four minutes before sunrise. We started our motors. We were pouring water into the radiator, and some of that fell, overflowed the pipes and froze. The temperature was 20 degrees... When Maynard started the engine, the radiator burst. No one at the airfield could repair it, seemingly necessitating a delay of at least 24 hours. "Maynard and Kline removed the radiator, took it into town and found a plumber to repair it, a process that delayed them only seven hours. Then, just as they were taxiing for takeoff, Trixie jumped out and ran around barking until she was put back aboard.

Perhaps she sensed that hostile terrain lay ahead."[73]

Maynard told an Elmira reporter that the trip from Reno to Sacramento was the most beautiful and dangerous.

The mountains were covered with trees and snow. There was hardly room to drive an ox cart through... I was invited to lunch by the King of Belgium. He was late and I didn't have time to wait... We found Battle Mountain, Nevada, the most enthusiastic town in the West (the home of one of the other racers). The whole place turned out at the schoolhouse that night and they gave a dinner at a dance in our honor. I did not dance...

During the flight Trixie helped to keep me warm... Ask if Trixie dipped her head over the sides as dogs do when riding? in

---

[73] Friedman, H. M., and Friedman, A. K. (January 2018). The Great Transcontinental Air Race, *Aviation History Magazine,* https://www.historynet.com/great-transcontinental-air-race.htm History Net; *Chicago Tribune,* October 19, 1919, page 1, 2.

automobiles, the Lieut. replied, "yes, she stretched her nose out into the wind all the while"[74]

He arrived in San Francisco after twenty-five hours and sixteen minutes, which worked out to an average speed of 108 miles an hour. His closest westbound competitor did not reach the Presidio until Monday.

As he coasted to a stop, the crowd enveloped Maynard's plane. Trixie was the first to alight, plying her way out of the cockpit as Maynard and Kline unbuckled their safety harnesses. Well-wishers practically pulled them up from their seats. Reporters and photographers swarmed, smiling "until my cheeks became cramped," Trixie in his arms and gamely filled questions on his journey. "It was a great trip," he said while acknowledging that he was still a little deaf. "I enjoyed it immensely."[75]

Maynard's wife, Essie, learned of his arrival late Saturday afternoon at Roosevelt Field, where she'd been waiting for the first eastbound flyers, "the children are very happy to know you landed safely," she wrote in a telegram...
But her relief was tinged with fear. She been shocked by the death toll the race and closed her message with a heartfelt plea, "I hope so much you will not try to fly back." Maynard shrugged it off. "I have heard that before I left home," he told a reporter. "It is not news to me."[76]

We had three days in San Francisco and got away about 1:20 in the afternoon on Tuesday. We found Battle Mountain, Nevada... We made record time from Rawlins to Cheyenne and landed at Sidney that night, finding the field covered with snow. I don't believe I could have found it if I had not been there before. We left the next morning while it was snowing, but we flew out of the storm.[77]

---

[74] *Star Gazette*, October 20, 1919, page 1, 15; "At San Francisco, Maynard invited the King of the Belgians, who was there with his queen, but Albert said he was sorry he couldn't go, being very busy. Then he invited Maynard to lunch, but the 'Flying Parson' turned the King down, telling him that he was a very busy man. The *Indianapolis Star*, September 8, 1922, page 5.

[75] Lancaster, J. (2023). *The Great Air Race: Glory, tragedy, and the dawn of American aviation*. Liveright Publishing Corporation, New York, page 166.

[76] Lancaster, J. (2023). *The Great Air Race: Glory, tragedy, and the dawn of American aviation*. Liveright Publishing Corporation, New York, page 167.

[77] *Chicago Tribune*, October 19, 1919, page 2.

Between Rawlings and Cheyenne, we encountered five mountains. While crossing the mountains we saw ahead of us two heavy banks of clouds. Between the two clouds was a light streak, into which we headed. It was about a mile and a half wide. The snow was falling on both sides, and we kept going on, when suddenly a snowcapped mountain loomed up in front of us. We were just able to clear it at 200 feet.... in spite of the weather, we made record time to Cheyenne in a light snowstorm and had pretty good going to North Platte.

Late in the morning on October 16, 1919, a de Havilland DH-4 dropped from the clouds and touched down silently in a pasture near Wahoo, Nebraska.

A tall man wearing riding breeches clambered out of its front cockpit, and from the rear a mechanic and a large dog emerged. The two men headed for the biplane's nose to gaze upward at their crippled engine. A broken crankshaft, unrepairable. Newspapers across America would carry the story that evening: U.S. Army Air Service Lieutenant Belvin W. Maynard, an ordained Baptist minister who had made headlines just two months earlier by besting a gaggle of aces and famous aviators in the International Air Derby, was down. But was the "Flying Parson" out of the Transcontinental Air Race for good?[78]

Maynard recalled, "While nearing Omaha, the motor was going good, and we were flying about 2500 feet up. Suddenly the motor quit."[79] *Hello Frisco* was flying a direct compass course above the clouds when Maynard reduced power and descended to check his position. As he advanced the throttle to regain altitude, the increased torque broke the Liberty engine's hollow crankshaft. The engine failure resulted in a dead-stick landing in a Nebraska pasture.

---

[78] Friedman, H. M., and Friedman, A. K. (January 2018). The Great Transcontinental Air Race. *Aviation History Magazine*, January 2018, https://www.historynet.com/great-transcontinental-air-race.htm History Net. This article presents a full history of the race's twists and turns, wrecks, and dangers. While featuring Maynard as he became the media star, it also accounts for many other pilots' stories of travail and triumph and the influence of various types of planes.

[79] *Star Gazette*, October 20, 1919, page 15.

Maynard turned to Kline, laughing, and said, "There is not another motor this side of Chicago." But then they remembered that Francis' wrecked Martin was only 10 miles away. A phone call later, and the engine and Francis himself were headed to Wahoo. "I'm still in the race," Maynard told reporters.

Race officials estimated it would take anywhere from two days to a full week to replace the engine—more of a delay than Maynard could possibly overcome. The replacement arrived late in the day, and the airmen convinced locals to encircle the biplane with their cars and shine their headlights on it. With the help of a farmer who had worked on the Liberty engines of the U.S. Navy's Curtiss NC-3 flying boat, Maynard and Kline pushed the DH under a tree, rigged a chain from a branch and removed the ruined engine. Kline and his scratch team worked all night while Maynard caught a few hours' sleep.

At 8 a.m. the next day the newly installed Liberty roared to life. The DH-4 crew had lost only 18 hours, and they were still in the lead."[80]

When asked if he had any difficulty taking off from such a small field he replied, "no we turned the machine around under the tree we had used to take the motor out and we put right off. We got to Omaha before anyone got down to the field.[81]

In Rock Island, Illinois, he was entertained by Mr. and Mrs. "Billy" Sunday.[82] "Sunday took special care of both the parson and his dog." On the mantelpiece of Maynard's home, "reposed the large photograph of Billy Sunday, which noted evangelists had inscribed to Maynard with the phrase "you lead, others follow."[83]

The biggest adventure of the remaining legs of the race, other than improved Chicago hospitality, was a repeat of the crossing of Lake Erie. He said, "It was too foggy over Lake Erie to make a direct cut. When

---

[80] Friedman, H. M., and Friedman, A, K. (January 2018). The Great Transcontinental Air Race, *Aviation History Magazine*. https://www.historynet.com/great-transcontinental-air-race.htm History Net, page 7-8.

[81] *Star Gazette*, October 20, 1919, page 15.

[82] Billy Sunday was widely considered the most influential American evangelist during the first two decades of the 20th century with his colloquial sermons and frenetic delivery. Sunday held widely reported campaigns in America's largest cities, and he attracted the largest crowds of any evangelist before the advent of electronic sound systems. https://en.wikipedia.org/wiki/Billy_Sunday.

[83] *Star Gazette*, October 20, 1919, page 1.

they got to Cleveland Friday afternoon a large crowd was on hand." The last hop home was "so rough that the fliers were almost thrown out of their seats."[84] After Buffalo it was on home to New York.

The most joyous member of the party, at least as far as demonstration went, was Trixie, the Belgian police Dog, who accompanied the flying parson as his mascot.

"Trixie's delight at feeling the solid earth under her once more knew no bounds, and she dashed around and around the place joyously barking."[85]

The New York Times, not to be outdone when supplying human (and canine) interest, wrote: "Trixie, the Belgian police dog which had accompanied her master on the hazardous flight, looked down on the field. She recognized home immediately, for a tail which had not done much wagging since it left Mineola two weeks ago came to life, slapping Sergeant Kline in the face."[86]

Upon landing "the first person to greet him as he stepped from his machine ... were his wife and two little girls who rushed across the field amid the frantic cheering of the hundreds of spectators who were marshalled at a safe distance...Mrs. Maynard was at the side of the airplane before it had come to rest and her husband leaned down from his seat and embraced her silently. His two little girls were lifted up one after the other to kiss their triumphant father.[87]

The United States Army sponsored the transcontinental race, having a strong interest in promoting the viability of aviation, often considered too new and unsafe by a skeptical public. "A successful showing could help persuade the public that airplanes had evolved into practical traveling machines." Promised such a day was coming "they were starting to get impatient."[88]

The transcontinental race in which nine pilots expired hardly improved the impression that flying is not hazardous. Lieutenant Maynard won the elapsed-time contest with 9 days, 4 hours, 25 minutes, and 12 seconds for the round trip.

---

[84] *Star Gazette*, October 20, 1919, page 15.

[85] *Chicago Tribune*, October 19, 1919, page 1.

[86] *The New York Times*, October 19, 1919, page 3.

[87] "Mrs. Maynard isn't "Crazy about Flight." *Star Gazette*, October 20, 1919, page 1, 15.

[88] Lancaster, J. (2023). *The Great Air Race: Glory, tragedy, and the dawn of American aviation.* Liveright Publishing Corporation, New York, page 36.

THE NEW YORK TIMES, SUNDAY, OCTOB

Lieut. Maynard With His Wife and Little Daughters

"...during the welcome, the Lieutenant spied a woman with tears in her eyes standing beside two little girls. Maynard jumped from his seat and took his wife in his arms." *The New York Times*, Oct. 19, 1919

"As an individual performance," General Mitchell[89] said, "Maynard's record stands second to none in the annals of the air in time of peace. His judgment, ability, grit, and determination exhibit the quality shown by our pilots in the European war and are typically American." The public agreed. The "Flying Parson" became the hero of the hour.[90]

---

[89] Billy Mitchell served in France during World War I and commanded all American air combat units in that country by the conflict's end. After the war, he advocated for increased investment in air power... Mitchell is widely regarded as the father of the United States Air Force. https://en.wikipedia.org/wiki/Billy_Mitchell.

[90] Maurer, United States Air Force Historical Research Center, *Aviation in the US. Army, 1919- 1939*, Office of Air Force History United States Air Force Washington, D.C., 1987, page 29-37. Maynard worked for the Army and knew his role in promoting aviation. Upon landing, Maynard held forth on viability and safety at an after-lunch news conference, couched in his personal hero's role. "I believe that landing fields should be established all over the country. At Battle Mountain [Colo.], a town of 500, the people constructed a flying field in ten days at a cost of $10,000 (Other sources said $2000) ... What the flight has brought out concerning the aerial defense of the country shows that it would be possible for a squadron of fighting machines to cross from coast to coast in three days... In any kind of machine there is always danger that the pilot may wreck it. As long as he keeps his head there is only one thing that can cause an accident—that is motor trouble... The airplane is

A TRAGIC END

The *Chicago Tribune* reported that September 7, 1922, "Lieut. Belvin W Maynard, internationally known as 'the flying parson,' and two other flyers, were instantly killed there this afternoon in the fairgrounds when the planes which Maynard was piloting crashed? to the earth at the termination of a tailspin and was completely demolished in Rutland, Vermont.[91] *The Tribune* noted the North Carolina native had learned the skills as an airplane tester in France, "the most dangerous job of all in that country at the time."[92]

No evidence was found that Maynard ever returned to complete his studies at Wake. He may have intended to return, but after a few days at the start of a semester, the Army called, and he was off again into the vast blue sky. *The News-Democrat* reprinted a story that claimed, "Although he hailed as the greatest airman in America and one of the foremost pilots in the world, Lieut. Maynard who left the Baptist ministry two years ago to enter the military service of his country, plans to obtain his discharge from the Army before Christmas and to reenter Wake Forest (N. C.) College, where he still has two years' work on his theological course.[93] These are essentially Maynard's words from statements after he landed.

John Lancaster's book *The Great Air Race* said Belvin Maynard never returned to the pulpit or Wake Forest College to finish his degree. "Essie, who knew her husband better than he knew himself, was disappointed but not surprised. She knew he could never stop flying."[94] *The New York Times,* in the story upon his crash in Vermont, noted after the Transcontinental race that Maynard was a frequent speaker at churches and was scheduled to speak that day at Rutland Baptist Church, where the bells tolled in his honor that evening.

---

built just the same as the Brooklyn Bridge. In time, it will be as easy to be a pilot as it is to be a chauffeur... It's unquestionable that this flight has demonstrated the commercial possibilities of aircraft.

[91] *Chicago Tribune*, September 8, 1922, page 6.

[92] *Chicago Tribune*, September 7, 1922, page 1.

[93] *News-Democrat* (Paducah, KY), October 19, 1919.

[94] Lancaster, J. (2023). *The Great Air Race: Glory, tragedy, and the dawn of American aviation.* Liveright Publishing Corporation, New York, page 256. Lancaster is not entirely correct; Maynard flew to many churches and gatherings where he preached sermons. He did not have an established church where he was pastor.

One of the "Great Air Race" succumbs to the cross winds and short runway in Rawlins, Wyoming. https://www.johnlancasterauthor.com/

After the Transcontinental achievement, he started an aerial photography business he claimed was successful. He used his ministerial credentials to perform weddings. Two weeks before the crash, he united Ms. Helen Virginia Lent and Lloyd Wilson Bertaud in his airplane above New York City's Times Square, a startling elevation.[95]

In the summer of 1920, after leaving the Air Service, Maynard attempted to monetize his fame by embarking on a speaking tour with a canned address entitled *The Motor Troubles of Society*. He settled with his family in Queens, where he "set up a business offering rides in a surplus Jennie."

In his book *The Great Air Race*, John Lancaster provides an account of Maynard's last flight:

> In the late summer of 1922, the owner of a flying Circus hired Maynard for a temporary job performing stunts and giving rides at a fair in Rutland, Vermont.
>
> A British trainer – a two-seat Avro – had been reserved for his use. To bring in more money, Maynard replaced the single seat in the rear cockpit with a makeshift wooden bench that could accommodate two passengers.
>
> At 1 PM on September 7, Maynard took off on a test flight with a pilot and mechanic who worked for the flying Circus. He climbed to 2000 feet, performed a few stunts, then tipped the plane into a spin – a

---

[95] *The New York Times*, September 8, 1922, page 3.

routine maneuver he had performed countless times. The Avro never recovered.

As fairgoers watched in horror, the biplane spiraled into a field at the edge of the fairgrounds. Investigation revealed that the bench Maynard had rigged in the seat rear cockpit had broken, the weight of the two passengers interfered with control cables right underneath. The two men in the rear cockpit died instantly. Maynard was still breathing when he was pulled from the wreckage, but he died before reaching the hospital. He was twenty-nine.

A few days later the Flying Person was buried beneath four oak trees on the family farm in North Carolina. More than 3000 people turned out for his funeral.[96]

Thus, three short years after Maynard and the governor buzzed the train station, Society Day was occupied by dedicating a plaque to the airman alumnus.

A Wake student editorialist noted, "He was a veritable figure of romance. But with it all he was a parson with all the simplicity of faith, the quiet absence of assuming, and lack of self-interest...A country boy from Sampson County, he never allowed his head to be turned

---

[96] Lancaster, J. (2023). *The Great Air Race: Glory, tragedy, and the dawn of American aviation.* Liveright Publishing Corporation, New York, page 257-258. An escort of American Legion members and the company of infantry will accompany the body of Lt. Maynard to the Pennsylvania station. The body will leave on the 5 o'clock train. *The Brooklyn Daily Eagle*, September 8, 1922, page 22.

by fame. With wonderful opportunity to amass wealth for himself, he preferred to risk his life in the interest of churches, hospitals, and orphan asylums." [97]

President William Lewis Poteat described Maynard as having a brief but brilliant career as a "cavalier of the clouds, the memory of Wake Forest's foremost airman in the hearts of his college acquaintances," and for thirty minutes, the undivided thoughts of the Society Day attendants were directed to commemorating his heroic and notable record.[98]

The plaque read:

Belvin W. Maynard, 'Flying Parson'
Pioneer in conquest of the air. Distinguish soldier in world war.
Servant of Christ.
Killed in flight at Rutland Vermont September 7, 1922.
Established world loop-the-loop record at Pomrantin, France, 1918
Winner Transcontinental Air Race 1919
Student Wake Forest College 1914-16
World famous but modest, brave but gentle
Honored above others his thoughts were always of others.[99]

Society Day Retreats as the Social Scene

Organizations are forever in transition, buffeted by social change and competing interests. Society Day's demise was an extended gradual drift. An essay published in a 1938 *Old Gold and Black,* written in a soft defense of society day, nonetheless previews its demise:

As Society Day rolls 'round again, the air is filled with the lamentations of "old grads" bewailing the fact that this literary Festival "ain't what she used to be."

As a matter of fact, she ain't! Society Day was for a number of years one of the two really big annual literary events on the campus. Now it shares a day with the Homecoming celebration.

---

[97] *Old Gold and Black*, December 1, 1922, page 1.
[98] *The News & Record*, November 25, 1922, page 2.
[99] *Old Gold and Black*, December 1, 1922, page 2.

FOOTBALL
HOMECOMING GAME—SOCIETY DAY
WAKE FOREST vs. CARSON-NEWMAN
FRIDAY, NOVEMBER 11
GORE FIELD AT WAKE FOREST
Kickoff: 3 o'clock   Admission $1.10 (incl. tax).

November 1932, *The News & Observer*, page 11.

Enough shreds of glory will still hang around its ghost, however, to make the occasion interesting. Bevies of lasses still trek to the campus from our sister college, although not on a special train, as once was the case, the voices of orators and debaters still roll forth upon the afternoon air, but those who spend their leisure time recalling the past days solemnly swear with tears in their eyes that these voices do not ring with as much elegant insincerity as they once did.

The rise of fraternities, "bumming" to Raleigh, and week-end dances contributed to the decline of Society Day. Enthusiasm for orations, debates, and banquets waned and football games became the major chief drawing cards. Society Days show a definite tendency to fizzle when held on a day on which no football game was played.

In spite of all this, however, ardent Eus and Phis still polished up orations and gargled mouthwash during the month of October. The voice of the bull shooter becomes more resonant and his steps spring here during the days preceding the festival. The occasion is still a big one for those who prefer the tongue to the pen or sword.

Society Day is not dead; only sleepeth![100] In the early Society Days, when students were somewhat confined to campus, the event soared. However, the holiday was soon diluted by the availability of

---

[100] Society Day Boasts Colorful Past – Only Shreds of a Former Glory Still Linger, *Old Gold and Black*, October 28, 1938, page 1.

cars, freeing the students to leave campus for home or other places and taking advantage of the Thursday to Monday break. Paschal described the debates and orations in Society Hall as "with few attendants other than parents and sweethearts."[101]

To correct "the evil" of deserting students, "the day was changed from Friday to Monday in 1920, but this did not reward the planner's intentions. Instead, the students left on "Friday afternoon and returned on Tuesday morning in time for the duties of the day. ... since the establishment of 'Homecoming Day,' about 1935, of which the chief attraction is, when possible, a game of football in the afternoon, while the debate and orations are in the Society Halls in the morning, sometimes both at the same hour."[102]

As early as 1919, cracks were beginning to show, at least from the society's traditional mission, which centered on students speaking. The *Old Gold and Black's* excitement for Society 'Day, aligned with sports and visitors relegated debate and oratories to background noise. "Yep, last week was Victory Week for Wake Forest. Of course, we are referring to the gridiron and tennis successes and the triumphal return of Maynard: About the attempted conquests of society Day, we can't tell."[103]

A 1925 issue of the student paper failed to commemorate the just passed event, leading with the headline:

Society Day Fails To Hold Students To Campus And Few People Attend.
MEREDITH STUDENTS FAILED TO SHOW UP
Euzelians Win Inter-Society Debate in Afternoon
Before Less Than 100 People

The article employed a handful of gloomy metaphors in its criticism:

---

[101] Paschal, G. W. (1943). *The History of Wake Forest College*, Vol. II, page 380. With attendance at the society days waning, a potential solution was holding the exercise on a Wednesday in the middle of the week to a "much larger crowd..." (it is unclear whether this adjustment took place or for how long).

[102] Paschal, G. W. (1943). *The History of Wake Forest College,* Vol. II, page 379-80. The students' "travel adjustments" to whichever Spring Break dates the college adopted sound quite contemporary.

[103] *Old Gold and Black*, November 7, 1919, page 21.

"An all-day drizzling rain, a mud-puddled and sloppy campus, a noticeable scarcity of the fairer sex, and quite a desolate college community were the characteristics that marked Society Day here Monday... According to the older ones of the college circle, it was an abominable degeneration of all past ones. Ever since literary societies were made non-compulsory, both the fall and spring celebrations have been on the downward slope until now they are nothing more than a mere conformity of the past. The day was given as a holiday, and most of the students took advantage of it by going home for the weekend.

Instead of meeting a special train overflowing with the fair damsels, numbers 12 and 20, were met with the utter torrents of not seeing a single skirt step off. It seemed as though Jupiter Pluvius[104] never intended the day to be "ladies," anyhow. For the past two years now Society Day on the most Pluvius day of the entire 365."[105]

"The Society Day program (1926), as rendered in Wingate Memorial Hall, was subpar with those of other years. By actual count less than a hundred heard the debate in the afternoon"[106] The students discussed *government ownership of coal mines*; the default to the national debate topic was not likely to draw a crowd.[107]

Forebodingly, an *Old Gold and Black* editorialist, A. M. McMillian, predicted:

Society Day will not be as gala an affair this year ...It was not possible to have it last week because of dramatic performance in the big city nearby; a varsity football game could not be arranged for this week-end – just a freshman game with Rocky Mount high school. Too many band members are leaving town and so the horns and drums will not lighten up the occasion.[108]

---

[104] Roman God, Rainmaker.

[105] *Old Gold and Black*, November 9, 1925, page 1.

[106] *Old Gold and Black*, November 6, 1926, page 1. The article provides a reasonably complete rendering of the debate and evening orations.

[107] The debate was judged by President W. L. Poteat, Dr. D. B. Bryan, and G. W. Paschal, who were in their customary roles of visible debate involvement.

[108] *Old Gold and Black*, November 9, 1925, page 4.

The next year's evening reception was canceled to make way for the noted lecturer John Cowper Powys, philosopher, poet, and novelist who "described himself as an anarchist" and was both anti-fascist and anti-Stalinist who regularly rubbed elbows with the prominent literary and entertainment names of the day.[109]

In 1921, the event could still merit headlines featuring the debate.

SOCIETY DAY WILL BE OBSERVED WITH APPROPRIATE CEREMONY BY WAKE FOREST STUDENTS
DEBATE TO BE MAIN FEATURE OF ENTIRE PROGRAM OF DAY[110]

A subsequent headline announcing the upcoming Society Day, which ran a week later, has a distinct tonal shift from Debate to theater.

PLANS COMPLETED FOR SOCIETY DAY AND JOY FESTIVAL.
Football Game with Guilford To Usher In Celebration Saturday Evening
Club House On The Golf Links Will Be Opened to all Students And Their Guests During The Entire Day.

By 1928, campus publications essentially ignored Society Day and the Literary Societies; in what was a huge year of accomplishment and activity in the intercollegiate debates, the debates received sparse mention.

In 1932, at least measured by newspaper coverage, Society Day had retreated into homecoming, with homecoming itself subsumed into the big football game between the Deacons and Carson-Newman.[111]

And it was not just the campus press that discounted the Society Day debate; so too the state papers. By 1933, *The News & Observer* was even more clipped. Society Day is listed in the third line of the headline and never again mentioned in a long feature story. From top to bottom, the printed text promoted the homecoming football game with NC State, reviewing present and past football games at great length.[112] In fairness,

---

[109] Klaus, H. G., and Knight, S. T. (2005). *To hell with culture: Anarchism and twentieth-century British literature*. University of Wales Press.

[110] *Old Gold and Black*, October 14, 1921, page 1.

[111] *The News & Observer*, November 11, 1932, page 9.

[112] *The News and Record*, October 21, 1933, page 1.

it appeared in the sports section, yet only tiny two-paragraph stories in statewide newspapers briefed the traditional speaking.

Society Day, at least for the majority, had become dramaturgy. Not only was there the most important football game before a "full stadium," there was the "added stunt between halves of the game, the great University of Southern Kalamazoo will defend their fame and honor in its heated, if brief gridiron contest with the equally great Nota Dam (sic)."[113]

Even with fading participation, arrangement and scheduling continued each year. In 1934, plans were "underway for a full afternoon of entertainment. George Copple, Eu president, and Clarence Hobgood, Phi President, report that the day expects to be one of the most enjoyable occasions ever on the campus with angels from Meredith, belles from St. Mary's, and Doves of Peace."[114]

The Philomathesian Literary Society's clean sweep of inter-society debates and the Baby Deacs football victory over Rocky Mount High School were the high spots of the Annual Society Day Celebrated on the local campus last Saturday.

WAKE FOREST, N. C., SATURDAY, OCTOBER 20, 1934

Society Day Program

| 10:30 A. M. | Debate | Eu Hall |

Resolved: that the electorate of N. C. Should adopt the proposed constitution as passed by the General Assembly.

Affirmative	Negative
H. A. Matthews, Eu	Al Martin, Phi
George Copple, Eu	Carl Ousley, Phi

Judges

C. P. West   Max Griffin   Gerald Grubb

2:30 P. M.   Football game. P. C. vs. Wake Forest College.
6:45 P. M.   Banquet to held at Miss Jo' Williams'.

After-dinner Speakers:

Carl Ousley, Phi   Ed Gambrell, Eu   W. R. Dixon, Phi   H. A. Matthews, Eu

8:15 P. M.   *Oratorical Contest*   Phi Hall

George Copple, Eu ...."The New South and the Old."
J. Glenn Blackburn, Phi ...."Personal Liberty."
Millard Brown, Eu..."The Sunrise of a New America."
Charles Guy, Phi..."A Soldier."

Judges:

Drs. D. B. Bryan   W. L. Poteat   A. C. Reid

---

[113] *Old Gold and Black*, October 21, 1933, page 4. In fairness, this article gives full coverage to the debaters and orators for the day.

[114] *Old Gold and Black*, October 27, 1934, page 1.

The Philomathesians, represented by Al Martin and Charles Guy, won the debating from the Eus, George Copple and H. A. Matthews. The topic was whether *The state of North Carolina should give financial aid to the denominational and privately endowed colleges within its borders.*

The climax of this lively contest came when Al Martin answered the claim of the affirmative that the allotment from this State treasury supplemented the relatively low salaries paid to the professors of Wake Forest. The affirmative would have prevailed with the popular argument of raising wages, an appeal to the immediate audience. Still, Al Martin, later the treasured Wake Forest philosophy professor, won the day declaring, "Gladly does Wake Forest furnish teachers that they may give back to the state a type of teaching that is distinctly different from that of the teachers trained in the State schools. Gladly has she done so in the past, and gladly will she continue to do so."[115]

The students were tightly linked to the faculty, most of whom showed up for the Society Day banquet, some of whom made remarks. "Their humorous talks generally concerned the age-old topics of love and pretty girls, both of which might well be considered suitable topics."[116]

A year later, at the 1936 banquet, "served in the school cafeteria amid decorating pumpkins and witches, Ed Knott, Society Day president, topped off... the afternoon with the gay program of after-dinner repertoire and paved the way for further celebration at a Presbyterian game in the evening."

In the evening orations, Earle Rogers, speaking on his topic, *The American Home*, charged that since the Civil War, the ratio of divorce to marriage has increased by 400 percent and that the breakup of the home is largely responsible for the survival of poverty and ignorance.[117]

By 1939, Society Day had grown into an entertainment event, and honoring of the society debaters continued to fade. The debaters were an afterthought as the public debate moved to the impossible hour of 10 AM to make room for sporting events[118].

---

[115] *Old Gold and Black*, November 9, 1935, page 1.

[116] *Old Gold and Black,* November 9, 1935, page 1.

[117] *Old Gold and Black* November 7, 1936, page 1; W. L. Poteat, then emeritus, spoke at the Society Day, as he seemingly did for decades throughout his long presidency.

[118] The move to mid-morning did not appear long-term.

The *Old Gold and Black* headline was direct: **Food, Speeches, and Meredith Gals.** On the " lighter side" of the day's festivities, the two societies clashed in a game of tag football on Gore Field. Entertaining the assembled was a vocal solo by Jean Bronson of the University of North Carolina and an intersociety quartet.[119] The Hon. Thad Eure, NC Secretary of State, spoke, and toasts were offered to the professors and the girls attending.[120]

Four years later, in 1942, *Old Gold and Black* headline begins to tell the story of Society Day's downfall; a two-hour program seems too long as fraternity dances and "no classes" conquered the students' fancy.

TODAY STARTS ONE OF THE BIGGEST WEEK ENDS (sic) OF THE YEAR, WITH NO CLASSES TOMORROW
Two Fraternity Dances Set for Tonight; SPE's And KA's Have One, Six Frats Another
SOCIETY DAY PROGRAMS WILL LAST FOR TWO HOURS[121]

The *Old Gold and Black* invoked their readers, "Homecoming promises to be gay and colorful, with all the fraternity houses in competition for the first prize in house decorations.... Society Day begins at 2:30 tomorrow afternoon in the Philomathesian Hall with the debates, and the following orations will be delivered in the Euzelian Hall. The program is timed to last two hours, allowing an hour for the four orations and the delivery of the judges' decisions. Such was the change in emphasis.

When Wake Forest's war session began at the end of September 1944, much changed at the school. Many of the students had left campus, and more were expecting their call-up. With an enrollment of 450 instead

---

[119] *Old Gold and Black*, November 11, 1939, page 2.

[120] *Old Gold and Black,* November 18, 1939, page 4; The 1940 pattern was similar, with the Phis Debate winners and Eus claiming the oratory division. Highlights included the "sensational freshman brother debate team from Erwin, TN," defending the Euzelian side of the question. Lee Copple, a future interim coach, "broke down his upperclassman competitors and won top honors in the oratorical class, speaking on *Wake Forest and Christian Culture." The News & Observer*, October 2, 1940, page 16. The afternoon featured Phis and Eus fighting for the title of society football. And why not two football games? Following the banquet speaker, Dr. Basil M. Watkins, Society members, and their guests will be admitted free to the Wake Forest-Marshall football game. *Old Gold and Black*, October 18, 1940, page 1, 4. It was a crowded schedule.

[121] *Old Gold and Black*, September 30, 1942, page 1.

of the usual thousand... and the Army Finance School on the campus, things had to be different.[122]

Graduation was held at the end of each quarter, not the kind of graduation with caps and gowns, but a small group of seniors gathered in the President's office, Dr. Kitchin, saying, "This diploma will mean more to you in the years to come." And the students thinking how much it meant to them then.[123]

The debate team's adjustments in travel and tone during World War II are chronicled in Chapter 13 – Intercollegiate Era Gives Way to Tournament Debates.

The story of this chapter is that the Society Day Debates continued, albeit as semi-public events. The debates were open, and many were alerted to their occurrence. By the mid-'40s, they were functionally an inter-fraternity contest, followed by a banquet for members and guests.

In the following years, many names surfaced as part of Society Day, individuals who were to become Wake Forest legends. By the fall of 1947, speaking was contested between societies with an in-house event. The

---

[122] *Howler,* 1944, page 26.

[123] *Howler,* 1944, page 26.

contests happened over four days, with various competitions happening each day, culminating at the end of the week with a joint banquet. Ed Christman, the future venerated Chaplain, was selected by the Euzelians to do After-Dinner Speaking. ADS is distinguished for speaking with a sparkle of humor; Ed Christman was a natural.

A year earlier, in 1946, *Nancy Easley* won the Society Day oration contest. Her topic was *Hope for Germany.* "Miss Easley, daughter of Dr. J. A. Easley of the college religion department, was chosen as Eu president during the spring elections, thus becoming the first woman to hold a literary society presidency in the history of the school."[124]

In 1947, *Bynam Shaw*, a famed Wake Forest Journalism Professor, was the student chairman of the arrangements committee for Society Day. He announced that the Phis reported that run-offs would be necessary in order to determine the Phi participants in the inter-society contests."[125]

The commemoration of Society Day as a "public" affair no longer held serious influence, even for a general campus audience. The *Old Gold and Black* referenced the interest in Society Day debates, "The debates, while heated on the part of the debaters, were presented before a small group of spectators, a group which barely filled the Euzelian hall."[126]

A 1947 reporter recognized, "In recent years, it has become less of an occasion part of the student body." Society Day debates and oratory were supplemented with impromptu, extempore, and after-dinner speaking events, as well as poetry reading and dramatic reading. "The latter two events have been added in order to give more people the opportunity to participate."[127]

Finally, it ended. Well, almost!

The student newspaper announced Society Day's downfall in 1959, with an account of an eye toward the sparring between the Phis and Eus over to whom the Debate Cup belonged. "The annual Society Day will not be held this year"… debaters did not show up to participate." The story of the downfall of Society Day involved inflated intersociety bickering and is chronicled in Chapter 15 – Transitioning from Society Life.

---

[124] *Howler,* 1946.

[125] *Old Gold and Black,* February 7, 1947, page 1.

[126] *Old Gold and Black,* December 7, 1945, page 1.

[127] *Old Gold and Black,* February 7, 1947, page 1.

CHAPTER 10

Planes, Trains, and Automobiles: Transportation Recasts Debate

Thirty Years of Isolation

As improved conveyances developed, the possibilities for debaters dramatically expanded. The activity found avenues to new areas, arenas, and audiences. Burgeoning from poorly heated halls to featured events at Southern Baptist conventions, from Raleigh holiday celebrations to the far-flung debates in Texas, and from a single audience evening to national tournament gatherings, technological advancements preceded and produced dramatic evolutions in debate. This chapter surveys the intriguing innovation story.

Before the Civil War, the University's Anniversary was celebrated with public student orations, beginning in 1854, and almost 20 years later, in 1872, on Anniversary Day, the first public debate was presented. These combined event days became possible after and the completion of the Raleigh and Gaston Railroad in 1840, allowing Raleigh easier access to the campus and vice versa. Not until 1874 was the rail station relocated to just outside the Arch on the Wake Forest campus. Before the convenience of a railroad from Raleigh, getting to campus was often a mixture of slow and unreliable transport; once on campus, one stayed.

An 1840 freshman claimed, "Among the many questions debated, one was, *Would the capital stock of the Raleigh and Gaston Railroad*

PUBLIC HOUSE.

The subscriber would inform his friends and the public, that he has opened a public house on the premises lately occupied by George Ryan, Esq. near the Wake Forest College, Wake county, where he will be happy to accommodate travellers or such as may wish a temporary location near the institution, and will pledge himself to do all in his power to make their situation pleasant.

ALLEN S. WINN

1839 – Advertisement in *The Biblical Recorder* offering accommodations near Wake Forest College

Company ever prove a paying investment?[1] One of the most prominent debaters selected the negative side and, in the course of his argument, said, " The road could never be profitable, as it was cut off at Raleigh like a cow's tail."[2]

Another early account, from student William E. Bond, Edenton N. C., illuminates the intricacies of setting foot on campus before rail. He was a student in Wake Forest Institute's first years in 1835 or 1836. Writing in *The Biblical Recorder,* Bond remembered:

We took passage from Edenton on a steamer up the Roanoke River, which must have been the old 'Bravo,' as that was the only steamer I had ever heard of up to that time. We landed at Halifax and went by stage through Weldon and Louisburg to Wake Forest. I recollect that the Roanoke River was so crooked as to justify the remark I heard made of it many years afterward, that "it was so crooked that a bird could not fly across it no matter where it started and in what direction it went, it invariably alighted on the same side." The antiquated and strangling appearance of Halifax is still fresh in my mind, whilst there was very little of Weldon except the name, though I remember the hearty laugh we had at a sign (hotel or mercantile,

---

[1] The topic does not appear in our compilation. It may have been an informal event, or a researcher missed a week, an easy mistake.

[2] Norwood, J. H. (1889). Wake Forest in 1840 and 1889. *The Wake Forest Student,* 9, October 1889, page 3.

I suppose) we saw there. It bore the euphonious and well-matched names of "Spriggins & Squiggins.[3]

A. G. Headen, an initial Institute student, recalled his journey as a 12-year-old from Hickory Mountain in Chatham County. "They traveled riding in a vehicle, called in those days a 'chair,' a kind of gig with two wheels and no springs, over the rough country roads... We forded Haw River ... and well do I remember the rocks in that ford; that night we reached the home of John Hackney, whose son... Joshua Hackney, was also a student of Wake Forest. Early the next morning we started in Raleigh, where we spent the night at a hotel... and drove out to college the third day."[4]

Dr. George Washington Paschal often presented lectures on the history of Wake Forest at Society meetings. During a 1934 Philomathesian Tuesday evening meeting, an *Old Gold and Black* reporter purportedly shared his words, "Practically isolated from the surrounding attractions by the slow, scarce means of transportation, the students of yesterday turned the restless energy expended today in week-end gallivanting, ... into their societies work."[5]

BUILDING THE ROADS

G. W. Paschal elaborates on the paucity of transportation in *History of Wake Forest College,* Volume I:

... the poor means of travel, which hardly improved at all before the Civil War, continued very bad for many years thereafter.

Baptist churches were in the country remote from towns; travel by rail was not to be thought of by one who undertook to reach them. He was under the necessity of journeying over dirt roads with such conveyance as he himself could provide. Raleigh and many of the various county towns were connected by roads known as

[3] *The Biblical Recorder*, February 16, 1887, Vol. 52, No. 34, page 1.

[4] Headen, A. G. (1901). Early Days at Wake Forest. *The Wake Forest Student*, page 85.

[5] *Old Gold and Black*, February 17, 1934, page 1. Other technologies were yet to be deployed. Telegraphic communication was unknown until 1844, when a line of forty miles from Washington to Baltimore was established, Norwood, J. H. (1889). Wake Forest in 1840 and in 1889. *The Wake Forest Student*, October 9, page 2.

Difficult North Carolina Road, Circa around the founding of Wake Forest

"stage roads" and kept in tolerable repair. Before 1860 numerous plank roads, most of them terminating in Fayetteville, had been constructed. Yet the roads in North Carolina during all of the nineteenth century were inexpressibly bad. In the rainy season many of them were impassable on account of the mud. Traveling was a weary process, whether one was "creeping over the red hills of Orange County at the rate of three miles an hour, driving a fretting horse through the deep sand of Harnett County roads, with the monotonous noise of the grinding wheels for mile after mile and with no break in the forest, or thridding the mazes of an eastern swamp where for miles on end the water came to the horses' knees and sometimes to his barrel. In the mountain section, a heavy rain would often render roads impassable. The roads were often only Indian trails, on parts of which the prudent traveler often dismounted and led his horse.

The most expeditious mode of travel was on horseback, with saddlebags thrown across the saddle and a traveling bag securely fastened behind it by rings and strap. But more comfortable for older or stouter men was a gig, a light two-wheeled vehicle drawn by one horse. … He who in 1839 was a hundred or two miles distant from his family in North Carolina was completely cut off from them.[6]

The *Wake Forest Gazette's* description was blunt: "Roads were dust in the summer, red clay bogs in the winter, and tree stumps still were a hazard to what traffic there was."[7]

Perhaps President Taylor, on the observation of Wake Forest's Seven-Fifth Anniversary, best summarized the transportation revolution, "We can now travel safely to New York or Florida in a single day. But in the early thirties of the last century a man started such a journey would make his will and leave his household weeping as he departs."[8]

With the Highway Act of 1921, the state government in Raleigh officially assumed responsibility for maintaining North Carolina's highways… In 1931, under the pressure of widespread economic failure of county governments during the Great Depression, the state added to its purview the upkeep of practically all roads in North Carolina. The federal government had completed U.S. 1 through town in the mid-1920s, paving North and South Main streets and the streets circling the east side of the campus.[9] In 1925, some of the downtown streets—White, Jones, Wait—were paved, but most streets were still dirt, dusty in the summer and muddy in the winter, with the dust and mud always mixed with the droppings of horses and mules.[10]

With these travel arrangements, debate staying home by necessity. With board and room secured, days filled memorizing Latin, and attending science classes, the young fellows undoubtedly sought diversion.

---

[6] Paschal, G. W. (1935). *History of Wake Forest College*, Vol. I, page 229-230.

[7] Wake *Forest Gazette*, June 9, 2021. https://wakeforestgazette.com/just-a-little-history-when-forestville-was-the-town/; "Plank roads vastly improved travel throughout the state. These early roads consisted of hewed or planed boards… placed side by side, giving wagons a smoother, more consistent surface than dirt. Only the section leading into town was planked, leaving the other side the same old dirt road." https://www.ncpedia.org/transportation/history. Archival efforts revealed no evidence that the Township of Wake Forest enjoyed a planked road, a conclusion confirmed by a specialist with the Wake Forest Historical Museum—personal correspondence with Terry Brock, Director, Cultural Heritage Archaeology Research Group.

[8] Taylor, C. (1902). The Times and The Men, *The North Carolina Baptist Almanac*, page 4.

[9] https://wakeforestgazette.com/just-a-little-history-lost-map-reveals-1925-wf/.

[10] https://www.ncpedia.org/transportation/history.

After 1840, choice was advanced with the purchase of a train ticket. Many students would not have the means for hotels, consigned to imposing themselves on friends when traveling. And who would you debate upon arrival?

Generating campus excitement was left mainly to the students, and their expression became the all-encompassing literary society. Although debates in the literary halls each week were at times repetitive, the students oversaw all facets of the debate setting, an environment involving competition and sparring among peers.

Trains Connect the World

EARLY TRAIN SERVICE

The first rail line through Wake Forest has had several names – CSX now, formerly Seaboard Air Line – but it began life as the Raleigh and Gaston Railroad, chartered in 1836 to connect with a new railroad that ran from near Weldon in North Carolina to Petersburg in Virginia.[11] This line was completed from Lake Gaston on the Virginia border to downtown Raleigh in March 1840.[12] It took four years to complete the 86 miles of track, described as "heavy wooden timbers laid parallel to form the track. On these timbers were spiked the flat iron rails, called strap iron."[13]

Wake County residents and businessmen raised construction funds for a railroad in early 1836, with assurances from their counterparts in Petersburg, VA (who would also benefit from the new rail) to contribute likewise. Slaves were leased to lay the rail.[14]

An alumnus, contrasting Wake environs 50 years earlier, when he first enrolled in 1840, wrote, "The Raleigh and Gaston Railroad had

---

[11] *Wake Forest Gazette*, Vol 17, Jan 6, 2019, http://wakeforestgazette.com/just-little-history-railroad-lifeline/.

[12] The first railroad in North Carolina was built in 1833 in downtown Raleigh to move granite blocks to construct the Capitol. Mules or horses pulled carts down the primitive track of what was known as the "Experimental Railroad." https://www.ncpedia.org/transportation/history.

[13] *Wake Forest Gazette*, Vol. 17, January 6, 2019, http://wakeforestgazette.com/just-little-history-railroad-lifeline/

[14] https://www.ncpedia.org/transportation/history.

not been completed. The track was only graded, and it was month afterward before it was finished. Well do I remember the first train, the 'Spitfire,' which went over the road, and the excitement and interest it produced among students and citizens. There were few railroads in that day... Twelve to fifteen miles per hour was a wonderful speed for a railway train... greater rapidity would have been attended with much danger."[15]

In 1905 or 1906, Seaboard Airline announced that a "Shoo-Fly" train would begin running from Weldon to Raleigh in the morning and return in the late afternoon. That train and perhaps another meant people could commute for business and shopping to Raleigh (or Richmond). The trains ran up through the 1940s and possibly later.

By 1905, "At least twice a day, sleek express passenger trains with dining cars, sometimes observation cars, came through town. The mail came in and went out by train. Good news, bad news and news about the country came into the telegraph office at the station."[16]

Trains became pervasive in the life of the Wake Forest community from 1840 through the 1930s, a lifeline for students leaving the campus confines. Train travel invited the extraordinary era of Intercollegiate Debates that dominated Wake Debate for the opening three decades of the 1900s.

Paschal refers to a college-sponsored advertisement that appeared numerous times in the 1840 *The Biblical Recorder*. In addition to the notable fact that there were three full professors, the yearly comprehensive expenses amounted to $137, "a railroad nearly completed with

---

[15] Norwood, J. H. (1889). Wake Forest in 1840 and in 1889. *The Wake Forest Student*, 9, page 1, 2.

[16] Wake *Forest Gazette*, Vol. 17, January 6, 2019, http://wakeforestgazette.com/just-little-history-railroad-lifeline/.

trains expected to run every day in full view of the College."[17] The hope of sighting a train may have been a superb attraction.

FORESTVILLE WAS THE TOWN

"Long before Wake Forest College began in Dr. Calvin Jones' house, Forestville was the notable village in what was called the Forest District... in the late 1700s and early 1800s. It grew up on a major north-south path used by Indians and settlers ... By the 1820s, Forestville... supported stores and businesses."[18]

The depot began operation in 1840 at Forestville... housing the area's post office. Calvin Jones was the first postmaster, appointed in 1823, using his house as the office. After Jones left North Carolina for Tennessee, the post office was moved to Alston's Store, located only in "The Forest of Wake," the township's name.

It was reported that the residents of Forestville beheld on March 19, 1840, "quite an entertainment" when the rail line was completed to that point. The traffic was not terribly heavy. Griffin recalled:

> They would advertise that the train would be due at a certain time if it didn't rain. Sometimes the agent at Forestville would go off squirrel hunting half a mile from the station, and they would have to blow the whistle for him to come back to meet the train." The trains needed to make frequent stops to get more wood for the fire and water for the steam.

The new college grew in popularity and enrollment, and those on or near the campus depended on the Village of Forestville for articles of everyday living.[19] Students and visitors had to descend from the train cars in Forestville and walk the mile to the campus. Most students walked down to watch the engines and get their mail almost daily.[20] Another

---

[17] Paschal, G. W. (1935). *History of Wake Forest College*, Vol. I, page 243.

[18] *Wake Forest Gazette*, Vol. 17, Jan 6, 2019, http://wakeforestgazette.com/just-little-history-railroad-lifeline.

[19] Just A Little History: How Wake Forest Went From Corn to Town, *Wake Forest Gazette*, June 16, 2021, https://wakeforestgazette.com/just-a-little-history-how-ake-forest-went-from-corn-to-town.

[20] *Wake Forest Gazette*, June 9, 2021. https://wakeforestgazette.com/just-a-little-history-when-forestville-was-the-town.

account of the long trek for their mail noted, "The students walked the mile to watch the engines puffing smoke from the fires in their bellies fed by wood. And it was a long and dusty or muddy mile south to board the trains to get the mail."[21]

Paschal's rendering of the mile-long routine was more romantic, capturing not hardship but the charm of the Forestville trek: "It seems that students and members of the faculty, who at that time comprised about all the population of Wake Forest, took great pleasure in their daily walk of more than a mile for the mail, except for those members of the faculty who had buggies, the walk furnished a pleasant exercise and was a kind of social promenade, and offered an opportunity to see the train, no little privilege in those days."[22] The stroll would have the promise of greeting friends and forging continual ties that certainly strengthened the nascent community. Likely, more than one conversation amongst those going and coming from Forestville would trade strategy for the week's upcoming society debate.

Despite the "lovely constitutional," the depot's residency in Forestville remained controversial for the College. From 1852 onward, the Wake Forest College trustees tried to persuade the railroad's owners to relocate the depot next to the small campus.

The railroad station was relocated in 1874, though there were still no buildings in Wake Forest east of the railroad tracks. The Railroad refused to finance two stations so close together, so the College paid $3,002.02 to move the depot from Forestville to Wake Forest[23]... The small building was loaded onto flatbed cars and carried north a mile, where it was placed on the west (college) side of the track.[24]

Forestville Baptist Church was the first church building in the area, completed in 1860. It was the church where Wake Forest professors, businessmen, and their families worshipped. Later, in 1874, the debate about moving the railroad depot from Forestville led to a rift in the church. That move was so contentious that the Church faced a congregational

---

[21] *Wake Forest Gazette*, January 6, 2019.

[22] Paschal, G. W. (1935). *History of Wake Forest College*, Vol. I, page 52.

[23] About $82,570 value in 2024 dollars.

[24] The Trustees paid the cost. At first, the station was called Wake, but in 1897, at the request of the College faculty, it was changed to Wake Forest. Paschal, G. W. (1935). *History of Wake Forest College*, Vol. I, page 52.

schism.[25] One casualty of the community's disunion was Wake Forest faculty member Dr. W. T. Brooks, the pastor of the leading church. As with the train depot, he returned to Wake Forest, whether by choice or upon being forced out remains unclear. For decades some of the members felt aggrieved at his favoring the station's moving.[26]

In a futile attempt to protect itself, Forestville became incorporated as a town in 1879 and maintained its incorporation until 1915. In 1984, the Wake Forest town board voted to annex a substantial area, including Forestville. A century after the controversy and court battles, the area became part of the Town of Wake Forest in 1988.[27]

By the time the Raleigh and Gaston line reached Forestville in 1840, the sound of a locomotive horn was heard throughout eastern North Carolina, signifying the arrival of trains and an era of prosperity.[28]

In 1904, Wake Forest remained a quaint rural community. One observed, "Wake is regarded a college village – and nothing more, but the visitor here sees the growth of industry felt elsewhere in the State. The population of Wake Forest in 1900 was 890. Today it is 1,500. New streets have been laid out, new buildings are in the course of construction... You will find no better population in North Carolina than this town and the surrounding country."

---

[25] *Wake Forest Gazette*, Vol. 17, January 6, 2019, http://wakeforestgazette.com/just-little-history-railroad-lifeline/.

[26] Paschal, G. W. (1935). *History of Wake Forest College*, Vol. I, page 52.

[27] Michelle Michael, historic preservation, History of Wake Forest, Town of Wake Forest. https://www.wakeforestnc.gov/planning/historic-preservation/history-wake-forest; Today all that remains of Forestville are two signs erected by the Wake Forest Historic Preservation Commission, Forestville Baptist Church, and its well-kept cemetery, and three old houses. Now it is just a little jog in South Main Street.

[28] After the Civil War, train travel suffered for several years. "The state's railroads were in a shabby condition, due more to lack of maintenance and overuse than wartime destruction. Recovery occurred relatively rapidly with the assistance of the federal authorities." From 1865 to 1875, the state government issued almost $18 million in bonds to 13 different railroads. The state witnessed the railroad expansion from 984 miles to 1,356 miles of track in the first postwar decade. https://www.ncpedia.org/transportation/history.

THE SOCIETIES DEBATE TRANSPORTATION

The centrality of railroads in the students' day-to-day lives not surprisingly led them to debate how best to develop the industry, topics that paralleled the unfolding national discussion.

Train Depot, Wake Forest, across the street
from the College entrance, circa 1920

The essence of transportation debates considered whether the government should own and operate railroads. In the very first instance, in 1846, the debaters affirmed that it would be in the interests of North Carolina to aid in the construction of a railroad rolling to Columbia, South Carolina. Government ownership was contentious, however. In at least five public debates, particularly intercollegiate debates of the 1910s, railroads were pivotal.

For five years (1850-55), the hall debates included five versions of the question: *Would a railroad from Atlanta to the Pacific enhance the welfare of the United States?* All the decisions were in the affirmative. A decade later, on May 10, 1869, the "Golden Spike" was placed at the Promontory Summit in Utah.

Even as the debaters analyzed significant public policy, they were also young, with shenanigans. One resolution debated passing rules for how the members should behave at the train station. The depot was, after all, the place in town where students squandered considerable time.

In 1886, the Euzelians drafted several resolutions "enforcing behavior" at the railroad station, apparently in response to complaints made by railroad authorities and backed by the faculty. The suggested rules would deny students the privilege of going to the trains unless better conduct can be obtained. It would apply to both the Eus and the Phis. In part, it read:

> 1st, that no student shall board any train; crowd the passage leading to or onto the same; disturb passengers by knocking on windows, or making slight remarks... or unbecoming conduct at depot or on grounds adjacent to within twenty minutes of arrival or departure of trains, or any other misdemeanor not designated herein.
>
> 2nd, that any student guilty of any of the above named offenses shall be fined fifty cents for each offense.[29]

Nearly a decade later similar concerns of disorderly students at the depot revived. In 1895 *The Wake Forest Student* recounted a reprimand placed on the newish (first-year) students. In their exuberance, it appeared the frosh boarded loading trains. "A number of students have been arrested for violation of city ordinance No. 20 regarding getting on S. A. L. Trains. It seems that a new kind of combine has been active, several of our most verdant Freshmen have been forced to 'cough up' the 'tin.' No allowances will be made for commencement week, and you must be content to stand off and talk to your best girl from the car window."[30]

Automobiles Expand Expectations

Cars connected the heretofore impossible. With the advent of readily available vehicles, debate tournaments proliferated in the 1960s and '70s. Everyone began hosting tournaments, and most participants would drive. Convenience and freedom of movement resulted. Of course, debate

---

[29] Euzelian Minutes, November 6th, 1886.
[30] *The Wake Forest Student*, Vol. 14, May 1895, page 416.

teams drove to tournaments before the '60s and still do today, but that era may have heralded the peak of copious tournaments.

As with any life-changing technology, the car brought new possibilities along with some complications. Few were feeling fully easy when careening down the highway in the middle of the night, looking forward to the early-morning sighting of the chapel's campus silhouette; always in the back of your mind was concern about an accident, the probability of which increased with the miles traveled. Even so, the first late-night glimpse of the illuminated Chapel thrilled us every time.

Bundled in a car, in conversation for hours on end, weekend after weekend, forms lasting bonds like few other activities undertaken in the college years. With the car came risks, but these were overwhelmed by the prospects. Debate squads multiplied, tournaments by the score were available,[31] and robust programs represented nearly every college and university. Merwyn Hayes' 1970 squad, for example, attended 33 tournaments, almost all of which involved automobile travel.

The auto also meant the world was a much smaller place. A 1956 *Rocky Mount Telegram* editorial commending the college's move to Winston-Salem wrote, "Let's not forget, amid the emphasis on the 'loss of Wake Forest' to this area, that it takes less time now for a student to reach the new campus at Winston-Salem then it took a student not so many years ago to reach the relatively nearby communities such as Warrenton or Tarboro or Fayetteville or Kinston."[32]

The introduction of the automobile aided the debate team's mobility, but this unfolding utility was a gradual improvement. The automobile's early days and uncertain infrastructure resulted in some intriguing growing pains.

Before yielding to the automobile's appeal, we can tip our hat to an earlier Wake Forest one last time. A description penned by a student in 1899 evokes a melancholy for the pre-auto world, then just outside the campus gates:

When the trains came they were greeted by an array of wagons, buggies, carryalls – some of which must have seen the Revolution.

---

[31] On a mid-January weekend in 1991, Wake attended three tournaments: Dartmouth, George Mason, and Samford in Birmingham, Alabama. Strong storms that weekend caused concern for the northern locations, but ironically, only the Samford team got snowed in.

[32] Hail to Wake Forest, *Rocky Mount Telegram*, May 24, 1956, page 4.

One carriage in particular, attracted general attention. Like an ugly woman, it showed itself everywhere, and seemed proud of its ancient origin.

But the horse and carriage, with its numerous colleagues, did good service keeping the feet of the sweet ladies dry.

In the evening, the hack acquitted himself like a man and brought a bigger crowd to hear the orations..."[33]

The serene landscape above harks back to that pre-automobile Wake campus. The train station (far left) was just off the welcoming Arch to the campus. The ubiquitous horse and buggy complement the scene. One can easily imagine the train pulling in from the great Randolph-Macon debate victory, where Johnson and Jones were swept onto a buckboard and toured the campus in celebration.

After the turn of the century, this nostalgic marriage of buggy and train began to wane as the public's delight with the automobile mounted. Converting from horse to horsepower involved infatuation and obstacles that consumed much of the next twenty years.

Relatively early on, "Between 1924 and 1926, the road through Wake Forest and Youngsville was paved. In 1926, the paved road went from Wake Forest to Cary. By 1929, US 1 was assigned to overlay with NC 50,

---

[33] *Wake Forest Student*, March 1899, page 417-418.

establishing the highway through both Wake Forest and Youngsville."[34] Still, it would be some time before most people had cars.

In the 1930s, the automobile began to assert its dominance. Railroads had held sway for decades, but people no longer had to rely on the railroad's schedules and were increasingly able to attend venues off the railway grid. If you could afford a car and find passable roads, a person could travel when and where they wanted.

The campus crowd was obsessed with the automobile. The *Old Gold and Black* observed in 1935, "Wake Forest may not be a big town, but it certainly has a few things in common with the big towns. To further

---

[34] U.S. Route 1A (Wake Forest–Youngsville, North Carolina), Wikipedia, https://www.wikiwand.com/en/U.S._Route_1A_(Wake_Forest%E2%80%93Youngsville,_North_Carolina)#History; The first highway to traverse the state stretched from Manteo, on the coast, to Murphy, along the Tennessee state line. The 1938 state road map listed these main early highways: Highway 17 (Elizabeth City–Wilmington); Highway 64 (Manteo– Murphy); Highway 70 (Atlantic–Asheville–Tennessee); and Highway 74 (Wilmington– Asheville). Along with others, such as U.S. 1 and U.S. 301, these highways connected the states along the eastern seaboard. Most were of a hard surface like concrete and had two lanes. Larry K. Neal Jr., *Acedia*, https://www.ncpedia.org/transportation/history; *The* August 1929 *Wake Forest Alumni News* boasted of the College's new highway connections. "With the approaching completion of the Wake Forest-Durham highway (State route No. 5) and the letting of the contract for the Wake Forest Zebulon route (No. 91), this little college town is beginning to assume the earmarks of a highway center. *Wake Forest Alumni News*, August 1929, Vol. 1, No. 4, page 2.

"Bumming Corner," Where students
thumbed a ride to Raleigh

reduce the excitement and curiosity, here's the explanation: In exactly one hour's time on Sunday afternoon, from 4 to 5 o'clock, there will pass by the 'wall' a total of 331 automobiles represented by 22 species, varieties, or "what have you?"[35]

It is very doubtful, however, that many students could afford cars in the 1920s and 1930s. Still, the debaters, who at the time embraced everyone, naturally would want to return home on occasion and almost certainly would desire to be in Raleigh to spoon a Meredith coed. In those days, "an era when hitching was so common the college boys had picked a spot near campus to use as a 'bumming corner'..."[36] Students took the short walk from the campus to US 1, simply extending their thumbs. Every so often, there was an adventure involved.

The main road running through Wake Forest was a busy "thoroughfare." In 1938, the *Old Gold and Black* reported that movie star Dolores Del Rio "is a dark, slender girl who works for some picture-taking people out of a town called Hollywood, California."

As the story goes, "a Wake senior from Henderson, Hodge Newell, was a fast-growing weary t'other day of thumbing Wake Forest bound

---

[35] *Old Gold and Black,* March 23, 1935, page 3; By 1909, the first year in which the state required auto licensing, 1,600 vehicles existed in North Carolina. In 1912, the number of registrations had reached 6,000, and by 1919, it had leaped to 109,000. With the rapid expansion after 1921 came a steady growth in automobile use, reaching 473,623 registrations by 1928. Robert E. Ireland, *NCPedia,* https://www.ncpedia.org/automobiles.

[36] Movie Stars in Cars. Wake Forest Historical Museum, https://wakeforestmuseum.org/2017/02/02/movie-stars-in-cars-in-1938-wake-forest.

motorists. He liked his hometown well enough but he was anxious to get back to school. He hardly noticed the car when it passed."

It was a dark and rather dirty limousine, and it came to a hesitant stop a few yards past the boy on the corner. The man in the front seat wore a chauffeur's cap and a gray suit. But it was the girl in the back who attracted Hodge Newell's attention.

He got in the backseat.

The girl smiled jokingly as she admonished Newell to leave his gun on the outside.

"Or aren't you all hitch-hikers holdup men?" she queried. The boy assured her that he at least was not, but was in reality a certain Mr. Hodge Newell from Henderson, a lad who had never shot anyone with anything more harmful than a camera.

"Do I need to introduce myself?" the girl said.

Newell knew he'd seen the girl elsewhere like this somewhere before, but was saved from the embarrassment only when he saw "Dolores Del Rio" printed on the registration card in the car.

Right then he began to fumble for the camera he almost always carries.

"May I have your picture?" He asked.

The movie star consented and at the filling station just outside Youngsville the Camera Touting Wake Forester snapped the picture...

"Dolores—she insisted that I call her by her first name—was very agreeable about everything. I think I made an impression on her. "She promised to drop me a card soon.

"She seemed inclined to talk a good bit, commented on the beautiful scenery, was interested in my account of Wake Forest's impressive football team."

"Had she heard of Wake Forest before?"

"She said yes, I'm afraid she had her fingers crossed. Like I did when I told her I'd seen her latest picture."

Newell must've had a good time: at any rate he went on to Raleigh with the actress, never stopping in Wake Forest. Once in Raleigh, he got out and hitchhiked back.

"But I would have gone on further if I'd had a reasonable excuse!" He said.

Who wouldn't?[37]

---

[37] *Old Gold and Black*, October 15, 1938, page 1.

Dolores De Rio, Photo 1838, the same year she gave a ride to young Hodge Newell

Hitchhiking had its distractors as well. The City of Raleigh's chief of Police, A. H. Young, told Bob Goldberg, president of the student body, "Wake Forest men have one week in which to show that they can behave themselves when hitchhiking from the city of Raleigh. Young said, "is it not the desire of the police to take such harsh actions," prohibition. Some citizens complained that students made loud noises while standing in the street. [38]

The automobile delivered excitement to campus mythology. Cars in the sleepy town were increasingly common from late 1920 to mid-1930 but remained a novelty. When hosting the 1920 declamation contests for state high schools, an occasion largely acknowledged as a recruitment event, taking a ride in the car was a perk. The student newspaper describing the entertainment for the high schoolers included, "So far as is possible that the contestants will be given automobile rides around the environs of Wake Forest."[39]

By 1939, the automobile was less of "an attraction," and there were enough cars to retrieve Raleigh ladies to populate the spring Society Day. "Hendlee Barnett, Eu President and in charge of the all-important transportation, states that a cavalcade of autos will make the journey to Raleigh about 1:30 PM today to bring the ladies here."[40]

In their weekly society meetings, the debaters argued issues connected to cars, often topics of interest to the general student body. On a November evening in 1926, the Philomathesians hosted a debate that drew attention, asking if *It was time the state of North Carolina to require North Carolina drivers for everyone, except those under seventeen, to*

[38] *Old Gold and Black*, October 11, 1940, page 1.

[39] *Old Gold and Black*, February 13, 1920, page 6.

[40] *Old Gold and Black*, November 11, 1939, page 1.

hold an individual license. The arguments, not surprisingly, revolved around improving inadequate roads. The affirmative held that the increased age limit would lead to a decrease of a third of accidents. The 18-year-olds also suggested that "no person under the age of seventeen is mentally capable of operating a motor vehicle under all circumstances." The negative reasoned that voters would not stand for another tax and held that young men were physically and mentally capable of operating a motor vehicle at the age of sixteen. The affirmative panel prevailed 2 to 1.[41] No one argued on behalf of licensing women drivers.

ON TO WICHITA

The debate team got into the automobile act early with its 1938 adventure to the Pi Kappa Delta nationals in Wichita, Kansas. This began the tournament era, which accompanied professional regional and national conventions. Wake's involvement in Pi Kappa Delta was central to its debating identity. Under the ambitious leadership of Coach Rice

Debaters and fans adorned the jalopy before departing Raleigh for the Western Tour. Photo: *The News and Observer*, April 1930

---

[41] *Old Gold and Black*, November 20, 1926, page 1.

Quisenberry, the debate team found a ride all the way to Kansas and back, perhaps the first Wake debate tournament by car.

"Leaving here the last week of April on an old collegiate Chevrolet painted up with 'Demon Deacons,' 'Bound for the Wild and Wooly West.' "Bull-buggy,' and other similar Insignia customarily found on a machine of this type, the young Baptists orators rolled out of Wake Forest."[42]

"In making the trip to the middle west, the car left Atlanta, Georgia,[43] and after 38 hours of steady driving by the team, reached Wichita, Kansas the following day, a distance of 1138 miles. On the return trip to North Carolina, the Car covered over 1500 miles in 43 hours of actual elapsed time."[44]

It was said, "that by traveling thirteen hundred miles in two days, and two nights the Old Gold and Dusty representatives reach Mars Hill last Monday where they met the mountaineers in a nondecision debate... It has been reported that "they were so exhausted by their exertions that one of the debaters fell asleep at the table while waiting his turn."[45]

Debaters Wade Bostick and Harold Deaton, along with extemper Raymond Long and orator D. E. Jester, made the Wichita trip.[46] The tournament dominated campus discussion for weeks. The relatively new

---

[42] *The News & Observer*, April 13, 1930, page 4.

[43] Debates were held with Furman and Emory on the way to Wichita. The starting point may have been Raleigh, or, as this *News & Observer* item suggested, Atlanta. An earlier report said Quisenberry, and crew started in Wake Forest. Regardless, it was a long haul in a "road-worthy" rattletrap.

[44] *The News & Observer*, April 13, 1930, page 4. The mileage numbers were guesstimates. The numbers varied from source to source and sometimes even changed in the same article, but the overall sense of distance and time reconciled.

The original picture was taken by the staff photographer of *The Beacon*, Wichita (Kan.) Daily, at Riverside Park during the Pi Kappa Delta tournament, it was printed in *The News & Observer*. The debate team is shown with several friends and the collegiate "Chevvy," which made the long trip possible for the squad. Over 4,000 miles were covered in approximately 98 driving hours while going to and coming from the convention. *Old Gold and Black*, April 12, 1930, page 2.

[45] *Old Gold and Black*, April 13, 1930, page 4, "At the Chapel, Thursday, the boys convulsed their fellow students with tales of their Western escapades."

[46] On their journey, the group was entertained at the home of three participants: Jester, Long, and Deaton. On the front page, *Old Gold and Black* shared, "The team reached Troy at noon and went immediately to the home of Harold Deaton, where his mother had waited for a repass fit for the delegation of Congressman. Not only were the boys entertained royally, but given a supply of sandwiches, roasted peanuts, and mints that lasted past the Mississippi River." *Old Gold and Black*, April 12, 1930, page 1.

coach, J. Rice Quisenberry, sent telegrams back to campus crowing about the debaters' success. They were commemorated for reaching the second round of the semifinals at the national contest, along with the individual event pair who also made it to the semifinals. It is unclear what the semifinal round meant.[47] Quisenberry reported, "By virtue of the fact that our debating team was not eliminated until the second round of the semi-finals they have the distinctive honor of enjoying a placement among the Top 14 of 147 entrants. This entitles them to a ranking among the upper 10% or above 90." The telegram also revealed "that the debaters had the best negative case on the subject at the tournament, but a very weak affirmative. It was the affirmative argument that lost for the team."[48]

The Wake Forest College Alumni News claimed the team was the only team from east of the Mississippi to get to the semi-final.[49]

The student paper, however, was not finished publishing follow-up articles on the glorious trip West. "Tuesday evening of the past week, about dusk, the college curfew rang out again at Wake Forest – a time-honored signal that Old Gold and Black had hung up another scalp. Not in athletic victory this time, but rather the distinction of having four platform artists, comprised of two debaters, an orator, and an extemporaneous speaker, which was the only school in the United States all of whose members reached the semifinals in the national forensic convention.

Eight years later, in 1938, Wake debaters again drove to Kansas, Topeka, this time for the Pi Kappa Delta Nationals, traveling with "[Zon] Robinson in his automobile to the National Tournament... and the fifth traveled by train![50] In an interview held by the Wake Forest ROTC Library Archives, Bobby Helm related that travel to tournaments was via car—usually Coach Zon Robinson's. If they had to go far, they went by train. Helm paid his own way to the national tournament in

---

[47] Reaching the semi-finals likely meant being in a certain percentage of the field with a particular win-loss record. There could multiple Superiors, undefeated or one-loss teams, and even more Excellence certifications. This may be what reaching the semifinals entailed.

[48] *Old Gold and Black*, April 5, 1930, page 1. A subsequent story indicated that the complete debate team at Pi Kap Nationals "debated Seven times, winning four negatives and one affirmative. They debated Huran (Wis.), Carthage (Ill.) Yankton (N.Dak.), Montana State, Wichita (Kansas), Tulsa (Okla.), and Northern Texas. The last-named team eliminated them." *Old Gold and Black*, April 12, 1930, page 1.

[49] *Wake Forest College Alumni News*, 1930.

[50] *Old Gold and Black*, April 15, 1938, page 1.

Topeka. It was the first time he had ever traveled by Pullman, and he was impressed by the dining car.[51]

The shift from train to the car as the principal transportation mode paralleled the transition from the Intercollegiate Debate to the tournament era.

AYCOCK'S 1940S

Atlanta-based debater of note in the early 1940s, Douglas B. Elam, wrote of his memories, sharing in a November 1999 letter that he had worked with Franklin Shirley as the co-member of the Winston Salem Board of Alderman, where they originated, although unverifiable, the source of the Wake Dixie Classic name.

His 1941 recollection also spoke of the heightened reliance on the automobile:

> The "Strawberry Leaf Festival" was held at Winthrop College, Rock Hill, S.C.... Our debate professor, Lewis Aycock, decided it would be more efficient if he drove our small group directly from Wake Forest to Rock Hill for this meeting. The railroads were being heavily

Downtown Wake Forest, Circa 1940

---

[51] Wake Forest ROTC Library accessed July 13, 2017.

loaded with excessive demands from the government and military and we were unable to use this superior method of transport on short notice.... We all crammed into Professor A's automobile and arrived safely at Rock Hill.

Although I was invited as a freshman member of this group, my two years of debating at R. J. Reynolds High in Winston Salem allowed me to feel fairly competent to be involved. On the morning of the first rounds, one of the team members became violently ill with an intestinal problem and was unable to report. I was hastily summoned to fill the void. As a team with John Dixon Davis, we debated a proposition Resolved: *That American railroads be nationalized by the U.S. Government.* John and I won the affirmative of this proposition in the morning. In the afternoon we debated the negative of the same proposition and we were winners of that contest... This tournament was a great moment in my young scholastic career. It was overshadowed, however, within two weeks by the Japanese bombing of Pearl Harbor which set the country into a tremendous upheaval and things have never again been the same."[52]

The most entertaining stories of Wake Debate and the automobile involved Franklin Shirley's "Bull-ship" era of driving adventures. Our narrative of the tools transforming how Wake debaters debate continues in volume II of this debate history trilogy.

---

[52] Doug Elam, Personal Correspondence, November 1999.

CHAPTER 11

Race Permeates Wake Forest (Debate) History

For nearly a year after the Civil War's guns blazed, the sounds of refutation and rebuttal continued uninterrupted from the society halls. The questions debated unexpectedly were not limited to archaic history, aesthetics, and literature topics but were replete with frequent instances of political intersections, including questions attending slavery.

This chapter offers snapshots into the campus climate that framed debating about race in the post-Civil War era. The chapter that follows Chapter 12, surveys the public instances in which pending national issues were tackled. The cursory topics typically debated may have amused, yet detachment from their lives surely frustrated the state's future leaders. They found ways to introduce a synchronous political tilt.[1]

Reconstruction

The Reconstruction Era was not easy for the Wake community. Following the school's reopening in 1866, the student body was decimated, the countryside was scarred, and poverty was palpable for nearly everyone.[2] Those fortunate enough to resume their education hunkered down,

[1] A strong case that the topic from the beginning favored political and contemporary topics can be supported.

[2] "The white people are reduced to poverty and have no means of sustaining schools… all were swept into the whirlpool of rebellion, and the people were left at the close

adopted a low profile, and pursued their studies. Each society quickly resumed weekly debates. As noted above the topics were generally not about their turbulent surroundings but returned to the prescribed tepid historical and philosophical topics.[3] However, there were notable exceptions, many of which are mentioned in this segment. Chapter 12, Debating Race Before Their People, more fully examines the holiday debates.

Reconstruction, the "Northern occupation," was personal in students' experience. Federal troops and the Ku Klux Klan, if not part of their daily lives, were foremost in State politics. On June 8, 1870, news accounts reported that then-Governor Holden "proclaims Alamance and Caswell Counties in a state of insurrection after the Ku Klux Klan perpetrates acts of violence, including several murders. Holden declares martial law and deploys troops." Although the troops fired no shots, more than 100 men were arrested, and some violence occurred. The situation becomes known as the Kirk-Holden War[4].

The political response was swift. By March 23, 1871, "Democrats, newly returned to power in the legislature, removed Republican Governor W. W. Holden. They impeached Holden on eight charges, which included "illegally raising troops to send to areas not in actual rebellion, arresting citizens illegally, and denying the writ of habeas corpus to those arrested. He is convicted on six charges."

By September of that year, Congress became alarmed about the unfolding events in North Carolina and investigated the role of the Ku Klux Klan in the state. Grant's response would end with nearly 1,000 men arrested by United States soldiers for alleged involvement with the

---

with simply their lands, and upon the very brink of ruin." Paschal, G. W. (1943). *History of Wake Forest College*, Vol. II, page 45. Paschal was quoting *The Biblical Recorder*, December 18, 1867.

[3] Occasionally, a topic would indirectly address issues of the war, such as *Whether war is ever justifiable*. This was debated not long after the war, on February 1, 1867. The Philomathesians were equally reluctant to address the war directly. It was not until February 20, 1880, when acceptance of having lost was more addressable, that a topic that contained the words "Civil War" was debated: *Was the South justifiable in fighting the late Civil War?* This portrayal, while descriptive overall, is misleading. The Societies, on many occasions, address slavery and the War. Details of in-house debates are provided in the Topic section of Chapter 4 – Debating in the Literary Societies.

[4] Colonel George Washington Kirk (Union Army) served as Holden's commander for the 1st and 2nd North Carolina Troops who undertook the Governor's intervention. https://en.wikipedia.org/wiki/Kirk%E2%80%93Holden_war.

Klan, and 37 were convicted."[5] Among the imprisoned was a young Wake student, D. S. Ramseur; the repercussions of his incarceration could not be foreseen by any onlooker.

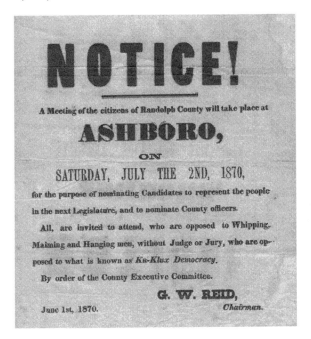

MURDERER AT EU

One of the enduring tales of Wake Forest's folklore is the story of a student caught up in President Grant's anti-KKK sweep across the South in 1871.[6] An Eu debater, "D. S. Ramseur, of Cleveland County... was

---

[5] https://www.ncmuseumofhistory.org/learn/in-the-classroom/timelines/nineteenth-century-north-carolina. This is a fascinating account of President Grant and the removal of the KKK, relevant later in this chapter. Full details of the Klan's "ending" in Reconstruction can be found in Bordewich, F. M., (2023) *Klan War; Ulysses S. Grant and the Battle to Save Reconstruction*, Alfred A. Knopf, New York.

[6] "On March 9, 1871, President Grant sent to Congress a call for support for an order for the "Army to take on the Klan." Grant wrote, "There is no other subject on which I would recommend legislation during the present session." Fergus Bordewich, in his *Klan War; Ulysses S. Grant and the Battle to Save Reconstruction*, observes: "He [Grant] stated his case forcefully: authority was collapsing in large parts of the South, life and property were at risk where the Klan was acescent, and for public officials even such basic functions and the delivery of mail and the collection of federal

arrested on Friday night, between the hours of nine and 10 o'clock, by the United States Marshal and five armed soldiers, while in attendance of the Euzelian Society. Soldiers were placed at the front and the back doors of the college building while the marshal entered to make the arrest."[7]

An essay in *The Wake Forest Student*, allegedly penned by Ramseur upon his eventual return to Wake Forest, gave life to his story and much more for forty years. The original entry is often referenced in historical accounts but rarely presented verbatim. Uncertainty lingers as to the essay's actual authorship. G. W. Paschal, in Volume II of his *History of Wake Forest College*, held that the unsigned article "shows unmistakable evidence of having been written by Ramseur," and subsequently, William Pate concluded that the essayist was most likely Ramseur.[8] Some hold, however, that the essay was loosely based on a letter that Ramseur sent back to the college from the prison in Albany and was written by another.[9]

In the Wake Forest Archives' Ramseur file is another letter commenting on the communique from the Albany cell. The handwritten letter, whose author appears to be Wake's President Charles Taylor[10] in September of 1872, reads in part, "Some years later Thomas Dixon, a student with literary aspirations, discovered Ramsour's (Sic) letter. When he read the Klansman's experiences, he was so impressed that he wrote an article for the papers entitled 'From College to Prison.' This was so well received that he wrote a book 'The Klansman' and a sequel 'The Traitor.' In each story, young Ramseur, under another name, was the hero. Finally, all these stories were condensed into a photo drama which proved the most successful moving picture ever filmed. It was David Ramseur's adventure that thrilled millions in 'The Birth of The Nation.'"[11]

President Taylor not only links Thomas Dixon as the author but directly argues that the essay recounting Ramseur's plight is the grounding

---

revenue were becoming a matter of life or death." Bordewich, F. M., (2023) *Klan War; Ulysses S. Grant and the Battle to Save Reconstruction*, Alfred A., page 175.

[7] *The Daily Journal* (Wilmington, NC), January 2, 1872, page 3.

[8] Pate, W. (1955). *Old Gold and Black*, January 17, page 2,

[9] Ramseur's original letter may have initially been preserved in the Wake Forest records but could not be located.

[10] Taylor was an early defender of Ramseur, seven years before becoming Wake Forest President. Taylor's Ramseur story appears below.

[11] University and N.C. Baptist Biographical Files Collection: https://wakespace.lib.wfu.edu/handle/10339/57793.

for the infamous *Birth of the Nation*. The recounting in "From College to Prison," especially "Ramseur's" college experience, feels more like Dixon's exalted rendition of himself. Dixon, as the hero, captures *his* robust college years, not the words of the scared, young, unpolished student. Others agree, claiming "From College to Prison" is Dixon's unsigned work. The table of contents in *The Wake Forest Student* lists the author as *Mac A Fee*, often assumed to be Dixon's coded mark.

Debated at length was the value of including the full version of *From College to Prison*.[12] The manuscript is insightful at many levels, often revealing subtleties of the Reconstruction Era. One is struck by the evident rhetorical skills of "Ramseur's" public surfacing, with appeals to sympathy and suffering, "Southern" patriotism, family ties and humble beginnings, and the audacious identification with Wake, his host institution. Dixon shares these themes throughout his writings and oratory.

Consistent with the times, the essay drips with racism when describing Ramseur's South Carolina "reconstruction jury" and unrepentant justifications for joining the KKK, which is not always an easy read.

He enlivens his essay with a romance from a chance tour of young ladies at the Albany Correction facility. William Pate, an *Old Gold and Black* historical chronicler,[13] questioned the romance and marriage to May Burton, "It may have been mainly Ramseur's [Dixon's] invention to give his story a romantic turn." Paschal in *History of Wake History College*, Vol. II is more generous, observing the "romantic turn probably had some basis in fact." Disbelief also seems reasonable, as Ramseur, who became a doctor, was subsequently married to Miss Sarah Logan, daughter of Sheriff Logan of Shelby, N. C., his hometown, disguised as Chessville in *The Wake Forest Student* narrative.[14]

Additionally, Ramseur's recollection intimated that May Burton's father, "who appealed directly to President Grant," was singularly responsible for his pardon; this, too, may have been imagined.

In addition to Professor Charles E. Taylor, the South Carolina judge, and Ramseur's immediate family, we could not locate any newspaper

---

[12] "From College to Prison: A Story of the Invisible Empire. *The Wake Forest Student*, January 1883, page 193-202.

[13] Pate, W. (1955). *Old Gold and Black*, January 17, page 2, and February 7, page 4, 1955, another similar piece appears in *The News & Observer*, July 31, 1955.

[14] Statement from an essay in Wake Forest Archives collection on Ramseur, author unknown. https://wakespace.lib.wfu.edu/handle/10339/57793.

mention of Mr. Burton's petition or Mr. Burton himself, for that matter. However, there was considerable press coverage of the contradictions between President Taylor's apologia on the young student's behalf and his father's appeals, which admitted the crime and invited compassion.

The Ramseur essay has been edited for excess loquacity and excludes extraneous sidebars, but it remains lengthy; some may consider bypassing it. The narrative is innately readable as it unfolds as if a thriller, packed with sentimentality and country-side values.

--*-*-*-*

Ramseur's testament

The original story "by David Ramseur" appeared in the January 19, 1883, *The Wake Forest Student*. Presented verbatim.

DR. DAVID RAMSEUR

FROM COLLEGE TO PRISON:

A Story of The Invisible Empire

COLLEGE

"All aboard!"

A moment of hurrying confusion, and the train is moving. On the rear platform of the hindmost coach stands a young man, gazing wistfully at the fast-receding depot.

Then the villages lost in the distance he looks mechanically, with eyes dimmed by tears, at the fleeting cross-ties over which he is whirling.

For the first time, he has bid farewell to home and sweetheart and is off to college. He is thinking—hence the tears. This means more than a temporary absence from loved ones. It means severance from old habits in introduction to a new world, a new life. The mother, in the future, will know her boy only as a visitor to the old homestead. He feels this and is sad.

On the next morning, we find him on the northbound express leaving Raleigh. He has been traveling for about 45 minutes, when Capt. Bear opened the coach door, and called out, "Wake Forest!"

Seizing his valise, our hero hastened from the car, and as he touched the ground, he was greeted with deafening shouts of "new-ish!" "leg' im!' "Leg'im!!"

After a struggle with many "friends" who wish to show him the way to the college (which was only 300 yards distance and in plain view), he succeeded in finding the young man to whom he had a letter of introduction. Under his guidance, after an hour's search, he found his trunk, which had been hurriedly borne by willing hands to regions unknown.

He then was shown to the bursar.

"Your name in full, sir?"

"David Summery."

"Your father's post office?"

"Chessville, South Carolina."

He then relieved himself of all his money but ten dollars.

At night we find him in his room alone, a travel-worn, homesick boy. He knows, however, that he must tough it out, and at length takes a more rational view of things. Wake Forest is a much smaller place than his mind had pictured. This is another sad disappointment. So taking his Bible he sits down and reads without interruption the entire book of Job...

This act came not so much from a spirit of devotion, as from a vein of dry philosophic humor which ran through his character.

His homesickness did not prove obstinate, The busy routine of college life soon left no time to pine for the impossible. He joined his chosen society. Charmed by the halo of fraternity which its secrecy throws around it and fascinated by the excitement of its heated debates within the struggle for supremacy without, he became at once a "society man."

Ambition whispers in his ear the luring story of honor and fame, and he is soon afire with and through. At Commencement he ascends the rostrum amid the cheers of friends and tender glances of admiration from pretty maidens, to receive the gold medal for improvement in oratory.

His career in college is destined to be a brilliant one. Vacation ended, he is back again and promptly at work....

Serious and thoughtful, he is sitting in his room a bleak day in December brooding over this trouble, when a friend calls to have a little chat... Read this letter from mother, and you'll understand." The letter ran thus:

My Darling Boy: * * * * U. S. troops are quartered at Chessville, and are making hundreds of arrests daily. Almost every young man in the country who has not been taken has gone to Texas or Arkansas. I need not ask you, my boy, why you joined the Ku Klux Klan. I know your reasons, as every true Southern woman does, and they were good. But oh, how terrible to think of your being arrested and thrown into jail! ... All my hopes are so bound up in your future that harm to you would be death to me..."Affectionately

MOTHER"

"So, they are liable to pounce upon you at any time, old fellow? And you don't feel comfortable under the circumstances?" " Oh! I don't care a straw what they do with me... But father and mother are worrying their life out; and if I am arrested there is no telling what will happen."

[David] "Shucks! they are not going to get you down here. Nothing so lively as that [is] going to take place around this old institution, I'm certain. Just imagine a boy being marched off at the point of the bayonet! Too romantic entirely!"

"Well, I only wish I were certain of it," was his companion's thoughtful reply." I joined that organization with my eyes open, though but a boy, and I am willing, if need be, to abide by the consequences. I would do the same thing again under similar circumstances. I believe the existence of that order, for a time at least, was absolutely necessary for the protection of our homes, our characters, and our lives. I have sown the wind: I am ready to reap the whirlwind, though it be the death knell of all the fond hopes and bright dreams of youth."

"Oh! you needn't get eloquent over it. I just know nothing will happen to you while stowed away in this old asylum. You are safe, old boy; so, save that eloquence for some debate..."

II. THE TRANSIT AND TRIAL.

...The shades of night were settling over the quiet little village of Wake Forest, as a rickety old ambulance drawn by two stacks of bones once honored by the name " horse," halted before the south campus gate.

In a few minutes the heavy tramp of soldiers could be heard as they marched up the walk-way leading to the college building. Not a boy was astir; for the bell had ceased to toll, and the last straggling Eu. and Phi. were in their seats.

In the Eu. Hall the debate had already opened and was growing warm. David Summey is on the floor defending, in his earnest and impulsive style, the character of Napoleon Bonaparte. A loud rap is heard at the door. The door-keeper announces to a startled Society: "A United States Marshal wishes to see officially the gentleman from Chessville."

Half the boys leaped to their feet with excitement at this announcement, but a rap of the gavel brought all to their seats.

"I move we adjourn!" cried a member. "Second the motion!" echoed a dozen voices.

The motion was carried, and in a moment the members had collected around Summey, who had not yet left his position on the floor. "Well, fellows, my hour has come," said he, in a half laughing way as he gathered up his hat from the centre-table."

We'll see about that, old chum," said a strong voice at his side. " There are only six soldiers out there. We can lick that crowd so quick there will be no fun in it. They are cowardly wretches, anyway, who have been mustered into Kirk's service. Dave, we'll rescue you in a twinkling, if you say so?

"That we will!" shouted every boy in the Hall...

In spite of all their protests he delivered himself up to the Marshal, who at once arrested him. With a heavy heart he bade adieu to his school-mates, and, casting a lingering look at the old college building, signified to the soldiers his readiness to depart.

Surrounded by six rusty bayonets, in the hands of six dirty scoun-drels, he was escorted through the campus; and, entering the waiting hack, was taken to Raleigh, where they arrived about midnight. He spent the remainder of the night, which was bitter cold, on the bare floor of the guard-house.

"With a heavy heart, he bade adieu to his schoolmates, and casting a lingering look at the old college building, signified his readiness to depart." (Illustration by Staff Artist Bill Ballard.)

The next morning he was informed by the United States Com-missioner that, as the charge of murder stood against his name, he would not be allowed to give bail.

"Who dares prefer such a charge!" indignantly asked David.

"That is immaterial at present, Mr. Summey. You will be tried in South Carolina, where the crime- was committed," replied the Commissioner.

" So, I am an alleged murderer," mused David, as he returned to the guard-house. "Rather an ugly thought. Though the charge is as false as the dastardly coward who has made it, I may hang for it. I can expect nothing better than to be tried by an ignorant negro jury. I see I have an enemy at work."

On New Year's Day he found himself lodged in the jail of Co-lumbia. The inmate of a prison, charged with the gravest offence known to law! The plate from which he was compelled to eat was an old wash-pan, so dirty that one could not tell of what it was made. So, he ate with his back to his plate, and felt for his victuals...

But as the days dragged themselves wearily along, these miserable, surroundings became familiar. Disgusting as they were at first, daily contact soon made all commonplace... His father was bending all his energy to his rescue, but without avail. There was a power behind the throne.

The jailor was a bitter Radical, and, at a safe distance behind strong bars, spent much of his time cursing and jeering at the prisoners.

At the end of a month David, handcuffed and chained to another prisoner, was removed to Yorkville, but thirty miles from his home. Here his condition was much improved. During his stay in the jail at Yorkville, he was visited by nearly all the young ladies of the town, who relieved the tedium of many a long hour by their jovial conversation and expressions of warm sympathy. He received numerous boxes from them containing the nicest edibles of every description.

One day a visitor in the person of Mr. Alvin Duncane was ushered into his presence. Mr. Duncane had some very important propositions to lay before his former associate. After informing him that he had been elevated to the rank of United States Marshal, he said with a confidential wink: " Now, Dave, if you will turn State's evidence against the Ku Klux, and pay me five hundred dollars, I'll manage this little charge of murder, and then see that you get a paying position besides."

David arose, and, with lips curled with scorn and eyes sparkling with suppressed rage, gazed for a moment at his visitor, and then said with burning emphasis:

"Alvin Duncane, do you know why I have not knocked your teeth down your lying throat? Because, traitor, I wished to see the depth of a black heart. Oh, no! You don't get out of this door yet [stepping between him and the door], I have something to say to thee.'

"You have proved yourself a villain of the deepest dye. The first and only raid in which I was ever engaged as a Ku Klux, you were with me. You were loudest in professions of everlasting fidelity to the order and its purpose. But when the crisis came, you were not only found wanting in all the principles of true manhood, but like a cringing hound licked the feet of the first Yankee officer you saw, acknowledging your guilt with the deepest humility. You even fell lower than the conquered hound... had rather die than gratify you with one dime. Methinks when you reach your final home below, the very flames of hell will recoil from contact with your foul carcass...

"Coward! I give you ten seconds to leave this room." It required but five...

At the expiration of two months more, our prisoner was removed to Charleston, where the United States Court was in session. He was arraigned before Judge Bond and tried as a simple conspirator, since there was not the shadow of any evidence to sustain the charge of murder. The jury consisted of eleven coal-black negroes (so slick they looked like they had been greased with meat skins) and another motley animal of uncertain color, who tried to pass for a white man. They retired for about five minutes and returned. There was silence in court as the dusky foreman, who was a sort of preacher, arose to render the verdict: " May hit please yer onuh, we fin's dat'pris'ner guilty—wurl widout en."

Even the Judge could not repress a smile at the solemn flourish attached to the decision, as he turned to the accused and slowly pronounced the sentence: Mr. Summey, by the authority in me invested, I sentence you to eight years confinement at hard labor in the United States prison at Albany."

III. PRISON

After the trial David's prison life began in earnest. His lodgings in jail were changed to a dungeon which admitted no fresh air. Life now was a burden indeed. His nature was not one that easily yields to melancholy but was rather defiant. He was too proud to ask any mitigation of the treatment. But the lack of fresh air and exercise, and the mental anguish caused by thoughts of his parents and his own blighted hopes, were finally too much for his constitution. He was taken suddenly ill, and in twenty-four hours became delirious. For weeks the fierce struggle between life and death continued...The sense of utter loneliness he experienced can only be understood by those who have wrestled alone with death in a strange land.

Upon learning of his condition, the ladies of Charleston took great interest in him. One especially (Mrs. Griggs) visited frequently the young sufferer, whose handsome face with its delicately cut features told her of gentle rearing... Every day she sent a negro with something nice to eat. When strong enough to be moved, she had him transferred to a room with windows, and provided him with a comfortable bed. David, however, remained dangerously ill until late in the spring when he began slowly to convalesce. The ninth day of June found him, with several other prisoners, aboard a steamer bound for Albany. The strong sea breeze seemed to infuse new life into his weakened blood. He soon felt strong and vigorous.

After four days on the water they arrive at Albany and were conducted at once into the presence of the Superintendent of the prison. They were told to choose a profession. David's name was called. He arose to reply. Casting a glance at the doleful countenances of his fellow prisoners, with a mingled smile of humor and pity, he said: "I'll make coffins, sir. I think we'll need several before long."

The officer looked up with an expression of astonishment which said plainly: " Rather an interesting specimen." He made no objection, however... David was conducted to his cell, and a cell it was in truth. Six feet wide, eight feet long, and walls of granite. The floor was one solid rock, and the ceiling the same. With the door closed, but one hole could be found, and that was a very small key hole.

As he sat there in the gloom on this Friday night in June, the terrible reality of a convict's life for the first time stared him full in the face. His mind (that power that cannot be imprisoned!), overleaping the solid masonry that confined the body, wanders back to his home in the Sunny South. Tears are falling as he sees the loved ones bowed with sorrow. He is at the old college again.

'Tis Friday night—the last one in the session, too! He sees the happy faces of old companions as they are smiling at the straggling " funny debate" which winds up the session's work.

He thinks of someone else, too. The windowed walls of Vassar College which he had seen in the distance that day, contains a little blue-eyed maiden whom he had learned to love. He had never declared that love, but he believed it was returned. May Burton was of Northern birth, and her father had removed from Chessville to his old home in New York since May had entered college. Few messages had passed between them, yet he believed that in her heart there was still a tender spot for him. But how she would receive the news of his arrest, condemnation, and imprisonment as a member of the dread Invisible Empire, he knew not; for May was a thoroughbred Yankee in all her ideas. So he says, with a sigh: " Better I should forget her. Eight years ' at hard labor' will not leave much poetry in my nature anyway." To him the future is as dark and cheerless as the cell in which he sits.

...All the days were alike, no variety, no change—all monotony. When not at work in the shops, he could be found sitting in his den, with one boot in his hand, battling manfully for life with the vermin which infested the place. The prison was noted for cleanliness—still they were there.

When about three months had passed, one day a friend, who had entered with him, stepped up and with a " furlough grin" that overspread his entire anatomy, said: " Dave, I'm a free man!"

"What!"

"Here is my pardon, if you don't believe it."

Then hope revived.

"Mine next" was the thought that thrilled David and gave his step a new spring. But alas! He was doomed to disappointment. He saw the last of his associate conspirators bid a joyful adieu to the dingy prison, and still no pardon came.

At last he knew the cause. Mr. Alvin Duncane, the United States Marshal, was at Washington specially interesting himself in his case. " The cursed villain!" muttered David, as he heard of it. " David still had hope that his friends would triumph over his enemy and obtain his release, but he had the benefit of an extensive doubt on the subject.

"I have no faith in the integrity of the National Government," he would say " I believe it as corrupt and villainous as the scoundrel whom it has favored with power."

On New Year's Day, the anniversary of his prison career, as he was driving his plane along a coffin lid, a party of joyous school girls, guided by the Superintendent, entered the shops. When within a few steps of his bench, one of their number suddenly stopped and gazed at him as if rooted to the spot.

Another girl noticing it, tittered out: " Heigho! May, do you recognize a friend. The girls all turned inquiringly to May Burton to hear her reply.

The prisoner's heart stood still as she waited breathlessly for the answer, which to him would mean worlds.

"Yes, I do," replied May, in a tone that showed she meant it. And turning to the Superintendent, she said: " I would like to speak to that prisoner?"

"Certainly."

Without a moment's hesitation, before her laughing and amazed companions, she walked straight up to David, and, extending to him her pretty little hand, asked, not without some agitation, " What does this mean, Mr. Summey?"

"It means, Miss May, that I am a member of the Ku Klux organization. My reasons for joining that order I have told you before. And, owing to the villainy of one I once trusted as a friend, I am still a prisoner while all others are released." Averting her face from his earnest look, she returned to the party, and was gone.

... Oh! Isn't it so funny!" said another. "May's lover—her true lover, remember—is in prison. How romantic! We must write it up for the Miscellany."

"Tut! Hush your foolishness, girls. I only know him as a friend. He never spoke a word of love to me in his life," said May, blushing...

The next train carried May home. Bursting into Judge Burton's room, she exclaimed:

"Father, what do you think?"

"Really, daughter, I don't know, but I rather think you have seen something interesting. What is it, little one?" ..."To please you, Daisy, I'll go. Though I am inclined to the opinion the young rascal ought to serve his time out."

"Oh! father, you don't believe that. You were in the South at the time and know the circumstances."

"Bless me, if I don't believe the little huzzy's in love with the scamp," ejaculated the Judge, as he hastened to the depot to catch the train. "He's a fine boy, though, without a doubt. These confounded Southern affairs are always in a mess."

On the twentieth day of January the doors of the old prison swung open once more, and David Summey stepped out a free man. The supreme joy of that moment can be better imagined than written.

* * * * * * *

Two years and a half have rolled away. On the deck of a steamer ploughing the waters of the Hudson, one beautiful evening in June, stands a young physician with his newly won diploma projecting from his pocket. He is enjoying the changing scenery, and from the expression of his face we know he is going to see her.

In due time we find him seated in Judge Burton's cosy (sic) parlor with the little one by his side. He had been there often before....

"Miss May, I have something of a serious nature to say to you." He received no answer and continued: " Since the day we first met, I believe —I know I have loved you. And this love has grown stronger and deeper with the years, until it has become a part of my being...

There was a moment's silence. She raised her drooping head, and in spite of a tear or two there was a mischievous twinkle in her eye, as she asked:

"Can I marry a released convict?"

"If you love him, May..."

Enter Professor Charles Taylor

Prof. of Latin and German, Dr. C. E. Charles Taylor[15], Wake Forest College's 6th president (1884 -1905), was an active, some would say

---

[15] Taylor's primary contribution to the college was his (begun in 1875 while he was still a Professor) increasing its endowment. As president, he made a steady appeal to the Baptist people to help Wake Forest. In 1883, he made an extensive trip among the Baptists in the North and was successful... donations formed the basis on which the college grew and no doubt contributed to his Presidency following the resignation of short-termed Thomas Pritchard. During Taylor's administration, the endowment increased from about $100,000 to more than $300,000.

A Taylor newspaper appeal in 1883 counseled, "The returns of the last census reveal the startling fact that nearly one-third of the white people of North Carolina cannot read or write. Still more startling is the other fact that the number of whites who cannot read or write is greater by 25,635 than it was in 1870. The masses of the people of North Carolina, white and black, belong to the Baptists more than to any other denomination. There are more than 100,000 white Baptists in the State. For much of this illiteracy, therefore, we are, as Baptists, responsible." *The Wake Forest Student*, Vol. 2, No. 5, January 1883, page 231-232, given by Taylor to *The Examiner* of January 11, 1883. "Dr. Taylor's administration marked a distinct epoch in the life of the college and Southern education as well." The school's curriculum grew as Taylor introduced the elective system in 1887. The School of Law was organized in 1894, and the School of Medicine in 1902. Several departments were added: Modern

activist, leader. In his first year as a professor, seven years before his selection as president, he engaged in a meaningful way to seek the release of Ramseur.

Taylor sent a letter to the Richmond, Virginia, *Religious Herald* in 1872. The professor and student relationship, corroborated by Paschal's account and written up by enterprising student William Pate recorded:

That the young man came to his room at "about Christmas of 1871" and informed him that there was a warrant out for his arrest on the charge of conspiracy of murder.

"With much feeling and youthful ingeniousness, wrote Dr, Taylor, "he told me that some time before, while at his home in Cleveland County, N. C. he had, with a few companions, ridden a few miles in the night and returned without molesting anyone."

1905 Engraving of Charles Elisha Taylor, Wake Forest's 6th President

Dr. Taylor described the earlier incident as being done "in that spirit of frolic, or desire for adventure, which would lead any boy of his age to do the same."

Dr. Taylor, the ardent worker on Ramseur's behalf, warned in the public letter to the "'Herald" that if Ramseur was left to serve his

---

Language in 1888, Religion in 1896, History and Political Science in 1898, Physics in 1899, and Education and Physical Culture in 1900. The faculty increased from seven professors to seventeen, and the student enrollment increased from 150 to 328. Three new buildings were erected with adequate lighting, running water, and comfortable classroom seats. Special attention was paid to the campus by planting magnolias and other trees and shrubs and building a rock wall around the property. After a grateful Board of Trustees lauded his long and impactful tenure, they also forced the aging Taylor's resignation in 1905. Jenny Puckett (2020). *Thine ancient days: A WFU history*: page 181-196.

entire sentence, "A whole life will be blasted," and condemning the boy's trial as a "mere farce,"[16]

Dr. Taylor carried his measures even further. Perhaps his personal appeal to President Ulysses S. Grant ultimately secured Ramseur's release after almost one year in the Albany prison. Some held that Taylor's appeal triggered a backlash from the Grant Administration, prolonging his Albany jail time.[17]

Others supported Ramseur's release. The Richmond paper that originally printed Taylor's letter said, "Young Ramseur ought at once to be released from prison. We have not a doubt."

South Carolina U. S. District Judge George T. Byron, perhaps trying to compensate for the "hanging judge" that oversaw Ramseur's trial, wrote to President Grant, "This is very much to invite and vindicate the prerogative of mercy confided to the President put forth in favor of the useful and unhappy prisoner. I would feign belief that such an exercise of clemency would not weaken or strengthen the administration of the law and is wholly consistent with justice I earnestly commend the petitioner to the tender consideration of the President." [18]

His father's letter, which acknowledged guilt, is moving in its appeal to compassion. In the letter to President Grant published in the *Richmond Herald,* signed "For which your petitioner will forever pray, F. S. Ramseur." He beseeches:

In your petitioner's deep distress, he humbly prays your Excellency graciously to extend mercy and pardon to his said son. His crime your petitioner does not pretend to justify or excuse but he was very young at the time he committed it, his older brother, who could and would have restrained him, was absent from the home. He is not naturally disobedient or evil disposition, and this is a first offense against the laws of the country. He did not know the purpose of the said raid

---

[16] Pate, W. (1955). *Old Gold and Black*, Jan. 17, page 2, and Feb. 7, page 4.

[17] An editorial quip written opposition to Grant's reelection pondered, "The *Baltimore American* says: If a certain Prof. Charles E. Taylor, of Wake Forest College, North Carolina, preceptor to this interesting youth (D. S. Ramseur, a young lad now in the Penitentiary at Albany) had not written a letter scandalous and outrageously false, it is probable that he would before this time, have been pardoned by the President. *Wilmington Journal*, October 25, 1872, page 1.

[18] United States Court, June 6, 1872. Obtained through Wake Forest Archives.

when he joined it, and after joining it, though he had not the moral courage to leave it, he did not personally aid in the unlawful acts either by personal dissipation then therein or by his approval. He now bitterly repents his hasty unlawful conduct and is deeply sensible of the disgrace and the grief he has brought upon himself and his aged father and mother. Your petitioner desiring to educate his said son for better things has sent him to college, where he was arrested.... But if the heart of your Excellency be moved graciously to forgive his youthful crime and grant him a free pardon, his gratitude for the clemency... cannot fail to make him here after a good, peaceable, and law-abiding citizen.

There were hostile responses to the young professor's defense of Ramseur, the social media blowback of the day. A letter "To the Editor" of Raleigh's *Triweekly Era* shared his outrage, characterizing Taylor as an apologist for Ku Kluxism:

Sir – Has it come to this in our country's history that a professor of a college, a Christian gentleman, clothed with the profession of a Divine Teacher, should condescend to apologize for a known violation of law. Has it come to this remarkable past that a minister of godly things should call the laws of the United States in the ministration of the same a mere farce.... Surely our land has had enough suffering, enough of the horrors of war and its sequel... Prof. Taylor says, "that in giving such counsel, it is to enable thinking and Christian men in all sections of the country to form an idea in regard to the operation of the Ku Klux law." By so doing he becomes lawmaker, statesman, politician, and loses sight of the calling for which he ought of all others to prize. ...Prof. Taylor would have the Christian world to believe that this young man just took a jolly ride, with a few companions at night without molesting anyone.... Ku Klux act a monstrous farce.... Prof. Taylor says that he is no apologist for crimes committed under lynch law. Then why charge that Ramsour had been maltreated, that he had the semblance of a trial... Prof. Taylor, according to his own logic, prefers lynch law to civil law. He would have Ku Klux continue their hideous midnight prowling's, to arrest without warrant, try without a jury and hang without evidence.

Woodknoll, Raleigh, Oct. 3, 1872.[19]

---

[19] *Triweekly Era* (Raleigh), October 5, 1872, page 3.

The backlash was plentiful and vocal in condemning Taylor's letter. The *Baltimore Commercial Advertiser* lashed out in an ensuing article:

A professor in a Baptist College in North Carolina has gotten himself into a most unpleasant predicament. The young man named Ramseur, who attended the college, was arrested in December 1871... Prof. Taylor, one of his former teachers, has addressed a letter to the editor of *The Richmond Herald* which is intended as an appeal to the Baptists of the United States on behalf of the young convict, who is a member of that denomination.

In this letter the facts connected with the arrest trial and conviction of Ramseur are so outrageously misstated that we felt compelled to publish the petition addressed to the President by the young man's father asking for the pardon of his son. After reading Mr. Ramseur's sworn petition and comparing it with Prof. Taylor's letter there are many pious Baptists in the country who will begin to think that there ought to be a vacancy in the Faculty of Wake Forest College.[20]

Confederate Symbolism

The reaction to removing Ramseur from the Euzelian Hall reflected the general white South's disdain with Reconstruction and revealed an ugly measure of resistance: the KKK revival. Wake students would echo regional attitudes in their debates and attitudes well into the 1900s.

As debaters trained in recognizing more than one point of view, an ambivalence sneaks into their commentary with indications of more

---

[20] Reprint from The *Baltimore Commercial Advertiser*; *Triweekly Era* (Raleigh), October 5, 1872, page 2. The paper further intoned: "There was no defense made for him [Ramseur]... because none could be made... Roundtree was an industrious colored farmer, who owned a plantation the upper end of York County, South Carolina. He was a quiet, peaceable, upright man, but his prosperity excited the wrath of the Ku Klux who determined to kill him. The raid was made by a party of masked was surrounded in the night and his family aroused by a terrible pounding at the door. He seized a gun and fired from the window, wounding one of the raiders, named Elijah Ross, in the arm. He then took refuge in the garret, but was driven from there, and finally in desperation he jumped from a second story window and ran toward the woods. Before he got 30 yards away from his house he fell, pierced by a dozen of bullets. A brother of the wounded Spaugh ran up and cut the dying man's throat."

progressive opinions. Attitudes were not solidly opposed to equal rights or hardened as historical harangues might imply. This is not to say, however, that Wake students were above the fray, as their expressed points of view were often less than tolerant. A continued romance with the "lost cause" held sway in the debating halls, even as more moderate positions were also spoken.[21]

HONORING THE WAR – ROBERT E. LEE, STONEWALL JACKSON, AND JEFFERSON DAVIS

Three years after Wake resumed, the Secretary's minutes of the Philomathesian December 1868 meeting named the new honorary members: Confederate President Jefferson Davis, Confederate generals D. H. Hill and James H. Clanton, and Gov. H. A. Wise of Virginia, a leading successionist.

Two years later, in 1871, the minutes recorded a resolution of condolences "be sent to R. E. Lee's family concerning his death."[22] Subsequently, four months later, the secretary was instructed "to seek the Best Life of R. E. Lee" for the library.[23] In 1906, President Poteat presented to the Societies library, on behalf of an alumnus, *Life of Gen. Lee*, $5.00 and *History of the War between States*, 2 vol., $9.00. In August 1866, the Philomathesian Society Minutes Mr. Hicks presented to the society the prison life of Jeff Davis, which was accepted on motion of Mr. Coates."[24]

A decade later, identification with their Civil War heroes was very much alive. On May 1st, 1875, the Philomathesian minutes reflected that Mr. Wright had "a committee of three be appointed to purchase three pictures, with frames, for the Society, consisting of those of Lee, Jackson

---

[21] In several spheres, as suggested by topics debated and votes, the Wake students were often progressive in their era: Women's suffrage, NC Public education, Women's access to higher education, Tariffs, etc. Recommended: an enlightening *Atlantic* piece that explores our retrospective judgments of figures in history and their often simultaneously firmly held progressive and conservative/racist agendas. Uncancel Woodrow Wilson, *The Atlantic*, March 2024. https://www.theatlantic.com/magazine/archive/2024/03/woodrow-wilson-racism-civil-rights/677174/.

[22] Philomathesian Minutes, October 29, 1870.

[23] Philomathesian Minutes, February 17, 1871.

[24] Philomathesian Minutes, August 17, 1866.

A Society Secretary's drawing on the final entry, 1880
Euzelian Ledger. J. W. Denmark's drawing labeled "Gen. T.
J. Jackson C.S.A., Lee's Right-Arm (Stonewall)"

Inscription above: "A Second Napoleon; Yea, and greater in many
respects than a Napoleon Bonaparte." *Inscription below:* "May God
have mercy on every soul that fell in that holy struggle. Honor to every
man that bit the dust, and honor to every arm that was raised. Amen.

and Yates."[25] Mr. Scott further moved the inclusion of Jeff Davis.[26] After
the summer break, during a fall 1875 meeting, Mr. Wright read "A commemoration with regard to the picture of Jefferson Davis. On motion, the

---

[25] Matthew Tyson Yates was a Baptist missionary in Shanghai, China. Yates and his
wife served under difficult conditions due to the Taiping Rebellion, isolation from
America during the Civil War, occasional cholera scourges, and Yates's bad health.
They began Sunday schools, churches, outstations, and chapels throughout Shanghai.
https://www.ncpedia.org/biography/yates-matthew-tyson.

[26] Philomathesian Minutes, May 1, 1875.

committee is directed to purchase the life-size at the cost of ten dollars."[27] This was a princely sum in the post-war depressed South.[28]

Presentations of Lee in seminal places continued well into the 20th century. In January 1906, *The Wake Forest Student* dedicated the full issue to the memory of Robert E. Lee. "Dr. Archibald Anderson, of the University of North Carolina, once said that *The Wake Forest Student* was the best college literary magazine in the South, an issue dedicated to the memory of Gen. Robert E. Lee has been used by scholars and biographers in the preparation of estimates and lives of the great southerner."[29]

The January 1907 issue of *The Wake Forest Student* opened with a poem composed by an alumnus "of distinction in the fields of literature poetry," Mr. McNeill. Excerpts elevate Lee's memory:

> His name is one in equal Trinity
> With these, whose glory more and more shall be,
> Our Washington, our Lincoln, and our Lee.
>
> A Victor's wreath: in ruin wrought through blood,
> Where wars events recorded ill for good,
> A king o'vr fortune's fallen flag he stood.
>
> Long since two faithful fields were lost and won.
> In these far days, be equal justice done.
> Our Lee, our Lincoln, and our Washington.[30]

The regular meeting debates demonstrated more than a passing interest in the Civil War heroes. On April 9, 1875, the Philomathesians argued the resolution asked if *R. E. Lee was a greater general than Stonewall Jackson* (Negative 12 to 11).[31] A comparative question considered was, *Which is the greater General Lee or Washington?* Phi debated this

---

[27] Philomathesian Minutes, October 30, 1875.

[28] The $10 "life-size" picture would be worth about $180 today. In those years, expenditures were the responsibility of the members.

[29] Philomathesian Minutes, April 14, 1906; *The News & Observer*, May 7, 1934.

[30] *The Wake Forest Student*, Vol. 26, No. 5, January 1907, page 291. Mr. McNeill, an 1898 graduate, has won the Patterson Cup presented to the North Carolina writer who contributed best to literature the preceding year.

[31] On September 5th, 1874, a motion was raised to replace the picture of Judge John Owen, a former governor, with that of Stonewall Jackson. Phi Minutes.

assessment eight times from 1872 to 1886 and the Eus eight times from 1874 to 1880. Some of the repetitiveness reflects the mechanical selection process from the topic list, but the topic remained on the list well into the late 1880s.[32] A three-decade reminder of Robert E. Lee's revered status .

Moving into the 20th century, racial bias in weekly hall debates remained. A 1904 Junior debate resolved *That the public-school funds of the South should be apportioned between the two races according to the amount of tax paid by each*.[33]

An in-meeting Phi debate in 1914 took up the topic, *Resolved, That the segregation of the Negro would be in the best interest of both races in the South*. While one side defended the practicality and economic advantages and the other side the impracticality and economic costs, in the end, they both essentially took positions aligned with radical segregation solutions. "The affirmative advocated segregation into districts within the several states, while the negative contended that the query meant the Negro would have to be removed to a territory and dealt with in the same manner that the Indian is. The judges rendered their decision two to one in favor of the negative."[34]

Yet change was afoot, however slow. Latin professor H. M. Poteat's[35] Archival file contains collections of sympathetic background notes concerning the Negro's plight in America, primarily quotations he had noted from newspapers. Debates examining the inequitable treatment of Blacks were well underway in the national conscience.

Poteat helped bring that conversation to the Wake campus.[36] *The Wake Forest Student* noted that in 1918, Hubert Poteat and Dr. R. Bruce

---

[32] See the chapter "Historical Resolutions About Race, Civil War, Reconstruction, & Immigration" in volume 3, *Milestones: Defining Lists of Wake Forest Debate, 1835-2022*.

[33] *The Wake Forest Student*, April 8, 1904.

[34] *The Wake Forest Student*, January 1915, page 291-292.

[35] W. M. Poteat, Wake Latin professor for 44 years, international Latin poetry expert, Cicero translator, national head of the Masonic and Shriners, musician, and long-term supporter of the debating societies, as well as Wake Forest President W. L. Poteat's son. https://www.ncpedia.org/biography/poteat-hubert-mcneill.

[36] This 1930s campus dialogue did not call for an end to racial segregation; it was more a call to live up to the "Equal" from the phrase "Separate but Equal," authorized in the *Plessy v. Ferguson*, 1896 Supreme Court ruling. This reading is based on a conversation with American historian Andrew Canady, Averett College, VA, in May 2024.

White, "though neither speaker had the audience that their messages deserved," were the featured speakers for the Young Men's Christian Association. Through its mission study classes, taught by members of the faculty, Poteat announced that the Association would introduce a study of Negro's problems. "Special text-books have been secured and many students are enrolled in the classes."[37]

The following year, 1919, "Under the efficient leadership of Dr. H. M. Poteat, a six-week course in the study of the Negro problem was begun on October 19th. The class meets every Sunday after the evening church service and is largely attended."[38]

Despite educational efforts as late as 1936, on-campus sensitivities to racial discrimination were weak. H. M.'s father, Wake Forest President W. L. Poteat attended the first of a series of four Wake Forest-Meredith Sunday school socials with 100 members of his class. The entertainment included a stunt night under John Ezell (Society Day orator) and C. V. Roebuck of Wake Forest, who appeared in a Negro impersonation and recitation skit.

Wake racial attitudes would change over time, and in many venues, campus personalities became leaders in the Civil Rights movement. That heartening story is told, in part, in Volume II of this sequence.

CELEBRATING GENERAL LEE – THE NATION'S STATUARY HALL

Well into the 20th century, a precocious and likely gifted Wake Forest Student body President, Ed Harrell, speaking before the revered Euzelian Society, made it his cause to ensure that Robert E. Lee retained his proper place in the US capitol's Statuary Hall. "Harrell declared that Lee was not merely a southern hero, but the finest type of American citizen." Harrell's program, given in the Phi society Monday night, March 16, 1931, was declared by the *Old Gold and Black* reporter "to be the best entertainment given this year in the Monday night group."[39]

Under the original 1864 authorizing law, each state could commission two statues "in marble or bronze of deceased persons who have

---

[37] *The Wake Forest Student*, March 1918, page 379.

[38] *The Wake Forest Student*, December 1919, page 144.

[39] *Old Gold and Black*, March 21, 1931, page 1.

been citizens thereof." The bill called on the states to honor citizens who were "illustrious for their historic renown for distinguished civic or military services such as each state may deem to be worthy of this national commemoration."

In 1909, Virginia, along with other states, got around to authorizing its selections. The state found consensus in George Washington, but after extended debate, it chose Robert E. Lee as the second honoree over such patriarchs as Jefferson and Madison.

News of Virginia's plans prompted outrage elsewhere in the country. Kansas legislators threatened to place a statue of John Brown, the hardline abolitionist executed by Virginia for organizing a slave revolt there in 1859, to join Lee in the Capitol if the Old Dominion placed him there. "I do not know about John Brown, but I do know there is one man who will fight against putting Lee's statue in the hall," Kansas Representative Charles Curtis said in 1903, referring to himself. "I think it will be a disgrace. He was a traitor to his country, and I will not sanction an official honor for a traitor."[40]

Lee's statue was installed in the Capitol without fanfare, dodging the controversy surrounding it. Lee quietly resided among the National Hall's statues until the controversy was again inflamed in 1931 when Mississippi sent the Jefferson Davis sculpture, the Confederacy's only president, to the Capitol. The already overcrowded Statuary Hall led lawmakers to authorize the distribution of lesser statues around the Capitol building, with rumors that Lee and one other would be sent to the crypt. Such allegations sparked their own national outrage.

It is unclear how young Harrell became interested in memorializing Lee's former glory. Still, in January 1931, he found himself speaking in the Chapel before the assembled commemorating Lee's birthday with recitations and his original oratory. He first gave a reading "from Thomas Dixon's *The Man in Gray* and from an oration on Lee."

The reading from *The Man in Gray* was taken from the account of the visit of Bleyer to Lee to tell the Colonel that President Lincoln had offered him the command of the Union army. Harrell skillfully portrays the effect of this message upon Lee and his refusal of the offer. The oration was one written by Harrell and delivered five years earlier in Wingate Hall in a high school oration contest that the college

---

[40] Matt Ford, *The Atlantic*, The Statues of Unliberty: Eight Confederate leaders are honored with sculptures in the halls of Congress. August 14, 2017. https://www. theatlantic.com/politics/archive/2017/08/confederate-statues-congress/536760/

Robert E. Lee statue transferred from Nations
Capitol to Virginia Museum in 2020

sponsored. It defends the right of Virginia to place a bust in Statuary Hall in Washington."[41]

It is also doubtful that Harrell's priming of public opinion changed many minds, as his audience's preference was already set to idolize Lee's legacy, an endorsement of their own shared culture. The *Old Gold and Black* seemed assured that Harrell's bass singer's voice and oratorical skills would carry the day,[42] however, Lee's bequest became increasingly associated with denoted racism. Harrell's appeal in the Literary Societies and then to the larger Wake Forest community is testimony to the endurance of political feelings that persist for years, decades, and often longer.

Lee retained a place in the Hall of Statues, perhaps a bit more in the background than before, from 1909, 44 years after the Civil War, until 2020. The Bronze Commission by Edward Virginius Valentine was then transferred to the Virginia Museum, replaced in the capitol by a statue of Barbara Johns, who, at sixteen, led student protests against segregated schools in Virginia.[43]

---

[41] *Old Gold and Black*, January 23, 1932, page 1, 3.

[42] *Old Gold and Black*, March 21, 1931, page 1.

[43] Davis-Marks, I. (2020). Statue of Civil Rights Activist Barbara Rose Johns Will Replace U.S. Capitol's Likeness of Robert E. Lee, *Smithsonian Magazine*, December 23.

Thomas Dixon – "Wake's Most Famous Graduate"

Thomas Dixon, a central Wake hero for 50 years, was intimately involved with the campus Literary Societies. He spoke to evening smokers and recruited new members. He attended, judged, and endorsed, often in person, debate and oratory presentations, from public expositions to special sessions in the Literary Halls. He had a serious medal bearing his name, which several times was presented by the namesake himself. He established and edited Literary Society publications[44] and was President of the Euzelian Society in 1882. He was a gifted debater in college, selected to debate immigration before a full-house audience on Anniversary Day in 1882 and again in 1884.

His contemporary popularity was shown in 1904 when the *Howler*, Wake's College yearbook, opened with a four-page dedication to Thomas Dixon, Jr.[45] The page drawing on highlights of his life, applauded, "Of all her sons Wake Forest has none who has reflected more honor upon his Alma Mater."

The yearbook wrote that Dixon graduated with the highest honors in 1883. "A year later, at the early age of twenty, before he himself could wield a ballot, he was elected to the State Legislature." He trained in Law Greensboro and became a barrister in 1886. Later, he attended Johns Hopkins University on a scholarship for History and politics but did not finish. He did, however, become friends with fellow student Woodrow Wilson,[46] remaining a lifetime acolyte.

In 1886, he entered the ministry and received his first pastorate at Raleigh. Dixon then moved north to a pastorship in Boston, and soon after that, he was ministering to the "People's Church in New York City,

---

[44] The *Old Gold and Black*, wrote "Dixon, one of the men who started the first long-lived publication on the campus, *The Wake Forest Student* (May 24, 1946, page 2). Strangely the start coincided almost to the day with discussion by the Publications Board to revive the literary magazine after a three-year suspension." Dixon died on April 3, 1946, at the age of 82, at his home in Raleigh, North Carolina.

[45] *Howler*, 1904, page 4-7.

[46] Gillespie, M. K., and Hall, R. L. (2006). *Thomas Dixon Jr. and the Birth of Modern America*. Louisiana State University Press, page 4. Wilson screened The *Birth of the Nation* in the White House, offering, "It is like writing history with lighting. And my only regret is that it is all so terribly true." Gillespie and Hall (page 12) attribute the quotation to Raymond Allen Cook (1968). *Fires from the flint: The amazing career of Thomas Dixon*, Winston-Salem, Blair.

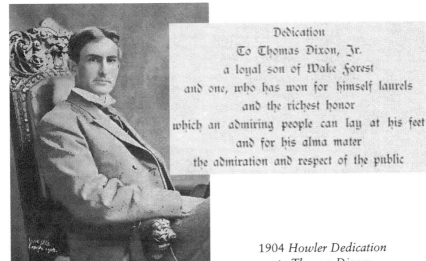

Dedication
To Thomas Dixon, Jr.
a loyal son of Wake Forest
and one, who has won for himself laurels
and the richest honor
which an admiring people can lay at his feet
and for his alma mater
the admiration and respect of the public

1904 *Howler Dedication*
to Thomas Dixon

where he preached to larger throngs of people than any other preacher in America."[47] He resigned in 1899, becoming a public lecturer, skyrocketing to national acclamation.

Dixon is most remembered for his trilogy of novels, *The Leopard's Spots* (1902),[48] *The Clansman* (1905) and *The Traitor* (1907). The second of the trilogy, *The Clansman-A Historical Romance of the Ku Klux Klan*, was produced as a play.[49]

Mr. Dixon also wrote a script for a motion picture, *The Birth of a Nation*, destined to make history and bring its author more fame and fortune. "His subsequent income from the picture and rights to 'The

---

[47] Claims of Dixon's fame and reach should be read with some skepticism. He also stirred up many detractors.

[48] "Thomas Dixon, Junior, says that his book *The Leopard's Spots* has reached 99,000 copies and is selling faster than ever. He also declares that it is the most faithful presentation of the race problem that he is capable of." 1903 *The Biblical Recorder*, February 11, page 4.

[49] Adapted for the stage, it opened in Norfolk on September 22, 1905, and toured the South with great commercial success. "Contemporary newspaper and religious criticism, even in the south, was less favorable. Journalists called the play a 'riot breeder' and an 'exhibition of hysterics,' while an Atlanta Baptist minister denounced it as a slander on white southerners as well as blacks. The Clansman played in New York in 1906, again to an enthusiastic audience and critical panning." https://en.wikipedia.org/wiki/Thomas_Dixon_Jr.

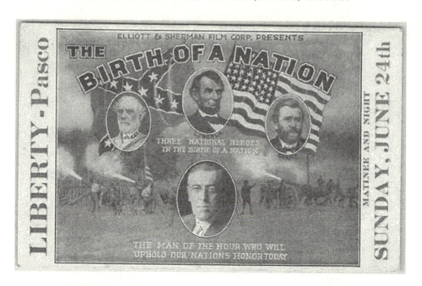

1915 handbill advertising D. W. Griffith's *The Birth of a Nation.*

Birth of a Nation' ran well over a million dollars."[50] Thomas Dixon
wrote twenty-two novels as well as many plays, sermons, and works of
non-fiction, but his literary success primarily stemmed from these first
three novels.

The Birth of a Nation originally premiered as *The Clansman: An
Historical Romance of the Ku Klux Klan* in 1915. It met with rousing
approval and indignant condemnation; attempts to block the film were
common.[51] The film offers a "racist portrayal of savage black men as
sex-starved villains and lion-hearted Ku Klux Klansmen as national
heroes"[52] in the South reclaimed from the "horrors" of Reconstruction.

---

[50] *Old Gold and Black*, May 24, 1946, page 5.

[51] Willis, C. E., Other Artifacts and Controversial Works, *The First Amendment En-
cyclopedia.* https://www.mtsu.edu/first-amendment/article/792/the-birth-of-a-nation.;
The entire first edition was sold before it was printed—"an unheard of thing for a
first novel"[65]. It sold over 100,000 copies in the first 6 months, and the reviews
were "generous beyond words." https://en.wikipedia.org/wiki/Thomas_Dixon_Jr

[52] Gillespie, M. K., and Randall, R. L. (Eds) (2006). *Thomas Dixon Jr. and the birth
of modern America*, Louisiana State University Press, Baton Rouge, page 1; Poster
photo credit: Michael T. Martin, Revisiting (As It Were) the "Negro Problem" in
The Birth of a Nation. https://iu.pressbooks.pub/thebirthofanation/front-matter/
revisiting-the-negro-problem/.

A more generous Wake student summarized that his fame resulted from, in part, his "interpreting the spirit of the Confederacy and the post-war South."[53]

After the general society rejected the movie *Birth of a Nation*, Dixon gradually became a shameful figure, disgraced and spurned, generally forgotten or put out of sight.[54]

This volume's purpose is not to debate the historical place of Dixon's book and Griffith's movie, a sordid tale better told by many historians and critics, but rather to document Thomas Dixon's place in defining and reflecting an era of debate and, by implication, his alma mater.

THE WAKE FOREST MAN

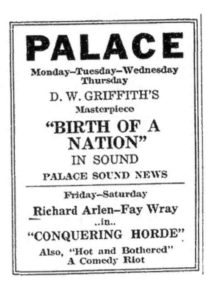

1931 – the Wake Town's
Palace movie House Ad.
Old Gold and Black

Dixon's "exalted" career began in the Euzelian Hall, where, as a sophomore, on December 16th, 1882, T. Dixon from Shelby, NC, was elected president of the Euzelian Society.

Over the years, Dixon often returned to campus, speaking at humble Society events to full-throated community assemblies. Not five years after his graduation, already of national importance, a Winston-Salem reporter summarized that his 1890 commencement talk was, "This most eloquent and brilliant living

---

[53] James, M. L., Student revival coincides with the death of its founder, *Old Gold and Black*, May 24, 1946, page 1, 5. The reference is to the revival of the publication *The Wake Forest Student*. For a discussion of Dixon's ability to define the South see Mcgee, B. R. (2009), Thomas Dixon's the clansman: Radicals, reactionaries, and the anticipated utopia, *Southern Journal of Communication*, 65, page 300-317.

[54] In April 2003 Wake Forest hosted a major symposium on "Thomas Dixon Jr. and the Making of Modern America." The symposium hosts also subsequently published this volume: Gillespie, M. K., and Randall, R. L. (Eds) (2006). *Thomas Dixon Jr. and the birth of modern America*, Louisiana State University Press, Baton Rouge Press, Baton Rouge.

1926 *Old Gold and Black* Advertisement for Birth of a Nation.

North Carolinian delivered the annual address before the literary societies of Wake Forest College last week. His subject, 'The Restless Masses' was presented in such a style and with such force and power as only the genius of Dixon could do it. THE PROGRESSIVE FARMER always a friend of the young man, is proud of Thom. Dixon... North Carolinians never fail to admire this brilliant and eloquent young divine. [55]

Raleigh's *News & Observer* offered a more insightful accounting. The reporter observed, "At 11 o'clock, Memorial Hall is packed to its utmost to hear Tom Dixon's speech. He is conducted to the rostrum by the chief Marshal amid the wildest cheers from the entire audience. Dr. Carter of Raleigh, who led the audience in a most fervid prayer, said, 'In 1883 I was walking with a distinguished divine in New York as we returned from the hall where we had listened to a lecture by the most celebrated lecturer on the continent. I told him I thought we had a boy at Wake Forest who was a better speaker than the one to whom we had just listened. He was incredulous and my partiality for the student had biased my judgment. Today ten thousand people in the United States, without prejudice or partiality, confirm this opinion. That boy will address you today.'"[56]

---

[55] *The Progressive Farmer* (Winston, NC), June 17, 1890, page 2.

[56] *The News & Observer*, June 12, 1890, page 2; Other papers fawned over the speech. *The State Chronicle,* when characterizing the speaker, was expressly fulsome. The copy introducing the speech content began: "He spoke earnestly, eloquently, impassionedly. Words flowed for his heart and lips in a resistless current, carrying everyone along with the sentiments he expressed. The speaker's whole soul and being

Mr. Dixon rose and in a pleasant and humorous manner referred to his college experience here while a student. He paid a high tribute to the literary societies, and, said he, "there is only one college in all of this country whose society halls compared to those of Wake Forest."

His gifts for fomenting division and offering inclusion through identities are well exhibited in the address...

Beginning in an easy strain, Mr. Dixon proceeded to say: there never has in the history of the world been a time when the masses were so restless.

REV. THOMAS DIXON.

The farmer is organizing. There is conflict in... all the professions; the only man who succeeds is he who never lets up or turns back.

We are in a transition state for good or evil. The old homes are being broken up and are now no longer homes at all. In the great cities, men have no home; they are living in great bee-hives and the club rooms. The little boy in the city of New York came into his mother's room crying because, as he said a man has boxed his jaws, and when he was asked who heard him, all the child could tell was that "he was the man who stays here Sundays." He didn't know his own father. It seemed as if the intellectual and the moral and social world had broken from their mooring were drifting at sea.

The speaker said amid all the innovation is a great central principle which we may hold, there is one and only one force to cure these evils,

seemed to be dissolving itself into what he was saying. His words seem to burn into the very hearts of his audience... they sat and gazed and listened as though they were under the influence of a mesmeric spell. At times, the pathos and eloquence of the speaker were so deep—so strong—so impassioned that the irrepressible tears welled up and glistened in thousands of eyes. Then, by the very magic of eloquence, the speaker would send them from the realm of sympathy into the regions of spontaneous and uncontrollable laughter. Never have the walls of Wingate Hall sent back to the echoes of a grander, nobler eloquence than was heard at Wake Forest to-day." *The State Chronicle,* June 12, 1890, page 1.

and this is not seen by the unthinking, nor cared for it is the necessity for men to recognize the brotherhood of man. Tammany Hall is the most merciless and cruelest of all the organizations controlling social influences... Behind them stands the power of the Priest himself.

Mr. Dixon said: he proposes to hold up the life of our Savior separate from his spiritual nature, whose example on earth offers a solution for all of our troubles. He taught men *how* to pray. He said, "*our father.*" The world never heard this. Now if you will tell me how a man prays, I'll tell you how high he can rise.

We have the same father; therefore, we are brothers. Everything that concerns me concerns my brother. His joys are my joys, his sorrows are my sorrows.

After rendering fragments of political philosophy, the reporter praised the address to pointedly flatter North Carolina Governor Daniel G. Fowle, the following speaker. The governor spoke:

"It is always gratifying for me to be at Wake Forest on these occasions. But I can truthfully say that I have never been so gratified on any occasion as I have today. Heard here last year the great speech of Mr. Wilson, and the year before the elegant address of Sen. Vance; but I thank God that today I have heard the best speech of my life."

... Mr. Dixon's speech was in entire accord with that of the vast assemblage who were thoroughly carried away by the fine eloquence and finished declamation... Mr. Dixon received an ovation that must have rejoiced him to his heart's core. [57]

Dixon often joined in campus pageantry. Returning to a packed Memorial Hall in 1891 aroused intense reverence from the students. The writer penned, "Reader, do not leave it to the weak and humble pen, which grows unsteady with emotion, while thinking of this towering genius to tell you of his wonderous persuasive, dramatic and oratorical powers...He is the incomparable North Carolinian, the phenomenon of the age."[58]

Dixon returned in 1901 to deliver the Address to the Literary Societies before a packed house. One newspaper headline summarized the speech as **Thomas Dixon on Modern Sodoms**. The actual title of the speech was

---

[57] *The News & Observer*, June 12, 1890, page 2.
[58] *The Wake Forest Student,* March 1891, page 39.

Thomas Dixon played roles in Stage production
of *The Clansman* – circa mid-1910s

"A Message to a Country Boy," in which Dixon compared the virtues of country life to the degradation of Metropolitan cities like New York and Chicago. He opened, "I remember well when I came here a Green, country boy, so green, so country... Everything was good and great... I believe the world was kind and good. But I have been disillusioned of the dreams of my college days."

In the cities "I saw squalor, filth, thousands of hungry men and women...a modern monstrosity... The great curse of city life is saloons they are the open slaughter pens in which soul and character are butchered... There are over 10,000 saloons licensed in New York City, and 4,000 unlicensed... New York has no asylums, no libraries, no schoolhouses, no wash houses, but has 10,000 saloons, the finest ever built."[59]

In 1931, late in his career, the charter member of the Kappa Alpha social fraternity, founded in 1881, his sophomore year, was invited by the KAs to address its 1931 banquet.[60] Earlier in his career, just visiting campus swelled adulation in the State press. One Raleigh paper noted as a sidebar, "Rev. Thos. Dixon, Jr. and his wife are attending Commencement... the most brilliant graduate of recent years... he is nothing less than a genius, and by a genius, I mean a man who has wonderful natural abilities and application. Don't tell the genius it is labor. I know a hundred men who work as hard as Mr. Dixon but who

---

[59] *The News & Observer*, May 30, 1901, page 1.
[60] *Old Gold and Black*, January 9, 1931, page 1.

shine in comparison to him as a tallow candle to an electric light. He has genius, innate." [61]

One student obtained an interview with Dixon during his 1934 campus visit. Wyan Washburn wrote Dixon's greeting, "'Come in sir,' said an exceptionally tall and handsome grey-headed, kindly-faced to me as I tapped uncertainly one recent Sunday morning on the door of President-emeritus W. L. Poteat's house, and 'have a seat here in the library:'" [62]

> The speaker was none other than Thomas Dixon, Wake Forest graduate, playwright, author of some 20 or more popular novels, biographer, historian, politician par excellence, minister of the gospel, orator without peer, citizen of the world, and at present time official speaker for the NRA [63] under Pres. Franklin D Roosevelt...
>
> Whether all the good or bad thing said by anyone about Thomas Dixon be true or false, it matters little.... His admission of the fact that perhaps he and the Hon. J. W. Bailey, now Sen. in the U. S. Congress, might have had something to do with putting boards over the chimneys to the rooms of the members of the Phi society 50 years ago and unmercifully smoking the boys out of the old dormitory.
>
> The Bible is still by far the most popular and most modern of all books... Oratory will live with civilization; nothing can take the place of the spoken word... I owe my oratorical success to training in Euzelian literary society... [64]

Fifty-four years after his 1883 graduation, the *Wake Forest College Alumni News* told of a late-career Dixon's return to college grounds, an ode to his influence and the preeminence of the Literary Societies. "Tom Dixon came back to Wake Forest again last week and made the Euzelian

---

[61] *The State Chronicle*, June 9, 1887, page 2.

[62] Wyan Washburn, Dixon expresses himself on his collegiate career, *Old Gold and Black*, February 7, 1934, page 1.

[63] National Recovery Administration, established by Franklin D. Roosevelt in 1933. Designed to eliminate "cut throat competition" by bringing industry, labor, and government together to create codes of "fair practices" and set prices. https://en.wikipedia.org/wiki/National_Recovery_Administration

[64] Washburn, W. (1934). Dixon expresses himself on his collegiate career, *Old Gold and Black*, February 7, page 1, 2. This citation provides an extended account of Dixon's life.

Literary Society Hall resound once more with oratory. Over 300 jammed the room where he was speaking, and others listened in adjoining rooms where he talked was carried by special amplifying system." The Alumni News resumed:

> He ended his speech on American Heritage by declaring, "You are the richest people in the world; your destiny is in your own hands." The speaker was introduced by Robert Simms (class of '97), father of Albert E. Simms, proud president of the EU society… According to Simms Senior, Dixon was like a meteor, never declining but ever in the ascendancy, "marking every pause with a triumph in every career with a crown."
>
> "The impoverished South asked the federal government for Bread and were given stones, but they took these stones and built even greater institutions than those destroyed. When former slaves came back to rule over them, the Clan was organized to ride out at night in defense of life, liberty and womanhood." [65]

Other speakers on the program included Dr. William Lewis Poteat, who commented on the men whose portraits line the walls of society… During the meeting, 72 men signed up to join the Euzelian society. All three principal speakers agreed that training in the literary societies had proved… more valuable than classroom work.[66]

The Euzelian Society established long-standing medals bearing his name in 1896[67]: The Thomas Dixon, Jr. Medal, given to the best orator of the Senior class, and the Thomas Dixon, Jr. Medal for the best essay.

Presentations of the medals, including the principal Dixon medal, were noteworthy events, necessitating the invitation of outside dignitaries to make the presentation an event worthy of an audience (athletic or commencement), with full newspaper coverage.[68]

---

[65] *Wake Forest College Alumni News*, October 1937, No. 1, page 6.

[66] *Wake Forest College Alumni News*, October 1937, No. 1, page 6. At least some tolerance continued into the 1940s. Kay Williams led a presentation in the 1945 program that appraised Dixon's life. *Old Gold and Black*, March 16, 1945, page 2.

[67] Thomas Dixon, Jr., Medal was awarded as early as 1896. The last newspaper reference found was 1927.

[68] *The Charlotte Observer*, May 21, 1906, page 3; Thomas Dixon, Jr., Medal was awarded as early as 1896. The last newspaper reference found was 1927.

A curious case occurred in 1900 when "The Rev. J. Q. Adams, pastor of the Baptist Church of Reidsville, was here today on his return from the Wake Forest commencement. He was accompanied by his two sons, who are the principal contestants for the Tom Dixon medal... The contest between them was so close that the committee was unable to render a decision. The matter was determined by Rev. Mr. Dixon himself, who was present."[69]

The aura of Wake Forest's arguably most famous, now infamous, alumnus has long faded, actively sidelined from institutional memory. Surely an apt exile, yet it is also the case that Dixon held sway with Wake Forest debaters and Wake Forest for over a half-century. The Wake Debate history would be unfinished without allowing for Dixon's impact.

Dr. Tom, Wake's Most Loved Citizen

TAYLOR'S GARDENER

The revered (and earned) position of "Dr. Tom" has long been part of Wake's legacy. Over forty-seven years, Thomas Jeffries transformed the campus from a pasture to a park, serving as each Deacon's friend. "Dr' Tom befriended generations of Wake debaters, greeting them at the campus gates in victory and defeat, and odds-on witnessed parts of the Memorial Hall debates after he "had prepared the seats and lights and heat in the College chapel at the appointed time" for the grand public debates.[70]

It is said that Jeffries, who grew up enslaved in Virginia, moved South after the Civil War. Walking south, his journey took him "down the winding dirt road that led from the north into the college town of Wake Forest sometime in 1880."[71] He encountered a resident tending his home

---

[69] *Greensboro Telegram*, June 1, 1900, page 5.

[70] Paschal, G. W. (1943). *History of Wake Forest College*, Vol. II, page 223.

[71] *Wake Forest Gazette*, February 21, 2018, Vol. 20, No. 23. From a speech by Ed Morris, the Wake Forest Historical Museum Director. https://wakeforestgazette.com/just-little-history-dr-tom-jeffries-scholar-teacher-floriculturist. Paschal's account is not nearly as romantic and leaves one wondering about Jeffries' Virginia departure. Paschal related that Tom lived in Virginia for many years where "he married his first

"Dr. Tom" Jefferies with Wake Students Circa early 1920s

garden along the "main" street. A conversation took place, and Jeffries "offered' his services as a gardener. From that time forward, the two men were fast friends."[72] In time, the distinguished gentleman, Wake President Taylor, offered Jeffries the college job.[73] One chronicler suggested Presi-

---

wife, Jennie Hayes, by whom he had eight children. While in Virginia he was a tenant farmer." Paschal, G. W. (1943). *History of Wake Forest College*, Vol. II, page 222.

[72] *Wake Forest Gazette*, February 21, 2018, Vol. 20, No. 23. From a speech by Ed Morris, the Wake Forest Historical Museum Director. https://wakeforestgazette. com/just-little-history-dr-tom-jeffries-scholar-teacher-floriculturist. It is likely the relationship was generally professional, where they trusted and depended on each other, but dealings would also have been bracketed by racial one-sidedness. It is also likely Morris' account of the Wake Forest initial encounter was not with Taylor, as implied, but then with President Pritchard. Paschal's account is "When he reached Wake Forest, he found Dr. Pritchard, president of the College. Tom worked as a day laborer for several years." It was years later when Taylor hired him at the college. They were friends throughout Taylor's presidency.

[73] Jeffries did not immediately become the Wake landscaper. Pres. Taylor's daughter, Ethel Crittenden, recalled in a letter accessed in the Wake Forest University Archives, "My father, then president of the college, had brought the Negro to serve as a "yard man" on our home grounds, but Tom soon showed such superior qualities that he was made head janitor of the college." Crittenden added, "with a firm hand he [Dr. Tom] wielded authority over what he called his 'sub-men,' seeing to the cleaning of classrooms, the chopping wood and the drawing of water. Since for many years the

dent Taylor "often took pride that while Columbus discovered America, he discovered Dr. Tom."[74]

"Together, Tom Jeffries and Dr. Taylor planned and worked together to transform what Jeffries referred to as a 'stock pastur' into a place of beauty. Over a span of 40+ years, Tom Jeffries planted over 3,000 flowering trees and shrubs on the campus." Dr. Tom has long been credited with his signature rock wall, which to this day surrounds the original campus.[75]

> The old wooden fence, used to control foot traffic and to keep in the sheep that kept the grass mowed around the college buildings, was in poor condition and in constant need of repair. Jeffries wanted a stone wall to replace it. When he approached Dr. Taylor, the president was skeptical. Taylor explained that the college did not have funds for a wall. Tom said it wouldn't cost anything! The local farmers would supply the rocks for free and Tom was willing to build the wall on his own time. Given the nod by Dr. Taylor, Tom put out the word that he needed large rocks. As the local farmers came to town for provisions, they would bring him rocks. Over the years the wall grew until it surrounded the entire 22-acre campus: a lasting monument surrounding the dogwoods, azaleas, camellias, and magnolias planted by Dr. Tom.[76]

Undoubtedly, Jeffries was not always "Dr. Tom," but the title, organic from a student comment, lasted for most of his years at Wake Forest. It was won out of respect and familiarity with the students, not a proclamation from the administration or trustees.

---

college boasted no heating plant, at least 25 fires must be kindled daily. No wonder the installation of central heating was, as the old janitor described it, 'De mos' gloriful dis college.'"

[74] Pate, W. (1955). Old Doctor Tom served college for many years; built rock wall, *Old Gold and Black*, March 14, page 2.

[75] Comments offered by historian Andrew Cannady point out that the wall was a collaborative project with many involved, sometimes with Jefferies directing the work. Cannady indicates he helped build the wall section on the East side of campus. The wall's legacy, regardless, has been accredited to "Dr. Tom."

[76] *Wake Forest Gazette*, February 21, 2018, Vol. 20, No. 23. From a speech by Ed Morris, the Wake Forest Historical Museum Director. https://wakeforestgazette.com/just-little-history-dr-tom-jeffries-scholar-teacher-floriculturist.

Dr. Tom received the students' sincere affection as an emissary; he was, for many, "their friend, mentor, philosopher, and trusted advisor. For students, often far from home, Tom was the one they turned to when they needed some parental advice."[77] An excerpt from a yearbook's ode decreed:

> The student secret with him stays,
> Their Confidence he keeps,
> And many a prank of other days
> with him securely sleeps.

Dr. Tom's Campus Wall --'From Pasture to Park'

The students were protective of "Doctor" Tom... but the quick-witted gardener could more than hold his own. "One such example is the story of a freshman student who made fun of his color while Tom was burning some overgrown grass on the campus. The student remarked that the

---

[77] *Wake Forest Gazette*, Vol. 20, No. 23, February 21, 2018. The speech was given by Ed Morris, the Director of the Wake Forest Historical Museum. It also entertained some magnified renditions of Jeffries' place on campus. For example, he stated: "To say his degree may have been earned is an understatement. Tom Jeffries was allowed to sit in on classes at Wake Forest College. This went on for 47 years. By death, he arguably was the most educated man on campus." The illiterate Jefferies undoubtedly gleaned much, but Morris' speech was in evident celebratory mode. https://wakeforestgazette.com/just-little-history-dr-tom-jeffries-scholar-teacher-floriculturist.

grass was as black as Tom. Jeffries retorted, "Yes, it's black now but come spring it will be as green as you is." Chastised by his classmates for his disrespect, that student was never again entirely accepted by fellow students on campus.[78]

CAMPUS, STATEWIDE CELEBRITY

"Dr. Edgar E. Folk described Tom Jeffries as '...an unforgettable personality. Once you met him, you knew him... he had the gift of original language, colorful, poetic in its own way, allusive, and always arrestingly expressive.'"[79] Over his long career, he grew into an authentic personality. In addition to meticulously tending the campus, he spoke to frequent assemblies.

In 1916, Jeffries was asked to give the address at an event called "The Marshall Setup," a smoker held by each senior class shortly before commencement, one of many times he was the principal speaker. According to the campus newspaper, "It was the most 'Magnolius' talk of the many magnolius talks he has delivered... After the deafening applause that greeted his appearance, he addressed the students."

He instructed the graduates, "You see, gentlemen, in accordance with my prayers we is de champions of North Carolina and all de various places in de world. We should feel proud and submissive on all occasions an'de los fo' de gain of another. Do not be discouragious fo' Wake Forests is de champions in skillery of education in de world, which is de ingredients of life, and you should feel praise to God."[80]

Caretaker Jeffries' speaking engagements ranged from casual remarks to invitations to talk around the State. In the fall opening meeting of 1920, the College Young Men's Christian Association (Y.M.C.A.), heard from University Pres. Poteat and football and basketball coach James White. "Dr." Thomas Jeffries followed, "that aged darky who has been entertaining the students at various gatherings for the past 40

---

[78] *Gazette. The* account is drawn from G. W. Paschal's *History of Wake Forest College,* Vol. II, page 222-224. Appendix to Chapter XVI, "Doctor" Tom Jeffries.

[79] *Wake Forest Gazette*, Vol. 20, No. 23, February 21, 2018. The speech was given by Ed Morris, the Director of the Wake Forest Historical Museum. https://wakeforestgazette.com/just-little-history-dr-tom-jeffries-scholar-teacher-floriculturist.

[80] *Old Gold and Black*, May 5, 1916, page 3.

years, talked for a few minutes giving advice that he is well qualified to give."[81]

The following year, *The News & Observer* announced, "'Dr. Tom' Jeffreys (sic)... will be the principal speaker at the annual banquet of the Wake County Alumni Association at the Bland Hotel at 8 o'clock tonight... During recent sessions, the janitor's oratory has been in frequent demand at college gatherings of all sorts, and those in charge of tonight's banquet feel the speech from the 'Doctor' will be the surest means of achieving the desired purpose of freshening memories of college days."[82]

Jeffries also spoke when intercollegiate debate teams left or returned. In 1916, the *Old Gold and Black* column "Cracks from the Campus," citing perhaps an interview, connected the custodian with the excitement of the Richmond debates. Dr. Tom advised that if the debaters were lacking in spirit to conquer Richmond in the upcoming debates, they could turn to Wake basketball coach Dr. Cozier to guarantee a victorious outcome.[83]

The story in the campus paper reassured the students:

---

[81] *The News & Observer*, September 21, 1920, page 4.

[82] *The News & Observer*, August 23, 1921, page 2; Other examples include a summer school welcome "social" given by the Wake Forest Community. "The feature of the occasion was an address by "Dr." Tom Jefferys, veteran colored janitor. "Dr." Tom gave the members of the summer school a hearty welcome in the name of "we faculty members." *The News & Observer*, June 25, 1922, page 6; "One of the interesting features of the [Wake Forest Law Students] smoker was the twenty minute speech of "Dr." Tom Jeffreys, aged college janitor, who has taken part in student gatherings at Wake Forest since 'the time when the memory of man runneth not to the contrary.' Dr." Tom in his characteristic manner, advised the prospective lawyers in various and sundry forms, declaring "that when you take dat 'xamination Monday, think three times befo' you put anything down den put it down right." *The News & Observer*, January 29, 1922, page 15; "As a special number on the program of the occasion [Wake County Alumni Association] President Williams Louis Poteat introduced "Dr." Tom Jeffries... who spoke some ten or fifteen minutes to the enjoyment of all present... President Poteat stated that the venerable old darkey had been with the institution during its darkest days and had contributed considerably to the extensive progress." The linguistic choice in *The News & Observer* entry points out how racist the society remained in 1921. Evidence of Jeffries dining with those he kept amused was not found; likely, he did not.

[83] *Old Gold and Black*, January 29, 1916, page 12. *The News & Observer*, August 24, 1921, page 3.

DOCTOR TOM IS CONFIDENT OF SUCCESS
Aged Don Declares Debate with Richmond at Easter Time will be Triumpherous

"De query," said the Doctor, "don't 'mount to nuthin' a'tall. Dese here boys of ours has been whoopin' everything dey kin git dere han's on here lately and the attitude towards a magnolius victory grows as de time draws near. ... De fact is, since I been here longer 'an you is an' has seen the spell-bound orators dat de College has had, I has always been very gregarious towards dem all, an' you kain't tell me dat dese here Wake Forest young gen'lemen is too depreciated to mek wrong 'pear right an' right 'pear wrong. Jus' let Mtr. Crozier coach 'em three weeks an' dey can denominate de skillery of odder organashun dat de Richmonds or the Norfolks or Bailley kin turn out by next July.[84]

Dr. Jeffries often became the campus cheerleader, stirring debaters and athletic teams and sometimes simply offering condolence. When the Wake boys return from Raleigh following the fourth debate with Trinity (Duke), having been denied the victory, tail between their legs, a crowd

---

[84] *Old Gold and Black*, January 29, 1916, page 12; The dialect reported as Dr. Tom's needs to be read with appropriate reserve. The vernacular inevitably varies depending on who reported his comments. Ability, accuracy, and motive would color the reporting of Tom's words. These excerpts of heavy dialect could be read as pointing to a foolish or dull-witted person or, minimally, one lacking proper education. It is also instructive to consider the nonstandard language as an unfavorable reflection of the times and, perhaps, on his part, an artifact of the customs in which Jeffries grew up. Minimally, the vernacular carries a stubborn racial hierarchy. It is plausible that over his four-decade career, Dr. Tom's words also reflect a dose of performance. Paschal said Jeffries was "not obsequious or servile. Tom, after all, was a man. No one ever thought of him as a clown. He had a modest self-respect and was respected of others." Paschal, G. W. (1943) *A History of Wake Forest College*, Vol. II, page 223.

Tom's student friends seemed genuine in their regard, yet still held deep racial prejudices. When the students returned for the fall semester after Jefferies's passing, they lamented missing the "greeting of our old College janitor." Yet an editor would write in a brief "tribute," which was sullied with the most offensive enunciation of racial conventions. "The quaint humor, the unfailing politeness and chivalry of the old southern negro were well represented in him. We caught in him a vision of the old South, with white columns, expansive fields of cotton, log cabins, and singing darkies, the twanging banjo and shuffling feet, picaninnies with white teeth buried deep in the tempting meat of huge watermelons, or a merry group of darkies scouring the forests in search of the 'possum." *The Wake Forest Student*, Vol. 45, No. 1, October 1927, page 422.

of enthusiastic well-wishers met them at the campus gates. Leading the chorus with good wishes and his specific "life lesson" was Dr. Tom. *The Wake Forest Student* detailed, "Last of all, but not least, came prof Tom Jeffries. Mounted upon the campus wall, he uncovered his dusky head, and while cheer followed cheer, the tears rolled down his ebony cheeks."

> "Gentlemuns, I'se proud o' my most noblest boys. I hev claimed ter be er Virginianum, but I'se been cunnected wid des instituootion fer many yurs. I'se been er member uv de faculty fer some time. (Cheers) And, gentlemuns, I hev sont several crouds out dere ter Raleigh ter ripresent de cup; but, gentlemuns, dis waz de best. I's proud uv de way dey permantly addressed de audience. (Cheer upon cheer.) Gentlemuns, all I'se sorry ter regret is is I waz not dere to hev saws it. An, gentlemuns, what I say is, hit's injustice, dat's all, injustice." [85]

As Wake's "Number 1 cheerleader, he often elevated athletic teams before the big game. Dr. Tom was a reliable source as he possessed insider insight into the teams gained through his cross-campus conversations. When interviewed about Wake's Baseball team, "Dr. Tom waxed eloquently and praised the team that could make twenty-five runs in one game. 'We shore are comin' in dese athalakties' was the Doctor's first remark. And when asked his opinion of our pitching staff, he said, 'An' since dat Mr.' Long" Smith is back wid us, Car'lina will hab to go down in the dust of our glorifous team'" [86]

As Tom aged and students changed, his speaking presence diminished. The student paper wrote in 1919, "We wonder why 'Doctor' Tom is not called on more now for speeches. Some years ago, it was a campus custom to call on him on every occasion, and a celebration could hardly be held without a speech from him. He always replied in a way to delight his hearers. We won't have 'Doctor' Tom and his quaint juggling of the English language much longer, and it seems that we should take full advantage of his presence among us." [87]

---

[85] Jeffries' rally speech would have taken place on the very wall he built. "Doctor" Tom Jeffries, the well-known College servant, died at his home in Wake Forest on July 4, 1927, after an illness of four weeks.

[86] *Old Gold and Black,* March 25, 1916, page 3.

[87] *Old Gold and Black,* November 29, 1919, page 2.

A late career encounter was reported after Governor Thomas Bickett (class of '90) who had just closed his address promoting the League of Nations before a gathered 500 students spoke with Jefferies. The Governor remarked, "Why we seem to be getting younger all the time," Yassir, yassir dat's right, yassirr," Dr. Tom replied.[88]

All was not applause, of course, as Tom labored hard for nearly five decades. He was married three times, not always the happiest of affairs, and near the end of his long career, at 2:30 pm on the 13th of January 1923, his house was destroyed by fire. "The village fire department rushed to the 'wrong side of the track's' scene but was unable to do more than keep the fire from spreading. Dr. Tom had no insurance on his furniture, but the house was insured for $1000."[89] The "college generalissimo for forty-five years …standing among his household goods, which kind neighbors helped to save, he viewed the smoldering debris of his comfortable cottage with the fortitude of a true philosopher.[90]

At the 1933 Commencement, one witness wrote in the *Greensboro Record* as touching an account of Dr. Tom's character and influence as may exist:

At the south entrance of the campus wall, Willis Johnson, old Negro brick mason, was carefully setting in his form a bronze marker of compatriot and fellow slave, the late college janitor, "Dr." Tom Jeffries which was to be unveiled with fitting ceremony here this afternoon.

Thousands of Wake Forest alumni can relate almost as many different tales about "Dr." Tom, but this one has an appeal which those who knew him say is characteristic: a member of

---

[88] *The News & Observer*, October 17, 1920, page 11.

[89] *The Charlotte Observer*, January 16, 1923, page 15.

[90] *Old Gold and Black*, January 16, 1923, page 2.

the faculty who recently appeared before a body of alumni was reminiscing about the old times. He told of a certain Christmas holiday period years ago when apparently all the students had gone to their homes. A heavy snow had fallen and night was fast approaching when Old Tom was making his final round of the buildings. He ran across the freshman who appeared lonely and crest-fallen, "Ain't you goin' home to see your ma and pa?" Tom asked. "I'd like to the lad replied, "but...

"I kin let you have some money," Tom broke in.

So, the freshman boarded the "shoofly and went home.

The eyes of the presiding officer at this alumni gathering, who is a prominent attorney now, clouded up with tears, and he told the speaker afterward that he could vouch for the authenticity of the story, because he himself was the freshman concerned.[91]

PASSING THE TORCH

"Dr. Tom is dead." The message flashed over the telephone wires, from office to office, from classroom to classroom. "Have you heard that Tom died this morning."[92]

The Charlotte Observer, in a full-page tribute, led with the headline:

Patriotic Old Negro Gets His
Final Call on July Four
"Dr. Tom" Gave 50 Years
of His Life In Service
Of The Great Wake Forest College
Quaint Negro Character Honored on Wingate Memorial Hall
With Biggest Funeral Ever Accorded Anybody, White Or Black, In
All The History of The Village Wake Forest. Had His Own Particular Niche In Life, Which Nobody Else Will Be Able To Fill.

An old Negro cemetery lying somewhere across the tracks that divide the village of Wake Forest is the quiet little grave of "Dr." Tom

---

[91] *The Greensboro Record*, May 31, 1933, page 2.

[92] Thompson, T. (1928). Patriotic Old Negro Gets his final call on July four, *The Charlotte Observer*, June 24, page 26. A full description of the funeral and delightful remembrances from his campus life is found in this article.

Jeffries, for nearly 50 years a mere servant at Wake Forest College, but one who, at his death on July 4, 1927, was honored with the grandest funeral ever accorded anybody white or black in all the history of the village.[93]

... In the vestibule of the college chapel one of the college servants carefully groomed for the ceremonial occasion, gave directions to those who entered;' white folks go to the right, please su-hus colored folks is to sit to the lef'.

The standing-room assembly shared tears, having left their jobs, stores, and farms in the busy afternoon, many of which you came from across the state for "a black man's funeral. There were the families of the faculty, the alumni, many of whom had come from other sections of the state; the students—Tom had always called them his boys and more than one member of the board of trustees.

The principal speaker was the pastor of the colored Olive Branch Church, followed by Dr. N. Y. Gulley, Dean of the law school, who spoke on behalf of the campus and Dr. J. H. Correll, head of modern languages speaking as his friend "in a voice which he could scarcely control because of emotion, Dr. Correll spoke of his own love for Tom.

When the funeral procession crossed the railroad and turned into Faculty Avenue, the college bell, which Tom had tolled on so many occasions, began to toll for him. As they crossed the threshold, the funeral march wailed forth, and the mixed assembly rose to do him honor. After the coffin came the active pallbearers—the servants

---

[93] Faculty and students gathered for more than just Dr. Tom's funeral. President Taylor's daughter recalls a major campus event, "having been thrice married, Dr. Tom was well-versed in affairs matrimonial. The faculty and student body responded *en masse* to an invitation given by the janitor for his third wedding, with the result of not only were the Negroes house and porch overrun, but the yard as well. At the occasion of the ceremony, quite gravely Dr. Tom passed his hat for contributions to defray the expenses of the wedding trip. The newly-weds departed, but the bride went only as far as Philadelphia. Then, since his funds were diminishing, Dr. Tom sent her home, while he went on to New York. The latter city overwhelmed the janitor, who reported later that while he was there he "couldn' see fer lookin!." Wake Forest University Archives. "Although Dr. Tom lived his private life without aid from outsiders in a seven-room house by the power plant, students twice flocked to his house to serenade him and his new bride. McIlwain, B., and Friedenberg, W. (May 1959). The Legends of Baptist Hallow, *Wake Forest Magazine*, page 16-17.

who had worked with Tom—then his family, and then the college faculty, who followed as honorary pallbearers.[94]

The Wake Forest Magazine reminisced, quoting Dr. Tom, I "used all my exertions to make people like me so dat when dey leaves and meets me later on, dey looks as if the day is glad to see me and greets me as if I was President of Wake Forest College. 'Doctor' Tom had become as much a part of the College as the stone wall he built around it."[95]

In 1933, the senior class erected a bronze monument mounted on a granite boulder. The inscription written by President Emeritus W. L. Poteat reads: "Doctor Tom Jeffries 1850-1927, Janitor Wake Forest College, His Memorial, These Stones, These Trees."[96] A final monument was placed by the college on Tom Jeffries' grave.

---

[94] Thompson, T. (1928). Patriotic Old Negro Gets his final call on July four, *The Charlotte Observer*, June 24, page 26.

[95] McIlwain, B., and Friedenberg, W. (May 1959). The Legends of Baptist Hallow, *Wake Forest Magazine*, page 16-17.

[96] *The Biblical Recorder*, May 31, 1933, page 8.

CHAPTER 12

Debating Race Before Their People

Racism Saturates Wake's Ecology

Thirteen months after Wake celebrated the inaugural intercollegiate debate series with Trinity (Duke), on November 10, 1898, armed columns of white men marched into the black neighborhoods of Wilmington. In the name of white supremacy, the mob burned the offices of the local black newspaper, murdered dozens of black residents, and "banished many successful black citizens and their so-called 'white nigger' allies." Josephus Daniels, *The News & Observer* publisher, offered a "new social order was born in the blood and the flames, rooted in what was heralded as "permanent good government by the party of the White Man."[1]

The Wilmington riots exposed and exploited the disparate lives open to North Carolina's black citizens. Vestiges of slavery and Reconstruction tinted every aspect of life. Attitudes regarding segregation were not new. [2] From well before the Nation's birth and arguably to this day a heritage of racism continued to saturate.

---

[1] Tyson, T. B. (2006). The Ghosts of 1898: Wilmington's race riot and the rise of white supremacy, *The News & Observer*, November 17, 2006, Section H. Also see Zucchino, D. (2020). *Wilmington's lie: The murderous coup of 1898 and the rise of white supremacy*, Grove/Atlantic.

[2] Thomas Jefferson, for example, seventy years earlier, held that slaves should be returned to Africa, arguing that "tropical climates made the people uncivilized." Jefferson, T., *Notes on the State of Virginia*. In Gates, H. L. & Burton, J. (Eds.). *Call and response: Key debates in African American Studies*. 2011, New York: W. W. Norton & Co.

Echoes of Reconstruction continued well past the withdrawal of northern troops or the initial foundations for a robust economy. The rhetorical edge was intense following the Civil War, yet explicit racism continued in the students' oratories and debates into the Civil Rights decades.[3]

"THE LIMB OF THE LAW"

Law School Section, *Howler*,1911

At Wake Forest, and in the state, the temper may have been milder than in other parts of the South, but racism lived on. Subtle and not-so-subtle reverberations adorn the public speeches, adding to what Guelzo characterizes as the "manufactured myth of a glorious 'Lost Cause' to justify themselves and their continuing belief in the rightness of the Confederate project."

As late as 1900, Josephus Daniels, a North Carolina "progressive" who served in Woodrow Wilson's cabinet, tongue-lashed North Carolina's final Senator in the 19th century, Marion Butler:

It is a sad commentary upon the political conditions to have obtained in this state... That North Carolina should have the only Negro congressman... So far as that particular Negro is personally concerned, he may be dismissed as beneath contempt... The Negro in office regards himself as the enemy of the white man and is anxious to have his race share in that sentiment. Therefore he becomes a menace to the peace of the Commonwealth and a danger to the safety of both races... Venomous, forward, slanderous of the whites, appealing to

---

[3] "Reconstruction "had no official starting or ending date; it sputtered on well into the 1890s." Guielzo, A. C. (2018). *Reconstruction: A concise history*, Oxford University Press, 2018, page 1.

the worst passions of his own race, he emphasizes anew the need for making an end of him and his kind."[4]

In 1904, *The Wake Forest Student* editor, C. P. Weaver, writing in his column, reflected an anxiety about the South's future and how to come to terms with its racially polarized world. He writes the "So-called 'Race Problem' has been the theme of so much flighty oratory, the rallying cry of the politician and the demagogue, the all-absorbing question of much debate in the literary societies, and yet solution in the eyes of many is as far from being realized as ever."[5]

Track Team

Howler Yearbook, 1906

His further message is to ignore the intractable problem, allowing rising expectations to cause enough discontentment to lead to a solution. He argues that you pull yourself up by your bootstraps (implicitly, "as we did"). He follows the lead of the then-Governor Charles B. Aycock, whom he quotes, at a Baltimore speech at which he roared the crowd-pleasing guidance, "...let him alone; quit writing about him; quit talking about him; quit making him 'the white man's burden;' let him

---

[4] The colored member, February 5, 1900, in *Congressional Record*, 56 Congress, first session, 1865. As quoted in Guielzo, A. C. (2018). *Reconstruction: A Concise History*, Oxford University Press, 2018, page 122.

[5] Weaver, C. P., Editor (1904). *The Wake Forest Student*, April 23, page 465.

'tote his own skillet;' quit coddling him; let him learn that no man, no race ever got anything worth having who did not earn it himself..."[6]

The solution Governor Charles B. Aycock argued for was to deny suffrage to black citizens. Canceled in conciliatory expression, he gave voice to the widely shared belief that Blacks are best excluded from civic participation, a societal debate that callously continues today:

> There is a corresponding responsibility laid upon the Southern white man that racial antipathy must be put away, and the utterances of radical reformers must be checked... The disenfranchisement of the Negro, while seemingly an untoward event, will eventually work out for him his salvation, for his desire for suffrage will cause him to deplore his present condition, and dissatisfaction is the mother of amelioration. The task of helping him shake off the shackles will then fall in willing hands, and the way to citizenship will be made easy for him.[7]

This environs comprised the scene in which the Wake Forest public debates unfolded.

Public Debates About Race

This section takes up Wake Forest's noteworthy public debates on the question of race.[8] The debates were presented before an elite community, including the state's star politicians, drawing large audiences and favorable State press.

They are illustrative of an era. This evaluation is not an indictment of the individual debaters or Wake's public presentations *per se*. Our aversion to the debater's statements presented below is sensible. We, too,

---

[6] Weaver, C. P., Editor (1904). The Wake Forest Student, April 23, page 466, From Speech by Gov. Charles B. Aycock delivered at the first annual dinner of the North Carolina Society of Baltimore.

[7] Weaver, C. P., Editor (1904). *The Wake Forest Student*, April 23, page 467. A more extended discussion of debates focusing on the denial of the franchise can be found in Chapter 4 – Debating in the Literary Societies.

[8] Debates took place away from the public eye, of course, safely secreted in the respective halls. Some of these are discussed in the Topics section of Chapter 4 – Debating in the Literary Societies.

live in imperfect times, but also in greatly altered times from the setting in which these debates took place, and the debaters managed.

Yet, the debates *were sponsored* by literary societies and institutionally sanctioned, continuing for over seventy years after the Civil War. The rhetoric from these debates is often appalling, especially to the contemporary ear. Nonetheless, it is a defining part of Wake Debate's history.

Topics dealing with the United States' rapid expansion, the increasingly tense North-South friction, and what to do about the troubling question of slavery were added step-by-step to the debating calendar. The topics from the school's founding moved from "seeking solutions to slavery" to the various compromises mapping its westward expansion to an extended debate on the rightness of secession from the Union.[9]

In the pre-Civil War period, the college remained relatively inward-looking, isolated by transportation, curriculum, and religion. The school was small and geographically constrained. Opportunities to present their debaters to a receptive public audience did not occur until

---

[9] A quick survey of representative topics addressing slavery prior to the Civil War follows. Of note is the progression to pro-slavery support, paralleling the evolution of the debate nationally. **Euzelian:** September 1841, *Is it probable that the slaves in this country will ultimately be freed?* Affirmative 11 yeas to 9 nays. March and August 1843, *Is slavery a moral evil?* Negative 6 to 5 and Affirmative 7 to 3. May 1844, *Is it probable slavery will ever be abolished in the U.S.?* Negative 9 to 6. September 1844, *Is it probable a disunion will ever take place between the Northern and Southern States?* Affirmative 6 to 5. March 1850, *Is it probable that dissolution between the North and the South will ever take place?* Negative 10 to 9, debated again in 1845 considerable uncertainty, Negative 7 to 4, and, in September, the certainty of disunion was increasing, Affirmative 10 to 5; October 4, 1850, *Should slavery be tolerated?* Affirmative 13 to 5. *Did Daniel Webster or Henry Clay benefit his country more?* debated 25 times, beginning in 1854. **Philomathesians:** May 1836, *Is slavery as practiced in the United States incompatible with the spirit of free institutions?* Negative; March 1847, *Should Congress enact laws to prevent slaveholding men Jordan and Clark from settling our territories?* Affirmative 19 to 12. (Jordan and Clark appear to be society members); October 1850, *Would emancipation of slaves in the Southern States be a means of making them more happy?* Negative 19 to 8; April 1854, *Is slavery an evil pur se (sic)?* Negative 18 to 2; 1855, *Is slavery consistent with the principles of a free government?* In this instance, Affirmative 11 to 3. The same resolution or versions *"compatible with free institutions"* were debated numerous times; August 1859, *Has the institution of African slavery been beneficial to the U.S.?* Affirmative 11 to 8. September 3, 1859 – Which would be more dangerous to the South, a dissolution of the Union or the abolition of slavery? Decided in the Negative 13 to 4; September 1859 and February 1861, *Which would be more dangerous to the South, a dissolution of the Union or the abolition of slavery?* Negative 13 to 4, Negative 8 to 4.

the 1872 Anniversary Day event, eight years after the Confederacy's surrender. The more overt debates about race and slavery were to occur in the wake of the Civil War.

This segment delves into eight public debates in which race was addressed, as performed by Wake's literary societies.

Ten years after the first Anniversary debate, the 1882 topic (suffrage) was the first to openly argue race-related issues. Debates do not take place in a vacuum. In these instances, the eight debates occupied a post-Civil War society built, in no small part, on bigotry and intolerance—prejudice so thoroughly blended as to become almost obscured to white society. The debates mark the period from 1882 through 1906.

Becoming a public debater was a hard-earned distinction, attracting the most able among the student body. These bright, aspiring students were inculcated into a view of life and mostly spoke these intolerant sentiments with approval. Yet their speeches also contained moments of enlightenment and genuine struggles with how to make a better society. The times were turbulent.

The assigned side of queries mattered occasionally, resulting in a slightly more enlightened stance, but not always. The thoughts and arguments provide a distinctive depiction of the University's historical navigation of race.

*_*_*_*_*

1882 — ANNIVERSARY DAY — EXTENDING SUFFRAGE

*Is the system of suffrage conducive to the
best interest of the Republic?*

Affirmative, W. J. Ferrell & E. G. Beckwith;
Negative, E. E. Hillyard & Thomas Dixon

Suffrage debates, naturally, focused on a discussion of who was worthy of the vote. Celebrating the 1882 Anniversary Day, *The Wake Forest Student,* in introducing the scene, gushed:

In the great desert of college life there are occasional oases which refresh the weary, drooping student, as with a foretaste of the Elysian

Fields[10]. Such an occasion was the forty-seventh anniversary of the Euzelian and Philomathesian Societies... The forces of nature had combined to make the occasion one of rejoicing, and when at 2 ½ o'clock p. m., to the music of the Raleigh string band, the representatives of the two Societies marched down the aisle of the new chapel, an appreciative audience had already assembled to enjoy the feast of reason so shortly to be set before them.[11]

A Wilmington, NC, paper added that the resolution was "just the kind of question for a clever student to tackle. It was handled with good sense, good humor, and fine repartee."[12]

The Wake Forest Student observed the first speaker, Mr. Fleetwood, "proceeded to make a speech teeming with the good sense and good reasoning by which this gentleman is distinguished." He held... The principles embodied in universal suffrage have elevated humanity more than all other political systems, yet the political dyspeptics and democratic hypocrites are crying change! Change! and murmuring and sighing for the flesh-pots of England and the onions and garlic of the feudal ages. It is the embodiment of our national character."

The first negative, Mr. E. E. Hilliard, concluded his speech: "Men not qualified for a public duty ought to have no share in its privileges. Men are not born equal, are not born free, but in subjection to society and law. Natural rights are not political rights. No government can stand on such a foundation as sycophants and artisans make of such elements as they can purchase in the ignorant negro freedmen and the swarms of immigrants to our shores."

Mr. E. G. Beckwith, upholding the affirmative, wondered, "The negative says the people are too depraved to rule. Are the people more depraved than the [President] Grants who robbed them?... The people may be fools in many things, but are they fools on such questions as the promotion of the Republic? They have been closest to difficulties

---

[10] In the mid-1800s, New Yorkers' refuge for sport and leisure was Elysian Field, across the river in New Jersey. The Park was especially popular, sometimes referred to as the "Birthplace of Baseball," a disputed claim. At the time, baseball was king in all of America.

[11] *The Wake Forest Student*, March 1882, Vol. 1, No. 3, page 144-145. A partial transcript of the debate is at the same citation, page 145-147.

[12] *The Daily Review* (Wilmington), February 20, 1882, page 4.

and have learned that political wisdom which life teaches in its sternest school. At the appearance of a people's government, despotic kingdoms vanish."

1882 Anniversary Debaters and Marshals: First Row: O. L. Stringfield, E. E. Hillard, D. W. Herring, C. A. Smith, Thomas B. Wilder. Second Row: E. G. Beckwith, H. G. Holding, W. T. Llewellen, J. W. Fleetwood, W. J. Ferrell. Not Pictured: Thomas Dixon

Not surprisingly, the second negative, Thomas Dixon, carried the evening "in a manner no report can do justice to. His clear enunciation and animated style gained him the closest attention of the audience. Dixon's insights, while not mentioning race, were thinly veiled.

He argued the principle that "'all men are born free and equal,' is erroneous." ... The man who votes is a sovereign. The system that declares ignorance and sloth entitled to equal consideration with knowledge and virtue is erroneous... No Man deprived of the advantage of the press can vote intelligently... Universal suffrage gives its sanction to corruption, opens the grandest field in the world for the demagogue, by supplying him with nearly two millions of ignorant voters upon whom to operate. Require these men to read and write, and the power of the demagogue is destroyed."

"During the debate, the utmost excitement and enthusiasm prevailed. By a vote of the audience, the question was decided in the negative by a majority of 70."[13]

*_*_*_*_*

1883 — ANNIVERSARY DAY — PROHIBITING IMMIGRATION

Ought immigration be prohibited?

Affirmative, L. L. Jenkins & W. F. Marshall;
Negative, D. M. Austin & H. B. Folk

(The Euzelian orator in the evening presentation was Thomas Dixon.)

The vitriol surrounding immigrants in the 1880s was more than a match for our acerbic contemporary politics. The question of prohibiting immigration, often debated in society meetings, was brought to the public for the second consecutive year with the celebration of Wake Forest's 48th Anniversary. Immigration disputes were understood in the context of race, often featuring a comparison of unknown foreign-born strangers with our own (un)acceptable known, the former slave population.

The first affirmative, Mr. L. L. Jenkins' words, divested of context, read more like a dogmatic rant. The affirmative, while acknowledging America as a melting pot, concluded:

The castaways of Europe come here, and in their hands will soon be the balance of power. Old Worldism and superstitions are destined here to corrupt both society and government. The influence of Catholicism imported from abroad is to be looked on with dread. The Roman Catholic Church is only a club for the accommodation of its members. They contaminate society and politics... The nation seems safe; but if immigration goes on, the sons of the Republic will soon set in a sea of blood....[14]

The negative offered familiar points, economic and moral, "Immigrants have become assimilated with our people. [Immigrants] became patriotic,

---

[13] *The Wake Forest Student,* March 1882, Vol. 1, No. 3, page 146.
[14] *The Wake Forest Student,* Eu. Sr. Editor, March 1883, Vol. 2, page 320.

fought and died for our country." And more critically, "the spirit of liberty is energizing and vitalizing. Let us go out to all lands and say that there is truth in liberty, power in liberty, life in liberty."[15]

The last speaker, H. B. Folk, concluded, "Isolation is a suicidal policy. Prohibition violates social and divine law."

The vote was taken, Folk's argument was persuasive, and the question was decided in the negative by 117 to 51.

--*-*-*-*-*-*

1886 — ANNIVERSARY DAY — FREE EDUCATION FOR ALL

Ought governments furnish free education by taxation to all classes of their citizens?

Affirmative, J. D. Boushall, Eu & J. B. Carlyle, Phi,
Negative, Jacob Stewart, Phi & W. P. Stradley, Eu

On a day "cold, dark, and dreary," the Wake debaters "of youthful heart" gathered with the Wake faithful for the 51st Anniversary of the society's founding. [16]

The Affirmative speaking in Wingate Memorial Hall, before students and town persons, politicians, and reporters, claimed, "it is a sacred duty of every government to take effectual means for the protection of life, the property, and the happiness of the people and since ignorance is dangerous to life and property, the education of the people must be part of their government." They reasoned, "the safety of the State depends upon the intelligence of the citizens." They cited counties with free schools, claiming they had better citizens.

The negative interjected a more nefarious interpretation that Blacks were essentially uneducable. They held that free public schools "violated well-recognized principles of taxation in that it taxed the many to educate the few; illustrated here in the South by the case of the Negro – the white paying four-fifths of all the expensive free schools for the Blacks; and

---

[15] *The Wake Forest Student*, March 1883, page 320-321.

[16] *The Charlotte Observer*, February 23, 1886, page 4. The reporter is quoting Longfellow.

Debaters, 1886. Top row: J. T. White; C. E. Brewer. Bottom row: J. B. Carlyle; J. D. Boushall; Tayloe; Stuart; and Stradley. Another note on the back of the photograph reads "Dr. Chas. E. Brewer"

that too, when these are only two possible solutions to the great African problem, either one of which involves the destruction of Southern civilization, and the debasing of the Caucasian race in the South." [17] The negative rebutted the affirmative's assumption that governments had this responsibility by answering "that the State could give education which would fit its citizens for duties of citizenship was false, since the State could not teach religion, the only foundation of morality."[18]

The audience agreed, voting with the Negative 115 to 55.[19]

*_*_*_*_*_*_*

---

[17] "The Negro will either overpower the whites by superior numbers – increases far more rapidly than the whites – or the races will amalgamate." The destruction comes from taking the 'superior' down to the 'inferior' by the use of taxes."

[18] *The Torchlight* (Oxford, NC), February 23, 1886, page 8.

[19] In truth, the debaters' recorded arguments in *The Charlotte Observer* were more nuanced than this reporter's retelling.

1887 – ANNIVERSARY DAY –SLAVERY'S INTRODUCTION

*Was the introduction of the Negro into the United States
productive of more good than evil?*

Affirmative, W. F. Watson, & J. W. Lynch;
Negative, L. R. Pruitt & D. O. McCullers

52nd birthday of the literary societies

By 2:00 PM, on a chilly February afternoon, an unusually large audience had assembled in the spacious Memorial Hall to listen to the Anniversary Day debate. The contestants filed in and took their place at the front, ready to inform and entertain. Their reasons generally endorsed the existing late 1880s Southern thought. Although not verbatim text, the following excerpts are drawn from the debaters' words as preserved by an editor of *The Wake Forest Student*, a rendition that appears faithful to the speakers' stances.

Undergirding speakers on both sides of the question was an hierarchical social system grounded in deeply held views of inferior and superior races, with shades of the more and less human. One is also struck by the white culture's missionary "White Savior" hue. One speaker muttered that, even after 300 years of white man's tutelage, the Negro "was still unfit." The final speaker went as far as blaming the slaves for the Civil War. Voices of retrenchment from Reconstruction are evident throughout.

(1st Affirmative) Mr. Watson opened the debate by saying he was conscious of representing the unpopular side of this question. So he begged the audience to dismiss all prejudice as far as possible. The Negro was taken from the wilds of Africa, a barbarian, raised to the elevation of human slavery, and finally given the right of a free citizen in the higher state of civilization than he had ever dreamed of. He was put under the purifying and elevating influence of Christian people, and today, the Negro has the same God and religion as we have. So that he had lost nothing by becoming a slave in the United States, but had gained much... After showing what rapid progress the Negro was making with an education and how the States helped him, he told us that the Negro had cleared the forest and made our beautiful Southland prosperous and productive.

(1st Negative) Mr. Pruitt met the argument of the gentleman by saying that the Negro came from the "Dark Cotton nut" without morality, without education, without civilization, without Christianity, and could not have otherwise been a cog in the wheels of progress. He claimed that the Negra (sic) was still unfit for many of the industrial pursuits. Although he had been under the influence of the white man for nearly 300 years, it was still a doubtful question whether he could be made an intelligent citizen. Slavery disorganized the Union and involved the country in a bloody war. The emancipation and freedom of ballot to the unprepared recipients was an enormous failure... The Negro intensifies the illiteracy in the South. The new girl [Negro] without the white man is like the Mockingbird without the song of other birds.

(2nd Affirmative) Mr. Lynch claimed not to belong to the ultra-class of persons denominated "Negro worshipers," nor to the other extreme known as Negro "they grow haters"; but he believed the African was a man with a soul and mind, with a mission, and that the temperament and capacity of the black man were particularly suited to the country and situation he occupies. The South would not exchange laborers with California or with New England. The Negro is lazy and careless, but he never boycotted a store, stopped a factory, or threw a bomb of dynamite. We have been freed from the scum and poisons of Europe by the presence of the black man. There is no danger of amalgamation, nor any foundation for fear of the Negro as a factor in our social system... He touchingly reviewed the "Lost Cause," followed the slaves into freedom, and showed how our people had accomplished the greatest mission work in the history of Christianity. The ultimate outcome of the movement is the salvation of Africa.

(2nd Negative) Mr. McCullers said that from the time of the introduction of the Negro until now, he had been a source of trouble. He said that the "Negro Problem" was the most difficult, dangerous, and uncertain the American people have ever had before them; that slaves caused the late four years' war, and now the black man continues to be the occasion of great disturbance... Politically, the black voter is a curse to the land. The majority of them are illiterate and possessed of little character; these are led to the polls to cast a vote they cannot read, and often, they do not know or care for whom they are voting. He claimed that there was danger of amalgamation, and that "Negro Rule" might oppress the South.[20]

One should assume that not all racial attitudes were as hardened as those expressed before the 1887 audience. Following the debate, the audience was asked to vote based on the arguments presented, not their personal views. The affirmative, who pleaded they were assigned the unpopular side, must have felt some relief when the vote was taken, resulting in favor of the affirmative, standing 132 to 33.[21]

*_*_*_*_*_*_*_*

1899 – ANNIVERSARY DAY – LIMITING IMMIGRATION

Foreign immigration should be further restricted.

Affirmative – William Parker Etchison & Arthur Weiland Cook;
Negative – William Alexander McCall & Oscar Leonidas Powers

With snow and sleet underfoot, the 1899 debate at the 64th anniversary explored the question of "further restricting" immigration. One finds obvious precursors to today's bombast of terrorists and drug dealers illegally crossing the US borders.

Phi debater William Etchison contended, "New York, Chicago, Philadelphia, and others of our largest cities are American only in name. They have just as much right to be called Jewish, Italian, or Irish cities as American cities… the horde of undesirable foreigners are not only here and continuing to come here in great numbers, but they are not in sympathy with our Constitution and freest nations. A great proportion of them are Anarchists, deserters from imperialism and militarism."

Etchison's Eu opponent, W. A. McCall, countered, "The laws in operation have slain the great immigration tiger whose growls and mighty paws once threatened the happiness of the American people. The present laws exclude all Chinese immigration, prohibit contracts for labor in foreign countries, and prevent transportation companies from inducing foreigners to come. All criminals, paupers, lunatics and persons likely to become a

---

[20] Stradley, W P., Editor, *The Wake Forest Student*, March 1887, page 282-285.
[21] *The News & Observer*, February 15, 1887, page 2.

1889 Anniversary Debaters: Front: W. A. McCall, 1st Deb., K. D. Stephenson, Pres., W. O. Speer Sec'y, W. P Etchison, 1st Deb., (Back) W. O., Powers, 3d Deb., P. S. Carlton, Phi Orator, J. C. Turner, Eu Orator, A. W. Cooke, 2nd Deb.

public charge are prohibited. The laws permit only the British, German and Scandinavian stock. To further restrict will necessarily exclude some whose presence would be a benefit to a large part of our national prosperity... He has built canals and railroads and furnished us with mechanics, laborers, and statesmen."[22]

The negative Won. Yet one of the interesting features of the discussion was how evenly divided were the sympathies of the audience. "When the vote was taken, there was little difference in the number of votes cast for each side."[23]

--*-*-*-*-*-*

[22] *The Morning Post* (Raleigh), February 19, 1899, page 6. This source provides a more complete account of the speakers' arguments.

[23] *The Biblical Recorder*, March 1, 1899, page 3.

1903 — ANNIVERSARY DAY — DEPORTING
THE "NEGRO PROBLEM"[24]

*Deportation is the best solution of the Negro
problem in the United States.*

Phi, Affirmative, T. A. Allen & Wm. H. Whitehead;
Eu, Negative, E. M. Harris & Isaac N. Loftin

For decades, the Anniversary Day Debates were a distinguished event on the state's social and political calendar. Wake alumni increasingly occupied leadership roles among the clergy, educators, and politicians. The ever more effortless proximity to the State capital, Raleigh, filled Memorial Hall with legislators, Supreme Court justices, and often senators and governors. The 1903 judging panel was "composed of His Excellency Governor Chas. P. Aycock, State Auditor Dixon, and Mr. Archibald Johnson, editor *of Charity and Children*... giving the palm of victory to the negative."[25]

The centrality of the topic debated corresponds fully with this chapter's subject matter – Race – thus sharing more from the students' words which provide distinct insights.[26]

The first speaker for the Affirmative was Mr. Thomas A. Allen. He spoke as follows: "The United States is leading in the civilization for humanity. The population of the South is 16,000,000; 10,000,000 whites and 6,000,000 blacks. We have a nation within a nation. It is impossible to keep two races together yet separate and distinct. Amalgamation is impossible. Every law of humanity and civilization prevents extermination. Then, the only solution is deportation.

---

[24] The same topic was chosen for the second 1903 Richmond intercollegiate debate on Thanksgiving Day. Records of the content of that debate were not found.

[25] Editorial, *The Wake Forest Student*, 1903, May, Vol. 22, No. 6, page 385. In one respect, today's debate struck out a new policy. Instead of submitting the question to the audience, the debaters asked the judging panel to decide. *The News & Observer* account also listed about twenty-five other notables in the audience, including professors from several colleges, ministers, and numerous legislators." (February 15, 1903, page 11; In a special post-debate release, Raleigh's *Morning Post* boasted that it is in the societies that a Wake man "learns all the arts of public speaking, learn how to grapple with a strong and wary opponent, and how to express himself elegantly, clearly, vigorously, forcefully." *The Morning Post*, February 14, 1903, page 6.

[26] *The Morning Post* (Raleigh), February 14, 1903, page 6.

Mr. Allen moves next to questions of the feasibility of deportation, asking his audience to be open-minded; he reminds his listeners that "the American Revolution did not seem feasible." "There must be a responsible time in which to deport the negro; 20 years will be sufficient. There is a place to which the negro can be deported. Conditions are favorable for their prosperity. The climate is tropical, the soil is fertile. It is in Liberia that they could find freedom."

The first speaker on the negative, Mr. Ernest M. Harris, opens with his definition of racial prejudice and interdependence. He then enumerates circumstances that make deportation not only ludicrous but counterproductive: a policy misguided for Blacks rooted in the community and for Whites, presenting threats to their economic interests. Harris intoned:

Race prejudice is friction between groups of people. It is the difference in aim, in feeling and in ideals of different races. If the differences exist touching territory, laws, language or religion, then there is no reason why in the same country two great races might not thrive and develop, especially when each race is dependent upon the other.

He argued that [deportation] was not desired by the negroes; (1) Because hundreds of thousands of them own their own homes that

1903 Anniversary Officers – The Debaters, Phis, standing, Wm. H. Whitehead &. T. A. Allen, Eus Right, E. M. Harris & Isaac N. Loftin. Also pictured standing center: Wayland A. Seagrave. Sec W. Harry Stephenson, Pres. Seated, Orators, Earl Broadus Fowler, and William Scott.

do not want to give up. (2) The negro cannot rule for himself – some race must guide him. (3) Their surroundings in the South are more favorable to their development than could be secured anywhere else. It is not desired by the whites: (1) We need them as laborers. (2) They keep the foreign immigrants from the South. [F]oreign immigration would bring contamination to the Anglo-Saxon blood, strife and industry, disorder to the government and atheism to religion. (3) It would cause an economic crisis in the South and retard the development of the entire country.

The second speaker for the affirmative was Mr. W. H. Whitehead, who revealed a learned chronic antipathy between the races, reinforcing, however indirectly, the superiority of whites:

Nearly 40 years ago, slavery was abolished in the South, and the authority under which it exists was removed from our statute books and the organic law of the land. The proclamation of Lincoln and subsequent amendments to the Constitution did not settle the Negro problem but created a new problem but equally perplexing situation.

The granting of the elective franchise to the negro followed hard upon his emancipation, arraying the two races against each other, and a conflict ensued, which terminated in the subversion of the negro.

The gift of the ballot led him to believe that the North had a particular love for him, that the ballot was given to him to dominate former masters and rebels and plot with impunity his deeds of darkness. This made him lawless and developed in him a spirit of insubordination to the social order. Crimes of violence against the whites were the natural fruitage.

The whites assumed the negro was a human being, and had taxed themselves to educate him. But education is doing the negro harm. The time will come when they will refuse to pay taxes to educate him. Emboldened in this is a germ of revolution which must separate the races.

The non-slave owners looked upon the negro as an inferior element, and the evident contempt of the negro... the competition they were forced to meet in slave labor, created a revengeful hostility to the negro...

The common people…hated the negro because he claimed to be a citizen of the state and the Republic. This class of non-slave owners, who hate the negro, is rapidly increasing in number and influence.

The last speaker of the negative was Mr. Isaac N. Loftin, reinforcing the feasibility and economic limitations of deportation. His comments, however, drip with condescension. He argues:

Though the negro belongs to an inferior race, and by nature is repulsive to us, he has some rights which we, the proud representatives of the aristocratic South, must respect. Besides, the negro has some latent powers which it is our duty to cultivate, from the fact that he was loyal in slavery, patriotic in freedom, and because he has a subtle sense of song, poetry, pathos and humor…

The increase in negro population is 18 percent over 10 years; then, allowing a proportional decrease for those deported, we can

1907 *Howler* Drawing – contributed student artwork

with safety calculate a 9 percent increase on the 9 million for the next 150 years, which, at the end of that time, will give us 3 million more negroes than at the present day, for whom we have counted no cost of transportation nor time within which to do it.

The deportation of the negro from the South is neither desirable nor feasible from industrial considerations:

1st. He is an indispensable factor in the woods of the turpentine section and around our lumber plants.

2nd. We need him to dig the canals and harness our water-power.

3rd. We need him to make brick and mortar, of which our mills are being built (sic)

4th. We need him in our cotton fields.

5th. The negro is best suited as an employee for the temperament of the southern white man.

6th. Every people must have a servile class, not to be oppressed, but to be protected.

7th Our race problem with the negro is not so great as the north has with its mixed and Mongol races of the globe.

With them [the Negro], the South is developing her resources so fast that some will persist in speaking of the new South, when it is really the same old south, beautiful ever, but more so dressed in her modern garb of industrial activity, moved on by southern enthusiasm, her people learning that beyond the bounds of leprous prejudice there is a mutual dependence between the races; and that it is our duty to raise the negro to the highest possible stage of development, teaching him the way of light until the millions in one grand chorus saying with Phyllis Wheatly:

> *'Twas mercy bought me from my pagan land.*
> *Taught my United soul to understand.*
> *That there's a God – that there is a savior, too.'*

The seconding speeches followed and were characterized as "short, incisive, and striking fire." In revealing the judges' decision, Gov. Aycock said, 'I have heard a great many debates in my time, and, speaking frankly, I never before heard a debate by any college students which equaled this one. Every speech showed the ability to think.'" The decision, not unanimous, was in favor of the negative.[27]

*_*_*_*_*_*_*_*

---

[27] *The Morning Post* (Raleigh), February 14, 1903, page 6.

1904 – INTERCOLLEGIATE DEBATE – RICHMOND – CONTROLLING BACKWARD RACES

Advanced nations should control, for the world's benefit, the territory occupied by backward races.

Richmond, Affirmative, B. M. Simmons & F. G. Pollard; Wake, Negative, J. Patton & Alfred H. Olive

"As the audience assembled, lively music was rendered by Leven's orchestra, and as 'Dixie' sounded, there was a volume of applause."[28]

The 1904 debate, held on the Richmond campus, did not directly address race in America; however, the topic's wording, mandating control of "backward races," had obvious implications for Blacks on the home front.

Richmond was assigned possibly the more difficult expansionistic stance to save other nations from themselves. Mr. Pollard opens in the affirmative for the home team. "Control by advanced nations meant the mental, moral and physical disenthralment of backward nations, and that this was the duty of the world powers, that backward nations should not harass and make millions to suffer if this could be stopped." Among his main points

JO PATTON, of Morganton, Debater for Wake Forest.

2. That such advancement can only come from advanced nations.
5. That backward peoples benefited and improved by contact with higher races.
7. That no other possible method remains except colonization.
9. That colonization, when accessible, becomes the highest manifestation of civilization.[29]

---

[28] *The Farmer and Mechanic*, November 29, 1904. page 3.

[29] *The Farmer and Mechanic*, November 29, 1904, page 3.

Wise and just control were urged, of course. The examples of a more enlightened "helping hand" were East India and the Philippines, with particular stress claiming that Roman control of Teutonic nations and the Anglo-Saxon of the negro, were cases in which real advance and benefit were shown.

A. H. OLIVE, of Thomasville, Debater for Wake Forest.

Mr. Joe Patton (Wake's 1st Negative) was greeted with a roar of applause as he spoke without notes, vigorously and earnestly, and for eighteen minutes held his audience by his able argument. He held forth, "That by natural methods backward nations will become civilized without being controlled by advanced nations." As to the effect of such control, he cited India and told how it was hampered by English control, brought by greed, similar cases being England's treatment of Egypt, Spain of Mexico and of the Philippines, Belgium of the Congo Free State. He ironically referred to Good King Leopold of Belgium, who allowed mutilation of bodies and slavery in Congo and most sarcastically talked of the treatment of the Filipinos by the United States, saying this country, in a perversion of justice, was trying to work out salvation for the Philippines with ninety-nine percent of fear of those people to one of salvation, called such "missionary politics."

He declared that progress in the United States came after we threw off the English yoke, a sentiment that was cheered. He closed with a strong argument for the negative amidst great applause.

The Farmer and Mechanic claimed that Richmond's 2nd Affirmative (Simons) expressions:

...were peculiar and he brought many a laugh." He cited the case of the control of the Indians and said that the United States was now doing good work in Porto Rico (sic) and the Philippines. You can no more give a backward nation independence without control than you could give a June bug a watermelon, as neither would know what to do with the gift. He said, and later that "Roosevelt may look on the Negro as free, but he does not so regard the Filipino, who is held in subjection... He urged there was a call to the advanced nations to help the backward ones, and that "if they fail to do so God himself would take a hand in it.[30]

Olive (2nd negative – Wake Forest). He held that control of backward nations would be a return to the feudal system of the Middle Ages... The strong have no right to trample on the rights of the weak who bear the stamp of the Divine image."[31]

The Farmer and Mechanic tendered the final word, "So came the glorious victory to Wake last night. The students are proud, so are the faculty, so is Raleigh, so is the State, for we be North Carolinans and Wake Forest's success is North Carolina's success."[32]

*_*_*_*_*_*_*_*

1906 –INTERCOLLEGIATE DEBATE – MERCER – INVITING IMMIGRANTS SOUTH

Southern States should encourage foreign immigrants admitted into this country to settle within their borders.

Mercer, Affirmative, O. C. Griner & C. A. Wells; Wake, Negative, Thomas B. Ashcraft & Jesse B. Weatherspoon

The North Carolinian newspaper assessed the mid-April crowd assembled for the debate headlining Mercer vs. Wake in Raleigh: "Besides a large representation of the cultured people of Raleigh, many students were present from the Baptist University for Women, St. Mary's Schools, and Peace Institute."[33]

---

[30] *The Farmer and Mechanic*, November 29, 1904, page 3.

[31] *The Farmer and Mechanic*, November 29, 1904, page 3.

[32] *The Farmer and Mechanic*, November 29, 1904, page 3.

[33] *The North Carolinian* (Raleigh), April 19, 1906, page 8.

1906 Mercer Debate, Thomas Ashcraft

Perhaps the "cultured people of Raleigh" appreciated both the economic and social disorder arguments allied with the affirmative. The immigration argumentative premises often sound familiar.

Mr. Griner, in opening the affirmative (Mercer), said, "The query raised the question, who are immigrants, and what shall constitute encouragement. 'Immigration,' he said, 'will enable this South to realize the possibilities of its wealth. ... The Negro is a failure, and the Italian or any other nationality is better than the black man, on the farm and in the factory. The quality of our labor is bad, the quantity insufficient.'"

Grinder expanded his argument:

The effect of our inefficient Negro labor is to restrict the South to a cruder type of agriculture. We need imperatively an efficient white labor supply. Foreign immigration is the only recourse the South has... In the South Atlantic States there are only eighteen white persons to the square mile; in the North there are 120. An increased white population would offer a solution to the Negro problem, for it would disperse and displace that race, sending the Blacks to the North and making that section share the burden with us.

Mr. Ashcraft, for the negative (Wake Forest), first observed that the South had not restricted immigration. "The hordes of old countries have not swept over this section" and yet the South prospers.

"The pride of race purity is stronger in the South than in any other section, but immigration would mean social degradation, bringing hordes to us from little Russias and little Polands in our big cities, cursing us with the slums of the North." Later in the speech, Mr. Ashcraft becomes animated:

It is repulsive to every Southerner to think of mixing his children's blood with the blood of the Roumanians (sic), Poles, Hungarians, Russians and Italians. Immigration is our largest contributor to the insane, deformed, criminal and pauper classes in this country. The children of immigrants are twice as criminal as foreign-born and three times as criminal as the children of native whites.[34]

Mr. Wells of Mercer (rebuttal) disagreed, "The greatest object of immigration is to preserve our Southern ideals of civilization, but we cannot do it by building around ourselves a Chinese wall of exclusion. The commingling of races brings out the best in all, and immigration is what has made America the greatest nation on earth. Isolation means stagnation."

Wells' position is steeped in slavery and the aftermath of the Civil War. Immigration helps revive the "Lost Cause." He contends:

Slavery kept the South isolated from the great liberating national movements and gave us crude agriculture instead of the profits from manufactured products. The Civil War was the result of the same force now operating in the South to retard our progress. The coming immigrants means our consequent independence of the Negro, and any labor is preferable to Negro labor. It will increase the white population, and then will Southern men and Southern ideals rule."

Wake Forest's Mr. Weatherspoon's rebuttal eerily reinforces racial prejudice, and he chooses to embrace the known set against the unknown. He maintained:

The negro is here, increasing in numbers, and is here to stay. What will become of him? The foreign immigrant will displace him. He is now performing the lowest work and he must go to our cities, to be the white man's burden, a criminal or a pauper. If we expose our children to these low races of the world, our religion, politics and social life would be prostituted with their base ideas. The South

---

[34] *The North Carolinian* (Raleigh), April 19, 1906, page 8.

would have to abandon for years to come the hope of an educated body politic.

Foreign immigrants bring with them dangerous diseases, they develop and spread, and are a constant menace to public health. Immigrants with their false conceptions of Christ, would prevent the prayers of our religion and mix with it their low morality and desecration of the Sabbath. A large per cent of them Are Roman Catholics, and in the North they are already driving the Bible from the public schools.

State Auditor Dixon, speaking for the judges, determined, "The arguments on both sides were absolutely unanswerable, but I want to say that the South, my friends, is safe, immigration or no immigration, so long as we have among us such young men as the gentleman who have addressed us tonight. We have heard much worse speeches made in the United States Senate... Dixon then stated that Wake Forest had won, and the applause was deafening. The winners were shouldered by enthusiastic Wake Forest students and paraded out of the Academy."[35]

*_*_*_*_*_*_*

FURTHER PUBLIC DEBATES ON RACE — 1911-2014

As public debates entered a more modern era, the public increasingly directed its attention to sports and entertainment. Newspaper coverage of public debates began to disappear. The debates listed below occurred with mostly an in-house audience. Extensive searches failed to uncover any record of manuscripts or traces of what was articulated.

1903 – Intercollegiate Debate – Richmond
  Deportation is the best solution of the Negro problem in the United States.
  Wake, Affirmative, J. N Loftin & J. W. Whisnant; Richmond, Negative, Holman Willis & D. M Simmons
  Wake Won. Held at Richmond Chapel[36]

---

[35] *The North Carolinian* (Raleigh) April 19, 1906, page 8.

[36] The debate seized enough attention that even the preliminary debate to select the debaters who would meet Richmond was covered in the *Richmond Times-Dispatch.*

1911 – Society Day – Sophomore–Junior Debate
The South should encourage the settlement within her borders of such immigrants as are lawfully admitted into the United States.
Jr. Debaters, J. W. Freeman & E. P. Yates, Decision Affirmative, 2–1.

1924 – Society Day Debate
Congress should be authorized to enact a uniform marriage and divorce law, with intermarriage between races prohibited.
Phi, Affirmative, D. D. Lewis, & J. W. King; Eu, Negative, S. L. Blanton & M. G. Stamey, Negative Won.

1965, December – International Public Debate – Britain
That the American dream is at the expense of the American Negro.
England, John Christopher Davies, & Norman S. H. Lamont; Wake, José Cabezas & Jerry Partney

1983, April – International Public Debate – Britain
This house would ban the Ku Klux Klan
Affirmative – Wake: Linda Hippler & David Cheshier; Negative, England: Mark Phillips, & Giles Kavanagh
"National debate team said no to the banning of the Ku Klux Klan and defeated the Wake Forest team." There is no indication of the basis for the decision, whether by a house vote or judges.[37]

2014, October – International Debate – Rwanda
The United Nations should be obligated to intervene militarily in situations of genocide and grave human rights abuse.
Wake: Joe LeDuc & Ryan Wash

The paper speculated that the winners, Loften and Whisnant, upholding the affirmative, would have the "harder side of the question, yet both faculty and students feel that [Wake] is represented by two men who are well able to sustain the college's enviable past record." *Richmond Times-Dispatch*. November 11, 1903, page 7. This 1903 contest debated the same topic as a Wake-Richmond affair held at the same time in Richmond. It would have generated a large audience.

[37] *Old Gold and Black*, April 15, 1983, page 5.

Orations and Race

Orations were part of the program for major events—Anniversary Day, Society Day, and Graduation. Public orations predate public debates by five decades. Not surprisingly, the orations in the post-Civil War years spoke first of tragedy (Civil War), eventually leading to optimism about regional pride (The "New South") and the ability of individuals to remake the world.

The oratorical theme of the "New South" ascending to its rightful place pervaded. Their vision was a future built on citizens whose character was forged in the crucible of the Civil War—brave, tested, exceptional. A relatively early Anniversary Oratory, 1885, by A. T. Robertson, *Rip Van Winkle Awake at Last*, offered lived memories of Reconstruction yet embraced an assurance that, in part, is uniquely reserved for college-age speakers. Robertson's tone, however, was laced less with blame and more with optimism, a prescription for the South's emergence. He holds that the last 20 years since the Civil War had been a "nap" and it was time to wake up. North Carolina [must] shame the loafers and encouraged into action, educate the children, induce native talent to stay at home, and to develop abundant natural resources.[38]

Even earlier, G. C. Briggs, a classmate of Thomas Dixon (valedictorian, commencement speaker in 1883) then editor of *The Wake Forest Student*, published "The Negro in America." The article was probably a version of his graduation speech, which was more enlightened than the position of his classmate, Dixon. He acknowledged the brutal problems facing former slaves and sought a solution. His commentary nevertheless retained intrinsic hints of collective racism. Briggs saw a way forward. He wrote:

> ... As he continues to improve it will give to the Negro material wealth; material wealth will give him influence and the means of moral intellectual culture, and moral, and intellectual culture will ensure the practice of virtue and the proper exercise of civil and political franchise without the detriment to the whites, and with honor and credit to himself.

---

[38] Robertson, A. T. (March 1885). *Rip Van Winkle, Awake at Last, The Wake Forest Student*, page 269-270.

Of course, this important transformation cannot take place at once. The Negro is not so far advanced in civilization as the whites, and hence the modern process of human development is not altogether so well adapted to his being an inherent nature as to the whites have grown up in, with, and by it, and, at the same time, have developed and given force and character to it. It will take generations....

Briggs concludes, "let us elevate the six million and a half of Negroes by a thorough and wholesome education. Education is the only remedy calming and education it must be."[39]

The increasing optimism and parochial celebration of the South's revival continued in the students' oratories. In 1902, one newspaper's coverage of A. J. Bethea, from his oration, *A New South in a New Century,* signals confidence. Nonetheless, the remnants of a War fought forty years earlier remain:

We are standing in the daybreak of a new century. An era of material and moral progress unequaled in the annals of history awaits us. Every section of our republic pulsates with new life. Amid these activities, in this national development in the 20th century, what part is the South to play? Her history of triumph in the past, the inspiration of the present, and her hopes for the future assert that she will stand for valor and virtue, for purity and patriotism, for loyalty and unselfish devotion to duty. The South is destined to become the leading section of this nation.

...No drop of blood poured out between Anastas and Appomattox was shed in vain. The thousands who sacrificed their lives on this country's altar will serve as steppingstones to higher things. The graves of her sons will continue to teach lessons of liberty and patriotism.[40]

Nearly twenty years after the turn of the century, the *Old Gold and Black* cheered in the hyperbolic style: "Lineberry introduced Mr. J. B Carlyle as the representative of the Philomathesian Society." The theme was '*The Lost Cause.*' "We have never yet heard a better speech on this

[39] *The Wake Forest Student*, June, Vol. 2, 1983, page 452-453.
[40] *The Morning Post* (Raleigh), February 15, 1902, page 6.

old theme than was delivered, by Mr. Carlyle. He sketched the cause of the war, dwelt a short while over the battlefields, surveyed the ruins of the old and the rising grandeur of the New South."[41]

More than occasionally, racist overtones clothed student oratories. Disputes continued as to what to do about the "Negro Problem," as with T. B. Ashcraft's untoward 1906 Anniversary Day speech, *The Fate of Inferior Races*.[42] For Ashcraft, civilization advances through inevitable conflict, including "fierce conflicts of races... The struggles for survival are an essential condition of progress and are destined to last long as humanity is to advance. The path of civilization is strewn with the wrecks of nations and their governments, melancholy memorials of the fierce conflicts of races."

Atlanta Race Riot, 1906, occurred the same
year as Ashcraft's Anniversary Day Oration

---

[41] *Old Gold and Black,* February 23, 1918, page 1.
[42] *The Wake Forest Student,* March 25, 1906, page 465-475.

"It is small wonder that the Anglo-Saxon will prevail in the foreseeable future…" He "documents" his certainly by enlisting the demise of the American Indian as evidence of an inevitable progression:

After a struggle of two and a half centuries, the Red Man has been driven to the centre of his hunting ground with the white man's civilization on every side. If he could pull back the silken veil of unborn time, the American Indian would be seen utterly exterminated or lost in the blood of his stabilizers. We may change him from a marauding robber and relentless butcher into a semi-civilized producer, we may take the string of beads from his neck and the feather from his hair, and put the white man's garment on him, and while he may stand 'close,' he is not 'in his right mind,' he has refused to accept the white man's burden." But the great inferior race, whose problem challenges our solution of the present time is the Negro race…Different from the Indian, he accepted servitude…"[43]

Ashcraft's characterizations reach increasing malice:

The Negro has been raised to the level of his master in the eyes of the law, and had been given the full right of suffrage; he has raised himself by education accumulated millions of wealth, but to the white race is inferior still. Inferior because he is imitative not initiative, and is easier to imitate vices than virtues; inferior in family life and social efficacy, possessing of the traits that make the world victorious races" … The contribution he has made to our civilization may be summed up in three words: "Nothing! Nothing! Nothing!" Like some wild animal domesticated, if left to himself he would escape the superior civilization and return to the barbarian whence he came. He is capable of knowledge, but not wisdom, prudence, nor virtue, regret, not remorse.[44]

After building a case of the relative weakness by population growth of the white race, orator John S. Thomas in a speech entitled *Racial Aspects of These Problems* considers solutions to the race problem. Without apology, he advises: "Amalgamation of races presents itself, but I thank

---

[43] *The Wake Forest Student*, March 25, 1906, page 467.
[44] *The Wake Forest Student*, March 25, 1906, page 467-468.

God that there are some things to which we find death preferable... Mexico, Cuba and Brazil well demonstrate this pitiable spectacled man robbed of his ways and stability by conflicting affiliations. Hence amalgamation and immigration must be prevented at all costs."[45]

By our current understanding, the 1899 view would not be described as enlightened (which is itself a reductionist view). Political opinion then, as it does now, gives voice to many expressed points of view. This was also a time when the celebrated Trinity-Wake Forest debates were happening in Raleigh, and a new awakening was arriving on campus.

The 1899 Anniversary celebration featured a highly praised student oration. Entitled *The English Speaking Brotherhood,* by Carlson, asks, "What is the English-speaking brotherhood? ...the kind of alliance we have is from the heart... to stand together in defense of the ideals of the Anglo-Saxon... Our common nationality, the common basis of morality, common forms of government, the common language and common interests," suggests for Carlson that in the "not-too-distant future they will have possession of the whole world in common."[46]

As the young man elaborated on the implications of the "special relationship," the outcomes became less comfortable. He arouses his audience: "I believe that the creator has chosen and united English-speaking people to evangelize the world. I believe this evangelization would be impossible without the English-speaking brotherhood."[47]

People of faraway countries were often thought of as uncivilized who would be saved by the intersection with the enlightened Anglo-Saxon race, armed with certainty and Christianity. It would have been unthinkable for a person of color, a foreign-born, or a woman to attend Wake Forest at that time. The attitudes toward race, however horrific, nonetheless were largely subscribed to in the South throughout the pubic-event debate era. Race as an issue never entirely fades, but campus attitudes profoundly change, as examined in Volume 2 of this series.

---

[45] *The Wake Forest Student,* January 1922, page 172. *The Wake Forest Student* editor noted that the oration "won first place in the Carolina Inter-collegiate Peace Oratorical Contest held in Burlington, NC, April 21, 1922." The speech also blamed Germany for the First World War's white-on-white struggle and held that Christianity is the only religion of peace, and it solely belongs to white cultures.

[46] *The Morning Post* (Raleigh), February 19, 1899, page 8.

[47] *The Morning Post* (Raleigh), February 19, 1899, page 8.

CHAPTER 13

Intercollegiate Era Yields To Tournament Debating

The long-term campus debate about Wake's Literary Societies' proper place in college life reached a crescendo in the early decades of the 20th Century. Many called to reform the "outmoded" Society stranglehold, while for others, the call to tradition appealed, a return to the "Glory Days" when the Phis and Eus oversaw nearly all social life.

Notwithstanding impassioned pleas, the scene in which the Societies conducted themselves was rapidly changing, often with their active support. The transition moved from debates tucked away in society halls, sprinkled with the occasional civic display, to intercollegiate debates connecting to an ever-expanding awareness. Oratorical styles also were changing, becoming more grounded and less bellicose. All of this took place in a reorganized campus curriculum and amid shifts in the progress of surrounding communities.

One astute student observer captured the cultural shift:

Our fathers of the 50s [1850s] were country-bred. For them argumentation meant sermons, Fourth of July orations, and political discussions, public and private. In response to the needs of the day the literary society trained lawyers and statesmen, orators and debaters who lead in the great crisis that tried the souls of men. There was a perfect adjustment between the work of the society and the needs of the nation. That day is past.

We are becoming a nation of dwellers in cities, we whose fathers met, say, once a week; we are hourly in one way or another influencing our neighbor's conduct and opinions. What are the channels of our influence? Least of all the old-time oration in the set debate. The most common of the new methods is the written argument.[1] In the new oratorical order, "the speaker's ideal is that of the 'heightened or animated' conversation."[2]

Debating squads, relatively independent among debating societies in the 1930s, began to carry the day.[3] Possibly the first tournament Wake Forest attended on April 23, 1929, was the regional Pi Kappa Delta Tournament, almost certainly under Louis A. Aycock's headship. The event was won by Wake debaters Joe Carlton and Wade Bostic, perhaps the first Wake tournament winners. A long line would follow.

In 1930, the transition to J. Rice Quisenberry as coach changed the program's tenor to a more active and competitive stance, featuring, for example, an end-of-the-year, ground-breaking, 3000-mile round-trip in a battered jalopy to the Topeka, Kansas, Pi Kappa Delta Tournament.[4]

With the Depression in '29, schools with limited funds met the challenge by "inventing" the common and soon-dominant debate tournament. The tournament drew various schools to one central location, allowing multiple debates at a lower cost. By 1942, Zon Robinson could summarize, "Most decision debating is done today at tournaments. Practically all schools have abandoned the practice of having decisions for single intercollegiate clashes."[5] As a result, the tournament format prospered; it survived depression and war.

Throughout the early 1900s, well into the 1920s, those who succeeded as intercollegiate debaters were campus gods. A 1914 yearbook entry describes one of the debaters, E. P. Stillwell. Their commentary is alive with hyperbole, capturing the attending adoration. The *Howler* narrated:

---

[1] Hubbell, J. B. (1912). The Opportunity of the College Literary Society, *The Wake Forest Student*, Vol. 31, No 6, page 541. The essay is an excellent exposition on the necessary fit between rhetorical training and the society in which it is practiced.

[2] *The Wake Forest Student*, Vol. 31, No 6, March 1912, page 547.

[3] Emerson, J. G. (1931). The Old Debating Society, *Quarterly Journal of Speech*, Vol. 17, page 368.

[4] This adventurous marathon is detailed in Chapter 10 – Transportation: Planes, Trains, and Automobiles.

[5] Robinson, Z. (1942). What happens to speech values in tournament debating, *Southern Speech Bulletin*, Vol. 7, page 123.

Ephram hails from the mountains and partakes in their characteristics, he stands at the front of the class in scholarship, and few rival him and his diligence. His presence, his voice, his looks—they are all persuasive. He stands for the right of everything. If you admire the gentleness and dignity of learning in the quiet reserve, you should make an acquaintance with Stillwell. Everybody recognizes him as a debater. He held the crowd in breathless awe while he delivered his Anniversary speech.[6]

While debaters were viewed as exalted, it was not without stipulation. The 1919 Junior Class historian penned, "Students, athletes, sports, leggers, ladies' men, blockheads, debaters, orators, big eaters—such men compose our class." In the same yearbook, the Ministerial Class History wrote of their membership: "They even ventured into the field of oratory and debate, and with their gas and brass they perplex their worthy competitors many times caring off honors, due only to great men."[7]

To persuade Wake Forest men to try out for the debates in 1914, a contributor to *The Wake Forest Student* wrote, "We make an appeal: Every man who knows how to roar, every man who knows how to bellow, every man who can bray, come out in the preliminary and show us what you can do. Let it not be said that those who represented us in those debates had an easy time to get on the teams. Make them believe that if they get on it they will have to get down and dig."[8]

As worshiped as the debaters were, eminence invites entitlement and exclusivity. Although likely unintended, a hierarchy among debaters developed, with a majority of students unselected for speaking acclaim. Once the top freshmen and sophomores arose, they tended to dominate through to graduation.

As often with such complaints, there resides a touch of "sour grapes." The early coaches worked diligently to expand opportunities with more events. Breaking into the tour's cadre nonetheless remained challenging. There were calls to break up the "cronyism" by opening Intercollegiate Debating to everyone. *The Wake Forest Student* editorialized in 1917:

---

[6] *The Farmer and Mechanic* (Raleigh), March 25, 1913, page 5.

[7] *Howler*, 1919, Junior Class History.

[8] The Open Door, *The Wake Forest Student*, Vol. 33, No. 3, December 1913, page 211.

The time has come for the debating system to be changed. Every student who can ably represent the College should be given a place on an intercollegiate debating team. The debates would be arranged with the view of developing and training as many students as possible in the art of public speaking, and not with the object of bestowing a singular honor upon any particular student or students.[9]

Varsity debaters were functionally picked from the two societies' membership for several years after compulsory membership ended. The top society debaters were skilled and familiar with the national topic debated in their intercollegiate contests. The first non-society-member debaters, William Grogan and Clarence Hyde, were selected for Intercollegiate debating in 1929-30, seven years after mandatory Society membership ended.[10]

The cracks in the intercollegiate debate edifice began appearing earlier, long before public debates were no longer scheduled or attended. As early as 1920, *The Wake Forest Student* called for a renaissance of debate and oratory, observing, "We pride ourselves upon enjoying an enviable reputation in forensic contests. We have been victors in this field far more often than losers, yet it appears that this heavy burden is to be borne by only a few. Poorly prepared speeches, fewer orations, negligence in attendance, and general indifference in both societies show where the winds lie. In some cases, the aspirants for medals given in oratory and debate are so few that the contest is barely interesting. The value of a medal is not intrinsic but extrinsic."[11]

Complaints about the societies' demise were posed both to keep the members in line and as genuine critiques. Cycles of dissipation and revival had a rhetorical rhythm, attempts to gather momentum even as the organizations' influence dwindled.[12]

---

[9] Even after mandatory society memberships ended, the societies still controlled the makeup of intercollegiate teams, each with representatives for the selection process.

[10] *The Wake Forest Student,* January 1917.

[11] *The Wake Forest Student,* Vol. 40, 1920, page 84.

[12] A pithy example of muted "revival," aimed at alumni in a 1929 *Wake Forest Alumni News,* is notable for its attempt to breathe optimism into Societies' contribution. Another perspective might be that the affiliation with Pi Kappa Delta National was a move away from Society dominance. "There has been so much said in recent years about the 'dying' Literary Societies at Wake Forest and the decay of oratory that it will be somewhat surprising to some to learn that three men, now students here

The charm of public debates was swiftly fading, as *The Student* suggests above. A 1934 "major" invited opponent (Vermont) emphasizes the ending enthusiasm: "Tuesday night in the Euzelian Literary Society Hall, two representatives of the forensic team of Wake Forest met in a non-decision contest with a team from the University of Vermont. There were present six people–the four debaters, the chairman, and the time-keeper. Students made themselves conspicuous by their absence. We wonder what impression was left on the minds of the visiting speakers."[13]

The transition story from intercollegiate debate to full tournaments requires a loose parsing. History seldom cooperates with clear-cut epochal shifts. The intercollegiate era lasted for nearly thirty years, with its final act drawn out over a decade. Proportions shifted slowly, a process often not altogether within a coach's control.

The unfolding transition is best told through the lens of "mini-epochs" defined by the Wake debate coaches' respective engagements. Four coaches are highlighted, along with an Interim coach and a sampling of consequential student debaters.

George Washington Paschal – "Coach" Indeterminate – 1928

George Washington Paschal, the father of Wake Forest history, was a guiding force for the debating societies for decades. He often spoke before the assembled students, judged tryouts for most every intercollegiate

---

have won the degree of special distinction offered by the Pi Kappa Delta Debating Fraternity composed of teams from two hundred colleges and universities. This degree is given to the student who has won sixteen intercollegiate debates; the three men are Cloyce R. Tew of Raleigh, Joe Carlton of Winston-Salem, and Wade Bostic of Japan. These men have made a record that has never been remotely approached by any man in the history of the college. Wake Forest has engaged this year in nineteen intercollegiate debates; winning some and losing some, the idea being to develop debaters rather than to win debates. One team debated four colleges and won each debate (but there were four teams sent out by the societies). Professor A. L. Aycock has rendered splendid service to the college as debate coach. *Wake Forest Alumni News*, Vol. 1, No. 4, May 1929, page 2.

[13] *Old Gold and Black*, April 7, 1934, page 2.

G. W. Paschal – Informal Coach

team, and served as an advisor and "coach" to debaters about to join a tour.[14]

There is no exact beginning date for his debate/Societies' mentorship. His involvement matured from joining the faculty to handing off the coach's role in 1928, across thirty years of continued participation in student debating.

Paschal is referred to as Coach as early as 1925, and likely informally held that role before.[15] A 1928 *Old Gold and Black* story left no uncertainty about his on-campus identity:

---

[14] For this volume, Paschal is best remembered for his impressive three volumes, *The History of Wake Forest*. Paschal, however, is more widely known for his extensive history writings in *The Biblical Recorder*, a multivolume history of North Carolina Baptists, among other historical books. He also was a busy man on campus, serving as a professor of Latin and Greek, the library curator, a college bill collector, and the college's first and longtime registrar. He even was, for many years, director of athletics teams, personally and financially responsible for the teams... Paschal was an 1886 Wake graduate. Lacking money for college, Paschal worked three years in Greensboro before entering Wake Forest College in 1889. While he was editor of *The Wake Forest Student*, a literary magazine, his writing ability became evident. The A.B. degree was conferred in 1892. He did his Ph.D. at the University of Chicago, returning to Wake Forest in 1896 as assistant professor of Latin and Greek. Laura Ann, his wife, and G. W. had ten children, all earning at least one degree from Wake Forest. *George Washington Paschal*, by Henry S. Stroupe, 1994, www.ncpedia.org/biography/paschal-george-washington; Paschal's three-volume history was said by competent critics to have "contained more details of people and events, activities of students, and relationships of denominational and private college to the state institution than any other college histories ever written." *Wake Forest College Alumni News*, Vol. 13, No. 1, October 1943, page 6.

[15] "It is true that the College has been represented by able men, but no little part of success has been due to the able coaching by Dr. G. W. Paschal." *Old Gold and Black*, May 18, 1925, page 1.

No résumé of Wake Forest debating would be complete without a few words about Dr. Paschal. Such successes we have must be attributed in a large measure to the untiring efforts of our coach. We feel it is not saying too much to class him as the best and most able debate coach in the State, yes, even in the South. It is certain that all men who have had an opportunity to work under him have emerged from the experience much helped by the contact with this able man.[16]

Paschal, writing in the third person, describes himself in his *The History of Wake Forest College,* Vol. III, as the "Debate Coach":

Each debater then proceeded to write his own speech and the team was ready for a hearing before the committee of the faculty appointed for the purpose. Almost invariably on this committee were President Poteat and Professor Paschal, the former of whom, being a master of debate himself, was especially helpful in all matters of composition and delivery, while Professor Paschal had nearly always read largely on the question debated and was able to give advice on choice and arrangement of arguments, and on this account came to be regarded as debate coach."[17]

In an early 1912 essay, G. W. Paschal outlines the factors that underlie successful debate training. "Having something to say is no less important than knowing how to say it, and to have something to say one must learn how to think... No one must suppose that he is thinking when he is only reproducing the thoughts of someone else, whether speech in his literary society or in a written thesis."

---

[16] *Old Gold and Black*, May 16, 1928, page 2. Major area newspapers also celebrated Paschal as coach. A 1927 *News & Observer* correspondent wrote: "The intercollegiate debaters and everyone else interested in the progress and success of Wake Forest in debating are very appreciative of the splendid and exceptionally thorough coaching of Dr. G. W. Paschal, who has been untiring in his efforts to coach Wake Forest men for the high standards of debating." *The News & Observer*, June 5, 1927, page 22.

[17] Paschal, G. W. (1948). *The History of Wake Forest College*, Vol. III, page 102; "Documenting that Paschal was the "debate coach" is undertaken here because it has generally been assumed that formal coaching began with faculty appointed for the task, perhaps Quisenberry and certainly Robinson. Paschal's status as the "debate coach" may have been informal, reflecting circumstances that he grew into without the College's formal acknowledgment.

He adds, "I do not mean that he must not make use of arguments made by others on the question for debate, but we must not make his speech a patchwork of arguments culled bodily from this source and that.... Borrowed plumage soon falls off."[18]

Paschal's era was more one of advisor for a time when only intercollegiate debate prevailed. [19] Soon, transportation, financial means, and an expanded vision would gel to make expansion to tournament debate inevitable, changing the mindset of the college itself.[20]

A. Louis Aycock – Interim Coach – 1928-1931

In 1928-29, Professor A. L. Aycock of the Department of English took responsibility for giving a more definite direction to the work of the society-chosen intercollegiate debaters.[21]

---

[18] G. W. Paschal, "A Bachelor of arts degree," *The Wake Forest Student*, Vol. 31, No. 7, April 1912, page 611-2. The Paschal essay lays out his advice for training public speakers.

[19] Paschal's interest in debate continued unabated throughout his busy life. He also continued as advisor, often addressing or judging at the Society events and meetings. Just as enduringly, Paschal was an advisor to the college. *Presenting at the Chapel session in 1935, he addressed the "attributes of a perfect gentleman."* He noted that Dr. Charles E. Taylor, former president, exemplified everything that a gentleman should be. He cited the qualities Aristotle considered necessary: self-confidence, goodness, frankness, courage, and adherence to the Golden Rule, *Old Gold and Black*, February 2, 1935, page 1.

[20] It is possible that for a brief period in 1927, following Dr. Paschal, Dr. H. B. Jones may have coached the team. Jones worked with the debaters without question. An English teacher, he is the same Jones who rode the celebratory buckboard following the victorious 1909 Randolph Macon debate.

[21] Andrew Lewis Aycock joined the faculty in 1920, a former Wake Forest undergraduate who served for 43 years as an English literature and composition teacher. From the beginning and for decades, he established a strong connection with art. From 1941 onward, he was the Curator of the Wake Forest College Museum of Art. He gave personal leadership to conserving the Simmons Art Collection on the old campus and its safe removal to Winston-Salem. Almost single-handedly, he maintained and greatly expanded the university's collection of art slides, which was then one of the best collections in the Southeast. Mr. Aycock's versatility led him briefly into administrative work. When the Office of Admissions was set up in July 1957, he became its first director. His colleagues saw in him the truth of Emerson's observation about the true scholar: "Character is higher than intellect."

Aycock's first tenure as coach was short-lived. His work primarily consisted of fulfilling the slate of Intercollegiate debates. For two years, his submitted records were primarily reports of tournament results and normal achievements, which placeholders provided to administrators. His more prolonged influence occurred later, during the challenging World War II years, when he stepped in from 1941 to 1948 to replace Zon Robinson as Director of Forensics, whose story is told

1943 Louis Aycock, Coach,
and Debater Bill McGill

below. Comments on Aycock's forensics contribution are reserved for that section.

J. Rice Quisenberry – The First
Selected Coach – 1930-1936

In 1930, Professor J. Rice Quisenberry of the Department of English took charge of the debating program at Professor Aycock's request. He hit the ground running, boosting Wake debate's aura.

Along with an ongoing Intercollegiate Debate schedule, including several tours, the tournament era begins under J. Rice Quisenberry. He announced the 1930 schedule,[22]... for the approaching spring semester will consist of about 30 meets.[23]

---

[22] *Old Gold and Black,* January 25, 1930, page 1.

[23] Quisenberry inevitably put the best spin on the team's activities. By "30 meets," he refers to 30 individual campus debates, many at other institutions, not 30 tournaments. The article indicates the planning for nine debates, two on the way to the Pi Kappa Delta Nationals in Wichita, Kansas, with Emory and Howard College of Birmingham, and seven on the return trip at Ottawa, Kansas, Westminster College, Bloomington, Illinois, Illinois Wesley and, Franklin College, Indiana, Marietta

This Photo's caption accompanying an *Old Gold and Black* story about the team's success: "Dr. J. Rice Quisenberry, wo will again act as puppeteer for the Wake Forest most successful extracurricular activity."

In the meantime, the Societies urgently requested that the College take responsibility for financing and directing the debate activity, feeling especially the pinch of funding extended tours, and the faculty approved. "During this year [1931], the Societies and the College shared the expense. About forty debates were held, and about 50% were won by Wake Forest teams; eight or ten of these contests all told eighteen or twenty men took part in these debates, most of the men debating in more than one debate.

A team of two debaters attended the Biennial National Tournament of Pi Kappa Delta fraternity, held in Wichita, Kansas, in the spring of 1930. About 140 colleges were represented. The Wake Forest team was the only team east of the Mississippi to reach the semifinals."[24]

Quisenberry had his ways of exerting pressure (even through others) for a better budget; in this effort, he was partially successful.[25] He appealed, "Because of a cut in the appropriation for the forensic endeavor, the size of the debate schedule was not quite that of last year, and the teams did not cover as much mileage. Also, some of the debates away from the campus were in tournaments. However, it has been found that

---

College, Ohio, University of West Virginia, and State Teachers College, Farmville Virginia, an ambitious trip for sure. A detailed description of the heroic trip and vanquished opponents can be found in Chapter 10, Planes, Trains, And Automobiles – Transportation Recasts Debate.

[24] *Wake Forest College Alumni News*, 1931, page 3-4.

[25] The College appropriated $300 for debating. This doubled the amount given the previous year. *Old Gold and Black*, October 11, 1930, page 2

Wake Forest teams get more support at tournaments than they are accustomed to at home. Let's try giving them a little more."[26]

Quisenberry's tendency to embellish is exhibited when he claimed that Wake Forest was the only school regularly recognized in debating circles as a leading challenger without a regular speech department and at least one full-time man in the department.[27]

The Wake Forest Alumni News officially characterized the financial situation: "The college has appropriated—on average—something less than $250 a year to finance this whole program. No student gets any pay or special financial consideration for his debating ability or any grades on his debating."[28]

The *Howler* was an apparent Quisenberry enthusiast:

A greater part of the phenomenal success of the Wake Forest Debate teams in the last few years of tournament debating is due to Dr. Quisenberry, who while carrying his full load of academic courses, has given himself whole-heartedly to the continuance of the tradition that a Wake Forest man should be able to think clean and fast, and talk from his feet fairly and with conviction. Dr. Quisenberry is unrequited for this service at Wake Forest except for the devotion of the men who have worked under his guidance. [29]

Quisenberry was not reticent to engage in the competition of his era. For example, double debates were held in Atlanta and Richmond on the same evening. The coach shared the telegram exchange:

"We have met the enemy, and they are ours!" Is the substance of the telegram sent to Dr. J. R. Quisenberry, Wake Forest debate coach, at Richmond when W. H. Ford. And W. M. Grogan won the decision for the negative side of the hotly contested debate on Free Trade with representatives of Emory University, Atlanta in the Eu Hall Wednesday night.

---

[26] *Howler*, 1933, page 176.

[27] This refrain was often offered in the Quisenberry, and later, eras but the claim is doubtful. Most teams operated with English department faculty, as at Wake.

[28] *Wake Forest Alumni News*, May 1934, Vol. 3, page 18.

[29] *Howler*, 1932, page 177.

Dr. J. R. Quisenberry, Wake Forest debate coach, and H. H. Deaton and E. L. Smith, Wake Forest first-team debaters, were in Richmond at the University of Richmond, leaving the task of defeating Emory to the second team. According to several witnesses, the debate was one of the season's closest and most interesting debates.[30]

In Atlanta, at the Southern Association of Teachers of Speech tournament, Dr. Quisenberry gained a distinction in judging debates as he was on five decision committees. Out of the 10 votes other than his own, eight agreed with him. All of Dr. Quisenberry's votes were for the winning team.[31]

Quisenberry often parlayed wins into assumed "championships," sometimes nearly the case, sometimes just good public relations. For example, the *Old Gold and Black* was prompted to include:

Although for several years in North Carolina, there has been no official championship series or title, Wake Forest has a clean slate in all three of her "Big Five" encounters. A difficulty in establishing a claim to the unofficial title is that Wake had not met North Carolina or Duke on the platform this year. Supporters of the Deacons, however, pointed out that Wake Forest offered contracts to both of these institutions early in the season and has won twice from State College, which in turn holds two debate decisions over the University.[32]

Tournament debate got its sea legs under Quisenberry in the early '30s. The team was contracted for fewer public debates and made more appearances at national tournaments, including the 1933 Pi Kappa Delta tournament in Tulsa, OK. Debating honors at Tulsa went to the team of Harold Denton and Leonidas Smith. As coach Quisenberry put it, "only 27 of the 102 entries went further in the contest." The news, however, was that "the office of Governor of the South Atlantic province was brought to Wake Forest by the election of its coach, Professor J. Rice Quisenberry, to this position."[33]

---

[30] *Old Gold and Black*, March 28, 1931, page 1.

[31] *Old Gold and Black*, May 2, 1931, page 1.

[32] *Old Gold and Black*, April 21, 1931, page 4.

[33] *The News & Observer*, April 7, 1932, page 3. Quisenberry was reelected as province governor in 1933, *Old Gold and Black*, April 8, 1933, page 1.

Quisenberry was also somewhat of a self-promoter, often quoted and pictured in stories about the team. One gets the sense he, understandably, was the source of the newspaper articles. One *Old Gold and Black* article featuring the then-upcoming national trip to Tulsa, Oklahoma, stated, "The debate team will be directed on the trip by Dr. J. Rice Quisenberry, the Wake Forest forensic coach. Dr. Quisenberry has been coaching here for the last three years and has made an immutable record as a Director of Speech."[34] To his credit, he understood media and campus reputations.

Quisenberry was not shy about sharing his sharp expectations and what it would take to reach those goals: "We do not have affirmative debaters and negative debaters, but just debaters." He also stated that speeches are not handed out neatly typewritten to the debaters, but that each man must write and deliver his own speech and succeed or fall on its merits."[35]

The key was hard work and originality. The neophytes reporting for debate work were warned by Dr. Quisenberry that "it was not a job for men who were not willing to expend plenty of effort and energy, stating that the only way men could advance on a team was "to do an analysis of the question, followed by the formation of a brief, then attack the brief for the location and strengthening of weaknesses, followed by repetition of the process."[36]

"Dr. Quisenberry assigns no readings to be done, he does not call the role, it requires no student work who does not want to work. However, if a debater was to become a member of the varsity debate team, and to be taken on the debate tours and to the forensic tournaments, he must work hard and faithfully."[37]

The Intercollegiate Debate Council principally regulated everything debate, with the core mission of negotiating upcoming intercollegiate debates. What is interesting here is that Dr. Quisenberry was a member of the Council and an active tournament coach. In the later Debate Council era, scheduling a tour featuring on-campus single debates was undoubtedly less complex than in the early days when cities and destination communities were more challenging to reach. A letter, albeit more official, is slow. Negotiations started a year or more in advance.

---

[34] *Old Gold and Black*, March 19, 1932, page 1.

[35] *Old Gold and Black*, November 25, 1933, page 1.

[36] *Old Gold and Black*, October 21, 1933, page 1.

[37] *Old Gold and Black*, October 21, 1933, page 1.

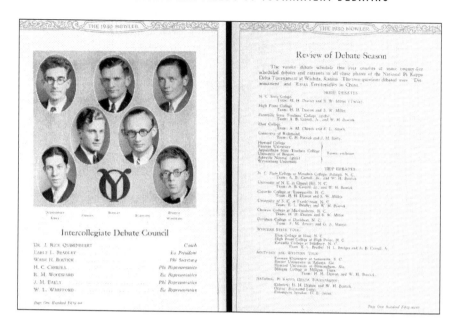

Intercollegiate Debate Council

Dr. J. Rice Quisenberry	Coach
Earl J. L. Bradley	Ex-President
Wade H. Bostick	Phi Secretary
H. C. Carroll	Phi Representative
B. M. Woodward	Eu Representative
J. M. Early	Phi Representative
W. L. Wrefford	Eu Representative

Until the mid-1930s, weekly meeting debates were reported in the school paper, sometimes in surprising detail. Most *Old Gold and Black* issues carried numerous debate articles, at times five or six on the front page. Covering a Phi meeting in 1934, hoping to inject some linguistic drama into a story, the reporter noted: "Despite the *vigorous onslaught* of the negative, H. R. Ellington and Russell Van Landingham, the judges awarded the decision to the affirmative."[38]

The weekly discussions were not as stolid as one might anticipate. During a 1934 meeting the debaters bantered over compulsory control of agriculture while an orator talked about the advent of "radio and the need for a revolution," John Peele reviewed Eugene O'Neill's play, "Days Without End." One imitated Emily Post advising speakers on etiquette while other speakers defended George Washington from the "cheap calamities with which a few modern biographers have tried to belittle the man who, Mr. Hewlett, insisted, still stands 'first in war, first in peace, and first in the hearts of his countrymen.'"[39] Poetry and impromptu speeches rounded out the meeting. Measured by length, some meetings must have been arduous.

---

[38] *Old Gold and Black*, February 24, 1934, page 6.
[39] *Old Gold and Black*, February 24, 1934, page 6.

The gatherings were indeed a potpourri of experiment and entertainment. Discussions outside the normal bounds were routine. And on rare occasions, the meeting did not convene, in favor of a more pressing agenda. At the same week's meeting in 1934, "Both sections of the society decided to discontinue meetings during revival week, and all members were exhorted to attend the services conducted by the Rev. John R. Sampey."

Sampey, a teacher of the Bible for 44 years, was to provide a ten-day series of Special services, twice a day. College classes were shortened to fit the revival's schedule and professors agreed to lighten the regular and required amount of work."[40] Deeply conservative strains still resided in the Societies and the college.[41]

Religious exultation was not the only interference vying for the busy debater's attention. In 1933 and 1934 the students busied themselves with tours and tournaments as well as hosting Intercollegiate Debates, then a two-year-long disturbance arrived in the form of arson.

"In the glare of the great fire which lighted up all the Campus, throngs of students, members of the faculty and town people looked on in sadness as the majestic old structure burned out. Perhaps the greatest emotion was aroused by the loss of the bell, the molten ruins of which were found in the ashes the next day."[42] On May 5th, 1933, a fire destroyed the old college building, Wait Hall.

"An engineer on a passing train saw flames arising from...Wait Hall. He immediately telegraphed the Raleigh Fire Department for help, but the truck came too late to save any of the structure. Ninety-six students living in the wing were able to get out with nearly all of their belongings, but Wait Hall burned completely down."[43]

---

[40] *Old Gold and Black,* February 24, 1934, page 1; John R. Sampey was Southern Baptist Theological Seminary's fifth president. He was three times president of the Southern Baptist Convention. https://archives.sbts.edu/the-history-of-the-sbts/our-presidents/john-r-sampey-1928-1942/.

[41] Quisenberry spoke on religion to various campus groups. For example, in 1928, "he addressed the Volunteer Band... on the general theme, "the Prerequisites of Mission Work."" *Old Gold and Black,* March 24, 1928, page 1.

[42] Paschal, G. W. (1948). *History of Wake Forest College,* Vol. III. As identified and appearing in Jenny Puckett's *Thine Ancient Days: A WFU History: 1818-1956,* page 166.

[43] Henry S. Stroupe, Professor Emeritus of History, in a conversation with Jenny Puckett, *Thine Ancient Days: A WFU History: 1818-1956,* page 166. The fire

Other fires followed, including a community-wide loss when the Wake Forest High School was destroyed in May. On February 14, 1934, one semester after the Wait Hall fire, another staggering fire occurred, destroying the Chapel and Wingate Memorial *Old Gold and Black* headline the next day read:

Early Tuesday Morning Blaze Causes Inmates of Dormitory to Move Out Belongings
FIRE SAID TO BE OF INCENDIARY ORIGIN.

Despite the fact that the blaze was a comparatively small one, boys in the vicinity the flames, distrustful of the efficacy of the local fire department, hastily girding up their loins, piled out of the student quarters within a few minutes.

Trunks bumped their torturous way down one, two and three flights of stairs behind the frantic tugs of their owners. Heavy baggage was lugged out by the joint efforts of the two. Still others were swirling bedclothes clutched in one arm and a load of shirts, ties, etc. and the other, vacated the building. Mounds of trunks, clothing and other belongings begin to pile up in the cold, frozen campus grounds, while the fire department made its most prompt arrival of the year.[44]

Discovery that the fire... seemed man-made, which strengthened the assertion of many students that the series of disastrous fires... were of incendiary origin. "I don't believe that many buildings could catch on fire by themselves all the same time of night," Dr. Thurman D. Kitchin, president of Wake Forest College, told the Associated Press."[45]

Finally, on March 2, a fire demolished the Wake Forest golf clubhouse. Using bloodhounds, a trail led to a sleeping student in Hunter dorm.[46] No one was ever arrested for the fires, but no more occurred after the late-night canine shakedown. The campus arson, certainly tragic, ultimately led to modernizing the campus, but it does remind the reader that

---

occurred less than a month after the Reichstag Fire in Berlin, which hastened the terror of Hitler.

[44] *Old Gold and Black,* February 24, 1934, page 1.

[45] *Old Gold and Black,* February 24, 1934, page 1.

[46] *Old Gold and Black,* March 3, 1934, page 1, 6.

debaters of that era (as with all eras) dealt with life's complexities even as they simultaneously excelled in the debate world.

Throughout the campus calamity, the Quisenberry era flourished, with the team hosting a sizable number of campus debates, eight in 1935. One was with UNC, as *The Daily Tarheel* reported. The affairs appeared gentle yet with import, meeting a U.S. Senator:

> Norman Kellar and Don Seawell, representing the University debate squad, journey to Wake Forest tonight to uphold the affirmative of the query: Resolved, that the nations of the world should agree to prevent the shipment of arms and munitions. Francis Fairly and Winthrop Durfee will accompany Kellar and Seawell...
>
> Next Sunday evening a group of Wake Forest debaters will be guests of the University. They will hear United States Sen. Gerald P. Nye of North Dakota speak on the munition's situation.[47]

Several styles of debate were experimented with during the Quesinberry years, including the "Carolina Plan" of debating with four debaters on each team.[48] "The affirmative presents one phase of the question in a speech of two minutes and the negative is given two minutes for rebuttal. This continues until the four speakers for each side have been heard. Then, three judges decided which team had the advantage in this phase. The winning side gets one point. The order is continued until one team scores at least four points, including a two-point margin over the opposition. If no team can secure the two-point lead, the contest is called a draw."[49]

Debating other colleges, particularly North Carolina State, employed the early application of the "Direct Clash Debate." "The plan involves a simple statement of the case, where each side's plan was presented before the debate proper started. The Affirmative initiates an argument in three minutes. Then there are six two-minute answers, alternating affirmative and negative. Then the negative assumes the initiation of argument and takes the defensive in every other clash. The form, which NC State

---

[47] *The Daily Tar Heel* (Chapel Hill), February 22, 1935, page 1.

[48] The Carolina plan of debating was used for the first time between intercollegiate teams when representatives from Wake Forest and State met in a non-decision contest at the Peace Institute on Thursday night, February 25, 1935.

[49] *Old Gold and Black*, February 27, 1932, page 1.

continued to promote for many years, was curious enough to be of interest in a general announcement in the *Old Gold and Black* (see insert).

There was some talk of using the "Oregon Plan" which employed direct cross-examination, distinct from the Oxford Style of dueling speeches. Contests using cross-examination became very popular at the University of North Carolina. *The Daily Tarheel* article noted a non-decision debate that "showed the value of the Oregon plan to bring out critical points of discussion." It was seen as better for "training speaking under conditions which prevail in the business and political world."[50]

irect Clash

State College's debate squad will present an exhibition of "direct clash" debating at seven o'clock tonight in the Euezlian Hall.

State originated this special form of forensics several years ago and has since taken the lead in popularizing it throughout the nation.

The public is invited to the event, which will last somewhat less than an hour, according to local debate sources.

Building an Audience – *Old Gold and Black*, March 1946

Scant evidence exists that Wake adopted the Oregon style. "Oxford Style" was not fully abandoned in the East until the late 1960s when most adopted the more interactive cross-examination format.

Over his tenure, Quisenberry became a fan of the "Non-decision" for Intercollegiate public campus debates.

In his first year, the coach had a strong mix of decision and nondecision debates; a preponderance of the former occurred with important events: Temple, Emory, and Davidson. We know other lower-profile debates also were decision affairs, specifically the Asheville and Farmville female team encounters, typically hosted on their campus, and which Wake routinely lost.

---

[50] *The Daily Tar Heel*, January 8, 1932, page 1. The original Oregon-style debate was elaborate with two twenty-minute constructive followed by two consecutive 10-minute cross-examinations. That would be interesting. Later the C-X was integrated with a more familiar sequence of speeches. See Stanley, G. J. (1926). The Oregon Style of Debating, *Quarterly Journal of Speech Education*, Vol. 12.

"Wake Forest has debated in decision contests only schools of reputation and importance." Large draws like Bates (Maine) in 1936 and Colgate in 1939 had decisions and were long-standing crowd pleasers, as were Richmond and Furman.

By the 1934-35 school year, the only decision debates were at tournaments they attended (three). The Intercollegiate debates were all non-decision (29 of them). Thus, the team's overall record was not placed in jeopardy.

At another level, some debates were simply "warmup debates" in preparation for the later tournament encounters. The annual series of nondecision debates with State College in Raleigh was "intended to accustom both squads to debating against intercollegiate competition without endangering either team's season record. Coaches Quisenberry and Paget [NC State Coach] feel that these debates have been very helpful in accomplishing this purpose."[51]

Quisenberry glorified the year's record in building support for his team. He bragged in percentage terms, claiming various victory margins, 60 percent, 70 percent. In 1931, he extolled, "The Wake Forest debating squad has engaged in 10 debates this season, losing only one decision, being defeated by the team of beautiful young ladies from Farmville Teachers College, Farmville, Va. They began the year by trouncing the State College debaters into consecutive trials.[52]

In a season summary report penned by Quisenberry, the paper reported, "Eight men have participated in fifty-seven debates, and over 20 men have been given training in the debate squad meetings. Of the total number of debates, thirty have been decision contests. Wake Forest won seventy-three percent of that number. This record beats the one set last year and the year's previous win when Wake Forest boasted of the famous Deaton-Smith combination."

Quisenberry not only protected his win percentages, but as mentioned before, he also had a penchant for defining a series of wins as championships. He told the student newspaper, "By reason of their double win over Davidson last week, the Wake Forest college freshman debaters won

---

[51] *Old Gold and Black*, January 23, 1932, page 3. In 1942-3 the team began the year with a tour of Western NC, TN, and VA. All debates were non-decision, "but were primarily to lay the groundwork for later direct clash decision contests."

[52] *Old Gold and Black*, March 21, 1931, page 1, 4.

the unofficial title of State Freshman Champions. Of the eight debates, the Baby Deacons lost only one."

He seemed to especially relish the contests with State College. A headline in 1934 read, "**National Champions**" Go Down in Defeat By 2-1... last night in Memorial Hall to the Wake Forest debate team, composed of Donald G Myers and Jack Murchison..." [53] Murchison and Myers were consistent winners.

Excerpts from a 1934 *Old Gold and Black* entry chronicling an extended trip for the Southern Tournament in Birmingham, AL, is a noteworthy instance of the team's mission and the celebration of its heroes:

> The Davidson Wildcats proved the first victim in the Deacon's first invasion of the South in four years. Murchison and Myers won a decision over Fitzgerald and Murphy and one of the most hotly contested debates of the season.
>
> Emory University was the scene for two novel debates. The Epworth League sponsored a debate on Humanism versus Theism. Methodism reeled and rocked as representatives of the Wesley Citadel told of the wonders of humanism. The defenders of the faith—Murchison and Myers—scored a technical debate knockout when they accused the Emory speakers of being technocrats. In a second non-decision debate held at the Atlanta school, the Deacon debaters didn't fare so well when they tried to defend a proposal for governmental ownership and control of radio.
>
> Wake Forest representatives were unusually honored when they were chosen with the University of Florida to stage a demonstration

---

[53] *Old Gold and Black,* February 24, 1934, page 1. Quisenberry often featured the exploits of Murchison and Myers to promote his program. For example, an extended article covering the Tenth Biennial Convention of Pi Kappa Delta, reported, "By virtue of five wins out of seven debates...Jack Murchison and Donald Myers...is now rated among the first eighteen teams of the United States. ...138 colleges and Universities from 32 states participated. The Deacon speakers conquered debate teams from Carroll College, Waukesha, Wisconsin; Illinois State Normal; University; Sioux Falls College; University of Akron; South Dakota State College. The school lost to were among the strongest in the nation. They were South Dakota State Teachers College, and Gustavus Adolphus College of St. Peter, Minnesota. The last-named school was declared national Champions when, in the tenth round of debate, they defeated Augustana College." In the mid-1930s, these were most likely exotic opponents. We can also note the level of detail the paper judged of interest to its readers. *Old Gold and Black*, April 14, 1934, page 1.

LAW SENIORS

JOHN C. MURCHISON, LL.B.
Rocky Mount, North Carolina
ΓΗΓ
Phi Society 1, 2, 3; Golden Bough;
Pi Kappa Delta; Class Historian 1;
Student Council 2; Old Gold and
Black 5; Debate Team 1, 2, 3, 4,
Manager 4; Society Day Debater 3;
Founder's Day Debater 3.

WOODROW H. PETERSON, LL.B.
Clinton, North Carolina

debate before the seventeen hundred Woodlawn High School students, at Birmingham. Indications are that those boys and girls were completely sold on the idea of debating. One radio program was given by the winners of the tournament in which Myers spoke on the subject: "A College Student Looks at the Recovery program."

The individual team record of Murchison and Myers is seventy-six percent.[54]

Murchison also received some light-hearted kidding in the student newspaper:

Jack Muchison's tongue has traveled about 3000 feet – more than a half mile – of gummed envelope acts during his five-year sojourn among us, arithmetic shows. The coeds, who usually smear on enough lipstick to cover several barns, have nothing on this son of Rocky Mount. He spurns sponges and wholesale methods when a whole batch of letters has to be sealed. "I like the taste he explains. His tongue has also helped make the Wake Forest debating team 70% successful during the year that he was a champion debater and extemp speaker. The News Bureau dictionary, North Carolina's postal guide, and the Wake Forest catalog are not necessary when Jack is around; he already has many of the important facts in his head.[55]

---

[54] *Old Gold and Black,* April 28, 1934, page 1.

[55] *Old Gold and Black*, February 8, 1936, page 6.

Quisenberry unknowingly entered his last year of coaching in 1936, and the student paper wrote, "This year's squad has intact the splendid record set by Deacon debate squads in the past six years. Over the period of years, teams coached by J. Rice Quisenberry have a grand average is slightly better than 65% somewhere between 100 and 125 debates in all."

Quisenberry's era was not always serious, and the quips in campus press suggest he was adored. In the 1930s, *The Wake Forest Student* interspersed brassy quotations to enliven the copy. A 1935 entry took a shot at one of the debaters, Mr. McMillan:

Archie McMillan: Dr. Quizenberry (sic), don't you think we could use this book on the debate?

Dr. Quizenberry: Maybe so. Last night I wanted to use the whole thing on your rebuttal[56]

Quisenberry was popular enough with students that he merited comments on monkey business in his class. "Between the rounds of speech-making in Dr. Quisenberry's public sleeping class, rounds of pantomimes are given. The professors here are the usual objects and I wonder whether they would take such great delight at the sight of their pupils attempting to reproduce their outstanding characteristics and numerous humorous oddities."[57]

On occasion, the paper was not above taking a shot at other schools (and the Wake debaters). Since the more esoteric national topic was used for nearly all intercollegiate contests, its appeal wore thin.[58] *The Old Gold and Black* noted, "Maryland and Carolina were to have a debate

---

[56] *The Wake Forest Student*, November 1935, page 13. Archie McMillian, a debater from Shanghai, China, became editor of the *Old Gold and Black* his senior year.

[57] *Old Gold and Black*, March 23, 1935, page 2.

[58] The 1921 Davidson debate illustrates how national propositions dominated the contested topics in the 1920s and '30s. The Friday evening topic asked whether *The U.S. should cancel loans and war debts from World War I allies*. Perhaps in a retrenchment mode, Wake, on the negative, argued that the US "had performed her full share in the winning of the war and that the victorious nations had received sufficient indemnities from the central powers to make cancellation unnecessary... 'They made the fur fly', *Old Gold and Black*, April 22, 1921, page 2. We did our part, and we expect to be compensated," page 1.

on the much-abused disarmament question, and not until the first speaker was announced was it discovered that all four of the speakers were on the affirmative side."[59]

The inclination for self-congratulation is hardly unique to Wake Forest debaters. The practice of lauding the college speaking tradition held constant throughout the program's history. As with most claims, the embellishments contain some truth, resulting in a guiding myth. An amusing overstatement from the 1933 yearbook declared, "It is highly improbable that any other school in the nation has traveled more miles, given more men experience, won more contests, and established a better reputation for clean, hard competition than has Wake Forest." Others might have happily taken the negative on this claim.

EDWARD LEONIDAS SMITH – 1929-1933[60]

One of Quisenberry's star debaters was E. Leonidas Smith, who shined in an era increasingly dominated by athletic heroes. Top debaters still achieved "big-man-on-campus" status, but the days were numbered. Leonidas did achieve some athletic fame as well when, in 1932, he became "the head cheerleader of Wake Forest, responsible for the megaphone at athletic contests, as voted by students.[61]

Opening the 1932 season, the then-debate team manager, E. Leonidas Smith, called for the team's starting salvo to be a decision contest with the University of South Carolina (which was accepted). Dr. Rice Quisenberry had "not yet announced which of his 17 men will be pitted against the Sandlappers, warming up orders having been given to Harold Deaton, Leonidas Smith, Sam Miller, Scott Buck, and Carl Ousley."[62]

Smith's debate career was prodigious. In addition to winning the notable Southern Association of Teachers of Speech, he represented Wake at the Tulsa, Oklahoma, Pi Kappa Delta nationals. He and longtime

---

[59] *Old Gold and Black*, May 3, 1930, page 4.

[60] E. Leonidas Smith was perhaps named after the Spartan King Leonidas, who famously led a small band of Greek allies at the Battle of Thermopylae in 480 BCE. At this battle, the Greeks valiantly defended the pass through which the Persian king Xerxes sought to invade Greece with his massive army.

The *Daily Times* (Wilson, N. C.) October 21, 1932, page 7.

[61] *The Herald Sun*, October 7, 1932, page 12.

[62] *The Daily Times* (Wilson, NC), March 2, 1932, page 4.

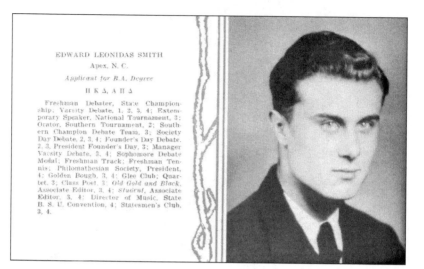

EDWARD LEONIDAS SMITH
Apex, N. C.

Applicant for B.A. Degree

Π K Δ, Λ Π Δ

Freshman Debater, State Championship; Varsity Debate, 1, 2, 3, 4; Extem-
porary Speaker, National Tournament, 3;
Orator, Southern Tournament, 2; Southern Champion Debate Team, 3; Society
Day Debate, 2, 3, 4; Founder's Day Debate,
2, 3, President Founder's Day, 3; Manager
Varsity Debate, 3, 4; Sophomore Debate
Medal; Freshman Track; Freshman Tennis; Philomathesian Society, President,
4; Golden Bough, 3, 4; Glee Club; Quartet, 3; Class Poet, 3; *Old Gold and Black*,
Associate Editor, 3, 4; *Student*, Associate
Editor, 3, 4; Director of Music, State
B. S. U. Convention, 4; Statesmen's Club,
3, 4.

partner Harold Deaton achieved an unusual record, winning 60 percent of their contests during a three-year period. In recognition of this record, Pi Kappa Delta bestowed upon them the degree of special distinction which permits them to wear a fraternity pin of white gold rather than regular yellow.[63]

He was a featured debater for sizable on-campus events, including the spring Society Day, in an era when the principal Raleigh citizens dotted the audience. In 1932, he won both the Edwards and Broughton debate medals.[64] A year later, he won the Charles Les Smith Debating Cup, which was awarded on Society Day.[65]

There was time enough for campus escapades, as when, for the 1932 pivotal presidential election, Leonidas and two other Wake students "Mounted the stump this morning before the student body and the faculty on behalf of their respective candidates for president, Roosevelt, Hoover, and Thomas."[66] E. Leonidas Smith... cornered for the Republicans, then a dicey political choice with Wake Students.[67]

---

[63] *Greensboro Daily News*, December 16, 1931, page 6.

[64] *The News & Observer*, November 13, 1932, page 6.

[65] *The Herald Sun* (Durham), January 9, 1933, page 9.

[66] *The News & Observer*, October 21, 1932, page 8.

[67] *The Daily Times* (Wilson, N. C.) October 21, 1932, page 7.

Earlier in his career, in 1931, E. Leonidas Smith, on the affirmative... met the Farmville State Teachers College women's team.[68] As was their record debating Women's Colleges, Wake, without protest, lost. The judge explained while he personally "was a free trader in agreement with the resolution's affirmative side; nonetheless, the young women debating for the negative had the better argument. It was the State Teachers College's 10th win in a row."

"Dr. Jay Rice Quisenberry, in responding to the [Farmville State Teacher's College] home loss, mused that 'he has long known that it was not only useless but unwise to argue with ladies.' He thinks that, in order to avoid embarrassing the judge, all debates with women should be non-decision."[69]

witness stand also. The court saw once it was the negro who was wanted, and not a prominent member of the junior class, who was perfectly innocent. The names were exactly alike."[70]

We presume Leonidas was not shot, and perhaps the identity mix-up was little more than a prank in the paper. The news clip, however, exposes a haughtiness associated with the racial climate of the 1930s.

---

[68] Now Longwood University, Farmville, VA.

[69] *The News & Observer*, February 7, 1931, page 3; Later that same year, Quisenberry exposed more of his 1930s sexist attitude. "Women love good-looking men, flowered speeches, and a decided amount of elocution, even in debating." Referencing an Atlanta trip at which "In the first three decision debates the Wake Forest team encountered five women judges and lost five women votes. Another obvious reason for the fact women judges are bad luck to real debaters is that during the tournament, Dr. Quisenberry judged five debates, casting his vote for the side that won each time, and of the two other judges who cast votes opposite Dr. Quisenberry, one was a women. Further proof that women judges are a jinx is that the team went into the tournament with practically all male judges and went to the last round." *Old Gold and Black*, April 25, 1931, page 1. The coach's comfort in airing these comments indicates acceptable attitudes at the all-male institute.

[70] *Old Gold and Black*, January 23, 1932, page 4; It was hard to trace Leonidas after Wake. He likely become an English Professor at Elon. He was a Recorders Court Judge in the town of Elon College, NC, and stood for reelection without opposition in 1956. He was nominated during the town's traditional mass meeting. *The Herald-Sun*, May 8, 1956, page 3 and April 26, 1956, page 5. Thanks to the Elon College Archives in attempting to trace Smith.

GEORGE COPPLE — 1937-1939

In a letter to the Wake Debate program of October 6, 1992, George Copple wrote, "The coach throughout my three years (I graduated in 1936) was Dr. J Rice Quisenberry. He was a wonderful human being. He became gravely ill in the spring of 1936 (leukemia) and died after a rather brief illness. I was put in charge of presiding over our weekly discussions and practice sessions, and we made a trip to the annual convention in Houston. We went by bus and had no stopovers after leaving Charlotte. Remember that our travel budget was exceedingly limited during the entire time I was at Wake. We were given a small daily allowance for food.

GEORGE ELLIS COPPLE, B.A.
Albemarle, North Carolina
K A
Sigma Pi Alpha; Pi Kappa Delta; Eu Society 1, 2, 3, Vice President 2, President 3; Statesman's Club 3; English Club 2, 3; Vice President Summer School 3; Old Gold and Black 1, 2, 3; HOWLER 2; Debate Team 1, 2, 3; Golden Bough; Society Day Debater 2, 3; Orator 2, 3; Founder's Day Debater 2.

In the fall of 1938, I was invited to return to Wake Forest as an English professor and public speaking instructor and debate Coach. I was there two academic years and the intervening summer. During those years we had no female students except the immediate family members of faculty and administration, and no female debaters.

Our squad during the two years I was coach had considerable success. I remember that Eugene Worrall (sic) won the national championship at the tournament in Knoxville in the spring of 1940 his oration was a rousing one supporting the New Deal and FDR."[71]

Copple was the perfect short-term replacement to cover Quisenberry's death and Zon Robinson's leave to finish his MA at Syracuse.[72] Before

---

[71] George Copple, personal correspondence to the debate program, October 6, 1992.

[72] George Copple, personal correspondence, October 6, 1992. After his Wake year, Copple earned a Ph.D. in clinical psychology at Vanderbilt, became a practicing

becoming interim coach during the Robinson leave, Copple was a mover and shaker on Quisenberry's debate squad, and reading between the lines, one gets the impression that he also was a "student-coach." It was clear, however, whose program it was. *The Old Gold and Black* mused, "Dr. Quis and K. A. Copple had a run-in at the Tri-State Debate Tournament last week . . . Copple forgot his speech... Tough luck..."[73]

During his Wake debate years, Copple was elected president of the Euzelian Literary Society, "Chosen by acclamation. On Society Day last fall, Copple won the oration contest with his speech on 'The New South' and, teaming with H. A. Matthews, copped the decision on the annual debate."[74]

A year later, Copple attended the 11th national convention of Pi Kappa Delta. They "ranked in the upper third of the debate finals along with partner Hugh Matthews. "Copple and Matthews also represented Wake Forest in a nondecision debate with William Jewell College held in Wait Hall. The girls who compose the William Jewell team are engaged in a six-week tour that includes 14 states...[75]

As Copple assumed the interim reins from Quisenberry, *The Wake Alumni News* was beating the drums for the new season among alums, lifting expectations.[76] The "Alumni News Flash" lead with the banner: **THE COLLEGE STILL TRAINS GOOD SPEAKERS.** The *Alumni News* elaborated:

> It has been traditional at Wake Forest to send out men who could be counted on at any time to "hop up on their hind legs and talk on any subject from Napoleon's war to the cotton crop. That this tradition is still being followed is shown by the fact that all of last year's Southern championship debate team is back in school to defend their

---

psychologist, often went to court, and gave depositions as a vocational expert. He notes, "No other college experience or phase of his college life could have prepared me as well for forensic psychology."

[73] *Old Gold and Black*, March 16, 1935, page 2.

[74] *Old Gold and Black*, April 13, 1935, page 6.

[75] *Old Gold and Black,* April 18, 1936, page 2.

[76] "Wake will hold five tournaments and 87 debates with other colleges for the 1937-8 school year. Also, Wake is one of three Southern colleges permitted to have a senator in the Student Congress at the national tournament this year. Coach Robinson's legacy was left for Copple to manage." *Old Gold and Black*, November 6, 1937, page 1.

place from over thirty members of the squad; that the literary society halls are crowded with new men seeking admittance...

Last year's varsity debate quartet consisted of juniors and sophomores. In fact, only one senior is on the entire squad of over thirty. This can be a peak and glorious future for Wake Forest in this extracurricular activity. The appropriation is twice last year's, and with $400 available, a much fuller program is being planned.[77]

During Copple's time, and well into the 1960s, tournaments held competitions in individual events and debates. This arrangement was based on the economy of travel and a prevailing philosophy that held individuals profited from a broad range of speaking experiences. At the 1937 Winthrop debate meet in Rock Hill, South Carolina, the premier event was the debating, but of notable importance were the individual events. The debaters were expected to enter at least one of the other events, including oratory, extempore speaking, after-dinner speaking, impromptu speaking, problem-solving, and replying to harangue.[78] One might think the rebuttals would qualify as an alternative for the last event.

Wake's event winners at the 1938 Southeastern and South Atlantic Forensic tournaments read as a future Wake Forest *Who's Who*: "First place in 'Stimulating Group Discussion,' Eugene Worrell, first place in 'Problem Solving,' Robert Costner, first place in 'Formulating Group Opinion,' Bobby Helm, second place in the Southeast 'In Speech To A Hostile Audience,' Phil Highfill, second place in 'Extempore,' Eugene Worrell, 3rd place in 'South Atlantic oratory,' Bobby Helm, and 1st place in 'North Carolina extemp,' Eugene Worrell, qualifying in North Carolina oratory Bobby Helm, etc.[79] It is intriguing to imagine how one staged the "Speech to a Hostile Audience." Instructionally, it appears animating.

The debate team made two trips and engaged in numerous practice debates. The first trip was one over North Carolina and Virginia, where the debaters spoke at eight schools over a week. Also, a northern tour was made. This journey was through the State of New York, where the College of the City of New York and others engaged in debates. These

---

[77] *Wake Forest College Alumni News*, Vol. 7, 1937.

[78] *Old Gold and Black*, December 4, 1937, page 1. One wonders if an event labeled "replying to harangue" might be appropriately reenacted in the partisan politics of the 2020s.

[79] *Old Gold and Black*, March 10, 1938, page 1, 4.

were tours of goodwill, and the debate contests were non-decision. The *Old Gold and Black* happily added, "The group will be in Gotham for the opening of the New York World's Fair."[80]

Also, fifteen debates were hosted on campus, the Colgate entry being the most prominent. It was a radio debate over WPTF in Raleigh. Three college professors living in different parts of the state—Buies Creek, Chapel Hill, and Guilford College—determined the decision. After listening to the radio, they made their decisions via telephone.[81] Wake Forest won by a two-to-one vote.

In the 1938 *Howler*, Coach Copple shared, "The team traveled about 5000 miles attending three tournaments." They also hosted the large High School tournament where director Copple "announced that "no debate team would be eliminated before having the opportunity of debating at least six times."[82] This was the tournament at which Copple presented the J. Rice Quisenberry Trophy to the debate winners. The team also attended the State-wide Student Legislative Convention at the State House in Raleigh. On the side, Copple directed a play.[83]

Zon Robinson – 1936-1938, 1940-1941

A letter of recommendation from Dr. J. Allen Easley, from Mars Hill, opined, "[Zon Robinson] is tremendously interested in having something to do with the debating and speaking teams here and to give that little course in argumentation that Quisenberry gave. Zon thinks this a real advantage to him in his religious work with the students."[84] Despite his short tenure at Wake, the letter underestimated Robinson's impact on both counts.

---

[80] *Old Gold and Black*, March 10, 1938, page 1.

[81] *Old Gold and Black*, March 24, 1929, page 1. The topic was *That the United States should stop spending public funds for the stimulation of business.* Eugene Worrell and Ralph Brumet upheld the affirmative.

[82] *The News & Observer*, April 5, 1940, page 9.

[83] Of course, the debate team was not the only group that held public debates on campus. The law school had two societies that, from time to time, held debates. It seemed that the Republicans and Democrats wanted to mix it up publicly, particularly in presidential years. *The News & Observer*, August 5, 1936, page 16.

[84] Dr. J. Allen Easley, Mars Hill, July 23, 1936.

Pres. Thurman Kitchen announced the Quisenberry replacement on August 4. 1936. "Mr. Robinson will teach courses in argumentation and public speaking and coach debating... In addition to his teaching duties Mr. Robinson will serve as secretary of student religious activities in the college and educational director in the Baptist Church."[85]

As a Wake undergraduate, he was active from the outset. Soon after arriving from Boiling Springs Junior College, he was elected as the Euzelian president. The campus paper observed, "The new president is a junior college man, coming to Wake Forest in the fall and immediately becoming active in society work. His outstanding ability is shown by the fact that in junior college, he had the distinction of being a state champion debater... As an active leader this year, the society agreed that it could have hardly chosen a better man to direct the affairs of the Euzelian society next year."[86]

Even as a student, Robinson was noticeable to the State Baptist Association, a relationship he cultivated as a faculty member five years later. The first-year transfer took it upon himself to defend the rhetorical traditions of the Societies in a 1932 letter to *The Biblical Recorder*, carefully contextualized within the Baptist cultural surroundings:

> The statement that the Literary Societies at Wake Forest are no longer training public speakers, that "the training given by the Societies is not given at all" is incorrect.
>
> For the past several years I have been actively connected with Literary Society work, and I know the contrary to be true. Everyone admits that this form of activity does not occupy the pinnacle it once occupied; but an unqualified assertion that students, particularly young ministers, are not being trained at all is not tenable in view of actual conditions.
>
> The fact that one of our young preachers trained in the societies was offered the pastorate of the First Baptist Church of Hendersonville, immediately after graduation last fall disproves that statement.

---

[85] *The News & Observer,* August 21, 1936, page 16; He had been Dean of men, professor of history, and debate coach at Campbell College, where he served as president of the North Carolina Speech and Forensic Society in 1933. *The News & Observer*, August 5, 1936, page 16.

[86] *Old Gold and Black*, May 14, 1932, page 1. He was also president of Dr. Reid's Sunday school class, assistant in two departments, and assistant in the college library.

Also, the debate team of Wake Forest College, every member of which was prominent in Society work, won the Southern debate championship...

The societies at our institutions are offering training in public speaking that could not be gathered at any other college in the State. Increased interest is being taken in our work, and indications point to the largest enlistment in years.

I assure the Baptist people of North Carolina that the noble tradition that has produced able public speakers at Wake Forest is being perpetuated with added vigor.

Yours for a greater Wake Forest College.

ZON ROBINSON,
President, Euzelian Literary Society.[87]

CAMPUS RELIGIOUS EXPONENT

Robinson, in his position as Social Secretary at the school, was responsible for the spiritual welfare of the students. His religiosity was always apparent, coupled with his more serious style. A quick throwaway barb in The *Howler* says as much:

Ted Phillips tells us that a fuse blew out in the church t'other night and Zon Robinson and his boys held "Vespers in the Dark."[88]

Addressing Wake Forest college students for the first time after becoming Student Secretary[89], Zon Robinson declared that "religious leaders throughout the ages have placed too much emphasis on the worship of God and personal purity and up-righteousness."

---

[87] *The Biblical Recorder*, September 9, 1932.

[88] *Old Gold and Black*, September 23, 1937, page 4.

[89] Robinson was succeeded in the position of Student Secretary following his departure in 1939 by Mr. Al Martin, one of his main debaters. Martin had graduated from Wake Forest in 1937. While a student at Wake Forest, he served as president of the local and State BSY Organizations and as president of the student body in 1937 (defeating Hubert Poteat, Jr., 469 to 283 in the election, *Old Gold and Black*, April 4, 1936. Later in his career, Al Martin became Wake's long-term, beloved philosophy faculty member. *The Biblical Recorder*, October 20, 1939.

He stated that religious leaders, "in an effort to maintain personal morals, often withdrew from the world, allowing it to "go hang." The chief aim of everyone in his religious life," he continued, "should be to seek out men who are in need and to sacrifice to help them."[90]

He often published long pieces on youth religion and theological essays in *The Biblical Recorder*. Early on, he made a name for himself by orchestrating summer religious programs.

Zon Robinson and Prof. A. L. Aycock (pictured)
conducting Daily Vespers for summer students.

Pictured is the scene on the Wake Forest College campus, showing summer session students attending the Daily Vespers, at which Prof. A. L. Aycock is speaking. "These meetings, as well as most of the other services, were held at the beautiful out-of-doors amphitheater, formed by a semicircle of wooden benches." Here, the students and faculty members gathered after supper for daily devotions and twice a week for chapel exercises, often led by Robinson.[91]

Robinson became widely known as a religious lecturer around the State. For instance, Zon Robinson, addressed the Sandy Run Association

[90] *Old Gold and Black*, September 26, 1936, page 1.

[91] Campus religious observations were overseen by a Baptist Student Union Council of 12 members, on which served representatives of Wake Forest, Meredith, Mars Hill, Campbell, and E. C. T. C. (East Carolina Teachers College). Members of the Council included Wake faculty adviser Zon Robinson.

on Christian Education at its meeting at Concorde Church on October 7 (1937). "Mr. Robinson is a home-grown product of the Sandy Run Association. He got his academic start at Boiling Springs, and there is no telling how far he is going, but his excellent address indicates that he is going in the right direction. Next week, Zon Robinson will attend the BTU training school at Meredith. He will teach the book, "Planning Life."[92]

An excerpt from a letter to Wake Forest President Dr. Thurman Kitchin from Zeno Wall, Pastor First Baptist Church, captures his appeal:

> Last week, the Kings Mountain Association held its annual meeting, and it looked like a state Convention. At this meeting Mr. Zon Robinson appeared and spoke, and he delivered a timely, stirring, and dynamic message. It was, in fact, the most inspiring message delivered during the meetings of the association. He thrilled you and made us all proud that we have Wake Forest College and all of the other Christian colleges in this country of ours. I was proud of him. We also heard the finest echoes from Sandy Run and Gaston County Associations where he spoke. He ably represents "Old Gold and Black."

Speaking before the assembled Chapel crowd, in 1940, the year before departing for his war role, he juxtaposed his opposition to war with his religious convictions tailored to his denominational college. Speaking on the 22nd anniversary of The Great Armistice, Robinson reminded the chapelgoers:

> We fought the war to make the world safe for democracy, and yet this has not been accomplished. It is true that the Hohenzollerns have been removed in Germany, Romanoffs in Russia, and the power of Victor Manuel in Italy, but in their place have risen Hitler, Stalin, and Mussolini.
>
> We can no more end war with war than we can end drunkenness with drunkenness...
>
> We, who are in a Christian college, ought to seek out the opinions of Jesus, Prince of Peace, on this matter of war. One of the first persons we conscript in a war is Jesus. We shouldn't have to coscript

---

[92] *Old Gold and Black*, November 6, 1937, page 2.

Him.... On this Armistice Day, we must keep peace with them, though they sleep and poppies grow on Flanders Field. [93]

MAN-ABOUT-THE-STATE, ROBINSON'S DEBATE PROGRAM

Legendary Wake Forest Professor Robert Helm, one Robinson's debaters, recalled, "The debate Coach at that time, Zon Robinson, was a very interesting character... He was a handsome guy, but he looked like an elegant fox. He had a very good speaking voice and was very demanding as a debate coach."

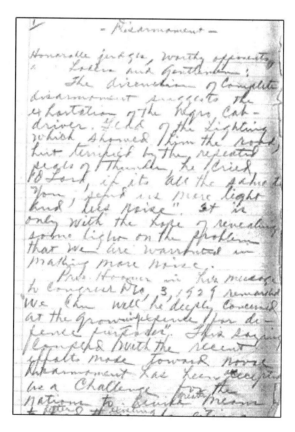

1930- The First page of Zon Robinson's Speech for a debate on "Disarmament" with Wingate Jr. College.

---

[93] *Old Gold and Black,* November 15, 1940, page 1, 4.

Robinson's successor as coach, Professor A. Lewis Aycock, commented, "He had a very strong personality. When I first took over his speech work, I found on tours that Zon had made a good reputation for both himself and Wake Forest, wherever he had been. Many teams asked that the Wake Forest Coach judge their debates, thinking that Zon was still with us. He was always successful in human contacts."

Robinson's debate life was a whirlwind. He judged, spoke, organized, and hosted with assurance. His debate services were in high demand, and he complied.

Campbell College's rival literary societies sponsored a public debate highlighting Homecoming Day in 1938, with Zon Robinson as the critic judge.[94] Among other honors, he joined President Kitchin as a "featured speaker" introduced by alumnus Governor-elect Broughton at the Mecklenburg alumni banquet in Charlotte. The following morning, he supervised a radio program with Wingate. [95]

One debate request was curious in its assumptions regarding debate's purity contrasted with sport:

Debate Coach Robinson this week received an invitation from a college in another state requesting a date for a debate, with the definite provision that the contest be non-decision. 'We do not want debating to become an intercollegiate sport,' said the coach of the other team.[96]

Robinson's response was not recorded, but given his competitive side, he may have seen the team as more akin to sports than intellectual diversion.

A short recounting of debaters and results provides the flavor of the Robinson era. Robinson hit the ground running, following the established circuit with a young but talented crew who spent the year growing into winning ways. The initial breakthrough was winning the debate division

---

[94] *The News & Observer*, November 19, 1938, page 12.

[95] *The News & Observer*, November 27, 1940, page 5; Robinson seems to specialize in overseeing radio debates. Earlier in 1938, Robinson refereed (over WPTF in Raleigh) a clash between State College and the University of Pennsylvania. The referee's task was to call a decision when either side had a distinct advantage. *Old Gold and Black*, February 18, 1938, page 1.

[96] *Old Gold and Black,* February 18, 1938, page 2.

at the Spring 1937 Pi Kappa Delta regional. The players were of note then and into the future: Robert Costner, Robert Helm, James Hayes, and Eugene Worrell. (Picture below)

The coach promised their second year would include "Five tournaments, in addition to debates with about 87 American colleges and universities."[97] The 1937 fall tryouts saw six returning debate team members. "These six candidates will face stiff competition for positions on the team from 26 new men, most of whom have had wide forensic experience and won honors in high school debating."[98]

The team with Robinson at the helm also conducted debate tours, as in 1937. "Zon was off on 'a four-day Jaunt,' a tour with seven stops for intercollegiate debates. With him were his core squad, Affirmative Jimmy Hayes and Robert Costner and Negative Eugene Worrell and Robert Helm."[99]

Robert Helm humorously recounted during an interview, speaking in the third person, "In the 1930s, the award medal was given to the best oration at commencement time. If you won the award, you didn't have to take final exams. Bobby [Helm] won it and didn't have to take finals. Public speaking can give you all sorts of ways to avoid unpleasantness." He also noted before you could earn a Letter for debate; that's not done anymore. He's disappointed in that fact... The whole debate project was sort of an exercise in rhetoric in the Greek sense – rhetoric and logic combined."[100]

For 1938, Coach Robinson indicated that large numbers forced selection contests for debate and oratory to be judged by outstanding students in these events like Gene Worrell. Up for the 1938-1939 season was "Twenty-four speech contests and 91 intercollegiate debates... traveling 3623 miles.[101]

---

[97] *Old Gold and Black*, November 6, 1937, page 1. It is not clear what Robinson means by "debates with 87 American Colleges and Universities." Perhaps he counted the schools entering the five tournaments. Regardless 87 dominated the article's headline.

[98] *Wake Forest College Alumni News*, October 1937, page 7.

[99] *Rocky Mount Telegram*, February 2, 1937. Robinson was every bit the promoter as was his predecessor Quisenberry.

[100] Interview with Bobby Helm, ROTC Archive, July 13, 2017.

[101] *Old Gold and Black,* May 20, 1939, page 1. The report was released this week by Coach Zon Robinson.

In Zon's last year, 1941, "the crack Wake Forest college speech and debate squad ... took top honors in the Dixie Forensic Tournament at Rock Hill, South Carolina. Debate coach Zon Robinson accompanied 13 members of the squad to the tournament. Out of the nine contests in the meet, Wake Forest placed first in eight.[102]

The program's steady rise continued through Quisenberry, Copple, and Robinson's span. Miles traveled shot from 2,450 to 3,623 and then 4334. The percentage of decision debates won rose steadily from the lower 60s to 76.[103]

Robert Helm, 1939

Newspapers added further praise in Zon's last season, 1941. Picking up again on the 3000-mile theme, the *Herald Sun* in Durham ran a long feature that began, "this month, Wake Forest college debaters made a 3000-mile tour of nine states, bringing home among other laurels from the South Atlantic championship. But that's not surprising since the first Wake Forest debate 106 years ago, 140,000 miles have been traveled by college speakers to participate in over 750 debates.

Robinson, while enormously competitive, also had an eye toward educational aims beyond the tournament format, a stance testified to by the variety of speaking venues and styles he promoted. In a 1942 academic article, he laid out potential limitations of tournament debating, which included:

> [Often] the good tournament debater makes little attempt to communicate an idea or an emotion. Rather, what he does try to do is

---

[102] *The Biblical Recorder*, January 1, 1941.

[103] *The Herald-Sun*, April 20, 1941, page 10. Some estimates and hard figures vary across the sources, as cited in the text. When unable to discern which was a more authoritative belief, the sources are quoted faithfully, acknowledging that most sources touting success and triumph often courted exaggeration.

Wake Debaters Emerge From Tournament Smiling, Victorious

1927 Winners of the Pi Kappa Delta Bi-Provincial
Tournament. L-R: Zon Robinson, Coach, Robert Costner,
Robert Helm, James Hayes, & Eugene Worrell

to display his knowledge of the query and his skill in the technical aspects of debate... The nature of the speaking situation encourages the debater to resort to such devices as trick cases, technical maneuverings, and the parade of vast accumulations of evidence.[104]

The *Howler* was left to summarize Robinson's shortened coaching career: "On the Debate Squad and Prof. Zon Robinson rests much of the reputation of Wake Forest College. It is said that as soon as one announces that he is a student or graduate of the Baptist institution, he is expected to arise and make a soul-stirring oration and when one

---

[104] Robinson, Z. (1942). This does not imply that Robinson was not a fan of tournaments. He certainly was. In the same article, he writes, "In no other way can a student engage in a greater degree of speech activity in so short a time and at so low an expense. The average tournament has from six to eight rounds of debate. This number is equivalent to a full year's program of home debates... If the debater can objectively analyze , his own performance, or if the judge presents an oral criticism of the debate, he is able to eliminate bad practices and remedy mistakes as he advances from round to round." What happens to speech values in tournament debating. *Southern Speech Bulletin*, Vol. 7, page 123.

examines the record of this year's Debate team, it is not hard to believe that all this is not a legend."[105]

CONTINUANCE AND INNOVATION

Robinson initiated several innovations that kept the program at the forefront while also demanding the students' attention. In 1941, the debaters made ten radio roundtable discussions and debates, ranging from Asheville's WWAC to Raleigh's WBT and Charlotte's WBT.[106]

On campus, the debaters were no less active. For the first time in the college's history, they inaugurated a two-week summer Debate Institute.[107] In the spring, the team sponsored the Third Annual High School Debate Tournament.

Discussed in length in the next chapter, Early Tournament Hosting, Robinson reinvented the Wake High School tournament. He promoted the tournament for "modern types of extempore for debating as opposed to the stilted declamatory debate style..."

In the Robinson years, the society meetings were often lighthearted. A resolution introduced in 1936 argued that "No freshman shall be allowed to win more than 10 consecutive games of 'Eightball' [pool], for such would deplete the upperclassman's pocketbook and complete his inferiority complex."[108]

Robinson's campus acuity was such that the student paper felt obliged to inform the student body in 1938 that "Prof. Zon Robinson... was confined to the infirmary for several days this week with a severe cold, but much improved and now has returned to his class."[109]

WAKE DEBATE'S GREATEST MYSTERY: THE DISAPPEARANCE OF ZON ROBINSON

Zon's early successes on campus with debate and his religious roles signaled a man of great potential. Unfortunately, Zon did not have the

---

[105] *Howler*, 1941, page 195.

[106] *Howler*, 1941, page 195.

[107] *Howler*, 1941, page 195.

[108] *Old Gold and Black*, October 10, 1936, page 1.

[109] *Old Gold and Black*, November 19, 1938, page 1.

advanced degrees required to secure a permanent spot as a Wake Forest faculty member. He set out to rectify that barrier on May 24, 1939, when he requested and received one year's leave of absence to study at the legendary rhetoric program at Syracuse University. Syracuse University created its Department of Oratory in 1910 and offered one of the nation's first academic programs dedicated to the study of rhetoric.[110]

1939 Radio Debate – Eugene Worrell vs Colgate

Zon joined the Syracuse graduate program and obtained a master's degree in one year with his thesis examining the Congressional Record's accuracy for floor speeches in Congress.[111] He returned to Wake Forest in the Fall of 1940, teaching through the Spring of 1941. He was then invited back to Syracuse University to join the Ph.D. program. President Kitchin supported Zon and wrote in his recommendation letter, "I'm sure that Mr. Robinson intends to make this his life's work…"

In March of 1942, Zon wrote President Kitchin and asked for permission to stay at Syracuse for an additional year to complete his doctorate. Given

[110] Communication and Rhetorical Studies-All Scholarship, *SURFACE*, https://surface.syr.edu/crs/.

[111] Robinson, Z. (1942). Are speeches in Congress reported accurately? *Quarterly Journal of Speech*, 28, page 8-12.

the onset of WW II, Zon mentioned in his letter to President Kitchin that he had received a limited-service draft classification (I-B), "I had a physical examination and received this classification because of poor vision in my right eye." His family would later say that he was "practically blind" in his right eye. President Kitchin approved the additional leave time and noted that the university was cutting staff because of the war.[112]

With his future at Wake Forest secure and a path to completing his doctorate, Zon continued life in New York as the world descended into chaos. He attended academic conferences, had a steady girlfriend, and served as a best man in the wedding of his close friend John Parker. By all accounts, Zon was living as happily as one could during the global war. Zon's consistent progress toward his career and seemingly favorable life with close friends and a romantic relationship makes what happened next even more surprising for his family and friends.[113]

Zon Robinson Coaching – 1941

In December 1942, Zon attended a conference on speech in New York City. At the conference, he met up with this old friend J. C. Herrin, who

[112] Davis, C. (1960). What 'secret' mission called Zon Robinson? Wartime disappearance still unsolved, *Journal and Sentinel* (Winston-Salem), March 13, page 27.

[113] Davis, C. (1960). What 'secret' mission called Zon Robinson? Wartime disappearance still unsolved, *Journal and Sentinel* (Winston-Salem), March 13, page 27.

was then the Baptist student secretary at the University of North Carolina at Chapel Hill. As the lifelong friends were catching up, Zon told J. C. he was about to be called into military service. He told J. C. that he had been offered the position of Captain in a branch of the military that he was not free to discuss. He made it a point to say that if he accepted this position, he would not be able to correspond with friends or family, and they would not be permitted to inquire as to his whereabouts.

In December 1942 and January 1943, Robinson told close friends and family a similar story. Some mentioned that Zon had used the phrase "intelligence service" but others simply said that he was very guarded about the specific nature of his plans. His girlfriend confirmed that she, too, was aware of Zon's plans to join something secret. She would later recount that she had been looking forward to seeing Zon when the war ended but did not expect to hear from him in the interim.

On January 11, 1943, Zon wrote a handwritten letter to President Kitchin (his other letters were all typed). In it, he wrote, "In a few days, I am planning to enter an officer's training school and, like so many others, will be away for the duration. At the close of the war, I should like to return to Wake Forest if conditions permit and if there should be a need for a man in my field."[114]

Immediately after sending this note, Zon packed up his things and left Syracuse "on very short notice," according to his landlady. He drove his car from Syracuse to his parents' home in Mooresboro, N.C.[115] On January 13, 1943, Zon spent time with his parents and reiterated that he was leaving for a branch of the military that he could not discuss. He emphasized that they would not be able to write to him and that he would not be able to communicate with them until after the war.[116] His last words to his parents were, "Always remember, no news is good news."

After that day, Zon drove to his sister's house in High Point, N.C. He arrived unannounced, explained his plan to leave, and said he was leaving his car with her for the duration. He asked her for a ride to the High Point train station that day. She agreed and brought her two daughters,

---

[114] Davis, C. (1960). What 'secret' mission called Zon Robinson? Wartime disappearance still unsolved, *Journal and Sentinel* (Winston-Salem), March 13, page 27.

[115] Davis, C. (1960). What 'secret' mission called Zon Robinson? Wartime disappearance still unsolved, *Journal and Sentinel* (Winston-Salem), March 13, page 27.

[116] Jenkins, J. (1952). Case of the missing professor. *The News & Observer*, August 17, page 41.

Penny and Gerry. At the station, one of the girls began to cry, and Zon told his sister not to wait any longer.

His last words were, "Be kind to your mother. I won't see you for a long time."[117] In reality, Zon would never see them again. The last time his family or friends saw Zon Robinson was standing at the High Point train station on January 13, 1943. After the war ended, Zon's family, colleagues, students, and debaters at Wake Forest and his professors at Syracuse waited with great anticipation for Zon's triumphant return. It never came.

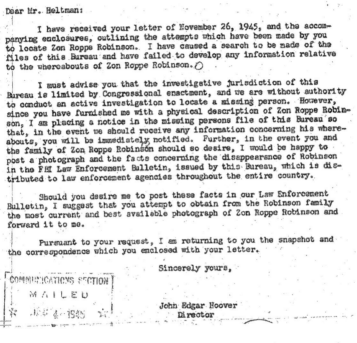

Dear Mr. Heltman:

I have received your letter of November 26, 1945, and the accompanying enclosures, outlining the attempts which have been made by you to locate Zon Roppe Robinson. I have caused a search to be made of the files of this Bureau and have failed to develop any information relative to the whereabouts of Zon Roppe Robinson.

I must advise you that the investigative jurisdiction of this Bureau is limited by Congressional enactment, and we are without authority to conduct an active investigation to locate a missing person. However, since you have furnished me with a physical description of Zon Roppe Robinson, I am placing a notice in the missing persons file of this Bureau so that, in the event we should receive any information concerning his whereabouts, you will be immediately notified. Further, in the event you and the family of Zon Roppe Robinson should so desire, I would be happy to post a photograph and the facts concerning the disappearance of Robinson in the FBI Law Enforcement Bulletin, issued by this Bureau, which is distributed to law enforcement agencies throughout the entire country.

Should you desire me to post these facts in our Law Enforcement Bulletin, I suggest that you attempt to obtain from the Robinson family the most current and best available photograph of Zon Roppe Robinson and forward it to me.

Pursuant to your request, I am returning to you the snapshot and the correspondence which you enclosed with your letter.

Sincerely yours,

John Edgar Hoover
Director

COMMUNICATIONS SECTION
MAILED
JAN 4 1945

J. Edgar Hoover's 1945 letter regarding the Zon Robinson search

The search for answers as to what happened to Zon Robinson has spanned decades but produced few substantive leads. Initially, the Robinson family asked for the help of Reverend T. H. Parris of Pilot Mountain, N.C., who agreed to enlist the aid of a retired Army Chaplain to dig into Pentagon military records. They found no record of Zon serving in any military capacity. When those efforts were unsuccessful, the family sought

[117] Davis, C. (1960). What 'secret' mission called Zon Robinson? Wartime disappearance still unsolved, *Journal and Sentinel* (Winston-Salem), March 13, page 27.

the help of Senator Clyde R. Hoey and Congressman Harold Cooley. They agreed and reached out to the Pentagon, Office of Strategic Services, and Department of Justice for any records related to Zon. Their efforts returned no clues. There was no indication that Zon had any role with the United States military or the O.S.S.[118]

Both Syracuse and Wake Forest University got involved in the search efforts. In 1945, H. J. Heltman, the Director of the School of Speech and Dramatic Art at Syracuse, wrote to J. Edgar Hoover asking if the FBI had any files on Zon and to see if he would assist in the investigation. Director Hoover wrote back and confirmed that the FBI had no files on Zon and no indication of where he might be. The FBI did post a missing person report for Zon in December 1945.[119] At Wake Forest, a professor named Johnson Hagood, who had served as an Army Captain, attempted to use his connections to spearhead a search but found nothing substantive.

Several investigative journalists took up the charge. In 1952, Jay Jenkins with the Raleigh *News & Observer* wrote a report on Zon that was picked up by the Associated Press but produced no new leads.[120] In 1960, Chester Davis wrote a comprehensive story in the *Winston-Salem Sentinel* but did not have any new information. The Wake Forest *Old Gold and Black* has published several articles on Zon. These articles include a basic review of the mystery and quotes from people who knew Zon, but no new information on his potential whereabouts.

In 2018, "Mr. Wake Forest" Dr. Ed Wilson reached out to his friend Elaine Tooley, who served as the Assistant Vice President of Advancement Communications at Wake Forest University. Dr. Wilson explained that when he was an undergraduate student at Wake Forest, Zon Robinson was a faculty member. He expressed that Zon Robinson's disappearance had captured the community's attention at the time, and he had always wondered what happened to Zon. Dr. Wilson asked if Elaine would be willing to take another look at the existing research. Elaine reached out to Jarrod Atchison, the Director of Debate, and the two of them dug back into the case.

Elaine and Jarrod tracked down and visited Zon's niece, Penny, who had been with him at the train station on that fateful day in 1943. Even

---

[118] Pate, W. (1953). *Old Gold and Black*, October 26, page 5.

[119] *Zon Roppe Robinson FBI File.* Obtained January 4, 2019.

[120] *The News & Observer*, August 17, 1952, page 41.

though she had been young at the time of the disappearance, she remembered Zon fondly and confirmed that the mystery had been a struggle for their family for decades. Elaine and Jarrod confirmed with the National Archives and Records Administration in College Park, Maryland, that there is no record of Zon Robinson serving in the O.S.S. Additionally, there continues to be no record of Zon Robinson with any branch of the United States Military.

The Wake researchers could categorize a series of theories ranging from the idea that Zon defected to the Germans to the possibility that he lived as a grocer on the Outer Banks of North Carolina. Although the categorization was helpful, they found no new evidence supporting any theory.

In the fall of 2021, a First Year Seminar class at Wake Forest, taught by Atchison and Tooley, was dedicated to the search for Zon Robinson. Sixteen first-year students spent the semester reviewing the existing research, examining Zon's writings and materials in the Wake Forest archive, reaching out to experts related to various theories, contacting Zon's surviving family members, and assessing the theories related to his disappearance. In the students' final assessment, two theories have the most potential for explaining Zon's disappearance.

The simplest explanation is that Zon intentionally used the war as cover and disappeared. The students struggled with the likelihood that Zon would be willing to give up his known life. Still, they admitted that we never know what is going on in another's mind or personal life, which could make the opportunity to disappear and start over again appealing.

The second theory is that the British recruited Zon to serve in clandestine operations behind enemy lines, where he was either captured or killed. A series of coincidences support this theory, but no hard proof exists. Before the United States entered WW2, Americans had been a part of an "off-the-books" class designed to link British and American operatives in secret since the Neutrality Act prohibited the United States from formally engaging in military operations.

Americans would make their way to a Canadian facility known as "Camp X," where they were trained in the techniques necessary to be spies and saboteurs.[121] They would then be dropped behind enemy lines

---

[121] Stafford, D. (1986). *Camps X: OSS, "Intrepid," and the Allies' Northern American Training Camp for Secret Agents, 1941-1945*, New York City: Dodd, Mead & Company, and Hodgson, L. (1999). *Inside Camp-X*. Ontario: Mosaic Press.

to serve as spies. Most importantly, the Americans would forfeit their identities and be given new Canadian identities, complete with new paperwork and uniforms; they would travel across the Atlantic as Canadian soldiers before rendezvousing at a safe house in London. They would then be dropped behind enemy lines.[122]

The students found this theory persuasive. They recalled that Zon mentioned to his lifelong friend J.C. Herrin that he was entering a secret military branch in December of 1942. In November of 1942, one month earlier, Zon was permitted by his draft board to attend a Speech Conference in Toronto, Canada. Camp X was less than 100 miles from Toronto. Additionally, the British used an office in New York City to recruit Americans into the program and arrange their logistics for going to Camp X. Zon attended a conference in New York City when he told J.C. his plan to serve in a secret military branch.[123] The students found it a strong coincidence that Zon first disclosed his plan to do something secret within a short time after visiting Toronto and New York City.

Zon spoke fluent German and Russian, making him an ideal candidate for clandestine work. The students discovered that Camp X was the site of a significant communication hub that transmitted telegraph information worldwide. Codenamed "Hydra," this communication system was instrumental in collecting and distributing intelligence.[124] Even if Zon were not tasked with sabotage, his language skills in German and Russian would make him an asset for collecting and returning intelligence from behind enemy lines.

Unlike the 50-year seal used by the Americans, the records of participants in the British clandestine services are sealed for 100 years. This provision would explain why there have been no successful record searches. Zon would have been working for the British but assumed a new Canadian identity for travel. If he were captured or killed behind enemy lines (or died trying to cross the Atlantic in a U-boat attack), his identity would have come back as a fictitious Canadian soldier...and not Zon Robinson.

---

[122] Interview with Lynn Philip Hodgson, September 30, 2021.

[123] Hyde, M. (1962) *Room 3603: The Story of the British Intelligence Center in New York during World War II*, New York City: Farrar, Straus, and Company.

[124] Stafford, D. (1986). *Camps X: OSS, "Intrepid," and the Allies' Northern American Training Camp for Secret Agents, 1941-1945*, New York City: Dodd, Mead & Company, page 136.

We can hope that the British records or some other clues will, in time, shed new light on the enduring mystery of Zon Robinson's disappearance. The notion that Zon Robinson could have transitioned from a small college debate coach to James Bond is romantic. Everyone encountering Zon's story ends up rooting for him to be a hero. With his dynamic presence, Zon was a successful debate coach, an adored professor, and an active Wake Forest and State Baptist community member.

A. Louis Aycock -The War Years[125] – 1941-1948

World War II amended the rhythms of the debate activity, accelerating the transformation to invitational contests complete with championships, permanent coaching, recruiting, and fast-tracked competition. The conversion would occur from the end of the War through the late 1940s. A. Louis Aycock's second appearance as coach was destined to manage this transition's beginnings.

Even before America entered the war, the landscape offered to Aycock included challenges in the form of altered schedules and restricted travel. In his annual report, Coach Aycock wrote, "In the interest of economy, the forensic program was curtailed to some extent during the 1941-42 season. The Wake Forest team did not attend the Pi Delta Kappa meet as they usually do; nor did they take any long or expensive trips. Many out-of-state debates scheduled at Wake Forest were canceled by the visiting schools."[126] A limited schedule in 1941-42 included "Six debates held at Wake Forest, eight at other colleges (Intercollegiate Debates continued to be scheduled), and 30 at the two tournaments in which Wake Forest participated: the Dixie and the Grand Eastern at Rock Hill, S. C.[127]

Aycock also advised at an opening meeting in 1944, "The strength and success of our team will depend wholly on the interest shown by the students. Although interest has not been any too strong, debating at Wake Forest has definite possibilities this year, if only the ones who are

---

[125] The United States entered WW II following the Pearl Harbor attack of December 7, 1941, and ended the war with VJ Day on August 14, 15, 1945.

[126] A. L. Aycock, *Report on Forensic Activities for 1941-1942* (submitted to the University President).

[127] A. L. Aycock, *Report on Forensic Activities for 1941-1942.*

interested will stick with it and work hard."[128] There were no tournaments to attend that year.

For the first part of the war, the team continued participating in customary tournaments within a day's turnaround drive. These included one of Wake's main staples, the Winthrop Grand Eastern Tournament. In 1942, Bynum Shaw and C. C. Hope won 1st and 2nd in After Dinner Speaking.[129] Wake's 1943 squad swept the men's divisions of Winthrop's Grand Eastern Tournament.[130] The competition held enough import to be the lead story of the second section of *The Charlotte Sunday Observer*,[131] a newspaper where the first 18 pages covered the ongoing war in Europe.

The debaters acquitted themselves nobly in entering competitions when travel was challenged. Who could travel, what tournament would be held, and would travel be restricted by "Homefront" resources or edicts? It was in mid-April 1943 that Wake entered the "local" South Hill, SC, tournaments, the Grand Eastern and Pi Kappa Delta. The college paper claimed that this was the "first time in the 109 years of Wake Forest's forensics that a feminine name appeared on the roster of the debate team:" Martha Ann Allen.

The paper praised Wake Forest's traditions and coach, Lewis Aycock. "Their speaking was a credit to Wake Forest tradition. The entire squad,

---

[128] *Old Gold and Black*, February 25, 1944, page 1.

[129] Bynum Shaw later serves as a legendary professor of journalism at Wake Forest and author of Vol. 4 of the *History of Wake Forest, 1943-1967*.

[130] Wake won seven of 13 events, competing with 27 colleges and universities. The rounds were held at the Selwyn Hotel and the First Methodist Church.

[131] *Charlotte Sunday Observer*, April 11, 1943, Section 2, page 1. Even as Florida won the debate competition among the 27 colleges, Wake Forest champions included C. C. Hope, Address Reading and After Dinner Speaking, Brunette Harvey, Oratory and Poetry Reading, J. D. Davis, Problem-Solving, Bill McGill, Radio Interviewing and Radio Newscasting, and Henry Huff, Response to Occasion and Situation Oratory. The latter represented a unique twist in oratorical competition. *The News & Observer* (Raleigh), April 11, 1943. Experimentation occurred more often in debate and individual events until the modern era (post-1980s) when events were increasingly codified to produce "level playing fields;" Dr. Warren G. Keith of Winthrop College, founder of the Strawberry Leaf Society which sponsored the meet, said that "despite wartime transportation problems and the paring of budget allowances for events of this nature by many of the nation's educational institutions, the 15th annual Grand Eastern was one of the most successful in the history of the tourney." *Charlotte Sunday Observer*, April 11, 1943, Section 2, page 1.

both those making the trip and those remaining behind, and their advisor, Professor Aycock, deserve the praise and approval of the student body."[132]

The Grand Eastern was combined with the Pi Kappa Delta Provincial Tournament in 1943. There is no record of the team entering the 1942, 1944 or 1945 events. Following a governmental request to eliminate all but essential travel, the forensic group canceled participation in forensic tournaments away from the campus for the [Spring] semester.[133]

Aycock and his debaters nonetheless participated in some speech contests independent of the tournament or Intercollegiate structure. The North Carolina Student Legislature was a regular supplement to the team competitions and continued through 1943. Speakers of the House and President pro tem of the Senate were regularly won by Wake.[134] In 1942, a contingent (Bruce Brown, Sam Behrends, Bynum Shaw, and Paul Bell) attended a Duke roundtable and extempore-discussion contest competing for summer tours through Latin America.[135] They also attended the 7th annual North Carolina Legislative Assembly in Raleigh at the State Capitol building. In 1942, Larry Williams, a first-year law student, was speaker of the House, and major debaters were Sam Brehrends, president pro tem of the Senate, and Burnette Harvey, parliamentarian of the House. [136] These happenings took place before the fully restricted period of the War.

In 1945, when all travel was interdicted, the speech group, under the guidance of A. L. Aycock announced in April "an intramural forensic tournament, open to all students and including 12 types of speech activities, to be held April 11-14.[137] The campus event was "to replace trips

---

[132] *Old Gold and Black,* April 16, 1943, page 2 (Unsigned Editorial).

[133] *Old Gold and Black,* March 9, 1945, page 1.

[134] *Howler,* 1943, page 118.

[135] *Old Gold and Black,* March 6, 1942, page 4.

[136] *Old Gold and Black,* November 5, 1943, page 1.

[137] Speaking events included address reading, after dinner, declamation, dramatic reading, extempore, oratory, poetry reading, radio newscasting, radio commercial, radio address, response to the occasion, and situation oratory. The last two events sound alike. Furthermore, via the last event listed, it is unclear why all oratories are not situational, yet the idea of specialized venues holds intrigue. The prize for first place was the three-volume set of Dr. Paschal's *History of Wake Forest College* and a recording by the Band and Glee Club featuring the Wake Forest College songs. One area newspaper noted, "The tournament created considerable interest among the student body and the competition was stiff in the events." *Henderson Daily Dispatch,* April 27, 1945, page 8.

to intercollegiate tourneys." The societies heard the winners' speeches, but the event did not receive the attention of former traveling teams.

The *Old Gold and Black* claimed, "This will be the first time any tournament of this kind has been held on campus."[138] The squad planned another intramural contest in the fall 1945 semester (November 28-30) but also suggested the return to tournament competition.[139] The "annual" intercollegiate event announced over twenty winners in the various events.

Problems did not disappear with the War's conclusion. The Pi Kappa Delta Nationals, which Wake planned to attend, was canceled. However, they were able to enter the joint regional tournament of the Southeastern and Lakes Provinces at Georgetown College, KY, in April 1946.

With the war's buildup in 1943, campus routines were reimagined:

Life at Wake Forest was changed this year... There was no doubt about it. From the moment Dean Bryan announced in chapel that

---

[138] Individuals or groups could compete. Organizations signing up included Euzelians and Philomathesians, the Little Theater, and the International Relations Club. *Old Gold and Black*, March 9, 1945.

[139] The Strawberry Leaf Society of Winthrop College tournament and regional and national Pi Kappa Delta tournaments. *Old Gold and Black*, October 12, 1945, page 4.

a division of the Army Finance School would settle down here in August, we knew that we were in for a new kind of experience... And when the soldiers did arrive, we saw that we faced still another new experience – the feeling of sacrifice.

By December, we had given up our cafeteria, our gymnasium, our dormitories, our just completed music-religion building, and two of our classroom buildings. Five fraternities, forced out of Simmons, had to find new houses. We found ourselves deprived of home basketball, taking physical education outdoors, eating in restaurants downtown, and rearranging our mode of life.[140]

The *Howler* of 1945 was dedicated to the Wake Forest men who are fighting for their country, their world, and a better day:

Most of you we have never seen, but we feel that we know you because a few years ago, last year, last month, you too were students at Wake Forest. You hurried into the same classrooms at the sound of the same bell. You joined the same fraternities, studied the same books, looked into the same mailboxes, bummed rides at the same corners.

Now you are the 2,800 Wake Forest men in uniform. You are generals and privates, commanders and gobs, leathernecks, coast guardsmen and merchant seamen. You march in deep snow. You fight in the steaming jungle. You watch endless days crawl by at sea. You dodge enemy flak among the stars.

We are frequently reminded of you when a draft board summons one of us to join you. We know that the story behind the headlines and the news flashes is your story... You who once like us arose reluctantly for an 8:30 history class (or slept through it) now awake at dawn, or earlier, to make history.

*_*_*_*_*_*

Buried at the end of a 1908 article, chiefly focusing on the "game-changing" upcoming Wake Forest-Randolph Macon Raleigh College debate, was the following addendum: "President Poteat received a letter from a

---

[140] *Howler*, 1943, page 11.

young Japanese student now in New Haven, Connecticut, who has graduated from the University of Tokio (sic) and has also spent two years at the University of Berlin, saying that he would like to finish his education at this college.[141] That was the extent of the "announcement." The same trailer appeared similarly submerged in numerous newspaper articles, suggesting it was likely Poteat's trial balloon to prepare the ground for the admission of a non-white Japanese student.

Konosuke Yakiama attended Wake Forest for two years, graduating in 1910, thirty years before WWII. While at Wake, he became close friends with future North Carolina Governor J. Melville Broughton. Broughton said at one point, "I took a great many walks with Akiyama (Sic), and while he talked freely of his country, I always gained the impression that he was never being entirely frank, although he was unfailingly polite."

As the *Howler* summarized, alongside Yakiama's senior picture, "he has made friends of us all, and we hope to hear of him as a bright and shining star in the political arena of his country, and also to hasten 'Sunrise' in the Sunrise Kingdom."[142]

"At the time he was at Wake Forest, there were only 12 students from outside North Carolina and one (Akiyama) from outside the United States. Those 12 students formed an 'Alien Club' in which Akiyama was voted 'Minister of

---

[141] *The News & Observer*, November 25, 1908.

[142] This entry is indebted to Nancy Sullivan for the additional details provided in her Wake archives entry: https://zsr.wfu.edu/2020/wake-forest-revisits-wwii/. Yakiama served commendably with the Japanese military during World War II. Testimony was obtained from Colonel K. Akiyama, who said he was "a Japanese military spokesman" and often issued dispatches from Tokyo during World War II.

Foreign Affairs.' He was remembered for his athletic tennis prowess and for his excellence as a student of English."[143]

The connection between a long-ago former student and the exploding war appeared in an October 1942 article in *The News & Observer*, headlined, **Jap Militarist Educated Here**.[144] War hysteria was at its height, yet one does not get the impression that any fallout reached campus when examining the 1942 issues of the *Old Gold and Black*. The student's print world was absorbed by campus social life and politics. War mentions were scattered, without recalling a former friend, now enemy, Yakiama.

POST-WAR REBUILDING

Bynum Shaw, in his *History of Wake Forest University,* celebrated the efforts of A. L. Aycock, who stepped in for his second time as the debate coach.

> In 1946 intercollegiate debating, a casualty of the war, was revived under the coaching of Prof. A. L. Aycock... Veteran oratorical performers Samuel Behrends, Jr., Henry Huff, Kermit Caldwell, and Daniel Lovelace were joined by bright young talents like T. Lamar Caudle, J. B. Scott, and Vernon Wall, Jr., and they fielded the premier teams of the national debating circuit. So prestigious were the titles and awards they brought home that Old Gold was prompted to ask editorially, "Mr. Aycock, how do you do it?"[145]

Returning to tournament competitions following the war, "Several girls indicated their interest in special speech events as well—some in debate—and, according to Aycock's statement, a girl's debate team is a possibility this year."[146]

The Wake Forest forensic squad left early on a 1946 Wednesday morning for Georgetown, Kentucky, for the regional Pi Kappa Delta tournament.

---

[143] Nancy Sullivan, January 9, 2020. Wake Forest Special Collections & Archives. https://zsr.wfu.edu/2020/wake-forest-revisits-wwii/.

[144] *The News & Observer*, October 19, 1942, page 18.

[145] Bynum Shaw, Ed., (1988), *History of Wake Forest University -1943-1967*, Vol. IV, page 55.

[146] *Old Gold and Black,* October 4, 1946, page 2.

Prof. Aycock made the trip. "This is the first important meet a Wake Forest group has participated in since 1943".[147]

An *Old Gold and Black* editorial, written upon the resurrection of intercollegiate debating following the World War II pause, extolled debate's worth:

ENSIC WINNERS Wake Forest college won a majority of th events of the men's division of the 15th annual Eastern Forensic tourney, held in Charlotte this year, and Virginia Inter college duplicated it in the women's division. Seated, left to right, are x group C. students who helped put their school on top, Elizabeth Hickman Branch, and Emilie Brownlie. Behind are representatives of Wake For [ ]ining group, C. C. Hope of Charlotte, Bob Smith, and Burnette Harvey [ ]ver Staff Photo.)

> When the drums of war began their beat, forensics joined many rather worthwhile activities and went into mothballs. But the need for producing men of oratorical abilities and proficiency in thinking on their feet did not become non-existent. Debating is still a requisite for well-rounded campus-building men and women capable

Wake Forest 1943 Winners
Grand Eastern Forensics Tournament

of expressing themselves... Debating is not a stuffed-shirt form of boredom; it is a fascinating lively battle of wits. The world lies at the feet of the man who can think straight and put his thoughts into words.[148]

At a regular 1946 Wednesday afternoon meeting, two teams staged the first squad debate since 1943. Dick Williams and Kermit Caldwell articulated an affirmative proposal for the *expansion of reciprocal trade agreements*... Sam Behrends and Al Copeland replied."[149]

Perhaps Wake Forest's strong debating team turned in one of the most brilliant debating performances a month later in April: "Competing in

---

[147] *Old Gold and Black,* October 4, 1946, page 2; During the immediate post-war years, debaters traveled to the University of North Carolina for what were essentially dual meets, and in 1948, had two Duke teams over where two debates took place in the respective Literary Society halls.

[148] *Old Gold and Black,* March 1, 1946, page 2.

[149] *Old Gold and Black,* March 15, 1946, page 1.

the Pi Kappa Delta's National Intercollegiate Tournament at Bowling Green, Ohio, Wake Forest finished in a three-way tie for the national championship with Baylor University..., and Nebraska Wesleyan University... These three teams went through a weeklong tournament without a defeat...[150] 78 teams from all sections of the country competed. The Wake Forest team consisted of Sam Behrends, a Wilmington Senior, and Henry Huff, a Washington, D.C., law student."[151]

Forensics at Wake Forest enjoyed a successful year, likely enticing the *Howler* to poke fun with the team:

> At Wake Forest, generally speaking, the team has been pretty generally speaking, generally. Behrends spoke. So did several other fellows. The team debated quite a lot."
>
> Several of the fellows got prizes for stuff. Debating, speaking, talking, stuff like that. Several others didn't. One-time old Behrends got a prize. For something, I forget. Hocked it, though. Didn't bring much. Lots of times the fellows debated and talked and such at different woman's colleges. And then, after the debates were over, everybody would get a date and sit around and drink cokes and talk about life. Girl debaters are very intelligent, especially from V.I. (Vir. Inst.), because they all come from Oklahoma and are very pretty and eight feet tall and they take your mind off debating.[152]

In 1947 Sam Behrends and Henry Huff received an invitation to the soon-to-be-prestigious, West Point tournament. The invitation was for an exclusive 32-team tournament, the First Annual National Invitational Debate Tournament (later known as the NDT).[153] The pair reached the elimination rounds before falling to Notre Dame. The claim to fame was a win over the University of Southern California.[154]

---

[150] Three teams 8-0. The team defeated Ottawa, KS; Howard Payne, TX; Monmouth, IL; Illinois Wesleyan, IL; Illinois State Normal, IL; Bowling Green State Univ.; Kent State, OH; and Heidelberg, OH. Three were top seeds.

[151] *Wake Forest College Alumni News*, Vol. 51, No. 4, May 1947, page 2.

[152] *Howler*, 1942, page 107.

[153] Pi Kap Nationals was a bi-annual affair, without qualifying requirements, open to the Honorary's member schools.

[154] *Old Gold and Black*, May 9, 1947, page 1. "Aycock emphasized the triumph over Southern California climaxed the personal hopes of the squad. ...This win completed

1947 Wake Forest National Co-Champions Debaters
Bottom row, from left: E. M. Britt, Lumberton; Sam Behrends, Willington;
Henry Huff, Washington D. C.; Larry Williams, Canton. Top Row: Kermit
Caldwell, Maiden; Hubert Humphrey, Columbia, S. C.; Robert N. Smith,
Wilmington; Daniel Lovelace, Raleigh; Professor A. Lewis Aycock, Coach.

It is not clear how the relative worth of the two tournaments would
have been weighed at the time, but one suspects the National Pi Kappa
Delta Convention win counted more. Professor Aycock, who accompanied the team to West Point, took the opportunity to promote the
debaters; in an article, he acclaimed each debater by name, expressing
"great satisfaction at the outcome of both the West Point tournament
and the overall results of the squad this year. He pointed out that of all
the 51 Tournament debates participated in by the squad in 1943, Wake
Forest teams have won 41.[155]

Of course, Aycock received praise for winning Nationals. President
James Ralph Scales added at his commemorative, "The printed catalog

---

wins over top teams from every section of the country," *Old Gold and Black*, May
9, 1947, page 3.
[155] *Old Gold and Black*, May 9, 1947, page 3.

has announced a Department of Speech for only a generation or so, and that too fails to reflect the fact that Lewis Aycock was the coach of a national championship debating team long before formal studies in forensics existed."[156]

Closing the Intercollegiate Epoch

Close to the turn of the century in 1908, *The Biblical Recorder* bragged about its premier Baptist College, Wake Forest. The *Recorder* reported that the student "enrollment has swelled to 371, the teaching force to 32, and the list of graduates to 1,134, including some of the leading men of the country in all professions." The Church exponent certified, "It is prepared to give a training of genuinely collegiate standard amid exceptionally favorable circumstances." Describing the school with access but safely distanced from Raleigh, Wake Forest *"is as free from unwholesome moral Influences as any village in the country."*[157]

Sam Behrends – Wake -1942-1946

Regardless of the State Convention's view of isolation as a component of spiritual health, distances shrank, and the mission grew. Wake Forest was very different by the end of the Intercollegiate era. Its Baptist ties lingered, but the school's era of focusing on missionary work and primarily producing preachers had passed.

Although the numbers sound modest in modern terms, the *College Bulletin -1928-29* reported that the total student fees collected from the entire student body (Approx. 525 undergraduate

---

[156] James Ralph Scales, Wake Forest President, April 12th, 1978, Funeral for Andrew Lewis Aycock.

[157] *The Biblical Recorder*, September 2, 1908, page 1.

students) were $66,894.95, less than the tuition of a single student today. The salary for the entire faculty in 1928-29 summed to $85,634 (for approximately 30 faculty members), a remuneration less than that of a single instructor presently.

Almost all students, 651 of 668 (including professional and graduate programs), were from North Carolina, with only one or two students from each of 16 other states. By 1929, the student body had grown 50% since the turn of the century.[158]

Campus dancing ended in 1957 when the banned was lifted. Dancing on campus happened throughout the history of Wake Forest, from the earliest days.

There were fractures as the college grew to become a 21st-century "regional college," but more traditional directions prevailed during the first five decades under the Baptist Convention's proprietorship.

As the years unfolded, the partnership between Wake Forest and the Baptist Convention became increasingly strained, with symbolic quarrels

---

[158] 1928-9 *Wake Forest Bulletin.*

appearing frequently. An indicative episode was the ongoing 40-year culture war regarding dancing on campus.

When Wake debate was undertaking multiple debate tours, *The Biblical Recorder* warned in 1936 that "the largest contributors to the endowment were not contributing to promote worldliness..."

In a 1936 Commencement story, *The Biblical Recorder* went off its usual laudatory script to lambaste a move that would allow dancing at Wake, a one-year experiment. They editorialize:

> The one action of the Trustees that will incite most interest was the authorization of the use of the college buildings by the students toward dances. There were some safeguards thrown around the grant: it was to be temporary, for only one year, and experimental; the dancers were under faculty supervision. Doubtless, the Trustees, in voting this permission, thought they were acting in the best interests of the College and the Baptists of the State whose entities they are... We know also that they were in a hard situation when asked to vote on a proposition which purported... to be the wish of "ninety-seven percent of the students (970 of the thousand students), and a predominant majority of the faculty."[159] And yet we would be false to our sense of duty if we did not take this occasion to say that in our view by authorizing dances at Wake Forest College, the Trustees made a serious mistake and that their action does not have our approval...[160] [Contributors] had in their hearts the fact that

---

[159] A fascinating group of interviews from the major Wake Forest Faculty members (N. Y. Gulley, Dean Emeritus of the School of Law, J. H. Gorrell, 42 years professor, J. W. Lynch, 71-year-old famous religion Prof., and W. R. Cullen, 40 years religion teacher, who taught perhaps the majority of ministers in Baptists Pastorates in NC), responding to the editorial in defense of the Dance experiment, their comments can be found at *The News & Observer*, July 19, 1936, page 30. A major argument was it is better to dance supervised in a Christian campus atmosphere than off to unsupervised venues in "nearby cities and resorts." Al Martin, President of the student body, famous debater, and later faculty member, called the Convention's decision to oppose the dance experiment a "militant attack" against the decision of the trustees.

[160] "... Many Baptists will think that faith has not been kept with those whose prayers and tears and sacrifices founded the college and have supported it through all the years. These men and women, including Mr. Jabez A. Bostwick, the largest contributor to the endowment, were not contributing to promote worldliness; they were contributing to promote the causes of religion. The students, while defending that campus dances were better than Raleigh soirées, backed off and

the primary purpose of Wake Forest College from the first day until now has been to give our Baptist people an educated ministry for their churches; and that all else is secondary.

... Would Jesus endorse dancing?[161]

Dancing on campus would continue, as before and after the State Baptist objections but would have to wait nearly 30 years to be fully sanctioned.[162] G. W Paschal's volume III, *History of Wake Forest College*, provides a noteworthy account of the decades of student pressure, Baptists' intransigence, Board of Trustees' hesitations, and a personal defense of his opposing dancing.[163] The debate team, as they typically align, was with progressive forces.[164]

Debater Robert Helms'[165] appears prominently in all the accounts of the squad's success in 1936-1939. His teaching career, which followed, spanned sixty-three years at Wake. In the spring of 1979, the admired

---

passed a resolution, "Although the vast majority of the student body thought and still thinks that supervised dancing was the best solution to their problem, at no time did the students wish or intend to cause a disturbance among the Baptists of the state or to disrupt the work of the denomination." *Asheville Citizen-Times*, September 19, 1936. page 6.

[161] *The Biblical Recorder*, June 10, 1936, page 6.

[162] The Intervening years were densely populated with Fraternity and Sorority dances.

[163] Paschal, G. W. (1948). *History of Wake Forest College*, Vol. III, page 444-451. The newspaper reported that only G. W. Paschal, also an associate editor of *The Biblical Recorder*, opposed. Paschal, in a footnote (*History of Wake Forest College*, Vol III, page 446,) offered this less-than-convincing rebuttal: "The representation in *The News & Observer* of July 19, 1936, that only one professor at the College was opposed to the action of the Trustees in authorizing dancing is inaccurate. Several others assured the 'one' that he was not alone."

[164] In addition to debating, debaters often commented on the Academia v. Convention religious culture wars. More attention to debater activism is taken up in Vol. 2 of this series.

[165] Robert Helm was an internationally acclaimed philosopher. He passed away in Winston-Salem in 2019 at the age of 102, remaining sharp until his passing. A quotation in his obituary is instructive, "When I became a student at the 'old campus' at the age of eighteen, I found myself in an environment so classically and romantically attuned to my idealized image of a college, that I have never been able to break the bond that holds me to Wake Forest. Now, more than six decades later, I still feel a deep sense of pride in the intellectual integrity that is its historic heritage, the beauty of a campus that I have known from its beginnings, and the richness of a spirit that draws its strength from the dedication of generations of faculty and students."

Philosophy professor offered remarks that made visible what a debater's life was like in the late 1930s and provided a delightful account of how they sidestepped "dancing rules" in the Big Band era:

> Images of the Wake Forest of that day are still sharply etched in my memory. The physical setting of the College seemed ideally suited to the expansion of the mind. A stone-walled campus, enclosing ancient magnolia trees and ivy-covered buildings, stood athwart U.S. Highway number one, which led northward and southward to the busy world. That world of the thirties was, in some ways, quite different from the present one. We were not worried about an impending recession. We had a depression. There was no thought of inflation. Dollars were sound but scarce. We were not suffering the debilitating aftereffects of an unpopular war. The clouds of our conflict were just beginning to gather over Europe and many of us would be caught up in the coming storm. What is surprising is that we were, on the whole, an optimistic generation. The world seemed improvable, and the eternal verities were still in place.
>
> The College, too, was different from the one you see today. With a student body composed almost entirely of male pedestrians, we were quite free of parking problems and disputes over inter-visitation. Our social life was pleasant, but it represented a perennial triumph of ingenuity over inadequacy. We were free to honor eight of the nine Muses at Wake Forest, but we had to go to Raleigh to pay proper homage to the ninth, Terpsichore,[166] for her devotees did not hold the reins of power in the Baptist State Convention. For our dances, we invited girls from our home communities and found lodgings for them in local boarding houses, or if transportation problems were acute, in accommodations nearer the scene of the festivities. The dances were black-tie affairs. On Saturday afternoons, buses, trains, and the cars of charitable southbound motorists were filled with penguin-like figures resplendent in the dinner jackets, starched shirts and stiff collars of the period, all headed for capital city ballrooms and the siren sounds of the big bands. Then, in the pre-dawn hours of Sunday, the weary revelers would board the Seaboard local train

---

[166] Terpsichore, in Greek mythology, is one of the nine Muses, patron of lyric poetry and dancing.

affectionately known as the Hoot Owl for the sixteen-mile trip back to Wake Forest.[167]

Talk was an essential part of the Wake Forest tradition. In the days when I had still been undecided as to which college to attend, a distinguished alumnus had tried to help me map my future. "Go to Wake Forest, my boy," he had advised, "and join the Euzelian Literary Society – the Euzelian, mind you, not the Philomathesian." His tone of voice when he said "Philomathesian" had been the one with which a Southerner of his political persuasion would have said "Yankee" or "Republican," and I am afraid I was a trifle prejudiced when I arrived on campus. I dutifully joined the Euzelians but learned that the two societies were equally reputable and that they had historically been at the very center of the life of the College... They were the proud custodians of elegantly paneled and carpeted halls, with specially designed furniture and paintings of formidable-looking public figures who had learned to think and speak under "Eu" or "Phi" auspices.

It would be difficult to exaggerate the contribution made by those societies to the life of the College. Tangle-tongued young men entered their halls and left the campus four years later articulate and self-confident speakers. Under pressure of criticism and debate, emotional advocacy gave way to rational discourse, and the horizons of our intellects were greatly expanded.[168]

By the end of Aycock's era and the 1948 handoff to Franklin Shirley, debate competition had moved from the Intercollegiate era to nearly fully tournament oriented.[169] Chapter 15, Transition from Society Life, provides absorbing details of the late stages of the Literary Societies' eroding scaffolding. But before that departure, there remains an equally intriguing narrative of reaching out to secondary schools. The coaches featured in this chapter hosted decades of invitational tournaments.

Wake Debate entered the "Modern Era."

---

[167] Robert Helm, Jr., The Spring of Learning, Remarks at Opening Convocation, Wake Forest, September 6, 1979.

[168] Robert Helm, Jr., The Spring of Learning, Remarks at Opening Convocation, Wake Forest, September 6, 1979.

[169] See Milestones, Vol. 3 of this series for entry on "International and Non-Literary Society Public Debates."

CHAPTER 14

Tournament Hosting in the Pre-Shirley Era

Declamation

Declamation presentations and contests were common in the American scene of the 1800s and early 1900s and still exist in local speech forums.[1] From civic organizations to Grange Halls it was not unusual for a speaker to portray the words of some past political or social icon. At its simplest, declamation is a memorized presentation that renders another's words for a local audience. It often involves delivering a well-known speech, poem, or piece of oratory with a strong emphasis on **impassioned** expression and powerful delivery.

From the beginning, Wake's Literary Societies accommodated weekly student declamations. Such practices, although downplayed, survived for much of the literary years. Criticism especially resided among those who self-identified as debaters, who characterized declamation as an empty rendition. Their preference held that presentations emphasizing invention (original oratory or debate) were superior training. The Eus in 1853, Phis in 1881 dropped declamations as a required meeting staple, yet they continued.

---

[1] The author's grandfather, in his younger days, was often called up to deliver a long narrative story of the rural life at the community gatherings in Alberta, Canada, as part of the evening's entertainment, guaranteed to bring tears among those enthralled. Declamations were the element anchoring their shared culture for civic and social groups of every stripe.

Focusing on declamation's shortcomings alone would be to miss the import of the communicative form. Delivering the words of another may strike contemporary speakers as merely derivative, an exercise in the repetitive and superfluous, yet that ignores the reasons declamations were broadly embraced.

The period, emerging from England's Elocution movement, emphasized delivery, gestures, and intonation, and was more justified as science than as rhetorical invention. These attractions were delivered to audiences in local and intimate settings for intellectual enhancement or escapism. Interpretations of the great speeches and thinkers of the era were channeled through speakers at small local gatherings, frequently transferring those grand ideas to illiterate audiences. The importance of sharing and building this cultural consensus can hardly be underestimated. While newspapers were the foremost form of mass communication, they were of little value to the majority who could not read.

In the early 1900s, college and high schools appropriated increasingly detailed "scientifically" based interpretations of what practices best conveyed a message.[2] The "declamation contest" innovation was an obvious outgrowth of widespread community promotion. It was offered as a valuable tool for educating high school students about the culture and importance of people and events in the past, all the while enhancing their confidence in public speaking.

In this same period, the academy was carrying on a parallel discussion of which is the more worthwhile: an emphasis on presentation and effective communication versus honing the skills of invention and logic (see Chapter 4 -Debating in the Literary Societies). Everett Lee Hunt, one of the founders of the National Communication Association, in a 1922 New York University convention, addressed the then National Association of Teachers of Speech, offering a derisive judgment surveying debate in opposition to declamation:

> But when a teacher of elementary courses in oral expression and extempore speaking also has elementary courses in dramatic art, and then hastens to meet some elementary debaters, and then must conduct a spasm of training for a declamation contest . . . what has such a man to do with scholarship? The teacher of argumentation and debate who will eagerly investigate the field of logic and rhetoric, who can speak upon the great debates with the background of a student of history or politics has no time for staging plays or coaching declamation contests.[3]

The Societies were aware of their choice, even as they infused meetings with declamations. Early in January 1851, they debated whether *Public declamation at College should be dispensed with*. The debate was decided

---

[2] Cohen, H. (1994). *The history of speech communication: The emergence of a discipline, 1914-1945*. National Communication Association, Washington, DC.

[3] Hunt, E. L. (1923). Rhetoric and literary criticism. *Quarterly Journal of Speech, 21*, pages 67-76. Before the 1890s, the merits of recitation vs invention were a flourishing debate. In 1891, *The Wake Forest Student* wrote, "It is no longer the object of elocution to make a man an imitator, but to develop the original power with which he is endowed," *The Wake Forest Student*, March 1891, page 115. The campus hosted HS declamation contests for decades. Declamation was felt to be an accessible mode for the high school student. Debating and competitive speech events would enter shortly before World War II.

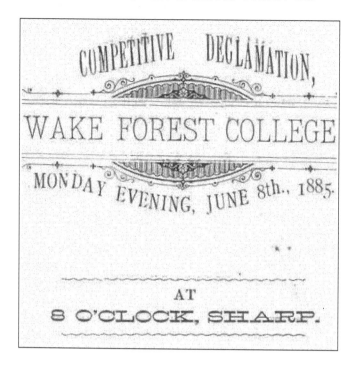

by the chairman's tie-breaking vote (the direction of the vote was not recorded in the ledger). Even earlier, in February 1842, the Phis debated Whether *The exercise of declamation was favorable to elocution.* They judged declamation superior, 19 to 6.

Despite the academic and Literary Society's ambivalence, declamations remained a hosted tournament staple as late as the mid-1920s. Declamation's competitive attraction endured for sensible reasons (visited below), with support from the college and high school communities.

Students' competitive declamation selections had a familiar ring to them, indirectly revealing societal standards. The 1917 Wake HS tournament found that Boston's Bunker Hill was not to be overlooked; neither was the audience allowed to forget the stormy Civil War days of '61-'65 or Napoleon's conquests: "They live on in the minds of the high school declaimers, the brave deeds of the Greeks and Spartans, the 'Fathers of His Country,' as well as Benedict Arnold, vividly recalled to the imaginations of the several hundred college students and townspeople who attended the declamations."[4]

---

[4] *Old Gold and Black,* January 6, 1917, page 1.

Popular subjects in a 1922 Wake-hosted North Carolina High School tournament included Presidents Woodrow Wilson and Warren G. Harding and newly elected North Carolina Governor Bickett, each of whom furnished several speeches. There were also abundant poems, "the only one of which reached the finals: The Cremation of Sam McKee" ... [5]

High School Declamations

Around the First World War, Wake's declamation content was introduced. The student newspaper recognized it as: "The first High School Disclaimers contest ever held at Wake Forest ... it will welcome over 25 students representing the leading preparatory schools in the state.[6]

In the inaugural year, 1916, the *Old Gold and Black*'s optimism showed:

The Euzelian and Philomathesian Literary Societies of Wake Forest College, realizing the need of a feeder, are now preparing for a State High School Declaimers Contest to be held here next April, to which each accredited high school in the state is to send a representative to compete for the first prize, consisting of a $50 scholarship in the college, a handsome gold medal bearing the emblems of both Societies and a second prize, in the form of a gold pin, which will bear the emblems.[7]

This contest is expected to be the means of getting a number of the best speakers from the various high schools of the State to enter college here and thus come into the Literary Societies. "Wake Forest has been slow in realizing the need for such a contest, and it is due to the efforts of Mr. A. Clayton Reid that the present movement is on foot."[8]

The declamation contest, readily welcomed as a "modern" entry into the high school contests scene, became Wake Forest's exponent,

---

[5] *Old Gold and Black,* March 24, 1922, page 2.

[6] *Old Gold and Black,* January 6, 1917, page 1.

[7] The school newspaper bragged that "the medal was worth $12.50, and the pin was $5... The second-place man was presented with a pin. *Old Gold and Black*, January 13, 1917, page 4; By 1920, the value of the medals increased to a substantial $25 gold medal and $50 scholarship [tuition waiver] for the contest winner, $12.50 gold pin for second. *The Wake Forest Student*, December 1920, page 41.

[8] *Old Gold and Black*, September 16, 1916, page 1, 3.

establishing a link with high schools throughout the state. It served the high schools' interests as well, offering proper training for the "uninitiated" high schoolers.

The transparent purpose was the unabashed promotion of the college. "What Wake Forest needs is more advertising and advertising of this sort is at once effective and attractive...It gives the contestants a view of the Wake Forest spirit and the aims of the institution. It makes friends for them among the students and exerts a wholesome influence on the whole institution...It is the best way to get the people of the State acquainted with Wake Forest because it makes Wake Forest mean something to them."[9]

1923 *Howler* illustrates the prominence placed on Wake's Declamation Tournament

It was not clear that the initial 1917 competition would happen. Wilmington's *Daily Advance* shared some inside info. "For the past six months, the committee on arrangements, of which A. C. Reid Eu is secretary, has been corresponding with the various high school principals in the hope that enough entrants might be secured to secure this contest. At present, forty-four schools have already entered the contest, and more are entering every day..."[10] Eventually, 53 prepa-

---

[9] *Old Gold and Black*, December 4, 1917, page 4.

[10] *The Daily Advance* (Elizabeth City, NC), March 6, 1917, page 4.

ratory schools participated, representing practically every section of the state and Cluster Springs of Virginia.[11]

Despite apprehension about the event's planning, the 1917 event did take shape, offering unique attractions for the guests, including the societies arranging "free entertainment," a basketball game, and attending the Wake Forest-Colgate Intercollegiate debate in the evening.[12]

By 1919, *The Wake Forest Student* reported that "any accredited school could send one representative to speak in the declamation contest. … Apparently, some schools were reluctant to send students to the 1919 Declamation contest for fear of then-serious ailments.[13]

The contest preliminaries were held in two society halls and Memorial Hall. Ten speakers were selected to compete in the finals. After the prelims, an informal reception was held in the society halls to honor the visitors. Finals took place the following afternoon in Memorial

---

[11] *Asheville Citizen-Times* March 9, 1917, page 1.

[12] *Old Gold and Black,* January 6, 1917, page 1.

[13] *Old Gold and Black,* February 22, 1919, page 1; Estimates varied, but most were in the low 50s. In 1919, the Philomathesian Constitution and bylaws codified the rules for hosting the Annual High School Declamation Contest, held jointly with the Euzelian Society.

1. Every accredited high school in North Carolina is invited.
2. The duty of the societies is to provide entertainment for the contestants.
3. Friday and Saturday nights in April.
4. For the best speaker in the contest, the college agrees to give a scholarship.
5. Gold medals for the best speakers, bearing the emblems of both Societies and costing not less than $10 nor more than 12 ½ dollars.
6. The second speaker gets a pin.
7. Arrangements to be handled by the bursar and the joint committee.

A 1922 version of the contest rules added constraints and specificity.

1. Any North Carolina High School is entitled to one male representative.
2. No declamation shall contain more than eleven hundred words.
3. Ten speakers shall be selected who shall enter the final contest.
4. The winner of the first prize shall receive a scholarship worth fifty dollars and a gold medal valued at twenty-five dollars.
5. The winner of the second prize shall receive a gold pin, bearing the emblems of both societies, valued at twelve and one-half dollars. The remaining eight shall receive a gold pin bearing the emblem of the college seal.
6. All contestants must arrive at Wake Forest and register by 6:30 P. M. March sixteenth.
7. Each representative shall be furnished free entertainment while at Wake Forest, Old Gold and Black, February 22, 1919, page 7.

SOME FUTURE TAR HEEL ORATORS GATHERED AT WAKE FOREST FOR DECLAMATION CONTEST

Wake Forest College, long famed as a training center for orators, has just closed another declamation conetst, in which the 59 high school boys shown above showed themselves to be possessed of forensic talent of no mean order. S. L. Blanton, of the Piedmont High School, wone the first prize with "Harding's Farewell Address to the Disarmament Conference." The first prize was a scholarship to Wake Forest College, and a gold medal. John Yonan, of the Charlotte High School, took second prize—a gold medal—with his declamation "At the Grave of Napoleon."

Hall.[14] It is not hard to imagine the reception as a major recruiting event for the college. However, World War I and the Spanish Flu dampened participation and numbers fell during the war.[15]

In the second year of the declamation contest, literary societies added an essay contest with a whopping prize of $80, nearly $1500 in current value, offered in three categories, in gold coin. The major portion, however, was not a gold coin but a scholarship redeemable at Wake Forest. Eventually, awards were extended to the other eight declaimers in the final round, all of whom were awarded college seal pins.[16]

---

[14] *The Wake Forest Student*, April 1920, page 270.

[15] *Old Gold and Black*, February 4, 1921, page 1.

[16] *The Wake Forest Student*, February 1922, page 243 : In the 1922 contest, "S. L. Blanton got first place; came to school here and debated here." The contests with fifty-dollar scholarships worked their will.

Unlike the declamation contest, essays could be awarded to "girls," not only "boys." The caveat was that "if the first prizes was won by a girl, she will place a scholarship at the disposal of the principal of her school to be given by him to a male member of the graduating class."[17] After all, Wake was then safely an all-male enclave. Little evidence emerged that the essay contest lasted long term.

In 1923, the contest became known as the Annual Inter-Scholastic Tournament or, as the student paper referred to it in 1927, the "Eleventh Athletic Tournament and Declamation Contests."[18] The new name reflected an expansion of the contests to include track for the first time.[19] Each school was invited to send five representatives for track (but continued to be restricted to one in the declamation contest).[20] Plaques were awarded to the winners of the first three places in each of the events, and a cup was awarded to the school making the largest number of points in the tournament. 1923 also added a gold medal for third place in the declamation contest.[21] Wake alumni around the state often sponsored HS teams or individual entries to introduce the young men to the campus.[22]

Until 1930, the Societies Declamation Contest Committee administered the HS tournament. That year, faculty member A. L. Aycock became director of the annual declamation contest and track meet.[23]

Spanish Flu

In the summer of 1918, Wake Forest was a quiet college town with 1,443 residents (1910 Census) and 1,536 (1920 Census). The streets were still unpaved, and two or three town-maintained wells were in the middle of South White Street. The town commissioners kept muttering... that hogs were not allowed in town.

---

[17] *Old Gold and Black*, February 16, 1918, page 1.

[18] *Old Gold and Black*, January 8, 1927, page 1.

[19] *Old Gold and Black*, January 16, 1923, page 1.

[20] In 1927 the ratio of track to declamation contestants changed such that "each school may be represented by as many as five contestants, not more than two of which may take part in each event." *Old Gold and Black*, December 17, 1927.

[21] *Old Gold and Black*, January 30, 1923, page 1.

[22] *Old Gold and Black*, January 8, 1927, page 1.

[23] *Old Gold and Black*, January 25, 1930, page 1.

That communal diseases would impact the College was not new. Before the Spanish Flu, prevalent infections caused people to stay close to home. In 1901 grave disappointment was registered when the Anniversary Day event was held with a "shadow of sadness cast over it." The problem was that the university girls in Raleigh could not attend, restricted by their president. Of course, *The Wake Forest Student* writer thought, "We should've been willing to risk the smallpox in order for the girls to come....to wear their new evening dresses..." [24]

The devastating world came to Wake Forest on Sept. 14, 1918, registration day at the college: "Students began falling ill during the day, and by nightfall all the College Hospital beds were full. The Euzelian dormitory in the old College Building was taken over as a hospital ward. That fall, 60 percent of the students and eight faculty members fell ill, cared for mostly by the three doctors on the School of Medicine faculty. Six patients later developed pneumonia, and one student died."

Paschal documented that the student who died "Was James L. Hedgecock of the vicinity of High Point.[25] The epidemic continued, with much abatement in the later weeks, until after the Armistice. In this period there were no church services nor other public gatherings in Wake Forest; among the citizens of the town there were many cases of the disease and not a few deaths."[26]

What was called the "Spanish Flu" had arrived in the township.[27]

A February 1918 headline from the *Old Gold and Black* acknowledged fewer attendees at the Anniversary Day celebration without once revealing why a quarantine was in place.

FEW VISITORS HELP LITERARY SOCIETIES
CELEBRATE EIGHTY-THIRD ANNIVERSARY
Marked Decrease in Attendance of out-of-town Visitors Noticeable.
Celebration More Serious than Usual.[28]

---

[24] *The Wake Forest Student*, March 1901, page 417.

[25] *The Wake Forest Student* note assessed that his death "was likely due only indirectly to influenza. Certainly, everything was done to save him." The note thanked the nurses and Professors of Medicine Aiken, Kitchin, and Buchanan. *The Wake Forest Student*, February 1919, Vol. 38, page 36.

[26] Paschal, G. W. (1948), *History of Wake Forest College*, Vol. III, page 95.

[27] See Katie Lawrence, Wake Forest College, and the Spanish Flu. ZSR Library Blogs, https://zsr.wfu.edu/2020/wake-forest-college-and-the-spanish-flu/.

[28] *Old Gold and Black*, February 23, 1918, page 1.

By October, the town board had banned all public meetings, including the moving picture shows, public schools, churches, and classes at the college. In February of 1920, all public meetings were again banned except for regular college classes and Anniversary Day exercises. The student newspaper, the *Old Gold and Black,* was closed at the end of April 1918 with no further issues that year, and there were fewer issues in the 1919 Spring semester. Mention of Wake Forest's experience with the pandemic in the Raleigh newspapers was sparse.[29]

Despite being referred to as the "1918 influenza pandemic," four pandemic waves occurred between 1918 and 1920.[30] It was estimated that approximately 1,000,000 of North Carolina's 2.5 million inhabitants had caught the disease. The state sent 86,457 soldiers overseas to fight for the United States. In only five months of combat, 624 North Carolinians were killed in battle, while 3,655 were wounded. In addition to the battle casualties, another 1,542 North Carolinians died of disease while serving in the army, mostly from influenza. Even more died of influenza back home.[31]

Eu. Minutes of January 22, 1918, entertained a motion to make changes to the Wednesday night section due to insufficient members. A reason was not provided, although WW I and the Spanish flu may have contributed.

Only eight schools responded to the declamation contest in 1918, a month out, and the secretary of the committee, A. C. Reid, raised the alarm. He claimed schools should attend without mentioning the flu: "No school should fail to send a representative because it cannot be as good as it did last year, since all schools are affected alike by the war."[32]

A year later, in an attempt to convince high schools to send representatives, the *Old Gold and Black* wrote in 1919, "No high school need fear sending a representative because of fear of the influenza or any other

---

[29] Just a little history: Wake Forest's first pandemic, *Wake Forest Gazette*, July 29, 2020. https://wakeforestgazette.com/just-a-little-history-wake-forests-first-pandemic/

[30] https://exhibits.lib.unc.edu/exhibits/show/going-viral/north-carolina

[31] https://www.ncpedia.org/nc-wwi; Influenza killed almost 500,000 Americans – ten times the number of American soldiers who died in combat during the war. American troop ships returning home with sick soldiers brought the flu to the home front. In a single week in October 1918, an estimated 21,000 Americans died. In North Carolina, 13,644 people died before the epidemic finally went away. During its peak in October and November, there were only two kinds of people in the state—those who were sick with influenza and those who were trying to save them.

[32] *Old Gold and Black*, February 16, 1918, page 1.

epidemic because Wake Forest is absolutely free of every form of disease and has been ever since the Christmas holidays."[33]

A slender comeback began in 1920. "A large number of contestants in the Inter-Scholastic Declamation Contest are now on the Hill, and the contest is well underway. The declaimers began coming in early Thursday morning, and by the time set for the preliminaries, about twenty-five were here Thursday evening. The preliminaries were held in Wingate Memorial Hall, and a large audience of town people and students was out to hear the contestant." The *Old Gold and Black*, 1920, indicated that the numbers at the Scholastic declamation contest were smaller than anticipated due to the influenza epidemic's effects.[34]

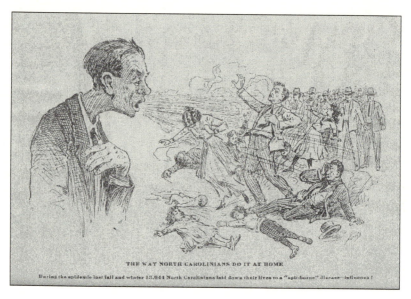

"The Way North Carolinians Do It at Home, 1919
NC State Bd of Health – *The Health Bulletin*

Despite the influenza ravaging the East Coast... neither *The Howler* yearbook nor the *Old Gold and Black mentioned* the Spanish Flu explicitly.[35]

---

[33] *Old Gold and Black*, February 22, 1919, page 1.

[34] *Old Gold and Black*, March 12, 1920, page 1.

[35] Suspending the publication of the *Old Gold and Black* in 1918 surely accounts for, in part, the OGB's retreat from acknowledging the flu. There were vague references

Remarkably, in 1919, little mention was made of influenza. *The News & Observer* offered the following lead to its coverage of the Anniversary Debates. "Under the most favorable weather conditions, and attended by a host of out-of-door-visitors, consisting chiefly of Meredith and Oxford college girls, the 84th annual celebration of the founding of the Philomathesian and Euzelian literary societies was celebrated today... The absence of classwork and the uninterrupted program rendered the celebration equally as delightful as those have been held in previous years."[36]

The following year, 1920, the 85th anniversary, was again affected by influenza as the *Greensboro Daily News* reported, "Although the customary large numbers of fair visitors from Meredith and Oxford college are absent owing to the quarantine in those schools on account of the Influenza epidemic, Wake Forest in a celebration of Anniversary Day Friday... A few guests made the occasion preventing it from becoming wholly a 'stag party. The few kindhearted young ladies, for the most part, from the town, realized our sad predicament."[37]

Across the state, the *Daily Tarheel* reported that 180 schools and 250 participants took part in the NC high school debating union.[38] The paper estimated the Wake Forest declamation contest in 1920 to have 25 entrants, the "blue epidemic" continuing its influence.

In a 1921 effort to rebuild the Contest, three separate letters were sent to "every Wake Forest alumnus who is teaching in the high schools of the state. A letter has been mailed requesting him to boost the contest and recommend some contestants. The second letter is one to the high school principal stating the rules and asking for his cooperation. Also, letters have been mailed to many students at the high school telling them of the contest, the prizes, and generally arousing interest."[39]

In 1921, 53 schools entered. *The Greensboro Record* chronicled, "Friday afternoon, the ten disclaimers who had been successful at night before assembled at Wingate Memorial Hall, and before a large audience, engaged

---

in *The Wake Forest Student.*

[36] *The News & Observer*, February 15, 1919, page 3.

[37] *Greensboro Daily News*, February 16, 1920, page 2; The article indicates the event was primarily outdoors. The year 1919 was also the break year between the 1918 and 1920 infection heights.

[38] *The Daily Tarheel*, February 28, 1920, page 4.

[39] *Old Gold and Black*, January 28, 1921, page 1.

in the final battle for the championship title and the medal which evinces the honor. Pres. Poteat was chairman. The first prize, a scholarship given by the college, and a gold medal given by the two societies, was awarded to C. W. Seller." His subject, the "*The Confederate Dead.*"[40]

Two year later, 1923, the *Old Gold and Black* would report that "once again the dreaded 'flu' made its appearance in and around the College community… So far there have been about fifteen… cases among the student body… Dr. Kitchin states that there are no indications of having to curtail classes."[41] Quietly normality was restored.

World War I

The 1920 *Howler's* "Senior Class History" section unfolded with a chronicle of World War I's impact on campus, year by year. Subtly, the active literary members viewed the war with patriotic poise yet also kept alive their anticipation for resuming Intercollegiate Debates:

> The latter part of our first year saw the opening of the bloodiest struggle the world has ever known, and it is but just to say that there were no slackers among us. From the rank and file of our college life we answered the country's call to "Make the world safe for Democracy."
>
> To a class with such a brilliant beginning the Sophomore year added continuous successes. Though our numbers had grown smaller during the months, we were still active in all college activities.
>
> When we returned to the campus in September 1918 – as Juniors, our ranks still more depleted – we found our beloved college temporarily converted into a military training camp, our campus a drill field. But we were proud to be of aid to our government in battling with autocracy. And then came that glorious day, November 11th, which brought to us news of the close of the mighty conflict and the triumph of Democracy.
>
> The opening of the spring term brought us again to real college life and we furnished to all varsity teams men who made our college

---

[40] *Greensboro Daily News*, March 20, 1921, page 10.
[41] *Old Gold and Black*, January 16, 1923, page 1.

1913 – *Howler* – The Deacon before the "Deacon"

athletics famous... In the intercollegiate debates, the Class of '20 sent out men who brought back unanimous decisions in their favor.[42]

A more visceral account by student "Re. Q" in 1919 talks of the displacements, including in society life, even as signs of normalcy remained:

Dormitories were constituted barracks, and the ivy-clad walls of the old dormitory, for almost a century the silent sharer of whispered society secrets, now furnished shelter to both Eu and Phi alike. The mellow tones of the college bell gave way to the more commanding notes of the bugle. Kitchen police, reveille, and other military terms became painfully familiar, and soon the realization that we were at war was brought about. Debates were adjourned, studies were adapted to the demands of the government, and the student quickly applied himself to the mastery of the "soldier's bible."

[42] Senior Class History, *Howler*, 1920, Vol. 18, page 72.

Life in the Halls was altered due to fewer members. Several Eu minutes in late 1919 "set aside the roll call on account of some many men being away."[43]

President Poteat headed a ceremony honoring the Wake War dead following the War, related: "Twenty in number were the lads who left the wall of their alma mater to face the din of a mighty war never to return. Upon these loyal heroes of Wake Forest... is confirmed the greatest honor a nation can bestow..."[44]

World War I restricted the flourishing Intercollegiate debate culture, adding uncertainty to hosting and traveling. The reconstructed Debate Council in 1917 dealt with "resignations of its officers, who left College in response to the call of the National Government," and newly elected officers continued to negotiate with other colleges.[45]

They succeeded in 1917 with contracts reached before—Colgate, Randolph Macon, Baylor—which proceeded when the US declared war on Germany in April. Debates were again held with Randolph Macon and Baylor in 1918[46] and 1919, with the addition of Emory and Henry in the latter year; the year 1920 brought additional clashes with Colgate and Baylor.[47] Undoubtedly, the number of Intercollege Debates was reduced, without fresh opponents, yet the activity continued throughout the war period.

Declamation Tournament Recovers

By March of 1921, the High School Declamation Contest was running again. The contest grew in the number of schools participating from a couple of dozen to over 50 at its height. The *Old Gold and Black* excitedly asserted, "Eloquence and the oratory exhibited by these young speakers held the attention of large crowds and gave proof that oratory will mean a North Carolinian art for at least another generation."

---

[43] *Old Gold and Black,* October 10, 1936, page 1.

[44] *Old Gold and Black*, November 18, 1921, page 1.

[45] *The Wake Forest Student*, 1917, page 232. Intercollegiate Debates held during the war years are noted in Chapter 6 – Intercollegiate Debate Goes On The Road.

[46] In 1918 the Council lost its president and secretary to the war effort and recommended just two Intercollegiate events. January 15, 1918, *Old Gold and Black,* page 1.

[47] These debates are reviewed in more detail in Chapter 6 – Intercollegiate Debates Goes on the Road.

"The contestants were lodged in rooms of the dormitory and village and boarded at the Hodnitt House. The committee was on the job when it came to caring for the disclaimers." Five preliminary contests were held... members of the faculty and citizens of the town served as judges. Refreshments included ice cream, cake, and punch, which "brought the smile of satisfaction ... many of the Wake Forest's host of pretty girls, assisted by visiting girls, enlivened the evening as only the fairer sex can."[48]

The 1920 "royal welcome" was even more effusive, promising to engage "the entire campus for this student recruitment." ... "At a Thursday night reception, they will meet the faculty and the students. They will find at the reception conclusive proof that Wake Forest has her full quota of the fair sex." And even more temptation was on hand as "The baseball management has arranged to entertain an inter-collegiate baseball game to play here that day."[49]

[48] *Old Gold and Black*, March 25, 1921, page 1, 3.

[49] *Old Gold and Black*, February 13, 1920, page 1.

A year later, the hyped campus newspaper promised the entertainment was... Automobile rides around the city and the surrounding country, with moving picture parties and group pictures taken of all the contestants."[50] A special committee met all arriving trains.[51]

The next year, 1922, the number of schools entered had jumped to 56. An intact pattern of events and ancillary activities unfolded for several years. A typical winner commentary was flattering, as was the *Old Gold and Black's* 1922 announcement of the winner:

> To S. L. Blanton, of Piedmont High School... the first prize of the declamation contest... The main advantage Blanton had on his fellow contestants was due to his seniority over the great majority of them in age. But not only did his age contribute to his victory but the fact that his bearing on the floor was credible... Blanton's subject of declamation was *Harding's Farewell Address to the Disarmament Conference*, it was asserted by a number that heard the contest that the speaker got off the president's speech better than the chief executive could have himself.[52]

The *Old Gold and Black* listed every winner in the 1920s high school tournament, and the results were important enough to also be listed in major State newspapers, especially Raleigh and the towns in which the high schools were located. The declamation challenge generated considerable publicity.

Mathematics Prof. J. G. Carroll managed the tournament for a short period around 1925. He boasted that over 1000 letters had been sent inviting high schools (over 300), high school principals, and students and that over 600 copies of the *Old Gold and Black* were also mailed. Carroll cautioned, "I see only one difficulty and that is in providing the lodging place for all these high school visitors."[53]

---

[50] *Old Gold and Black,* March 3, 1922, page 1.

[51] *Old Gold and Black,* February 24, 1921, page 1.

[52] *Old Gold and Black,* March 24, 1922, page 1; From a large personage to another small in stature, another winners' description informs: "In the 10th Annual Declamation content, Caskin Norvell carried off the first honors... His rendition of 'The Shooting of Dan McGraw,' together with his small size, made him a favorite in the contest." *Old Gold and Black,* April 10, 1926, page 1.

[53] *Old Gold and Black,* March 14, 1925, page 1; In 1925 "Pres. W. L. Poteat presided over the finals", as he did in most years. That year, students from Winston-Salem

Carroll confronted his own challenges in managing the 1926 declamation event. A new precedent was nearly established when two young ladies applied for admission to present their declamations. It was feared, however, that these fair speakers might have used rather unfair means of swaying the judges to their side, and admissions were denied to them by Prof. Carroll.[54]

In the same year, 1926, the *Old Gold and Black* article promoting the upcoming interscholastic Declamation Tournament (and track meet) concocted an odd mixture in the author's attempt to highlight both the declamation and the athletic event. Writing with an "every-other-paragraph-style," the author would praise the immediate past winner of the declamation and, in the next, list the winners and who broke records among the runners and jumpers. The article, while praising traditions, lionized athletic competition in the end. The scholastic emphasis shifting away from speaking to physical prowess continued.[55]

By 1929, some of the steam was going out of the declamation event. The paper reported that only 35 or 40 boys entered the declamation contest whereas the promotional story hailed potentially 100 entering high schools. A further disappointment was that the contest could not be held in conjunction with a track meet. The track facilities were not adequate, so it was canceled. President Gaines presided in the afternoon when the elimination contests were held.[56]

Professor A. L. Aycock was appointed director of the Annual Declamation Contest and Track Meet in 1930.[57]

High School and Durham High School were the winners. *Old Gold and Black*, April 20, 1925, page 1.

[54] *Old Gold and Black*, April 2, 1926, page 3.

[55] *Old Gold and Black*, February 12, 1926, page 1, 2; The paper later reported sixty schools entering the declamation contest and thirty the track meet. *Old Gold and Black*, March 20, 1926, page 2; The cup presented to the declamation winner, some would say ironically, was sponsored by Athletic Supply Co of Raleigh, *Old Gold and Black*, April 2, 1927, page 1.

[56] *Old Gold and Black*, April 27, 1929, page 1; Wake was not alone in hosting tournaments. Carolina reportedly hosted 225 high schools in the 23rd Triangular Debates in 1923. The number reported was more likely the number of participants, not schools. These were debates, not declamation contests.

[57] *Old Gold and Black*, January 25, 1930, page 1.

Zon Robinson Reinvents the HS Tournament

Major changes were undertaken in the first year Zon Robinson hosted the High School tournament. *The Biblical Recorder* bore witness with its typical embossing, "The youthful debaters, some boys and some girls, got a chance to debate, not once but four times... It was a delight to see them and hear them. There is more noise at football games but the interest and earnest zeal at these debates was far greater than any other college event we have ever attended."[58]

Professor Zon Robinson announced that the 1939 contest was the first high school debate tournament held in North Carolina using extemporaneous techniques. A regional newspaper, *The Robesonian* (Lumberton, NC), described the tournament as an attempt to encourage high school debaters to do original work and depart from the traditional "canned" speech, too often written by adults.[59]

The President of the N. C. Association of Teachers of Speech commented: "Repeatedly, high school principals and debate coaches have suggested that steps be taken to improve the status of organized speech and debate work in high schools. The criticism that the present system encourages stilted, declamatory speeches and discourages extemporaneous, direct-clash debating has come from many quarters. To meet the need so many have felt, the North Carolina Association of Teachers of Speech, in which twelve colleges and universities held membership, decided to sponsor this high school tournament at Wake Forest."[60]

Mr. Zon Robinson... worked out the numerous details of organizing the event.[61] He first sought the approval and financial support of the college trustees for the undertaking. Then, he submitted the plan for the

---

[58] *The Biblical Recorder,* April 19, 1939.

[59] *The Robesonian* (Lumberton. NC) February 24, 1939.

[60] Professor Edwin H. Paget, Director of the Division of Speech at N. C. State College, then President of the N. C. Association of Teachers of Speech, was one of the most ardent advocates of the new tournament. After its establishment, he and his debaters continued to contribute greatly to its success.

[61] Robinson also contended with more tedious hurdles. He pleaded to the Wake Forest community for help "in providing free housing to the students." The visiting boys could be provided accommodations "in the gymnasium and student rooms but they needed to secure a place for the young ladies who would be attending." Robison's letter assured the faculty and townspersons "that the students be involved in the competitions, did not need to be entertained."

ZON ROBINSON   **WAKE FOREST COLLEGE**   GENE WORRELL
FACULTY DIRECTOR   SPEECH AND FORENSICS   STUDENT MANAGER

WAKE FOREST, NORTH CAROLINA

October 26, 1938

To the Principals and Superintendents of Group I High Schools:

The North Carolina Association of Teachers of Speech, in which twelve colleges and universities hold membership, is planning to sponsor a high school debate and speech tournament at Wake Forest sometime in March or April. (The date will not conflict with any other tournament. Due to the fact that it is impossible for an affair of this sort to be successful if it is too large, we are limiting our invitation to the sixty-four Group I Standard high schools in the state. This arrangement will have the added advantage of permitting larger and stronger schools to compete against schools of their own standard rating.

We should like for you to remember that this will not be just another tournament; it will be a DIFFERENT type of Tournament. Actual debate conditions will prevail: that is, an affirmative and negative will be placed in a separate room for the debates. Also, the judging will be done by experts, many of whom will be college debate coaches. After the debates the judges will give oral criticisms, thereby letting the debaters know WHY they won or lost.

The tournament is to be held on a week-end and will begin on Friday afternoon and run through Saturday. Each high school will be permitted to enter one or two teams, that is either an affirmative or negative or both. The national high school query on an Anglo-American alliance will be used. No pre-tournament debates are to be required, although schools are urged to hold as many as possible. It is our plan to let all of the teams debate four times in the meet before any are eliminated. In addition to the debates there will be contests in oratory and extempore speaking, in which the debaters may be entered. Lodging will be afforded free of charge. Meal may be secured in the college dining rooms for 20¢ or 25¢.

The purpose behind the tournament is the encouragement of a better type of debating in the high schools. All of us agree that we should get away from the stilted, "canned" speeches which many times pass for debates. We hope we may have your cooperation in this matter. If you are interested in having your school participate, please check the enclosed card and return it as soon as possible. Any comments or suggestions you wish to make will be welcome.

Sincerely yours,

Zon Robinson
Director of the Tournament

1938 letter Zon Robinson sent to HS Principals in conjunction with the State's Department of Public Instruction and the Association of North Carolina College Teachers of Speech announcing many new innovations.

proposed tournament to many leading high school officials and coaches for their reactions.[62]

Several features of the tournament made it distinctive. "Constructive training," [a guaranteed four rounds], instead of mere elimination of losing teams was stressed... Each debate was judged by a single critic judge who rendered a decision and gave a brief criticism of each team's strengths and weaknesses. Males and females both attended the tournament.[63]

The winning teams must win three out of four debates to advance. They met in the semi-finals until all but two were eliminated. These two battled in a final radio debate broadcast by Radio Station WPTF. The resolve was that *the United States should establish an alliance with Great Britain*. In addition to the debates, oratory and extempore speaking contests were included in the first tournament.[64]

"This tournament will make 'canned' speeches worthless, Prof Zon Robinson, announced this week, because debates will be judged on the basis of response to the argument set up by the opposing team."[65]

As a recruiting strategy, the tournament held sway. The *Old Gold and Black* suggested that "Ten of the sixteen highest-rated debaters enrolled in Wake Forest this year."[66] This claim is not verifiable due to the reporter's unspecified method of reaching the estimate, but it does shore up one of Robinson's goals, recruiting effective debaters.

Other Tournament Hosting

For an undetermined number of years, the Wake Forest College debate team provided coaching for the Wake Forest High School Debaters Club.

---

[62] Typical of the overwhelmingly favorable response is the following from Superintendent L. E. Andrews of the Lexington high schools: "I think the plan of the speech tournament to be held at Wake Forest more nearly meets the needs of our high schools than anything we have had in the state heretofore. The plan will furnish a genuine incentive for real speech work."

[63] *Old Gold and Black*, April 7, 1939, page 1.

[64] *Old Gold and Black,* February 4, 1939, page 1, 4. By 1942, contests in Declamation, Impromptu and After Dinner speaking, and Radio Announcing had been added.

[65] *Old Gold and Black*, March 24, 1939, page 4.

[66] *Old Gold and Black*, September 23, 1939, page 1.

In April of 1932, the high schoolers participated in a Triangular Debate; one of the high school debaters was Hubert Poteat. One must assume that faculty children were a big part of the program. Clippings also indicate that strong women debaters and all-women teams were part of the high school program's fame. [67]

Wake hosted the State Debate Tournament for at least four years (1939-1942). "Approximately 100 students representing 20 North Carolina high schools will be in Wake Forest on April 4, 5, and 6 for the college-sponsored Annual High School Debate and Speech Tournament, director George Copple and student manager Bob Goldberg announced today. The tournament originated last year." [68]

Former Wake Debater and lifelong supporter, Governor Melville Broughton begin his Senate campaign in 1947 Photograph by Hugh Morton photographs and films, North Carolina Collection, UNC Chapel Hill Library

---

[67] *Old Gold and Black*, January 23, 1932, page 4.

[68] *Old Gold and Black*, March 9, 1940, page 1. A later article reported that 156 high school debaters and speakers from 39 class A schools in North Carolina are attending, *Old Gold and Black*, April 6, 1940, page 1.

"No debate team will be eliminated before having the opportunity to debate at least six times," Dir. George Copple announced. The final debate was broadcast over Raleigh Station WRAL, tackling the query: *Should the federal government own and operate railroads?* Also contested was an event not mentioned before, Poetry Reading for Girls. The extempore subject was *America and the European War*.[69] The school presenting the best outline of speech activity for the entire year was to be awarded the J. Rice Quesinberry trophy, given in memory of the late coach.[70]

The 1940 *Wake Forest College Alumni News* added that the two winning debate teams clashed in a radio match. Needham Broughton (Neg. team) won for the second year over Asheville High.[71] In addition, there was an exhibition between North Carolina State and Wake Forest debaters at a local Baptist Church, plus a Wake Forest College band concert.

The North Carolina Forensic League for high schools organized a special meeting of debate coaches on Friday afternoon of the tournament.

At the 1941 event, two queries were debated: *That the United States should adopt a policy requiring military training of all able-bodied men before they reach the age of 23* and *That the power of the Federal government should be increased*. It was the first year to add oratory, extempore, impromptu, declamation, and after-dinner speaking to the competitive repertoire.[72]

The 1942 tournament final debate, with 23 North Carolina Senior High Schools participating, featured Winston-Salem Reynolds HS, the defending champion, versus Wilmington High School, the affirmative, who prevailed on a 3 to 2 decision.[73]

---

[69] *Old Gold and Black*, March 9, 1940, page 1.

[70] *The News & Observer*, April 5, 1940, page 9; Joseph Melville Broughton, a Wake Forest student in the early 1900s, he then began law school in 1910. He worked briefly at the *Winston-Salem Journal*, was a school principal, and then went to Harvard in 1918. He was appointed to the Wake Forest College Board of Trustees, a position he held his whole life. Broughton was governor from 1941 to 1945 and served in the US Senate from 1948 until his death from a heart attack in 1949. One of Broughton's children, Melville, of Broughton High School in Raleigh, had won the high school tournament and was a freshman at Wake Forest.

[71] *Wake Forest College Alumni News*, Vol. 9, 1940, page 9.

[72] *The Greensboro Record*, March 19, 1941, page 12.

[73] *The Wilmington Morning Star*, April 7, 1942, page 3.

In addition, the 3rd State Tournament featured Governor J. M. Broughton, aiding the proceedings' credibility. He attended the WPTF radio station, which broadcast the finals, where he presented the loving cup, originally awarded by him three years earlier to the first winning teams.[74]

No evidence was found that Wake hosted the State tournament after 1942. Franklin Shirley reestablished a high school tournament that moved to Winston-Salem in 1957, and Merwyn Hayes revived it in 1968. These developments are discussed in volume 2 of the Debate History series. Wake was a continual host of the declamation contest, beginning in 1916 until 1942. The declamation conte st constituted an integral part of the debaters' spring term for nearly four decades.

---

[74] *Old Gold and Black*, March 7, 1942, page 1.

CHAPTER 15

Transition from Society Life

Societies Subside – Compulsory Membership Ends

Wake Forest's Literary Societies continued their unbroken supremacy for nearly ten decades, a remarkable run. As the retelling in this volume revealed, this journey, while amazingly dynamic and beneficial, also underwent ebbs and flows. This chapter concludes by providing a closing look at the societies' slow but fated dissolution.

By the early 1920s, the college was busting at the seams, claiming an enrollment of 554.[1] Most college entrants were destined to gladly or grudgingly join the Philomathesian or Euzelian Society. The Societies became unwieldy, and students increasingly had available alternative pursuits. Inadequate physical space, strained management, and the call of sports and fraternity life further diluted the societies' claims on fellow students' loyalty.

COMPULSORY MEMBERSHIP

The dominating issue in the early twentieth century was the compulsory membership requirement, with opinions varying predictably and broadly.

---

[1] *Bulletin of Wake Forest College – 1920-1922*, Eighty-Fifth Session, page 155. "The session, 1920-1921, opened September 7th, with an unusually large enrollment. The present registration is 554." The subsequent *Bulletin, Eighty-Sixth Session*, page 157, put the next year's enrollment at 577.

1939 – Literary Society Debaters

Passionate feelings supporting either abiding by customs or breaking them up became commonplace.

A critic of compulsory membership, writing in the 1920 *Wake Forest Student*, did not hold back: "If attendance should be made optional, the societies would cease to exist. This is proven by the fact that approximately half the members are absent under the present compulsory system."[2]

Frustrations heated up, resulting every so often in sharp attacks. Absent the usual backpedaling or currying favor found in most commentaries, a year before mandatory membership was outlawed, one student lashed out:

> All are agreed that the literary societies are at present "mock institutions." All know that the majority of the members who do attend, do so simply because they find it too expensive to do otherwise... Why is it that men graduate every year who have never spoken in either of the societies?... Where is the student who is willing to put in the hard work on a speech so that he may have the high privilege of delivering it before empty chairs and an audience composed chiefly

---

[2] *The Wake Forest Student,* December 1920, page 138.

of dejected youths who groan inwardly and long to be listening to sounds other than the orator's eloquence? [3]

Expanding memberships strained the societies' efficacy. The Euzelian society, with swelling rolls, "has found it expedient to have five debating sections, one meeting every night of the week except Sunday and Monday. This makes it possible for those to have a debate each time without such a long list of men to speak, and it is their testimony that they find this to be a good plan to prevent the lagging of interest because of long sessions." The Philomathesian Society maintained three debating sections as established the year before.[4]

Others maintained that the societies' larger size was a strength needed to finance their work. They warned against voluntary affiliation: "With compulsory membership and attendance, the societies have been able to challenge for debates some of the largest and best-known institutions in the country... Assuming that these debaters could have been picked from a minority of the student body... the expenses of such debates would be prohibitive since there would be not sufficient membership to finance their cause."[5]

The year before required alliance was abandoned, *The Wake Forest Student,* in a student editorial, held that interested volunteers would better fill any void than learners who did not want to be in the hall: "In the interests of the college which they serve, some seem to be afraid that if society duties were not required of all men... we believe that far better work will be done without the necessity of fighting off the 'bear' of protest. Men who want to be speakers will still develop their powers, and the College will still have debaters and orators for public occasions."[6]

In the fall term of 1921, the tumult in society relations reached its peak. intersociety politics ruling the day. An *Old Gold and Black* headline cautioned:

SOCIETY ADOPTS A MORE LENIENT ATTENDANCE
Optional Attendance Law...
Opposers of the Amendment Hope That the Faculty or the
Trustees Will Interfere and Annul the New Law

---

[3] *Old Gold and Black*, February 4, 1921, page 2.

[4] *Old Gold and Black*, October 29, 1920, page 5.

[5] *Old Gold and Black*, February 18, 1921, page 1.

[6] Student Editorial, *The Wake Forest Student*, 1921, page 238.

At the Saturday morning session of the Euzelian literary society the original Mauney proposal, which would make attendance optional for all members of the freshman class, was adopted as an amendment to the Constitution by a substantial majority...

During the week feelings ran rather high among the members of the literary organization when the question was mentioned. Both societies did ... "politicking" outside of the society halls as each contended that theirs was a side of righteousness...

Now the optional attendance is invoked at the Eu Society, the question for discussion is whether or not the Philomathesian society will amend their Constitution. Both factions and the Euzelian society agree that unless the society also adopts the optional attendance system it will be an utter failure. Opposers... are hoping that the faculty or trustees will intervene and annul the new law.[7]

A year later, both societies adopted a resolution and recommended to the faculty that "only such students as desire to engage actively in debating and the other activities fostered by the literary societies will become members."[8]

The faculty endorsed the students' suggestion in a special March meeting, leaving the societies to manage Intercollegiate debates and the publication The Wake Forest Student. They suggested that the entire student body support the Howler. The faculty called for adding a member to the English faculty, who would, in part, cooperate with the societies in training men in public speaking [the seed of formal coaching].[9] The move would help the Societies, an Old Gold and Black article argued, because the slackers no longer interrupted meetings, failed to show up, or attempted to get out of debates. "At the time members in both societies were required to debate once every fourth week."[10]

The final policy passed in October 1922:

---

[7] Old Gold and Black, March 11, 1921, page 1.

[8] Nelson, J. R. (January 1922). In and About College, The Wake Forest Student, page 305.

[9] Nelson, J. R, (1922). In and About College, The Wake Forest Student, April 1, page 431.

[10] Old Gold and Black, October 20, 1922, page 1.

SOCIETIES ADOPT RESOLUTION RECOMMENDING THE ABOLITION OF COMPULSORY MEMBERSHIP

MEASURE PASSES WITHOUT FIGHT
Committee Will Present Notice of Action to Faculty at Early Date

----

WILL GO INTO EFFECT IN SEPTEMBER NEXT YEAR[11]

With no voice of protest and scarcely a word, the Philomathesian Society passed last Saturday morning in about two minutes time a resolution similar to the one presented in the Euzelian Society on the same day, as a result of which action there will be conveyed to the Faculty of the College the societies recommendation the students entering Wake Forest in the fall of 1922 and thereafter no longer be forced into one of the ancient literary organizations, and that those of the present membership who desire to be released at that time from the obligations of membership.

Opinion in the societies has long been decidedly against anything looking toward optional membership, and it was surprisingly to no small degree that the resolution passed so easily. When... F. Hester arose ... he said... "It is not necessary for me to describe in detail the conditions existing in our two societies, We recognize ourselves that the societies have reached a very degenerate state, and certain

[11] *Old Gold and Black*, January 13, 1922, page 1.

Euzelians have for some time been insistent with me... that the society should take steps not only to put them back on the basis of sound development and growth, but, as a first step to that end, to release from duties a large number of men who cared nothing for society work."[12]

This chapter recounts the various attempts at the revival of societies, pressures pointing toward their irrelevance, and puzzlements that had subtly confounded the debaters for many years. At a lumbering pace, "the sword of Damocles" would eventually fall. Despite the protests and revivals, the Literary Societies were destined to fade in influence and from students' lives.

CURRICULUM DEVELOPMENT

The Societies were always an academic safety valve to the routine of rigid class work. Thomas Harding, in his *College Literary Societies: The Contribution to Higher Education in the United States 1815-1876*, advised, "They offered respite from the classical curriculum; they were an opportunity for fraternal gatherings; as one extracurricular activity, they were a release for youthful enthusiasm and energy as they were the only available means by which experience in speaking could be obtained."[13]

---

[12] *Old Gold and Black*, January 13, 1922, page 1; Mr. Hester then read the resolution... "The provisions were simply that society should recommend to the faculty that beginning with the next session, membership would be optional to all students and that the College bursar be asked to take over the financial obligations in connection with college publications heretofore assumed by the societies... it was proposed that the expenses of Intercollegiate Debate be included in the financial obligations suggested transferred to the bursar... was unanimously carried." Less than a year ago, that body[faculty] urgently recommended societies that no change be made in attendance or membership requirements and offered as an inducement to continue supportive societies by all students and certain academic credits for literary work done in those organizations.

[13] Harding, T. S. (1971). *College Literary Societies: The Contribution to Higher Education in the United States 1815-1876*, Pageant Press International Corporation, New York, page 88; For Wake's first century, on her 100th birthday, the enrollment was around 1000. Across those years, 15,000 men had received instruction. Trained were, by some estimates, 2,500 businessmen, 1,440 lawyers, 1,400 ministers, 500 physicians, 2,500 teachers, and the rest engaging in an assortment of occupations, *Old Gold and Black*, March 30, 1935, page 1; Graduation programs (e. g., 1874) suggest the slenderness (some would say rigidity) of the curriculum. The students

The dance between curricular development and the flourishing of society life took several turns, most of which resulted in deferring to the informal society system for the instruction of public speaking., Toward the middle of the century, nationally, "the caliber of extempor disputations was so high in the societies that several colleges dropped exercises from the curriculum. Thus, at Columbia, on January 4, 1837, the trustees were informed that 'no exercise in extemporaneous speaking or debating required from the students, as there are two Societies... To which these exercises constitute the principal objects.'"[14]

With the Wake faculty's blessing, public speaking was entrusted to the Societies. The 1928-1929 *Bulletin of Wake Forest College* summarized the faculty/administration's outlook: "The faculty regards Societies as important aids in the work of education and the preservation of wholesome sentiments among students it would be difficult to overestimate their importance in imparting a knowledge of parliamentary law, and cultivating and directing the taste for reading, and in the formation of correct habits of public speaking."[15]

Often, the Societies made requests to the faculty that impacted curricular matters. The 1900 Phi minutes, for example, asked, "On motion the vice pres. is empowered to appoint a committee to confer with the faculty of the College and asked them not to put their examinations on Saturday as it competes with the workings of the society."[16] The faculty complied.

The development and added depth of the faculty afforded new classes by the beginning of the new century's second decade. In 1912, *The Bulletin of Wake Forest College* listed a new class by Prof. Hubbell, an argumentation class offered over two semesters. The *Bulletin's* write-up

---

who graduated represented Latin (three), Greek (three), mathematics (six), and moral philosophy (one), two each for Bachelor of Philosophy and Arts. In fairness, the number of graduates was still impacted by enrollment declines following the Civil War

[14] Porter, D. (1954). The Literary Societies, in *A history of speech education in America*. Karl Wallace, Editor, page 245; The contention that Literary Societies, in fact, generally offered superior training to formal curriculums was offered not in terms of Societies *per se*, but rather due to the nature of the training: "The nub of the matter is, not that the literary society itself, but the sort of speaking activity in it—the give and take of full and free discussion with a minimum of faculty interference—is the best sort of platform training." Hellman, H. G. (1942). The Influence of Orators on Public Speaking, *Quarterly Journal of Speech*, 28, No.1, page 14.

[15] *Bulletin of Wake Forest College*, 1928-1929.

[16] Philomathesian Minutes, November 24, 1900.

for the class reveals the framing of the class as a supplement to society training and examining only areas beyond their expertise.[17]

The 1917 editorialist writing in *The Wake Forest Student* reasoned that a more formal curriculum was needed to aid the society's work, not as it had been historically, but the other way around. Specialization led to establishing curricula that augmented the Societies' work:

> The matter of preparation is not so simple; it lies deeper than a man's willingness to work. The mere placing of material on the open shelf for the use of debaters is not enough; they need special training in the use of material, training which the society cannot give. THE STUDENT, therefore, advocates the immediate establishment of a course in Public Speaking and Debating, which shall be required of every man in either society who shows himself the least deficient in preparing and delivering speeches. Such a course could not but

---

[17] Course a.—Elementary Argumentation. One hour a week. Elective for B.A. degree. Open to all students, but designed primarily for first and second-year men. Professor Hubbell.

> The purpose of the course is to supplement the work of the College Literary Societies. The work consists largely of debates, both oral and written, with particular attention to the questions debated in the Societies; but some attention is given also to declamation, reading aloud, and preparing speeches for special occasions. Foster's Essentials of Exposition and Argument and Shurter's Public Speaking, supplemented by parallel reading, are the text-books; but the emphasis is on the writing and delivery of speeches.

4a.—The general purpose of this course is to give the student a knowledge of the principles of speech-writing. The instructor endeavors to supplement the work of the Literary Societies; hence the emphasis is on the preparation and writing rather than the delivery of speeches. Professor Hubbell.

> The Fall Term. – Argumentation. Foster's Argumentation and Debating, Baker's Specimens of Argumentation, and Bouton's Lincoln and Douglas Debate are studied carefully. Many written and oral exercises are required; and a considerable amount of parallel reading is done in the speeches of Webster, Calhoun, Lincoln, Burke, and others.

> The Spring Term. – After a brief study of the Oration, with Shurter's The Rhetoric of Oratory as the text, the work of this term is given to the study of the special forms of public speech other than the argument and the oration. Knapp and French's The Speech for Special Occasions and Baker's The Forms of Public Address are studied. Frequent oral and written exercises are required; and Sears's The History of Oratory and the speeches of the great orators are read as parallel. *The Bulletin of Wake Forest College*, 1912.

work toward the best interests of the societies and members; and if Wake Forest is to maintain her standing in the inter-collegiate debating world, it is imperative that the work of the societies be supplemented in this way.[18]

Two years earlier, Dr. Hubert Poteat, the prominent Latin scholar, professor, and Wake Forest alumnus, wondered if a faculty takeover was advisable. He called attention to the creation of "an efficient speech department which has removed much of the Society's original purpose in speech."[19]

The consistency of curricular accessibility took time to shake out. It is unclear when Professor Hubbell's classes ceased. By 1920 there were again calls for additional classes. A 1920 *The Wake Forest Student* entry recommended, "We have courses teaching us how and what to think. We need a course teaching us how to say what we think. Such a course could be established as a Chair of Public Speaking, making public speaking a course and a requirement for a B.A. degree. It could be connected with the work of the literary societies and be prescribed for the B.A. degree."[20]

---

[18] Editor's Portfolio, *The Wake Forest Student*, November 1917, page 123.

[19] Freeburg, V. O. (1915). Debating in the college curriculum, *The English Journal*, 4, page 578.

[20] *The Wake Forest Student*, December 1920, page 138; In the early 1920s, rumors circulated that the Board might terminate the societies, producing overwrought gossip, but the rumors solicited correctives in the student press:

Perhaps *Old Gold and Black* in its eagerness to publish news has... created... in the minds of some alumni that there is a danger that the literary societies could be abolished at Wake Forest College. At least one alumnus, Mr. W. I. Francis, probably had this in mind which prompted him to write an article of concern printed in the *Old Gold and Black*. The paper later countered the rumor, responding to Francis: "There is not one iota of danger of the Literary Societies being abolished at Wake Forest. But some of its requirements, especially the compulsory membership... not only should but will inevitably be dispensed with. This change does not deserve the title of being radical because no other college in the State exacts such similar requirements on its students. Even in our own confines, where things of a conservative nature flourish, this movement cannot justly be called radical... Anyone acquainted with the college activities cannot imagine Wake Forest maintaining her high prestige without a debating team. More than anything else is the compulsory membership of Societies and payments of dues. If this is a sore spot in our student body and the source of troubled waters, why not eradicate it? Societies are all right. The crux of the whole situation is attempting to compel an Anglo-Saxon to do something against his will." Correcting Misconceptions, Editorial, *Old Gold and Black*, February 17, 1922, page 2.

Eventually, in 1921, the College devised a "1 hour of elective credit"… for Freshmen and Sophomores to complete a total of four written and memorized speeches of seven minutes each. The delivery of the speeches by the men claiming credit was certified by society secretaries, and copies of the speeches were turned over to the English department. "This is the first year the college has offered credit for society work."[21]

"IBID."

Howler 1912 – Society Speaker

This symbiotic relationship between forensic participation and class-work may have been more a mirage than separate instruction, perhaps a cover for the coach performing his coaching duties. A quip from the *Wake Forest Alumni News* in 1934 suggests as much: "The faculty director of this work has… a full-time teaching load including one three-hour course in public speaking, in which there is rarely ever more than one debater registered. The special training for debate is done in "bull sessions" at which any interested student is welcome – 15 to 25 usually attend."[22]

---

[21] *Old Gold and Black,* October 14, 1921, page 1. Currently, a limited practicum credit is given for work undertaken as a debate team member.

[22] *Wake Forest Alumni News,* May 1934, Vol. 3, No. 4, page 18; Professor Shirley, in his "Historical Notes," recalled, "In the Spring term in 1926, one course in Argumentation was taught by Professor Henry Broadus Jones. This was a course in the theory and practice of debating." Jones was also listed in 1926 as the Faculty Advisor to Pi Kappa Delta. *Howler,* 1926. E. L. Roberts, President of Pi Kap, was on the Pan-Hellenic Council, which had eight members.

Later, in 1928, the *Wake Forest Alumni News* wrote, "Alumni who are especially interested in society work will be glad to learn that the college now offers two courses that are especially designed for the benefit of society workers. One is a course in public speaking, the other a course in argumentation. These courses are given by Prof. A. L. Aycock who comes to us for the first time this year as a member of the English Department."[23]

Formal classes in debating and argumentation became permanent offerings in the 1950s. Formal debate training classes were often offered by faculty members with debate backgrounds.

WHAT IS A SOCIETY'S PURPOSE?
– A DECADES-LONG DEBATE

Intercollegiate athletics, social fraternities, specialized clubs catering to focused interests (e.g., music and drama clubs, enlivening the curriculum giving equal standing to scientific fields, and ambitious student-managed publications "all hastened the decline and inevitable demise of the Literary order."[24]

The roots of divisions, apart from debates, were innocently embraced when *The Wake Forest Student* was established in 1877. This worthy endeavor provided students with a literary outlet they relished. By the turn of the century, and likely earlier, some clamored to focus on the scholarly and avoid the daunting prospect of speaking in public. The Philomathesian in 1902 entertained the motion which allowed "students interested in 'The Student' versus those interested in oratory to have fewer obligations for the one they were not interested in."[25]

While sports leagues and event scheduling foretold a newfound emphasis on athletics, the literary societies, and debates remained, for

---

[23] *Wake Forest Alumni News*, Vol. 1, No. 2, October 1928, page 4; Around the same time, the debate team was undoubtedly aware of outside voices shaping debate. In particular, George P. Baker of Harvard, first mentioned in Chapter 4, advised: "Productively channeling the excitement around debate meant constructing a curriculum that focused more on rhetoric and argumentation and less on the specific techniques one might employ to win a debate." Presumably, the Societies' piece offered superior instruction in strategies and refutation.

[24] Williams, D. E. (1966). College Literary Societies and the founding of Departments of Speech. *Journal of the American Forensics Association, 3*, page 29.

[25] Philomathesian Minutes, January 11, 1902.

some, central to Wake Forest's core, even as late as 1916. An *Old Gold and Black* editorial, in anticipation of the double-Richmond debates, thundered:

> With the basketball championship of the State secured so firmly as to make ridiculous any dissenting parlay, attention remains to be fixed upon two other events of intercollegiate importance during the months of spring term. One of these, our hope of presenting a bold front in baseball, needs no comment to become a center of interest. The other, equally an object of quiet, less demonstrate concerns, is the double debate with Richmond College. The superiority in which devotees of Wake Forest chiefly pride themselves is again to be submitted to the task of cold logic and hot air.
>
> There is at least no occasion for pessimism over the issue. Without doubt, Richmond College is a worthy and courteous opponent, one whose defeat can only be secured by thorough and passionate labor, but at the same time we retain our faith in Wake Forest's traditional mastery of debate...our hope that our recently celebrated representatives will end the whole affair in a blaze of glory...
>
> No, the Philomathesian and Euzelian Societies are not dead, but "living, breathing," and, if not growing every hour, at least holding their own. And in the approaching Richmond debates the summation of their energy and life will not be put to shame.[26]

Even a decade later, the Administration still waved the society's flag.[27] On more than one occasion, University president Dr. Francis P. Gaines (1927-1930 – shortest Wake presidency) spoke to the Literary Societies

---

[26] *Old Gold and Black*, February 26, 1916, page 3, 4. A full accounting of the Richmond Debates can be found in Chapter 6: Intercollegiate Debate Goes on The Road.

[27] "There has been so much said in recent years about the 'dying' Literary Societies at Wake Forest and the decay of oratory that it will be somewhat surprising to some to learn that three men, now students here, have won the degree of special distinction offered by the Pi Kappa Delta Debating Fraternity composed of teams from two hundred colleges and universities. This degree is given to the student who has won sixteen intercollegiate debates; the three men are Cloyce R. Tew of Raleigh, Joe Carlton of Winston-Salem, and Wade Bostic of Japan. These men have made a record that has never been remotely approached by any man in the history of the college. Wake Forest has engaged this year in nineteen intercollegiate debates; winning some and losing some, the idea being to develop debaters rather than to win debates. One team debated four colleges and won each debate but there are four teams sent out

for opening fall sessions, giving the administration's blessing. Despite the societies' fading, the case continued to be made for learning oral competencies, as it is today.

The *Old Gold and Black* had not given up the ghost, as late as 1931, then faculty member Dr. Herbert Poteat, with the help of the evening's student orators, soon converted their message to a description of what Wake ought to be:

> The characteristics of a good speaker today are the same as in the days of Cicero and are to stand up to speak up and shut up. These are the words of advice given by Dr. H. M. Poteat in his lecture to the Euzelian Society at the annual "Smoker" on October 3, at which time 34 new men joined the society.
>
> Dr. Poteat explained that there was a great need for speakers today, that though he couldn't think of what they would say, speakers are always used for road and bridge openings and numerous other public and political functions. [28] The point is, continued Dr.

---

by the societies. Professor A. L. Aycock has rendered splendid service to the college as debate coach." *Wake Forest College Alumni News*, May 1929, page 2.

[28] Poteat's inability to adequately give examples to sustain his own argument would surely profit from rhetorical refurbishment

Poteat, "that speaking is still one of America's favorite indoor and outdoor sports."

A short history of the society was given...after which all present were entertained at an informal "smoker" in which sandwiches, lemonade, cigarettes and cigars were furnished.[29]

Well into the tournament era, the tentative relationship between the societies and the traveling team was maintained, at least at face value.

The Robesonian newspaper editorial, written by Wake's J. L. Memory, Jr. admitted that "campus organizations made inroads, and popular interest in literary societies slackened. There were crack debating teams, to be sure, but none of that old-time 'special train' interest."[30]

REVISION AND REINVENTION

Touting a "we are relevant" narrative was an annual ritual as the societies sought to adapt to the changing campus culture. A segment of students who thrived in literary highlights remained, but they were a smaller minority. In the 1930s through the 1950s, innovation was the mantra of the meetings. Debates and original oratories continue but with less frequency. In place of the evening debate, many curious and sometimes remarkable evenings ensued.

The scheme for a 1931 Tuesday night program was "several five-minute talks on the timely subjects. The materials for these discussions were obtained from current magazines with the aid of the *Readers Guide*. W. Goal Rosser told of *The New Morality in the Colleges*, giving some striking examples of how college morals appeared to other folks."[31]

In 1934, the South, including Wake, was forcefully segregated. While scarcely liberal, there was a building resentment on campus with the malice of racial separation, a trend which continued till Wake assumed statewide leadership on behalf of Civil Rights in the 1950s and '60s.

In 1934, the Euzelians extended an invitation that was perhaps progressive for the times. The newspaper's lead was rhetorically sensitive, with the announcement clothed in religion and precedence: "The popular

---

[29] *Old Gold and Black*, October 10, 1931, page 1.

[30] Reprinted in the *Old Gold and Black*, October 13, 1944, page 1.

[31] *Old Gold and Black*, November 12, 1931, page 1.

local colored quartet will be the highlight of the program of Thursday night section of the Euzelian literary society next week. The singers have been well received in several religious programs on the campus, and will give several selections as part of the regular program. The public is cordially invited to attend.[32] Of course, the invitation to colored singers was limited to an entertainment role, any mixing that occurred with society members is only speculative.

A full program of society "rebirth" in 1936 included highlights of the Tenn. Valley Admin. . Supreme Court decision, a description of the German set-up of the Winter Olympic games, and a brief history of the Western Union Telegraph Company. In addition, "John Sykes gave readings on *Two Tickets for a Twain Ride* and the *Well Undressed Skier*. These readings were humorous, intending to add a light touch to the program."[33]

By 1950, a Phi meeting featured typical assembled fare. The members continued to prepare and speak, retaining some of their original mission, but preparation and extended discussions were not on the agenda:

> Tom Clark, program Chairman, presented a very timely and interesting program which was centered around Abraham Lincoln. Fred Billups gave a declamation, B. I. Henderson an extemporaneous speech on "Abe Lincoln's influence today" and Rose Bullard gave a dramatic reading. Shirley Schellenberg then gave an impromptu speech on "All Men Are Created Equal" *Cecil Arnold, Rec. Sec.*[34]

Later that month, Mr. Redwine gave an extemporaneous speech on *Wake Forest Should have remained the college for men.* Mr. Matthews gave an equally entertaining extemporaneous speech on *Wake Forest should not have remained the college for men.*[35]

In 1954, the societies served refreshments at meetings to improve attendance and offered various speaking programs, from comic debate and impromptu to declamation and oration. It was not that students were not debating in meetings; they were…but the committed debating was

---

[32] *Old Gold and Black*, April 13, 1934, page 1.

[33] *Old Gold and Black*, February 29, 1936, page 1.

[34] Philomathesian Minutes, February 12, 1950.

[35] Philomathesian Minutes, February 20, 1950.

less under the literary banner; the "serious" debate was happening on the competitive circuit.[36]

Several outside speakers, some more controversial than others, adorned the programming. The Philomathesian Literary Society heard Sgt. C. C. Peters, of the ROTC program and wrestling coach, speak about the "beat generation." His advice was exceedingly traditionalist, even for the times:

> Peters... described the causes of the "beat generation," to the disintegration of the traditional American family structure. The typical 'Beatnik,' said Peters, assumes and I don't know nuttin' and don't care about nuttin attitude. They are defeatist mentally, he charged, and do not want anything to do with what that which requires thinking. He recommended a return to the traditional family structure, in which the woman is docile and the man master, in order to cure the present problems.[37]

---

[36] *Howler*, 1954, page 74.

[37] *Old Gold and Black,* December 8, 1958, page 1.

At the 1957 bi-monthly meetings, members heard guest speakers like Dr. David Smiley (Wake's legendary "History of Wake Forest" professor).[38] A 1958 "debate" entry "featured a humorous takeoff on classical debating: David Hughes as the southern demagogue, James Peterson as the intellectual, Marjorie (Thomas) Warlick as the sexy feminine debater and Joe Grubbs as the auctioneer."[39] A year later, the program included a parody of classic debating in a study of Verdi's Opera "Rigoletto."[40]

The Philomathesian Literary Society began the year 1962 by "undergoing a reorganization" (the "new" formula sounding remarkably familiar). A new set of bylaws was adopted to complement the New Constitution. Emphasis has shifted from "book reports" to original work. Society life has returned to a greater emphasis on impromptu work.[41]

It is not that inventing "exciting" new content is unusual. Each set of officers seeks their own legacy, yet the Societies were fighting a rearguard action to maintain attention. In the last two active decades, the Society leaders were clever (the same folks active with the tournament scene), but students' consumption of literary fare was sated, or attention diverted.

The *Howler*, in its description on the Literary Society pages, took a hopeful tone, reasserting the same methods that societies had found disappointing in their three-decade struggle for relevance:

> Realizing that great opportunity and advantage lie ahead of them at Reynolda, the societies have been taking steps to overcome their weakness and ensure their continual existence; the year's efforts have been concentrated on getting more people into the societies, on creating more interesting programs, and on making more profitable the societies' influence on the members' bearing and speech. They even once forgot their traditional rivalry and held a joint meeting per purpose to foster interest in the works of the groups.[42]

The *Howler* exhibited politeness and encouragement, but each society's fame and power had already faded.

---

[38] *Howler*, 1957, page 46.

[39] *Howler*, 1957.

[40] *Howler*, 1958, page 169.

[41] *Howler*, 1960, page 163.

[42] *Howler*, 1955.

SPORTS AND FRATERNITIES ARISE

> 1888 Wake's First football game – Defeated North Carolina (6-4)
>
> 1906 Wake's First Basketball Game – Defeated Trinity (24-10)

Most commentators who feted sport simultaneously gave lip service to preserving the school's debate roots. A few, however, were upfront in their preference for sport. These critics chafed, holding debates as lacking entertainment value and asking openly for additional sports. In an item in the last year of the Trinity intercollegiate debate series, 1902, one student editorialist argued that sports unify, whereas societies bicker:

> Another reason the college spirit is not as alive as it ought to be is that some students allow society loyalty to come between themselves and their fellow-students. Their loyalty, especially at the beginning of the college term, degenerates into a kind of partisan rancour, which estranges students of different society affiliations, and prevents the formation of friendships. This is not true of all students, but it is true of some in both literary societies.[43]
>
> There are other things that might be mentioned as an explanation for the lack of enthusiasm and loyalty among the students. One is that we have nothing in the fall term to arouse college spirit except the annual debate. This event generally receives good support, but it alone is not sufficient for a whole college term, for only a few men can possibly participate in it. We need football and tennis and other athletic contests, where the Muscle that is manufactured by compulsion in the gymnasium may be utilized for increasing the reputation of Wake Forest men as men physically as well as mentally. The two things go hand in hand.[44]

While the inter-society competition at the turn of the century was sharp, by 1930, their fierce competition opposition had generally dissolved. Under a headline that promised **The Rivalry Between Literary Clubs Becomes Milder** the student reporter, with more than a little irony, writes:

---

[43] The argument sounds suspiciously like those aimed at freshman Greek life at Wake.

[44] Craven, H. E. (1902). Editorial, *The Wake Forest Student,* October, page 97-99.

Literary societies have twice their former membership, but the rivalry they once aroused on the campus died out with the advent of Social Fraternities and football competitions, according to Dr. W. L. Poteat. Remembering the days when campus politics lived only in society elections, Dr. Poteat tells us that "The most active campaigns, leading to desperate rivalry, held the college in their sway."[45]

The discussion on the relevance and sustainability of literary societies continued in various forms for decades. During the height of the World War II years, when Wake enrollment was halved, it seemed the societies enjoyed a resurgence of interest.[46]

The Robesonian (Lumberton, NC) picked up on Wake's student newspaper editorial wishing the revision well, adopting an "optimistic" yet sardonic tone. Sure, there was a loss, but that was an inevitability with the erosion of the Societies' raison d'être:

> The pendulum of interest in literary societies at Wake Forest college has taken a backward swing. Backward in the right direction toward the year 1900 when there was keener rivalry between the two colleges two historic societies and now exist at a Big five football game. So reports the Wake Forest College News Bureau. ...we wonder if football hasn't contributed to the livelier interest...
>
> The main thing is that there seems really to be a resurgence of interest in debates and such. [We] recall the good old days when representatives of Wake Forest's literary societies were to appear in debates in Raleigh against some college... A student would rather win a debate or oratorical contest for his society in the college or for dear old alma mater... than win almost any other honor. That was the road to college fame.
>
> But we have made progress since then. Literary societies have been relegated to the rear, and football stars are the heroes. No one gives a thought to the best orator or debater. No admiring crowd shouts his name. He is ignored—at least outside a small circle on the campus... The pendulum has taken a backward swing that indicates a forward move. [47]

---

[45] *Old Gold and Black,* November 7, 1931, page 1.

[46] *Old Gold and Black,* November 7, 1931, page 1.

[47] *The Robesonian,* October 18, 1944, page 4.

The decline in status embraced an inevitability. As scholar James Emerson of Stanford noted in 1931, "The whole character of American Life has changed. ... now the automobile, the movie, the radio has brought within the reach of hosts of individuals, entertainment, amusement, and even instruction... now less and less individuals and groups have had to rely for entertainment, upon themselves."[48]

The Societies fully embraced intramural sports competition. While, in part, this was a ploy to stay relevant in a sports-mad culture, more likely, they, too, were caught up in the excitement. Sport provided some of the same competitive drive that underwrote the appeal of debating. However, there remained reservations about open-participation sports, which echoed the inherent tensions, the choice of elitism/excellence as opposed to unceremoniously widely shared activities.

A year later, in 1927, the emphasis on sports continued within the societies. The yearbook claimed that Phi and Eu innovation was renewed with the intramural "big event." On this field, the Phi's performed admirably. Athletic highlights were the two football games with the Eu Society, both of which were won by the Phis.[49] The two major events of the year for the Phis were their 26-6 football victory over their Eu rivals and winning of the Speaking contests of Founders Day celebration.[50]

The problem of drawing in new society members remained, and the answer was "what does the majority want." In 1942 the Phi claimed in the yearbook that "Emphasis was placed this year on programs in which a large number of the members could participate. In line with this plan, such features as mock legislatures, quiz programs, impromptu speeches and debates, and conversational forums found their place in the regular Monday night meetings. All the time, however, they vocally embrassed their the main purpose of the 'Society, was to train students in the art of speaking."[51]

---

[48] Emerson, J. G. (1931). The Old Debating Society, *Quarterly Journal of Speech*, Vol. 17, page 366.

[49] *Howler*, 1942. page 45.

[50] *Howler*, 1947, page 117.

[51] *Howler*, 1942, page 45; The new wrinkle for selecting topics for the Phi debate in 1941 was preparing programs "where the programs were built around topics selected by the individual members themselves and coinciding with special interests." It is unclear what that meant in practice. Most likely, some enterprising soul assembled the meeting's agenda.

Independent scholar Claudia Kennan surmised, "Poor attendance plagued debate events right from the start, and while debate victories fostered school spirit, the real fun lay with athletics and fraternities. In an era when college students giddily sought entertainment and escapades, it is remarkable that an enterprise as cerebral as debate drew the student body's interest at all."[52]

For some time, fraternities tried to forge an opening at Wake, but faculty and Society opposition kept them at bay until 1922. In February 1909, *The Wake Forest Student* could still write, "The fraternity, which is a deadly foe to the literary society, has never dominated the college life. A desperate effort was made by the 'frats' to gain a footing, but they ingloriously failed, thank God, and the two literary societies still stand preeminent among the factors of college life and power."

In part, "the literary societies grew out of a desire for social prestige and social urge... It was something for him to belong to, to identify himself with, or what was more important to be identified with and by his fellows."[53] Social fraternities, however, did so with far fewer obligations.

Societies Traverse the 1940s and '50s.

At the end of the intercollegiate debate era, with expressive sarcasm, academic George Jackson suggested barrenness among the organizations and events that displaced literary societies:

There was the apparent shift in opinion as to what was an honor., A man would give his last dollar (and often did) to belong to some futile body known perhaps as the Humpy Dumpty Club (an organization which did absolutely nothing but parade around in a peculiar looking hat for a few days), but they would disdain the literary societies. To be a Humpy Dumpty was to be a big man on campus; to be in the literary societies was apparently an admission of defeat.[54]

---

[52] Keenan, C. J. (2009). Intercollegiate: Reflecting American culture, 1900-1930, *Argumentation and Advocacy*, 46, Fall, page 50.

[53] Emerson, J. G. (1931). The Old Debating Society, *Quarterly Journal of Speech*, Vol. 17, page 367.

[54] Jackson, G. S. (January 1939). Reinvigorating Moribund Literary Societies, *Southern Speech Bulletin*, Vol. 4, page 9.

By 1939, the reign of the orator as "big man on campus" had closed.

▶ *"Covers The Campus Like The Magnolias"*

Wake Forest, N. C.. Monday, December 11, 1950

Society Day Winners

1950 winners Annual Society Day Contest. L-R: Billie Parrish, Best Woman Debater, Doris Ann Link, Impromptu, Doris Greene, Clara Ellen Francis (Debated with Ann Kelly, not present), Back Row: Graham Weathers, After Dinner, John Oates and Dave Clark, Debate, Bill Cramer, Poetry, Allen Johnson, Declamation, Roy Snell, Extemp, Tom & Dave Clark Impromptu, Joe Mauney, Oratory. Phi's won 20-17.

Nonetheless, in the decades of the 1920s and '30s, and for bursts in the '40s, the societies remained reasonably healthy. As late as 1944, the *Howler* recorded that the clubs' members "have reached unprecedented numbers in recent years. Over 100 were enrolled. For a time, there was standing room only, and the society finally had to close its doors to new members. Girls became increasingly active in the society and its work."[55]

The Phi's started the new school session in the same year, 1944, customarily, with: "A guest speaker, a smoke-filled hall, freshmen gazing at the portraits of bearded alumni, gleaming cups on the stately officer's stand.[56]

---

[55] *Howler*, 1944, page 88.

[56] *Howler*, 1944, page 90.

Two years later, the Phi membership boasted about a sizable 80 active members at the close of the term. Several former Phis who had left school to enter military service returned to the society following discharge.[57]

Early in World War II, women were granted admission and were soon vital players in the societies. Miss Nancy Easley, daughter of Dr. J. A. Easily of the college religion department, was chosen as Eu president during the spring of 1945, thus becoming the first woman to hold a literary society presidency.[58]

Debates at regular society meetings rhythmically endured. Sporadically the *Old Gold and Black* attended to weekly meetings as in a February 1952 debate. The paper advertised that Kay Arant and Carwile LeRoy would uphold the affirmative on the topic: *The Woman's place is in the home*. Clara Ellen Francis and Graham Weathers defended the negative. Two prominent women debaters merited notice with non-gendered admissions barely a year old.[59]

Literary societies did not become motionless in the late 1940s and '50s, even as tournament debating eroded much of their luster. The Societies adapted to the times, increasingly recruiting their membership from beyond contest debaters.

In the 1940s and '50s, the societies sponsored the "Forensic Founders Day Contests," which lasted nearly a week, beginning on Monday and culminating with the announcement of winners at the Phi-Eu joint Thursday night banquet.[60]

---

[57] *Howler*, 1946, page 141.

[58] *Howler*, 1946, page 141; "It was spring 1942... when Wake Forest... First admitted women to the residential student body in an effort to alleviate financial challenges presented by World War II. Marina Hawkins began classes in June. As it happens, two women had preceded her by four months: Beth Perry and Anna J. Moore had enrolled in February 1942 for the spring semester. In May, Wake Forest College hired its first Dean of Women, Lois Johnson." Puckett, J., https://magazine.wfu.edu/2022/06/29/the-first-coeds-marina-hawkins-nowell-43/

[59] *Old Gold and Black*, February 25, 1952. The paper did not carry who won in the next week's paper.

[60] The Eu-Phi banquet sported "an April showers theme throughout decorations. The place cards at the speakers' table were the form of umbrellas, while a giant multicolored rainbow formed a background for the speakers' table." *Old Gold and Black*, May 7, 1948; during part of this period, Society Day also had inter-society speaking events. These detailed inter-society contests were no longer public celebrations on the Spring and Fall Founders and Society Days, although the inter-society debates retained the Founders and Society Day titles until 1958.

During the contest week 1948, head-to-head finals were conducted, including Debate (held during Chapel, Best Debater Ed Christman), dramatic reading, impromptu speech, and declamation. After dinner speaking and poetry reading finals were banquet entertainment. Wake's future esteemed Chaplain, Ed Christman, speaking on *How to Cram for an Exam*, won the after-dinner contest, defeating Bill Joyner.[61]

Banquets were the societies' currency of the period, with newspapers listing multiple events, seemingly one for every organizational stripe. The Literary Societies managed these shared meals with genuine care, reaching out to speakers, faculty, and guests, seeking to make their gathering one of the favorites.[62] Occasionally, banquets took place in Raleigh, as at the Bon Air Club, a 1950 affair, at a not insubstantial cost of $1.75 per person ($22.30 today). One year the Phi Literary convened at the popular Raleigh Hen House Restaurant.[63]

The Final Breakup

The Societies' concluding action arrived when the annual Founders Day Contests were untenable due to a lack of entrants. The failure to field speakers soon developed into a full-fledged controversy, including blame, name-calling, and capricious competitors.

Ironically, the opening Society event of 1958 featured an inter-society debate examining the resolve: *That the literary societies of Wake Forest should be abolished.* Don Schoonmaker upheld the Affirmative and George Pruden the Negative.[64] Given the unfolding drama of the next two years, Schoonmaker's side assignment was itself prescient.

---

[61] *Old Gold and Black*, May 7, 1948, page 8; There were men's and women's debate divisions at the height of the annual contests. Philomathesian Minutes, April 10, 1950. Cecil Arnold and Elva Lawrence were long-time loyal alumnae who, in several instances, kept in touch with the coach.

[62] Phi's and Eu's held the first joint banquet in 1947. The societies had been hosting separate banquets since 1939; the 1951 banquet sparkled with eminent guests. "The debaters were entertained at a banquet that featured United States Congressman Joseph Martin, minority leader of the house, as principal speaker. Several notables followed Martin, including Sec. of the Navy J. M. Matthews." Wake debaters also met with both North Carolina US senators. *Old Gold and Black*, March 19, 1951, page 3.

[63] Philomathesian Minutes, March 13, 1950.

[64] *Old Gold and Black*, October 20, 1958, page 5; Schoonmaker, D. (1958). The Literary Societies, *The Wake Forest Student*, October 1958, page 2-3.

Don Schoonmaker, then an important Wake Faculty member,
Roasts Franklin Shirley on his retirement.

By November of the same 1958 season, "The Euzelian Literary Society voted ... to discontinue one of the two traditional speaking contests held each year (Founders or Society Day), pending discussion of the matter by its neighbor society, the Philomathesians.[65] The Phis then failed to field a team for the scheduled Society Day contest, and an altercation was about to ignite. The *Old Gold and Black* dutifully reported in 1959, "The annual Society Day will not be held this year."

According to Bill Horne, president of the Phis, the competition rules were not followed, and naming a winner was moot. Euzelian president, Don Schoonmaker contested Horne's decision, "charging that the Phi's simply were not ready to debate."[66]

Schoonmaker said the Eu's have been ready "for several weeks" and that the statement by the Phi president constitutes a default.

---

[65] *Old Gold and Black*, December 8, 1958, page 1.

[66] *Old Gold and Black*, May 18, 1959, page 1; Don Schoonmaker became a treasured Wake Forest faculty member, an expert on German politics. As a former debater he always followed the teams until his untimely passing in 1993 at age 55. His papers reside in ZSR Library including a sizable collection on Dr. Edwin G. Wilson.

Schoonmaker, in referring to the Eu's as the "rightful owner" of the Society Day cup, said in a statement that, "I would at this time claim the Society Day cup for Eu's by virtue of default of the Phi's."

In answer to Schoonmaker's reasoning, Horne contended that the Phi's did not default, because they were merely following the rules.

"Nobody, neither the Eu's nor the Phi's, paid any attention to the rules," Horne said, "and so we think it would be better to forget the whole thing."[67]

The controversy spilled over into 1960, as evidenced by an *Old Gold and Black* editorial. The headline read, **No Society Day This Year**, but the story's text, motivated by the controversy, inadvertently chronicles how organizations dissipate. The Debating Societies had given up their festival and the attendant speaking contest. The very heart of the Societies' public profile was disappearing. The editorial is investigative, showing how the Societies had become hollow in the ever more varied milieu:

Society Day has heretofore been a much anticipated occasion once each semester when the Euzelian and the Philomathesian literary societies pitted themselves against each other in strong contention for the coveted Society Day trophy.

Now, there is no trophy. The trophy got lost last year in a squabble between the two societies over which of them was entitled to it.

There was no Society Day last year. The Euzelian Society announced itself ready to participate; the Philomathesian Society made no obvious preparations except to defend itself against the Euzelian charge of "default."

Don Schoonmaker, then president of the Eu's, charged the Phi's with default and claimed the trophy for the Eu's. But Bill Horne, president of the Phi's, contended that neither of the societies was entitled to the trophy since neither society had observed the rules for competition.

Schoonmaker then charged the Phi's with "an exploitation of technicalities and rules that have traditionally been honored more in breach than in observance."

The issue was taken to the Student Relations Committee.

---

[67] *Old Gold and Black*, May 18, 1959, page 1.

The upshot of the whole matter was that neither society got the trophy, the trophy, was "placed in the hands of the Dean" and has since been retired.

This year, however, the Eu's observed all the rules in preparing for Society Day. They even went so far as to ratify a revised, up-to-date covenant that had been primarily a "technicality" a year earlier and to have members "prepared" for six phases of competition.

But now? No competitor.

The Philomathesians have even forgotten their traditional regular meetings. Nobody has admitted it officially but the real proof that the organization is inactive blossomed forth when not enough members showed up this year to have their pictures made for the *Howler*.

"I can't understand it." Bill Horne told the photographer. "The meeting was announced." He was 20 minutes late for the picture.

Don Schoonmaker echoed Horne's words almost exactly last week, though in a different context. "I can't understand," Schoonmaker said. "Why the Phi's objected so strongly last year when the Eu'", claimed the cup by default, causing us to go through all this technical procedure of revision, etc., when now they have shown no interest at all in Society Day." It is difficult to understand why the titular leaders of the Philomathesians continue to pretend the organization is active. Or why, if recognizing the ineffectiveness of their leadership, they do not relinquish their positions to persons more capable and/or more interested in observing the ideals on which the Philomathesian organization is founded.

Persons within the organization recently did admit the organization is serving no useful purpose. They went so far as to suggest the Philomathesian Society be dissolved.

The rival organization, the Euzelian Society, is effective. It has met regularly. Members are enthusiastic in defense of its existence. The ineffectiveness of the Philomathesian Society seems to lie then, not with the organization itself, but with the elected leaders themselves.

And we question the assumed prerogative of the Philomathesian officers to do away with the organization merely because they are unable to handle it.

R. R.[68]

---

[68] No Society Day This Year (Editorial), *Old Gold and Black*, May 9, 1960, page 5.

Schoonmaker wrote in *The Wake Forest Student*: "It is true that the societies have themselves notable histories. It is equally true that the histories... the last three decades have been conspicuous by the fact that they have lacked average qualities which would justify their continuance." A group with a membership so small they cannot elect officers, "has to stretch the term, literary society...Why not drop the Euzelian or Philomathesian and form literary groups ... Face the fact that only a small percentage of students at Wake Forest need any intellectual stimulation.[69]

Even with the demise of the Intersociety Day competition, the thrill of tournament success was closely followed on campus and in State papers.[70] The debate did not expire with the Societies but rather entered a new era of enthusiasm. The debaters were "on the road," living the narrative to which we turn next in volume 2 of the Debate history series.

---

[69] Schoonmaker, D. (October, 1958). The Literary Societies, *The Wake Forest Student*, page 2-3.

[70] From time to time, the literary societies revived, tending to take on a more literary or discussion format rather than acting as debating societies. These organizations' modern revivals are noted in Volume 2 of this series.

ABOUT THE AUTHOR

Allan Louden (Ph. D. University of Southern California) was a long-term professor at Wake Forest University, serving thirty years as the Director of Debate. This is his sixth book and the first Volume 1, in a three-book series on the History of Wake Forest Debate. Volume 3, *Milestones*, will soon be reissued. He is a former chair of the Department of Communication. He has worked as a political campaign consultant and was often a commentator for TV and newspapers during election cycles, specializing in political debates and advertising.

Made in the USA
Columbia, SC
18 October 2024

44460564R00402